Facility Design and Management
for Health, Fitness, Physical Activity, Recreation, and Sports Facility Development

Eleventh Edition

Thomas H. Sawyer, Editor-in-Chief

©2005 Sagamore Publishing, L.L.C.
Production Manager: Janet Wahlfeldt

Developmental Editor: Cindy McNew

Copy Editor: Susan Moyer

Proofing Editor: Mark Zulauf

Cover Design: Meghan Daly Sawyer Rosselli

Cover Pictures and Drawings: Hastings and Chivetta Architects, Inc.

ISBN: 1–57167–565–5
        978-1-57167-565-1

Library of Congress Catalog Card Number: 2005928533

Printed in the United States.

Sagamore Publishing L.L.C.
804 N. Neil Street
Champaign, IL 61820

www.sagamorepub.com

10 9 8 7 6 5 4 3 2 1

This book is dedicated to all the
professionals who work daily with
students and clients to develop new or
renewed health, fitness, physical activity,
recreation, and sports facilities worldwide.

Contents

Section I
Facility and Event Management

Section II
Common Facility Components

Section III
Field and Court Specifications

Section IV
Recreational Spaces

Section V
Specialty Areas

Section VI
Trends

Glossary of Terms (on-line www.sagamorepub.com)
Meet the Authors (on-line www.sagamorepub.com)
Appendixes (on-line www.sagamorepub.com)
A—Facility Specification Guide
AA—Listing of Skatepark Builders, Consultants, and Designers
B.1—Planning Checklists Indoor and Outdoor
B.2—Existing Facility Assessment and Future Planning Checklist
B.3—Indoor Activity Area Planning Checklist
BB—Cleaning and Maintenance Equipment Record Sheet
C.1—Surface Selection Process
C.2—DIN Standards
D—Indoor Activity Dimensions
DD—Park and Recreation Open Space Standards
E.1—Sample Strategic, Operational, and Other Plans
E.2—Sample Operational Plan
E.3—Planning to Succeed
F—Metric Conversion Formulas
G—General Resources for Planning Facilities
H—Associations Pertinent to Planning
I—Associations Pertinent to Planning for Accessibility
J—Track and Field Layouts
K—Retrofitting or Replacing Facilities
L—Sample ASHRAE Standards
M—Leadership in Facilities and Equipment since 1920
N—History of the CFE
O—Facility Maintenance
P—Winter Sport Activities
Q—Academic Classrooms and Laboratories
R—Boxing Facilities
S—Equestrian Spaces
T—Dance Spaces
U—Orienteering
V—Business Plan for Promotions
W—Business Plan for Public Relations
X—How to Deal With Complaints
Y—Writing a Press Release
Z—Interviewing Process

Foreword

As the cost of construction for sports- and health-related facilities skyrockets, it becomes ever more paramount for those who plan, design, construct, and use these facilities to have access to a comprehensive facilities guide. The 11th edition of *Facility Design and Management for Health, Fitness, Physical Activity, Recreation, and Sports Facility Development,* is a tool for all professionals involved in facility planning and construction use.

The 21st century is a time of increased interest in health, fitness, recreation, physical activity, and sport. A synopsis of the historical development of this text is important. In 1945 at the board of directors' meeting of the American Alliance for Health, Physical Education, Recreation, and Dance (AAHPERD) in Washington, D.C., support was given to a proposal submitted by Caswell M. Miles, AAHPERD vice president for Recreation, to prepare a grant to finance a national workshop on facilities. Subsequently, a request for $10,000 was submitted to and approved by Theodore P. Bank, president of the Athletic Institute, to finance the first workshop. The December, 1946, workshop at Jackson's Mill, West Virginia, resulted in the publication of the premiere edition of the *Guide for Planning Facilities for Athletics, Recreation, Physical and Health Education.*

The 1956 edition of the guide was a product of the second facilities workshop, held May 5-12, 1956, at the Kellogg Institute, and was held again January 15-24, 1965, at the Biddle Continuing Education Center, Indiana University in Bloomington. Two years later, April 29-May 8, 1967, another workshop was held at Indiana University. Among those invited were a number of outstanding college and technical personnel engaged in planning and administering programs of athletics, recreation, outdoor education, physical education, and health education. Other planning authorities and specialists receiving invitations included city planners, architects, landscape architects, engineers, and schoolhouse construction consultants.

The 1974 guide was reconstructed in such a way that it would serve as a more practical tool for school administrators, physical education heads, architects, planning consultants, and all others interested in planning new areas and facilities or checking the adequacy of those already in use.

The Athletic Institute and AAHPERD Council on Facilities, Equipment, and Supplies initiated the 1979 revision of the guide. A blue-ribbon steering committee was appointed by the Council. Edward Coates from Ohio State University and Richard B. Flynn from the University of Nebraska at Omaha, were appointed as coeditors and contributing authors.

Professionals well known for their expertise in facility planning, design, and construction were invited to assist in a complete rewrite, which resulted in *Planning Facilities for Athletics, Physical Education, and Recreation.*

The 1985 edition of *Planning Facilities for Athletics, Physical Education, and Recreation* represented a continuing effort on the part of The Athletic Institute and AAHPERD to keep the text current and relevant. Richard B. Flynn was selected to be editor and contributing author. Many of the contributors to the previous edition updated their chapters, and some new material was added.

The American Alliance for Health, Physical Education, Recreation, and Dance published the 1993 edition, entitled *Facility Planning for Physical Education, Recreation, and Athletics,* and Richard B. Flynn again was asked to serve as editor and contributing author. Again, many of the contributors to the previous edition updated their chapters, and some new material was added.

The AAHPERD Council on Facilities and Equipment selected Thomas H. Sawyer of Indiana State University to serve as chair of the editorial committee and editor-in-chief of the 1999 and 2002 editions of *Facilities Planning for Physical Activity and Sport.* Many new contributors were selected to complete a major revision of the text, which resulted in a great deal of new material and many fresh ideas and concepts. The editorial team for both the 1999 and 2002 editions was: Thomas H. Sawyer, EdD (Indiana State University); Michael G. Hypes, DA (Indiana State University); Richard L. LaRue, DPE (University of New England); and Todd Seidler, PhD (University of New Mexico). There were 21 authors involved in writing 29 chapters in the 1999 edition and 21 authors involved in writing 37 chapters in the 2002 edition.

The revised 2005, 11th edition, with Thomas H. Sawyer again serving as editor-in-chief, fulfills the intent of the Council on Facilities and Equipment to update and revise the text on a regular basis. Regularly revising and updating a text of this magnitude is no easy task. Basically, at the completion of one edition, the planning for a new edition begins—therefore never-ending work for the editor, editorial board, and authors. I would like to commend these selfless individuals. With rapid changes in both technology and construction methods, the regular updating of this text is a necessity. This new edition now adds a number of new chapters, including financial management, promotions, public relations, merchandising and ticket operations, programming, facility and event risk management and shooting areas.

It should be noted that much of the material in this text reflects the composite knowledge of many professionals who have contributed to past AAHPERD text editions, as well as of those individuals who were solicited to serve as authors, editors, and reviewers for the current text. The American Alliance for Health, Physical Education, Recreation, and Dance, the American Association for Active Lifestyles and Fitness (AAALF), and the Council on Facilities and Equipment (CFE) have endorsed this book as one of the best on the topic of planning facilities for sport, physical activity, and recreation.

Having had the pleasure to work closely with Thomas H. Sawyer and the editorial board (10 years) and the Facilities and Equipment Council (23 years) and having been an author in four editions of the text, I would at this time give my sincere thanks and appreciation to all of those involved in this 11th edition of this text—a job well done! I recommend this edition of *Facility Design and Management for Health, Fitness, Physical Activity, Recreation and Sports Facility Development* as the most comprehensive source guide for planning, designing, constructing, and managing facilities related to health, physical activity, and sport.

From its inception, this text has been a milestone resource for sports and physical activity facility designers, users and managers.

Each edition builds on and adds to the field of knowledge in sport and physical activity facility design, planning, and construction. I give my highest endorsement to this 11th edition of the "bible" for facility designers and planners.

With gratitude,

Edward (Ed) Turner, PhD
Professor Emeritus
Department of Health, Leisure and Exercise Science
Appalachian State University

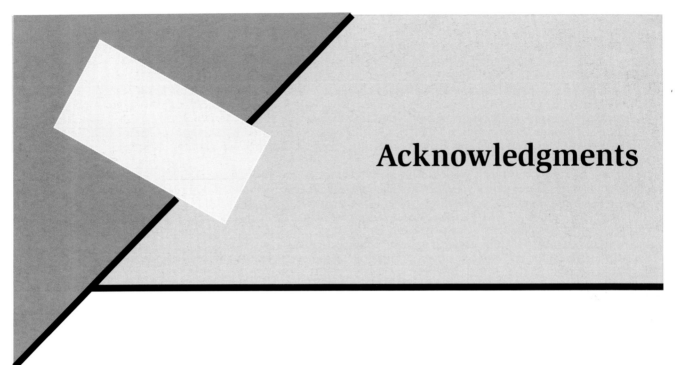

Acknowledgments

Appreciation is expressed to the Editorial Committee members of the Council for Facilities and Equipment (CFE) for assuming initial responsibility for outlining the content and chapters for the text and selection of the chapter authors. While some served as authors/editors for specific chapters in the text, all served as reviewers for assigned chapter drafts. The Editorial Committee members include:

Dr. Thomas H. Sawyer, chair and editor-in-chief, 1999-2008 (9th, 10th, and 11th editions), Indiana State University, chair CFE, 1995-97
Dr. Bernie Goldfine, Kennesaw State University, chair CFE, 1999-2001
Dr. Michael G. Hypes, Indiana State University, chair CFE, 2001-03
Dr. Richard J. LaRue, University of New England, chair CFE, 1994-95
Dr. Todd L. Seidler, University of New Mexico, chair CFE, 1991-92
Dr. Jan Seaman, American Association for Active Lifestyles and Fitness (AAALF), Executive Director
Dr. Thomas Horne, United States Military Academy, chair CFE, 2003-05

We are indebted to a number of authoritative sources for permission to reproduce material used in this text:

—The National Collegiate Athletic Association (NCAA) for permission to reproduce drawings from selected 1997 NCAA rulebooks. It should be noted that these specifications, like others, are subject to annual review and change.
—*Athletic Business* for permission to reprint selected drawings.
—Selected architectural firms for supplying photographs, line drawings, artists renderings, and other materials.

Special recognition is due to those professionals who served as chapter authors or editors, including: Kimberly Bodey, Joe Brown, Payna Brown, Ned Crossley, Michael Edwards, John Gartland, Bernie Goldfine, Tom Griffiths, Tom Horne, David Hoffa, Susan Hudson, Julia Ann Hypes, Michael Hypes, Richard LaRue, David LaRue, Hervey Lavoie, John Lentz, Dan McLean, John McNichols, John Miller, Arthur Mittlestaedt Jr., Jeffrey Peterson, Donald Rogers, Gary Rushing, Richard Scott, Todd Seidler, Steven Smidley, David Stowe, Donna Thompson, Jack Vivian, Hal Walker, and Jason Winkle. These individuals worked diligently to present chapter material in an informative and useful manner.

Without great assistance from a number of very special and important folks, this book would not have been possible: Julia Ann Hypes, who was responsible for the glossary and author information; Meghan "Muffin" Sawyer Rosselli for her graphic and photography expertise; Sagamore Publishing for invaluable advice, counsel, patience, and encouragement during the final edit of the manuscript.

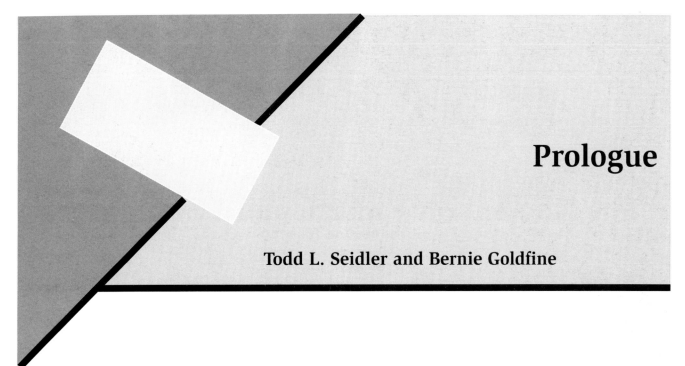

Prologue

Todd L. Seidler and Bernie Goldfine

Have you ever seen a facility with so many design problems that it left you shaking your head in disbelief? Each facility presents its own unique design challenges; if these challenges are not addressed and overcome, the result is a facility with design problems. Typically, the larger a building project, the greater the likelihood that mistakes will be made in the planning and design process. Often, details are overlooked, and sometimes even major mistakes are made in the planning process and not discovered until after the facility is built and opened for use. For example, most of us have seen buildings with poor lighting, ventilation, or access control that could have been prevented with appropriate planning. In particular, one of the most common design flaws in recreational, physical education, and sports facilities is a lack of proper storage space. Surely, we have all visited buildings where hallways, classrooms, and even activity spaces were used for temporary or permanent storage of equipment.

Inadequate planning has resulted in countless design flaws in sports and recreation facilities. Can you imagine a high school football team playing on an 80-yard football field? What about a recreation center with access to the locker rooms available only by crossing the gym floor? Do you believe a facility designer would locate a locker room toilet one foot lower than the septic field it was supposed to drain into? How about a gymnasium with large picture windows directly behind the basketball backboards? And how safe is an indoor track constructed as part of a pool deck that has water puddles present in every running lane? Impossible? Unfortunately not.

These "building bloopers" are real and not as uncommon as we would like to believe. Such mistakes can be embarrassing, expensive, amazing, and sometimes humorous (if it is not your facility). These and many other design errors can usually be traced to insufficient planning. An example of an outrageous building blooper is Olympic Stadium in Montreal. Constructed as the track and field site for the 1976 Montreal Olympics, it has yet to be completed satisfactorily. Originally estimated to cost about $60 million, the price thus far is in excess of $1 billion.

Building bloopers are often caused by devoting insufficient time, effort and/or expertise to the planning process. The earlier in the process that mistakes are discovered and corrected, the less they will cost to rectify. It is inexpensive to change some words on a paper, somewhat more expensive to change lines on a blueprint, and outrageously expensive or even impossible to make changes once the concrete has been poured. Furthermore, the impact of a poorly designed building is staggering when compared with other management problems. Problematic staff can be relieved of their responsibilities. Funds can be raised for underfinanced programs. However, the consequences of a poorly designed building will have to be endured for decades. Therefore, it is essential to devote all available resources early in the planning process.

All too often, facilities are planned without in-depth consideration of the programs that they will support. Basically, a facility is a tool. The better it is planned, designed, and constructed, the better it will support the objectives of the programs it will house. Strange as it may seem, sport facilities often are designed without a great deal of consideration given to programming and user desires. Aesthetics, the interests of one popular sport or program at the time, or the personal desires of decision-makers may, in fact, dictate the design of the facility. Implementing a new program in an existing or poorly planned facility often requires designing the programs based on the limitations of the facility. Poorly designed venues may limit or even prevent some activities from taking place. Conversely, a well-designed facility will support and enhance the desired programs. Planning and building a new facility is a great opportunity to ensure that it will optimally support these programs. Furthermore, well-planned venues allow for flexibility when the popularity of activities and user demand fluctuate. Planned with an eye toward future trends, these facilities are designed to be easily altered so that new activities can be added as needs change.

This book is intended to provide a basic understanding of the planning and design process as well as the unique features of many different areas and types of facilities. Although there is no such thing as a perfect building, with significant time, effort, and expertise devoted to the planning and design process, future building bloopers can be kept to a minimum. It is hoped that those of you involved with the planning of sports facilities will find this book to be a significant resource.

The Council on Facilities and Equipment
Founded in 1946

Since 1946 the Council on Facilities and Equipment published and endorsed *Facility Design and Management for Health, Fitness, Physical Activity, Recreation, and Sport Facility Development*. This book has been used worldwide by design specialists and facility and event management professionals. The expanded and updated 11th edition will continue the tradition established in 1946. It is the leader in the field. Its authors are well known for their expertise in the design and management fields.

Thomas Horne, PhD
United States Military Academy
Chairperson

Jeffrey Petersen, PhD
Ball State University
Chair-Elect

Section

I

Facility and Event Management

Facility Design/ Event Leadership and Management[1]

Thomas H. Sawyer

Facility management is critical in keeping any organization operating smoothly and efficiently. A facility that is well maintained and managed is one of the best public and consumer relations tool in an organization's arsenal. Further, event management is intimately related to facility management. They go hand in hand and cannot be separated easily. An organization's facility and event manager must become involved in many tasks, including, but not limited to, leadership, facility and event admission access control, crowd control and security, emergency operations, facility maintenance, operational policies and procedures, and human resources.

Instructional Objectives

After reading this chapter, the student should be able to

- understand the role and function of a leader in facility and event management;
- develop a facility/event policy and procedure manual;
- plan an appropriate communication strategy; and
- develop crowd control, emergency management, and security plans.

Leadership

Attila the Hun, Napoleon, Marshall, Eisenhower, Patton, and Rommel each believed that, under the right circumstances, every soldier in his army had the potential to be a general and lead the army in his absence. Whether you hold that belief or not, the plain fact is that "natural" leaders do not just happen, nor does anyone have a divine right to lead or rule.

You do indeed have a marshal's baton in your own knapsack. The first step toward leading others is recognizing your leadership potential. The second is being able to manage yourself before trying to manage others. Finally, a third, as noted by Bennis (1989), is self-expression. The key to self-expression is understanding one's self and the world, and the key to understanding is learning from one's own life and experience.

Bennis based his bestseller *On Becoming a Leader* (1994) on the assumption that leaders are people who are able to express themselves fully; "... they know who they are, what their strengths and weaknesses are, and how to fully deploy their strengths and compensate for their weaknesses." Further, "... they know what they want, why they want it, and how to communicate what they want to others, in order to gain their cooperation and support" (Bennis, 1994, p. 37).

Norman Lear's success was based on four very simple yet complex steps: (1) becoming self-expressive, (2) listening to the inner voice, (3) learning from the right mentors, and (4) giving oneself over to a guiding vision (Bennis, 1994).

Leadership and the Facility and Event Manager

Leadership has been defined by many and many continue to redefine it. For the purposes of this chapter, leadership will be defined as a set of qualities that causes people to follow. Leadership requires at least two parties, a leader and a follower. Many experts have argued over what exactly causes a group to follow one person and not another, but the decision to follow a leader seems to come down to a few common traits (see Table 1.1).

---

[1]This chapter has been reprinted with modifications with permission from Sagamore Publishing. It represents Chapter 12, Facility and Event Management, from Sawyer, T. H. (1999), *The Management of Clubs, Recreation, and Sport: Concepts and Applications*. Champaign, IL: Sagamore Publishing.

Table 1.1
Ten Characteristics of a True Leader

The following are the 10 characteristics of a true leader:

- eager
- cheerful
- honest
- resourceful
- persuasive
- cooperative
- altruistic
- courageous
- supportive
- assertive

Leaders have the ability to inspire people to go beyond what they think they are capable of doing, making it possible for a group to attain a goal that was previously thought unattainable. Leaders carry their followers along by (1) inspiring their trust, (2) acting consistently, and (3) motivating them by words and deeds.

Leadership boils down to a willingness to accept responsibility and the ability to develop three skills that can be acquired through practice—elicit the cooperation of others, listen well, and place the needs of others above your own needs. When you properly put these skills together, people begin to turn to you when they need direction.

Responsibility and Accountability

Leadership begins with the willingness to embrace responsibility. You cannot be a leader if you are afraid of responsibility and accountability. With responsibility comes the concept of accountability. If you cannot answer yes to the following question, you are not ready to become a leader. Do you have enough confidence in yourself to accept responsibility for failure?

One of the realities about placing the needs of others above your own is that you cannot blame other people. If you are the type of person who looks outward for an excuse instead of inward for a reason, you will have a hard time earning the trust of others. An absence of trust makes eliciting their cooperation more difficult, which, in turn, makes it more difficult for you to lead, even if you have been given the title of leader.

On the other hand, the leader receives most of the accolades and rewards when things go well. No matter how hard your followers work, no matter how modest you are, no matter how much you attempt to deflect credit to your entire team, yours is the name that people will remember. That is the great benefit of being the leader. Can you handle the limelight of success?

The Basic Ingredients of Leadership

Leaders come in every size, shape, and disposition. Yet they share some of the following ingredients (Bennis, 1994):

- guiding vision
- passion
- integrity (i.e., self-knowledge, candor, and maturity)
- trust (i.e., constancy, congruity, reliability, and integrity)
- curiosity
- daring

Key Leadership Abilities

The trick to becoming a leader is to be able to elicit cooperation, to listen to the needs of others, and to put other people's needs ahead of your own with great consistency. After you decide that you can and want to embrace responsibility, leadership requires that you be able to do three things very well (see also Table 1.2):

- Elicit the cooperation of others. You must be able to get others to buy into your vision of the future and the right way to get there.
- Listen well. You have to be able to gather many kinds of information from others in order to lead; doing so requires that you hone your listening skills. The old adage, "*listen* and *hear* before you speak," is very important when dealing with people.
- Place the needs of others above your own needs. Leadership requires that you be willing to sacrifice for a greater good.

Table 1.2
Ten Ways to Master Leadership Skills

- prepare
- volunteer
- keep an open mind
- give speeches
- develop discipline
- meet deadlines
- stay in touch
- listen
- cooperate
- do things for others

Characteristics of Leaders Coping With Change

There are 10 characteristics for coping with change and creating learning organizations (Bennis, 1994):

- Leaders manage the dream.
- Leaders embrace errors.
- Leaders encourage reflective backtalk.
- Leaders encourage dissent.
- Leaders possess the Nobel Factor (optimism, faith, and hope).
- Leaders understand the Pygmalion effect in management (if you expect great things, your colleagues will give them to you—stretch, don't strain, and be realistic about expectations).
- Leaders have the Gretzky Factor (a certain "touch").
- Leaders see the long view.
- Leaders understand stakeholder symmetry.
- Leaders create strategic alliances and partnerships.

Building Leadership Tools

John F. Kennedy once said, "Leadership and learning are indispensable to each other." Learning about the job, the employees, and yourself is very important to a leader and his/her leadership ability. There are a number of leadership traits that need to be developed by the leader. The remainder of this section will discuss these traits:

1) Learn to use what you have. Intelligence is critical to leadership because synthesizing information is often necessary in order to create a vision.
2) Respond to situations flexibly. Gathering new information and adjusting a response to a particular situation requires intelligence. Instead of responding in a knee-jerk way, an intelligent person responds flexibly based on circumstances and needs.
3) Take advantage of fortuitous circumstances. You not only have to be smart enough to adapt to new information with flexibility, but you also have to have the courage to seize opportunities when they present themselves.
4) Make sense of ambiguous or contradictory messages. A good leader listens to all the information and then sorts through it. You test contradictory messages by asking for more information in order to find the truth.
5) Rank the importance of different elements.
6) Find similarities in apparently different situations. One of the normal characteristics of intelligence is a talent for analogies. Analogous intelligence in leaders is the ability to draw on prior experience, no matter how tenuous the connection is, to find a similarity that you can use to solve a problem.
7) Draw distinctions between seemingly similar situations. You can find differences among situations just as often as you can find similarities, and a good leader learns to recognize when A is not like B and emphasize the differences over what the two have in common.
8) Put concepts together in new ways. Along with analogies, one of the components of intelligence is the ability to synthesize new knowledge by putting together time-tested concepts in new ways.
9) Come up with novel ideas.

Communicating Effectively

First and foremost, a leader has to keep the vision in the minds of his or her followers in every conversation, whether in a spoken or unspoken manner. When a leader is speaking as a leader and not as a friend or confidante, he or she needs to remind people in a simple and straightforward manner and without a lot of additional explanation why they are being asked to turn the vision into reality. The responsibility of leadership is to communicate the vision so clearly that no room is left for doubt among those who must execute it. Finally, leaders must not only explain, they must also motivate their followers.

Assessing the Situation

Your first challenge is to listen carefully to what you are being told about the position and situation. You need to gather information about the responsibilities your superiors are asking you to assume. Long before you meet your team, you need to make a quick but detailed examination of the group you are expected to lead and the current situation. The questions to ask as follows:

- What has the group's past performance been?
- Does management care about the group?
- Has the group's success or failure been short-term or long-term?
- Have there been many personnel changes in the team or is it stable?
- What are the group's goals?
- How does the group compare to similar groups in its ability to command resources?
- What is the commitment of the larger organization to the group?

Leaders are calculated risk takers. They get ahead by knowing when to say yes, and they stay ahead by knowing when to say no.

Leaders Are Not Managers

A leader is not a manager and a manager is not a leader. There are enormous differences between leaders and managers, including:

Manager	Leader
↓	↓
Administers	Innovates
Copies	Original
Maintains	Develops
Focuses on systems and structure	Focuses on people
Has short-range view	Long-range perspective
Relies on control	Inspires trust
Asks how and when	Asks what and why
Watches the bottom line	Eye on the horizon
Imitates	Originates
Accepts status quo	Challenges status quo
Is the classic good soldier	His own person
Does things right	Does the right thing
Wears square hats	Wears sombreros
Learns through training	Learns through education
Can be described as:	Can be described as:
deductive,	inductive,
firm,	tentative,
static,	dynamic,
memorizing,	understanding,
facts,	ideas,
narrow,	broad,
surface,	deep,
direction,	initiative,
left brain,	whole brain,
common sense,	imagination,
rules,	risk,
rigid,	flexible,
reactive	active

Both leaders and managers are crucial in any large undertaking. A leader has the vision and communication to dream the large project (e.g., a new stadium) and the inspiration and determination to put together the right group to make it a reality. A manager's job becomes most vital once the project is complete and the day-to-day operations and events commence. The following discussion centers around the job of the facility manager.

Policies and Procedures Manual

There are any number of reasons why it is important to have written policies and procedures for governing facility/event management. The primary reasons are to (1) provide a formal policy that guides administrative decisions, (2) reduce the organization's vulnerability to litigation, and (3) clearly communicate to staff and customers/clients a set of uniform and standard practices to guide decisions and behaviors.

A well-designed policy and procedure manual for facility/event management can assist in answering questions, such as these:

- What type of reports, records, or documentation are staff required to file and keep?
- What are the due process procedures?
- What are the staff's legal responsibilities and procedures for implementing them?
- What is the policy regarding requisitioning, purchasing, inventorying, servicing, maintaining, and inspecting equipment?
- What is the recruiting, hiring, and evaluating process?
- What are the emergency procedures?
- What are the crowd control procedures?
- What process is utilized for inspecting and maintaining the facilities?
- What procedures are employed for program evaluation?
- What process is implemented to control admission?
- How is the facility scheduled?
- What are the procedures for evaluating whether or not a person can return to activity after injury or illness?

Suggested Contents

A facilities/event policies and procedures manual should delineate general as well as specific program guidelines. The kind of information that should be contained in the policies and procedures manual will vary from one organization to another. In general, the policies should reflect; (1) the rights of all participants; (2) the philosophy of the organization and the rationale for the existence of the program; (3) such legislative dictates as Title VII (sexual harassment), Title IX (gender equity), and the Americans with Disabilities Act (equal access for disabled participants) (Conn & Malloy, 1989). Figure 1.1 outlines a suggested table of contents for the policies and procedure manual.

Steps for Developing a Policies and Procedures Manual

The steps for the development of a policies and procedures manual (Conn & Malloy, 1989; Conn, 1991) are described below. This manual should be a flexible, dynamic document that guides employees. Further, the document should be reviewed and revised annually after implementation. Finally, the primary reasons for a policies and procedures manual for facility/event management are to (1) provide a formal policy that guides decisions, (2) reduce the organization's vulnerability to litigation, and (3) clearly communicate to staff and customer/clients a set of uniform and standard practices to guide decisions and behaviors.

Step 1: Developing a policies and procedures manual is a long, arduous task that requires management's complete involvement and support. It is important that all personnel (management as well as staff) are involved in the development of the policies and procedures for the organization. The typical approach is to appoint a committee to carefully research and ultimately recommend policies and procedures. Management must be prepared to allocate resources (e.g., time and funds) and encourage the involvement of all staff members. Policies and procedures must be carefully researched and synthesized before being written. Therefore, it is extremely important to involve people who look at policies and procedures from many different angles. The more widespread the involvement, the greater the chances are that the manual will be used and maintained after completion.

Several factors should be considered when deciding who will be appointed to the committee:

- Size of the staff—every member of a small staff will have intimate involvement on the committee; however, larger staffs should be divided into subcommittees that will prepare specific sets of policies and procedures.
- Administration and board—the manual must be approved by management and the board (if one exists); therefore, it is important that management and the board are represented on the committee.
- Customer/client/student-athlete—it is important to involve those most affected by the policies and procedures on the committee that develops them.
- Community interest—most organizations have links with the community and community representation could be very useful in future activities; therefore, it is important to involve community members on the committee.
- Diversity or inclusiveness—the committee should be a mirror image of the organization and the community as a whole.

Figure 1.1
Suggested Table of Contents for a Policies and Procedures Manual

- **Accountability**: annual financial audits, facility and equipment maintenance audits, facility and equipment inspection audits, inventory control, personnel evaluation, program evaluation, risk assessment survey, and ticket inventory control and sales audits
- **Sports/Athletics Council**: purpose, function, structure, and operating rules
- **Governance Structures/Authorities**
- **Equipment**: acceptable supplier or vendor list, requisition process, purchasing process, bidding procedures, inventory process, inspection audits, and maintenance procedures
- **Budgeting**: formulation, accountability, and control
- **Events**: staging, concessions, entertainment, scheduling, traffic, and parking
- **Computer Operations**
- **Conduct and Ethics**: staff and participants
- **Courtesy Car Program**
- **Disbursements**: goods and services, payroll, and travel expenses
- **Employment Conditions**: educational benefits, hiring, holidays and vacations, leaves of absence, parking, and performance evaluation
- **Expansion and Curtailment of Programs**
- **Expansion/Renovation of Facilities**
- **Facilities**: maintenance, inspection, risk assessment, usage, and key distribution
- **Film Office**: equipment and operations
- **Fundraising and Booster Organizations**
- **Advertising, Marketing, and Promotion**
- **Media Relations**: events, news releases, publicity materials, television and radio programs, and printed media
- **Philosophy, Mission, Goals, and Objectives**
- **Printing**
- **Receipt, Deposit, and Custody**
- **Scheduling**: events, practices, sports officials, and personnel (e.g., ushers, ticket sellers and takers, program sellers, concession workers, police, emergency personnel)
- **Summer Camps**
- **Telephones**: Fax machines, mobile phones, and beepers
- **Ticket Office**: distribution, operations, sales, complimentary tickets, and auditing
- **Concessions**: sales, inventory, and licenses
- **Alcohol**: sales, inventory, and licenses
- **Leasing and Contractual Agreements**: advertising, signs and posters, ticket office service, program development and distribution, staging, traffic, parking, concessions, alcohol, security, insurance, and emergency management

Step 2: The format of the manual must be flexible. It is suggested that (1) a three-ring binder be used to store the information; (2) the information be divided into logical sections and subsections with appropriate paginations (e.g., section 1—1.1, 1.2, 1.3; section 2—2.1, 2.2, 2.3); (3) a table of contents, definition section for acronyms and terms, and index be included; and (4) the various sections be color-coded.

Step 3: The committee should assign one person to write the manual after collecting the appropriate data from the various task groups. The committee needs to adopt an outline and structure for the manual as well as a timeline for completion of the various sections. The writer should be using a computer and appropriate word processing software.

Step 4: The completed manual is dynamic in nature and must be reviewed periodically. A procedure for reviewing the manual must be established. All staff members should be encouraged to periodically review the policies and procedures within their domain and then recommend any changes to the appropriate authorities. Making policy and procedure changes a regular agenda item at staff meetings sensitizes the staff to the importance of the manual and maintains its currency.

When One Manual Will Not Do

Depending on the size of the organization, one thick manual may not be the most efficient way to operate. This is particularly true if there are a large number of specialists working within the program who do not need to know everything. What may be more efficient is a series of special manuals. One or more manuals may be given to employees as needed. Here is a listing of possible policy manuals to be used by an organization:

- the scheduling manual
- the fitness manual

- the operations manual
- the emergency manual
- the in-service training manual
- the risk management manual
- the sales and marketing manual
- the repair and maintenance manual
- the human resources manual
- the fund raising manual
- the employee benefits manual
- the special event manual
- the membership retention manual
- the recruitment/motivation manual for volunteers

Insurance and the Facility/Event Manager

Are you worried that bad weather will cancel the event you have spent months planning, or that the star athlete will suffer a career-ending injury, or a patron will slip on a spilled soft drink or ice on the sidewalk and break a leg? Today's litigious environment and tight budgets mean managers and owners must take a closer look at insurance and risk-management strategies. In the past 10 years, there has been a dramatic increase in the number of companies specializing in insurance for the fitness, physical activity, recreation, and sports industries.

A survey, completed by *Athletic Business* (1993), of companies specializing in this type of insurance shows a wide variety of coverage available:

- **For professional teams, athletes, and events**—liability and accident medical coverage, high-limit accidental death and disability insurance, contractual bonus and performance incentive programs.
- **For amateur athletes and events** (e.g., Olympic Festivals, USOC, National Governing Bodies, Pan American Games, World Games).
- **For college and high school teams, athletes, athletic associations, club/recreational sport activities, sports camps, and facilities**—sports liability and accident medical coverage, disability insurance, play-practice coverage, transportation insurance, catastrophic injury coverage.
- **For youth/adult recreational teams and leagues**—liability and accident coverage.
- **For health clubs, fitness centers, and sports clubs**—property, accident and liability insurance for participants/members and staff, day-care facilities, tanning beds, diving boards, whirlpools, weight rooms, trampolines, food and liquor services.
- **For venues** (e.g., stadiums, arenas, recreational facilities, water parks)—spectator and participant liability, property insurance, casualty insurance.
- **For promotions and special events**—event cancellation, sponsorship/prize guarantee, special events liability, weather and non-appearance insurance.

The most necessary coverage is catastrophic injury insurance for fitness, physical activity, recreational activity, and sports. Beyond this coverage, the manager should add liability insurance that includes participant legal liability. It is important to select a carrier who has a stable, long-term knowledge of this industry. Investigate the insurance company because there are companies out there that are not experienced in the fitness/sport/recreation field.

What do insurance companies consider before determining if a facility or event is insurable? The insurer reviews information regarding five basic areas: (1) security, (2) maintenance and housekeeping, (3) emergency services, (4) parking and traffic control, and (5) concessions. The company is concerned as to how these areas are managed. Premiums are based on how these areas are managed. The only thing that makes insurance inexpensive is good loss experience, and if year after year a facility or event or team has good loss experience, then all the insurance company needs to collect the premium for is the inevitable "what if?" If the experience is consistently good, the insurance company does not have to build in premiums to pay losses and take care of routine claims.

The cost of premiums can be reduced by opting for higher deductibles or taking the initiative of hiring a risk management expert to survey the facilities and programs for unsafe conditions. Some insurance companies offer on-site safety inspections as a value-added service that can help facilities develop ongoing risk management strategies.

Principles for Establishing an Effective Maintenance and Housekeeping Program

In establishing an effective maintenance and housekeeping program, it must be realized that each organization has unique problems and needs. The maintenance and housekeeping operations of any two organizations will not be exactly alike. The maintenance and housekeeping program plan should abide by principles that include

- establishing objectives and standards, such as: all facilities should (1) have a clean, orderly appearance at all times, (2) be maintained to create a safe and healthful environment, and (3) promote good public relations by providing facilities where people have an opportunity for an enjoyable experience;
- performing all tasks with economy of time, personnel, equipment, and materials;
- implementing operations based on a sound, written maintenance plan;
- scheduling maintenance and housekeeping based on sound policies and priorities;
- placing a high emphasis on preventive maintenance;
- developing a sound organizational plan for the maintenance and housekeeping department;
- providing adequate fiscal resources to support the program;
- furnishing adequate personnel to implement the maintenance and housekeeping functions;
- designing the program to protect the natural environment;
- assuming the responsibility for both customers/clients, visitors, and staff;
- designing renovation or new construction projects with maintenance and housekeeping in mind; and
- accepting responsibility for the public image of the facility.

Communication Technology Role in Facility/Event Management

Communication is a key to successful facility/event management. The communication must be total and instant for it to be of any value. All facilities should have the following tools for enhanced communication: a radio system; mobile phones; beepers/pagers; a telephone system with minimum capabilities of automatic busy redial, automatic call return, call forwarding, special call forwarding, call waiting, special call waiting, speed calling, three-way calling, VIP alert, dial data link service, and caller ID; a fax machine; and computer capabilities such as electronic mail and internet. If the facility sells a large number of tickets for numerous events, then an 800 service needs to be installed.

Radios and beepers/pagers should be for business only. The Federal Communications Commission (FCC) regulations govern all language on the air; use of profane and/or obscene language and derogatory remarks should be strictly forbidden. A code system to communicate critical information should be developed and all security personnel should be required to memorize and use it.

Controlling Building and Event Access

Facilities should have controlled access. Only people who have purchased a ticket or have been given authorized passes should gain entry into the facility. Most facilities do not allow entry unless the person is a member or has an authorized visitor pass.

Admission control begins in the box office with the ticket itself. Tickets must be clearly printed on a safety stock to prevent counterfeiting. The ticket must be designed for easy recognition (i.e., event, date, performance time, section, row, seat) by the admissions-control staff (e.g., ticket takers, users). Tickets should be published by a reputable and bonded ticketing company that ships them with the audited manifest directly to the box office to be counted, racked, and distributed under direct control. An alternative to this process is computerized ticketing, which offers the greatest control. All unused tickets should be either stored in a secure location (e.g., safe within the main office) or destroyed using a shredder.

There are two basic categories for admission-type events: (1) "general admission," which permits a person to sit in any available seat on a first-come, first-serve basis, and (2) "reserved seating" which provides patrons with a specific seating location.

It is advisable to open the doors to the facility approximately 75 minutes prior to the scheduled starting time. This allows patrons adequate time to locate seats, use the restrooms, visit the concession stand, socialize, and become settled before the event begins. It is important to constantly monitor the size and mood of a crowd in the lobby and outside the facility before the doors are opened.

There should be a system for admitting people to the facility who do not have tickets. Many facilities use a photo identification system, which provides one of the best means of identifying persons with legitimate business (e.g., employees, media, show personnel, security, and service contractors).

Entrance into facilities that are not spectator venues require proper identification. In large facilities, that is most often accomplished with the issuance of photo identification (ID) cards that can be scanned by computers. Cards do have many uses for fitness, physical activity, recreation, and sports facilities that relate in some way to security. They are most often used to ensure that the person coming to use the facility is an actual member/customer/client, which can be verified visually or by swiping the card through an electronic reader (scanner), and then the user is admitted into the facility. This can be done (1) manually by a member of the staff who reads the display of relevant information that appears on the screen and then buzzes users through the door or turnstile or (2) the card can automatically allow entry to users by buzzing the door latch or freeing the turnstile, mechanism. Finally, ID cards can be used to track users, notify users of an emergency, alert users to messages, or notify users of misuse of the card.

Current software has many uses such as: (1) storing information about the user's past medical history, purchasing records, rental records, fitness program progress, results of last workout or stress test; (2) alerting the user to messages; (3) informing staff of certain user restrictions; (4) flagging unpaid accounts; and (5) alerting staff to special announcements for the user such as birthdays or anniversaries.

There are a number of small facilities that cannot afford a computer card ID system. The "low-key" solution is simple. The use of fluorescent, plastic ID wristbands, free to all users. They are numbered sequentially and each user is expected to wear the band. The bands can be clipped to a gym bag or sneakers, so "I do not have it with me" no longer works as an excuse. A replacement band costs the user $5.

Crowd Control

Facility/event managers are responsible for crowd control and are liable for injuries caused by crowd violence. No facility/event manager can anticipate all the situations that might lead to disorder. A key to crowd control is cooperation between the facility management staff and promoters, agents, performers, admission control staff, security, police, fire, and government officials. This cooperation will do a great deal to minimize risks.

The International Association of Auditorium Managers (IAAM) recommends the following in regard to crowd control (Lewis & Appenzeller, 2003):

- There should be clearly defined and published house policies which should be implemented for each event. The facility management staff should be clearly in charge and ensure compliance with all laws, house rules and regulations, health standards, and common sense practices.
- Carefully evaluate the effects of the sale of alcohol.
- Clearly define the chain of command and the duties and responsibilities for the facility/event manager, as well as all policemen, security guards, ushers and usherettes, ticket takers and first-aid personnel. Be sure they are constantly trained on how to properly react in an emergency situation.
- Encourage patrons to report dangerous and threatening situations.
- Avoid general admission ticketing and seating if at all possible.
- Carefully plan the sale of tickets, especially when the demand will greatly exceed the supply. Develop a fair and equitable distribution system, mechanisms to control lines, and policies requiring personnel to treat the crowds well and courteously.
- Conduct search and seizure to confiscate bottles, cans, and other items, that may be used to injure others.
- Establish legal attendance capacities for each event set up and obtain the written approval of the fire marshal and building inspector.
- Pay close attention to the architectural plans and designs of the facility. Do not allow illegal or dangerous obstructions. Be certain that the graphics system works to the facility's advantage and to the crowd's advantage by helping them to their seats and other conveniences and exits as quickly and safely as possible.
- Develop an emergency evacuation plan.
- Make sure the public address system works and that its volume and clarity are adequate.
- Keep aisles clear.
- Keep people without floor tickets off the floor.
- Do not turn the lights off completely; maintain at least three-foot candles of light to illuminate aisles and emergency exits.
- Play soft, soothing music before and after an event and during intermission.
- Control the stage and the attraction and do not allow the attraction to overly or dangerously excite the crowd.
- Insist on a clean, well-maintained building and a hassle-free atmosphere.

Procedures for Security and Emergencies

There is no substitute for well-trained security and emergency medical personnel. The most basic training tool for security and emergency medical personnel is a security and emergency medical handbook. The handbook can be used to orient and indoctrinate the security and emergency medical personnel. The main function of the personnel is to provide professional service on behalf of the facility for the patron's health and safety. The handbook should provide personnel with guidelines for providing appropriate service and assist them in becoming aware of potential trouble and increasing their safety awareness. Further, the handbook should contain a clearly written outline of the appropriate chain of command in the facility.

The handbook should describe what is expected of security and emergency medical personnel, such as

- knowing where and how to obtain help when necessary;
- being alert at all times on duty;
- watching for activities, conditions, or hazards which could result in injury or damage to person or property;
- having an attitude that supports good public relations;
- being helpful;
- being courteous but firm at all times;
- obeying and executing all directives from management;
- taking pride in their duties;
- maintaining a keen interest in their job;
- acting without haste or undue emotion;
- avoiding arguments with visitors, customers, employees, or management;
- reporting on time and ready for work;
- wearing a proper, complete, and neat uniform;

- following instructions by reading and implementing posted directives;
- remaining at an assigned post until relieved;
- refraining from eating, drinking, or smoking while on duty;
- assessing injuries appropriately;
- administering immediate and temporary care;
- implementing the appropriate emergency medical procedures necessary;
- activating the emergency medical response plan; and
- completing all necessary reporting forms.

Special Event Planning

The key to a successful event is planning, planning, and planning. Developing and implementing successful events requires great attention to detail and organization. It also requires discipline and patience on the part of the key organizers.

This section will refer to a charity special event to illustrate the planning process for event development and management. This event takes place annually in Terre Haute, Indiana to raise funds for the American Red Cross of the Wabash Valley. The event is organized and managed by volunteers. There is no paid staff.

Defining the Event

The American Red Cross of the Wabash Valley partnered with a local Chrysler/Jeep dealership to develop an annual charity golf tournament to raise money for local disaster victims. This event is defined by its participants (supporters of the American Red Cross), geographical reach (Terre Haute and Vigo area), and local financial needs (providing support for local single family fire victims) of a not-for-profit agency with national name recognition. Most events are defined by one of three factors. The organizers, like the American Red Cross in this example, will decide which of these factors apply to the event being planned. The three common factors are participants, geographical reach, and sanctioning by a governing body (i.e., the parent organization and/or sport).

In the example at hand, the organizers chose a worthy, highly recognized, national organization with strong local ties, the American Red Cross, as the key participant. They clearly defined the geographical reach as the City of Terre Haute and Vigo County, Indiana. Finally, the organizers gained approval of the American Red Cross chapter's board of directors as well as the marketing department for Chrysler/Jeep.

What Factors Should Be Analyzed

The planning committee should study a number of factors prior to making the final decision to hold the event. Any one of these factors could spell disaster for the event. The factors include weather, competition for sponsors and participants, market to be targeted for this event, attitudes of the target audience and the prospective sponsors toward the event, availability of facility or facilities, community support for the event, charity recognition, and availability of potential sponsors.

The planning committee for the Annual American Red Cross Charity Golf Tournament took all of these concerns into account when planning the event. Since a golf outing is always vulnerable to bad weather, the planning committee decided to hold the event, rain or shine, providing a luncheon and completing the planned raffle. All participants would receive their goody bag and an opportunity to participate in a raffle for a set of fitted golf clubs with bag and shoes.

The committee had reviewed carefully all the major events in the community and selected a date in the very early spring when the golfers are "chomping at the bit" to get out and play. The committee also began contacting prospective sponsors in late November for next year's budget before the competition began knocking on the door.

The target market is sufficiently large enough and golf is very popular in this community as well as the adjacent communities. The facility was available. Further, the community has strongly supported the charity (American Red Cross) for many years. It is well recognized in the community for its efforts with disaster victims and armed forces families. Based on the above analysis the community determined that the event was feasible and should be developed.

The Motivation for the Event

Solomon (2002) emphases that, "The first rule of event planning and management is to figure out why you are doing this event in the first place." (p.5) It is extremely important for the organizers to clearly understand the motivation behind the event. The motivation will provide a road map for the direction of the event. The focus of the Annual American Red Cross Golf Tournament is to raise money to assist single family fire victims as well as other local disaster victims in their time of need.

The primary objective of the organizers of the event is to make a profit. A secondary objective is to expand the American Red Cross's network of future supporters. Finally, the organizers want to develop some goodwill among the participants and new friends and to have some fun.

Gaining Sanction or Approval

A sanction is an official approval for an event. This sanction is granted by a governing or regulatory body of an organization or agency and/or a sport. It is vitally important to gain this approval. Sanctioning by a sport regulatory body requires making application to the body in a timely fashion. Most sport regulatory bodies have policies and procedures governing the sanction process.

What Causes Poor Events?

The planners of special events should seriously consider the common pitfalls for special events. These pitfalls can cause an event to fail. These pitfalls include, but are not limited to: "But we've always done it that way!", lack of creativity and innovation, uninspired marketing, poorly selected and trained personnel, too much, too often, not enough money, timing! timing! timing!, event of poor quality, and poor physical conditions (e.g., insufficient parking, poor traffic control, lack of signage).

Steps in Creating an Event

There are 11 simple steps that should be considered when organizers are creating an event. These should be done early in the planning process. The 11 simple steps are as follows:

- Get organized (i.e., establish a steering committee and work committee including event production, accounting/audit, communications/marketing/promotions, decorations, entertainment, facilities, equipment and supplies, maintenance/clean-up, risk management/security, signage, transportation, vendor, sponsorship, and volunteers).
- Determine why this event should be organized.
- Define the event with a short and direct mission or motivation statement.
- Determine who the participants should be.
- Learn about the organization and/or sport governing bodies.
- Determine who needs to sanction the event.
- Define the focus of the event.
- Determine the identity for the event.
- Define the geographical area for the event.
- Develop a budget for the event.
- Design a marketing and promotional plan for the event.

The Budget

A budget is a blueprint for financial success (see Chapter 6 for greater detail relative to budgeting). It is also an estimate for revenue and expenses. No event should move too far down the road without a budget in place.

The typical revenues for events include title (major) sponsor, presenting sponsor, official sponsors, ticket sales, merchandising, program, domestic and international television, commercial sales, ancillary events, donations, and concessions, while the typical expenses include personnel, office space, office supplies/equipment, insurance, travel/hotel, entertainment, trademark search, trophies, gifts, officials, facility rental, portable toilets, refreshments, production costs, talent costs, sales and marketing, and television production.

The budget for the Annual American Red Cross Charity Golf Tournament is as follows:

Revenues

Title Sponsor	$5,000
Gold Sponsors (10)	5,500
Hole Sponsors (54)	5,400
Beverage Sponsor	3,000
Beverage Cart Sponsors (4)	600
Cart Sponsors (4)	600
Shirt Sponsors (2)	3,000
Luncheon Sponsor	1,500
Raffle	800
50/50 Closest to the pin	350
Mulligan	720
Teams	6,800
In-Kind Donations	5,000
Total	$33,270

Expenses

Green and Cart Fees	$7,320
Luncheon	1,440
Shirts (150)	4,550
Beverage	3,000
Gifts	2,000
Trophies	200
Signage	1,500
Advertising	1,500
Printing	500
Total	21,410
Net Income	11,860

Sponsorships

A sponsorship is when a company or organization pays a promoter or organization a fee for the right to associate itself and its products with an event. Sponsorships come in all sizes and shapes as companies and organizations look to achieve vastly different objectives within their sponsorship budgets. For a sponsor, an event can do the following (Schmader & Jackson, 1997, pp.1, 67):

- Create positive publicity.
- Heighten visibility.
- Set sponsor apart from its competition.
- Complement other marketing programs.
- Enhance image.
- Drive sales.
- Shape customer attitudes.
- Improve customer relations.
- Sell or sample products/services directly.
- Drive traffic.
- Increase employee morale/quality of life.
- Contribute to community economic development.
- Combat larger advertising budgets of competitors.
- Promote image of sponsor as a good corporate citizen.
- Reach specifically targeted markets.

A sponsorship package includes, but is not limited to: exclusivity, television, signage, entertainment, display/merchandise, promotions/public relations, advertising, sponsor benefits, cost, term of contract, and option to renew. Sponsor benefits, for example, include product exclusivity, 30-second commercial spots, on-premises signage, tickets to each session, hotel accommodations, free or reduced parking, VIP parking, invitations to all social activities, point-of-sale display, on-site promotion, name and logo on materials produced, radio spots, player appearances, and an ad in the event program.

There are commonly four types of sponsorships offered. They are title (primary or exclusive) sponsor, presenting (secondary) sponsor, media sponsor, and official product sponsor. There is another category called associate, partner, or other levels. The title sponsor is the lead sponsor of the event.

The presenting sponsor is the second biggest sponsor of the event. This sponsorship costs less and proportionately fewer sponsor benefits are provided. The third type of sponsorship is official product sponsors. This category has the greatest opportunity for corporate clutter. For example, Coca-Cola (soda category), Verizon (telecommunications), UPS (shipping), Miller (beer), Ben & Jerry's (ice cream), Kodak (film), Wells Fargo (banking), etc. Too many sponsors can kill the golden goose. These sponsors receive approximately a third less than presenting sponsors who receive about 25% less than the title sponsor.

The media sponsors usually provide a predetermined amount of advertising support for the event. They may also provide some cash support and publicity. Finally, they may provide celebrities for the event. The committee should consider selecting three media sponsors including print, radio, and television.

Another sponsorship category includes associate, partner, and specialty sponsorships. An associate sponsorship might fall in between the title and presenting sponsors. A partner sponsorship might be at the title level with multiple title sponsors. Finally, a specialty sponsorship could be what is often found at golf tournaments such as hole sponsors, cart sponsors, and beverage/refreshment cart sponsors.

A word of caution regarding sponsorships: Be careful about what benefits are provided for each type of sponsorship and make sure that the price for a sponsorship is high enough to cover all sponsor benefits as well as provide for a nice margin of profit for the event. Finally, make sure the contract is clear to all parties. The following are the components of an agreement for sponsorship: identify the parties involved, term of the contract, description of the event, site, date, sponsor benefits, obligations of the sponsor, warranties, indemnity, insurance, assignment, waiver, employer/employee relationship, notices, confidential terms of the contract, governing law, severability, force majeure, and option for renewal.

Sponsorship Lists

It is important to carefully develop a prospective sponsorship list. The committee should start with a list of categories and companies that could be interested in sponsoring the event. Further, the committee needs to spend time researching the various companies. (See Schmader & Jackson, 1997, pp. 69-79) In developing the list, Schmader and Jackson (1997) suggest posing the following questions for each prospective sponsor. Those prospects that receive a "yes" to all probably would be the most likely to become involved.

- "Does the prospective sponsor sell or operate in the event's host community?
- Does the prospective sponsor's history include past or present sponsorship? If so, what kind?
- Does the prospective sponsor advertise in the host community?
- Does the prospective sponsor maintain a high profile in the host community?
- Is the prospective sponsor's name mentioned with some frequency in the news media? (Is it mentioned for positive or negative reasons?)

- Does the prospective sponsor provide a commercial function that is customer- or client-driven?
- Is the prospective sponsor noted for the support of at least some altruistic or community betterment efforts?" (p.66)

The following is a sponsorship checklist for the event organizers:

- Seek sponsorships aggressively.
- Develop a sponsorship proposal.
- Design a marketing and sales strategy to sell the sponsorships.
- Determine the competition for sponsorships.
- Concentrate on building relationships.
- Determine the optimal number of sponsorships in each category developed.
- Research potential sponsors.
- Develop a plan for advertising and promotion that will add value to the sponsor's participation in the event.
- Make sure the final contract protects all parties.

Building the Customer Base

A special event can be a one-time affair, but generally, they develop into annual events. The initial year is the most important in developing a solid foundation for customer loyalty. The planners must make sure the event is done very well in order to guarantee customers will return next year and bring a friend.

Planners must know their customers and the market for the event. This will require some research to be done by the organizing committee or a research company. Some of the information can be gathered by questionnaire and other information can be gleaned from the internet. The type of information includes age, marital status, number and age of kids, income range, unemployment, likes and dislikes, what products they like, and their feelings about the proposed event. The survey can be by mail or phone or at the local mall.

Once the planners have determined the market, a mailing list should be created. As the event grows so will the mailing list. This mailing list could be sold to sponsors, so make sure you gain permission to use the customers' names and share them with others.

Getting the Word Out

Once the planning committee has completed its plans for the event, it is time to develop the media plan for informing the selected market. The advertising outlets for getting the word out include print, direct mail, internet, radio, and television. The ad copy should communicate the following information about the event: date, time, location, how to register, who the stars will be, who the funds will support or charity affiliations, open to all interested parties, where tickets can be purchased, and cost of registration or tickets.

Working With the Participants

The focus of the Annual American Red Cross Charity Golf Tournament is to make it a player-friendly tournament. The planning committee approached the tournament with a player-friendly mentality. The mind-set of the committee should be to design an event with the participants in mind. The following key planning points should be considered during the planning of a special event:

- Review the community event schedule and find a date and time when other major events are taking place, and set the event in a place readily accessible to the market you hope to capture.
- Assure that ample and convenient parking or other transportation is available.
- Arrange for prizes, gifts, and other benefits that will be interesting to the participants who will be attracted to the event.
- Design the entry fee so that at least 50% of the fee can be deducted as a charitable contribution.
- Provide a welcoming luncheon or social gathering to be held no matter what the weather may be.
- Design a few games of chance for participants (e.g., raffles, 50/50s, prizes for hole-in-ones, etc.).
- Provide souvenirs as a remembrance of the event, such as, for a golf tournament, bag tags, a sleeve of balls with tournament logo, a quality golf shirt, golf tees, etc.
- Create an atmosphere of fun.

For example, the Annual American Red Cross Charity Golf Tournament has done the following for its participants:

- Provided a welcoming luncheon prior to tee off
- Provided courtesy beverage stations at key locations on the course

- Provided prizes for 1st through 3rd place
- Arranged for three hole-in-one prizes (e.g., two cars and a four-wheel sport package)
- Provided a goody-bag for all participants that included a sleeve of golf balls with charity logo, package of tees, a quality golf shirt with the logos of two shirt sponsors and the charity logos, a free test drive coupon for a Chrysler/Jeep vehicle, and a coupon for 50% off the next round played
- Arranged for a raffle to be held with the following prize: a custom set of clubs with a bag and shoes
- Arranged for a 50/50 closest to the hole contest
- Provided a follow-up thank you letter for participating
- Provided a card indicating what portion of their fee was tax deductible

The planning committee needs to be aware that if professional players are involved in the charity, then sports agents become involved in the process. If this is the case, the committee should then enlist the assistance of an attorney to assist in the negotiations and draft what the athlete's obligations and promoter's obligations will be for the event. This can become very complicated when advertising and promoting the event (i.e., group rights, endorsements, media rights, indemnification, warranty, and releases).

Summary

Facility management is critical in keeping any organization operating smoothly and efficiently. A facility that is well maintained and managed is one of the best public and consumer relations tools in an organization's arsenal. Further, event management is intimately related to facility management.

The primary reasons for a written policy and procedure manual are to (1) provide a formal policy that guides administrative decisions; (2) reduce the organization's vulnerability to litigation; and (3) clearly communicate to staff and customers/clients a set of uniform and standard practices to guide decisions and behaviors.

Insurance is no longer a luxury; it is a necessity. Today's litigious environment and tight budgets mean managers and owners must take a closer look at insurance and risk management strategies. In the past 10 years, there has been a dramatic increase in the number of companies specializing in insurance for the fitness, physical activity, recreation, and sports industries.

A strong maintenance and housekeeping program is built upon the following principles: (1) guidelines for establishing a sound program, (2) standards to measure the effectiveness of an existing program, and (3) a basis upon which the entire program should be developed.

A standard procedure should be established for requesting use of facilities. The organization should create and adhere to a standard request form and establish priority guidelines for authorizing use.

Communication is a key to successful facility/event management. The communication must be total and instant for it to be of any value.

Facilities should have controlled access. Only people who have purchased a ticket or have been given authorized passes should gain entry into the facility. Most facilities do not allow entry unless the person is a member or has an authorized visitor pass.

Facility/event managers are responsible for crowd control and liable for injuries that are caused by crowd violence. Cooperation between the facility management staff and promoters, agents, performers, admission control staff, security, police, fire, and government officials will do a great deal to minimize risks.

There is no substitute for well-trained security and emergency medical personnel. The most basic training tool for security and emergency medical personnel is a security and emergency medical handbook. The handbook can be used to orient and indoctrinate the security and emergency medical personnel.

Human Resource Management

Thomas H. Sawyer

2

The most important asset in any organization is its human resources. People are the key to a business's success or failure. The goal is to obtain competent employees and provide the means for them to function optimally. Sport organizations are service-oriented operations. Therefore, the management of human resources, whether it be a manager of the human resource department in a large organization or the owner or manager of a small organization, plays a primary role in the organization. Further, the human problems of management are often the most complex because of the variability of human nature and behavior. This makes the management of human resources of the organization a key to its success.

Instruction Objectives

After reading this chapter, the student should be able to

- Describe the various types of employees;
- Understand the human resource role; and
- Describe the hiring, performance appraisal, in-service, termination, compensation, and grievance processes.

Management of human resources involves all the policies and procedures developed for employees to interact with the organization both formally and informally. The common components of human resource management are

- hiring competent and qualified employees,
- assigning and classifying employees effectively,
- motivating employees to perform optimally,
- stimulating employees' professional growth and development,
- evaluating and compensating employees fairly,
- rewarding employees for their efforts, and
- providing in-service education opportunities.

Types of Employees

There are basically two types of employees—professional (salary) and hourly. These employees can be paid, volunteer, or independent contractors. The professional employees are paid a salary, have a college degree, hold higher-level positions, do not have fixed work schedules, do not punch time clocks, and perform specific duties that do not fit into fixed day/hour schedules (e.g., club manager, program director, marketing director, and instructors). The hourly employees usually have specific day/hour schedules, punch time clocks, may have specified lunch and rest breaks, receive specified vacation time and sick leave, and are not expected to work after hours without additional compensation (e.g., custodians, secretaries, maintenance personnel, equipment managers, security officers, and other office personnel).

Some special types of employees include part-time and seasonal employees, volunteers, and independent contractors.

Every organization at one time or another has the need for *part-time personnel*. In determining personnel needs, the manager should decide which work tasks can be clustered into jobs that can be accomplished by part-time employees. Part-time positions may include: aerobic dance instructors, fitness instructors, professional trainers, instructors, day care personnel, janitors, secretaries, accountants, lifeguards, ticket sellers, ticket takers, concessions personnel, post-event cleanup to name a few. These positions need to have job descriptions developed the same as full-time positions.

---

[1]This chapter has been reprinted with modifications with permission from Sagamore Publishing. It represents Chapter 1, Managing Human Resources, from Sawyer, T. H. (1999). *The Management of Clubs, Recreation, and Sport: Concepts and Applications*. Champaign, IL: Sagamore Publishing.

Some organizations employ *seasonal employees* to meet the demands of its clientele. The need for seasonal employees depends on the time of year (e.g., summer, June or/to August, and winter, November or/to March), activities (e.g., water sports, winter sports), and region of the United States (e.g., Southeast, South, Southwest, Northeast, Upper Midwest, or Northwest). The summer increases the need for personnel in organizations that cater to school-aged children. Many fitness centers need to employ more personnel for day care centers during the summer months because the younger children are out of school and during the first quarter of the new year to meet the demands of the increased number of clients after the holiday eating binges.

Many tasks and services can be accomplished by *volunteers*. Managers have to determine the specific work tasks (e.g., answering the phone, working the registration desk, working in the day care center, assisting in raising funds). All volunteer positions should have job descriptions. A volunteer service program should be considered and initiated.

When selecting volunteers the organization should expect that the volunteer will

- like people;
- accept the clients of the organization and treat them with respect as individuals rather than maximize their shortcomings;
- be dependable, sincere, thoughtful, and cooperative;
- have a strong sense of responsibility;
- be able to take action;
- be creative;
- be able to take initiative within the limits of the assigned responsibility;
- be appropriately dressed for the work to be performed;
- enjoy the work assignment in the organization;
- be able to stimulate participation; and
- be physically, mentally, and socially fit to perform the assigned responsibilities.

Finally, many organizations use *independent contractors* to provide services. An independent contractor is someone from another organization who contracts with the primary organization to provide a specific service for a specific amount of time and for an agreed upon amount of money. Traditionally, these contracts are for services including: aerobic dance, clerical, custodial, trash collection, laundry, lawn, professional trainers, snow plowing, marketing, advertising, concessions, etc. The organization pays for the service, and the individual or other organization is responsible for paying employment taxes, fringe benefits, and liability insurance. It is imperative that the independent contractor carry liability insurance to cover errors of commission and omission. Another caution is to be certain that the aerobic dance instructor has gained copyright permissions on all the music used in the performance of the contracted service. The organization should not be responsible for the independent contractor's infringement upon the artist's copyright on the music.

All organizations should have a chart that provides a graphic view of the organization's basic structure and illustrates the lines of authority and responsibility of its various members. All employees should be familiar with this chart and understand how their positions and duties contribute to the overall structure.

The limitations of an organizational chart include: (1) it is easily outdated; (2) it fails to show precise functions and amounts of authority and responsibility; and (3) it does not portray the informal relationships that exist.

Hiring Process

Every organization needs to have a manual outlining policies and procedures for recruitment and appointment of personnel. The manager of human resources must have appropriate hiring procedures in place. The components of a hiring process should be: (1) gaining approval for the position, (2) establishing a search and screen committee (i.e., appointing/selecting a committee chair and outlining the responsibilities of the chair and the committee), (3) informing the search and screen committee of the appropriate Affirmative Action and Equal Opportunity Employment statutes, (4) developing a job description, (5) preparing a position announcement, (6) establishing a plan for advertising the position, (7) screening the pool of candidates, (8) verifying the candidates' credentials, (9) interviewing the candidates, (10) selecting the final candidate, and (11) negotiating the appointment with the selected candidate.

Gaining approval for the position is the first step in any hiring process. Human resource managers and owners are faced with replacing vacant positions or determining whether a new position is appropriate. In either situation, a case must be built to justify a replacement or new position. It is best to develop a five-year plan for human resources. The plan is developed based on future business projections and consideration of turnover in personnel (e.g., retirements, emergency leaves, sick leaves, and resignations). This will assist in justifying the need for a replacement or new position or even a redefined position.

Once approval for a replacement, redefined position, or new position has been gained, the next step is to *appoint a search and screen committee*. This may not be necessary in small organizations. You can never be too careful when it comes to recruiting and selecting personnel. The committee should be composed of three to seven people. The members of the committee should be as diverse as the employees and clientele or customers of the organization.

Before the committee begins its work, there should be a meeting to *review the Affirmative Action and Equal Employment Opportunity guidelines* (Executive Order 11246 mandates nondiscrimination and affirmative action in public and non-public institutions that receive federal monies over a specified amount). The committee is to develop the job description, the position announcement, search strategy, and to screen the candidate pool down to three to five final candidates. The committee may be asked by the human resources manager to either recommend three to five final candidates with no priority, with a priority order, or select the number-one candidate.

Developing the job description should be the responsibility of the search and screen committee. The job description should include, but not be limited to: (1) a position title (i.e., the position title should describe generally the responsibilities of the position), (2) the qualifications for the position (i.e., experience, education, certifications), and (3) the responsibilities and duties for the position.

When developing the qualifications for the position, do not be too prescriptive. An example of an overly prescriptive set of qualifications would be: *The candidate must have earned a MA/MS. degree in exercise physiology, have five years experience in a club setting, current certification in CPR, and currently hold a director's certification from the ACSM.* This set of qualifications may narrow the pool of qualified candidates. A set of qualifications like the following, however, is less restrictive and allows for a larger candidate pool: *The candidate will have a BS in physical education, adult fitness, sport sciences, recreation and sport management, prefer an MA/MS in physical education, adult fitness or cardiac rehabilitation; have three to five years experience in a clinic, club, college/university, corporate, or hospital setting; have completed a class in CPR from either the American Red Cross or the American Heart Association, prefer current certification; and a fitness instructor or exercise technician certification from the ACSM, prefer director certification.* If you are truly searching for a strong candidate, the larger the candidate pool, the better.

The duties of any position have four basic components: duty period, tasks to be accomplished, ethical practices, and expectations. Policies concerning responsibilities and expectations common to specific employee groups should be found in a human resources handbook. All organizations should have a human resources handbook.

The job description will not be used only for the search process. Every position, whether it is full-time, part-time, or volunteer, should have a job description. It will become the basis of the performance appraisal document. Therefore, it is imperative that the job responsibilities and duties be very detailed and can be evaluated objectively after the candidate is employed. Further, include a statement toward the end or at the end of the responsibilities section that allows the employer some flexibility, such as "and any other responsibilities or duties assigned in writing by the immediate supervisor."

After the job description is completed the committee will *design an appropriate position announcement.* A position announcement includes: (1) the position title, (2) a short description of the organization, (3) a summary of the job description, (4) qualifications, (5) the application procedure, (6) the deadline, and (7) an AA/EEO Employer designation. It is important to be flexible in establishing the deadline. A statement such as, "the review of applications will begin September 1, and continue until the position is filled" allows the committee to review later applicants who qualify.

The application procedure should request the following from the applicant: letter of interest; completed application; résumè, copies of all current and appropriate certifications; and names, addresses, email addresses, and phone numbers of three to five professional references. Once the names and addresses are received, a letter should be prepared asking specific questions about the candidate for the reference to respond to in detail. A phone call can be made to clarify answers or ask other questions. Each candidate should be asked for current copies of all certifications. Candidates may be required to provide an official copy of all college transcripts upon employment.

Once the position announcement has been completed, the committee must decide *how, where, and when the position will be announced.* The following are a few common ways of communicating a position announcement: (1) referral and employment agencies, public and private; (2) college and university placement services and bulletin boards in departments of exercise science, kinesiology, physical education, recreation, and sports management; (3) professional journals and newsletters; (4) job marts at professional conventions (e.g., American College of Sports Medicine [ACSM]; American Alliance for Health, Physical Education, Recreation, and Dance [AAHPERD]; International Dance Exercise Association [IDEA]; National Strength and Conditioning Association [NSCA]; National Recreation and Park Association [NRPA]; and the annual Athletic Business Convention); (5) local newspapers, (6) national/regional newspapers; (7) employee referrals; (8) cooperative fieldwork, internship, or work study programs with colleges and universities; and (9) job listings on the internet, World Wide Web or Listservs. It is customary to allow at least 10 to 20 working days for people to respond to the position announcement.

When developing the recruitment strategy, the committee must be conscious of preparing a realistic budget. The search budget will include not only the recruitment aspects but also costs related to advertising, long distance calls, postage, transportation, lodging, and meals. Therefore, it is important to establish early financial benchmarks for the entire hiring process.

As the deadline nears for the initial screening to begin, the committee should establish a procedure for *screening the pool of candidates.* The first step in screening candidates is organizing each candidate's file to determine which files are complete. Only those files that are complete are to be reviewed by the committee. A complete file would include, for example, a letter of application; a current rèsumè with names, addresses, email addresses, and phone numbers of references; copies of certifications; and possibly a valid high school or college transcript.

Next, each member of the committee will review all completed candidate files and select their top 10 to 15 candidates. The review will be based upon required and desired qualifications as well as best fit for the position and organization. After this process is complete, the committee will meet to narrow the pool to 10 to 15 potential semifinalists. Each of the semifinalist's *credentials will be verified,* and the candidate will be called to see if he or she is still interested in the position. At this time, letters will be sent to each continuing candidate's references to gather more information, and each candidate will be interviewed over the telephone by the committee. The interview questions must be appropriate (see Appendix Z for examples of appropriate and inappropriate questions). At the conclusion of this process, the committee will narrow the field to three to five finalists to be interviewed on-site.

The above process is appropriate for all professional employees but may not be for other employees such as clerical, receptionists, and housekeeping. The process for non-professional personnel would not be as elaborate. For example, when hiring a person for housekeeping the applicant would complete a standard application and complete any appropriate pre-employment tests. The human resources manager would check all references from the application, review the results of the test(s), and interview the candidate with the housekeeping supervisor.

All candidates must be *interviewed* prior to hiring. The interview is for both the candidate and the organization. The candidate is deciding whether or not the position and organization are a match for his or her skills and personality. The organization is concerned about whether the candidate is a good match for the organization. See Appendix Z for interviewing procedures.

The on-site interview can range from a few hours to a few days. The length of time will depend on the position, whether it be professional or support staff. The more influential the position, the longer the interview. An on-site interview should include time with the committee, others who will interact with the position, and completion of any tests required (e.g., strength, flexibility, computer skills, keyboard test, etc.). After the interview has been completed, the committee will meet to discuss and rank each candidate. At the conclusion of this meeting, a recommendation should be forthcoming to the human resources manager. The facility/event manager will make the *final selection* based on the committee's information and recommendation. After the selection has been made, the facility/event manager will *negotiate the appointment* with the selected candidate.

The use of a written contract or letter of agreement is recommended so that obligations of the employer-employee relationship are explicitly stated. The contract or letter of appointment should be developed in consultation with legal counsel.

Recruitment

Recruiting strong, effective employees is the key to the success of any organization. The efforts in the area of recruitment are critical to the future of the organization. One mistake can spell doom for an organization.

An important question to be answered when filling positions is whether it is desirable to fill the positions from within the existing staff through promotion or transfer or to seek outside applicants. It is the philosophy of many organizations always to look first within to promote loyal and competent employees as a preference to bringing in new, outside personnel. This practice has the advantage of building staff morale and a conscious effort by employees to achieve and thus earn their way to more desirable positions. It rewards loyalty and provides a strong base for tradition and standardization of operation. However, outsiders may have qualifications superior to any current members of the organization. They will be more likely to provide new ideas and approaches to their assigned duties. In most cases, it is best to solicit applicants from both within and outside the organization. Careful judgment will then produce the best selection from the potential candidates. If the internal candidate is selected, in the end he or she will be stronger because of the process.

In-Service Training

Training personnel is not a luxury. It is a necessity. Personnel can never be too well trained to perform their responsibilities. The training program should be for all personnel. No employee should be exempted from training.

Providing regular, planned, and systematically implemented in-service education programs for the staff can only benefit the organization and staff member. The education program(s) should be based on the needs of the individual(s) in relation to the demands of the job. The employee and employer should see the process as career development designed to make the employee a more effective member of the organization.

The human resources manager should develop an ongoing staff development program. This program should be composed of the following elements: (1) new staff orientation, (2) safety training (e.g., C.P.R. and first aid), (3) career development, and (4) technology upgrades. A few examples of staff development seminars or workshops are time management, communication skills, risk assessment and management, or computer skills. These are only a few examples of the need for staff development, which will continue to increase in a rapidly changing society.

The new staff orientation should include a discussion of

- organization history, structure, and services;
- area and clients served by the organization;
- organization policies and regulations;
- relation of managers and human resources department;
- rules and regulations regarding wages and wage payment, hours of work and overtime, safety (accident prevention and contingency procedures), holidays and vacations, methods of reporting tardiness and absences, discipline and grievances, uniforms and clothing, parking, fringe benefits, identification badges, office space, key(s), and recreation services; and
- opportunities for promotion and growth, job stabilization, and suggestions and decision making.

Common Errors Related to In-Service Education Programs

It is important for the human resources manager to avoid the following errors when designing an in-service education program:

- feeding too much information at one time
- telling without demonstrating
- lack of patience
- lack of preparation
- failure to build in feedback
- failure to reduce tension within the audience.

Evaluating Employee Performance

All employees should be evaluated. The evaluation period varies from six weeks for new employees to annual performance reviews for established employees. The evaluation should take the form of a performance appraisal. The performance appraisal is drafted by using the job description for the position as well as the mutually agreed upon annual performance objectives.

A performance appraisal (i.e., work plan, progress review, and annual performance review) is a systematic review of an individual employee's job performance to evaluate the effectiveness or adequacy of his or her work. Performance appraisals are the essence of human resources management. They are the means for evaluating employee effectiveness and a basis for producing change in the work behavior of each employee. Performance appraisals should be used as learning tools.

The task of assessing performance is a difficult and extremely complex undertaking. For this reason, significant planning and supervisory time should be devoted to the appraisal process. All organizations should require annual performance appraisals of all employees. In every case, they provide the opportunity for employee and supervisor to discuss the employee's job performance and to identify any desired redirection efforts. The human and financial resources devoted to conducting performance appraisals pay-off in the long haul. It is valuable for both large and small organizations.

Other purposes for performance evaluations are to

- provide employees with an idea of how they are doing,
- identify promotable employees or those who should be demoted,
- administer the salary program,
- provide a basis for supervisor–employee communication,
- assist supervisors in knowing their workers better,
- identify training needs,
- help in proper employee placement within the organization,
- identify employees for layoff or recall,
- validate the selection process and evaluate other personnel activities (e.g., training programs, psychological tests, physical examinations),
- improve department employee effectiveness,
- determine special talent,
- ascertain progress at the end of probationary periods (i.e., new employees or older employees with performance difficulties),
- furnish inputs to other personnel programs, and
- supply information for use in grievance interviews.

Personnel Records

A personnel file should be established as a depository for all pertinent information concerning the employment status and productivity of each employee. These files serve the purpose of recording all aspects of employment status including, but not limited to: position title, job description, contract provisions, an accounting of benefits, accumulated sick leave, vacation time, awards received, performance appraisals, disciplinary actions, letters of commendation, salary history, home address and phone number, person(s) to contact in case of emergency, name of spouse and children, social security number, income tax data, life and/or disability insurance, and family physician.

Personnel files are confidential. When an item is placed into a personnel file, the employee must be notified. The employee may have access to his or her personnel file at anytime under the guidelines established by the Freedom of Information Act. The employer cannot maintain a secondary personnel file that contains information that the employee is not aware of its existence. It should be general practice that only an employee's supervisor(s) has access to personnel files. Care must be exercised to protect the confidentiality of the employee. There should be policies and procedures established for the handling and accessibility of personnel files. Files should be retained a specific number of years to meet statute of limitations requirements, which differ from state to state. Always check with an attorney before destroying files. Finally, all files should be stored on a computer with appropriate backup.

Reward System

A rewards system, whether intrinsic or extrinsic, is essential to maintain employee morale. People need to feel that their efforts are appreciated or they will seek appreciation elsewhere. An intrinsic reward is personal—"I know I am doing a good job." The person feels good about him- or herself, whereas extrinsic rewards are tangible and provided by the organization. Common extrinsic rewards are salary increases above the average provided, promotional opportunities, bonuses not attached to salary, payment for attendance at conferences, special recognition dinners, and newspaper recognition.

The rewards system should be developed by the human resources manager. The system should concentrate on celebrating personnel for jobs well done. There should be a specific line item in the annual budget to cover all costs for the system.

Fringe Benefits

It is essential that a fringe benefit packet be established for all personnel in the organization. Fringe benefits typically include group health insurance (including prevention coverage, doctor visits, surgical interventions, drug purchases, and eye and dental coverage), group term life insurance, disability insurance (Rehabilitation Act 1973, Veterans Readjustment Assistance Act 1974, Vocational Rehabilitation Act 1973), retirement programs, contributions to social security, leaves of absence for various reasons (e.g., personal emergency, death in the family, and jury duty), vacations, sick leave, holidays, and tuition assistance for advanced education.

The health benefits program should be administered by the human resources manager. The fringe benefits packet needs to be budgeted. The organization should not pay for the entire program but share the costs with the employees (e.g., the organization will pay 80 percent of the medical plan and the employees will pay 20 percent).

Termination

Termination, like appointment, is a two-way street: the person may choose to leave the organization or the organization may decide that the person must leave. Whichever the case, policies and procedures need to be established and placed in the human resources policy and procedure manual. There are two policies that need to be developed. The first relates to when an individual is considering termination (i.e., quitting). This policy might say, "All personnel are expected to give due notice, in writing, of intention to leave the organization whether by resignation or retirement. Due notice is construed as not less than_____for supervisory personnel, and _____ for all other personnel."

Procedures for terminations by the employee should include, but not be limited to

- an indication of the persons to whom written notice should be sent;
- a statement regarding turning over such items as reports, records, and equipment; and
- completion of an exit interview.

The second policy, which is the most sensitive of all human resources policies, is organization termination of the employee. The policy might read: "Termination of a staff member is based upon consideration of quality of performance in relation to achievement of the goals of the organization. The judgments of peers and supervisors are taken into account by the executive when recommending terminations to the board."

Procedures for terminations by the organization might include:

- How is quality performance considered?
- What are the roles of the peers and supervisor(s)?
- When is notice given?
- How is notice given?
- What, if any, severance pay?
- What about the employee's due process?
- How are the specific reasons for termination communicated?

Either the human resources manager or immediate supervisor will complete the dismissal.

Grievance Policy

All organizations need to establish a grievance policy and appropriate procedures to guarantee the employee's due process rights. The individual who is either terminated or disciplined has the right to due process. This aspect is generally covered by a policy on grievance and provides detailed procedures of implementation. The policies and procedures developed should have the intent to resolve differences at the lowest level of the professional relationship and as informally as possible.

Sexual Harassment Policy Development

Sexual harassment is the imposition of unwanted sexual requirements on a person or persons within the context of an unequal power relationship. There are many forms of sexual harassment in the workplace, including but not limited to: unwelcome physical touching, hugs, and kisses; physically cornering someone; sexual jokes, derogatory sexual names, or pornographic pictures; promises of reward or threats of punishment coupled with sexual advances. A man as well as a woman may be the victim of harassment and a woman as well as a man may be the harasser. The victim does not have to be of the opposite sex from the harasser.

Since 1976, the courts and the U.S. Equal Employment Opportunity Commission (EEOC) have defined sexual harassment as one form of sex discrimination. As such, it violates Title VII of the 1964 Civil Rights Act (42 U.S.C. §2000e-5-9) which guarantees that a person shall not be discriminated against in an employment setting because of race, color, religion, sex, or national origin.

In the workplace, sexual harassment occurs when a person who is in a position of authority or influence or can affect another person's job or career uses the position's authority to coerce the other person (male–female; female–male; female–female; male–male) into sexual acts or relations or punishes the person if he or she refuses to comply.

It is important that the organization's human resources handbook have policies and procedures to assist employees faced with this type of action. Such policy might read as follows:

> Unwelcome sexual advances, requests for sexual favors, and other verbal or physical conduct of a sexual nature constitute sexual harassment when (1) submission to such conduct is made either explicitly or implicitly a term or condition of an individual's employment, (2) submission or rejection of such conduct by an individual is used as the basis for employment decisions affecting such individuals, or (3) such conduct has the purpose or effect of unreasonably interfering with an individual's performance or creating an intimidating, hostile, or offensive environment.

Note: All policy statements developed should be reviewed by legal counsel before implementation of the policy.

The policy rests on three conditions established by the EEOC:

- Submission to the conduct is made as either an explicit or implicit condition of employment.
- Submission to or rejection of the conduct is used as the basis for an employment decision affecting the harassed employee.
- The harassment substantially interferes with an employee's work performance or creates an intimidating, hostile, or offensive work environment.

A sexually hostile work environment can be created by

- discussing sexual activities,
- unnecessary touching,
- commenting on physical attributes,
- displaying sexually suggestive pictures,
- using demeaning or inappropriate terms, such as "babe,"
- ostracizing workers of one gender by those of the other, or
- using crude and offensive language.

If you are sexualy harrassed, what should you do? Hoping the problem will go away or accepting it as "the way things are" only perpetuates and encourages such inappropriate behaviors. It is important that the organization outlines a similar procedure as follows: (1) report the incident immediately, (2) know your rights and the organization's policies and procedures, (3) keep a written, dated record of all incidents, and any witnesses, (4) consider confronting the harasser in person or writing the harasser a letter (i.e., outlining the facts of what has occurred, how you feel about the events, and what you want to happen next), and (5) evaluate your options and follow through.

False accusations of sexual harassment can be prevented if the following suggestions are taken seriously:

- Schedule one-on-one meetings in businesslike settings, preferably during the daytime.
- Leave doors open.
- Focus on the purpose of meeting.

- Respect the personal space of others.
- Limit touching to the conventional handshake.

The charge of sexual harassment is not to be taken lightly by a charging party, a respondent, or any member of the organization. Both the charging party and the respondent may anticipate a confidential, impartial review of the facts by the human resources manager.

Finally, all staff in positions of authority need to be sensitive to the hazards in personal relationships with subordinate employees. When significant disparities in age or authority are present between two individuals, questions about *professional responsibility* and the *mutuality of consent* to a personal relationship may well arise.

Americans With Disabilities Act

The Americans With Disabilities Act (ADA) Public Law 101-336 (July 26, 1990) provides certain protections for those with statutorily defined disabilities in the areas of: employment, government services, places of public accommodation, public transportation, and telecommunications. Health clubs, fitness and exercise facilities, health care provider offices, day care or social service establishments, as well as gymnasiums, health spas and other places of exercise or recreation are all covered under the ADA.

Disability means, with respect to an individual, a physical or mental impairment that substantially limits one or more of the major life activities of such individual, a record of such an impairment, or being regarded as having such an impairment. The phrase physical or mental impairment includes, but is not limited to, such contagious and non-contagious diseases and conditions as orthopedic, visual, speech, and hearing impairments, cerebral palsy, epilepsy, muscular dystrophy, multiple sclerosis, cancer, heart disease, diabetes, mental retardation, emotional illness, specific learning disabilities, HIV disease, tuberculosis, drug addiction, and alcoholism.

The phrase *major life activities* means functions such as caring for one's self, performing manual tasks, walking, seeing, hearing, speaking, breathing, learning, and working.

The phrase *has a record of such an impairment* means an individual has a history of or has been misclassified as having a mental or physical impairment that substantially limits one or more major life activities.

The ADA is a federal antidiscrimination statute designed to remove barriers which prevent qualified individuals with disabilities from enjoying the same employment opportunities that are available to persons without disabilities. Like the Civil Rights Act of 1964 that prohibits discrimination on the basis of race, color, religion, national origin, and sex, the ADA seeks to ensure access to equal employment opportunities based on merit. It does not guarantee equal results, establish quotas, or require preferences favoring individuals with disabilities over those without disabilities. Rather, it focuses on when an individual's disability creates a barrier to employment opportunities; the ADA requires employers to consider whether reasonable accommodation could remove the barrier. The ADA establishes a process in which the employer must assess a disabled individual's ability to perform the essential functions of the specific job held or desired. However, where that individual's functional limitation impedes such job performance, an employer must take steps to reasonably accommodate, and thus overcome the particular impediment, unless to do so would impose an undue hardship. Such accommodations usually take the form of adjustments to the way a job customarily is performed or to the work environment itself. An accommodation must be tailored to match the needs of the disabled individual with the needs of the job's essential functions.

Guidelines for Managing AIDS in the Workplace

HIV/AIDS is a serious health problem. Many people do not understand the disease and make certain inappropriate judgments. It is important for organizations to develop a response to AIDS in the workplace. The following principles are a starting point for the development of a policy relating to AIDS in the workplace (developed by the Citizens Commission on AIDS for New York City and Northern New Jersey):

- People with HIV/AIDS infection are entitled to the same rights and opportunities as people with other serious or life-threatening illnesses.
- Employment policies must, at a minimum, comply with federal, state, local laws and regulations.
- Employment policies should be based on the scientific and epidemiological evidence that people with HIV/AIDS infection do not pose a risk of transmission of the virus to coworkers through ordinary workplace contact.
- The highest levels of management and union leadership should unequivocally endorse nondiscriminatory employment policies and educational programs about HIV/AIDS.
- Employers and unions should communicate their support of these policies to workers in simple, clear, and unambiguous terms.
- Employers have a duty to protect the confidentiality of an employee's medical information.
- Employers and unions should undertake education for all employees in order to prevent work disruption and rejection by coworkers of an employee with HIV/AIDS.

- Employers should not require HIV/AIDS screening as part of general pre-employment or workplace physical examinations.
- In those special occupational settings where there may be a potential risk of exposure to HIV/AIDS (e.g., health care, exposure to blood or blood products), employers should provide specific, ongoing education and training, as well as the necessary equipment, to reinforce appropriate infection control procedures and ensure that they are implemented.

Summary

Human resource management is the key to a successful organization. A strong impartial set of human resources policies and procedures is critical to the health of an organization. This chapter has identified the steps to be taken when recruiting, hiring, training, motivating, and evaluating personnel; the appropriate policies to be developed regarding sexual harassment, ADA, and AIDS in the workplace; and the steps to improve employee and employer communication.

The Planning Process[1]

Thomas H. Sawyer

Planning is the process of determining an organization's goals and objectives and selecting a course of action to accomplish them within the environment inside and outside the organization. Its primary purpose is to offset future uncertainties by reducing the risk surrounding the organization's operations. It requires the organization to review its internal accomplishments (strengths) and challenges (weaknesses) and external opportunities and threats. During this process the organization will develop a SWOT chart (i.e., the depiction of internal strengths and weakness and external opportunities and threats) and identify internal and external connections that will allow the organization to become strategically competitive in the future (see Figure 3.1). Planning is essential for facility and event managers. The planning process is best facilitated by the use of brainstorming.

Instructional Objectives

After reading this chapter, the student should be able to

- describe the planning process,
- appreciate the planning process,
- identify the different types of plans that might exist in a typical enterprise,
- recount the importance of strategic planning,
- assess an enterprise's strengths and weaknesses
- recognize the 10 biggest pitfalls to successful planning
- recount the characteristics of a goal and an objective, and
- list some benefits of objectives.

Brainstorming

Brainstorming, developed by Alexander F. Osborn (1888-1966), involves forming a group of six to eight members who are presented a problem and asked to identify as many potential solutions as possible. The session usually lasts from 30 minutes to an hour. At least two days before a session, group members are given a one-page summary of the problem they are to consider (Hussey, 1991). There are four rules of brainstorming: (1) Criticism is prohibited—judgment of ideas must be withheld until all ideas have been generated. (2) "Freewheeling" is welcome—the wilder and further out the idea the better. It is easier to "tame down" than to "think up" ideas. (3) Quantity is wanted—the greater the number of ideas, the greater the likelihood of an outstanding solution. (4) Combination and improvement are sought—in addition to contributing ideas of their own, members are encouraged to suggest how the ideas of others can be improved or how two or more ideas can be combined into still another idea.

Business leaders all over the world have used brainstorming techniques to solve problems for many years. Brainstorming is time consuming. If you only have a short period of time to loosen up a group and get everyone talking about solutions to a problem or inventing new initiatives, the answer is "fun and games" brainstorming (Ensman, 1999).

Ensman's (1999) humorous, slightly offbeat techniques can be used to stimulate out-of-the-box thinking and discussion. They can be used to overcome marketing obstacles and productivity problems. They can help identify ways to enhance customer service, lower costs, improve an organization's image, and position an organization's operations for the future. Here are a few examples of "fun and games" brainstorming activities:

---

[1]This chapter has been reprinted with modifications with permission from Sagamore Publishing. It represents Chapter 17, Planning, Evaluation, and Control from Sawyer, T. H. (2001). *Employee Services Management: A Key Component of Human Resource Management.* Champaign, IL: Sagamore Publishing.

- **Castles in the sand**—The participants physically build a solution to the problem using blocks, putty, sand, or other materials.
- **Communication gaps**—Seat the participants in a circle. Whisper some variation of your current business problem into the ear of the first person sitting on the right in the circle. Ask that individual to repeat what was heard to the next person and so on until the message comes back around full circle. By that time, it will have changed—and the group may have a new perspective on the situation.
- **Detective work**—Appoint members of the group as detectives and charge them with solving the crime at hand. Group members must conduct an investigation, seek clues bearing on the problem, identify suspect causes of the problem, and eventually, pose a resolution of the case.
- **Make it worse**—Invite members of the group to imagine all the possible ways they could make the solution worse. In stark contrast to this humorous exercise, prospective solutions will probably abound.
- **Playmates**—Invite participants to bring a partner not connected to the group along to the brainstorming session and become part of the proceedings. Or invite members of the group to select imaginary playmates such as historical figures, celebrities, or competitors and conduct imaginary discussions about the issues at hand with these individuals.
- **Pretend**—Invite the members of the group to portray the customers, employees, or vendors involved with the issue at hand. Then, let these characters address the issue in their own words.

Figure 3.1
A Connections SWOT Chart

Internal Strengths List (accomplishments)	Internal Weaknesses List (challenges)
External Opportunities List	External Threats List

The best way to identify items under each category is through the use of brainstorming with the organization's employees and others outside the organization. The category "external opportunities" relates to those unique favorable circumstances that the organization might be able to take advantage of in the future. Whereas the external threat category refers to those circumstances that might be harmful to the organization if not carefully understood.

Conducting a Needs Assessment Survey

The success of a facility or event thrives on its ability to fulfill the needs of its employees. Many facility and event managers administer needs assessment surveys to gauge client or community needs. Needs assessment surveys can help pinpoint the factors that determine everything from if employees plan to use employee services programs to whether or not the programs fit their needs. Use needs assessment surveys to evaluate current services or to predict if patrons will use new programs. The most difficult aspect of coordinating a needs assessment survey is determining which information is needed to plan for the future of your facility or event (Busser, 1999).

Categories of Needs Assessment Information

Busser (1999) indicates there are eight major categories of information that can be collected through a needs assessment. Consider these categories of data collection to determine the information that will be needed: demographic data, user participation patterns or current levels of use, attitudes of employees, barriers to participation, predictions of future participation, appraisal of existing facilities and programs, health hazard appraisal, and areas of improvement.

Demographic Data—This includes all relevant information regarding the demographics of employees. Demographic data includes age, gender, marital status, residential location, number of family members living at home, number and ages of children, work shift, and job classification. Demographic data is useful in constructing a profile of the needs for particular groups of users or participants. For example, single users or participants may be interested in fitness activities while others with children may desire family programs. Use this information to focus your program development on the needs of that particular audience.

User Participation Patterns or Current Levels of Use—This category assesses the frequency of participation in existing programs and services. These data are useful in determining participation trends, i.e., examining if existing programs and services are under- or overutilized given the allocated resources and tracking changes in participation from year to year. This information is also valuable when you are faced with the need to purchase additional equipment or to justify requests for new facilities. Registration data is often used to construct participation trends. However, the patterns of facility and equipment use usually are not contained in registration data.

Attitudes of the Consumer—It is essential to identify the attitudes and beliefs of consumers regarding the prominent aspects of program plans. Attitudes are the consumers' feelings related to the importance of various issues or services. Consider addressing consumers' attitudes such as the value they place on family programs, child care, elder care, and the opportunity to socialize with fellow users (Busser, 1999). The determination of these attitudes may be beneficial in setting objectives and establishing priorities for the facility or event.

Barriers to Participation—Busser (1999) suggests the barriers to participation are the constraints that consumers perceive as preventing their participation in programs or services. One significant barrier to participation revolves around consumers' lack of awareness or knowledge that a program or service exists. Other potential barriers include work schedules, family responsibilities, lack of interest, and lack of convenience. If these and similar perceived barriers to participation are explored in a needs assessment, the programmer can resolve those issues that may prevent consumers from participating in programs and services and thereby increase the effectiveness of the facility or event.

Predictions of Future Participation—If the provider is more concerned with long-term planning, ask the respondents to project their future needs. This is a very useful category of needs identification when considering equipment purchases, constructing new facilities, or deliberating contractual arrangements to supplement the existing services and programs.

Appraisal of Existing Facilities and Programs—Give the consumers the opportunity to rate the quality of existing facilities, services, and programs. Use the feedback and evaluation data to prove the need for appropriate changes. In addition, this information provides insight into the current level of consumer satisfaction with the association.

Health Hazard Appraisal—Health hazard appraisals are standardized instruments used to evaluate the current health status of consumers and to estimate the presence of potential risk factors that are predictors for disease. Risk factors include smoking, stress, family history of disease, high blood pressure, high cholesterol, and poor nutrition. The health hazard appraisal evaluates a respondent's risks compared to national statistics on the causes of death, the consumer's medical history and lifestyle. Comparisons are then made with others in the same age and gender group. Use the results of the appraisal to explain specific recommendations to an employee. Results can also indicate potential areas for the development of services and programs.

Areas for Improvement—This component of a needs assessment provides employees with the opportunity to share suggestions or issues related to the association and its programs, services, facilities, policies, and procedures. This willingness to go to the employees for their opinions fosters a dialogue, which indicates a commitment on the part of the association to resolve problems and to provide quality programs (Busser, 1999).

Collecting Data on Needs

Once the facility or event manager has determined the kind of information he or she would like to uncover from the needs assessment, the next step is to collect the data. There are many research methods available to collect data on needs. Using research methods to conduct a needs assessment requires specific knowledge and skills in order to ensure that the data collected is valid and reliable. The validity of a needs assessment refers to the degree to which the information collected accurately portrays the needs of employees. For example, a needs assessment that focuses only on satisfaction with special events is not a valid assessment of overall satisfaction with the facility or event and should not be used as such.

Reliability is concerned with the consistency of the data. Consistency indicates that the information obtained through the assessment truly represents the employees' perspective and is not influenced by outside factors. For example, a needs assessment that asks for overall program satisfaction may obtain different responses if conducted in the summer versus the winter, especially if a strong summer activities program is offered and no activities are provided in the winter. If the planner wants to determine comprehensive levels of satisfaction, the reliability of this assessment is doubtful. While several methods of data collection are appropriate for needs assessment, we will focus on the survey (Busser, 1999).

Surveys

Surveys provide the greatest opportunity to solicit consumer input and to generalize the findings from a smaller group of consumers to the community as a whole. Surveys require expertise from knowledgeable individuals to implement them successfully. Consider consulting the local and state chamber of commerce or a market research firm. There are five steps in the survey process: (1) an operational definition of the purpose of the survey, (2) the design and pretesting of data collection instruments (e.g., the questionnaire or the interview guide), (3) the selection of a community sample, (4) the data collection, and (5) an analysis of the data (Busser, 1999).

The design of the questionnaire includes the development of the specific questions to be answered by consumers and decisions concerning the form of the questions (e.g., multiple choice, fill in the blank). At this stage, determine the directions for completing the survey, the procedures for carrying out the survey, and the method of returning completed questionnaires. Pretesting the data collection instrument is essential to uncovering and eliminating any difficulties that may exist in the data collection procedure. Pretests are mini-surveys you can conduct with a small group of employees by administering them the questionnaire and asking them to identify any difficulties in understanding directions, questions, or the type of information solicited (Busser, 1999).

Sampling is the use of particular procedures that allow you to generalize the findings of a representative small group of consumers to the whole corporate workforce. By selecting employees through a random process (e.g., selecting every 10th person from a random listing of employees), the results of the assessment are likely to be representative of the needs of all employees, even though all consumers were not surveyed (Busser, 1999).

In collecting the data from consumers, it is important that the cover letter of the questionnaire explains the purpose of the survey and indicates that the contributed information will be kept confidential. It is the ethical responsibility of those individuals conducting the survey to ensure anonymity for respondents. After sending the questionnaire to consumers, follow up with phone calls, memos, or other methods to continue to solicit the return of surveys. To be considered sufficiently representative, at least 35 percent of the surveys must be completed and returned. Try offering incentives to increase the return rate. For example, the organization could offer consumers a discount on programs or purchases in the pro shop for completing and returning the survey (Busser, 1999).

Once the provider has collected and tabulated the data, it can be analyzed. The frequencies and percentages of responses to particular questions may reveal significantly desirable information. The data should be carefully analyzed to answer the questions and purpose of the survey. These results, then, become the basis for decision-making regarding the needs of employees and the provided programs and services.

Developing a Needs Assessment Report

Compile a needs assessment report and present it to management. The most appropriate method of sharing this report is to compile tables, graphs, and statistics in a manner that is easily understood. Provide a comprehensive report to management and an executive summary to interested consumers. The report should consist of the following components (Busser, 1999):

- Title page
- Executive summary (i.e., a short introductory summary of the entire report to allow the reader a quick overview of the report prior to reading the entire report)
- Introduction to the needs assessment study purpose
- Overview of methods and procedures
- Results
- Conclusions and recommendations

The Steps in the Planning Process

Six steps involved in the planning process are identifying internal and external connections and relationships, establishing objectives, developing premises, decision-making, implementing a course of action, and evaluating the results (Wright, 1994).

Step 1: Identifying Internal and External Connections and Relationships
The initial step in the planning process is identifying internal strengths (accomplishments) and weaknesses (challenges), and external opportunities and threats (concerns). This information is placed into a SWOT analysis chart, which will assist in the identification of connections and relationships relating to the internal organizational environment and external environment.

Step 2: Establishing Objectives
The next step in the planning process is the establishment of organization objectives. Objectives are an essential starting point as they provide direction for all other managerial activities. Objectives are generally based on perceived opportunities that exist in an organization's surrounding environment.

Step 3: Developing Premises
Once organizational objectives have been established, developing premises about the future environment in which they are to be accomplished is essential. This basically involves forecasting events or conditions likely to influence objective attainment.

Step 4: Decision-Making
After establishing objectives and developing premises, the next step is selecting the best course of action for accomplishing stated objectives from the possible alternatives. There are three phases of decision-making: (1) available alternatives must be identified, (2) each alternative must be evaluated in light of the premises about the future and the external environment, and (3) the alternative with the highest estimated probability of success should be selected.

Step 5: Implementing a Course of Action
Once a plan of action has been adopted, it must be implemented. Plans alone are no guarantee of success. Managers must initiate activities that will translate these plans into action.

Step 6: Evaluating the Results
Plans and their implementation must be constantly monitored and evaluated. All managers are responsible for the evaluation of planning outcomes. Comparing actual results with those projected and refining plans are both necessary.

Classification of Plans

Plans can be viewed from a number of different perspectives. From the viewpoint of application, plans can be classified in terms of functional areas (e.g., marketing plans, production plans, human resource management plans, financial plans). Plans may also be classified according to the period of time over which they are projected (e.g., short- or long-range) or with respect to their frequency of use (standing versus single-use). The nature of functional plans is evident. However, further explanation is needed for period of time and frequency of use plans.

Short- and long-range plans are the most popular classification of plans. In practice, however, the terms short-range and long-range have no precise meaning, but rather express relative periods of time. These plans are interrelated in at least two respects. First, they compete for the allocation of resources. Consequently, there can be a dangerous tendency to sacrifice long-term results for short-term gains. Second, short-range plans should be compatible with long-range plans. It is usually difficult, if not impossible, for long-range plans to succeed unless short-range plans are accomplished. Thus, both are important in achieving an organization's objectives.

The term short-range is often titled "operational" in many organizations and long-term has been changed to "applied strategic." These terms will be used interchangeably throughout the remainder of the chapter.

There are three criteria most often used in determining the length of a plan: (1) how far into the future an organization's commitments extend; (2) how much uncertainty is associated with the future; and (3) how much lead time is required to ready a good or service for sale (Paley, 1991).

Planning by most effective organizations is often done on a "rolling" basis. This simply means that those organizations that develop applied strategic plans for a five-year period and two-year operational plans are updating both plans on an annual basis. As the current year of a five-year plan closes, it is extended or rolled forward to include a new fifth year. This procedure allows an organization to revise its plans on the basis of new information and to maintain a degree of flexibility in its commitments. A general guideline is to refrain from formalizing plans until a final commitment is absolutely necessary (Fogg, 1994).

Standing plans are used again and again. The focus is on managerial situations that recur repeatedly. Standing plans include policies, procedures, and rules.

Policies are general statements that serve to guide decision-making. They are plans in that they prescribe parameters within which certain decisions are to be made. Policies set limits, but they are subject to interpretation because they are broad guidelines. Table 3.1 provides examples of policies. Notice that each example is purposefully broad and only provides a general guideline subject to managerial discretion. However, each statement does prescribe parameters for decision-making and, thus, sets limits to the actions of organization members.

A procedure is a series of related steps that are to be followed in an established order to achieve a given purpose. Procedures prescribe exactly what actions are to be taken in a specific situation. Procedures are similar to policies in that both are intended to influence certain decisions. They are different in that policies address themselves to single decisions while procedures address themselves to a sequence of related decisions. Table 3.2 shows how an organization might write procedures for processing a bill of sale.

Rules are different from policies and procedures in that they specify what personal conduct is required of an individual. Stated differently, rules are standing plans that either prescribe or prohibit action by specifying what an individual may or may not do in a given situation. Therefore, the statements "eye goggles must be worn," "no swimming alone," "no smoking," "no drinking on premises" are all

Table 3.1
Examples of Policies

Customer Service:	It is the policy of this organization to provide customers with the finest service possible within the limits of sound financial principles. [Interpretation = What are the limits of sound finance?]
Employee Benefits:	It is the policy of this organization to provide its employees with acceptable working conditions and an adequate living wage. [Interpretation = What is acceptable and adequate?]
Promotion From Within:	It is the policy of this organization to promote qualified employees from within organization ranks whenever possible. [Interpretation = What is meant by qualified or possible?]
Gifts From Suppliers or Vendors:	It is the policy of this organization that no employee shall accept any gift from any supplier or vendor unless it is of nominal value. [Interpretation = What is nominal?]

Table 3.2
Procedure for Processing a Bill of Sale

Step 1:   Prior to recording, all non-cash sales will be forwarded to the credit department for approval.

Step 2:   Following necessary credit approval, all bills of sale will be presented to production scheduling for an estimated product completion date.

Step 3:   Subsequent to production scheduling, all bills of sale will be delivered to the accounting department where they will be recorded.

Step 4:   Pursuant to their processing in the accounting department, all bills of sale will be filed with the shipping department within 24 hours.

examples of rules. Rules are usually accompanied by specifically stated penalties that vary according to the seriousness of the offense and number of previous violations. Unlike policies that guide, but do not eliminate discretion, rules leave little room for interpretation. The only element of choice associated with a rule is whether it applies in a given situation. Of the three forms of standing plans discussed, rules are the simplest and most straightforward. They are without question the narrowest in scope and application.

Single-use plans are specifically developed to implement courses of action that are relatively unique and are unlikely to be repeated. Three principal forms of single-use plans are budgets, programs, and projects.

A budget is a plan that deals with the future allocation and utilization of various resources to different activities over a given time period. Budgets are perhaps most frequently thought of in financial terms. However, they also are used to plan allocation and utilization of labor, raw materials, floor space, machine hours, and so on. A budget simply is a tool that managers use to translate future plans into numerical terms. Further, they are a method for controlling an organization's operations.

Programs are typically intended to accomplish a specific objective within a fixed time. Table 3.3 offers six guidelines for effective program development.

Table 3.3
Guidelines for Effective Program Development

1. Divide the overall program into parts, each with a clearly defined purpose.
2. Study the necessary sequence and relationships between the resulting parts.
3. Assign appropriate responsibility for each part to carefully selected individuals or groups.
4. Determine and allocate the resources necessary for the completion of each part.
5. Estimate the completion time required for each part.
6. Establish target dates for the completion of each part.

Projects are usually a subset or component part of a specific program. Accordingly, projects often share some of the same characteristics with the overall programs of which they are a part. Projects are less complex than their supporting programs and are, by definition, narrower in scope. Table 3.4 summarizes the various standing and single-use plans.

Strategic Planning

Strategic planning, unlike operational planning which focuses on more direct aspects of operating an organization, focuses on an organization's long-term relationship to its environment (Wright, Pringle, Kroll, & Parnell, 1994). The strategic plan should be developed through the participatory involvement by all members of the organization and its clients. By focusing on an organization as a total system, strategic planning recognizes that all organizations face many uncontrollable elements within the environment. Competitors' actions, economic conditions, regulatory groups, labor unions, and changing customer preferences represent factors over which an organization achieves its objectives. Therefore, strategic planning concerns itself with shaping an organization so it can accomplish its goals. A strategic plan attempts to answer such questions as (Antoniou, 1994):

- What is the organization's business and what should it be?
- What business should the organization be in five years from now? Ten years?
- Who are the organization's customers and who should they be?
- Should the organization try to grow in this business or grow primarily in other businesses?

Table 3.4
Summary of Standing and Single-Use Plans

Type	Definition	Example
Standing Plans		
Policy	A general statement that guides decision making.	"Preference will be given to hiring persons with disabilities."
Procedure	A series of related steps that are to be followed in an established order to achieve a given purpose.	Filing for travel expenses reimbursement.
Rule	A statement that either prescribes or prohibits action by specifying what an individual may or may not do in a specific situation.	"No eating at work stations."
Single-Use Plans		
Budget	A plan that deals with the future allocation and utilization of various resources to different enterprise activities over a given time.	The allocation and utilization of machine hours.
Program	A plan typically intended to accomplish a specific objective within a fixed time.	A membership recruitment program.
Project	A subset or component part of a specific program.	A telemarketing project.

Objectives

Objectives are those ends that an organization seeks to achieve by its existence and operation. There are two essential characteristics of an objective: (1) objectives are predetermined, and (2) objectives describe *future* desired results toward which *present* efforts are directed. There are eight key result areas in which all organizations should establish objectives—market share, innovation, productivity, physical and financial resources, profitability, manager performance and development, worker performance and attitude, and social responsibilities (Drucker, 1988).

There are two ways to establish objectives. The first is the entrepreneurial method. Entrepreneurs establish objectives in the entrepreneurial method (top management or stockholders). An organization's objectives are defined as the entrepreneur's objectives. The entrepreneur ensures that employees' actions are consistent with these objectives by paying them salaries, bonuses, or pensions to support the goals.

The second method is the consensual method. In this method the objectives of an organization are established by the general consent of those concerned. Organization members share in setting the objectives and, thus, eliminate conflict by identifying common or consensual goals.

The Planning Premise

Once enterprise objectives have been established, developing planning premises about the future environment in which they are to be accomplished is essential (Hoffman, 1993; Hamel and Prahalad, 1994). Unfolding environmental conditions almost invariably influence enterprise objectives, forcing modifications in both current and anticipated activities. Premises, which attempt to describe what the future will be like, provide a framework for identifying, evaluating, and selecting a course of action for accomplishing enterprise objectives.

The applied strategic plan is composed of a situational analysis; highlights, introduction; vision statement(s); value(s); mission statement; internal environment; external environment; connections; major action plans; major action priorities; monitoring and evaluating; and review, approval, and commitment (Goodstein, 1993). The *situational analysis* has five sections including a description of the geographical location and pertinent demographics (e.g., population, economic indicators, industry, average income, etc.), a description of the organization, a SWOT summary, an overview of major strategies and plans, and an organization progress since last review.

The *highlights* section describes major challenges, customer/client needs, and major accomplishments. The *introduction* provides the reader with a brief description of the planning process and the people involved in the process. The *vision statement* describes the dream of the future for the organization. The *values* section describes that which is desirable or worthy of esteem by the organization (e.g., fostering a "we care" image with our clients). The *mission statement* is a statement outlining the purpose and mission of the organization. The *internal environment* is composed of a description of the organization's strengths (accomplishments) and weaknesses (challenges) and the *external environment* consists of a description of the organization's external opportunities and threats (concerns). After the internal and external environments have been analyzed, a series of *connections* are established based on the relationships found in the analysis. From the connections, a series of *major action plans* are established. The actions plans are then translated into *major action priorities.* These major action priorities are the foundation for the one- or two-year operational plan. The applied strategic plan must have established *monitoring and evaluating* procedures in place to assure the proper implementation of the plan. Finally, there must be *review, approval, and commitment* steps established for the final acceptance of the plan.

The operational plan includes the following components: major action priorities, problems, project summary, priority issue(s), background, vision of success, goals and objectives of the plan, and action plans (strategies, objectives, baseline data, and action steps).

Each major action priority will have a specific *problem(s)* that will be resolved at the completion of the project. The *project summary* describes briefly the project that will be undertaken by the organization. Each project will have one or more *priority issues* to be tackled during the project. Each major action priority will have a section that outlines the historical significance of the issue(s) relating to the action priority. This section is called *background.* The authors of the operational plan will describe a *vision of success* for each major action priority. Each major action priority will have one or more *goals* and a series of *objectives* for each goal.

Each major action priority has an *action plan.* The action plan can have one or more strategies, which can have one or more objectives. Each action plan has baseline data to be used to compare what was with what is. This comparison over the years will establish progress. For each action plan, there will be a series of action steps. Each action step will outline the resources to be used to complete the step, who's responsible for the completion of each step, and when the project will start and end.

Pitfalls of Planning

Strategic planning is a process requiring great skill (see Table 3.5 for tips for writing plans). It can be frustrating and require a great deal of time. An inability to predict the future can create anxiety and feelings of inadequacy. The 10 biggest pitfalls to successful planning are (Nolan, 1993; Poirier, 1996):

- Top management assuming that it can delegate its planning function and, thus, not become directly involved.
- Top management becoming so involved in current problems that it spends insufficient time on planning. As a consequence, planning becomes discredited at lower levels.
- Failing to clearly define and develop enterprise goals as a basis for formulating long-range goals.
- Failing to adequately involve major line managers in the planning process.
- Failing to actually use plans as a standard for assessing managerial performance.
- Failing to create a congenial and supportive climate for planning.
- Assuming that comprehensive planning is something separate from other aspects of the management process.
- Creating a planning program that lacks flexibility and simplicity and fails to encourage creativity.
- Top management failing to review and evaluate long-range plans that have been developed by department and division heads.
- Top management making intuitive decisions that conflict with formal plans.

A Guide to Benchmarking

Hauglie (1997) described benchmarking as a process used to identify gaps between company A's performance and other industry "best practices." Practitioners across the world are continuously improving their programs and processes to create more value for their customers. If employee services programs align with the company's vision, mission, and values and identify customer's needs, the programs are usually successful at making incremental improvements. However, if benchmarking is used as a tool, process improvements can be greatly accelerated to achieve superior performance and enhance the company's ability to gain a competitive edge.

It is recommended that those interested in benchmarking as a tool for making change answer the following questions:

- Are there key services or processes that require accelerated improvements?
- What is the cost in time and resources to benchmark?
- What is the cost of not doing it?
- Are management and employees ready and willing to make substantial changes based on benchmarking results?
- Can a dedicated team be assembled with the right skills and enthusiasm to take on a project of this magnitude?

Table 3.5
Tips for Writing Plans

The following are a few tips that may assist the organization planner in preparing the applied strategic or operational plans:

✓ Include a table of contents describing the overall content and organization of the plan, including page numbers.

✓ Format the plan consistently using the same style for sections, subsections, headings, and subheadings, etc., with a consistent use of numbers or letters for headings.

✓ Number all pages. Number the pages consecutively.

✓ Spell out and define all acronyms so that readers unfamiliar with the organizations, programs, and operations will understand the plan.

✓ Write clearly and concisely, with short declarative sentences and active verbs.

✓ Order the plan elements, provide cross-references when necessary, and develop a topic or subject index so that a reader can follow major ideas and themes throughout the document.

✓ Make all references to other documents, plans, or reports clear and specific enough to allow a reader to easily find the item or section referenced.

✓ Include in an appendix any information that is not critical to understanding the plan, but which provides useful background or context.

✓ Structure the plan in a way that will permit sections to be excerpted and distributed to specific audiences, and that will permit changes, edits, or updates without revising the whole plan.

✓ Test the understandability of the document by having it reviewed by individuals who were not directly involved in its development.

✓ On each section, type its computer file name (to speed retrieval in the future). In addition, during the draft process, include date/time code (to keep track of the most up-to-date revision). During the draft process, it helps to also hand-write the draft (revision) number in the corner as each revision is printed or to establish a watermark (Draft Document 1).

There are six common steps in benchmarking and they are: determining what to benchmark; preparing to benchmark; conducting research; selecting with whom to benchmark; collecting and sharing information; and analyzing, adapting, and improving. The first step, determining what to benchmark, is critical to the entire process. The manager must review carefully all products and services provided to ascertain which ones need to be compared to benchmarks for purposes of improvement. The manager answers seven basic questions in this process: (1) Which aspects of the service are excellent? (2) Which aspects are above average? (3) Which aspects are average? (4) Which aspects are below average? (5) Which aspects are poor? (6) Which aspects are very important? (7) Which aspects are not important?

The second step is to prepare to benchmark. It is important to baseline current services for two reasons: (1) to identify weaknesses or gaps that can be concentrated upon, and (2) to identify strengths.

Next, the manager or team conducts research to select the organizations that are comparable in size and function and that have outstanding services in this specific area and to gather information about each of these companies and their services.

In step four the benchmark companies and programs will be chosen from the list prepared in step three. In this step a short questionnaire (pilot study) is prepared to ascertain which companies have excelled in this particular service. After reviewing the returns, the benchmark group will be selected from the results.

The next step is to collate all information about the benchmarked companies and programs, visit the companies and programs (on-site) to gather additional information, and share all the information gathered with the team, management, and the other companies.

Finally, the data is analyzed and discussed among the team members and recommendations for modification are prepared and communicated.

Effective Delegation in the Planning Process

Do any of these statements sound familiar? "If you want something done right, do it yourself!" "It will take me more time to explain it to you than if I do it myself!" "It is easier and faster for me to do it, so I will do it!"

One of the traps a manager falls into is *perfectionism* (i.e., feeling as though he or she is the only person who can work with a special supplier, handle a ticklish situation or create the promotional materials for a program). A manager is much more effective if he or she teaches others how to do various tasks and then supervises their efforts. It is impossible to do everything equally well when one is spread too thin.

Effective delegation requires that the delegator: (1) state a clear objective, (2) determine guidelines for the project, (3) set any limitations or constraints, (4) grant the person the authority to carry out the assignment, (5) set the deadline for its completion, and (6) decide the best means for the person to provide regular progress reports (e.g., oral or written; weekly, monthly, semi-annually, or annually). Further, the manager can employ any one of seven levels of delegation: (1) Decide and take action, you need not check back with me. (2) Decide and take action, but let me know what you did. (3) Decide and let me know your decision, then take action unless I say not to. (4) Decide and then let me know your decision, but wait for my go ahead. (5) Decide what you would do, but tell me your alternatives with the pros and cons of each. (6) Look into this problem and give me the facts. I will decide. (7) Wait to be told.

Finally, there are five common reasons why managers fail to delegate. They are: (1) nobody does it better, (2) guilt, (3) insecurity, (4) lack of trust, and (5) takes time.

Planning Teams ... Friend or Foe?

If a planning team is formed the right way it can accelerate the planning process, reduce the time to complete a plan, and reduce operating costs. But if it is done incorrectly, just the opposite can happen. There are number of wrong reasons for initiating a team approach to planning, including (1) a belief that teams will produce better results automatically; (2) it is the popular thing to do; (3) we have downsized and have fewer managers; and (4) we have downsized and have fewer employees (Wilbur, 1999).

However, there are a number of right reasons to consider utilizing teams including (1) an organizational belief in creating an environment where people can give their best, (2) an increase in the flexibility of the organization, and (3) an organization's structure is already suited to a team approach.

There are two categories of teams—performance and problem solving. Performance teams are structured around work processes. The members are employees who have been hired to do the work. It is a permanent structure of the organization and operates on a daily basis. Participation on the team is mandatory. The team establishes its mission, identifies key performance indicators, measures and monitors performance, solves problems, removes barriers to performance, and holds itself accountable for high levels of performance. Further, the team is empowered to change work processes and has decision-making authority within boundaries. Finally, the team requires training in identifying customers, performance measurement, work process evaluation, team leadership, problem solving, group dynamics, and coaching.

While the problem-solving team is structured around expertise in the problem area, its members are hand selected for their expertise in the problem area. It has a temporary structure that is disbanded after the problem is solved. It represents extra work for those assigned. Participation is voluntary. The team is provided a mandate outlining the problem to be solved. It uses a systematic approach to problem solving. Further, the team makes recommendations for change and has no decision-making authority. Finally, the team requires training in complex problem solving.

Transforming a group of people into a team requires the following:

• Management values individual initiative and high levels of employee participation versus maintaining the status quo.
• Employees are eager to learn and welcome the opportunity for training.
• Employees have a "we can solve anything" attitude.
• Accountability is based on process and results.
• Performance management systems are aligned with and support teams.
• Management is willing to walk the talk.
• Strong team values are established.

Sample team values include: perform with enthusiasm; share time, resources, and ideas with each other; consult together to achieve unity of thought and action; listen to each other, encourage, clarify points of view, ask questions and support other coworkers' opinions; continuous improvement in work and in learning; do things right the first time; will not initiate or receive gossip; use appropriate channels to express disagreement/concern; work through problems and look for win-win solutions; and be tough on problems, easy on people.

In Chart 3.1, Wilbur (1999) describes common team problems and how to solve them.

Chart 3.1
Common Team Problems and How to Solve Them

Problem	Solution
Too much time spent in meetings	One hour a week set aside for a meeting
Lots of responsibility, no authority	Clarify boundaries and level of authority
Lack of direction	Management sets clear direction
Over/under-empowerment	Empowerment tied to competency level
Unclear purpose	Clarify mission and performance objectives
Lack of training	Provide necessary training
Withdrawal of management support	Build team structure to sustain itself

Summary

The need for planning stems from the fact that virtually all enterprises operate in a changing environment. The uncertainty resulting from environmental change makes planning a necessity in all but the simplest circumstances. This chapter has identified the phases of the planning process, commented on the importance of planning, examined the scope and application of different types of enterprise plans, introduced the concept of strategic planning and discussed pitfalls in planning.

The planning process is composed of six repetitive and interactive phases that must be considered simultaneously. During each phase, an enterprise should look ahead and back to determine how other phases affect implementation at a particular time. The six phases of the planning process are: (1) identifying internal and external connections and relationships, (2) establishing objectives, (3) developing premises, (4) decision-making, (5) implementing a course of action, and (6) evaluating results.

Planning is important for at least four basic reasons: (1) it helps enterprises succeed, (2) it provides direction and a sense of purpose, (3) it helps managers cope with change, and (4) it contributes to the performance of other managerial functions. Plans can be classified in terms of (1) functional areas (i.e., marketing plans, production plans, personnel plans, financial plans, and so forth); (2) period of time (i.e., short- versus long-range); and (3) frequency of use (i.e., standing versus single-use). Strategic planning is important because it serves to define an enterprise's overall character, mission, and direction.

The assessment of an enterprise's strengths and weaknesses involves considering a range of factors related to a specific industry and the positioning of a company within the industry.

Objectives are predetermined and stated in advance and describe future desired results toward which present efforts are directed. Objectives serve as: (1) guidelines for action, (2) constraints, (3) a source of legitimacy, (4) standards of performance, and (5) a source of motion.

Chapter 4

Planning Facilities: Master Plan, Site Selection, and Development Phases

Thomas H. Sawyer and Michael G. Hypes

Anyone who has been involved in facility planning and development understands that errors are common during the planning and development process. The challenge is to complete a facility project with the fewest number of errors. Before becoming too deeply involved in the planning and development process, it is important to review some of the common errors that have been made in the past (Conklin, 1999). Conklin (1999); Farmer, Mulrooney, & Ammon (1996); Frost, Lockhart, & Marshall (1988); and Horine & Stotlar (2002) suggest these errors include, but are not limited to (see photos on next page): (1) failure to provide adequate and appropriate accommodations for persons with disabilities throughout the facility; (2) failure to provide adequate storage spaces; (3) failure to provide adequate janitorial spaces; (4) failure to observe desirable current professional standards; (5) failure to build the facility large enough to accommodate future uses; (6) failure to provide adequate locker and dressing areas for both male and female users; (7) failure to construct shower, toilet, and dressing rooms with sufficient floor slope and properly located drains; (8) failure to provide doorways, hallways, or ramps so that equipment may be moved easily; (9) failure to provide for multiple uses of facilities; (10) failure to plan for adequate parking for the facility; (11) failure to plan for adequate space for concessions and merchandising; (12) failure to provide for adequate lobby space for spectators; (13) failure to provide for an adequate space for the media to observe activities as well as to interview performers; (14) failure to provide for adequate ticket sales areas; (15) failure to provide adequate space for a loading dock and parking for tractor trailers and buses; (16) failure to provide adequate numbers of restroom facilities for female spectators; (17) failure to provide adequate security and access control into the facility and within the facility; (18) failure to provide adequate separation between activities (buffer or safety zones) in a multipurpose space; (19) failure to provide padding on walls close to activity area, padding and/or covers for short fences, on goal posts, and around trees; (20) failure to plan for the next 50 years; (21) failure to plan for maintenance of the facility; (22) failure to plan for adequate supervision of the various activity spaces within the facility; and (23) failure to plan to plan.

Instructional Objectives

After reading this chapter, the student should be able to

- appreciate the process used for designing a facility,
- understand the composition of a master plan,
- prepare a program statement,
- understand the roles of selected professionals in the planning process,
- discuss the function of the predevelopment guide,
- describe the process involved in site selection,
- understand the various facility development stages,
- describe what construction documents consist of,
- outline the bidding process, and
- describe the construction phase.

Planning Facilities/Venues for Health, Fitness, Physical Activity, Recreation, and Sports

The planning process defined in this chapter should be used for planning any of the following facilities/venues: stadiums for baseball, football, soccer, softball, or track and field; arenas for basketball, football, or ice hockey; gymnasiums for public schools, colleges and universities, YM/WCAs; or Boys' and Girls' clubs; natatoriums; outdoor aquatic centers; municipal parks and recreation areas; skateboard parks; adventure areas including rope courses, challenge courses and climbing walls, and combative areas. Further, the process should include a planning committee, a master plan, predevelopment review, a facility checklist, site selection, and development phases.

Do's

This is an example of proper use of safety fencing for a baseball or softball shelter. Notice the four-foot fence is covered with a protective cover.

This is an example of proper use of a protective covering for a short fence that provides a greater measure of safety for the players.

This is a good example of proper design with a warning track, eight-foot fence with protective covering and a wind screen.

Don'ts

This is an example of an unsafe fence without a protective covering for a short fence.

This is an example of a proper 10-foot safety buffer zone, but with an unprotected wall. This wall should be covered with mats under the basket.

This is an example of poor planning with the exit doors located directly behind the basketball.

Development of a Master Plan

Master planning is a decision-making process that promotes changes that will accommodate new needs and search for ways to improve existing conditions. The master plan is very critical during periods of limited resources. The process of planning can and does change attitudes about the needs and utilization of current assets, as well as provides a way for communicating with the stakeholders (Hewitt, 1997).

The master planning process requires coordination and integration of program, financial, and physical planning. Such planning is cyclical in nature and requires the development of procedures and schedules implemented by the expertise of strategic and master planning staff to ensure that the various activities occur in the proper sequence (Hewitt, 1997) (see Figure 4.1).

Figure 4.1
Facilities Master Plan

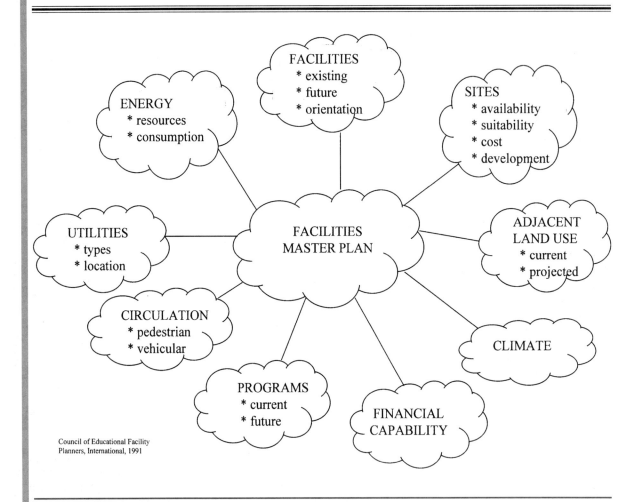

Council of Educational Facility
Planners, International, 1991

Another important characteristic of the master planning process is its ability to respond to changing needs. It must be a flexible and dynamic plan so that it is easy to amend, taking into consideration future projections as reflected by the realities of the present. This means the process is more important than the product (Hewitt, 1997).

Master planning is a process structured to promote cost-effective development decisions that best serve the goals and objectives of the organization. The process operates on the premise that the development of facilities and their ongoing management can best serve specific program needs if the organization's standards of space planning, facilities programming, design, and construction management are closely linked (Hewitt, 1997).

Typical Phases of a Master Plan

The master plan can be used to answer three common questions often raised: Where are we? Where do we want to go? How do we get there? This approach is flexible to allow the individual organization to reflect local conditions, priorities, and emphases.

Establishment of an Ad Hoc Program Committee and a Plan for Planning

The organization's ad hoc planning advisory committee (sometimes called the program committee) should be composed of the following members:

- program specialists
- end users
- financial consultants
- maintenance personnel
- community representatives
- management representatives
- facility consultants

The role of the planning advisory committee includes representing all the organization's constituencies; overseeing and reviewing the ongoing work; communicating with the various stakeholders the work in progress, findings, and results; validating the process; resolving unsettled issues; and endorsing the results and forwarding the master plan for approval.

The committee should be assisted by the office staff within the organization, who should keep the senior administration advised of the ongoing work, coordinate and schedule the planning efforts, serve as committee recorder, assist in communicating the ongoing work to the stakeholders, and represent the committee at planning work sessions and related meetings.

Organization Briefings and Initiation of Organization Master Plan Studies

The committee should organize and schedule information meetings to (a) notify the organization and the community of the organization's planning activity, purpose, method, and schedule; (b) solicit immediate concerns, comments, and suggestions; (c) encourage participation in the planning process and identify organization or community issues; and (d) identify the planning staff who will be available for further discussions of these and related matters.

Identification and Confirmation of the Organization's Goals and Objectives

Now detailed planning can begin with three concurrent studies—development of an organization profile, identification of capital improvements, and analysis of existing conditions. The development of the organization's program statement is intended to generally describe the organization's niche (see Figure 4.2). The statement should include, but not be limited to: brief history of the organization; organization's mission; organization's programs, products, and services; administrative structure; critical issues and strategic responses; goals and objectives for the organization; details about clientele; an outline of short-range planning, mid-range planning; and long-range planning, and other programmatic features that help describe the organization as a distinctive operational entity (see Figure 4.3). Finally, the statement should conclude with a descriptive overview of how the existing situation is expected to change strategically during the period covered by the proposed organization master plan and the implications and consequences such changes may have on the physical development of the organization.

It is important to compile a 10-year listing of projected capital improvements for the organization. Capital improvement items should include buildings, landscape, circulation (i.e., pedestrian and vehicular traffic), infrastructure (i.e., chilled air, electricity, roadways, sewage, sidewalks, steam, telecommunications, water, etc.), land acquisition, and actions that will change and modify the existing physical plant (e.g., new state highway right-of-way).

The objective of the survey of existing conditions is to discover and describe elements that, in combination, typically help create, inform, and/or express the organization as a physical place designed and operated as an organization for a specific purpose and located in a setting that has tangible physical characteristics. Certain items should be identified and defined in graphic and narrative formats so as to describe location, function, and physical character of elements. Such items include land ownership, land forms and topography; microclimate, soils and related subsurface conditions; recreational, social, and cultural patterns; land use; building use; buildings rated by physical condition; building entrances, exits, and service points; pedestrian and vehicular circulation systems; public transportation; parking; landscapes; ecological and natural settings, views, vistas, and related design features; major utilities by location, type, and condition; site history and heritage; site and building accessibility; and site and building problems.

Synthesis and Evaluation of Findings

After establishing an ad hoc planning advisory committee, completing briefings and initiating plan studies, and identifying and confirming master plan goals and objectives, it is time to synthesize and evaluate those findings. This effort should begin to clarify issues and opportunities that should be addressed by the organization and should establish and confirm the direction of the master plan. The issues and opportunities that should surface during the synthesis and evaluation effort relate to the following:

- The organization's image.
- A sense of place for the improvements.
- Existing and new initiatives that may require new building(s) and infrastructure, improvements and revitalization of existing physical resources, and potential demolition.

Figure 4.2
Program Statement

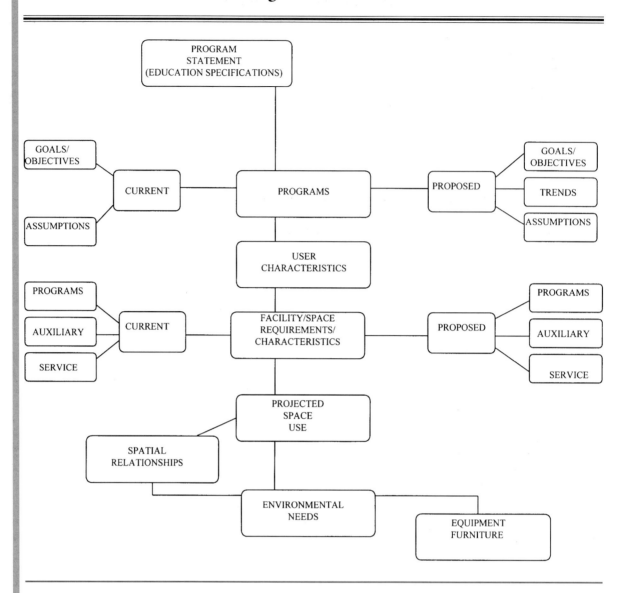

- Expansion of present facilities should occur only after careful and thorough evaluation of projected needs and capabilities of existing facilities.
- Once needs are established, the following approaches, listed in priority order, are generally considered the most appropriate way to proceed with the program requirements: (1) higher usage of existing space, (2) renovation of existing structures, (3) infill (i.e., adding vertically or horizontally to existing structures), and (4) expansion of facilities into new areas on the organization's site.

The master plan, during this phase, needs to take into consideration generally accepted land use guidelines such as (1) the highest and best use should be made of all land, (2) avoid land use conflicts (i.e., neighboring residential and commercial areas), (3) areas should complement each other and promote a visual interest and functionally fit the remainder of the organization's site, (4) facilities should be constructed only on sites that best meet programmatic and environmental objectives of the organization, and (5) the organization should develop a no-build policy relating to the preservation of historic sites or open spaces.

Further, the master plan should contain goals and objectives for circulation and transportation on the organization's site. These goals and objectives should include, but not be limited to: (1) general access to the organization, (2) vehicular circulation, (3) parking, (4) pedestrian and bicycle circulation, and (5) transit.

Another extremely important aspect of the master plan will be the utilities and service elements. A consolidated utility system consistent with the projected needs of the organization should be developed. This system should be designed for simplicity of maintenance and future needs for extension or expansion of the utility network.

The master plan should consider the landscape design. The primary landscape goal for the campus should be to present an image with a high degree of continuity and quality. The landscape design should take into consideration the organization's buildings and grounds, accessibility issues, fire, security, energy conservation, and desired development beyond the organization's property line.

Figure 4.3
Sample Building Program Statement Outline

Part I. Objectives of the Programs
      a. Instructional (professional service)
      b. Recreational sports
      c. Adapted activities
      d. Athletics (interscholastic and intercollegiate)
      e. Club sports
      f. Community/school programs
      g. Others

Part II. Basic Assumptions to be Addressed
      a. Facilities will provide for a broad program of instruction,
        adapted activities, intramural and other sports
      b. Demographics of the population who will use the facility
      c. Existing facilities will be programmed for use
      d. Basic design considerations. "What's most important?"
      e. Facility expansion possibilities will be provided for in the planning
      f. Outdoor facilities should be located adjacent to indoor facilities
      g. Consideration will be given to administration and staff needs
      h. Existing problems
      i. Others

Part III. Comparable Facility Analysis
      a. Visit comparable facilities that have been recently constructed
      b. Compare cost, design features, etc.

Part IV. Factors Affecting Planning
      a. Federal and state legislation
      b. Club sports movement
      c. The community education or "Lighted School" program
      d. Surge of new non-competitive activities being added to the curriculum
      e. Expansion of intramural sports and athletic programs
      f. Sharing certain facilities by boys and men and girls and women (athletic training
        rooms and equipment rooms)
      g. Coeducational programming
      h. Emphasis on individual exercise programs
      i. Physical fitness movement
      j. Systems approach in design and construction
      k. New products
      l. Others

Part V. Explanation of Current and Proposed Programming
      a. Instructional
      b. Intramural sports
      c. Club sports
      d. Adaptive programs
      e. Community/school
      f. Recreational programs
      g. Priority listing of programs
      h. Others

Part VI. Preliminary Data Relative to the Proposed New Facilities

The following steps assume an organization planning a new facility from the ground up.

Regional Analysis

Sufficient data must be gathered about the off-site surroundings to ensure that the project will be compatible with surrounding environments, both man-made and natural. This part of the design process is referred to as the regional analysis. It should include:

- Service area of the facility under construction (i.e., major facilities such as parks, large commercial areas facilities, and minor facilities, such as children's playgrounds, senior citizen centers, local library, etc.).
- User demand (i.e., determining the kind of use desired by clients, activity interests, demographic makeup of residents, local leadership, and calculating the number of users).
- Access routes (i.e., major and secondary routes).
- Governmental functions and boundaries (i.e., contact the local planning agency and local government offices).
- Existing and proposed land uses (i.e., gathering information about abutting land ownership, adjacent land uses, land use along probable access routes, off-site flooding and erosion problems, offsite pollution sources, views [especially of aesthetic and historic interest], and significant local architectural or land use characteristics).
- Regional influences (i.e., check for anything unusual or unique that could either enhance or cause problems to the project).

Site Analysis

The planning committee will need to consider various pieces of information prior to selecting the building site. The considerations for site selection (Fogg, 1986; Miller, 1997) include:

- Access to the site (i.e., ingress and egress, surrounding traffic generators, accessibility via public transportation).
- Circulation within the site (e.g., roads—paved and unpaved, bicycle trails, walks and hiking trails).
- Parking.
- Water supply.
- Sewage disposal.
- Electrical service.
- Telephone service.
- Other utilities including oil/natural gas transmission lines, or cable TV.
- Structures to be constructed.
- Environmental concerns and conditions on and off property (e.g., noise, air, water, and visual pollution).
- Easements and other legal issues (e.g., deed restrictions, rights of way, and less-than-fee-simple ownership).
- Zoning requirements (i.e., changing the zoning is usually time consuming and expensive and frequently not possible).
- Historical significance.
- Any existing uses (activities) on the site.
- Climactic conditions prevalent in the area by season (e.g., temperature; humidity; air movement velocity, duration, and direction; amount of sunshine; precipitation—rain, sleet, snow; sun angles and subsequent shadows; special conditions—ice storms, hurricanes, tornadoes, heavy fog, heavy rain storm, floods, and persistent cloud cover).
- Nuisance potentials (e.g., children nearby, noise, etc.).
- Natural features (e.g., topography, slope analysis, soil conditions, geology, hydrology, flora and fauna).
- Economic impact of a site (e.g., labor costs, growth trends, population shifts, buying power index, available work force, property taxes, surrounding competition, utility costs, incentives, area of dominant influence [ADI], designated market area [DMA], and established enterprise zones).
- Natural barriers and visibility.
- Supporting demographics (e.g., age, gender, occupation, martial status, number of children, expenditures, education, income, number of earners in the family, ethnic background, etc.) and psychographics (e.g., lifestyle data or lifestyle marketing).
- Security concerns (e.g., proximity of police, fire, emergency medical personnel, hospitals).

The most important aspects of site selection are location, location, and location. If the site is not in the most accessible location with a high profile for people to recognize, it will have a negative effect on the success of the venture.

The following seven steps apply to both new ventures and established organizations planning major overhauls:

1. Master Plan Agenda

The master plan agenda is a specific list of issues, opportunities, and projected physical improvements. The plan will include the number and type of structures to be constructed or renovated, the estimated capital costs over a set period of time, approximate locations of new structures, and probable priority to be considered in the preparation of the master plan (see Figure 4.4).

Figure 4.4
Developing a Master Plan

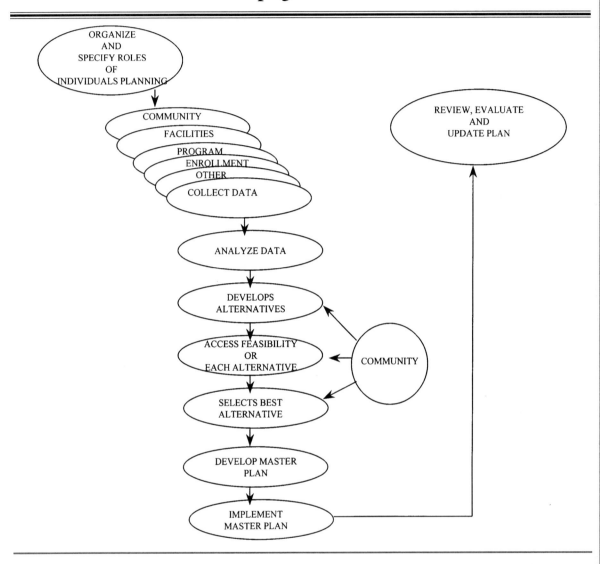

2. Review and Discussion

This step offers the organization and its stakeholders the opportunity to review and comment on the work completed on the master plan to date. The planning committee should be present at these open forums to answer questions and understand the issues and concerns raised. The presentations for these open forum meetings should include
- a description of the process,
- a summary of the organization's profile,
- a review of the projected capital improvements,
- a summary of the surveys and analysis of existing conditions,
- an accounting of issues and opportunities,
- a list of items on the master plan agenda, and
- a description of the next steps in the planning process.

The committee should review and evaluate all reactions and concerns raised at the meeting(s). Then the committee should determine appropriate modifications to the master plan.

3. Preparation of the Draft Master Plan

The preliminary master plan should be expressed in both general and specific terms. The former is intended to communicate the major features of the campus plan. The latter view enriches the vision by showing in greater detail the character, justification, feasibility, and phasing of selected significant improvements. The following components typically appear in a master plan: (1) new construction;

(2) building and site reconstruction, renewal, and demolition; (3) revisions to and extension of the circulation systems; (4) new and improved landscape projects; (5) parking patterns; (6) transportation proposals; (7) infrastructure projects; (8) joint organization and community development; (9) drawings and illustrations; (10) block models; (11) organization design guidelines for buildings and building materials; and (12) landscape guidelines including views, boundary identification, major entrances and exits, service entrances and exits, building sites, vehicular and pedestrian circulation systems, parking, water features, rock formations, gardens, open spaces, and passive or recreational spaces.

4. Review of Preliminary Plan

The planning committee will present the preliminary plan to the organization's constituencies, administration, board, and community at large. These groups will review the preliminary plan. After careful review a combined report will be generated with any suggested modifications and justifications for the modifications.

5. Revision of the Master Plan to Obtain Consensus and Approval

After the preliminary plan review has been completed, the master plan should be revised to include any recommended changes from the stakeholders. The revised plan should be published and distributed as a draft master plan for use in the plan approval process. The master plan remains a dynamic and flexible document even after approval.

6. Documentation and Dissemination of the Master Plan

The ad hoc planning advisory committee is transformed into a standing planning advisory committee with the following responsibilities: (1) serve as a conduit for the organization's community to present issues and suggestions regarding the master plan; (2) review all capital expenditure projects; (3) confirm conformance to the campus plan; (4) expedite the resolution of nonconformance; (5) review, resolve, and recommend plan amendments; and (6) participate in an annual review of the master plan and cyclical master plan revisions.

7. Master Plan Amendment Process

The master plan will need to be amended periodically to stay current with new trends and developments. The standing planning advisory committee should plan to revise the master plan every five years. The process would be the same as the original process that established the master plan.

The standing planning advisory committee will annually review the master plan. If a major new initiative has been approved by the administration and requires modification of the master plan or a major failure of a structure or utility occurs, the committee can request that a modification be made in the master plan. This recommendation would be forwarded to the administration and board for approval.

Implementation of Plan

After the master plan has been approved as a guideline for the organization's future planning, it is important to remember that the master plan is a guide for the entire organization. It is not a specific plan for a particular structure. Once approval and funding have been gained for a specific structure, then the developmental process begins for that structure.

The common components that compose a development process for a single structure or complex include research; regional analysis; site analysis; program; functional analysis; combined site, function, land use; refinement and site plan/overall design; construction documents; bidding; construction; and review.

Design Team

The design team (see Figure 4.5) is composed of the project planning committee, architect(s), engineers, facility consultant(s), interior designer(s), construction manager, acoustical consultant(s), and turf management specialist(s). Generally, the architectural firm selected by the organization employs engineers (e.g., civil, electrical, mechanical, and structural), interior designers, acoustical consultants and turf management specialists. The organization often hires a facility consultant to work with the program committee and architect. However, in some cases, the architectural firm as part of the design team may employ the facility consultant.

A facility consultant can provide numerous services. If the consultant is part of the owner's team rather than the architectural team, this individual should serve as a liaison between the project planning committee and the architect. It is important to understand that the majority of architects employed by an organization have little or no experience in designing these types of facilities. It would be preferable to select an architectural firm familiar with these types of facilities. If this is not possible, then the facility consultant becomes very important to the process.

Selecting an Architectural Firm

The selection of an architectural team should be based solely on the reputation and experience of the company and a formal review process. Once a project is approved then an advertisement (a request for qualifications [RFQ]) should be placed in the news media seeking qualifications of interested architectural firms for the specific project. Later, a letter would be sent to specific firms who qualify, inviting them to submit proposals.

Figure 4.5
Project Planning Committee

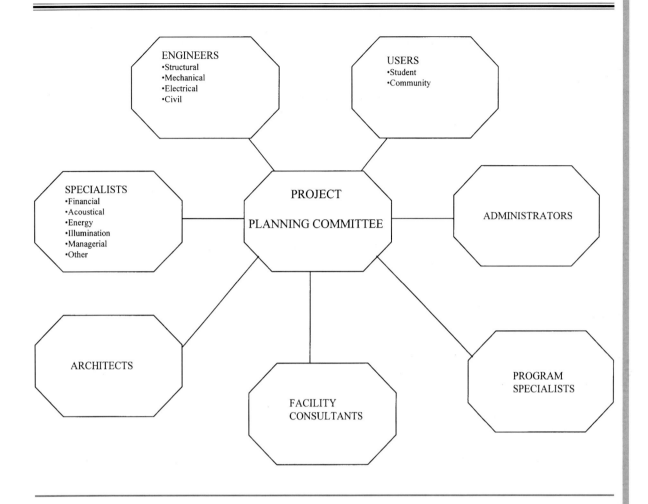

Tips for Drafting the Request for Proposal

The request for proposal, (or RFP), is composed of the following components: (1) Prepare an RFP and send to a broad list of applicants to ascertain their qualifications for this particular type of project (Noyes and Skolnicki, 2001). (2) Draft an evaluation sheet to be used by the selection committee to determine who is qualified. (3) Based on your responses to the RFQ, select no more than 20 firms to which to send the RFP. (4) Draft a second evaluation sheet to narrow the pool to three to five finalists for the selection committee. (5) Provide the applicants adequate time to prepare a proposal—between three and four weeks, and longer if holidays are involved. (6) Request the firms include in their proposals the following: a list of recently completed projects (last 10 years), the estimated budgeted costs and actual costs for each project, and in-house professionals available to work on the project. (7) The owner needs to provide the applicants with adequate background for the project. (8) The finalists will participate in an interview process.

Prior to the Interview

Prior to interviewing the finalists, the program committee, facility consultant, and administration representatives should travel to at least two facilities built by each firm and review the final result of their efforts. The travelers need to speak with the facility manager and users and ask about the best features of the facility and the worst features. What would they do differently? After completing the tours, draft a number of questions to ask the architect during the interview.

The Interview

After the field of applicants is narrowed to three to five, the firms should be interviewed. Each firm should demonstrate their competence and philosophy in the following areas (modified from the American Institute of Architects suggestions):

- client's role in the design process
- number and type of consultants required
- design or build versus conventional design versus fast-track process
- extent of engineering services
- construction supervision
- number of sets of plans or specifications to be provided
- construction costs

- factors that may influence construction
- time schedule and target dates for completion
- architectural fee and payment schedule
- development of a budget

Criteria for Selection

The successful firm should be open and flexible with the program committee and facility consultant, be experienced with this type of project, and be able to demonstrate that they have completed facilities within the budget developed (Noyes & Skolnicki, 2001). The firm should be able to demonstrate awareness, a user-friendly process, past success with other similar projects, and past fees as related to similar projects. Finally, the firm should be willing to provide accessibility to the architects and engineers during the planning and building phases.

Research for Facility Development

In its research, the planning committee should be concerned with (1) knowing and understanding the current and future needs and desires of the people who are involved in and/or affected by the proposed project and (2) knowing everything reasonably possible about the project function and/or activity and the space requirements.

Designers Design for People

At least four groups of people may need to be involved in the research and to be eventually satisfied, including clients (board of directors, etc.), users, affected neighbors and/or public, managers and operators, and possibly others. Each of the relevant groups must be identified and its needs, concerns, and desires understood. There will almost certainly be some conflicts between the various groups. Understanding these problems in advance may make it possible to resolve them during the design phase.

Maintenance and Operations

Maintenance and operational needs, small but significant, must be clearly understood. They can make a project successful or doom it to future failure. The following are some specific items to consider:

1) *Maintenance*
- Will maintenance be by in-house labor or by contract?
- Is special equipment used or needed (e.g., riding lawn mowers, etc.)?
- Does maintenance staff have any requirements for any standard equipment (e.g., motors, lights, shower heads, pumps, etc.) used or preferred by the maintenance staff?
- How capable is staff to maintain sophisticated equipment?
- What are maintenance space requirements, such as equipment clearance around motors and pumps, so routine maintenance can be performed, etc.?
- Are there any special fire protection requirements?
- What special storage requirements are needed for flammables and chemicals?

2) *Operations*
- Security—Is it needed? If so, what type (patrol, electronic, entrance only, dogs, by whom)? If patrolled, how—by foot, car, motorcycle, horse, bike, or boat?
- Hours of operation—Is night lighting required?
- Trash pickup—In-house? Contract? Kind of equipment used?
- Deliveries—Food, supplies, etc. When are separate entrances and exits needed?
- Communications system—Speakers, phone, radio, bell system, public address system?
- Safety/first aid—Are special facilities needed? Where? Extent? Emergency vehicle access?
- Peak use—How handled? Restrict use or provide overflow capacity?

3) *Special Programs*
- Will there be any? If so, what kind (e.g., concerts at noon, employee training, visitor information and/ or education, arts and craft shows, special exhibits)?
- Any special space requirements for programs? Lighting? Service areas? Other utilities?

Facilities and Their Requirements

Most facilities have specific site requirements. Technical data must be gathered on all the proposed facilities. At a minimum, the following must be known:
- Size (actual dimensions plus any buffer spaces or required accessory space)
- Grade requirements (i.e., maximum and minimum)
- Any special construction requirements (e.g., tennis courts, ice hockey rinks)
- Utility needs (i.e., type and amount)

Predevelopment Review

Along with the master planning process, a thorough review of facility needs should be completed for a proposed new or renovated facility. This review should be completed before an architect or consultant is brought on board. This can save time and money as well as assuring that the structure will fit the proposed program. It is important to develop a checklist at the beginning, not the end, of the planning process. This will help focus and guide the dream and planning process. See the appendixes for examples of specific checklists as a guide in developing your own checklist for the proposed project.

Program

Program, as used here, is the organization of the information needed for planning a project to provide an appropriate facility to meet the needs of the affected people (client, users, neighbors, and staff). Program needs should include a list of activities, facility needs for each activity listed, number of participants in each activity during peak periods, size of each facility ranging from minimum to ideal, and a description of the relationship between activities and facilities (i.e., can certain activities coexist with other activities at the same time in one facility?).

Functional Analysis

Functional analysis is the process of analyzing and organizing the information provided in programming and relationships by translating that analysis into graphic symbols. It establishes the preferred or ideal physical relationships of all the component parts of a project. The process commonly consists of four parts: space diagrams, relationship charts and/or diagrams, bubble diagrams, and land-use concepts. All the elements contained in the activity/program must be considered and their desired functional and physical relationships accommodated.

Combined Site, Function, and Land Use

Two issues are key to land use: people needs and site constraints. At this point, the various constraints and opportunities presented by the site must become integrated with people needs. It is also the time when the reality of the site constraints may require changes in the program. This step combines the site analysis with the functional analysis. If changes are made in the program, the changes must be incorporated throughout the functional analysis phase. This step in the site design process is where analysis of the site data is most completely utilized.

If the site selected is too small, the following options should be considered:

- Physical modification of the site. This may be the least desirable option because it is almost always undesirable from an environmental standpoint. It frequently is not aesthetically pleasing and it is usually expensive.
- Expand the site if adjacent land is available. This is frequently not possible and can be expensive.
- Change to another site. This can be expensive, and alternate sites may not be available.
- Cancel the project. This is not usually desirable or possible.
- Creatively look at new ways of solving the problem.

The location is the most difficult choice. It is always difficult to abandon the proven acceptable way of designing and operating facilities. When successful, however, it can often lead to outstanding, innovative solutions.

Refinement and Site Plan/Overall Design

After the land-use step has been completed, the planning committee needs to refine the focus of the building project before it moves to the site plan/overall design step. After the refinement is complete, then, and only then, should the planners consider site planning and overall design.

A site plan shows the entire existing and proposed site features superimposed on a topographic base map at an appropriate scale. It functions as the coordinating plan that ensures that all the project parts fit together. This is the point in the site design process where imagination and creativity are really important. In addition, this plan is almost always the feature part of any presentation to the client and other interested parties.

Accompanying the site plan will be a number of drawings, including utilities (e.g., water sources, sewer lines, and electricity/communication lines), grading and drainage, circulation, scale drawings, relationships, and three-dimensional aspects.

Construction Documents

Construction documents control the actual constructed results and consist of two separate parts: working drawings and specifications, the written companion to the working drawings. Upon completion of the working drawings and specifications, the project is bid and, if the bids are satisfactory, the contract is awarded.

Working Drawings

All working drawings must be clear, concise, and understandable to the people who are going to construct the building. Only as much detail as is necessary to build the project should be included. More detail might give the client more control but will definitely cost more money for design and will result in higher bids. All pieces must be clearly presented in such a manner that will allow accurate building.

All construction drawings must be accurate, clearly labeled, and dimensioned. If in doubt as to the need for a label or a dimension, include it! Normally, written numbers on the plan take precedence over field-scaled distances.

A useful tool in outlining the numbers and kinds of construction drawings is a plan control list. Each drawing expected to be needed is listed by description. This enables the designer(s) to coordinate work and helps to ensure that all aspects of the project are included.

With the completed list of plans, an estimate of time required to complete the working drawing and the necessary scheduling of work assignments can be carried out. This plan control document will probably be revised during the preparation of drawings. In its final form, it will become the drawing index listing for Sheet 2 of the working drawings package.

The more detailed and elaborate the working drawings, the higher the cost of preparing them, and very frequently, the higher the cost of building the project. A rule of thumb: The smaller the job, the fewer the construction documents. Small contractors do not like excessive control and paperwork. They frequently will not bid on projects with elaborate specifications, and if they do, they bid high. Frequently, too much control will cause bids to be higher, but does not result in an increase in quality.

The construction drawings must be reviewed by the maintenance staff to 1) ensure compatibility of parts with existing facilities, 2) see if the project can be effectively maintained at reasonable cost, and 3) determine if alternative materials or design modifications would reduce the costs and/or simplify maintenance. A detailed cost estimate is almost always necessary at this point in the design process. If costs estimated for the time of construction are too high, then the project may have to be reduced in scope and/or redesigned. Be certain that lifetime operations and maintenance costs are also considered in the estimate.

The construction drawings should include the following: demolition and site preparation, utilities, landscape and site improvements, structural, architectural, mechanical/HVAC, mechanical/plumbing, mechanical/fire protection, and electrical/telecommunications.

Specifications

The written portion of the construction documents comes in three parts: bidding and contract requirements (including the bid documents)—Division 0; general requirements—Division 1; and construction specifications Divisions 2-16.

This part of the design process is often most disliked by designers because of the massive detail required. It is, however, of the utmost importance in ensuring that the design is actually built according to the way it was envisioned.

Specifications should be organized in the 16-division format developed by the Construction Specifications Institute (CSI) as follows:

Division 0:	Bidding requirements, contract forms, and conditions of the contract
Division 1:	General requirements/special conditions
Division 2:	Site work
Division 3:	Concrete
Division 4:	Masonry
Division 5:	Metals
Division 6:	Wood and plastic
Division 7:	Thermal and moisture protection
Division 8:	Doors and windows
Division 9:	Finishes
Division 10:	Specialties
Division 11:	Equipment
Division 12:	Furnishings
Division 13:	Special construction
Division 14:	Conveying systems
Division 15A:	Mechanical (HVAC)
Division 15B:	Mechanical (plumbing)
Division 16:	Electrical

General Notes

- Include everything in the specifications that you want to see in the final constructed product.
- Make sure that Division 1 includes the contractor providing "as built" drawings, catalogue cuts, and, where appropriate, an operation manual and training of operating and maintenance staff.
- Include only information necessary to the specific project—especially if it is a small one. As with plans, small contractors don't like and frequently don't understand long, involved specifications; therefore, they will not bid or may increase their bids accordingly. The heavier, thicker, and more complicated the specifications are, the higher the bid.
- Conversely, the less detail you have in the specifications, the greater the opportunity for misunderstandings between the owner and contractor.
- All phases of specifications are readily adaptable to computerization and/or word processing. Much time can be saved if "canned" specifications are used, thus speeding up this tedious but crucial task. Computerization will probably lead to standardization of details and format.

Schematic Design Phase

In the schematic design phase, the architect prepares schematic design documents, which consist of drawings and other documents illustrating the scale and relationship of project components. These are based on the mutually agreed upon program with the owner, the schedule, and the construction budget requirements, and they are submitted to the owner for approval.

The products from this first phase of the project consist of the following: renderings (architects conception of the building) and models, floor plans and elevations, narrative (a description of the project with sufficient detail to allow an initial review by the organization), outline specifications (e.g., exterior materials, interior finishes, mechanical and electrical systems, identification of significant discrepancies between the project requirements and the budget), and cost estimates.

The project management issues for this phase consist of cost and budget, program expansion, schedule slippage, design review, quality assurance, use of design and estimating contingencies, code compliance, and building committee(s).

Design Development Phase

Based on schematic design documents and any adjustments authorized by the owner in the program, schedule, or construction budget, the architect prepares further design development documents for approval by the owner. These consist of drawings and other documents to fix and describe the size and character of the project as to architectural, structural, mechanical, and electrical systems, materials, and other appropriate elements.

The products for this phase include: drawings (site and landscape, utilities, structural, architectural, mechanical, electrical, and special equipment), narrative, specifications, and cost estimates.

The project management issues for this phase consist of cost and budget, scope creep (common elements previously eliminated from the project reappear in design development), design review, technical review (specific reviews initiated by the owner to ensure the organization's guidelines for design and construction are being complied with), and use of design contingencies.

Construction Approaches

The traditional approach is commonly known as the *lump sum contract*. In this method a general contractor is selected based on the lowest bid. The general contractor is responsible for selecting all subcontractors and selection of all construction materials. It is not advisable to enter into this type of contractual relationship because the general contractor has too much control of the profit and loss for a job.

Many public projects employ a *construction manager* to oversee the progress of the construction through all phases. This method allows for multiple bids such as one for mechanical, another for electrical, and another for general construction of the structure.

Another approach is called *design and build*. This method places the responsibility for completion of the project on the architect and builder who work for the same company. This option sets a fixed price, encourages interaction, and eliminates additional costs arising from design changes. A variation of design and build is called *fast tracking*. It is used in large projects in which contracts are let incrementally or sequentially so that the construction time may be reduced. This variation may be not be allowed in public projects due to federal or state mandates.

Construction Document Phase

Based on the approved design development documents and any further adjustments in the scope or quality of the project or in the construction budget authorized by the owner, the architect prepares construction documents for the approval of the owner. These consist of drawings and specifications setting forth in detail the requirements for the construction of the project.

Construction documents (developed by the American Institute of Architects [AIA] and the Associated General Contractors of America [AGCA] consist of the following: invitation to bid, instructions to bidders, information available to bidders, bid forms and attachments, bid security forms, construction agreement, performance bond, payment bond, certificates, contract conditions (i.e., general conditions, and supplementary conditions), specifications (Divisions 1-16), drawings, addendum(s), and contract modifications.

The program management issues for the phase consist of: code compliance, scope creep, schedule slippage, design review, technical review, quality assurance, use of design and estimating contingencies, design contract interpretation and enforcement, bidding and construction strategy (i.e., a lump-sum bid for all components or multiple bids for general contractor, mechanical, electrical, and add-ons or reductions), cost overruns or under runs, design-bid-build (i.e., project designed by an architectural firm and bid out to construction firms to build), design and build and a variation of design and build called fast tracking.

All designers must keep current on the latest product information available in their field of expertise. When the plans and specifications are completed, the project is ready for bid.

Bidding

Bids are opened in front of witnesses, usually the contractors or their representative(s), and an attorney (normally required by a government agency). The bidding process includes (a) bidding and advertising, (b) opening and review of bids, and (c) award of contract. The bid documents include invitation to bid, instructions to bidders, the bid form, other sample bidding and contract forms, and the proposed documents (e.g., drawings and specifications).

Bidding and Advertising

Bidding is the process of receiving competitive prices for the construction of the project. A bid form should be provided to ensure that all bids are prepared in the same manner for easy comparison. The bids can be received in many ways. The most common are

- lump sum (one overall price),
- lump sum with alternatives (either add-ons or deletions), and
- unit prices.

All bids on large projects should be accompanied by some type of performance bond, ensuring that the contractor will perform the work as designed at the price bid in the time specified. This ensures that bidders are sincere in their prices.

The time and place of the receipt of the sealed bids must be clearly shown on all bid packages. *No late bids can be received without compromising the entire bidding process.*

Small Projects (Up to $25,000)

A bid of this size can normally be handled informally. The process of calling a selected list of local contractors will usually be sufficient and will probably result in obtaining the best price.

Larger Projects (Over $25,000)

A formal bid process is usually necessary to ensure fairness, accuracy, and a competitive result. The process starts with advertising for bids. Advertising frequently is initiated prior to the completion of the plans with an effective date for picking up the completed plans and specifications. The larger, more complex the project is, the wider the range of advertising necessary. Governmental agencies usually have minimum advertising standards. They advertise in the legal advertisement section of the local paper and papers in larger nearby cities and in professional construction journal(s). In addition, designers or clients frequently have a list of contractors who have successfully built past projects and/or who have indicated an interest in bidding on future projects.

As a minimum, the advertisement should consist of

- a description of the project and kind of work required,
- the date and place plans can be picked up,
- the cost of plans and specifications (usually only sufficient to cover printing costs),
- the bid date and time, and
- client identification.

The approximate value of the project is sometimes included although some designers and clients do not wish to give out this information. With complex projects, it is desirable to schedule a pre-bid conference to explain the design and bidding process to prospective bidders. During the bidding period, one or more prospective bidders frequently raise questions. If the questions require design modifications or clarifications, the questions must be answered in writing in the form of an addendum to all holders of plans.

Opening and Reviewing of Bids

The designers or their representatives are usually present at the bid opening. After the bids are opened and read, it is necessary to analyze them and decide to whom the contract is to be awarded. The technical analysis is usually by the designers who consider whether the bid is complete, the prices are reasonable, and the contractor is able to do the work. A recommendation is then made. The legal analysis by the attorney is conducted concurrently with examining whether bonds are attached, all necessary signatures are included, and all required in formation is provided.

Award of Contract

Assuming favorable analysis by all involved and that the bids are acceptable to the client, the contract will be awarded. Most contracts are awarded to the lowest qualified bidder. Sometimes, however, the low bidder is not large enough or does not have the expertise to do the work required. Occasionally some bids are improperly prepared. In these situations, they may be rejected and the next lowest qualified bidder will be awarded the contract, or the project is re-bid. This can lead to problems with the disqualified bids or bidders and is why an attorney should be present.

Construction Phases

The architect should visit the site at least twice monthly at appropriate intervals during the construction stage and make the owner generally familiar with the progress and quality of the work in writing. The architect has other responsibilities including certifying the payments represented to the owner for payment.

The construction step of a project goes through several phases. The number of phases depends upon the scope of the project and the contracting agency. Two general guidelines govern the construction step: (1) the larger the project, the more steps required, and (2) governmental projects usually have more contractual controls. At least some, and perhaps all, of the following steps will be required during construction.

Pre-Construction Conference

A meeting between the contracting agency and the contractor(s) prior to the commencement of construction to review the contract items and make sure there is an understanding of how the job is to be undertaken.

Construction

The actual construction begins this phase, which could take as much as five years depending on the scope of the project. However, generally construction can be completed in 18 to 24 months on an average project.

Change Orders

Defined as an official document requested by either the contractor or the contracting agency that changes the approved contract documents. These changes usually include an adjustment of the bid price and a benefit to the contractor. It is better to avoid all change orders. Where this is not possible, be prepared to pay a premium price and to accept delays in contract completion.

Pre-Final Inspection and Preparation of Punch List

The initial review of a completed construction project is called a pre-final inspection. This inspection should have all the affected parties' decision-makers present including the owner or his or her representative, the architect, the contractor(s), and any subcontractors. At this time, it is also desirable to have the facility operation supervisor present. During this review, a "punch list" is prepared of any work that needs to be completed by the contractor prior to a final inspection. All items that are not completed or are not completed according to specifications should be included on the list. The punch list is then agreed upon and signed by all affected parties. The contractor must then correct and/or finish all the items on the list. When the punch list is completed, it is time to call for a final inspection.

As-Built Drawings and Catalogue Cuts

Defined as the drawings prepared by the contractor showing how the project was actually built. These drawings will be of great value to the operations and maintenance staffs. They must know exactly what facilities were actually built and their locations to be able to maintain the project effectively.

Catalogue cuts are printed information supplied by the manufacturers on materials and equipment used in the project construction. This material is necessary so that the operating staff will be able to learn about the material and equipment. In addition, it is needed for locating necessary replacement parts. It must also be included in working drawings and specifications of future renovations and/or expansion of the project.

Preparation of an Operations Manual

An operations manual contains written instructions on how to operate and maintain special equipment. The minimum data included should be how to start up, how to shut down, inspection(s) time intervals and what should be inspected, schedule of required maintenance, safety precautions, and who to contact for specialized repair assistance.

Training on How to Operate the Project

This contract item is usually included only for larger projects that are unfamiliar to the people who will operate them.

Final Inspection

The final inspection should concentrate on items not found acceptable during any previous inspections. The same review team that made the pre-final inspection should be assembled for the final inspection.

Acceptance of Completed Project

Assuming all the work has been completed as shown on the plans and described in the specifications, the project should be accepted and turned over to the owner or operator. Further, if the contractor has posted a performance bond guaranteeing the work, it should be released by the contracting agency.

If at all possible, avoid partial acceptances. Sometimes it is necessary to take over a part or parts of a project prior to completion of the entire project. If this becomes necessary, the contractor will have the opportunity to blame future problems and/or delays on having to work around the people using the project.

Maintenance Period

When living plants are involved, many contractors have a maintenance period included after the acceptance of the project. This can last anywhere from 30 days or more (for lawns) to 90 days for flowers and, frequently, one full growing season for ground cover, vines, shrubs, and trees.

Bond Period

Most government projects and some larger projects require the contractor to post not only a performance bond, but also a one-year (or some other specified period) warranty on the quality of the work. Usually the bond requires the contractor to replace or repair any defective or damaged items during the time covered by the bond. Typical items would be leaking roofs, infiltration of ground water into sewer lines, puddling of water in parking lots or tennis courts, etc.

Bond Inspection and Final Acceptance

At the end of the bond period, the original final inspection team holds another inspection. Prior to release of the bond, any problems that have been uncovered during this inspection must be rectified at no cost to the contracting agency. It is important to note that when the bond is released, the contractor no longer has any responsibility to the project.

Review

The project has been completed and turned over to the client. Does the project do what it was designed to from the standpoint of the (a) client, (b) user, (c) affected neighbors and/or public, (d) manager and operator, and (e) design team? There are two basic kinds of information to be gathered: information on people and on physical conditions.

Summary

A very important process in the construction of a facility is the selection of the most appropriate site. Many variables must be considered when selecting a site, including research, regional analysis, site analysis, program, functional analysis, combine site and function, land use, refinement, site plan/overall design, construction documents, bidding, construction, and review. If the site selection process is successful, the building project will be well established.

Programming and Scheduling Process[1]

Thomas H. Sawyer

The term *program development* as used in this chapter refers to the total learning experiences provided to consumers to achieve the objectives of health, fitness, physical activity, recreation, and sport. It is concerned with the component parts of all the programs in each of the five areas as well as with the resources (e.g., facilities, financial, human, and technological) involved in implementing those learning experiences. The overwhelming trend in American society today is to provide carefully planned programs based on the following considerations: (1) the abilities, needs, and wants of the customer/client, (2) the needs of society in general, (3) the practical usefulness of the various knowledge bases and physical skills, (4) the social-psychological aspects of society that influence learning, and (5) the marketability of the products or services developed to meet the needs and wants of the customer/client.

Instructional Objectives

After reading this chapter, the student should be able to:

- understand the dynamics of developing a program,
- understand the dynamics of developing a schedule,
- describe the most common tournaments available for scheduling,
- comprehend the process required for expanding or reducing a program, and
- perform a program evaluation.

Program Development

The responsibility of program planning falls on the shoulders of a number of people and organizations. The planners include, but are not limited to: management personnel, staff, professional organizations, customers/clients, parents, community leaders, and other professionals such as medical personnel, lawyers, architects, and corporate leaders.

The *management personnel* play a vital role in the planning process. They serve as the (1) creators of the catalytic force that sets the planning in motion, (2) facilitators for the planning process, and (3) sustainers of the development process. Further, they provide the leadership that encourages and stimulates interest in providing optimal experiences, clears the barriers (e.g., time, place, space, and resources) that might impede the accomplishment of the task, and implements the appropriate recommendations for a program plan. Finally, management is responsible for pulling together a team who can work cooperatively and effectively together, provide them with a charge or challenge, and supply them with the necessary motivation as well as adequate financial, human, and technical resources to accomplish the task of designing a quality program.

The *staff members* are at the grass-roots level of program development. They will be key members of the team that develops programs. The staff member contributes experience and knowledge and provides data to support the directions of program development. Staff input and perceived ownership are necessary before a program is designed and implemented.

The *professional organizations* are the many groups and agencies that can help in program planning. These groups may provide program guides, consulting services, and advice that will prove to be invaluable in the planning of any program. Before embarking on a program development adventure, you should first consider what professional groups or agencies can be of assistance and contact them early on in the process. There is no need to reinvent the wheel. The old wheel may only need a small amount of adjustment to meet your needs.

---

[1]This chapter has been reprinted with modifications with permission from Sagamore Publishing. It represents Chapter 3, Programming for Success, from Sawyer, T. H. (1999). *The Management of Clubs, Recreation, and Sport: Concepts and Applications*. Champaign, IL: Sagamore Publishing.

The *customers/clients* should play a part in program development. Their collective thoughts on what constitutes desirable activities for program delivery are important. Customers/clients today are more actively involved in expressing their program needs or desires. They want to be heard and identified as part of planning the various activities and experiences that a quality program should provide to its customers/clients.

The *parents* and *community leaders* can assist in communicating with the public what an organization is trying to achieve. These two groups can make significant contributions by supplying information regarding desired outcomes. It is important to include representation from these two groups in order to develop any program in an effective and efficient manner.

Program Development Elements

There are eleven elements that either directly or indirectly influence program development: (1) climate and geographical considerations; (2) economic and social forces; (3) population demographics; (4) the community; (5) federal, state, and local legislation and regulations; (6) professional organizations; (7) attitudes of managers and consumers; (8) staff; (9) research; (10) facilities and equipment; and (11) competition.

Components of the Planning Process

The components of the planning process for effective program planning are: (1) establishing that a need exists for program development, (2) appointing a diverse planning team to specify the areas of need, (3) organizing for planning, (4) identifying program objectives, (5) generating program solutions, (6) selecting the program design, (7) implementing the program design, and (8) evaluating the program.

Steps in Program Development

The major steps involved in program development include (1) determining the objectives, (2) analyzing the objectives in terms of the program, (3) analyzing the objectives in terms of activities, (4) providing program guides, and (5) assessing the program based on predetermined outcomes.

In *determining the objectives,* the planning team should consider studying such factors as the nature of society, developmental program trends, needs and wants of the consumers, competitors' programs, and technological advances so that objectives may be clearly formulated to meet market demands. Every program should consider the following four goals or purposes when determining program objectives:

1. *Self-realization* goals include the inquiring mind, speech, reading, writing, numbers, sight and hearing, health knowledge, health habits, recreation, intellectual interests, aesthetic interests, and character.
2. *Human relationship* goals consist of respect for humanity, friendships, cooperation, courtesy, appreciation of home, conservation of the home, home-making, and democracy in the home.
3. *Economic efficiency* goals concern work, occupational information, occupational choice, occupational efficiency, occupational adjustment, occupational appreciation, personal economics, consumer judgment, efficiency in buying, and consumer protection.
4. *Civic responsibility* goals embrace social justice, social activity, social understanding, critical judgment, tolerance, conservation, social applications of science, world citizenship, law observance, economic literacy, political citizenship, and devotion to democracy.

After the objectives have been determined based on the understanding of the consumers' characteristics, needs, and wants, they should be *analyzed in terms of the program and activities.* The analysis should consider the various constraints associated with the objectives and assign relative emphases to the various phases of the program. Further, the analysis must focus attention on the activities needed to achieve the set objectives. Do these activities allow for the objectives to be met?

Each program developed needs to have a *program guide* for its participants and its marketing endeavors. Program guides offer opportunities to achieve objectives. Further, they provide opportunities for marketing products/services to the organization's various markets.

All programs need to be *assessed* based on predetermined outcomes. Evaluation represents the culmination of the program development process. It defines the end result of the program and compares it with what the program expected to achieve during the developmental stages. Evaluation, like program development, is a dynamic process that helps to determine the progress being made in meeting program objectives. It should identify strengths, weaknesses, and omissions and show where needed resources or emphases might be shifted in order to improve the program. Further, it assists the consumers in determining their own progress within the program and is useful to the management for interpreting and reporting program outcomes to its consumers and board.

Five Common Program Approaches

There are five common approaches to programming. They include programming by (1) objectives, (2) desires of the participants, (3) perceived needs of the participants, (4) cafeteria style, and (5) external requirements.

Programming by Objectives

This is the most contemporary approach. Inherent in this approach are these assumptions:

- The programming team/programmer is able to conceptualize the activity process.
- The programming team/programmer is skilled in writing performance objectives.
- The objectives so stated are consistent with the objectives of the participants in the activity.
- The program's success or failure will fairly be evaluated by whether or not the program has realized its objectives.

This approach to planning should be based on four solid planning principles. These include:

- The needs of the consumer—activity should be designed to meet the anticipated needs and wants of the consumers.
- Life enhancement—programs should enhance education and quality of life.
- Evaluation—programs should be formally and regularly evaluated in terms of their planned purposes.
- Participant readiness—programs should be related to participant readiness and abilities.

Programming by Desires of the Participants

This approach is a very popular method. It allows for consumer/participant involvement in the process. The following assumptions are inherent in this approach:

- Desires of the participant groups can be ascertained.
- Health, fitness, and recreation programs are an important need-reduction milieu.
- Programming teams/programmers are able to understand which activities meet which desires in most individuals.
- Programming team/programmers are able to know when desires have been met or satisfied.

The planning principles involved in this approach are:

- All programs should be designed to meet the needs and interests of the consumer/participant.
- All programs should encompass a variety and balance in substance and organizational patterns. This diversity should embrace a variety of skill levels relating to both genders, noncompetitive to highly competitive activities, and a variety of financial arrangements (e.g., free to special costs, time offering, and format for participating in terms of size of activity groups).
- All programs should be set in a safe environment.

Programming by Perceived Needs of the Participant

This approach makes the following assumptions:

- The programming team/programmer is a professional in the fields of health, fitness, physical activity, recreation, and sport, and knows and understands what others will want and need.
- The programming team/programmer is in a better position to know what others want than anyone else.
- Consumers/participants are unable to identify program-activity desires.
- Consumers/participants are anxious to be told what they are interested in.
- Generally, people are much the same, and time and money are saved by avoiding an expensive input system while the programming team/programmer designs what will be satisfactory.

This approach uses the following programming principles:

- All programs should be designed to utilize creatively all facilities and areas available.
- All programs should be efficiently organized and planned so that maximum participation is available.
- All programs should be nondiscriminatory and allow for true diversity (inclusion).
- All programs should be staffed by top-quality leaders who understand and accept their role in providing these services.
- All programs should have an interrelationship and progress sequences from one level to another.

Programming Cafeteria-Style

This approach is based on the ensuing assumptions:

- Consumer/participant interests are constantly changing, and the least expensive way to satisfy these interests is to offer a wide variety of programs and let consumers indicate their preferences by their own selection. The programming team/programmer cannot know every possible interest area. Therefore, this smorgasbord is a useful approach to discovering interests in a participant group.
- Guiding principles of programming can be met by offering diverse programs through which any potential participant can find at least one attractive activity.

- Many people do not know what they want, and the programming team/programmer is unsure. This approach provides a useful compromise.

     The guiding principles to employ with this approach are:

- All programs should tap the total possible resources within the area of their jurisdiction.
- All programs should provide an opportunity for adventure and new, creative experiences.
- All programs should be compatible with the economic, social, and physical abilities of the potential consumers/participants.

Programming by External Requirements (Standards)
     This approach is based on the following inherent assumptions:

- If the external standard is met, the program is good, i.e., satisfying to the users.
- Those persons involved in setting the standards are able to make quality judgments about the local situation.
- Standards generally represent minimums; therefore, to exceed the standard would indicate higher quality in the program experience.

     The guiding principles of programming by external requirements are:

- All programs should have diversity and internal balance
- All program planning should adhere to carefully developed standards for both design and administration.
- All programs should be delivered through a system of highly qualified leadership.
- All programs should utilize the full resources available to the planning agency.

Components of Program Evaluation

     The programming team/programmer must complete a thorough evaluation of the program(s) developed on a regular basis. The following questions need to be answered prior to embarking on the evaluation journey:

- What is the philosophy behind the program developed?
- What personnel and customer/client behaviors represent the minimum acceptable competence for the program?
- Can you verify that all of the personnel make safety a priority?
- Do the personnel maintain appropriate, proper, and accurate records?
- Are the facilities safe, adequate, and cost effective for the program offerings?
- Is equipment maintained, distributed, collected, and stored properly and safely?
- Does the program offer equal access to all persons regardless of gender, race and ethnicity, and socio-economic status?
- Are the program offerings the best use of financial resources?

     The approach taken in evaluating the program(s) should be dictated by the needs of the organization and its customers/clients. Effective and efficient program evaluation requires careful planning. There are six steps that will lead you to a successful evaluation:

1. Reflect on organizational philosophy(ies).
2. Identify key roles.
3. Assess evaluation needs.
4. Develop an evaluation plan.
5. Implement the evaluation plan.
6. Review and revise the evaluation plan.

Process for Expanding or Reducing/Eliminating a Program

     The programming team/programmer, after completing the evaluation, has a number of options regarding the future existence of the program. These options include maintaining, expanding, reducing, or eliminating the program. Before any of these options can be selected, the following must be considered:

- the human resources available or affected
- the financial resources available or affected
- the facility resources available or affected
- the equipment resources available or affected
- the effects on other related or tangential program offerings
- the effect on overall programming
- the effect on the customer/client base.

Any time a program is modified in any way, it has a domino effect on all other activities within the organization. It may appear to be a simple modification on the surface, but it could cause major problems with other related and non-related activities within the organization. Any recommendation for modification must be reviewed carefully in the context of the whole organization, not merely the area of suggested change.

Scheduling

It is important for the programming team/programmer to understand the calendar patterns of the customer/client who the organization serves. Scheduling has at least four distinct and different patterns: (1) seasons; (2) block periods such as 2, 3, 4, or 8 to 10 week periods; (3) monthly or weekly; and (4) daily time frame, such as sessions held during the early morning (6 to 9am), morning (9am to 12noon), early afternoon (12 to 3pm), late afternoon (3 to 6pm), early evening (6 to 9pm), and late evening (9 to 11pm).

Considerations When Scheduling the Facility or Event

A standard procedure should be established for requesting use of facilities. The organization should create and adhere to a standard request form and establish priority guidelines for authorizing use. The following is an example of a priority list used by a major university. Strict adherence to priority guidelines and request protocol should be stressed to all groups using facilities. In smaller organizations, scheduling may be less complicated; however, there is still a need for protocol and proper authorization for facility use. Computer programs for facility management are available to assist in scheduling.

Priority Listing for Facility Usage
1. scheduled academic classes
2. scheduled non-academic classes
3. recreational sports
4. athletic practices and contests
5. other campus groups—academic
6. other campus groups—non-academic
7. off-campus groups

Effective Scheduling

Effective scheduling is a distinguishing characteristic of every successful sports program, whether it be at the youth, interscholastic, intercollegiate, or professional level. Scheduling impacts every aspect of the sports program. Unless a high level of agreement between the mission of the organization and the schedule(s) generated is obtained, the sports program will suffer the consequences of less than adequate performance. The success level of each team within a sports program rests, in a great part, on the construction of a well-planned schedule.

The following questions should be used as a guide for the development of successful and competitive schedules for all teams involved in a sports program:

- What is the standard of competition sought for each sport? What is the expected level of success for each team?
- What is the participation level? How should participants be grouped—by age, gender, experience, size, or skill?
- What are the financial parameters governing the construction of the schedule?
- What geographical/travel limitations exist? Are there conference affiliations to be considered? What is the policy governing the mode of transportation utilized for trips?
- Is it necessary or desirable to arrange schedules to enable two different teams from the same institution to travel together to a common opponent?
- Relative to some sports, is there a limit on how many contests per week are academically permissible? How many contests can be played during one day? Is there a difference or a preference for weekday versus weekend day contests? Can contests be played on Sunday?
- Are contests permitted to be scheduled during vacation periods which fall within a sport's season?
- Are teams who qualify permitted to participate in postseason tournament competition? What are the ramifications if postseason participation falls during examination periods or after the academic year is concluded?
- What considerations are given to vacation periods—Christmas, New Years, Easter, summer?

If an institution is a member of a conference, there will most certainly be guidelines and agreements relative to scheduling that should be understood by those making the schedules. Likewise it is quite important for the sports director/coordinator to be aware of scheduling parameters set forth by the national or state governing bodies to which the institution belongs.

Once a scheduling policy has been established and adopted by the organization, other questions need to be considered before the scheduling team/scheduler can draft the schedule:

- What facility considerations exist? Is the facility shared with others? If the facility is shared, what priorities for usage have been established so that equity exists and conflicts can be avoided?
- What are the goals of the program? How many contests, if any, should be scheduled in different divisions? If scheduling against a lower-division opponent, how strong is the opponent? What effect would a defeat to a lower or higher-division opponent have on the morale or team ranking?

- What days of the week are preferred for scheduling of contests? Is spectator attendance an important factor and how is it affected by day or time of contest?
- Should contest days and times be consistent from week to week? Do the participants on the team tend to have one day per week when it is better not to schedule contests because of academic reasons?
- Does the organization have a policy about scheduling a contest on the Sabbath? Are there participants that cannot play on certain religious holidays or days?
- Is Monday a good day to schedule a contest if it follows a weekend of no competition or practice?
- When should away trips be scheduled (e.g., short trips during the week and longer trips over the weekend)?
- What are the vacation periods and holidays that fall during the season? How should the schedule relate to these?
- When is the first permissible contest date of the season?
- What national or state sport organizations' rules may impact non-educational institution scheduling?
- Which opponents should be scheduled early in the season?
- How should the strong opponents be spread throughout the season?
- What kind of home and away balance is desired?
- How does a long trip affect the next competition? What are the considerations of a long trip and how should long trips be balanced from year to year? How many contests should be played during a long trip?
- What considerations exist for contest starting times?

A Good Schedule

A good schedule is the end result of meeting the stated philosophy and policies of the organization. The following is an example of a good educational institution schedule:

- Includes all members of the conference (if the institution belongs to a conference).
- Includes a few non-conference games that encompass:
    — at least one probable win,
    — at least one ranked team, and
    — at least one respectable opponent with name recognition and the possibility of a toss-up competitive situation are;
- Includes at least a 50/50 split between home and away contests.
- Generates maximum financial rewards.
- Includes no more than two games at home or two on the road consecutively.
- Creates fan interest.
- Gives a fair chance to:
    —have a winning season, and
    —gain postseason opportunities.
- Is reasonable in terms of travel.
- Includes opponents who have reasonably similar academic standards
- Maximizes geographical, institution, and individual player(s) exposure.

Mechanics of a Sound Schedule

Organization is the key to success in almost any administrative function and scheduling is no exception to the rule. Scheduling at best is a complex task requiring a great deal of patience. The greatest assets a schedule team/scheduler must possess are patience, the ability to negotiate, and attention to detail.

The following records must be kept regarding the schedule: records of ideas, thoughts, phone calls, correspondence, past schedules, future schedules, agreements to play, contest contracts (e.g., actual contracts, when sent, received, and returned), officials' contracts, officials' roster, and details of successes and concerns.

All contests within a schedule should have contracts or agreements, even in youth league operations. The following is a checklist for what should be included in an agreement:

- dates the agreement is entered into
- site of the contest
- date of the contest
- time of the contest
- eligibility regulations of participants
- financial agreements, if any
- auditing requirement, if required
- complimentary ticket arrangements for both teams
- number of sideline passes for both teams, if appropriate
- number and location of visiting teams
- number of seats for team parties

- admission of band and cheerleaders, if appropriate
- control of ticket prices
- admission of game workers
- media agreements
- programming concession rights
- game officials
- special event rights (e.g., Band Day)
- additional games to be played as part of the original contract agreement
- conditions of failure to comply with the contract
- terminations of the contract clause
- additional miscellaneous agreements (e.g., meals, lodging, guarantees, etc.)

The development of a good schedule requires good sound planning, good communication, and attention to detail. The greater the number of sports to be placed on the calendar, the more important these elements become. It is possible for a scheduling team/scheduler to accomplish this task well, especially if a reasonable timetable is established early in the process.

Fundamentals of Booking Events

A facility without a schedule of events has little purpose. A public facility has an obligation to provide for scheduling community events. A private facility may limit charitable and non-profit activities. Regardless of the facility's purpose and mission, its manager is encouraged to book a well-rounded schedule of events geared to satisfy the desires of the market. Since rental income is such a major portion of annual operating revenue, this is an extremely important process.

Booking is the act of engaging and contracting an event or attraction to be held at the facility on a specific date. Scheduling is the reservation process and coordination of all events to fit the facility's annual calendar. There are two types of reservations: *tentative* indicates that an organization requested a specific date and time on a tentative-hold basis, and *confirmed* refers to an organization that has placed a deposit for the agreed upon date and time (contracted reservation).

Facilities that are successful in scheduling events have made a good first impression on the tenants and the ticket-buying public. These facilities are clean, well-maintained, well-lit, environmentally comfortable, and staffed by friendly, courteous, and professional people.

There are a number of fundamentals to be considered when attracting, booking, and scheduling a facility, including:

- Developing a level of confidence others have in the quality of services available at the facility.
- Establishing trust on the part of the promoter and the ticket-buying public in the professionalism of the facility manager and staff.
- Advertising the facility in various trade publications such as *Amusement Business, Variety,* and *Performance.*
- Attending appropriate trade and convention functions and networking with other facilities.
- Maintaining visibility with local and national promoters.
- Producing a facility informational brochure detailing the specifications of the building, staff, types of events, and event suitability.
- Preparing and making available a current financial report for the facility.
- Assigning responsibility of booking and scheduling to one person.
- Preparing contracts for the event and follow up to make sure the contracts are executed and returned with the necessary deposits and certificates of insurance.

Types of Tournaments and Selecting a Particular Type of Tournament

This will be a brief description on how to organize a successful tournament. For greater detail refer to. *Organizing Successful Tournaments* (Byl, 1990). *Tournament Scheduling: The Easy Way (Gunsten, 1978).* There are also numerous software programs available such as Tournament Pro.

The selection of a tournament is based on the goals of the program. The programming team/ programmer should answer the following questions before selecting a particular type of tournament:

- Should all players or teams play an equal number of contests?
- Does it matter whether the number of contests is the same per player or team?
- Should all the contests to be closely contested?
- Does it matter if there are a few lopsided contests?
- How important is it to know who comes in first, second, third, fourth, or fifth?

The common types of tournaments used in programs are: single elimination, double elimination, round robin, and extended. There are variations to these such as multi-level, round robin-double split, -triple split, and -quadruple split.

The single elimination tournament is best used for postseason competition after the completion of a round robin tournament. The advantages of a single elimination tournament are: format is easy to use and understand, accommodates a large number of entries, requires few games, and requires few playing areas. The disadvantages are: each participant is guaranteed only one game, accurate seeding is crucial, and does not maximize use of multiple playing areas.

The double elimination tournament is best used when time and playing areas are limited and final standings are important. The advantages of a double elimination tournament are: each participant is guaranteed two games, a participant who loses once can still win the championship, requires few playing areas, and is a better measure of ability than a single elimination tournament. The disadvantages are: some players participate in many games and others in few, takes many rounds to complete, and does not maximize use of multiple playing areas.

A *round robin* tournament is best used for league play and whenever standings are essential. The advantages of a round robin tournament are: all players play each other so true standings result, seeding is unimportant, uses multiple playing areas effectively, and no one is eliminated. The disadvantages are: it requires many games and several games may be lopsided.

Extended tournaments are best for individual sports in recreational settings. The advantages of extended tournaments are: they can be conducted over any length of time, the number of games per entry can be limited, they require little supervision, and no one is eliminated. The disadvantage is: the number of contests depends upon participant's initiative in challenging.

Summary

The program development players (programming team) are management personnel, staff members, professional organizations, customers/clients, and parents and community leaders. There are eleven factors that impact program development, they are: (1) climate and geographical considerations; (2) economic and social forces; (3) population demographics; (4) the community; (5) federal, state, and local legislation and regulations; (6) professional organizations; (7) attitudes of managers and consumers; (8) staff; (9) research; (10) facilities and equipment; and (11) competition.

The components for the program planning process are: (1) establishing that a need exists for program development, (2) appointing a diverse planning team to specify the specific areas of need, (3) organizing for planning, (4) identifying program objectives, (5) generating program solutions, (6) selecting the program design, (7) implementing the program design, and (8) evaluating the program. The major steps in program development are: (1) determining the objectives, (2) analyzing the objectives in terms of the program, (3) analyzing the objectives in terms of activities, (4) providing program guides, and (5) assessing the program based on predetermined outcomes.

There are four goals every program planning team/planner should consider—self-realization, human relationship, economic efficiency, and civic responsibility. Further, there are five program approaches that can be used in the development of programs—programming by objectives, programming by desires of the participants, programming by perceived needs of the participant, programming by cafeteria style, and programming by external requirements.

When scheduling, the scheduler needs to consider at least four distinct and different patterns - (1) seasons such as fall, winter, spring, and summer; (2) block periods such as 2-, 3-, 4-, or 8-to-10-week periods; (3) monthly or weekly; and (4) daily time frame such as sessions held during the early morning [6 to 9am], morning [9am to 12noon], early afternoon [12 to 3pm], late afternoon [3 to 6pm], early evening [6 to 9pm], and late evening [9 to 11pm]. There are four commonly used tournament types—single elimination, double elimination, round robin, and extended.

Finally, there are six steps in program evaluation—reflect on organizational philosophy(ies), identify key roles, assess evaluation needs, develop an evaluation plan, implement the evaluation plan, and review and revise the evaluation plan. After the evaluation is complete, a decision is made to either maintain, expand, reduce or eliminate the program. Any recommendation for modification must be reviewed carefully in the context of the whole organization, not merely the area of suggested change.

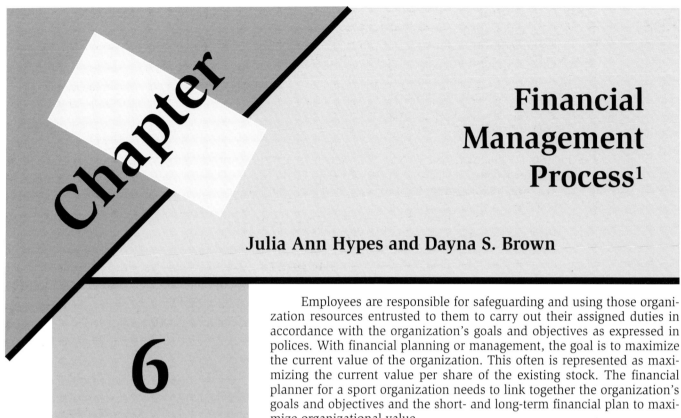

Financial Management Process[1]

Julia Ann Hypes and Dayna S. Brown

Employees are responsible for safeguarding and using those organization resources entrusted to them to carry out their assigned duties in accordance with the organization's goals and objectives as expressed in polices. With financial planning or management, the goal is to maximize the current value of the organization. This often is represented as maximizing the current value per share of the existing stock. The financial planner for a sport organization needs to link together the organization's goals and objectives and the short- and long-term financial plan to maximize organizational value.

Budgets are an integral part of financial management process designed to help guide an organization through a financial calendar year, budget cycle, or a fiscal year. Budgets aid an organization in determining what funds are available after fixed costs and routine or annual expenses. They also express how much money may be available for special projects and are tied to the goals and objectives of the financial plan. Budgets help an organization utilize available funds in the most effective and efficient manner possible as well as help eliminate wasteful spending practices.

Accountability is the culmination of the organized summarization of transactions representing economic events taking place within various business operating cycles throughout the organization. Employees working in financial areas are therefore responsible for appropriately managing and safeguarding the organization's assets that contribute to the preparation of reliable financial information.

In addition to an organization's specific policies, certain assertions are generally recognized as being embodied in all summarized financial data up to and including financial statements. Employees contributing to financial reports at any level are therefore making implied representations to all users or potential users of the data concerning the financial information they worked with. Users throughout the organization and outside the organization have a reasonable expectation to rely on the representations made. These representations then become the minimum goals and objectives of the organization regarding financial reports. This chapter will assist the future sport manager in understanding the importance of accountability and how to guarantee financial accountability.

Financial analysis is designed to aid sports managers through the process of evaluating past and current financial data. This analysis is necessary to evaluate performance and estimate future risks as well as financial potential. By reviewing balance sheets, income statements, and cash flow statements, a manger can obtain an overview of the financial solvency of the organization and its ability to withstand economic hardship. By properly analyzing revenue and investment potential, along with costs, the manager can better utilize the financial resources of the organization.

This chapter will review accountability issues, basic financial statements, cash flow, and the financial analysis process. In addition, it will review the traditional budgeting process, preparation of budgets, revenues and expenditures, and the components necessary for sound financial planning and provide the sport manager with the necessary tools for a successful contribution to the financial future of an organization.

Instructional Objectives

After reading this chapter, the student should be able to

- describe what accountability is in general,
- understand the concept of financial accountability,
- understand the role of financial planning and financial analysis within an organization,
- explain cash planning,

[1]This chapter is a combination and modification of Chapters 3, (Financial Accountability and Analyses, and 4, Financial Planning, in Sawyer, T. H., Hypes, M. G., and Hypes, J. A. (2004). *Financing the Sport Enterprise*, Champaign, IL: Sagamore Publishing.

- discuss profit planning,
- explain short- and long-term financial needs of an organization,
- understand the role of the financial manager,
- discuss the impact of financial planning on an organization,
- explain how to prepare a financial plan,
- design an internal audit process,
- understand the role of the budget within an organization,
- discuss the budgeting process,
- explain how to prepare a budget,
- identify revenue sources,
- explain expenditures, and
- discuss capital budgeting.

Accountability

Accountability is defined as the state of being accountable, subject to the obligation to report, explain, or justify something; responsible; and answerable. Most academicians use a narrow definition that involves the not-for-profit answering to a higher authority in the bureaucratic or interorganizational chain of command.

The public and the media tend to use a broader definition of accountability. Generally, this definition holds the organization accountable to the public, media, donors, customers/clients, stockholders, and others. The public and media have a greater expectation that the organization will have a certain level of performance, responsiveness, ethics, and morality.

The organization's views on accountability will play a key role in developing an organization's standards of accountability. The manager should answer two questions when defining accountability for the organization: To whom is the organization accountable? For what activities and levels of performance is the organization held responsible?

Financial Accountability

The financial manager makes the following assertions regarding the execution and summarization of financial transactions that are found in various financial reports.

Existence and Occurrence

The assets and liabilities actually exist at the report date and transactions reported actually occurred during the reporting period covered. There is physical security over assets and transactions are valid.

Completeness

All transactions and accounts that should be included in the reports are included and there are no undisclosed assets, liabilities, or transactions.

Rights and Obligations

The organization owns and has clear title to assets and liabilities, which are the obligation of the organization. Transactions are valid.

Valuation and Allocation

The assets and liabilities are valued properly and the revenues and expenses are measured properly. Transactions are accurate.

Presentation and Disclosure

The assets, liabilities, revenues, and expenses are properly classified, described, and disclosed in financial reports.

Internal Control

Since employees and management involved with financial processes are making (implying) the above representations (assertions), management, at various levels, needs internal controls to ensure that financial data compiled is not false, misleading, incomplete, or inaccurate.

Users have every reason to believe the data and reports you give them are accurate and reliable. These minimum financial reporting objectives therefore become the objectives used in designing an effective system of internal control that ensures reliable financial reporting. The uniquely designed internal control procedures within the organization are there to achieve these objectives.

Everyone in the organization has some responsibility for internal control even though it is often supervisors and/or managers who design the internal control procedures within their area of influence. This is true from two perspectives. First, almost all employees play some part in effective control. They may produce information used in the control system or take other actions needed to affect control. Any weak link in the organization's structure can create a weakness in the control system. Second, all employees are responsible to communicate problems in operations, deviations from established standards, and violations of the organization's financial policy.

By definition, internal control is a process designed to provide reasonable assurance regarding the achievement of the organization's financial reporting objectives. Within this definition there are fundamental concepts relating to internal control, including: (a) it is not one event, but a process or series of actions that permeate the organization's activities and are inherent in the way business is transacted, (b) it is affected by the people of the organization in what they do and say and they must therefore know their responsibilities and the limits of their authority, (c) it provides reasonable, not absolute, assurance regarding the achievement of objectives and should be cost effective, and (d) it is geared to the achievement of the organization's objectives.

Components

In determining the control procedures to achieve the objectives, the process usually starts with a management-directed self-evaluation at the business operation cycle level and applies the "objectives" to groups of similarly processed transactions (types of transactions). The objectives for each group are achieved by a judiciously determined mix of procedures from the following five major components of internal control. The mix may be different for each type of transaction within a financial area based on the relative risk and significance of the amounts involved. Also, some components cover a number of transaction types. The overriding purpose is that there is not a high risk of significant errors getting through the accounting process that would not be caught by a control procedure performed by an employee performing his or her regular duties.

The process used to fulfill responsibilities and determine the level of internal control necessary should adhere to the following steps and be documented.

Control Environment

It is the responsibility of the financial manager to establish an environment that encourages integrity and ethical values. The financial manager's leadership philosophy, competence, and management and operating style communicate to the employees a sense of control consciousness in the organization.

Risk Assessment

Risk assessment is the process of identifying financial risks and the consequences of such risks as related to control activities.

Control Activities

Control activities are those procedures designed to see that objectives are met and the risks identified in step two are reduced to a reasonable level. These techniques include procedures to ensure that transactions are

- These executed in accordance with management's general or specific authorization, and;
- These properly recorded to permit the preparation of financial reports in conformance with generally accepted accounting principles and to maintain accountability for assets.

Information and Communication

Surrounding the control activities are information and communication systems. These enable the organization's employees to capture and exchange the information needed to conduct, manage, and control operations. A large part of the communication system is the accounting system, which consists of methods and records established to identify, assemble, analyze, classify, record, and report the organization's transactions in accordance with generally accepted accounting principles and maintain accountability for recorded assets and liabilities. At a minimum, the system must be able to

- identify types of transactions executed (revenues, expenses, assets, and liabilities),
- accumulate (record) economic events in the appropriate accounts at the correct amounts, and
- record the economic events in the correct accounting period.

Monitoring

The entire process must be monitored and modified as necessary to react to changing conditions. The monitoring process should be performed at several levels. A supervisory review of activities should be on a regular basis as part of the normal management function. Periodic special reviews should be by management, internal auditors, and external auditors.

Not-for-Profit Organizations' Accountability

Not-for-profit organizations are defined as private, self-governing organizations that exist to provide a particular service to the community (e.g., American Legion Baseball, AAU Basketball, Boys Clubs, Community Soccer Leagues, Girls Clubs, Little League Baseball, YMCA, YWCA, and many more). The word *not-for-profit* refers to a type of organization that operates without the purpose of generating a profit for owners. As government continues to decline in providing services due to legal and budget constraints, not-for-profits have been filling the void by providing these needed services; but unlike government agencies, not-for-profits have not always been held to the same public scrutiny.

As scandals over not-for-profit accountability (e.g., American National Red Cross, United Way) make their way to the headlines of widely read newspapers, not-for-profit credibility wanes. As a result, not-for-profit organizations' images suffer, causing much of the public to decrease donations to all not-for-profit organizations; although, many of the accusations against not-for-profits are spurious. Today, not-for-profits face powerful accountability pressures and are asked by donors and the public to justify their delivered services and operations.

What Is Financial Planning?

Effective financial planning is the foundation upon which an organization can build a successful future. It is much easier for decisions to be made in a proactive manner rather than as a reaction to unplanned situations. Risks are reduced and the organization's competitiveness is increased (Horine and Stotlar, 2003).

An organization must develop a sound strategic plan which includes establishment of the organization's objectives, design of the organization's structure, recruitment and selection of qualified employees, inducing individuals and groups to cooperate, and determining whether or not the organization's objectives have been obtained. Financial planning is an integral part of any strategic plan. A strategic plan specifically for financial planning should be developed to integrate into the overall organizational strategic plan. All revenue and expenditures need to be planned for well in advance in order to ensure success of the organization.

When planning for financial success, the manager must consider many facets of finance, including cash planning, profit planning, capital budgeting, long-term planning, short-term financing, asset management ratios, forecasting, evaluating the environment, and risk management. The manager must be able to determine revenue streams and flow in order to cover expenditures in a timely fashion.

Financial planning can also help provide appropriate solutions for many of the problems that a business may face every day, such as:

- funding of capital projects
- developing new products and services
- retiring products and services
- selling assets
- purchasing assets
- protecting assets
- moving an organization to a new location
- covering tax liabilities

The financial staff's task is to acquire, and then help, employ resources so as to maximize the value of the organization. Here are some specific activities:

- forecasting and planning
- major investment and financial decisions
- coordination and control
- dealing with the financial markets
- risk management

Cash Planning

Determining the amount of cash needed at a particular point in the budget year can be accomplished by gathering data from both internal and external sources. Internal data are generated by the organization itself and may include areas such as past budgets, sales records, and human resources reports. This type of data is primary data. The organization generates the data, analyzes it, and compiles reports from the data gathered within the organization. Internal data can also be gathered from personal observation or conversations as well as customer and employee surveys.

External data may be gathered from resources outside of the organization to help determine the impact of factors such as the local, state, national, and world economy and demographic and geographic information. These external factors may impact sales and trends within the industry and the organization must be able to respond to the changing consumer needs. External data are often referred to as secondary data because such compilations have been published by another organization.

Because the nature of a sport is seasonal, the manager should utilize previous budget records to determine how much cash will need to be on hand during particular points in the budget year. During times of revenue prosperity, cash should be held back to pay for expenditures during the off-season or other low revenue points. Cash planning should also include capital projects, those projects that require large sums of money to complete, as well as daily operation expenses. Cash is any medium of exchange that a bank will accept at face value including bank deposits, currency, checks, bank drafts, and money orders.

Cash Flow

Cash flow is the difference between the number of dollars that came in and the number that went out. For example, a manager would be very interested in how much cash the organization expended in a given year to anticipate future cash needs.

Operating Cash Flow

Operating cash flow is an important number because it tells the sport manager whether or not an organization's cash inflows from its business operations are sufficient to cover its everyday cash outflows. For this reason, a negative operating cash flow is often a sign of trouble.

Cash Flow Budget

The cash flow budget is a forecast of cash receipts and disbursements for the next planning period. The cash flow budget is a primary tool in the short-run financial planning. It allows the sport financial manager to identify short-term financial needs and opportunities. Importantly, the cash flow budget will help the manager explore the need for short-term borrowing. The concept behind a cash flow budget is simple. It records estimates of cash receipts (cash in) and disbursements (cash out). The result is an estimate of the cash surplus or deficit.

Profit Planning

Profit is the sum remaining after all costs, direct and indirect, are deducted from the revenue of an organization. In general, revenue is the amount charged to customers for goods or services sold to them. There are alternative terms used to identify revenue including sales, fees earned, rent earned, or fares earned. The bottom line for an organization is the ability to generate revenue at such a pace that continued growth could be both sustained and achieved. If an organization has shareholders, this growth should include rewards, or dividends, for those shareholders.

While making a profit is the ultimate goal of any business, the mission, goals, and objectives of the organization should not be forsaken in order to obtain profit. By determining the short- and long-term goals of an organization and keeping them in mind during all phases of financial planning, resources can be better allocated to achieve these goals. Short-term goals are those goals that you want to achieve in the near future. The time frame for short-term is no more than 1 to 2 years. Long-term goals are priorities that are set for a 3-to-5 year period in the future and they often require more time and resources to bring to reality. These goals should move to the short-term goal list as their deadline approaches and resources become available. By properly planning where an organization's profits will be allocated, the manger can allocate funds for these various short- and long-term projects.

To properly plan for where and when profits will be spent, a person must first know where they are obtained and how stable that revenue generation will be over a longer period of time so the manager can better determine the profit margin. Revenue generation is not the only area of concern when determining profits. The manager must also forecast costs and plan for unforeseen emergencies in order to determine profit margin.

There are several commonly used measures of profitability. These include profit margin on sales, return on total assets, return on common equity, and return on investment. Profit margins, gross and net, are determined by dividing profits by revenue. Net profit margins use net income or income after taxes and interest and gross profit margin uses earnings before taxes and interest have been paid. Margin is the difference between the cost and the selling price of goods produced and services rendered. This is sometimes called a margin on sales or sales margin. Profit margin is a profitability measure that defines the relationship between sales and net income. The result is a percentage of profit. Some items have a high percentage of profit margin and others have a lower percentage. The sport manager uses the profit margin measure to determine what the price of the service or product should be to be competitive and allow the organization to make a profit.

Common equity is the sum of the par value (i.e., the principal amount of a bond that is repaid at the end of the term), capital in excess of par, and accumulated retained earnings. Community equity is usually referred to as an organization's book value or net worth.

Return on assets (ROA) is another profitability measure of profit per dollar of asset. The ROA is determined by dividing profits by average assets for a given reporting period. The average assets (i.e., an average of an organization's assets over a prior period of time) can be located on the balance sheet. The return on investment (ROI) is often referred to as the ROA because it reflects the amount of profits earned on the investment in all assets of the firm. These terms are interchangeable.

The return on common equity (ROE) is similar to the ROA; however, it is concerned with stockholder equity. The ROE is determined by dividing the net income by the average stockholders' equity in the organization. The ROA and the ROE can be effective in comparing the financial statuses of businesses of similar size and interest.

The balance sheet is a snapshot of the organization. It is a convenient means of organizing and summarizing what an organization owns (i.e., assets), what is owed (i.e., liabilities), and the difference between the two (i.e., equity) at a given point in time. If the difference between assets and liabilities is positive then the organization is profitable. The ROE is yet another profitability measure of how the stockholders did during the year. It is the true bottom-line measure of performance.

A fixed or permanent asset is one that is long-lived. These assets are tangible in nature, used in the operations of the business, and not held for sale in the ordinary course of the business. They are classified on the balance sheet as fixed assets.

Long-Term Planning

Long-term planning is considered any type of planning that is at least 5 years into the future. All sport managers need to establish a long-term plan for the organization. This plan can be 5 to 15 years in length. The plans need to be revised annually and extended for one additional year into the future. Each department within the organization needs to be involved in the long-term plan and each department's plan needs to be an integral part of the overall organization's long-term plan. Those organizations who do not plan well into the future generally are not around for the long haul. An organization cannot plan too much. Planning must be an integral part of the organization's culture.

Short-Term Financing

Most sport organizations in the private sector use several types of short-term debt to finance their working capital requirements, including bank loans (e.g., line of credit, revolving credit agreement, promissory note), trade credit (i.e., accounts payable), commercial paper (e.g., unsecured promissory note issued by the organization and sold to another organization, insurance company, pension fund, or bank), and accruals (i.e., accrued assets). Short-term credit is generally much less expensive, quicker, and more flexible than long-term capital; however, it is a riskier source of financing. For example, interest rates can increase dramatically and changes in an organization's financial position can affect both the cost and availability of short-term credit.

The Financial Manager

A common feature among all large sport entities is that the owners (the stockholders) are usually not directly involved in making decisions, particularly on a day-to-day basis. Instead, the corporation employs managers to represent the owner's interests and make decisions on their behalf. Those managers would include, but not be limited to: general manager, facility and grounds manager, concessions manager, human resource manager, risk manager, and financial manager.

The financial manager has the responsibility to answer key questions, including:

- What long-term investments should the organization consider?
- What lines of business will the organization be in?
- What sorts of facilities, machinery, and equipment will the organization need?
- Where will the organization secure the long-term financing to pay for investment?
- Will the organization bring in additional investors?
- Will the organization borrow the funds needed?
- How will the organization manage everyday financial activities such as collecting from customers, paying suppliers, and meeting payroll?

The financial management function is usually associated with a top officer of the firm such as the chief financial officer (CFO) or the vice president of finance. The top financial officer may have two key subordinates called controller and treasurer. The controller's office handles cost and financial accounting, tax payments, and management information systems. The treasurer's office is responsible for managing the firm's cash flow and credit, its financial planning, and its capital expenditures. In small organizations the responsibility for financial accountability, budgeting, and planning becomes the duty of the executive director or general manager.

The Role of Financial Analysis

An organization must review and revise its financial status just as it reviews its programs and facilities. Through financial analysis, managers can review financial statements, assess cash flow, and determine if the organization is financially sound. There is no real difference in reviewing your own personal finances and the finances of an organization. An organization will have more and different categories to review, but the purpose of the analysis is the same.

Financial analysis allows an organization to determine when, and if, capital projects may be undertaken, as well as take advantage of investment opportunities. Capital projects are often defined as a major building project, building acquisition, or major equipment purchase. Missed opportunities or great financial risk can result from poor financial analysis. Budget reductions often occur during economic downturns and knowing and understanding your financial status is essential in maintaining organizational solvency.

When analyzing financial statements, it is essential that good judgment prevails. It is more appropriate to compare the financial statements of similar organizations to obtain realistic information for present and future financial growth. The current performance of an organization should be compared with its performance in previous years. This will aid the manager in setting realistic goals and objectives for future growth.

Evaluating the Environment

Evaluating the environment in which your organization competes is vital to its long-term financial stability. From terrorist activities that may affect event planning to advances in food preparation for concession sales, the competitive environment in which an organization operates must be monitored to avoid missed opportunities as well as financial disaster.

There are numerous ways to evaluate the environment of an organization. The manager must first look internally for components that may be easily altered to bring about a more profitable future. Internal aspects may include employee benefits, workloads, staffing, and policies. All of these areas work together to provide a pleasant work environment, which, in turn, increases productivity. By reviewing benefit expenses, it can be determined, for example, if less expensive health coverage could be provided to save both the organization and the employee money without reducing services. Workloads may be reassigned or new staff hired to reduce overtime and tension of overworked employees. Policies may need to be altered as an organization grows both in size and as its financial status changes. All of these components are controlled within the organization and requires little effort to monitor, evaluate, and change.

The external environment in which an organization operates is not as easy to monitor and therefore necessary change may be slow; however, its importance is vital to the future financial success of an organization. The international political environment such as terrorism, war, and government stability must be monitored to determine if events must be moved or cancelled. The marketing environment for sports products and services must be analyzed so opportunities in the marketplace will not be lost. Demographics and geography should be reviewed to determine new market potential and current market change. Such information can be found in census reports conducted by the government. Market research is the foundation for reviewing the environment in which an organization operates.

Forecasting Sales

Financial planning is often based on the successes and failures of previous years' sales. Along with the present market analysis, managers can use previous sales to forecast future sales. A market analysis will include a strengths, weaknesses, opportunities, and threats, (SWOT) analysis of the organization and its competition. When properly conducted, a SWOT analysis can show the position of a product within the market and can help the manager realize future market potential and opportunities within the market place. Strengths and weaknesses are internal components that can be controlled and corrected within the organization whereas opportunities and threats are external factors that are influenced by areas such as the economy, trends, fads, culture, and the environment. By realistically forecasting sales, an organization can better plan for cash flow and conduct both short- and long-term planning.

Financial Risk Management

As sports enterprises become increasingly complex, it is becoming more and more difficult for the sports manager to know what problems might lie in wait. The sports manager needs to systematically look for potential problems and design safeguards to minimize potential damage. There are 12 major sources of risk common to sports organizations including business partners (e.g., contractual risks), competition (e.g., market share, price wars, antitrust), customers (e.g., product liability, credit risk, poor market timing), distribution systems (e.g., transportation, service availability, cost), financial (e.g., cash, interest rate), operations (e.g., facilities, natural hazards, internal controls), people (e.g., employees, independent contractors, training, staffing inadequacy), political (e.g., change in leadership, enforcement of intellectual property rights, revised economic policies), regulatory and legislative (e.g., antitrust, licensing, taxation, reporting and compliance), reputations (e.g., corporate image, brand), strategic (e.g., mergers and acquisitions, joint ventures and alliances, resource allocation, planning), and technological (e.g., obsolescence, workforce skill-sets) (Teach, 1997).

Preparing a Financial Plan

When preparing a financial plan, the manager must review all aspects of the organization and make decisions for its future stability and profitability. Financial planning will allow an organization to sustain itself through inflation, recession, cash flow shortages, and other economic situations that can be devastating to any business.

Building the Case

Without a sound financial plan, investors and lenders will not place their trust and resources into an organization. Research should be conducted by looking at both past and present budgets, revenue generation resources, and capital outlay projects. This research of both internal and external factors will provide the manager with an overview of the past and current financial condition and help to make future decisions for improved financial stability.

The Balance Sheet

The balance sheet, income statement, and cash flow statement all summarize some aspect of an organization's finances at a given point in time. The balance sheet summarizes the financial position of an organization at a particular point in time and is considered one of the most important financial statements. According to Parkhouse (2001), the four main uses of the balance sheet are that it shows (1) changes in the business over a period of time, (2) growth or decline in various phases of the business, (3) the business's ability to pay debts, and (4) through ratios, the financial position.

The balance sheet is a snapshot of the firm. It is a convenient means of organizing and summarizing what an organization owns (its assets), what an organization owes (its liabilities), and the difference between the two (the organization's equity) at a given point in time.

Auditing

Auditing is a field of accounting activity that involves an independent review of general accounting practices. Most large organizations employ their own staffs of internal auditors.

Internal auditing is an independent, objective assurance and consulting activity designed to add value and improve an organization's operations. It helps an organization accomplish its objectives by bringing a systematic, disciplined approach to evaluate and improve the effectiveness of risk management, control, and governance processes.

Internal control is a process affected by the board of directors, senior management, and all levels of personnel. It is not solely a procedure or policy that is performed at a certain point in time; but rather, it is continuously operating at all levels within the organization. The board of directors and senior management are responsible for establishing the appropriate culture to facilitate an effective internal control process and for continuously monitoring its effectiveness; however, each individual within an organization must participate in the process. The main objectives of the internal control process can be categorized as follows:

- efficiency and effectiveness of operations (operational objectives)
- reliability and completeness of financial and management information (information objectives)
- compliance with applicable laws and regulations (compliance objectives)

Operational objectives for internal control pertain to the effectiveness and efficiency of the bank in using its assets and other resources and protecting the organization from loss. The internal control process seeks to ensure that personnel throughout the organization are working to achieve its objectives in a straightforward manner without unintended or excessive cost or placing other interests (such as an employee's, vendor's, or customer's interest) before those of the organization.

Information objectives address the preparation of timely, reliable reports needed for decision-making within the organization. They also address the need for reliable annual accounts, other financial statements, and other financial-related disclosures including those for regulatory reporting and other external uses. The information received by management, the board of directors, shareholders, and supervisors should be of sufficient quality and integrity that recipients can rely on the information in making decisions. The term *reliable*, as it relates to financial statements, refers to the preparation of statements that are presented fairly and based on comprehensive and well-defined accounting principles and rules.

Compliance objectives ensure that all business of the organization is conducted in compliance with applicable laws and regulations, supervisory requirements, and internal policies and procedures. This objective must be met in order to protect the organization's reputation.

Internal control consists of five interrelated elements:

- management oversight and the control culture
- risk assessment
- control activities
- information and communication
- monitoring activities

The problems observed in recent large losses at organizations can be aligned with these five elements. The effective functioning of these elements is essential to achieving an organization's operational, informational, and compliance objectives.

Although the board of directors and senior management bear the ultimate responsibility for an effective system of internal controls, supervisors should assess the internal control system in place at individual organizations as part of their ongoing supervisory activities. The supervisors should also determine whether individual organization management gives prompt attention to any problems that are detected through the internal control process.

The Role of the Budget

The budget is a part of the foundation upon which an organization justifies its mission. It establishes financial parameters through which the organization can determine its objectives and attain its goals. The mission statement for the organization establishes guidelines that help construct the budget. It is the statement of purpose for the organization that establishes goals that the organization wants to achieve. Without a mission statement, an organization would not function in an effective and efficient manner. There would be no direction, goals, or means of obtaining those goals. An organization without a budget could be likened to someone setting out on a cross-country road trip to visit relatives without a map or plan for which direction to drive first.

A budget is an estimate of revenue and expenses for a given period of time, usually 1 to 2 years. Budgets anticipate or predict cash flow as well as control cash flow. Effective cash flow budgeting involves estimating when income and expenses occur to ensure that no times arise when a shortage of income means that an agency is unable to pay its expenses (Crompton, 1999). In sport, there are many periods when an organization may not be generating income sufficient to cover expenses. Monthly bills continue to become due and renovation projects are often undertaken during this off-season period. When cash flow problems are anticipated and planned for within the budget, the organization can easily attend to routine monthly bills as well as continue with maintenance schedules and renovation projects. The budget of the organization is determined by the organization's goals and objectives. Essentially, the budget is a restatement of the organization's goals and objectives in financial terms.

Budgeting Process

There are five steps that are commonly used in the budget process: (a) collecting data relative to the needs, strengths, and resources of the organization then applied to the mission of the organization and goals of the previous year, (b) analyzing the data collected and comparing it to past experiences and present requirements, (c) identifying other factors that may impact operations, (d) preparing the document according to stipulations and requirements of the organization's governing budget, including reviewing the document for accuracy and feasibility, soliciting a third party to review the draft document, and preparing for anticipated questions during the formal budget review, and (e) implementing the approved budget and auditing the budget at the conclusion of the fiscal year (Horine and Stotlar, 2003).

When collecting data for budget preparation, sports managers should use a variety of resources. Statistical information should be considered when preparing a budget. Statistics that a manager needs are: how income and expenses compare for a given period of time (variance analysis), usage and participation data, program evaluation reports, inventory levels, and other sources as appropriate (Sawyer & Smith, 1999).

Management must also look to employees for input on budgetary needs. Since employees are the users of equipment and supplies, they have firsthand knowledge regarding what is most effective and efficient in the production of goods and services. Management should provide all workers with the opportunity to share their knowledge and experience and to contribute to budgeting decisions.

To build a budget, management must be able to forecast, or predict with some degree of confidence, what expected revenues and expenses will be for the next fiscal period. Forecasting must be done for both existing programs as well as anticipated new programs (Sawyer & Smith, 1999).

When looking at other factors that may impact or have impacted the budget, we can explore trend analysis. Past budgets should be examined to attempt to identify financial trends that have developed. This can be accomplished by examining the financial statement for the current month and comparing with past months of the fiscal year, comparing the current month with the same month last year, comparing year-to-date with the same information of the previous year, and actual performance year-to-date with budget year-to-date (Horine and Stotlar, 2003).

There are internal and external factors that can also impact budget preparation. Internal factors are what come from within the organization, such as policy changes, personnel changes, and cost of living salary increases. These internal factors are within the organization's control. Those elements over which the organization has little or no control are termed external factors. These factors occur outside the organization and can include the economy, tax structures, trends, and changes in the law.

After all data have been collected and analyzed, dollar amounts should be calculated and applied to various accounts. Expenses should be based on input from the three methods of forecasting (i.e., employee, statistical, and managerial input). Revenue can be forecast using those methods as well. Most managers estimate expenses based on anticipated increases in the cost of living and/or suppliers' forecasts for price increases. Income, on the other hand, is usually projected to be somewhat less than actually hoped for (Sawyer & Smith, 1999).

After the budget has been completed, it should be reviewed with as much staff involvement as is possible and practical. The staff should be aware of the financial status of the organization for the upcoming budget year and management should feel confident that the budget appears reasonable and that justifications for expenditures are clearly stated. It is essential that questions and concerns be addressed at this level before the budget is sent forward to the governing board for approval. The budget should be sent forward for presentation and all staff should believe that the budget has been developed with the best available data, experience, and forecasting possible.

Budget Preparation

Effective budget management is the result of continuous long-range planning, review, evaluation, and preparation. Before one can begin to plan for the future of an organization, a budget must be prepared. A typical budget begins with the establishment of a budget calendar and manual. The calendar denotes the beginning and the end of the budget cycle (see Figure 6.1) and establishes a time schedule for completing each phase in the budget. Organizations operate on different fiscal calendars such as July 1 to June 30, October 1 to September 30, and January 1 to December 31. The approval process for the budget takes approximately 2 months, therefore the process needs to begin at least 6 months prior to the operational date of July 1, October 1, or January 1.

Figure 6.1

Sample Budget Cycle
July 1 to June 30 Fiscal Year Cycle

Implementation Phase	Monitoring Phase	Data Gathering Phase	Preparation Phase	Approval Phase
July 1 to June 30	July 1 to June 30	January 1 to February 28	March 1 to April 30	May 1 to June 30

The organization's CFO prepares the manual, and its main purpose is to facilitate a consistent understanding of what is expected from all involved in the budget planning process. The manual is distributed to all department heads so that there is a clear understanding of deadlines and expectations. Depending on the magnitude and scope of the organization, the process for developing a budget will be different and the number of staff involved will vary. The budget must still be established by the appropriate staff, approved by administration, and followed by all members of the organization. For example, a collegiate athletic budget would be prepared by the athletic director with input from all the head coaches; head athletic trainer; equipment manager; assistant athletic directors responsible for compliance, scheduling, and travel; facility and game management; and marketing and promotion. Once all data have been gathered and included in the overall budget and the athletic director reviews and makes adjustments, the budget is forwarded to the next level of administration for review, modification, and approval, then forwarded to the Board of Trustees for final approval. After the budget has been approved, it is implemented and monitored by the athletic director and the departmental staff.

The first step in preparation of a budget is the establishment of fiscal, operational, and policy guidelines that will affect the preparation of the budget. These include items such as salary increases, establishment of program priorities, personnel increases or decreases, and facility maintenance. These guidelines will be submitted to department heads. The department head, with consultation from the employees, will develop the details for the next budget year as well as for priority programs.

After the guidelines are received, the divisions (e.g., in a collegiate athletic program divisions might include each sport offered, sports medicine, facilities and equipment, game management, scheduling, travel, marketing, and promotion compliance) are asked to submit budget requests to department heads. These requests should include a rationale for the requested funding and be in a priority order. Funding for special programs and services should also identify sources for additional revenue and potential new markets for the program or service. Each department head is responsible for reviewing program requests and "pulling together" the priorities for funding to most efficiently and effectively utilize available resources. The department head is charged with submitting a comprehensive department budget that will encompass routine operating expenses (see Figure 6.2) as well as allow for growth and development of the department and the organization. The budget document should include a justification for expenditures so when presented to the governing body all questions and concerns regarding the budget can be effectively answered.

Figure 6.2

		Sample Explanation for an Expense
Printing	$45,000	25,000 football programs—5,000/game/5 games
		84,000 basketball programs—7,000/game/12 games
		10,000 baseball programs—500/game/20 games
		5,000 softball programs—250/game/20 games
		10,000 department brochures
		10,000 business cards

Preparation of the budget is a year-round process. While the director and agency staff may be involved formally in the mechanics of preparing and presenting the budget for only a six-month period each year, effective budget development is the result of continuous long-range planning, review, and evaluation (Crompton, 1999).

Revenue Sources

The types of revenue sources available will depend upon the type of organization and program involved. The primary sources of revenue generation are: (1) membership fees, (2) ticket sales, (3) admissions fees, (4) food and beverage concessions, (5) sponsorship agreements, (6) licensing agreements, (7) leases/rentals, (8) parking, and (9) merchandise sales (Sawyer & Smith, 1999). For detailed information refer to Chapter 7.

Expenditures

Expenditures are costs, or money paid out, that an organization encounters. Costs are those factors associated with producing, promoting, and distributing the sport's product (Shank, 2002). There are three types of costs: fixed, variable, and total. Expenditures are expenses (costs) that have been consumed in the process of producing income (revenue). Expenditures are often called expired costs or expenses.

Fixed costs are those expenses that do not change or vary in regard to the quantity of product or service consumed. A fixed cost used in breakeven analysis is that cost that remains constant regardless of the amount of variable costs. For example, fixed costs include insurance, taxes, etc.

Variable costs are those costs that are going to increase or decrease based on the increase or decrease in a product or service provided. For example, variable costs include advertising, utilities, postage, etc. If the facility will host a rock concert, a basketball game, and a beauty pageant this week, the cost for advertising events may increase. If only a basketball game is scheduled, the advertising needs may be less. Although an athletic team experiences very few variable costs in the total cost equation, a manufacturer of pure sports goods would encounter a significantly greater number of variable costs (Shank, 2002). As the number of units sold increases, the costs for packing and shipping the product also increase.

The total cost for operations is arrived at when the fixed costs (expenses) and variable costs (expenses) are added together. Costs are considered to be internal factors that can be largely controlled by the organization; however, they can have an external or uncontrollable factor. The costs of raw materials, league imposed salary minimums, and shipping of products are controlled by external factors. When establishing a budget, the sports manager must review the total operating expenses and consider both internal and external factors to forecast the expenditures for the upcoming year.

The common expenditures found in sports enterprise budgets include personnel, guarantees (e.g., dollars paid to visiting teams), advertising, team travel, recruiting travel, scholarships, costs of operation (e.g., postage, utilities, telephone, duplication, printing, office supplies, athletic supplies, sports medicine supplies, computer maintenance, etc.), association/league fees, officials fees, technology upgrades, capital projects, awards and banquets, insurance, and facility lease agreements.

Capital Budgeting

Capital budgeting deals with investment decisions involving fixed assets (e.g., equipment, buildings, accumulated depreciation for equipment and buildings). The term *capital* is defined as long-term assets used in production and *budget* means a plan that details projected inflows (amount of dollars coming into the organization) and outflows (amount of dollars leaving the organization to cover expenses) during some future period. Thus, the capital budget is an outline of planned investments in fixed assets and capital budgeting is the process of analyzing projects and deciding which ones to include in the capital budget.

Summary

Sports managers or their financial managers have a critical role in the management of revenue and expenses within an organization. Through proper analysis of financial records, a manager can determine cash flow and sales revenue and project future earnings. These reports and statements can help the organization realize capital budget projects and plan for the future.

Establishing a budget is a necessary process to help an organization keep sight of its mission, goals, and objectives. There are five frequently used budget types: the line-item, program, performance, zero-based, and entrepreneurial budgeting systems. A combination of two or more of these types is often used to effectively handle an organization's budgeting needs.

When collecting data for budget preparation, sport managers should use a variety of resources. A manager may need various statistics to aid in developing a budget. These statistics include how income and expenses compare for a given period of time (variance analysis), usage and participation data, program evaluation reports, inventory levels, and other sources as appropriate.

Effective budget management is the result of continuous long-range planning, review, evaluation, and preparation. Before one can begin to plan for the future of the organization, a budget must be prepared. Total costs are determined by reviewing fixed and variable costs, which will aid in determining expenses for a given budget cycle.

The task of the future sports manager is to seek out new resources that can help an organization achieve its goals. The unprecedented prosperity of sports in the 1970s and 1980s is gone and traditional revenue resources can no longer cover rising costs (Howard & Crompton, 2003).

Without adequate financial planning, organizations with continued limited resources will not be able to sustain economic stress. This stress can come from short-term issues such as cash flow or long-term problems such as litigation or national and international economic downturns. Every organization must be concerned with sound business practices and financial responsibility. The need to develop and follow such practices is essential to the current and future financial stability of the organization.

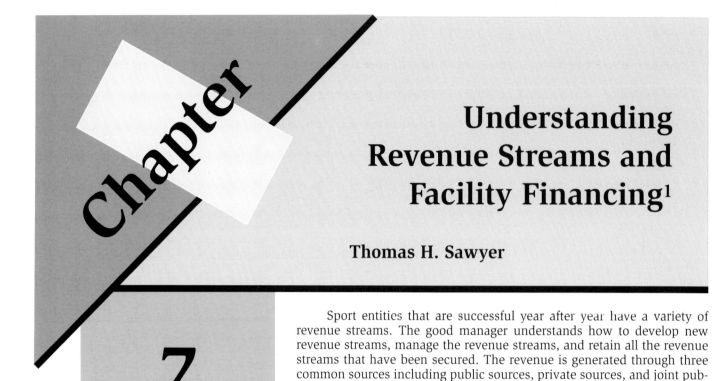

Understanding Revenue Streams and Facility Financing[1]

Thomas H. Sawyer

7

Sport entities that are successful year after year have a variety of revenue streams. The good manager understands how to develop new revenue streams, manage the revenue streams, and retain all the revenue streams that have been secured. The revenue is generated through three common sources including public sources, private sources, and joint public and private ventures. This chapter will focus on understanding the revenue streams available to sports managers.

Learning Objectives

After reading this chapter, the student should be able to

- understand how taxes can be used to finance sports entities,
- describe how tax abatements work in financing sports entities,
- describe the use of nontaxable bonds in financing sports entities,
- outline the value of taxable bonds in financing sports entities,
- understand how tax increment financing works,
- describe the use of luxury suites, club (premium) seating, and personal seat licenses to finance sports entities,
- outline the value of naming rights in financing sports entities, and
- understand the use of broadcasting rights in financing sports entities.

Public Revenue Streams

Since 1961 professional sports venues for Major League Baseball, National Basketball Association, National Football League, and National Hockey League franchises have cost, in 2003 dollars, approximately $24 billion (Crompton, 2004; Crompton, Howard, & Var, 2003). The public sector's share of this amount has been approximately $15 billion, which represents 64% of the total (Crompton 2004). Prior to 1950 the venues were almost totally built by use of private dollars.

Venue development has passed through four recognizable joint private and public funding eras (Crompton et al., 2003). Table 7.1 depicts the four eras and shows that there has been a substantial shift over time in responsibility for funding these types of facilities (Crompton, et al., 2003). It is clear that the public is growing weary of supporting venue construction for billionaire owners and multimillionaire players. The future funding for facility construction will require substantially more private funding and in some cases 100% private funding. According to Solomon, a New York City based journalist, for example, the St. Louis Cardinals' new $400 million stadium will be almost entirely privately funded.

Local, county, and state governments for over 50 years have played a major role in constructing and operating sports facilities for many programs including youth; interscholastic; community golf courses; community swimming pools; and professional ballparks, stadiums, and arenas. The financing often includes construction costs, infrastructure development (e.g., roads, sewers, water, and other utilities), equipment, and operations (see Table 7.2 for a listing of sports stadiums/arenas constructed in the United States).

---

[1]This chapter has been reprinted with modifications with permission from Sagamore Publishing. It represents Chapter 6, Understanding revenue streams, from Sawyer, T. H., Hypes, M. G., and Hypes, J. A. (2004). *Financing the sport enterprise.* Champaign, IL: Sagamore Publishing.

Table 7.1
Comparison of Public and Private Sector Financing by Funding Era

	Combined Costs for Stadiums and Areas	
Era	% Public	% Private
Gestation (1961-69)	88	12
Public Subsidy (1970-84)	93	07
Transitional Public-Private Partnerships (1985-94)	64	36
Fully-Loaded Public-Private Partnership (1995-2003)	51	49
Future Partnership (2004-2015)	33	67

Modified from Crompton, J. (2004). Beyond economic impact: An alternative rationale for the public subsidy of major league sports facilities. *Journal of Sport Management, 18*(1), 41.

Taxes

There are a variety of taxes that can be levied by local governments including so-called hard taxes and soft taxes. All of these taxes provide revenues to pay the public's share of costs for sports entities.

Hard Taxes

Hard taxes include local income, real estate, personal property, and general sales taxes. The burden of the hard taxes falls on all sales tax and a significant portion of local income, real estate, and personal property taxes on the taxpayers. The hard taxes often require voter approval.

Local Income Tax

Over the past two decades, local income taxes have been levied for economic development and other good reasons. The assessment ranges generally from .5% to 2.0%. In some jurisdictions, these taxes require voter approval.

Real Estate Tax

Local government (i.e., cities, counties, school districts, and in some states community college districts) for generations has been dependent on real estate tax revenue to cover operational and capital costs. Real estate taxes are based on the value of land and improvements (i.e., buildings and infrastructure). The current value (100% of market value) increases annually but generally is only reassessed every three to five years. Every time the owner improves the land or buildings he or she is required to report the improvements to the local tax assessor.

All property owners are required to pay the real estate tax except for churches, charitable organizations, educational institutions, and other government agencies. Some states exclude cemeteries, hospitals, and historical properties. The real estate tax serves as a benefit tax since its revenues are used primarily to finance local government expenditures for services that benefit property owners and increase the value of the property.

Personal Property Tax

The personal property tax includes tangible property (e.g., furniture, machinery, automobiles, jewelry, artwork, etc.) and intangible property (e.g., stocks, taxable bonds, and insurance). Many states have repealed the personal property tax for homeowners and collect taxes for motor vehicles through an annual licensing tax. Some states have eliminated all personal property taxes to encourage more businesses and manufacturing development within the state borders.

General Sales Tax

Sales taxes are the largest single source of state tax revenues and the second largest source of tax revenues for local governments after the real estate and local income tax. If a community is small but has a large retail center, the sales tax will very likely exceed real estate tax revenues. A sales tax is considered a user's tax and all taxpayers are taxed equally. However, it is also considered a regressive tax, which bears more heavily on lower income groups than on higher income groups. Many states reduce the regressive nature of the sales tax by exempting at-home food items and prescription drugs.

Notes

Table 7.2
Stadiums/Arenas in the United States

Stadium/Arena	Team	Capacity	Opened	Cost (millions) In 1995 $	% Publicly Financed	State	Sport Authority	League
Bank One Ballpark	Arizona Diamondbacks	48,500	1998	338	75	Arizona	Yes	MLB
Arizona Cardinals Stadium	Arizona Cardinals	73,000	2004	335	100	Arizona	No	NFL
American West Arena	Phoenix Suns	16,000	1992	97.7	39	Arizona	No	NBA
Coyotes Arena	Phoenix Coyotes	16,210	2004	210	85	Arizona	No	NHL
Anaheim Stadium	California Angels	64,593	1966	112.6	0	California	No	MLB
Dodger Stadium	Los Angeles Dodgers	56,000	1962	116	0	California	No	MLB
Network Associate Coliseum	Oakland Athletics	47,313	1966	120	100	California	No	MLB
	Oakland Raiders	62,000						NFL
The New Arena	Golden State Warriors	15,025	1966	120	100	California	No	NBA
PETCO Park	San Diego Padres	46,000	2004	456.8	49	California	No	MLB
Qualcomm Stadium	San Diego Chargers	71,294	1968	105	100	California	No	NFL
3 Com Park	San Franisco Giants	62,000	1960	126.5	100	California	Yes	MLB
	San Franisco 49ers	70,207						NFL
Staples Center	LA Lakers	18,500	1999	330	18	California	No	NBA
	Los Angeles Kings	16,005						NHL
Arrowhead Pond Arena	LA Clippers	17,250	1993	84.3	100	California	No	NBA
Arrowhead Pond Arena	Mighty Ducks	17,250	1993	84.3	100	California	No	NHL
ARCO Arena	Sacramento Kings	17,317	1988	90.15	0	California	No	NBA
HP Pavillion	San Jose Sharks	17,190	1993	179	82	California	No	NHL
Coors Field	Colorado Rockies	50,100	1995	215	75	Colorado	Yes	MLB
Invesco Field	Denver Broncos	76,125	2001	364.2	100	Colorado	No	NFL
The Pepsi Center	Denver Nuggets	19,309	1999	160	20	Colorado	No	NBA
	Colorado Avalanche	18,129						NHL
Civic Center Coliseum	Hartford Whalers	15,100	1975	86.4	100	Connecticut	No	NHL
RFK Stadium	Washington Redskins	56,454	1961	96.7	100	D.C.	No	NFL
MCI Center	Washington Bullets	20,674	1997	260		D.C.	No	NBA
	Washington Capitals	19,700						NFL
Pro Player Stadium	Florida Marlins	47,662	1987	154.2	3	Florida	No	MLB
	Miami Dolphins	74,916						NFL
ThunderDome	Tampa Bay Devil Rays	46,000	1990	171	100	Florida	Yes	MLB
Raymond James Stadium	Tampa Bay Buccaneers	65,647	1998	168.5	100	Florida	No	NFL
ICE Palace	Tampa Bay Lightning	19,500	1996	153	66	Florida	Yes	NHL
Jacksonville Stadium	Jasksonville Jaguars	73,000	1995	135	90	Florida	No	NFL
Miami Arena	Miami Heat	15,200	1988	68.3	75	Florida	Yes	NBA
Office Depot Center	Florida Panthers	15,200	1998	182	100	Florida	Yes	NHL
TD Waterhouse Centre	Orlando Magic	17,248	1989	125	100	Florida	No	NBA
Turner Field	Atlanta Braves	49,831	2000	235	100	Georgia	Yes	MLB
Georgia Dome	Atlanta Falcons	71,594	1992	232.4	100	Georgia	Yes	NFL
Phillips Arena	Atlanta Hawks	18,750	1999	213.5	100	Georgia	Yes	NBA
Wrigley Field	Chicago Cubs	38,765	1914	3.8		Illinois	No	MLB
U.S. Cellular Field	Chicago White Sox	44,321	1991	167.8	100	Illinois	Yes	MLB
Soldier Field	Chicago Bears	66,950	1924	20	100	Illinois	No	NFL
United Center	Chicago Bulls	21,711	1994	179.9	9	Illinois	No	NBA
	Chicago Blackhawks	20,500						NHL
RCA Dome	Indianapolis Colts	60,127	1984	139.3	50	Indiana	Yes	NFL

Table 7.2 continued
Stadiums/Arenas in the United States

Stadium/Arena	Team	Capacity	Opened	Cost (millions)	% Publicly Financed	State	Sport Authority	League
Conseco Field House	Indiana Pacers	19,200	1999	183	70	Indiana	Yes	NBA
Kauffman Stadium	Kansas City Royals	40,625	1973	73.7	100	Kansas	Yes	MLB
Arrowhead Stadium	Kansas City Chiefs	77,872	1972	78.3	100	Kansas	Yes	NFL
Superdome	New Orleans Saints	76,791	1975	379	100	Louisana	Yes	NFL
Camden Yards	Baltimore Orioles	48,000	1992	228	96	Maryland	Yes	MLB
Ravens Stadium	Baltimore Ravens	68,900	1998	200	100	Maryland	Yes	NFL
FedEx Field	Washington Red Skins	80,116	1997	250.5	70	Maryland	No	NFL
US Air Arena	Washington Bullets	18,756	1973	61.7		Maryland	No	NBA
	Washington Capitals	18,130						NHL
Fenway Park	Boston Red Sox	33,871	1912	6.5		Massachusetts	No	MLB
Gillette Stadium	New England Patriots	68,000	2002	325		Massachusetts	No	NFL
Fleet Center	Boston Celtics	18,624	1995	160		Massachusetts	No	NBA
	Boston Bruins	17,565						NHL
Comerica Park	Detroit Tigers	40,000	2000	300	38	Michigan	Yes	MLB
Ford Field	Detroit Lions	68,000	2002	300	50	Michigan	No	NFL
Palace of Auburn Heights	Detroit Pistons	21,454	1988	103		Michigan	No	NBA
Joe Louis Arena	Detroit Red Wings	18,227	1979	71.3	100	Michigan	No	NHL
H. Humphrey Metrodome	Minnesota Twins	56,144	1982	118.4	91	Minnesota	Yes	MLB
	Minnesota Vikings	63,000						NFL
Target Center	Minnesota Timberwolves	19,000	1990	136.3	72	Minnesota	Yes	NBA
Xcel Energy Center	Minnesota Wild	18,834	2000	130	100	Minnesota	No	NHL
Cardinals Ballpark	St. Louis Cardinals	47,900	2004	370	100	Missouri		MLB
Trans World Dome	St. Louis Rams	65,300	1995	299	96	Missouri	Yes	NFL
Savvis Center	St. Louis Blues	18,500	1994	138.8	46	Missouri	No	NHL
Giant Stadium	New York Giants	78,124	1976	200.8	100	New Jersey	Yes	NFL
	New York Jets							NFL
Continental Airline Arena	New Jersey Nets	20,039	1981	142.5	100	New Jersey	Yes	NBA
	New Jersey Devils	19,040						NHL
Shea Stadium	New York Mets	55,601	1964	117.8	100	New York	No	MLB
Yankee Stadium	New York Yankees	57,545	1923	28.3	21	New York	No	MLB
Ralph Wilson Stadium	Buffalo Bills	80,290	1973	75.5	100	New York	No	NFL
HSBC Arena	Buffalo Sabres	21,000	1996	125	45	New York	No	NHL
Madison Square Garden	New York Knicks	19,763	1925	200		New York	No	NBA
	New York Rangers	18,200						NHL
Nassau Vet Mem Coliseum	New York Islanders	16,297	1972	114	100	New York	No	NHL
Ericsson Stadium	Carolina Panthers	72,350	1996	247.7	20	No Carolina	No	NFL
Charlotte Coliseum	Charlotte Hornets	24,042	1988	67	100	No Carolina	Yes	NBA
RBC Center	Carolina Hurricanes	18,763	1999	158	88	No Carolina	Yes	NHL
Great American Ball Park	Cincinnati Reds	42,036	2003	297	100	Ohio	No	MLB
Paul Brown Stadium	Cincinnati Bengals	65,000	2000	400	100	Ohio	No	NFL
Jacobs Field	Cleveland Indians	42,400	1994	177.8	88	Ohio	No	MLB
Gund Arena	Cleveland Cavaliers	20,562	1994	159.3	97	Ohio	No	NBA
Nationwide Arena	Columbus Blue Jackets	18,138	2000	200		Ohio	No	NHL
Rose Garden	Portland Trail Blazers	21,401	1995	94	14	Oregon	No	NBA
Veterans Stadium	Philadelphia Phillies	62,382	1971	188	100	Pennsylvania	No	MLB
Phillies Ballpark	Philadelphia Phillies	43,000	2004	346	50	Pennsylvania	No	MLB
First Union Spectrum	Philadelphia 76ers	21,000	1996	206		Pennsylvania	No	NBA

continued

Notes

Table 7.2 continued
Stadiums/Arenas in the United States

Stadium/Arena	Team	Capacity	Opened	Cost (millions)	% Publicly Financed	State	Sport Authority	League
First Union Center	Philadelphia Flyers	19,519	1996	206	100	Pennsylvania	No	NHL
Lincoln Financial Field	Philadelphia Eagles	62,000	2003	285	50	Pennsylvania	No	NFL
PNC Park	Pittsburgh Pirates	38,365	2001	262	100	Pennsylvania	Yes	MLB
Heinz Field	Pittsburgh Steelers	65,000	2001	230	67	Pennsylvania	Yes	NFL
Mellon Arena	Pittsburgh Penguins	17,537	1961	112	100	Pennsylvania	No	NHL
Cumberland Stadium	Nashville Oilers	76,000	1998	292	100	Tennessee	Yes	NFL
The Coliseum	Tennessee Titans	67,000	1999	290	100	Tennessee	No	NFL
Gaylord Entertainment Center	Nashville Predators	17,500	1997	144	100	Tennessee	No	NHL
The Memphis Pyramid	Memphis Grizzlies	20,142	1991	65	100	Tennessee	No	NBA
The Ballpark @ Arlington	Texas Rangers	49,292	1994	196	71	Texas	Yes	MLB
Minute Maid Park	Houston Astros	42,000	2000	250	68	Texas	Yes	MLB
The Summit Arena	Houston Rockets	16,311	1975	51	100	Texas	No	NBA
Reliant Stadium	Houston Texans	69,500	2002	400	100	Texas	No	NFL
Texas Stadium	Dallas Cowboys	65,846	1971	131.6	100	Texas	No	NFL
American Airlines Center	Dallas Mavericks	19,500	2001	420	50	Texas	No	NBA
	Dallas Stars	18,000						NHL
SBC Center	San Antonio Spurs	18,500	2002	186	100	Texas	Yes	NBA
Delta Center	Salt Lake City	19,911	1991	100.6	26	Utah	No	NBA
Safeco Field	Seattle Mariners	46,621	1999	517.6	85	Washington	Yes	MLB
Seahawks Stadium	Seattle Seahawks	67,000	2002	430	100	Washington	Yes	NFL
Key Arena	Seattle SuperSonics	17,102	1995	114	82	Washington	No	NBA
Miller Park	Milwaukee Brewers	43,000	2001	400	78	Wisconsin	Yes	MLB
Bradley Center	Milwaukee Bucks	18,633	1988	116	42	Wisconsin	No	NBA
Lambeau Field	Green Bay Packers	60,789	1957	6.5	100	Wisconsin	No	NFL

The combined local and state general sales tax rates generally range from 3 to 10%. However, the portion most commonly collected by cities and/or counties ranges from 1 to 2%. It is not uncommon to find in a few northern states a general sales tax of 10% with 7% going to the state, 2% to the county, and 1% to the city.

The general sales tax has been used, in part, to finance sport entities and facilities since the early 1990s. The largest increases for sports facilities have been 0.5% (for Lambeau Field, Great American Ballpark, Seattle Seahawks Stadium, Paul Brown Stadium, Safeco Field, and Raymond James Stadium) and the lowest was 0.1% (for Invesco Field at Mile High, Miller Park, and Coors Field). In most jurisdictions, a voter referendum is required since the burden is borne by all residents.

Soft Taxes

The soft taxes include car rental, hotel-motel, player, restaurant, sin, and taxi. The soft taxes are borne by a select and relatively smaller portion (e.g., tourists generally) of taxpayers and are easier to levy.

Tourist Development Taxes

These are taxes imposed primarily on tourists. They include the cost of occupying a hotel or motel room and the cost of renting a motor vehicle. These taxes are easy to impose and cities are always ready to tax people who will not be there to take advantage of the taxes paid. Some might view this, like our forefathers did in Boston, as "taxation without representation."

Car Rental and Taxi Taxes

Many local governments have instituted a car rental tax to finance sport entities and recreational facilities. This mechanism has increased in popularity since the early 1990s. The average tax rate nationwide according to the American Automobile Association is 8%. Some communities have developed surcharges to be added to the base for a specific number of years to cover the cost construction of a sports facility (e.g., 3% in Atlanta for the Phillips Arena, 5% in Dallas for the American Airlines Center). The American Automobile Association and the car rental industry indicate that greater than 50% of the rentals are booked by tourists.

The taxi tax is similar to the car rental tax. The tax is calculated into the final fare the rider pays to the cab driver, limo driver, shuttle driver, or bus driver. The tax ranges from 2 to 5%. Approximately 30% of the taxes are collected from tourists.

Hotel-Motel and Restaurant Taxes

These taxes have been in existence for a long time and are the most commonly applied tourist taxes by local governments. Many communities use a portion of this revenue to support the development and operations of sports venues. The tax rate ranges from 6 to 15%, of which 2 to 5% is used to retire bond issues. The hotel-motel tax was originally called a bed tax.

Sin Taxes

There are four common sin taxes imposed on the sale of alcohol, tobacco, gambling, and prostitution (Nevada only). These taxes have partially been used to assist in financing the development and operations of sports facilities. Generally, the revenue is guaranteed for 15 to 20 years. In states where gambling has been legalized since the early 1990s, a portion of the tax revenue has been directed toward the development and operation of sports facilities.

Player Tax

In the early 1990s, state and local governments began to impose a tax on income earned by visiting players. Currently, there are 43 states that have imposed player taxes. The press has referred to this tax as the "jock tax." The tax is based on the right for states to tax nonresidents on income received for services performed within their boundaries. Many employees who live near state borders are taxed by the state they work in and again by the state they live in. For athletes, the tax is generally based on the number of days they performed in the state times their average per-game salary. However, there are states that define "duty days" as game days, practice days, days spent in team meetings, preseason training camps, and promotional caravans. In some jurisdictions, the state and the local government tax the player. Players have challenged this taxation but have failed to gain any ground. The real issue should be fairness. The question that should be asked is, "Do other performers such as actors, musicians, dancers, singers, and other entertainers who enter the state pay taxes?" If the answer is no, then maybe the player tax is unfair and constitutes taxation without representation.

Tax Abatement

Another tax strategy used by governments to stimulate private sector investment and create employment in the community is to offer property tax abatements (Howard & Crompton, 2004). Abatement programs exist in approximately two-thirds of the states (Severn, 1992). Typically, they are awarded whenever they are requested (Wolkoff, 1985); therefore, they often are part of a city's incentive package in negotiations with professional franchises (Howard & Crompton, 2004). Tax abatement will exempt an organization's assets from property taxation for a given period of time. It may be for all or a portion of the tax. The length of time varies according to the state enabling legislation.

Grants

Additional sources beyond taxes and bonding available from the public sector include state and federal appropriations and public grants.

Private Funding Sources

Most stakeholders as a result of declining public monies and questionable economic impacts prefer private sector investment (Miller, 1997). Private sector investments take on a variety of forms and degrees of contribution. The private sector regularly contributes to financing of sport facilities in ways such as the following:

- **Donation of Cash:** Cash is donated to the organization for general or specific uses in return for a personal tax deduction.
- **In-Kind Contributions:** An organization, business, or craftsman donates equipment or time to the project in return for a tax deduction.
- **Naming Rights:** Corporations vie for the right to place their name on the facility for a specific sum of money for a specific number of years (e.g., RCA Dome in Indianapolis, $2 million a year for 10 years; Conseco Fieldhouse in Indianapolis, $2.5 million a year for 10 years; Raymond James [Financial Inc.] Stadium in Tampa, $3.8 million a year for 10 years; Pacific Bell Park [Pacific Teleis Corporation], $50 million over 24 years) (see Table 7.3). The key elements of a naming rights agreement includes term or length of contract, consideration, signage rights and limitations, installation costs, marketing rights, termination upon default, reimbursement, and renewal option (Howard & Crompton, 2004).
- **Concessionaire Exclusivity:** Companies purchase the exclusive rights for all concessions within a spectator facility for a specific number of dollars over a specific time period.
- **Food and Beverage Serving Rights:** Companies purchase exclusive rights to soft drink, beer, and foods sold to spectators. See Chapter 8, Retail Operations, for greater details.
- **Premium Restaurant Rights:** Corporations purchase exclusive rights for all the restaurants within a spectator facility.
- **Sponsorship Packages:** Large local and international firms are solicited to supply goods and services to a sporting organization at no cost or at substantial reduction in the wholesale prices in return for visibility for the corporation.
- **Life Insurance Packages:** These programs solicit the proceeds from a life insurance policy purchased by a supporter to specifically benefit the organization upon the death of the supporter.
- **Lease Agreements:** These programs lease facilities to other organizations during the off-season or lease additional spaces within the facility not used for the sporting activity such as office space or retail space.
- **Luxury Suites (i.e., skyboxes):** Luxury suites are a dominant and universal feature in every new or remodeled stadium or arena. Luxury seating first became commonplace in stadiums (e.g., Astrodome was the first) and found in arena designs in the early 1990s. The luxury suite generally includes amenities such as carpeting, wet bar, restroom, seating for 12 to 24 guests, computer hook-ups, cable television, telephones, and an intercom. Table 7.4 depicts the number of suites as of 2001.
- **Premium Seating (i.e., club seating):** This is VIP seating located within the luxury suites or in the club areas of the stadium, which are the most expensive seats in the facility. See Table 7.5, which depicts club seat breakdowns, for a number of facilities.
- **Personal Seat Licenses (PSL):** Personal seat licenses became a widespread practice in sports venues in the early 1990s. The seat license is to the individual as the luxury suite is to the corporation. A seat license requires an individual to make an advance payment to purchase the right to secure a particular seat in the venue. After making the one-time payment, the buyer is provided with the opportunity to purchase a season ticket to that seat for a specified period of time. See Table 7.6 for average cost of a PSL in the professional leagues.
- **Parking Fees:** These fees are generated from parking lots that surround the spectator facilities. See Chapter 8, Retail Operations, for greater details.
- **Merchandise Revenues:** This income is generated by the sale of shorts, hats, pants, T-shirts, sweatshirts, key rings, glassware, dishware, luggage, sports cards, balls, bats, and other licensed goods. See Chapter 8, Retail Operations, for greater details.
- **Advertising Rights:** Rights are sold to various entities that wish to advertise to the spectators within the sports facility.
- **Vendor or Contractor Equity:** The vendor or contractor returns to the owner a specific percentage of the profit generated by the firms during the construction process.
- **Bequests and Trusts:** Agreements are made with specific individuals that upon their deaths a certain amount of their estates will be given to the organization.
- **Real Estate Gifts, Endowments, and Securities:** Agreements are made with specific individuals to give to an organization real estate, stocks, or mutual funds to support an endowment for a specific project. Only the annual income returned by the endowment would be used, not the principal.

Table 7.3
College Corporate Naming Rights

Venue	School	Total Value in Millions	Length of Contract
Save Mart Center	Fresno State Univ	40	23 years
Comcast Center	Univ of Maryland	20	25 years
Value City Arena	Ohio State Univ	12.5	Indefinite
Cox Arena	San Diego State Univ	12	Indefinite
United Spirited Ctr	Texas Tech Univ	10	20 years
Bank of America	Univ of Washington	5.1	10 years
Cox Pavilion	Univ of Nevada-Las Vegas	5	10 years
Wells Fargo Arena	Arizona State Univ	5	Indefinite
Papa John's Cardinal Std	Univ of Louisville	5	15 years
Coors Event Ctr	Univ of Colorado	5	Indefinite
Carrier Dome	Syracuse Univ	2.75	Indefinite
Alltel Arena	Virginia Commonwealth	2	10 years
Rawlings Stadium	Georgetown College (KY)	.2	4 years
Midwest Wireless Ctr	Univ of Minnesota-Mankato	6	20 years
U.S. Cellular Arena	Marquette Univ	2	6 years
First National Bank Ctr	North Dakota Univ	7.2	20 years
Reser Stadium	Oregon State Univ	5	10 years
Ryder Ctr	Univ of Miami (FL)	9	NA

Modified from Howard, D., & Crompton, J. (2004), *Financing sport* (2nd ed.). Morgantown, WV: Fitness Information Technology, p. 277.

Table 7.4
Luxury Seats in Sports Facilities

League	Suites in 2001	Teams	Annual Lease Price
MLB	2,286	30	$ 85,000
NBA	2,533	29	$113,000
NFL	4,294	31	$100,000
NHL	2,813	30	$ 77,000
Total	11,926	120	$ 93,750 average price

Modified from Howard, D., & Crompton, J. (2004), *Financing sport* (2nd ed.). Morgantown, WV: Fitness Information Technology, pp. 265-266.
Note: NBA/NHL shared arena annual lease price = $199,000.

Table 7.5
Sampling of the Number of Club Seats at Various Venues and the Prices Charged by Teams for Their Occupancy

Team	Facility	Club Seats	Price Range/Year
Lakers (NBA)	Staples Ctr	4,500	$12,995 to 14,995/season
Trail Blazers (NBA)	Rose Garden	2,500	$7,500 to 11,500/season
Nuggets (NBA)	Pepsi Ctr	1,854	$65 to 100/game
Knicks (NBA)	Madison Square	3,000	$175 to 1,350/game
Coyotes (NHL)	American West	1,651	$72/game; $3,250/season
Bengals (NFL)	Paul Brown	7,700	$995 to 1,900/season
Buccaneers (NFL)	Raymond James	12,000	$950 to 2,500/season
Ravens (NFL)	PSINet	3,196	$108 to 298/game
Indians (MLB)	Jacobs Field	2,064	$32/game; $1,905/season
Rockies (MLB)	Coors Field	4,400	$30 to 32/game
Rangers (MLB)	Arlington	5,700	$2,000/ to 3,000/season

Modified from Howard, D., & Crompton, J. (2004), *Financing sport* (2nd ed.). Morgantown, WV: Fitness Information Technology, p. 270.

Table 7.6
PSLs Average Cost by League

League	Average Price Range
MLB	$3,615 to 14,600
NBA	$ 900 to 5,000
NFL	$ 600 to 3,350
NHL	$ 750 to 4,000

- **Project Finance:** In 1993 the Rose Garden (Portland, Oregon) was the first facility financed using a new mechanism called project finance. *Project finance* is the Wall Street term that refers to the type of financing used to build arenas such as the Rose Garden, Delta Center, SBC Park, American Airlines Arena, and recently the St. Louis Cardinals' new home. The word "project" is used because traditionally this type of loan has been used to finance utility plants, factories, and other large enterprises. These entities have guaranteed revenues that provide comfort to the insurance companies and pension funds that lend the money. The recent Rose Garden bankruptcy case may leave insurance companies and pension funds reluctant to finance sports venues in the future.
- **Lexus Lots:** Atlanta's Turner Field and Miami's Office Depot Center, with the backing of area Lexus dealers, are carving out sections of preferred parking reserved for those fans who drive a Lexus. This new twist on sponsorship may be called exclusionary or elitist, but in the competitive marketplace it should be classified as creative thinking.

Private and Joint Public-Private Funding

Over the past decade, public-private partnerships have been developed to construct large public sports facilities. Typically, the public sector lends its authority to implement project-funding mechanisms while the private partner contributes project-related or other revenue sources. The expanded revenues generated by the facilities and their tenants have resulted in increases in the level of private funding (Regan, 1997). Recent examples of partnerships include the Alamodome (San Antonio), Coors Stadium (Denver), and Big Stadium (Saint Denis, France) (Regan, 1997). See Table 7.7 for some examples of joint funding efforts.

Broadcast Rights

There are 10 common types of broadcast media including networks as outlined in Table 7.8. The sale of broadcast rights is a major revenue source for professional sports, Division I intercollegiate sports, and many interscholastic tournaments. Television contracts are multi-year contracts worth millions of dollars to leagues and teams. For example, National Football League has a seven-year deal with ABC, CBS, ESPN, and FOX worth $17.6 billion; Major League Baseball has a five-year agreement with ESPN and FOX for $3.35 billion; National Basketball Association has a five-year contract with ESPN, ABC, and Time Warner for $4.6 billion; National Hockey League has a five-year contract with ABC and ESPN for $600 million; NCAA Men's Basketball has an 11-year contract with CBS for $6 billion; NCAA Football has a five-year contract with ABC for $500 million; and Professional Golf Association has a 4 year contract with ABC, CBS, ESPN, and NBC for $107 million (Schlosser & Carter, 2001).

Broadcasting executives link audience size and revenue together when deciding whether or not to broadcast a sporting event. The larger the audience size, the higher the potential for revenue production from advertising. Broadcasters seek programming that will appeal to larger, more valuable audiences. The contract for broadcasting rights is based on the potential for generating advertising and gaining high TV ratings. The greater the advertising revenue and the higher the average TV rating (e.g., the average five-year TV ratings for the NFL was 11.2; MLB was 2.8 for regular season, 12.4 for the World Series; NBA was 2.75; and NHL was 1.1 [Schlosser & Carter, 2001]), the greater the value will be for the short-term contract for the sporting entity.

Financial Team

All building projects need to assemble a proper financial team in order to design, organize, and finance a public, private, or public-private facility. A successful financial team should include the owner, facility manager, feasibility consultant, examination accountant, business plan consultant, financial advisor, facility consultant, architect, cost estimator, contractor, construction manager, senior underwriter, bond council, and owner's legal counsel (Regan, 1997). The financial team must work together to develop the goals and objectives of the community and/or owner. Successful facility financing is a partnership among the regional community, the owner, government, the financial institutions, and the investors.

Essential Points of a Financial Plan

The following are essential points of a financial plan. These points should be broken down for each year of the financial plan.

Table 7.7

Stadium/Arena/year	Public Financing	Private Financing	Total in Millions
Raymond James Stadium/1998	.5% sales tax		$168.50
The Coliseum/1999	$149.5 million thru hotel/motel taxes		$290
	$70 million from State		
	$55 million in bonds repaid by sales tax		
	$12 million for infrastructure		
	$2 million land donations		
MCI Center/1997	$60 million for infrastructure	Private loans	$260
Office Depot Center	$184.7 million thru 2% tourism tax	$42 million naming rights over 20 years	$212
RBC Center/1999	$22 million City and County	$20 million franchise	$158
	$48 million thru hotel tax	$80 million naming rights $4 million per year/20	
	$22 million NC State		
	$18 million State of N.C.		
Phillips Arena/1999	$130.75 million revenue bonds/arenas	$20 million from Turner Broadcasting	$213.50
	$62.5 million from 3% car rental tax		
American Airlines Center/2001	50% public financing	50% private financing	$420
America West Arena/1992	City bonds	Private debt	$90
Gaylord Entertainment Center/1997	City debt service	$26 million naming rights for 30 years	$144
	General obligation bonds		
Nationwide Arena/2000		Private financing	$200
United Center/1994	City contributed infrastructure	Private financing	$175
SBC Center/2002	City sales tax		$186
49ers new stadium		100% privately financed	$100
New Fenway Park	$50 million for traffic and infrastructure	$350 million design and construction	$545
	$80 million for parking garages (2)	$65 million for land	
Gillette Stadium/2002		$325 million	$325
Miller Park/2001	$310 million from five county .10% sales tax	$90 million	$400
FedEx Field/1997	$70.5 million by state	$180 million private financing	$250.50
Phillies Park/2004	$174 million	$172 million	$346
Safeco Field	$340 million .5% food tax and rental car tax	$75 million Mariners owners	$517.60
Minute Maid Park/2000	$180 million from 2% hotel tax and 5% rental-car tax	$52 million from Astros Owners	$250
		$33 million no-interest loan	
Heinz Field/2001	$96.5 million	$76.5 million by Steelers	
		$57 million for naming rights over 20 years	
PNC Park/2001	$262 million		$262
PETCO Park/2000	$225 million hotel-tax revenue	$153 private financing	$456.80
	$57.8 million project-generated redevelopment bonds		
	$21 million San Diego Unified Port Dist		
Great American Ball Park	$297 million		$297

Table 7.8
Ten Common Types of Broadcast Media

- ABC, CBS, NBC, FOX, Westinghouse Broadcasting, and Public Broadcasting Service
- Ultra High Frequency (UHF) Channels
- Superstations (namely, WGN in Chicago, and WTBS in Atlanta)
- Cable Channels (e.g., TNT in Atlanta, and USA Network in New York City)
- Sports Channels (e.g., Entertainment and Sports Programming Network [ESPN]; Sportsvision and Sports Channels in Chicago, St. Louis, Ohio, and Orlando; Prime Network in Houston; Prism in Philadelphia; and Sunshine Network in Orlando)
- Independent Producers
- Local TV Stations (local Very High Frequency [VHF])
- Cable Franchises
- Pay-Per-View
- Local AM and FM Radio Stations

- the mission, goals, and objectives for the overall plan
- an analysis of the organization's current financial situation
- an analysis of revenue projections versus expense projections, including dollars obtained through private fund raising and government resources
- an analysis of capital projections throughout the time period of the plan broken down into needs versus ideals
- specific information regarding the intended financial state at the end of the time period

Mechanisms for Financing Debt

Cities, counties, and states invest in capital projects by borrowing substantial amounts of money over an extended period of time. The loans or bond issues secured are backed by tax revenue streams such as real estate, personal property, personal income taxes, general sales tax, hotel-motel and restaurant taxes, sin taxes, and others. The downside, like personal loans to individuals to spreading out payments over a 15- to 30-year period, is the amount of interest incurred. However, politically debt financing is a desirable approach and, from an equity perspective, long-term debt financing makes good sense. The primary source for governments to secure long-term financing is through bonds. Bank loans are used for short-term loans of less than 5 years.

Bonds

The issuing of bonds is the most common way for a city or county to generate the needed money for recreation and sports facilities (Miller, 1997). A bond is defined as "an interest-bearing certificate issued by a government or corporation, promising to pay interest and to repay a sum of money (the principal) at a specified date in the future" (Samuelson & Nordhaus, 1985, p.828). According to Howard & Crompton (1995), a bond is "a promise by the borrower (bond issuer) to pay back to the lender (bond holder) a specified amount of money, with interest, within a specified period of time."(p.58) Bonds issued by a government or a subdivision of a state are referred to as municipal bonds. Municipal bonds are typically exempt from federal, state, and local taxes on earned interest. Bond buyers can include individuals, organizations, institutions, or groups desiring to lend money at a predetermined interest rate. However, according to Miller (1997), bonds are not a panacea for recreation and sports facility development for two primary reasons—debt ceiling or capacity and tax-exemption concerns by the public.

Tax Exempt Bonds Issued by Government Entities

There are basically two types of government bonds—full-faith and credit obligations, and non-guaranteed. A general obligation bond is a full-faith and credit obligation bond. The general obligation bond refers to bonds that are repaid with a portion of the general property taxes. There are two key disadvantages to issuing general obligation bonds—it requires voter approval and it increases local debt.

The second type of full-faith and credit obligation bond is a certificate of obligation. The certificate(s) is secured by unlimited claim on tax revenue and carries a low interest rate. Its greatest advantage to politicians is that the certificate(s) does not require a voter referendum.

Non-guaranteed bonds including revenue bonds, tax increment bonds, and certificates of participation have been the most common type of bonds used in funding sports facilities construction and operations (Howard & Crompton, 2004). These bonds are sold on the basis of repayment from other designated revenue sources. If revenue falls short of what is required to make debt payments, the government entity does not have to make up the difference. There are three main advantages for using this funding mechanism: voter approval generally is not required, debt is not considered statutory debt, and those who benefit the most from the facility pay for it.

Revenue bonds can be backed exclusively by the revenue accruing from the project or from a designated revenue source such as hotel-motel tax, restaurant tax, auto rental tax, or a combination of these taxes and others. Revenue bonds normally carry a higher interest rate compared to general obligation bonds (i.e., approximately 2%).

Certificates of participation are third-party transactions. It involves a nonprofit public benefit organization or government agency borrowing funds from a lending institution or a group of lending institutions to construct a new facility. Once the facility is completed, the organization or agency leases the facility to a public or private operator. This operator, in turn, makes lease payments to retire the certificates. There is no need for a voter referendum.

Taxable Bonds Issued by Private Entities

There are two types of taxable bonds—private-placement bonds and asset-backed securitizations. Private-placement bonds are sold by the sporting entity. The security for these bonds is provided by a lien on all future revenues generated by the sport entity. The asset-backed securitizations are also sold by the sporting entity. Its security is provided by selected assets, which are held by a bankruptcy proof trust.

In the mid- to late 1990s, local governments were inclined to provide less and less support for the construction and operation of sport facilities. Therefore, the private sector began developing a number of other financial strategies including luxury suites, premium or club seating, premier restaurants (i.e., high class restaurants), naming rights, and private-placement bonds. Facilities initially using the private-placement bonds included the FleetCenter (Boston) for $160 million, First Union Center (Philadelphia) for $142 million, and the Rose Garden (Portland) for $155 million. These private-placement bonds were issued for a long-term (20-30 years) with a fixed-interest-rate (6 to 9%) bond certificates to a large number of private lenders (e.g., insurance companies and venture capitalists). The private-placement bonds are secured by revenues generated from premium seating, advertising, concessions, parking, and lease agreements.

The asset-backed securitizations (ABS) are a variation of the private-placement bonds. The ABS is the newest debt financing mechanism in the private sector. It is secured by selling future cash flow through bundling such revenue streams as long-term naming rights agreements, luxury suite leases, concession contracts, and long-term corporate sponsorship deals. The following sports facilities have used ABS as the financing mechanism: Pepsi Center (Denver) and Staples Center (Los Angeles).

Tax-Increment Bonds

"Over half the states now have enabling legislation authorizing tax increment financing (TIF)" (Howard & Crompton, 1995, p.102). TIF is available when an urban area has been identified for renewal or redevelopment. Real estate developed with the use of TIF is attractive to stakeholders as tax increases are not necessary (Miller, 1997). The tax base of the defined area is frozen and any increases in the tax base are used to repay the TIF bonds. The economics of any TIF are dependent on the development potential of a chosen site and its surrounding land (Regan, 1997).

Special Bonding Authority

Special authority bonds have been used to finance stadiums or arenas by special public authorities, which are entities with public powers (e.g., Niagara Power Authority, New York State Turnpike Authority, or the Tennessee Valley Authority) that are able to operate outside normal constraints placed on governments. Primarily, this has been used as a way to circumvent public resistance to new sports projects (e.g., Georgia Dome, Oriole Park at Camden Yards, or Stadium Authority of Pittsburgh [Three Rivers Stadium]) and construct them without receiving public consent through a referendum. Without having to pass a voter referendum, the authorities float the bonds that are sometimes guaranteed or accepted as a moral obligation by the state (Howard & Crompton, 2004).

Summary

Successful sports entities have a variety of stable revenue sources to meet increasing expenses. There are three major categories of revenue sources including public, private, and a combination of public and private sources. It is extremely important for the sports manager to ensure that all varieties of revenue streams are maintained.

The public sources of revenue primarily include hard and soft taxes, tax abatement, nontaxable and taxable bonds, tax incremental financing, and special bonding authorities.

The private sources include grants, donations, in-kind contributions, naming rights, concessionaire exclusivity agreements, premium restaurant rights, sponsorship packages, lease agreements, luxury suites, premium (club) seating, personal seating licenses, parking, merchandise revenues, food and beverage serving rights, advertising rights, broadcast rights, vendor or contractor equity, real estate gifts, and bequests and trusts. The value of private-sector funding is best illustrated by the amount of revenue generated from private sources in the construction of The Ball Park in Arlington, Texas, which included $12.7 million from the ballpark's concessionaires, $6 million from first-year luxury suite revenues, and $17.1 million from personal seat licenses totaling $35.8 million (Brady & Howlett, 1996).

All sports entities should have a financial team in place to develop and implement a multiyear financial plan. The financial team is essential to bring together a partnership among the regional community, the owner, government, financial institutions, and the investors. Through these partnerships, the financial team will develop the goals and objectives of the community at large and the owner(s). It is a team effort to develop a sound financial plan to construct and operate sports facilities.

Retail Operations: Concessions, Merchandising, and Ticket Sales[1]

Thomas H. Sawyer

8

Sports organizations have known for years that retail operations can generate a significant and consistent revenue stream. If the retail operations are run well and selling the right products at competitive prices, they should be turning a handsome profit and saving the clientele money.

The most dramatic change for the food and beverage concession industry came in 1987 with the opening of Joe Robbie Stadium, which started the luxury suites and club seats era. The owners of Joe Robbie Stadium offered its customers a new level of service never before available in a sports facility: waiter and waitress service at their seats and a fully air-conditioned and carpeted private concourse featuring complete buffets from gourmet sandwiches to homemade pasta and freshly carved prime rib. A new level of culinary expertise would now be required of the concessionaire, and the concessionaire's skill would be instrumental in the success of the customer's total entertainment experience at the sports venue.

Successful retail operations accomplish the following: (1) feature prominent locations that require clientele to pass through the various sites; (2) offer personalized service and competitive pricing; (3) print catalogues for clients to share with friends; (4) merchandise their goods/products (i.e., displaying goods/products in an appealing way); (5) consider themselves retail outlets; (6) sell innovative goods/products; (7) concentrate on apparel, accessories, beverages, and food; (8) stock regularly needed convenience supplies; and (9) sell licensed merchandise.

The box/ticket office is the heart of a sports enterprise that fields teams. Its management is the key to financial success. Selling tickets to events is a major financial resource for any sporting team whether at the interscholastic, intercollegiate, or professional level. It is vital for sports managers to book a well-rounded schedule of events to satisfy the desires of the market and to ensure a major portion of the annual operating revenue.

Learning Objectives

After reading this chapter, the student should be able to

- understand the function of retail operations,
- prepare a store layout for a retail operation,
- understand a retail contract,
- appreciate the value of bonding personnel involved with collecting money and reducing theft, and
- understand the function and operation of a box/ticket office.

Retail Operations

Retail operations within a sports organization can include concessions such as beverage (alcoholic and non-alcoholic), fast food, and parking; licensed and convenience products; and full-service restaurants. Some operations (e.g., state and national parks) extend their offerings beyond products to include services such as rentals (e.g., bicycle, watercraft, ski equipment, golf equipment), downhill ski facilities and services, equestrian services, golf courses and services, photography services, marina services, shuttle bus services, theater productions, vending machine services, and aquatic facilities. Retail operations must stretch the discretionary income of the clientele. Some operations provide the organization a source of operating revenue separate from, but in addition to, a subsidy provided by the media rights and ticket sales. Others operate on a breakeven basis and serve strictly as a service to clientele.

---

[1]This chapter has been reprinted with modifications with permission from Sagamore Publishing. It represents a combination of Chapters 10, Box office operations, and Chapter 11, Retail operations, from Sawyer, T. H., Hypes, M. G., and Hypes, J. A. (2004). *Financing the sport enterprise*, Champaign, IL: Sagamore Publishing.

Concession Operations

The food and beverage concessions can be a gold mine if handled appropriately. Many stadiums and arenas are expanding their options from the traditional concession stand to include favorite fast food options (e.g., Burger King, McDonald's, Pizza Hut, Papa John's, Hardees, Taco Bell, Long John Silver, Kentucky Fried Chicken, Ballpark Franks, TCBY yogurt, Krispy Kreme donuts, TGI Friday's (Miller Park), Outback Steakhouse (PNC Park), Hard Rock Café (SkyDome), etc.) as well as the traditional hot dog, popcorn, peanuts, pretzels, and beer concessions. All stadiums have added, along with their luxury suites and club seats, full-service premium restaurants. Numerous concession companies have added regional favorites including a microbrewery and Rocky Mountain oysters in Denver, fish tacos in San Diego, cheesesteaks in Philadelphia, and dog-bone-shaped chocolate chip cookies in Cleveland. The greatest amount of profit in the food concessions business is from soda drink sales followed by popcorn, hot dogs, nachos and cheese, candy, and beer. See Chart 8.1 for a listing of 2003 soda and beer pouring rights for NFL stadiums.

A food concession open from dawn to dusk must be flexible, offering breakfast, lunch, and dinner favorites that are fast and convenient. People expect to pay more at a food concession than elsewhere because of the convenience factor. The food concession will be successful if the customers' needs and wants are known and a clean fresh atmosphere with friendly, convenient, and fast service is provided.

The food concession must be conveniently located to the customer. Many stadiums and arenas are now using portable concession stands as well as permanent locations to provide more convenient service to the customers. The food concession area should have plenty of counter space; hot and cold running water; adequate electricity to operate popcorn popper, microwave, refrigerator and freezer; a warming unit; and storage space. The floor and walls should be tile. The floor should have numerous drains for cleaning. On the customer side, there should be plenty of space to accommodate a large number of people quickly and efficiently.

The seven major concessionaires in the food service industry are:

- Aramark (largest concession company in North America)
- Compass (European, largest concession company in the world)
- Fine Hosts Corporation
- Global Spectrum
- Sodexho (European)
- Sportservice Corporation (Buffalo)
- Volume Services America (VSA), now known as Centerplate (Spartanburg)

Concessions

Myers and Jewell (1982) indicated a well-operated concession operation is more often than not the determining factor in the financial status of a facility. Rarely is an auditorium successful without a sound concession operation. The importance of good concession operation to the average facility cannot be overemphasized. The role of the concession operation is to generate revenue and provide good food and drink to the consumers.

The concession operation requires managers to understand the following: (1) how to serve good food at a reasonable price, (2) development of marketing strategy, (3) financial management, (4) business planning, (5) purchasing, (6) inventory management, (7) business law, (8) health codes, (9) OSHA regulations, (10) selection of insurance, (11) how to advertise, (12) selection of personnel, (13) stocking the concession area, (14) maintaining the equipment, (15) housekeeping requirements, (16) how to establish price, and (17) convenience foods.

The location and configuration of concession operations is extremely important to their success. There are four sources of good information about concessions operation: (1) International Association of Auditorium Managers (IAAM), (2) National Association of Concessionaires (NAC), (3) Don Jewell's book *Public Assembly Facilities Planning and Management* (1981), and (4) Steve Roger's article, *Avoiding Concession Design Problems* in *Managing the Leisure Facility* (1980).

Rogers (1980) listed the major shortcomings as: (1) not enough concession stands to serve the number of seats, (2) inadequate kitchen location and space, (3) no installation of floor drains in kitchen and stand areas, (4) no provision for a commissary for hawking (vending) operations, (5) service elevators on the opposite side of the building from storage areas, (6) no provisions for exhaust, (7) loading docks and storerooms on different floors than needed, (8) inadequate ventilation, (9) insufficient energy and water availability, and (10) lack of wide concourse areas to facilitate traffic flow.

Concession stands should be (1) conveniently located to all seats (a patron should be able to reach a stand in 40 to 60 seconds.); (2) well-organized with clear indications of where the patrons should line up for service; (3) bright, colorful, well-lit, and decorated with attractive pictures of food and beverage being served; (4) able to generate the aroma of food such as popcorn into the concourse; (5) designed so equipment, food, and cash registers are located so that items can be quickly served by a single person in each selling station; (6) constructed so that menu boards are appropriately placed indicating the products and prices; and (7) attention grabbers.

The National Association of Concessionaires (NAC) in conjunction with Coca-Cola USA and Cornell University published a study (1982) for NAC members entitled, "Creating and Handling Buying Fever," which discussed the basic elements of a successful concession operation. The key points of the NAC's

Chart 8.1
Beverage Contracts for NFL Stadiums 2003

NFL Stadiums	Soda Exclusive Pouring Rights	Beer Pouring Rights
Arizona Cardinals Sun Devil Stadium	Coke	NA
Atlanta Falcons Georgia Dome	Coke	NA
Baltimore Ravens M&T Bank Stadium	Pepsi	Budweiser, Bud Light, Coors Light, Miller Lite, Sam Adams, Killian's, Michelob Amber Bock, Red Hook
Buffalo Bills Ralph Wilson Stadium	Pepsi	NA
Carolina Panthers Ericsson Stadium	Pepsi	Miller Lite, MGD, Icehouse, Sky Blue, Miller, Budweiser, Bud Light, Michelob Ultra, Michelob Light, Red Hook, Widmer, Amstel Light, Heineken, Carolina Blond, Harp, Bass, Pilsner Urquell, Newcastle Brown, Coors Light, Foster's Miller, Miller Lite, Leinenkugel Red, Honkers Ale, Bass, Guinness
Chicago Bears Soldier Field	Coke	Budweiser, Bud Light, Michelob Light, Michelob Ultra, Miller Lite, MGD, Sam Adams, Warsteiner, Warsteiner Dunkel, Warsteiner Oktoberfest, Coors Light, Barrelhouse Red Leg Ale, Barrelhouse Vandermeer Strong Ale, Hudy Delight
Cincinnati Bengals Paul Brown Stadium	Coke	NA
Cleveland Browns Cleveland Stadium	Pepsi	Miller Lite, MGD, Budweiser, Bud Light, Coors Light
Dallas Cowboys Texas Stadium	Pepsi & Dr. Pepper	Budweiser, Bud Light, Coors, Miller, Miller Lite
Denver Broncos Invesco Field	Coke	Budweiser, Bud Light, Labatt, Labatt Light, Heineken, Amstel Light
Detroit Lions Ford Field	Pepsi	Miller Lite, MGD, Miller High Life, Rolling Rock, Labatt Blue
Green Bay Packers Lambeau Field	Coke	Miller Lite, Bud Light, Foster's, Michelob Ultra, Heineken, Shiner Bock, Sam Adams, Fat Tire
Houston Texans Reliant Stadium	Coke	St. Arnold, Sierra Nevada
Indianapolis Colts RCA Dome	Coke	Budweiser, Bud Light, Miller, Miller Lite, Coors Light
Jacksonville Jaguars Alltel Stadium	Pepsi	Bud Light, Budweiser, Miller Lite, Coors Light, Amber Bock, Michelob Light, Foster's
Kansas City Chiefs Arrowhead Stadium	Coke	Budweiser, Bud Light, Coors Light, Miller Lite, MGD, Heineken, Boulevard
Miami Dolphins Pro Player Stadium	Coke	Budweiser, Bud Light, Miller Lite, Icehouse, Michelob Light, Michelob Ultra, Michelob, Amber Bock, Foster's, Killian's, Yuengling, Heineken, Amstel, Bass, Beck's, Sam Adams, Coors Light
Minnesota Vikings Metrodome	Coke	Budweiser, Bud Light, Grain Belt Premium (contract requires a Minnesota brew) and lots of specialty beers, Budweiser, Coors Light, Bud Light, Heineken, Amstel Light, Guinness, Bass Ale, Sam Adams
New England Patriots Gillette Stadium	Pepsi	Budweiser, Bud Light, Miller Lite, Coors Light, World Select, Heineken, Michelob Ultra, Red Dog

continued

Chart 8.1 continued
Beverage Contracts for NFL Stadiums 2003

New Orleans Saints Superdome	Coke	Miller, MGD, Miller Lite, Coors Light, Heineken, Guinness, Budweiser, Bud Light
New York Giants and Jets Meadowlands	Pepsi	Bud Light, Coors Light, MGD, Heineken, Dos Equis, Tecate, Gordon Biersch, Pyramid, Deschutes, Guinness, Foster's
Oakland Raiders Network Associates Coliseum	Pepsi	Miller, Miller Lite, MGD, Budweiser, Bud Light, Coors Light, Pilsner Urquell, Labatt
Philadelphia Eagles Lincoln Financial Field	Pepsi	Michelob Amber Bock, Foster's
Pittsburgh Steelers Heinz Field	Coke	Rolling Rock, Green Light, Loyal Hanna, Iron City, Iron City Light, Coors Light, Budweiser, Bud Light, Miller Lite, Labatt Blue, Guinness, Bass Ale, Harp, Penn Pilsner, Yeungling, Michelob Ultra
St. Louis Rams Edward Jones Dome	Coke	Budweiser, Bud Light, Miller Lite
San Diego Chargers Qualcomm Stadium	Coke	Budweiser, Miller, Heineken, Corona and more
San Francisco 49ers 3Com Park	Coke	Miller, MGD, Miller Lite, Budweiser, Bud Light, Coors, Coors Light, Gordon Biersch, Red Hook, IPA, Sierra Nevada, Heineken, Foster's, Anchor Steam, Beck's
Seattle Seahawks Seahawks Stadium	Coke	Budweiser, Bud Light, Busch, Michelob Ultra, Miller Lite, MGD, Coors Light, Widmer's, Heffeweisen, Amber Bock, Heineken, Beck's, Pyramid
TB. Buccaneers Raymond James Stadium	Coke	Budweiser, Bud Light, Miller Lite and Icehouse, Coors Light
Tennessee Titans Coliseum	Coke	Budweiser, Bud Light, Michelob Ultra, Miller Lite, MGD, Michelob, Coors Light, Bohannon
Washington Redskins FedEx Field	Coke	NA

Modified from Kaufman, G. (December 2003). *Venuestoday*, 2(12), 28.

"Buying Fever Check List" are listed as:

- Review merchandising and menu boards for clarity. Communicate and make it easier to order.
- Cut down on inquiry time through effective menu board layout.
- Use combinations of menu items to reduce the number of customer decisions.
- Keep your equipment in good repair. Perform preventative maintenance checks regularly.
- Locate equipment and supplies for soft drinks and popcorn adjacent to the dispensers.
- Place the menu board so that it is easily visible to all customers.
- Ensure that employees check supplies during slack time and that additional supplies are easily accessible.
- Make lettering on the menu boards large enough so that it is easily readable for all customers. List all brands of soft drinks carried in their logo script and all the names of sizes and prices for all items.
- Provide containers or boxes for customers to carry large orders.
- If you do not have a cash register, place an adding machine or table of prices for popular combinations for the employees to use.
- Design the stand with promotions in mind. Build in space to handle premiums such as plastic cups and posters.
- Locate the stand in an accessible area with the right products, packages, and price.
- Keep the stand very neat and clean.
- Make sure the personnel are well trained and pleasant.

Further, all facilities should consider having "vendors" or "hawkers" take food and beverages to the people in their seating who are reluctant to get up and risk missing part of the event. Another contribution made by "vendors" or "hawkers" is that they relieve the pressure placed upon permanent concession stands during the intermission when customers swarm the concession facilities.

Finally, all facilities should have portable concession stands to be used during special events. These usually are attractive wagons that everyone has seen in shopping malls and airports.

Food Concession Guidelines

It is important for any food concession system to have operation guidelines. The recommendations address and include employee appearance, training goals, maintenance goals, operation goals, regulations, inspections, safety and sanitation certification , patron comforts, guest relations, professional signs and pricing, decorations, and food handler's guidelines.

National Organizations for Concessionaires

The sports manager should be aware of three national organizations that deal with food and beverage concessions. The first is the National Association of Concessionaires, which can be found on the web at http://www.NAConline.org. This organization offers a concession manager certification course and an executive concession manager certification course. The programs for these courses include the topics: management, profit planning, cost control systems, menu planning/branding, and event planning. The basis of the course and the textbook it is based on are also part of the curriculum at the School of Hospitality Management at Florida International University in Miami and the School of Human Sciences, Department of Nutrition and Food Science at Auburn University in Alabama. The second organization is the National Association of Collegiate Concessionaires whose URL address is http://www.NACC-Online.com. Finally, a third organization is the Outdoor Amusement Business Association (OABA) that can be reached at http://www.oaba.org. The OABA has guidelines for food and game concessions.

Alcohol Management

The focus on patron safety relating to alcohol consumption began in 1983 with Bearman v. University of Notre Dame. The Indiana Supreme Court determined that Notre Dame had a "duty" to its paid patrons. This was a landmark case because the court determined that intoxicated persons could pose a general danger to other patrons. This determination flew in the face of previous decisions that placed the responsibility of duty of care on the individual or group, not on the event organizers. The Court determined that foreseeability dictated that Notre Dame had a duty to protect its patrons from the potentially dangerous actions of intoxicated third parties. This case set the standard for duty of care for the management of alcohol at events.

In a number of states, there are dram shop statutes that allow injured plaintiffs to bring suit against restaurants, bars, and other establishments that allow the defendant to become drunk. In some states, the court allows recovery through common negligence actions. There are a few states that allow recovery using both methods.

In addition to the dram shop statutes, there is another liability known as the social host liability. This statute provides the injured plaintiff an opportunity to sue based on a social host knowingly serving alcohol to a minor who becomes intoxicated and causes injury or damage to property. In the jurisdiction where this line of thinking is embraced, the venue manager should be aware of this type of liability.

Alcohol Management Plan

Venue managers should have in their liability tool bags an alcohol management plan. This plan should be coordinated with the crowd control management plan. The plan should include procedures to check age restrictions, restrictions on the number of beers served, terminating beer sale at a specific point during the event (e.g., basketball, end of third period; football, beginning of third quarter; ice hockey, end of the second intermission; and baseball, end of the seventh inning), deploying trained personnel to watch for trouble, and incorporating a designated-driver program.

Alcohol Sales Strategies

In 1992, Miller Brewing Company, in combination with previous research and encouragement from its legal department, provided the following suggestions regarding an effective alcohol sales strategy (modified from Ammon, Southall, & Blair, 2004, pp.188-189):

1. Decide whether or not to sell alcohol. If the decision to sell alcohol is made, then an alcohol management plan must be developed.
2. Develop procedures to stop outside alcohol from entering the venue.
3. Establish crowd management procedures for alcohol management for day and evening events and for weather.
4. Install appropriate signage to inform patrons about responsible and irresponsible drinking and its consequences.
5. Establish a strong ejection policy.
6. Do not promote or advertise drinking during the event.
7. Make sure that security personnel are aware of the demographics of the crowd in each section of the venue (e.g., gender, white-collar, blue-collar, families, senior citizens, under 21, etc.).
8. All staff (not just security and servers) should complete regulated alcohol management training.
9. Establish consumption policies (e.g., number of beers per patron at one time, termination of sales prior to conclusion of the event).
10. Only permit tailgating in parking lots under strict supervision of security personnel.
11. Establish no-alcohol sections within the venue (i.e., family sections).
12. Develop a designated-driver program.

Parking Concession

The parking concession can be profitable, but it has liabilities. The manager, before charging for parking, must ensure that the following have been accomplished: (1) purchase adequate liability insurance, (2) provide adequate surfacing for the proposed traffic, (3) ensure safe entrance and exit areas, (4) provide adequate lighting, (5) plan for immediate snow and ice removal, (6) establish an emergency plan for the space, (7) ensure that adequate supervision and security is available, (8) provide for the safety of the pedestrians, (9) plan a graphic system that makes it easy to find customers' cars at the conclusion of the event, and (10) provide an adequate number of cashiers and attendants. After the manager has accomplished the above, it is time to decide how many spaces will be for persons with disabilities (i.e., review state and federal disability guidelines for actual number of spaces), VIPs, and regular customers. The greatest amount of money will be made from VIP parking.

According to Russo (2001), the following controls should be implemented to ensure a smooth operation: "(1) sensors or loops buried in each entrance line; (2) a single pass lane; (3) a cashier or checker watching the sellers and authorizing passes; (4) spot checks on sellers; (5) different colored tickets for different events, days, or hours; (6) cash registers; (7) TV monitors; and (8) clean graphics and signs indicating special entrances."

The parking operation is second only to the box office in terms of direct contact between the facility and the patron. A well-designed and managed parking operation will ease crowd tension and allow for sufficient time for patrons to buy snacks, enter the venue, and still be in their seats on time. There is no question that the ease of access and parking is a major factor in increased public acceptance and attendance at events.

Mercantile Operations

These are the stadium or arena gift or souvenir shops. They deal with licensed products and convenience items needed by patrons while attending a sporting event.

Finding a Retail Niche

Finding customers who value what you offer is difficult at best. Achieving customer approval is especially demanding in these uncertain times. It takes regular and consistent cultivation on several fronts. Every community is overwhelmed with retail shopping locations and merchants offering everything imaginable. What distinguishes your business from the rest? Developing a niche and working it could be the best answer.

Rigsbee (1997) suggests that the following questions are crucial to your success. Record your answers and you are sure to hit pay dirt. Your responses will indicate who your customers are and, more importantly, who they should be:

- How is my store special and unique?
- What groups of people would most benefit by what I offer?
- How have I physically set up my store to be user-friendly and to serve this group of people?
- Is my advertising targeted to the customers I desire to serve?
- What products do I like?

In your efforts to add value, a pitfall to avoid is that of adding the value you desire, rather than the value your niche customers want (Rigsbee, 1997). Become market driven, rather than product driven, by listening to your customers' needs, wants, and desires. Do this, and they will reward you with greater profitability than you have ever enjoyed before.

Using Cutting-Edge Retail Strategies in Merchandising and Buying

The world of retailing is changing at breakneck speed. These changes are driven by busy people who have too little time to shop, consumers who have new economic priorities, and the fact that too many stores are selling the same merchandise. All this is having a profound impact on when, where, and how merchandise is sold.

Ensman (1999) suggests there are nine steps to being a good buyer. He has put these nine steps under the umbrella of B-U-Y W-I-S-E-L-Y:

- **B**e specific in defining needs, identifying performance, and results.
- **U**nderstand the options that are available prior to purchasing the item(s).
- Tell the supplier, It's **Y**our move. Tell me why you can meet my needs better than anyone else.
- Aim for a **W**in-win situation between you and the seller.
- **I**mpose deadlines and conditions when necessary.
- **S**eek assistance from an outside consultant when in doubt about a purchase.
- **E**ducate the seller about your special needs.
- **L**ook for after-sale service.
- **Y**ell for help when necessary.

The Four Ms in Retail

Shaffer (1999) indicates that "operating a successful retail establishment comes down to the four Ms: merchandising, markups, marketing, and methodology." The basis for any success in a retail business comes down to merchandising the items placed on the shelves. Failing to carry what the customer wants and needs, they will breeze right past on their way to their destination; but capture their interest, and you have won a dedicated customer.

Merchandise must be visible. If nobody sees what merchandise is available, the store manager is setting him- or herself up to fail. The store should be positioned in a high-traffic area where the customers must pass by on their way to activities. If merchandise is not in their line of sight, customers will probably not be enticed to enter the store. Keeping goods in a high-traffic space will discourage shoplifting.

Basic Store Merchandise

The retail store does not require a great deal of space. Some of the most popular elements that will enable an organization to start even the most basic store are outlined in Table 8.1.

Most retailers agree that you should promote your retail store by offering clothes with the organization's logo. Embroidered items go so much faster than anything else. People like to wear items that look good and are crisp, sharp, and classy. Embroidery even dresses up a really nice T-shirt.

Retail Store Design

The retail manager needs to carefully plan the layout of the retail store. The store layout is as much a marketing tool as are the catalogues and merchandise on the shelves. The manager needs to work with a consultant and visit other employee stores before making the final decisions regarding store layout, space needs (including storage), and overall design.

Table 8.1
The Building Blocks

Clothing		
T-shirts	Shorts	Hats
Socks	Sweatshirts	Tank tops
Bike shorts	Gore-Tex running suits	Coolmax singlets

Effective Store Layout

When a customer enters an employee store, what do they see? Do they see a store that is cluttered and disorganized or one that is clean, attractive, and interesting? Do they see too much merchandise or too little? Do they see merchandise that is poorly displayed or do they see a well-designed store that shows off the merchandise at its best? Do they find it difficult to locate specific merchandise, brands, styles, sizes, and colors; or do they find a store with merchandise that is logically organized on racks and shelves so that it is easy to find and buy? Do they experience a dynamic shopping environment or just another store where they can occasionally buy a few items because it is convenient and the prices are pretty good? (Whalin, 1998)

Whalin (1998) indicates that customers expect more from every kind of store whether it is located in the mall or where they work. Influencing employee customers' buying decisions means knocking their socks off with a creative shopping environment where the merchandise is the star. Further, he suggests three main keys to an effective store layout—maximizing the space, controlling and directing traffic flow, and maximizing exposure.

- Maximizing the space—The key is to create an exciting, comfortable, and dynamic retailing environment for customers by using innovative layout and design software tools. The well-designed store maximizes every square foot of selling space. The manager needs to fine-tune the layout to minimize or eliminate "dead spots" and maximize a store's "hot spots" where almost anything will sell.
- Controlling and directing traffic flow—The customer's experience, according to Whalin (1998), starts in "The Decompression Zone." This is the all-important space at the very front of the store where customers first enter and sometimes stop for just a few moments to become acclimated. During the first few moments after customers enter, they begin to get a feeling for the store, even those who may have been in the store many times before. If everything stays the same month after month and year after year, the customer simply breezes in, buys what he or she wants, and leaves, never seeing all of the other merchandise. Therefore, it is important to re-merchandise and change the location of the merchandise frequently.

Further, it is important that the customers feel as though the store is comfortable, inviting, easy to shop, and that they are welcome. While it is nice to show-case new merchandise in the front of the store, it is more important to give customers a little space when they first enter the store to begin to feel comfortable.

After years of observing customers, researchers have discovered that more than 70% of people entering a store will either look or walk to the right. The simple explanation is that we have become a "right-handed" society. Researchers say even left-handed people frequently look or turn to the right. "What merchandise will customers find in the store when they look or turn to the right? Is there merchandise on the left side that is being ignored? Are the displays in the front of the store changed frequently so customers do not just come in and look past the merchandise?" (Whalen, 1998).

Another important research finding is that customers prefer shopping in stores where the aisles are wide enough to easily accommodate two or three people going in opposite directions. A growing number of the nation's most successful retail chains are discovering that wider aisles mean more sales and more satisfied customers.

- Maximizing exposure—Are departments easy to find and identified clearly with appropriate signs? Are the fixtures and displays arranged in nice, neat, symmetrical rows or are they angled to create open spaces that allow customers to see most of the merchandise? It is recommended by many retailers to arrange fixtures and displays at 45-degree angles that create soft corners that maximize customer exposure to merchandise. Fixtures placed at 45-degree angles and rounded corners are being used to display all types of merchandise.

King (1998) suggests the proper use of fixtures will make your life easier and your bottom line bigger, especially if you keep four things in mind: flexibility, convertibility, ingenuity, and simple common sense. A totally inflexible fixture should be used only for products that are sold in fixed quantities throughout the entire year (e.g., greeting card cases).

Further, King (1998) suggests the use of slatwall panels; wall systems; and fixtures like spinners, four-ways, and A-frames permits the arrangement of a seemingly endless array of slatwell accessories. In addition, using slatwall as a component in a fixture can totally change its function. Put a slatwall on the back of a window display and you have just created a two-sided fixture.

Steel shelving is found everywhere, usually with flat shelves. Yet you can create entirely new departments by removing the flat shelves and replacing them with a wide variety of inserts. They range from simple peg hooks and hang bars to spinner displays, units with glass doors, computer demo shelves, and even inserts for such items as fishing poles.

One of the simplest ways to incorporate flexibility into fixtures is to put them on casters. You can then alter traffic layout, move fixtures into position for seasonal promotions, or even take them out of the store for special sales. There are ready-to-assemble fixturing systems available that can be reconfigured depending on the need.

The following are a few useful tips to maximize sales dollars per square foot:

- Look at that empty space between the top of your wall fixtures and the ceiling.
- Use box displays of various sizes, stacking them in different configurations.
- Jamming as much as possible into a limited space may not always be wise.
- Gridwall is a simple and inexpensive way to add display capacity.
- If customers cannot find it, they cannot buy it.
- The simplest way to maximize the use of space is just to clean up the store.
- Research what is successful in other stores (Helson, 1998).
- Use conservative numbers when estimating future sales.
- Use logic when estimating how much money will be made (Helson, 1998).

Finally, Whalin (1998) has developed 15 questions to be used as a checklist for store managers to answer when preparing store layouts (See Table 8.2).

Table 8.2
Effective Store Layout Checklist

Would you answer yes, no, or needs improvement to these questions about the store?

- If I were one of your customers, would I enjoy shopping in the store?
- Is the store always clean and well maintained?
- Are the shelves always stocked with merchandise?
- Do the in-store signs clearly communicate the information the customers need and expect?
- Is the store laid out so that it is easy for customers to move around and find the merchandise they want?
- Are merchandise displays dynamic, attractive, fun, and interesting?
- Is the merchandise frequently rearranged to take advantage of seasonal events?
- Is the store regularly remodeled to keep it fresh and inviting for customers?
- Do display fixtures fit the overall decor of the store?
- Is the exterior of the store attractive and inviting?
- Has management done everything within the budget to make the interior and exterior of the store more attractive and inviting?
- Is the store bright and colorful?
- Are all the merchandise display possibilities taken advantage of in order to make the store a pleasant and enjoyable place to shop?
- Are the merchandise displays fresh and interesting, and are seasonal themes used to create excitement and keep customers coming back?
- Does the lighting in the store show merchandise at its best?

Adapted from Whalin, G. (1998). Effective store layouts. *Employee Services Management*, 41(2), pp.26-28.

The Most Common Mistakes Made by Retailers

A successful retail store is the outcome of constant planning and setting realistic goals. Yet many business people run their businesses without any direction. The following are the 10 most common mistakes that retailers should avoid (Azar, 1999):

- No business plan.
- No marketing plan.
- No sales plan.
- No advisory board.
- No cash reserve or real cash flow.
- Ignoring the numbers.
- Not being automated.
- Not knowing your customer.
- Ignoring employees.
- Being a lone ranger.

Staffing the Retail Store or Concession Stand

The dwindling pool of candidates, especially for sales positions, is of grave concern to all retailers and concessionaires. Store or concession managers are looking for a special type of retail salesperson who can perform a variety of tasks and build relationships with revisiting customers. To attract this type of person, you should know that surveys of employees show that the opportunity to do meaningful work, the feeling of being appreciated, and a sense of job security are as important to workers as the hourly salary and benefits. Of course, you should check to see what other stores are paying and offer as much as you can afford in order to attract the best candidates; but, you must look beyond money and benefits to create jobs that people will enjoy.

Where to Find Valuable Employees

Traditionally, most applicants discover retail positions by reading the classified ads section of a newspaper. To attract applicants in today's labor market, ads must be larger (which can be quite expensive) and more enticing. An effective ad should romance the job and the excitement of working in your store. Be sure to mention the salary and benefits, if they are attractive, and specify the experience and skills required for the position.

Colleges, technical schools, and local high schools often have placement offices that will post employment listings. Many schools even provide internship programs which allow students to earn credit hours for time on the job. Students placed with a store as part of a course in retailing business may be interested in permanent placement in the future.

The community may have a program for retirees looking for part-time work. Senior citizens often make excellent employees. The sports manager should network with friends and coworkers for potential candidates.

One of the best ways to advertise a job opening is to post a notice on the store door or prominently within the store. Customers who have shown an interest in your store and its merchandise may know someone who would like to work in your store. Avoid broadcasting that you are short-staffed or that an employee just quit and, out of respect for your current staff, don't post an hourly wage on the job opening notice. This is a matter that can be discussed with applicants later or mentioned in a memo attached to the application form. Also including a job description and the hours required in this memo will help applicants understand what type of experience and availability are necessary for the position.

Job Sharing

Consider having employees job share all specialized job functions such as bookkeeping, stocking, and managing the store. The store and the employees will benefit from this flexible arrangement and essential store responsibilities will not come to a halt if someone is ill or on vacation. Staff members will have someone to share the workload while parents can enjoy being home when children return from school or if a child is sent home ill from school. Usually those sharing a job build a close rapport, develop their own division of tasks, and even set their own schedules.

Typical Payroll Costs

The following are the typical payroll costs associated with retail operations and food and/or beverage concessions:

Concession Stand Workers	8 to 12% of concession sales
Food and Beverage Vendors	15 to 20% of vending sales
Catering/Restaurant Workers	18 to 30% of catering/restaurant sales
Sports Souvenir Vendors	12 to 17% of sports souvenir sales

The Vending Machine

What could be more low-maintenance than a retail effort that requires minimal staff? How about something that involves no store staff at all? Many facilities are finding that an effective way to sell small retail products such as convenience items, health foods, and beverages is by positioning at least one vending machine in a prominent spot in the employee services area.

There are two ways to become involved with the vending option: own or lease the machine, or contract with a vending company for a commission. The first option, that of owning or leasing a machine or a number of machines, is the most profitable and the ultimate way to go. However, it can become labor intensive and requires an up-front investment in merchandise; plus, merchandise can take up valuable storage space. In contrast, the second option requires no labor nor any investment in merchandise. The commission covers the cost of electricity, floor space, and the store's percentage of the net income.

A vending machine location is accessible and unattended 24 hours a day, 7 days a week. Another benefit is that vending machines virtually eliminate theft and facilitate inventory control. It is possible to vend such items as vitamins, minerals, protein supplements, sports drinks, socks, shirts, headphones, and almost anything else that will fit in a vending machine.

Financial Risk Management

An adverse event that is planned or unplanned can potentially impact an organization, operation, process, or project. It is usually defined, in negative terms, as a risk. If a risk has a positive outcome, it will be an opportunity. However, if it has a negative outcome, it will be a problem or loss.

If the activity is planned (i.e., defined, analyzed, and controlled), countermeasures can be put in place before the risk materializes. If unplanned, the risk can result in anything from minor consequences to severe catastrophes. The probability of outcome is part of the analysis as well as the financial impact. See Chapter 6 for a more detailed discussion of financial risk management.

Bonding

Bonding is an insurance agreement guaranteeing repayment for financial loss caused to the covered organization by the act or failure to act of a third person. Bonding is used to protect the financial operations of organizations. For purposes of the sports enterprise, bonding is intended to protect the organization from losses caused by acts of fraud or dishonesty by officers, employees, or other representatives.

To Catch a Thief

Shrinkage (theft) happens to retailers, large and small. Here are the top five ways of minimizing the damage: (1) Lock it up. Sounds obvious, but often at the end of the day, every item must be stored securely away behind a gate or glass. (2) Play traffic cop. Positioning the employee store in a high-traffic area not only encourages impulse shopping, it also discourages sticky fingers. (3) Watch who cleans up after the employee store closes. (4) Encourage employees. Establish an incentive program for employees that can financially reward them for low rates of shrinkage. (5) Keep an eye on the future. Technology is constantly changing in both equipment and in security. For those willing to make an investment, new practices similar to ink tags and computer chips can help prevent merchandise from leaving the store.

Ticket Sales and Box Office Operations

For sports organizations that depend on fan participation to generate revenue, the box office becomes a vital operation. If the box/ticket office is not operated efficiently and effectively, it could cause a serious financial dilemma for the organization. The box office is also the point of entry for your new and older reliable fans. The impression the ticket personnel leave with the customer is like a first impression at a job interview. Return purchases by fans can and will be influenced by the box office staff.

The Importance of Ticket Sales or Memberships

The importance of ticket sales varies greatly from one professional league to another and from one collegiate division to another (i.e., Division I-A to Division III). The media-rich NFL (i.e., long-term contracts with ABC, Fox, NBC, ESPN, and TNT) is the only professional league that ticket sales is not the most prominent revenue source. The amount of ticket revenue generated by sports organizations is dependent on two interrelated factors: the number of tickets sold and the unit cost of each ticket sold. The mission of the sports manager relating to ticket sales is to determine the optimal ticket prices that will maximize total cash flow per seat (i.e., general admission, club or premium seats, and luxury box seats). Pricing, in the past, has been based on the best, informed guesses of management. In the future, a successful sports manager must establish ticket prices based on market research, which provides an understanding of sports consumers' expected price threshold, or their willingness to pay. The manager must be knowledgeable about marketing techniques and strategies to effectively sell the product(s) to the general public.

While the mission of managers in club settings (e.g., golf, racquet, health and fitness, and multi-sport) focuses on developing optimal membership programs, selling and retaining memberships is the lifeblood of the sports club sector. The key challenge facing sports club managers is to sustain membership levels in the face of growing competition such as watching television, including cable and satellite, surfing the internet, renting a video tape or DVD, renting a video game, attending a movie, purchasing a CD, going out to dinner, attending a rock concert or Broadway play, or going to a child's sporting or other event. In the future, sports club performance will be based on how effectively clubs recruit and retain members as well as their ability to maximize income return from each member.

The challenges of selling tickets to sporting events for the athletic director at any level or president of a professional sports enterprise are very similar to those faced by the sports club manager mentioned above. Both groups of managers must sell their products to the general public more effectively than the competitors. Further, they must retain the customer from year to year or event to event, in order to be successful.

The Product of a Box Office

The primary product of the box office is the ticket. When selecting a ticket and the method by which the ticket will be sold, there are a number of factors to consider including the physical characteristics of the facility, seating plans, ticket system, ticketing software (e.g., BOCS, Data Factors, Haven Systems, Folio Box Office Management, Nortech Software, Smart Box Office, Software4Sport, and Tickets.com), outsourcing ticketing (e.g., TicketMaster, TicketWeb, 800BuyTickets), online ticketing, pricing structure, credit card service, group sales, discounted prices, advanced sales, and sales incentive plans utilized.

The ticket is a product. It is a souvenir for the patron. It can also be used to notify patrons of dangers by the inclusion of a warning on the backside of the ticket. Further, the backside of the ticket could include a safe harmless clause with the warning. This alerts the patrons to known dangers (e.g., when purchasing a ticket for a hockey contest, it could warn patrons seated in rows 10 and higher of the possibility of being hit by a puck).

Printing of Tickets

Tickets can either be purchased from an outside organization or printed internally in the ticket office through a computerized system. General admission tickets are easily controlled and can be purchased at any print shop, office supply store, or department store. Reserved tickets are more complicated.

If the box office is not computerized, tickets must then be purchased for every seat for each event. If the tickets are not sold, the remaining tickets must be destroyed. If there are 10,000 seats in the sports facility and there are 15 home games, the box office then needs to store 150,000 tickets for the season. The tickets need to be stored by each event and seat. This requires a large area and a number of cabinets with appropriate shelving to secure the tickets. Once tickets are received from the printer, they all need to be checked and inventoried. The tickets sold must be checked off the master-seating chart to avoid duplicating sales. This system is labor intensive, costly, and time-consuming and exposes the box office to seating errors.

In a computerized box office, there is no need for ticket storage and purchase of tickets from an outside vendor. The computer will generate the tickets and automatically record the sale. The manager will need to purchase ticket stock on a regular basis. Internal printing also enables the ticket manager to control how many tickets are printed for each event. This reduces waste and the need for storage space. Further, the computer will allow the box office personnel to print complete season-ticket packages with mailing labels. The tickets are separated for each season order, placed into envelopes for mailing, and mailing labels are attached. Printing and packaging tickets internally is preferable for the organization. Many organizations cannot afford this cost, however, and continue to use the manual reserved system or sell all seats as general admission.

Finally, one of the biggest problems for sports managers is the counterfeit ticket. The manager needs to consider the best method for reducing or preventing counterfeiting. Including any of the following within a ticket design can do this: bar codes, computer chips, watermarks, or holograms.

Types of Tickets

Typically, sports organizations use one or more of the following types of tickets: reserved, general admission, season and mini-season plans, individual event, complimentary, student, or rain check. What tickets are available depends on the organization (e.g., interscholastic, intercollegiate, or professional sports). The larger, more established organizations will offer all types of tickets.

The season ticket provides a guaranteed source of income before the season starts and does not depend on variable factors including weather, quality of opponents, or team record. The season ticket involves the sale of a particular seat and location in the stadium or arena for an entire season for a one-time fee.

The mini-season plans allow fans to purchase tickets for a portion of the season. These plans offer a lower financial commitment to individual game ticket holders who wish to become more active fans but are not ready to purchase season tickets. The plans are designed to encourage individual event purchasers to move up to a multi-ticket plan with hopes of making them season-ticket holders.

Individual tickets are tickets that are available for walk-in purchases the day of the event. The purchasers are generally in town for a convention, a business meeting, or visiting friends or relatives and want to experience a game.

Complimentary tickets (comps) are those given to individuals (e.g., visiting dignitaries, politicians, local heroes, donors, key clients, family and friends of players and coaches, etc.) or groups (e.g., Boy Scouts, Girl Scouts, youth sport teams, elementary school teams, etc.). There are two key strategies behind complimentary tickets: (a) to increase crowd size and (b) the organization hopes the "free" experience will be so positive that fans will want to return as paying customers.

Universities and colleges generally allocate seats for students. These tickets are often discounted, but not always. Many institutions require students to pick up their tickets early to control crowd size and to allow the athletic department to sell unclaimed student tickets.

Rain checks are tickets given to patrons when an event is cancelled due to weather or other reasons. The patron can return to the next event without paying an admission fee. Some organizations require the patrons to notify the box office one week prior to the event to control crowd size and to determine what additional tickets can be sold.

The Event

Before an event goes on sale, the ticket manager gathers important information about the venue, the organization, and the event itself and provides this information to all points of sale including individuals selling tickets on consignment. The ticket manager should be familiar with all aspects of the event that affect the patron. The ticket manager should visit the venue ahead of time, sit in different locations in the house, attend a rehearsal or performance, and be ready to offer feedback on the event based on firsthand experience.

Event Information

You will need to give the following information to box office managers and ticket outlets so that they are able to answer patron inquiries:

- Information obtained from the producer.
- A description of the event including featured performers.
- Number and length of intermission(s).

- Will any of the performances be ASL (American Sign Language) interpreted?
- Instructions for writing checks. When running an independent ticket operation, checks should probably be written to the producing organization. If you are selling tickets through an established box office or ticket outlet, they will instruct the patron.
- Your organization's tax ID number.
- Any information regarding connected events such as a black tie opening, pre- or post-event receptions, or lectures.
- Web sites with information about the event or producing organization.
- A statement from the producer regarding the suitability of the event for children.
- Description of the event. At the point of sale, the ticket seller may be asked to volunteer information about the performance or the performing group to aid the patron in their decision-making process.
- Information obtained from the representative of the venue, such as:
  —Directions to the venue both by car and public transportation.
  —Parking options.
  —Information for patrons in wheelchairs regarding parking, access to building, the house, the box office, restrooms, and location of wheelchair seating in the house.
  —Is there a teletypwriter (TTY) phone line at the box office? Does the venue have assisted listening devices?
  —The seating capacity and seating chart of the house. If you are using an established box office, they may already have this information.
- Web sites with information about the venue.
- Information obtained from the stage manager.
- An estimated running time for the event.

Setting Policies and Parameters

The following guidelines should be established in consultation with the producer, ideally two months in advance of the event.

Seating Configuration. General admission (unreserved) tickets are easier to sell and account for. They also make house management simpler. Remember to inform patrons that seating is on a first-come, first-served basis.

Reserved seating is used in special circumstances. It restricts seating options for patrons and house management, requires more work for the box office and usher staff working the event, and often delays the start time of an event.

Discounting Ticket Prices. Discounting tickets for special groups of people (e.g., students, seniors, disabled, etc.) can assist in filling the house and provide a nice community service. The discounted tickets can be used as a means of penetration marketing into a new customer base or to fill seats that may not be filled for the event. It is important for the manager to determine what number of individuals constitutes a "group." Further, it is important to decide prior to the season whether or not there will be discounted preseason games for all patrons.

It is the producer's responsibility to consider both the positive and negative impact of any special offers on the overall event budget. Special deals should be geared toward people who would not otherwise attend the event and for performances that would otherwise be undersold.

On-Sale Date. Tickets for undergraduate events generally go on sale one month before the event. Do not publicize or advertise an event before tickets are on sale. If necessary, the on-sale date should be included in press releases, brochures, and "save the date" postcards.

Tickets to Be Held. Before tickets are on sale to the public, the ticket manager and producer should discuss how many and which tickets should be withheld from sale. This is a good time to determine the best and worst places to sit. If an event is reserved seating, sit in several different seats to determine what the view of the stage is like from different sections of the house. Reasons for holding tickets include:

- **House Seats/Trouble Seats.** These are seats that are kept off-line for last-minute problems. The house manager may need to use these seats if an error leads to a show being oversold or, in a reserved seating house, a seat being "double sold." They may also be needed if there is damage or a spill that makes another seat in the house unusable. House seats are also kept available so that the producer can accommodate last-minute ticket requests from VIPs.
- **Usher Seats.** Consult with the house manager on how many and which seats need to be held for ushers.
- **Obstructed Seats.** The placement of lighting and sound equipment or the need for cameras and other video equipment in the house often necessitates removing seats from the capacity because the equipment is placed in the seating area. These decisions need to be made early so that the appropriate number of tickets can be pulled. In the case of a reserved seating house, the exact placement of such equipment must be established before a show can go on sale.

- **Obstructed View Seats.** Some seats may offer particularly bad sight lines to the stage or have views that are obstructed by architectural elements or production equipment. The producer and ticket manager should use their discretion in deciding whether to pull these seats or to sell them at a reduced price. Patrons must be informed by the ticket seller and by the text on the ticket that they are purchasing an obstructed view seat.
- **Seats Required for Performers.** A performer may need a seat if he or she is being "planted" in the house. Events with multiple performing groups may allow performers to sit in the audience for part of the performance.
- **VIP Seats.** A producer will often decide to make complimentary tickets available to performers; production crew; and VIPs such as college staff and faculty, donors, and other special guests. The ticket manager should have a list of such individuals.

    The producer and ticket manager should be very selective in offering complimentary tickets. If you offer someone a free ticket to one event, they are likely to expect free tickets to your next event.

    Set a policy as to when unclaimed complimentary tickets will be released for sale. Inform all recipients that their tickets will be released at the door for sale if these tickets are not picked up 30 minutes prior to the advertised start time.

    VIPs should be given a special invitation by the producer and asked to RSVP. The ticket manager can develop a list of VIPs for whom tickets should be held ahead of time and submit it to the box office.

    Producers and ticket managers may offer performers and production crew a certain number of complimentary tickets. Since the core audience for most student shows comprises friends and family of the performers and production crew, be aware that a generous complimentary ticket policy will diminish your primary income source.

    It is recommended that you create and use a complimentary ticket voucher that cannot be easily duplicated for cast and crew. Complimentary ticket vouchers simplify the process of complimentary ticket distribution for the ticket manager, especially for multi-performance events.

    Complimentary tickets for cast and crew are usually offered on an "as available" basis unlike VIP seats that are actually pulled from the pool of tickets put on sale.
- **Latecomer Seats.** Think about latecomers before you put tickets on sale. If you decide that it is unsafe or impractical to admit latecomers at all, you need to include a "no latecomer policy" in your advertising and press releases. If you decide that latecomers can be admitted only to a particular area of the house, you'll need to pull those seats before an event goes on sale.

Waiting Line Policy. When an event sells out, the ticket sellers should inform the patrons that a waiting line will be established at the door. It is not recommended to start a waiting list either by phone or for friends who did not buy a ticket in time. A clearly established policy set ahead of time should clarify when and where the waiting line will begin and at what time tickets will be released. It should be well marked and be out of the way so that it does not interfere with other patron traffic. If tickets can be released, start releasing them at 15 minutes before curtain.

People in the waiting line may be admitted only if

- complimentary tickets are unclaimed,
- unpaid reservations are unclaimed,
- standing room is available, and
- the producer and house manager decide to release house seats.

Preparing the Box Office for an Event

For each event there is a beginning and an end. The beginning commences after the event is scheduled and the tickets are offered for sale. The ending is after the books are closed and all sales are finished. The length of an event's promotion depends on the promoter. It could be as few as two weeks or as long as six weeks.

Pre-Event Preparations. Each ticket seller is assigned a specific number of tickets and a small bank in order to make change. The seller confirms the number of tickets and the amount of money in the bank by signing the section of the ticket seller's audit sheet. Each organization has a different set of audit or reconciliation forms as directed by the organization's controller.

During the Event. There should be a will-call window for spectators to pick up prepaid tickets, complimentary tickets, press passes, and tickets being held for someone. The ticket seller at this window will not have separate tickets to be sold nor a bank. The seller should have a list with the names of the people assigned to the tickets. Once a person identifies him- or herself with appropriate identification, tickets should be signed for on the master sheet. Finally, this seller would also be the troubleshooter to assist other ticket sellers with questions or complaints.

Post-Event Reconciliation. At the conclusion of the event, the ticket sellers will reconcile their banks and cash, checks, and credit card receipts received for the tickets they were assigned. The head ticket seller will verify everything is in order before allowing the ticket seller to leave. The head ticket seller will prepare a final event sales report and deposit the cash, checks, and credit card receipts in the bank. The final event report will include the total number of tickets sold, number of complimentary tickets provided, number of press passes provided, number of season patrons attending, total amount of income received, and the total number of people in the audience paid and non-paid.

The head ticket taker will confirm with the head ticket seller the total number of patrons present at the event. The ticket takers will collect the tickets and count all those that were collected or scan them into a small computer. If tickets are collected, they should be torn in half with half being retained by the patron (as a souvenir). If the ticket is scanned, the entire ticket can be given to the patron.

Box Office Design

The box office is the initial contact office for most patrons. Sales windows should be located on all sides of the facility and a drive-up window should also be considered for customer convenience. The box office manager can decide which window areas should be open on a daily and event basis.

This space should be easily accessible to all patrons. It must be compliant with the Americans With Disabilities Act (ADA) sections dealing especially with facility accessibility.

The main box office space should be large enough to accommodate such areas as office spaces for personnel, sales windows (at least 10) for walk-in traffic and a drive-up facility, storage area for office supplies and ticket paper stock, a small conference room, and restrooms. The smaller sales areas should have a minimum of six windows for sales and "will-call" tickets. These spaces should be protected from the elements and have a depth of at least 15 feet. All smaller auxiliary ticket sales areas should be facing the outside of the facility. The main ticket area should have inside and outside windows. The windows should be shatterproof. Computers to all sites should be networked to each other and to the main office computer. The ticket spaces should have environmental controls and telephone communication. The main office should have a safe built into the wall to store funds safely.

Summary

The retail store can generate a significant consistent revenue stream. If the retail store is run well and sells the right products at competitive prices, it should turn a handsome profit and also save the customers money. Successful retail stores accomplish the following: (1) feature prominent locations that require members to pass through the store, (2) offer personalized service and competitive pricing, (3) print catalogues for employees to share with friends, (4) merchandise their goods/products (i.e., displaying goods/products in an appealing way), (5) consider themselves retail outlets, (6) sell innovative goods/ products, (7) concentrate on apparel and accessories, (8) stock regularly needed supplies, and (9) sell licensed merchandise.

In your efforts to add value, a pitfall you will want to avoid is that of adding the value you desire rather than the value your niche customers want (Rigsbee, 1997). Become market driven, rather than product driven, by listening to your customers' needs, wants, and desires. Do this, and they will reward you with greater profitability than you have ever enjoyed before.

King (1998) suggests the proper use of fixturing will make your life easier and your bottom line bigger, especially if you keep these four points in mind: flexibility, convertibility, ingenuity, and simple common sense. A totally inflexible fixture should be used only for products that are sold in fixed quantities throughout the entire year.

Booking outstanding events does not guarantee high-volume ticket sales. The key to selling tickets is good information and easy, convenient access for the tickets. The personnel in the box/ticket office who provide sales services and serve as public relation folks must be user-friendly. As a result of the service, audience and performer are brought together with the dollars generated from the sale of tickets held by the box/ticket office until distribution of monies between those responsible for providing services (i.e., performer, promoter, agent, sponsor, and facility) is determined.

Promotions and Customer Retention: Keys to Financial Stability[1]

Thomas H. Sawyer

9

Promotions is a catch-all category for any one of a variety of marketing efforts designed to stimulate consumer interest in, awareness of, and purchase of the service, product, or program. Promotions is the vehicle that (1) carries the message about the services, products, and programs; (2) positions them in the market; and (3) develops the appropriate image for the services, products, and programs.

Promotions includes the following forms of marketing activities: (1) advertising, (2) personal selling (i.e., any face-to-face presentation), (3) publicity, and (4) sales promotion (i.e., a wide variety of activities including displays, trade shows, free samples, introductory free classes, coupons, giveaways, and exhibitions).

Customer (fan) retention is a key to overall financial stability for any sports enterprise. There are many competitors for entertainment dollars on any given day in the United States. A number of years ago there was an unlimited supply of new fans for sporting events. As the price of going to a sporting event has increased and the availability of more convenient and less expensive television opportunities have increased, many sporting organizations have seen a decline in their fan base. It is estimated it costs six times more to attract new fans than to keep existing fans. Sporting organizations' profits come from retention, not replacement, of fans. If the retention rate is improved, the organization can expect dramatic increases in profits due to the lower cost of retaining customers as opposed to recruiting new ones (Sawyer & Smith, 1999).

Sports managers at the interscholastic, intercollegiate, and professional levels understand how critical fan retention is in the real world. These sports enterprises, particularly minor league baseball and the former Continental Basketball League, cannot be successful unless fans continue to purchase tickets. The successful sports managers have learned that the fan comes first and the fans are never wrong. This chapter will assist the reader in understanding how to successfully retain fans and increase the fan base in the very competitive entertainment field.

Learning Objectives

After reading this chapter, the student should be able to

- understand why customers (fans) decide not to renew season tickets or increase the number of tickets purchased,
- describe how to gather knowledge from current customers to guide the renewal process,
- outline the costs of recruiting new customers,
- understand how to retain the customer,
- describe how to interact with fans and deal with angry customers, and
- describe how technology can connect with the customers.

Promotions

Many people consider *selling* and *marketing* to be synonymous terms. However, selling is only one of the many components of marketing. Selling is the personal or impersonal process of assisting and/or persuading a prospective customer to buy a commodity or a service or to act favorably upon an idea that has commercial significance to the seller (Mullin, Hardy, & Sutton, 2003).

Promotions is a form of selling but is the all-inclusive term representing the broad field. Selling suggests only the transfer of title or the use of personal salesmen while promotion includes advertising, personal selling, sales promotion, and other selling tools.

---

[1]This chapter has been reprinted with modifications with permission from Sagamore Publishing. It represents a combination of Chapter 6, Promotions and advertising, and Chapter 8, Membership retention, from Sawyer, T. H. (1999). *The Management of clubs, recreation, and sport: Concepts and applications.* Champaign, IL: Sagamore Publishing.

The two most widely used methods of promotion are personal selling and advertising. Other promotional methods/strategies are (1) sales promotion, which is designed to supplement and coordinate personal selling and advertising efforts (e.g., store displays, trade shows and exhibitions, and the use of samples or premiums); (2) mail-order advertising and selling; (3) automatic vending; (4) auctions; (5) telemarketing; (6) product differentiation; (7) market segmentation; (8) trading up; (9) trading down; (10) use of trading stamps or frequent flyer miles; and (11) branding a product or service.

The Promotional Campaign

A promotional campaign is a planned, coordinated, and integrated series of promotional efforts built around a single theme or idea and designed to reach a predetermined goal. The first step in developing the campaign is establishing the goals and determining the campaign strategies. The manager should answer the following questions when developing the campaign strategies:

- What is the relative emphasis to be placed on primary versus secondary demand stimulation?
- What balance is desired between the immediacy of the action-response and the duration of the response?
- Does the organization influence everyone a little bit or a few people intensively?
- At what point is the management targeting the organization's emphasis on the spectrum between brand awareness and brand insistence?
- What issues, products or services (e.g., both the organization's and the competitor's) will the organization stress?

Early in the course of planning the campaign, management should decide what selling appeals will be stressed. This decision will be based, to a large extent, upon the specific objectives of the campaign and the research findings concerning the buying motives and habits of the customers.

Most campaigns revolve around a central theme. This theme should permeate all promotional efforts and tends to unify the campaign. A theme is simply appeals dressed up in a distinctive, attention-getting form. As such, it is related to the campaign's objectives and the customers' behaviors. It expresses the product's benefits. Frequently the theme is expressed as a slogan (e.g., Nike's "Just Do It;" Ford "Quality Is Job One").

The key to success in a campaign depends largely on management's ability to activate and coordinate the efforts of its entire promotional task force and the physical distribution of the product or service. In a successfully implemented campaign, the efforts of all involved should be meshed effectively. The *advertising program* will consist of a series of related, well-timed, carefully placed ads. The *personal selling effort* can be tied in by having the salesperson explain and demonstrate the products or services benefits stressed in the ads. *Sales-promotional devices* such as point-of-purchase display materials need to be coordinated with the other aspects of the campaign. Personnel responsible for the *physical distribution activities* must ensure that adequate stocks of the product are available prior to the start of the campaign.

Determining the Promotional Mix

Determining the promotional mix (i.e., advertising, personal selling, sales promotions) can be difficult for management. However, if management takes into consideration such areas as (1) the factors that influence the promotional mix (e.g., money available for promotion, nature of the market [geographical scope, concentration, and type of customers], nature of the product or service, and stage of the product's or service's life cycle); (2) the questions of basic promotional strategy in order to illustrate the effect of the influencing factors (e.g., When should personal selling [see Figure 9.1] and advertising [see Figure 9.2] be main ingredients; when should promotional efforts by retailer be stressed; when should manufacturer-retailer cooperative advertising be used; is retailer promotion needed when manufacturer emphasizes advertising; if a retailer emphasizes personal selling, does he or she need to advertise; and should promotional activity be continued when demand is heavy or exceeds capacity); and (3) the quantitative data from a research study to show the practical applications of the analytical material.

Sales Promotion

Sales promotion comprises those activities, other than personal selling, advertising, and publicity, that stimulate consumer purchasing and dealer effectiveness such as displays, shows, and expositions; demonstrations; and various non-concurrent selling efforts not in the ordinary routine. Sales promotion (1) informs and persuades groups through tools and methods controlled by the organization itself; (2) deals with nonrecurring and non-routine matters; (3) exists as a plus ingredient in the marketing mix (i.e., an organization could exist profitably without sales promotion); and (4) serves as a bridge between advertising and personal selling to supplement and coordinate efforts in these two areas.

Effective Procedures in Personal Selling

There are five steps to effective personal selling including presale preparation, prospecting for (locating) potential buyers, pre-approach to individual prospects, sales presentation, and post-sale activities. **Presale preparation** makes certain that the salesperson is prepared. This means that the salesper-

Figure 9.1
When Should Personal Selling Be Main Ingredient?

Personal selling will ordinarily carry the bulk of the promotional load when

- the organization is small or has insufficient funds with which to carry on an inadequate advertising program,
- the market is concentrated,
- the personality of the salesperson is needed to establish rapport or create confidence,
- the product has a higher unit value,
- the product or service requires demonstration,
- the product or service must be fitted to the individual customer's needs,
- the product or service is purchased infrequently, or
- the product involves a trade-in.

Figure 9.2
Criteria for Deciding Whether or Not to Advertise

Advertising works best when the seller wishes to inform many people quickly (e.g., change in hours, a special sales promotion, or a new credit policy). There are five criteria that should be considered when deciding whether or not to advertise.

- The primary demand trend for the product or service should be favorable.
- There should be considerable opportunity to differentiate the product or service.
- The product or service should have hidden qualities.
- Powerful emotional buying motives should exist for the product or service.
- The organization must have sufficient funds to support an advertising program adequately.

son must be well acquainted with (1) the service, product, or program; (2) the market; and (3) the techniques of selling. The salesperson should know as much as possible about (1) the motivation and behavior of the target markets to be pursued, (2) the nature of the competition, and (3) the business conditions prevailing in the market.

Prospecting for (locating) potential consumers is the next step in the process. At this juncture, the salesperson is involved in establishing a profile of the ideal consumer for this service(s), product(s), or program(s). The salesperson should (1) examine past and present consumers; (2) ask present customers about new leads; (3) research consumers of competitors; (4) regularly read lists of building permits, real estate transactions, births, and engagement announcements; and (5) contact former consumers and/or alumni for new leads. The final product of this research is a list of potential consumers.

The next step is the *pre-approach to individual prospects.* Before calling on prospects, the salesperson should learn about the person or company (i.e., what services, products, or programs the prospect is now using; what the prospect's reaction is to them; personal habits, likes, and dislikes of the prospect) that is to be approached as a new consumer of the service(s), product(s), or program(s) offered by the organization.

The actual *sales presentation* of the salesman will start with an attempt to attract the prospect's attention. Next, the salesperson will try to hold the customer's interest while building a desire for the service, product, or program. Then, the salesman will try to close the sale. All through this presentation, the salesman must be ready and able to meet any hidden or expressed objections which the prospect may have.

There are four approaches to attracting a customer's attention. In the simplest approach, the salesperson merely greets the prospect, introduces him- or herself, and states what is being sold or the reason for the call. Another approach is to start the presentation with: "I was referred to you by . . ." The third approach has the salesperson suggesting the product benefits by making some startling statement, such as, "If I can reduce your cost by 25% on an introductory offer, and at the same time provide you all benefits and a free shirt, are you interested?" The final approach is simply to walk in and show the services brochure, product, or program brochure to the prospect.

The *post-sale activities* are important to an effective selling job. Normally, sales success depends upon repeat business. Satisfied customers will furnish leads. They are also the best salespersons for the organization. The salesperson should (1) reassure the customer by summarizing the service's, product's, or program's benefits and pointing out how satisfied he or she will be with its performance; (2) ascertain that all points in the sales contract and the guarantee are clearly understood; and (3) provide instruction for the new owner, if necessary.

Knowing the Customer

Wal-Mart has greeters, which is nice, but they do not know you. They are polite, welcome you to Wal-Mart, and provide you with a shopping cart. Ticket takers for the Colorado Rockies provide patrons with a souvenir Colorado Rockies pin in exchange for your ticket, which is nice; but, in most cases, they do not know you. Lynne Schwabe (2001) suggests customers (fans) want value, choices, the newest items, convenience, long open-for-business hours, one-stop shopping, a friendly personal touch in a clean and friendly place to shop, and they do not want hassles (the Wal-Mart philosophy developed by Sam Walton). Schwabe (2001) suggests the retail manager should focus on four critical areas with their customers, including (a) identify the customers, (b) differentiate the customers from one another, (c) interact with the customers, and (d) customize items for the customers.

Identifying Customers

Identifying customers can be a challenge, but it is a necessary one. Customer surveys are good ways for the manager to determine who are the customers and what are their personal needs, wants, and feelings toward what is sold beyond the ticket to the contest. This is very helpful in determining how to mail or market only to those who want or need what is being sold. Surveys assist the manager in determining which customers are mailed to, the frequency of those mailings, and what is offered to the customers. Finally, a dialogue develops naturally when the customers realize they are being contacted only about products and services they are interested in personally.

The customer is no different than the retail manager. The manager expects from other organizations such traits as a willingness to stand by their products, on-time delivery, knowing and remembering the customer, clearance racks, impulse items, size and selection, convenient and easy payment plans, speedy service, service with a smile, competent assistance, preferred customer notice, approachability, convenience, uncluttered and clean stores, and convenient refund policies (a hallmark at Wal-Mart, the largest retailer in the world). Guess what! The customers of the sports organization's retail store expect the same as the manager does of other frequently used retailers.

Schwabe (2001) indicates the manager should consciously create a system (see Table 9.1) that enables the manager to identify customers as individuals each time the manager comes in contact with the customer.

Table 9.1
Identifying Customers: A Store Information System

- Use drip irrigation: ask one or two questions every time you are in touch with them. The customers begin to think the retailer is interested in their needs and wants.
- Verify and update customer data and delete departed individuals. Have a "spring cleaning" day. Run the database through the National Change of Address (NCOA) file.
- Take inventory of all customer data already available in an electronic format. This should include not only the current database but also Web site, credit card information, etc.
- Locate customer-identifying information that is currently on file but not electronically compiled: customer books, files, special order file, etc.
- Devise strategies for collecting more information. Concentrate on identifying customers who are valuable and will be potentially valuable in the future.
- Gather by an employee store information system sources of information including, but not limited to: name, mailing address, business phone, home phone, fax number, e-mail, position and title, account number, credit card number, birthday, anniversary, spouse or significant other's name, children's names, buying history, preferences (wants and needs), and frequency of purchases.
- Include other sources of information: billing and invoice records, sweepstakes and contest entry forms, warranty records, coupon redemption and rebate forms, customer comment and research data, sales force records, repairs and service records, loyalty user card, frequency program with most valuable customers, user number groups, clubs and affinity groups involving the company or products, company newsletter, and list swaps.
- Verify information at least every two years. This means updating 5% of names in the database every month or so. Prepare sales associates to update automatically.

Schwabe, L.D. (2001). *Your store: The secret weapon.* ESM Association Annual Conference and Exhibit, New Orleans, LA. April 8-12, 2001.

Table 9.2 outlines the manager's customer identification task list that should be used by all managers to identify their customers.

Table 9.2
Customer Identification Task List

- Determine first how many customers are known.
- Devise programs or initiatives to increase the number of customers known, such as special contests for monthly or weekly giveaways.
- Establish a common format for identifying customers.
- Determine how to link customer ID with all of that customer's contacts and transactions across all divisions, departments, products, and functions.
- Make it easier for employees and managers to capture customer information.
- Allow customers to enter and update identifying information themselves. Determine how to collect non-transactional data (e.g., phoned-in inquiries that do not generate a sale).
- Develop a system to ensure that contact information is kept up to date.
- Track all "referred to" and "referred by" parameters for all prospects and customers.
- Consider programs to increase referrals by current customers.

Schwabe, L.D. (2001). *Your store: The secret weapon.* ESM Association Annual Conference and Exhibit, New Orleans, LA. April 8-12, 2001.

Differentiate Customers

Schwabe (2001) suggests every manager should rank customers by their value to the store including "(1) prioritize efforts and gain most advantage with Most Valuable Customers (MVCs), (2) tailor behavior toward each customer based on needs, (3) develop ranking criteria or a customer profitability and valuation model, and (4) categorize customers by their differing needs." Table 9.3 describes how to differentiate customers.

Table 9.3
Differentiating Customers

- Differentiate top customers. Take the best guess at the top 5% using sales.
- Add customers based on profitability, referrals, status in community, etc.
- Determine customers who cost money. Look for simple rules to isolate the bottom 20% of your customers and reduce mail currently sent to them by at least half.
- Find customers who have complained about the product or service more than once in the past year. Babysit them. Call and check up on how strategy is working. Get in touch with them as soon as possible.
- Look for last year's customers who have ordered half as much or less this year. Get in touch with them as soon as possible.
- Divide customers into As, Bs, and Cs. Decrease activities with Cs and increase with As.

Schwabe, L.D. (2001). *Your store: The secret weapon.* ESM Association Annual Conference and Exhibit, New Orleans, LA. April 8-12, 2001.

Ranking by Value.
The criteria for ranking value by managers might include: total dollars spent, frequency of purchase, profitability on sales, profits earned on referrals from customers, value of collaboration, and benefits of customer reputation with current or potential customers.

Ranking by Need.
The criteria to be considered for need might be for a community of purchasers' needs (e.g., fiction and nonfiction readers) and individual needs. Ranking customers by value and need allows the retail manager to prioritize marketing and sales efforts and treat customers individually in more cost-effective ways. Managers can and should rank their customers as follows:

- Most Valuable Customers (MVCs) is the customer base that should be retained with out question. The manager should reward the customers for their loyalty and make certain they receive the highest level of service.
- Most Growable Customers (MGCs) is the customer base that should be grown. The manager needs to recognize these as good customers and turn them into great ones.
- Below Zeros (BZs) is the customer who needs incentives to make it more profitable. The manager might want to consider encouraging them to shop elsewhere and be come an unprofitable customer for another retailer. (Schwabe, 2001)

Table 9.4
Reducing BZs

There are several ways to reduce the energy and resources that you devote to your BZs :

- Reduced service. Provide fewer options, less choice, and slower methods of shipping.
- Alternative service. Use virtual representatives for sales, customer service, or support.
- Charge for service. Charge for services that were once free.
- Reduce communication. Decrease the frequency of or entirely eliminate mailings to these customers.
- Encourage BZs to use the Web site. Seek opportunities to bill these customers less frequently, eliminate billing inserts, or identify other cost-saving avenues.

Schwabe, L.D. (2001). *Your store: The secret weapon*. ESM Association Annual Conference and Exhibit, New Orleans, LA. April 8-12, 2001.

Finally, the employee store manager should invest more in MVCs and MGCs and less in BZs. Table 9.4 describes ways to reduce BZs.

Interact With Customers

Schwabe (2001) encourages managers to engage customers in an ongoing dialogue that ensures that the manager will learn more and more about their particular interests, needs, and priorities. Interaction with customers can be good as well as bad (e.g., conflict resolution and the angry customer). Interactions should minimize the customer's inconvenience. The outcome of the interaction should be a real benefit for the customer. The employee store manager should adjust behavior toward customers based on the interaction. Interactions should take place within the context of all previous interactions with that customer. Further, the general rules regarding interactions include: do no harm, treat each customer as a best friend, and never do anything to the customer that you would not do to a best friend. Table 9.5 suggests how the retail manager should interact with customers and Table 9.6 outlines cus-

Table 9.5
How the Retail Manager Should Interact With Customers

- Have each salesperson call his or her top three customers. Say hello! Do not sell, just talk and make sure they are happy.
- Call the company. Ask questions. See how hard it is to get through and to obtain answers. Call competition. Find out same.
- Use technology to make doing business with the store easier. Gather customer e-mail addresses and follow up with them. Offer non-postal mail alternatives for all kinds of communication. Consider fax-back and fax-broadcast systems. Find ways to scan customer information into a database.
- Improve complaint handling. Plot how many complaints you receive each day and work to improve ratio of complaints handled on the first call.

Schwabe, L.D. (2001). *Your store: The secret weapon*. ESM Association Annual Conference and exhibit, New Orleans, LA. April 8-12, 2001.

Table 9.6
How to Interact With Customers

- *Direct sales calls.* Determine frequency and substance of calls, what products or services, and what percent of total sales are sold this way.
- *E-mail and electronic data interchange.* Determine what proportion of customers want to be connected electronically to the firm, what transactions and interactions can be accomplished online and which are online already, and what kinds of electronic commerce can be used profitably, such as invoicing, fulfillment, delivery scheduling, etc.
- *Fax messages.* Determine what link fax communication has within other media interactions (e.g., print, direct mail, phone), whether outbound fax messages are effective for dissemination of any kind of information, and how inbound fax messages are received, routed, and managed.
- *Mail (postage).* Establish frequency of direct mail campaigns and tenor of the campaigns, track which customers are most frequent recipients of mail, and establish testing mechanisms.
- *Point of Purchase.* Determine what customer information is captured at cash registers and points of product or service delivery to customer.
- *Telephone.* Establish method for scheduling, executing, and evaluating outbound calls and method of routing, handling, and evaluating inbound calls and for escalating calls from MVCs.
- *Web site.* See how easy it is to ask the company a question via the company Web site; determine what tools will be used to capture customer information through the Web site and how it can automatically be transferred to database; explore ways of tracking activities on the store site and observing behaviors of the customers; examine options for differentiating communications with the best customers so they are treated with special care; explore automated response options to frequently asked questions; be sure the customers can help themselves and are able to obtain all necessary information directly from the Web site; and ascertain how difficult it is for customers to update their own profiles, ascertain up-to-date product and service information, configure and order products or services directly, check status of order, and talk to other customers or users, perhaps with similar profiles or similar needs or problems.

Schwabe, L.D. (2001). *Your store: The secret weapon.* ESM Association Annual Conference and Exhibit, New Orleans, LA. April 8-12, 2001.

---

tomer interaction opportunities. Finally, Schwabe (2001) suggests there are five objectives for interactions: strategic value, customer needs, customer satisfaction and complaint discovery, do not use customer satisfaction and complaint discovery to excess, and recognize interaction opportunities.

Customize

Schwabe (2001) indicates that the employee store manager should act on what is learned about the customer. The manager needs to use the knowledge about individual customers to customize the way they are treated. The goal is to treat a particular customer differently based on something learned about the customer during the previous interaction. Finally, Table 9.7 describes how to customize things for the MVCs.

Why Do Customers Fail to Renew Their Season Tickets?

It is not hard to understand that the campaign to retain customers begins the day a person purchases the season ticket or sports product. The critical time period is the initial year or the first few games attended. This period of time is when most people decide whether they will stay and become a more frequent buyer or drop out. Table 9.8 outlines why sports teams lose fans. The information provided in Table 9.8 could be used by sports managers to develop strategies to eliminate the common barriers to retaining customers.

The Fan Comes First

Retaining sports fans is a challenging task in this day of high technology and multiple entertainment opportunities that can be enjoyed in one's own living room. What makes the sports fan want to

Table 9.7
Customizing

- Customize paperwork to save the customer time and the employee store money. Use regional versions of catalogues. Segment mailing lists.
- Personalize direct mail. Use customer information to individualize orders.
- Ask customers how often they want to hear from the employee store. Use fax, e-mail, postal mail, or in-person visits as the customer specifies.
- Ascertain what the customers want. Use focus groups and customer surveys to solicit feedback.
- Ask top 10 customers what the employee store can do differently to improve the product or service. The manager should do what the customer suggests. Follow up and do it again.

Schwabe, L. D. (2001). *Your store: The secret weapon.* ESM Association Annual Conference and Exhibit, New Orleans, LA. April 8-12, 2001.

Table 9.8
Why Sports Teams Lose Fans

There are a number of reasons why sports teams lose fans. Sports managers need to be aware of these reasons so that strategies can be developed to eliminate them:

- Fans did not feel as though they were important.
- Cost outweighs enjoyment.
- Dirty facilities.
- Boring food service.
- Poor seating.
- Inconvenient parking.
- No luxury seating.
- No picnic areas
- No nonsmoking areas.
- No nondrinking areas.
- No place to change young children.
- No daycare facilities.
- No playground for young children.
- Souvenirs too expensive.
- No other entertainment but the game itself.
- Team is not exciting.
- Team fails to win consistently.
- No opportunities to meet the players.

Sawyer, T.H., and Smith R. (1999). *The management of clubs, recreation, and sport: Concepts and applications.* Champaign: Sagamore Publishing, p.137.

return to the ballpark, stadium, arena, or rink contest after contest? What can be done to draw customers to events? Table 9.9 outlines a sample of ways to increase event attendance.

Sports teams are well-oiled entertainment businesses built by hard-driving sports entrepreneurs. The entrepreneurs have a deep respect for their customers. They offer amenities such as changing tables in restrooms for mothers or fathers with young children, more restrooms for women to reduce the waiting, daycare centers for mothers or fathers with young children, nonsmoking and nondrinking seating areas, seating for persons with disabilities area, barbershops, beauty shops, specialty foods, full-service restaurants, highly recognized fast food establishments (e.g., Arbys, Burger King, Hardees, McDonald's, Pizza Hut, Subway, Taco Bell, etc.), luxury boxes, club seats, mini-malls (e.g., clothing shops, shoe stores, souvenir shops, etc.), reasonably priced souvenirs and other licensed products, entertaining

Table 9.9
How Can the Audience Be Increased?

The following listing is a sample of what can be done to draw customers to the events:

- Pre-event entertainment.
- Youth games at half-time.
- Special group promotions (e.g., Boy Scouts, Girl Scouts, mother and son outing, father and daughter outing).
- Special rates for groups (e.g., senior citizens, ladies night, honor students, high school band members and families).
- Giveaways (e.g., miniature baseball bats, baseball caps, miniature basketballs, miniature footballs, T-shirts, pins).
- Scheduling doubleheaders.
- Reduced ticket fees.
- Shoot-out contests at half time.
- Event buses.
- Special days (e.g., hometown day, specific town day, specific school day).
- Student athletes visiting schools as role models.
- Clip-out coupons.
- Radio giveaways to listeners (e.g., tickets).
- Use of pep band at events.
- Team color night (e.g., offer half-price admission to anyone dressed in team colors)
- Face-painting contest (e.g., encourage students to come early and face paint each other in an area separate from the event area, and judge the painting jobs and provide prizes to the winners at halftime).

Sawyer, T.H., and Smith R. (1999). *The Management of clubs, recreation, and sport: Concepts and applications.* Champaign: Sagamore Publishing, p.137.

scoreboards, reasonable and accessible parking, health and fitness centers, playgrounds and entertainment rides, free parking for season ticket holders, car detailing services, and picnic areas.

Further, the owners provide special entertaining promotions including fireworks, celebrities during opening ceremonies or halftime or the seventh-inning stretch, contests for fans prior to the game or during halftime, free entrance for children wearing any kind of sport uniform, hat or bat night, team picture night, family picture with favorite player, and ladies night. These are all examples of how a sports manager can encourage his or her fans to continue their loyalty to the team (Sawyer and Smith, 1999).

The Function of Advertising

Advertising consists of all the activities involved in presenting to a group a nonpersonal, oral or visual, openly sponsored message regarding a service, product, or program. This message, called an *advertisement*, is disseminated through one or more media and is paid for by the identified sponsor.

There is a significant distinction between advertising and an advertisement. The advertisement is simply the message itself. Advertising is a process. It is a program or a series of activities necessary to plan and prepare the message and get it to the intended market. Another point is that the public knows who is behind the advertising because the sponsor is openly identified in the advertisement itself. Further, the payment is made by the sponsor to the media which carry the message. These last two considerations differentiate advertising from propaganda and publicity.

Fundamentally, the only purpose of advertising is to sell something—a service, product, or program. The intent may be to generate a sale immediately or at some time in the future. Nevertheless, the basic objective is to sell. Stated another way, the real goal of advertising is effective communication; that is, the ultimate effect of advertising should be to modify the attitudes and/or behavior of the receiver of the message.

The general goal of advertising is to increase profitable sales, but this goal is too broad to be implemented effectively in an advertising program. It is necessary to establish some specific objectives that can be worked into the program. A few examples of these more limited aims are to

- support personal selling program,
- reach people inaccessible to salesman,
- improve dealer relations,
- enter a new geographic market or attract a new group of customers,

- introduce a new product or a new price schedule,
- increase sales of products,
- expand membership sales,
- counteract prejudice or substitution, and
- build goodwill for the organization and improve its reputation by rendering a public service through advertising or by telling of the organization behind the service, product, or program.

How Is the Advertising Budget Developed?

The advertising program budget is developed by taking into consideration the following components:

- Expenses
  - (1) The number and size of printed advertisements (internal and external sources).
  - (2) The number and length of radio spots.
  - (3) The number and length of television spots.
  - (4) The number of billboards in use.
  - (5) Personnel.
  - (6) Office expenses.
- Income
  - (1) Advertisement space sold.
  - (2) Trade outs (It is possible to increase the advertising schedule for a program on a non-cash basis [trade outs—tickets or memberships for free advertising] if the attraction and manager are willing to allow a radio station [it is less common for television and the printed media to enter into trade out agreements] to be the program's official media sponsor. Never allow a media sponsorship to be construed as a sponsorship exclusive. Offer the media sponsor a promotional exclusive and clearly retain the right to advertise anywhere else it is appropriate).

The annual budget should include funds each year to advertise the schedule of services, products, and programs in local newspapers in a format which people can clip out and retain on a month-to-month basis. Many organizations also publish a weekly or monthly in-house newsletter which is used as a direct-mail piece as well as a handout at the facility.

Depending on the organization's philosophy, advertising can generate income by selling space for advertising in a variety of media throughout the organization's facility(ies). The possibilities include, but are not limited to: (1) scoreboard systems, (2) concourse display cases, (3) lobby displays, (4) point-of-sale displays, (5) Zamboni, (6) in-house publications, (7) message centers, (8) outdoor marquees, (9) upcoming program display cases, (10) membership packages, (11) concession product containers, (12) indoor soccer wall boards, (13) baseball/softball outfield fence, (14) scorer tables, and (15) contest programs. There are a number of potential advertisers for these spaces and, in particular, for concession products. Concession product vendors are willing to advertise their names and products on concession containers. This coupled with discount sale promotions will increase food and beverage sales for the organization as well as its vendors.

What Are the Steps to Selecting the Media?

Advertising strategy varies from program to program and season to season depending on the nature of the anticipated audience or market. Where to place an advertisement is governed generally by funds available.

Management must determine what general types of media to use—newspapers, magazines, radio, television, and billboards? If newspapers, local or regional? If television is selected, will it be local, national network, or spot telecasting?

Objective of the Advertisement

Media choices are influenced both by the purpose of a specific advertisement and by the goal of an entire campaign. If an advertiser wants to make last-minute changes in an advertisement, or if he or she wishes to place an advertisement inducing action within a day or two, he or she may use newspapers, radio, or television. Magazines are not so good for this purpose, because the advertisement must be placed weeks before the date of publication.

Media Circulation

Media circulation must match the distribution patterns of the service, product, or program. Consequently, the geographic scope of the market will influence the choice of media considerably. Furthermore, media should be selected that will reach the desired type of market with a minimum of waste circulation. Media used to reach a teenage market will be different from those used to reach mothers with young children.

Requirements of the Message

Management should consider the media that are most suitable for the presentation of the message to the market. Meat products, floor coverings, and apparel are ordinarily best presented in pictorial form; thus, radio is not a good medium for these lines. If a product, such as insurance, calls for a lengthy message, outdoor advertising is poor. If the advertiser can use a very brief message, however, as in the case of salt, beer, or sugar, then billboards may be the best choice. Television can be used to show pictures, but not detailed ones.

Time and Location of Buying Decision

The advertiser should select the medium that will reach the prospective customer at or near the time and place that he or she makes his buying decision. For this reason, outdoor advertising is often good for gasoline products and hotels/motels. For this reason, outdoor advertising (billboards) is often good for gasoline products and hotels/motels. Grocery store advertisements are placed in newspapers on Thursday nights or Friday mornings in anticipation of heavy weekend buying.

How Are Advertisements Created?

Before creating the advertisement, the people concerned should remember that the main purpose of advertising is to sell something and that the advertisement itself is a sales talk. The advertisement may be a high-pressure sales talk as in a hard-hitting, direct-action advertisement; or it may be a very long-range, low-pressure message, as in an institutional advertisement. In any case it is trying to sell something. Consequently, it involves the same kind of selling procedure as a sales talk delivered by personal salespersons. That is, the advertisement must first attract attention and then hold interest long enough to stimulate a desire for the service, product, or program. Finally, the advertisement must move the prospect to some kind of action. The desired action may lie anywhere within a virtually unlimited scope of possibilities ranging from an immediate change in overt behavior to a slowly changing attitude or thought process.

Creating an advertisement involves the tasks of writing the copy, selecting illustrations to be used, preparing the layout, and arranging to have the advertisement reproduced for the selected media.

The copy in an advertisement is defined as all the written or spoken material in it, including the headline, coupons, and advertiser's name and address, as well as the main body of the message. The illustration, whether it is a photograph, drawing, reproduction of a painting, cartoon, or something else, is a powerful feature in an advertisement. Probably the main points to consider with respect to illustrations are (1) whether they are the best alternative use of the space and (2) whether they are appropriate in all respects to the advertisement itself. The layout is the physical arrangement of all the elements in an advertisement. Within the given amount of space or time, the layout artist must place the headline, copy, and illustrations. Decisions are made regarding the relative amount of white space and the kinds of type to be used. A good layout can be an interest-holding device as well as an attention- getter. It should lead the reader in an orderly fashion throughout the entire advertisement.

What Is Important to Consider When Selecting an Advertising Firm?

If the organization is unable to maintain an in-house advertising operation, it is advisable to interview and select a local agency to serve the organization. If an outside agency is engaged, the performance must be constantly monitored so that more than simple advertisement placement is accomplished. The agency should advise the organization of the most appropriate advertising media plan for the organization. Finally, the agency should have a good sense of promotion and public relations. The average charge by an outside agency is a 15% commission for each advertisement placement.

What Is the Purpose of Consumer Relations?

The consumer (customer/client) is a person who buys services, products (goods), and programs for personal needs and not for resale. It is important to understand that your customers/clients are always right—whether or not they are right. The organization must develop a sound customer relations policy with appropriate procedures to provide outstanding customer service. The following are a few suggestions for the development of user-friendly customer relations procedures:

- All personnel should treat all customers as their friends.
- All personnel should give 110% to answer customer questions and meet their needs.
- Birthdays and other anniversaries of customers should be recognized by the staff.
- All staff should welcome members and guests with a hardy "hello" and a friendly smile.
- All telephone responses should be friendly and upbeat (management should prepare a script and monitor all phone calls).

Member (customer/client) retention begins the moment a prospect signs his or her name on the membership contract. After all, members or ticket holders only will renew their membership or purchase other tickets if they feel they are a valued part of the club. It is the responsibility of the consumer relations program to make the consumer feel at home from the "get-go."

Here are a number of ways that employeees should be integral parts of the organization's consumer relations program:

- Assist the consumers in designing their own programs, whether it be an exercise plan, a recreation plan, or a ticket purchasing plan.
- Encourage employees to invite prospective new consumers to club events, classes, or contests.

- Ascertain consumers' interests and link them to the interest areas or services available.
- Follow up by calling new as well as established consumers periodically to gauge the level of satisfaction.
- "Buddy up" new consumers with established consumers or a member of the staff—doing so helps personalize the organization and makes the consumer feel wanted.
- Organize a "welcome" party periodically for the newer consumers to introduce them more thoroughly to the facilities, staff, and other consumers.
- Last, but not least, foster a friendly environment: "Hi my name is_____, what is yours? Welcome to_____!"

Technology and the Customer

Technology is one key to successful operations in almost every aspect of the company, including the employee store. Technology makes operations more efficient and user-friendly. The manager needs to be aware of how technology can improve operations.

Making the Connection to the Customer

Managers need to begin taking advantage of the uses of e-commerce to enhance sales. Start by developing new ways to connect with suppliers and interact with customers. An example of a new approach to connecting with suppliers is the Collaborative Forecasting and Replenishment (CFAR) system used by Wal-Mart. Wal-Mart and its suppliers have become on-line partners in inventory control at the store level. An example of a new approach to interacting with customers is Amazon.com selling books and music over the internet.

Customer Needs

In 1998, the Georgia Institute of Technology conducted a survey that identified the average age of Internet users at 35 and stated that 81% of them had some college training. A significant 88% of those surveyed log on to the internet daily and 63% are able to make the connection from their homes. An impressive finding by this survey was that 76% of those surveyed have already made purchases using e-commerce (Penderghast, 1999).

Customers have four basic needs when ordering products over the internet:

- Security—the trust that the transaction will be honest. An Ernst & Young study reports that 87% of those surveyed stated that they would use e-commerce if security were improved.
- Support—the belief that the sellers will stand behind the products they sell.
- Information—both about the items offered for sale and about the use of an item after the sale is completed.
- Privacy—the hope that the demographic data collected as a result of the transaction will not be sold to someone else. (Penderghast, 1999)

The manager can turn the facility into a virtual store with the application of e-commerce, particularly during the offseason. Think of it as expanding offerings without the need to bring additional inventory into the facility and display it on shelves. Consider placing orders electronically and having the merchandise delivered either to the store or directly to the customer.

The provider can make agreements with suppliers to provide information about their goods and services online for the customers. When placing orders, customers can make their payments directly to the store and the provider can then forward the agreed wholesale price to the supplier.

Another aspect of the virtual store concept is that the store can offer goods for sale to employees who live and work in other geographic locations and to retirees who have moved away. The provider will be able to expand the employee customer base as well as expand the scope of products offered for sale (Penderghast, 1999).

Customers may have other needs that the provider can fulfill by using e-commerce. For example, consider providing access to items that might be important to the members of a hobby club. Why should the employees go elsewhere to buy these items when they can purchase them through the store?

The provider may also consider providing access to recreational resources. Foster Research predicts that by the year 2000, 25% of retail e-commerce will be related to tourism. Customers can go through you to make travel and vacation plans. Every time a customer makes travel plans through the store, the store earns a commission (Penderghast, 1999).

Making Preparations

Penderghast (1999) strongly recommends that managers need to plan to make an investment of managerial time and store resources to make e-commerce an operational addition to your store. The first thing the provider must do is to develop a Web site. This will require the contributions of personnel who are technically qualified to build your site and make it appealing to your customers.

The provider will also need to train the store personnel in the use of e-commerce. They should know how to search for and acquire information from the internet. They must learn to advise customers for this purpose.

One managerial issue to consider is the extent to which the provider wants to rely on e-commerce software to handle transactions. This can range from a browser, which can be used to search for information, to a full-blown package that can handle all aspects of catalogue purchases. Depending on the needs and complexity of the computer network, this software could range from $15,000 to $100,000 (Penderghast, 1999).

Another concern is the trade-off between glitter and download speed. The use of color, graphics, sound, and animation on your Web page may be appealing, but it also could result in an inordinate amount of time to transmit the page to your customers' computers. This is especially true when customers access the Web page at home on their computer through a telephone modem. Research the options and make the page as appealing as possible without making it too difficult to access.

E-commerce offers a challenge to all managers. There are significant advantages for the customers and a potential for increased profit, but to do it right will require an investment of both management time and store resources. E-commerce is a reality. The genie is out of the bottle and can no longer be ignored. The manager has an obligation to the organization served to meet the needs of its customers. If the manager does not, someone else will.

A Dozen Ways to Use the Web

Penderghast (1999) outlines 12 features the internet/intranet offers for increasing revenues, speeding customer service, and enhancing employee productivity at the retail store:

- Allows employees to browse items, place orders on the web, and then pick them up at the store.
- Integrates and allows employees to manage decentralized mail, phone and e-mail orders, Website sales, and the physical store's sales.
- Uploads the store data economically via the web.
- Empowers the POS with company information by exchanging data with a corporate website or Intranet site.
- Sends e-mail notification of overdue layaways and the arrival of back-ordered items.
- Facilitates inventory balancing. When one employee store runs low on an item or has a surplus of a product, the manager is able to visit a website to view the inventory of another store.
- Interfaces with suppliers' Web sites to check availability, place orders, and verify delivery dates.
- Provides access to your catalogues to display, compare, and order items not carried in the store.
- Displays vendors' websites to customers. This feature can be used to showcase the local attractions that offer discount tickets through the store.
- Shows event seating charts and allows customers to make online reservations.
- Provides access to the websites of letter carriers for shipping and tracking packages.
- Broadcasts online advertising and promotions from the POS system (Penderghast, 1999, p.33)

Table 9.10
Anger Triggers: What Sets Customers Off

As you ponder this list, ask yourself, "What steps am I able to take to prevent these problems from occurring in the first place?"

- Long delays.
- Service or sales problems that result in serious customer problems or emergencies.
- Uncaring or sloppy attitude.
- Wasted time, such as excessive trips back and forth to a retailer's location.
- Failure to listen.
- Failure to follow customer's instructions.
- Broken promises.
- Financial losses that result from poor service.
- Inability to provide needed answers or information.
- Impolite salespersons.
- Feeling that you are a number and not an important customer.

Modified from Ensman, R.G., Jr. (1998). Angry customers: A step-by-step guide to turning things around. *Employee Services Management, 41*(1), p.33.

Dealing With Angry Customers

Something has gone wrong. You can see it in the customer's face, which is turning beet red. She may be raising her voice or issuing veiled threats. Your knees feel weak at this verbal onslaught and you are frantically trying to compose a response while keeping your emotions in check.

Anyone could easily encounter this situation. In fact, you probably often do. Handling it effectively is easier than many think if you develop and practice anger response skills. The following is offered by Ensman (1998) as a step-by-step guide to turning things around with an angry customer:

First 30 Seconds

- First and foremost, listen. And listen immediately. No delays. Remember the triggers that can deepen customer anger—a seemingly uncaring attitude, argumentation, or officious bureaucratic behavior (see Table 9.10).
- What type of person is challenging you: a methodical inquisitor, an avenger, a bureaucrat anxious to catch someone breaking the rules, or a righteous victim? Try to understand the emotional type, and you will be able to gear your conversation accordingly.
- As the customer speaks, listen with your entire body. Arch forward a bit. Keep your head erect. Gaze at the customer and nod as she emphasizes key points.
- If you find yourself becoming defensive or angry, relax, and count to 10 or take a deep breath for a few seconds.
- After the customer gets the conversation going, signal your willingness to continue. Invite the person to sit down, step over to a more private location, or enter your office. This simple action on your part symbolizes your interest in the customer and sets the tone for a productive resolution of the problem.

The Conversation: 2-10 Minutes

- Allow the customer to blow off steam early in the conversation, and let the customer know you take all complaints seriously and you want to seek a resolution to the problem. Do not promise anything at this point.
- Let your customer know you are an impartial observer and that your immediate goal is to understand the problem as well as the circumstances that caused it. Then work with the customer to address it.
- When you must answer a question or respond to a comment, speak slowly and thoughtfully.
- When the customer raises her voice, nod and make a notation on your notepad. This is an expression of your attentiveness.
- Remember your customer's emotional profile; it is time to use this knowledge. If the customer is angry that some rule wasn't followed, for example, you might explore your procedures. If the customer feels her pride was insulted, you might praise and affirm the customer. Model your communication style in response to the customer.
- While you continue to actively listen, you can relax your body somewhat during this phase of the conversation. Here, you may put the customer at ease for the first time.
- Continue to acknowledge the legitimacy of his emotions and offer anecdotes about poor service or problems you have encountered in the past.
- Try to ascertain why the customer is bothered by the problem. A customer who encountered a late delivery, for example, actually might not be angry about the late delivery, but rather about having to change her plans as a result of the delay.

Attacking the Problem: 2-10 Minutes

- Up to this point you have said very little, preferring instead to let the customer speak. Apologize if that is appropriate. Outline in general terms how you will go about resolving the problem. If you can offer specifics, such as correcting the error, making an adjustment on the customer's account, or replacing merchandise, then do so; but, be sure to underpromise rather than overpromise.
- If you cannot firmly resolve the problem, indicate your next step, such as asking another individual to look into it, investigating further, or writing a letter to the manufacturer.
- Give the customer options, two or three ways you can address the problem. This symbolizes power to the customer.
- If you have discretion in resolving problems, simply ask: "What can I do to make things right?" While you might not be able to meet the customer's exact terms, those few words can begin a fruitful negotiation.
- Finally, this stage of discussion is often frustrating and aggravating; but think of it as an opportunity to sell your responsiveness. If you can indeed make a "sale" here, you may end up with a grateful customer for years to come (Ensman, 1998, p.32).

Summary

Customer/fan retention is the foundation for successful business operations in sports-related organizations. It is definitely important to maintain customers. The simplest way to complete this task is to treat each customer as if he or she were the most important person in the world.

Most often, customers do not return because they are not satisfied with the services or attention provided to them or their needs. A major key to maintaining customers is knowledgeable, reliable, friendly, and effective staff. The sports manager needs to work hard to continually train all staff in tactics to maintain customers. There are a number of customer strategies that need to be considered by all sports managers regarding customer retention. Not all will fit every situation or organization. The sports manager should make sure that all customers feel they are an integral part of the organization and important to the organization. The successful sports teams have loyal season ticket holders because they cater to the fan and his or her needs. The "fan comes first" attitude will make a sports franchise successful.

Advertising consists of all the activities involved in presenting to a group a nonpersonal, oral or visual, openly sponsored message regarding a service, product, or program. This message, called an advertisement, is disseminated through one or more media and is paid for by the identified sponsor.

The annual budget should include funds each year to advertise the schedule of services, products, and programs in local newspapers in a format that people can clip out and retain on a month-to-month basis.

Advertising strategy varies from program to program and season to season depending on the nature of the anticipated audience or market. Where to place an advertisement is governed generally by funds available.

Creating an advertisement involves the tasks of writing the copy, including the headline, selecting illustrations that may be used, preparing the layout, and arranging to have the advertisement reproduced for the selected media.

The manager and staff need to understand how to deal with customer complaints. The manager should be certain that strategies to deal with complaints are reviewed regularly. The complaints should be analyzed to determine the frequency of the common complaints and the resolutions practiced.

Finally, the manager must make technology an integral part of the customer relations strategy. The customer/fan of the future will be technically oriented and will expect to be able to use current technology to communicate with the organization. If the manager fails to keep abreast of the latest technology, the customers will migrate to where the technology is present.

Public Relations[1]

Thomas H. Sawyer

A *public relations* program is designed to influence the opinions of people within the targeted market through responsible and acceptable performance based on mutually satisfactory two-way communication. It has been noted that Abraham Lincoln once said, "Public sentiment is everything. With public sentiment, nothing can fail; without it, nothing can succeed." In order to gain public sentiment, programs must familiarize not only customers/clients but the public in general with all aspects of the services, products, and programs offered. An effective public relations program will open communication lines with the various publics and effectively utilize the media in a manner that competently presents the objectives of the organization to the public at large. Further, it will modify the attitudes and actions of the public through persuasion and integrate them with those of the organization.

Learning Objectives

After reading this chapter, the student should be able to

- understand how to develop a public relations plan,
- competently select a public relations agency,
- understand how to write a basic news release,
- define the difference between internal and external public relations,
- appreciate the function and importance of advertising,
- understand the value of soliciting advertising to raise funds to support the organization's advertising program, and
- decide whether or not an outside advertising agency needs to be employed.

Public Relations

A sport organization's public relations program should include, but not be limited to

- serving as an information source regarding organization services, products, and activities;
- promoting confidence that the services, products, and activities provided by the organization are useful and assist people in maintaining, gaining, or regaining their health and fitness;
- gathering support for the organization's programs and fund-raising appeals;
- stressing the value of active lifestyles and the positive impact they have on health and fitness;
- improving communication among customers/clients, staff, parents, and the surrounding community;
- evaluating the organization's services, products, and activities;
- correcting myths, misunderstandings, and misinformation concerning the organization's services, products, and activities.

Steps in Developing a Public Relations Program

It is important to first agree that a public relations program is necessary for the organization. Then resources to develop and implement a public relations plan must be provided. The primary resources required are human, financial,

---

[1]This chapter has been reprinted with modifications with permission from Sagamore Publishing. It represents Chapter 11, Public and media relations, from Sawyer, T. H., & Smith, O. R. (1999). *The Management of clubs, recreation, and sport: Concepts and applications*. Champaign, IL: Sagamore Publishing.

facility space, equipment (e.g., computers, printers, and scanners), and materials (e.g., funds for duplication, phones, postage, printing, software, etc).

Initially, a public relations program planning committee should be established with representation from all facets of the organization. This committee should follow the steps outlined in Figure 10.1, in the development of a public relations program plan.

Figure 10.1
Steps for the Development of a Public Relations Plan

- Develop a philosophy statement that encourages the belief that the foundation for any good public relations program is outstanding performance.
- Establish a mission statement that encourages the establishment and maintenance of two-way lines of communication with as many related publics as possible.
- Develop a sound, uniform public relations policy (i.e., All communication with the public will be handled through the Public Relations Office.).
- Establish a set of principles to guide the development of the public relations program, such as:
  —Public relations must be considered internally before being developed externally.
  —The public relations program plan will be circulated to all members of the organization for meaningful input and buy in.
  —The persons selected to implement the public relations plan must have a thorough knowledge of the professional services to be rendered, the attitudes of members of the profession and organization represented, and the nature and reaction of the consumers/clients and all the publics directly or indirectly related to the organization's services, products, or programs.
  —The public relations office must be keep abreast of the factors and influences that affect the program and develop and maintain a wide sphere of contacts.
- Identify the services, products, and programs that will yield the greatest dividends.
- Define the various related publics.
- Obtain facts regarding consumers'/clients' and other publics' knowledge level about the organization's services, products, and programs.
- Determine the following before drafting the program plan:
  —Is there a handbook or manual of guidelines or a newsletter to keep members of the organization informed (internal communication)?
  —Is there a system for disseminating information to the media?
  —Is there access to the internet and, if so, does the organization have a Web page?
  —Is there a booklet, flyer, or printed matter that tells the story of the organization?
  —Do the members (customers/clients) and staff participate in community activities?
  —Does the organization hold open houses, clinics, seminars, or workshops?
  —Are there provisions for a speakers' bureau so that civic and service clubs, schools, and other organization's may obtain someone to speak on various topics relating to the organization's services, products, or programs?
  —Does the organization have an informational video?
  —Is inter- and intra-organizational electronic mail utilized to its fullest capacity?
- Determine appropriate timelines for implementation and who or what group is responsible for the completion of the task.
- Establish a regular evaluation process for the plan.

Publicity

After the public relations committee completes the public relations plan, it is important for the committee to determine what the steps are to gain publicity for the organization. Every organization should have established a strategy for publicizing its programs and services. The basic tenet in effective publicity is developing a positive image for the organization and linking with other organizations with a similar philosophy. For example, a youth organization would not be wise to align itself with an alcohol or tobacco industry in sponsoring its events.

The primary objective of publicity is to draw attention to a person, the organization, or an event. An effective publicity program is required to obtain an individual's attention. Publicity will not sell tickets, raise funds, win supporters, retain members, or sell merchandise; however, publicity can be helpful in conveying ideas to people so that these ends can be more easily attained.

Effect of Publicity

Publicity should be planned with these guidelines in mind: (1) too much publicity can be poor public relations, because often at a given point people tend to react negatively to excessive publicity; (2) the amount of publicity absorbed is important, not the amount released; (3) the amount of publicity disseminated does not necessarily equal the amount received or used; (4) the nature of the publicity eventually tends to reveal the character of the organization it seeks to promote, for better or worse; (5) some publicity an organization receives originates from outside sources; and (6) not all public relations activities result in publicity (Bronzan & Stotlar, 1992).

Figure 10.2 outlines some basic steps for effective publicity.

Figure 10.2
Steps to Effective Publicity

Publicity is free; however, a sound plan for publicity does not happen by accident. It requires planning and careful execution. Consistent media attention is the overall goal of the publicity plan. There are a number of guidelines that should be followed when developing publicity materials for the media and others including, but not limited to:

- Focus the materials on specific objectives.
- Create materials that are interesting to the editors and the reader and are creative in nature.
- Make the materials newsworthy.
- Ensure the materials are accurate and neat.
- Fashion materials so they look professionally complete.
- Furnish background material regarding the submission.
- Provide artwork, graphics, or photographs with the submission.
- Focus manuscript (text) on intended audience.
- Develop and respect all relationships with media contacts.
- Reinforce all relationships with the media contacts by expressing appreciation for their efforts.

Finally, there are a few general pointers that should be considered regarding the interrelationship between the media and the organization's publicity practices:

- It is nice to know someone in the media, but it is not necessary to get free publicity. Editors have numerous pages and hours to fill, and in many instances your news release may be very helpful to them. Therefore, do not hesitate to send materials to a media source.
- The key to success with the media is to package the news release in such a way it attracts attention, allowing for a more in-depth examination by the editor.
- The best way to communicate with the media is by mail or electronic mail. Avoid using the telephone unless it is an emergency or to return a call.
- It should be understood that publicity efforts do not have to appear in the most influential media to be worthwhile.

Principles of Good Publicity and Media Relations

The sports manager can develop confidence and respect by adhering to some basic principles. These include the following:

1. Be honest.
2. Do not try to block the news by use of evasion, censorship, pressure, or trickery.
3. Be cooperative at all times; be accessible by telephone or in person at all times.
4. Be candid; do not seek trouble, but do not try to hide from it either.
5. Use facts, not rumors, although initially they may be more detrimental than the rumors. Remember, facts limit the story, rumors tend to remove all boundaries.
6. Do not pad a weak story; this practice tends to weaken credibility.
7. Do not stress or depend upon off-the-record accounts. Remember, the job of the reporter is to obtain facts and report the story. Asking the reporter to abide with off-the-record requests is unfair and costly.
8. Give as much service to newspapers as possible. When news occurs, get the story out expeditiously. Hot news is desired by newspaper reporters, so one must be willing and able to supply newspapers with the stories, pictures, and statistics they wish, as they want them prepared, and on time.
9. If a reporter uncovers a story, do not give the same story to another reporter. Treat it as an exclusive right.
10. Since news is a highly perishable commodity, remember that newspapers want news, not publicity.

Sports managers must become acquainted with the publishers, the highest ranking officer (the executive editor), the editor, the editorial page editor, and finally, the managing editor who is the working head of staff engaged in handling news. In addition to these individuals, a close working relationship is necessary with the sports editor, Sunday desk editor, and society editor. Of course, it is advantageous to also know the editors for the amusements, arts, and business sections.

Positive reinforcement is as important in public relations as it is in sports. One should act promptly to commend all persons involved in carrying a special story, promotional activity, or unusual action. Copies of the commendation should be mailed to all relevant members of the newspaper.

Seeking a Public Relations Agency

Olguin (1991) suggested the following 10 questions should be asked before an organization contracts with a public relations agency:

- Does the agency have experience in the health, fitness, physical activity, recreation, and sport industries?
- Do the account executives have experience in these industries?
- Does the agency have a good reputation?
- Will the agency give you a list of references?
- Will you have the senior-level management attention?
- Do they know the industry's publications and have media contacts at each?
- Are they a full-service agency with public relations, advertising, direct mail, and promotional capabilities?
- Are they creative? Ask to see other public relations campaigns completed for other organizations in the same or related areas.
- Are they results-oriented?
- Are they good listeners?

Once the questions have been answered and analyzed, it is time to narrow the field of prospective agencies to the top three to five. These agencies should be requested to make a presentation to the selection committee. After the presentations have been completed the committee should make a recommendation ranking the agencies and providing a narrative explaining the ratings for each agency.

Difference Between Internal and External Public Relations

Internal public relations is communicating openly and often with personnel and members. The best promotion for an event can be negated if one of the employees or members gives a disgruntled response to the media. The best promoters of an organization are its employees and members.

External public relations is communicating with the publics external to the organization and its employees and members. This communication is done directly with the public and through the media. These are prospective new members.

Outlets for Public Relations

There are numerous avenues for getting the message out to the internal and external publics. They include, but are not limited to: (1) printed media, (2) pictures and graphics, (3) radio, (4) television, (5) video, (6) posters, (7) exhibits, (8) brochures, (9) billboards and posters, (10) public speaking opportunities, (11) electronic mail, (12) internet (Web page), (13) direct mail, and (14) telemarketing.

The most valuable list the public relations professional has is the media list. The list is updated every day and compiled from three sources: (1) media who routinely cover the health, fitness, physical activity, recreation, and sport areas; (2) personal contacts; and (3) media directories.

The media directories most often used include:

- *Bacon's Publicity Checker* reports on the content of 5,000 trade and business periodicals in over 100 different categories.
- *Broadcasting Yearbook* lists every licensed radio and television station in the United States, Canada, and Central and South America.
- *Burrelle's Special Groups Media Directory*, an annual list of newspapers, periodicals, and electronic media classified by Black, European Ethnic, Hispanic, Jewish, Older Americans, Women, Young Adults, and Activists.
- *Communications Guide*, an annual guide published by local chapters of the Public Relations Society of America. It includes area broadcasts, print media, news bureaus, community publications, college publications, and special interest magazines.
- *Editor & Publisher Yearbook*, an encyclopedia of the newspaper industry.
- *Gale Directory of Publications*, an annual listing of over 20,000 publications including daily and weekly newspapers and all major trade and specialty magazines.
- *Standard Periodical Directory*, a guide to more than 65,000 U.S. and Canadian periodicals.
- *Working Press of the Nation* lists editorial staffs in newspapers, magazines, syndicates, broadcast news, and major free-lance writers and columnists.
- *PR Newswire and Business Wire* provides listing of subscribers in all types of media.

It should be understood that annual directories are roughly 20% inaccurate because of rapidly changing editorial staffs each year. Everything should be double checked for accuracy.

The news release can be distributed using a variety of electronic equipment and other means: (1) fax machine, (2) computers, (3) PR Newswires, (4) handouts, (5) messenger, (6) express mail, (7) U.S. Mail, and (8) telephone.

Public Speaking:
A Key to Achieving Good Public Relations

The sports manager needs to understand that public speaking, if done well, can be an effective medium for achieving good public relations. Addresses should be made regularly to civic and social groups, schools, professional meetings, government entities, and general gatherings.

If the organization is large enough, a "speakers bureau" should be formed and a number of qualified employee speakers recruited. Once the bureau has been established, a list of topics should be circulated and distributed to civic and social groups, schools, churches, and other interested parties. The bureau and speakers need to prepare a number of topic areas with appropriate overheads, slides, and videos. Finally, the bureau should prepare younger professionals to become effective and accomplished speakers.

What Is Necessary for Preparing Radio and Television Presentations?

Radio and television media are powerful and well worth the money spent for public relations. The largest obstacle is obtaining free time. The idea of public service will influence some station managers to grant free time to an organization. This may be in the nature of an item included in a newscast program, a spot public service announcement (PSA), or a public service program that might range from 15 to 60 minutes.

Sometimes a person must take advantage of the media on short notice. Therefore, it is important for an organization to be prepared with written plans that can be put into operation immediately. The following are a few guidelines for preparation:

- Know the organization's message.
- Know the program (i.e., style, format, audience participation, time).
- Know the audience (e.g., seniors, teens, up-scale, nonconsumers, gender).
- Tailor the message and presentation to the audience's interest.
- Practice—speak in lay terms, be brief and concise.

What Are the Four Essentials of a Great Communicator?

There are four areas in which audiences will not forgive speakers: not being prepared, comfortable, committed, and interesting. If the speaker concentrates on being prepared, committed, interesting, and making others comfortable, he or she will become an accomplished communicator in formal speeches as well as in interpersonal communications.

Preparation is essential. Your listeners (1) must have confidence that you know what you are talking about; (2) should feel that you know more about the subject than they do; (3) will feel that you spent time preparing your subject and analyzing your audience; (4) must feel there is a purpose to your message; and (5) must understand you are prepared to face a hostile or skeptical audience.

In Figure 10.3 there is a preparation checklist that will save you time in preparing your next speech.

Figure 10.3
Speech Preparation Checklist

1. Speech preparation
   * Evaluate the audience.
   * Consider the occasion.
   * Determine the length of the talk.
   * Determine the purpose of your speech—to entertain, inform, inspire, or persuade (good speeches often combine elements of all four).
   * Decide on a central theme. (If you cannot write your theme on the back of a business card, it is too complicated.)
   * Develop background knowledge.
   * Gather facts.
   * Consider the makeup of the audience.
   * Find a good opening line or story that relates to the speech. (If it does not interest you, it will not interest your audience.)
   * The speech can be in either past, present, or future tense. (Write down three to five questions the audience might ask you and answer them as the body of your speech.)
2. Speech outline
   * Introduction. (Tell them what you are going to tell them.)
   * Body. (Tell them)
   * Close. (Tell them what you have told them and close the door.)
3. Speech delivery
   * Be interesting—use some memorable phrases and quotes.
   * Support statements with facts and examples.
   * Practice speech out loud in front of a mirror (also use either a tape recorder or video recorder).
   * Time speech (add 20 seconds for actual delivery).
   * Consider size of audience and room (adjust volume).
   * Take your time in order to have the audience's attention.
   * Concentrate on good eye contact.

It is important for the speaker to be *committed* to the message. This is crucial. Very few speakers freeze up, unable to speak on what they feel strongly about. If you know what you are saying, why you are saying it, and care about what you are saying, you will say it well.

A speaker must be *interesting*. It is vital to the health of the audience. It is difficult to be interesting if you are not committed and vice versa. No audience will forgive you if you are boring.

It is essential to make others *feel comfortable*, but you must first be comfortable with yourself and your surroundings. People who are confident are usually comfortable with themselves. Others take their cues from you, so relax, keep things in perspective, and do not overreact. Maintain your sense of humor and take your work seriously but not yourself.

Summary

A public relations program is designed to influence the opinions of people within the targeted market through responsible and acceptable performance based on mutually satisfactory two-way communication. It has been noted that Abraham Lincoln once said, "Public sentiment is everything. With public sentiment, nothing can fail; without it, nothing can succeed." In order to gain public sentiment, programs must familiarize not only customers/clients but the public in general with all aspects of the services and activities offered.

An organization's public relations program should include serving as an information source, promoting confidence, gathering support, improving communications, correcting misunderstandings and misinformation, and evaluating the organization's services, products, and activities.

It is important to first agree that a public relations program is necessary for the organization. Then resources to develop and implement a public relations plan must be provided. The primary resources required are human, financial, facility space, equipment (e.g., computers, printers, and scanners), and materials (e.g., funds for duplication, phones, postage, printing, software, etc).

Internal public relations is communicating openly and often with personnel and members. The best promotion for an event can be negated if one of the employees or members gives a disgruntled response to the media. The best promoters of an organization are its employees and members.

External public relations is communicating with the publics external to the organization and its employees and members. This communication is done directly with the public(s) and through the media. These are prospective new members.

There are numerous avenues for getting the message out to the internal and external publics. They include, but are not limited to: (1) printed media, (2) pictures and graphics, (3) radio, (4) television, (5) video, (6) posters, (7) exhibits, (8) brochures, (9) billboards and posters, (10) public speaking opportunities, (11) electronic mail, (12) internet (Web page), (13) direct mail, and (14) telemarketing.

It is important to understand and remember that news is first what an editor or a broadcast news director thinks is news. If they are negative to any story, the public may never see or hear it. Publicity is the attempt by an organization or person to benefit from editorial coverage. Since the public believes editorial information is more trustworthy than paid advertising, there is incalculable value in published positive publicity.

Pictures and graphics are very important and effective mediums for public relations. When taking and/or selecting pictures for publication, look for action and people. Pictures that reflect action are far more appealing than stills. Further, pictures with people in them are more effective than those without people.

Public speaking, if done well, can be an effective medium for achieving good public relations. Addresses should be made regularly to civic and social groups, schools, professional meetings, government entities, and general gatherings.

Radio and television media are powerful and well worth the money spent for public relations. The largest obstacle is obtaining free time. The idea of public service will influence some station managers to grant free time to an organization. This may be in the nature of an item included in a newscast program, a spot public service announcement (PSA), or a public service program that might range from 15 to 60 minutes.

There are four areas in which audiences will not forgive speakers: not being prepared, comfortable, committed, and interesting. If the speaker concentrates on being prepared, committed, interesting, and making others comfortable, he or she will become an accomplished communicator in formal speeches as well as in interpersonal communications.

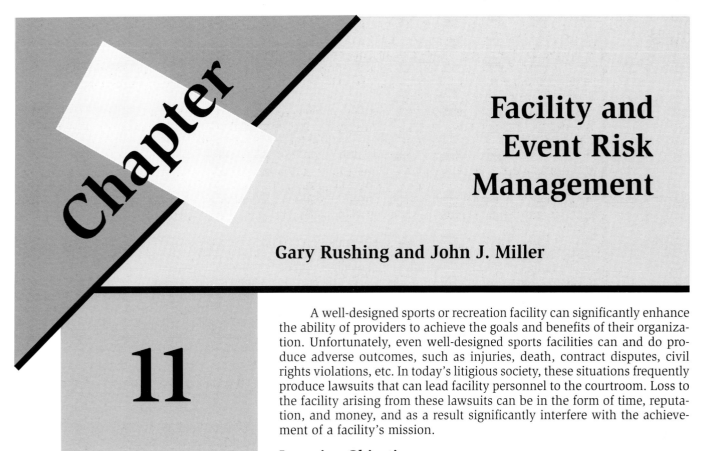

Facility and Event Risk Management

Gary Rushing and John J. Miller

11

A well-designed sports or recreation facility can significantly enhance the ability of providers to achieve the goals and benefits of their organization. Unfortunately, even well-designed sports facilities can and do produce adverse outcomes, such as injuries, death, contract disputes, civil rights violations, etc. In today's litigious society, these situations frequently produce lawsuits that can lead facility personnel to the courtroom. Loss to the facility arising from these lawsuits can be in the form of time, reputation, and money, and as a result significantly interfere with the achievement of a facility's mission.

Learning Objectives

After reading this chapter, the student should be able to

- develop a general risk management program for a sports or recreational facility, and
- develop a specific risk management plan for an event.

Risk Management

The most effective way for sports facility operators to avoid losses is to design and implement a strategy that identifies those situations in which legal or financial difficulties may arise and then take corrective actions that will either eliminate the exposure, significantly reduce the chances of the situation from occurring, or reduce the impact of the happening should it occur. This process is called *risk management* (Appenzeller, 2000; van der Smissen, 1990).

Risks are viewed broadly as physical injury or death, potential litigation, and financial loss (Jensen & Overman, 2003) and can be defined as those occurrences that expose a provider to the possibility of loss (van der Smissen, 1990).

Benefits of a Risk Management Program

Sawyer and Smith (1999) stated that a good risk management program increases the safety of the patrons, reduces the losses to the organization, and increases effective use of funds. Additionally, it serves as a deterrent to a lawsuit and demonstrates intent to act in a reasonable and prudent manner. Appenzeller (Appenzeller & Lewis, 2000) reinforced this notion when he explained "the law does expect that sport managers develop and implement loss control and risk management programs to ensure a safe environment for all who participate in the sport activities" (p. 314). The overriding benefit is that a good risk management program significantly enhances the achievement of goals and the mission of a facility.

Risk Management Manager

Safety and risk management are shared responsibilities; all workers in a venue should know their roles and be aware of the need to minimize risk. To clarify each employee's role in risk management, and to oversee the development and implementation of the risk management program, someone should be designated as the risk manager. This could be an individual who is a full-time professional risk manager or someone who has additional responsibilities. It should be noted that for a risk manager to be effective, he or she must have the support of the upper management in a facility.

Risk Management Committee

Further, it is very unlikely that one person would know all the risk exposures that a venue may encounter, nor can one person effectively manage a risk management program. Therefore, it is extremely beneficial to have a risk management committee to help provide guidance and oversight to a risk management program. The ideal committee should be composed of experts in insurance and law and have representation from the various units in the facility. Unit representation helps ensure support for the program and provide valuable input from those most familiar with risks in their department (Buisman, Thompson, & Cox, 1993). Ammon & Unruh (2003) recommended that at the very least, the committee should be composed of knowledgeable senior members of the organization.

Risk Categories

Although there are many ways that loss can occur within facility operations, most loss exposure can be categorized in one of four general areas. These include: 1) public liability caused by negligence, 2) public liability excluding negligence, 3) business operations, and 4) property exposures (Brown, 2003; van der Smissen, 1990). The extent to which a particular facility needs to be concerned with each area varies depending on the purpose of the facility, the unique situations of the facility, the types of programs and populations served, and specific injuries and incidents that have occurred in the past (Eickhoff-Shemek, 2002). Facility operators should familiarize themselves with safety and welfare concerns in each of these areas.

Public Liability Caused by Negligence

Negligence in a sports or recreation facility is *failure* on the part of the owner/operator to manage a facility in a reasonably prudent and careful manner and this failure results in damage to the plaintiff. This definition implies that facility management must provide a reasonably safe environment in which to work or participate. This general obligation can be translated into more specific duties such as: providing proper warnings and instructions to participants, providing proper supervision/security, providing proper equipment and facilities, providing medical/emergency precautions and care, and providing proper travel and transportation (Appenzeller, 2000). A claim of negligence could result from poor risk management caused by failure on the part of a facility operator to fulfill any of the above duties. Examples of claims in this area include injuries due to poorly maintained facilities (*Woodring v. Board of Education of Manhasset Union Free School District, 1981*) and attacks by third parties (*Bearman v. University of Notre Dame, 1999*).

Public Liability Excluding Negligence

This area is composed of circumstances in which facility personnel cause harm to patrons, fellow employees or volunteers in ways other than negligence. Tort law provides an avenue for people to be compensated for damages caused by these injurious situations. Examples of these situations include hiring and employment practices, professional malpractice, product liability, intentional torts, sexual harassment, and civil liberty violations. Examples of claims in this area include age, gender, disability and racial discrimination; wrongful termination; sexual harassment; invasion of privacy; and false imprisonment.

Business operations

Business operations include business interruptions, employee health, theft, embezzlement, and contract disputes. Examples of risks in this area include fraud by workers, such as cheating on hours worked, admitting people into events free of charge, stealing money, and work interruptions such as strikes and sickness of key personnel.

Property exposures

This category consists of risk exposures to equipment, buildings, and grounds as a result of fire, natural disasters (earthquakes, floods, blizzards, hurricanes, tornados), vandalism/terrorism, and theft.

Risk Management Program Development Steps

The foundation of effective risk management is taking logical and proactive steps to handle uncertain financial and other losses that may occur from the activities of a facility (Jensen & Overman, 2003). The following steps enable a risk manager to develop a program that identifies risks, eliminates the unacceptable ones, and manages the remainder:

- Identify applicable areas of concern (public liability excluding negligence, business operations, property exposures, public liability caused by negligence
- Identify specific risk exposures in each category.
- Estimate the probable impact of the risk and classify.
- Select the optimum method of treating the risk.
- Implement a plan to carry out the selected method, monitor and evaluate.

Step One: Identify Applicable Areas of Concern

The first step in developing a risk management program is to determine the areas or categories of risks with which the facility operator should be concerned. A reference outline can be developed from the previously mentioned general categories of risks (public liability caused by negligence, public liability excluding negligence, business operations, and property exposures) or more specific categories can be selected such as accidents, security, contracts, personnel, financial, natural disasters, speculative risks (strikes), terrorist threats, design and construction, etc. The purpose of selecting the areas of concern is to provide risk reviewers with a reference for brainstorming and finding more specific risk exposures.

Step Two: Identify Risk Specific Exposures in Each Category

After the general categories have been selected, risk managers can enlist the help of risk management committee members or unit heads in the facility to do a risk inventory and compile a list of specific hazards that they may face in each category. Research must be done; Moore (1995) recommended utilizing interviews with pertinent personnel, loss analysis questionnaires, physical site inspections or business plan reviews. He further suggested that those responsible for identifying risks should use their imaginations and conduct "what if" scenarios. Professional literature, knowledgeable professionals, manufacturer's recommendations, historical claims data, and professional standards and practices can also be consulted. Finally, equipment and facility checklists or audits designed to help expose risk situations can be utilized (Rushing, 2000; Seidler, 2000). Not all risks are identifiable; however, if the above suggestions are applied, a fairly comprehensive list of risks can be identified.

Step Three: Estimate the Probable Impact of the Risk

The next step in developing a risk management program is to assess each risk on the risk *master* list and estimate the level of loss that each risk occurrence may impose on the operation of a facility. Various assessment tools in the form of frequency and severity matrixes have been developed to assist risk managers with this task. Frequency is how often the risk could occur and the severity is the degree of loss resulting from the occurrence. The more frequent a risk occurs and the more severe the occurrence, the greater the potential impact on the facility (Ammon & Unruh, 2003; Sawyer & Smith, 1999; Mulrooney, Farmer, & Ammon, 1995).

Risk managers may wish to devise a matrix that reflects their own facility's specific needs. Table 11.1 provides one means of evaluating a risk.

Table 11.1
Impact Table

(Risk Occurrence)	1	2	3	4	5
Estimate the likelihood of occurrence					
Assess the potential human impact					
Assess the potential property impact					
Assess potential business impact					
Total score					

Each risk, should it occur, is rated 1 to 5 on four criteria with 5 being the highest. The first criterion is the likelihood of occurrence, which is an estimate of the probability that the risk will occur. The second criterion is the potential human impact, which deals with death or injury caused by the particular risk occurrence. The third criterion is the potential property impact and relates to the loss or damage of property and the cost to replace or repair it. The last criteria is an estimate of the impact of the loss to business resulting from business interruptions, employees unable to work, contractual violations, fines and penalties or legal costs, etc. The scores for each risk should be totaled and the risks classified according to estimated impact. For example, a score of 17 to 20 might be considered severe; 13 to 16, high, 9 to 12, medium; and below 9, low. The higher scores result in greater impact (adapted from Emergency planning assembly facilities. [1996]. *IAAM*, pp.111-118).

It is not critical that this process is exact; however, the assessment that is performed should enable the risk manager to classify the impact of the risk on the facility's operation. The example above is one means of classifying the impact (i.e., severe, high, medium and low). Knowing classifications of impact will provide some guidance in determining a strategy for managing each risk and will help determine planning and resource priorities.

Step Four: Select the Optimum Method of Treating the Risk

After risks have been identified and classified, the next step is to apply a strategy that will appropriately control the loss resulting from the risk occurrence. Controlling the loss of assets is the goal of risk management (Jensen & Overman, 2003; Wong & Masterelexis,1996) and can be accomplished in one or a combination of four general ways: avoid, retain, transfer, and reduce.

Avoid

The first way is through loss avoidance, which entails avoiding or abandoning activities that have been deemed to have a loss potential that is too great (catastrophic or high loss) and that are nonessential to the mission of the venue. Examples of the application of this strategy are the removal of trampoline competition at a high school gymnastic competition or not booking an unruly rock band that is known to create serious problems. These are situations where the potential loss clearly outweighs the value of the event.

Retain

A second strategy is to retain the risk and prepare for potential loss through budgeting, deductibles, or self-insurance. Some situations or activities are inconsequential, uninsurable, nontransferable, or the cost of insurance is prohibitive. Risks associated with these situations/activities may be assumed by the facility as part of the cost of doing business. An example of the application of this strategy is budgeting for the loss of game balls at sporting events.

Transfer

A third means of controlling loss is transferring or shifting the loss to another person or entity through insurance or contractually by way of waivers of liability, indemnity clauses, and use of an independent contractor. This transfer strategy is applicable in situations where loss potential is substantial and the entity does not want to eliminate the risk (Sawyer, 1999).

Insurance is an excellent way to control for loss; however, it is expensive and therefore should be a last resort and done in conjunction with risk reduction. Reduction of risk lowers the potential for loss, which translates into lower premiums.

Facility operators need to have coverage that protects staff, participants, volunteers, administrators and visitors. Typically, facilities need to have four major forms of insurance: 1) liability insurance for loss-related claims for damages to persons or to their property; 2) accident insurance, which pays medical expenses for injured patrons; 3) property insurance, which covers facilities against natural disasters, theft, vandalism, and other events; and 4) workers compensation, which covers injury claims of workers. Additional insurance may be needed for special events. Selection of the appropriate types and amounts of coverage should be prepared in consultation with a reputable insurance specialist.

Use of Waivers or Releases. Facility operators can use waivers or releases of liability as a means of transferring loss arising from negligent acts of the facility provider or its employees. These documents are contracts that relinquish the right of patrons to sue for ordinary negligence. It must be noted that they only provide relief for mere negligence and not for extreme forms of negligence such as reckless misconduct or gross negligence. Also, it is unlikely that the courts will enforce waivers signed by or on behalf of minors (Cotten, 2003a). Waivers can provide a valuable means for transferring loss to the participant; however, the use of these documents must adhere to legal restrictions of the jurisdiction in which the facility is located.

Indemnity Clauses. These are agreements that hold owners/landlords harmless for any negligent acts or omissions by rental groups or independent contractors, such as venders or concessionaires. These agreements have obvious value in that they relieve the facility owners from any negligent loss resulting from the use of their facility.

Independent Contractor. An independent contractor is a person or business that agrees to perform a specific job for a facility. They are not considered employees of the venue if they are only hired to perform a specific task and the venue does not retain control over the method by which the task is performed (Cotten, 2003b). As a result of this arrangement, independent contractors are responsible for their own unemployment and liability insurance and are, typically, solely liable for their negligent actions. As with any contractor, their references and credentials should be carefully checked. Also, make sure the firm is adequately insured. Security guards and some vendors at many facilities are independent contractors.

Reduce

The fourth and final way of controlling loss is managing risk through loss reduction (loss prevention and loss control). This strategy is most effective when performed in conjunction with transfer and retention and is achieved by employing prudent practices that eliminate or reduce the effects of risk occurrences. The following are a few general ways of reducing risk in all risk categories: hiring qualified personnel, educating and training them effectively, selecting appropriate venues, abiding by all laws and codes, and implementing standard operating procedures for all significant risks. Specific strategies should be developed in each risk category (public liability caused by negligence, public liability excluding negligence, business operations, property exposures).

Risk Reduction for Public Liability Caused by Negligence. There are many ways to increase safety and decrease public liability risk exposures related to negligence. Facility operators must apply the best option for each risk based on their resources and characteristics. Risk managers must consider the characteristics of their users (age, skill level, etc.) and the types of activities in which they engage. They also must know their legal obligations as an owner of property versus a renter or leaser of property. They must meet local, state, regional, and federal code requirements. They must develop regularly scheduled inspections of the facility (floors, ventilation, restrooms, equipment, food preparation areas, toxic materials disposal, and security). They must regularly schedule maintenance with safety concerns given priority; monitor visitors for security; supply emergency/crisis plans for natural disasters and terrorist exposures such as bomb threats; hire or select qualified personnel (lifeguards, aerobics instructors, etc.); supply appropriate signage; provide proper supervision; and insure proper transportation. Additionally, dram shop laws related to alcohol sales and use must be followed.

An example of a method for reducing negligence risk exposures is properly designing and constructing a facility (see Chapter 12, Planning Facilities for Safety and Risk Management). This strategic measure enhances supervision and security and, as a result, reduces risk exposures. Another application of a reduction strategy is illustrated by a facility that chooses to book a rowdy rock band knowing that it will create a very high-risk situation. They reduce the risk by increasing the quantity of security, limiting festival seating, and/or halting alcohol sales early. Both examples increase the safety of patrons and reduce the likelihood of loss through lawsuits.

Risk Reduction for Public Liability Excluding Negligence. There are a number of risk situations, exclusive of negligence, in which facility personnel can cause harm and expose the facility to loss. Examples of these risk exposures include: illegal searching of patrons, false imprisonment (retaining patrons), improper employment practices, sexual harassment, assault/battery, invasion of privacy and professional malpractice. Each of these areas should be evaluated for exposure and proper policies and procedures developed to mitigate them.

A major risk area that must be addressed is employment practices. Risk incidents that occur in this area usually allege some form of discrimination in employee recruitment, hiring and firing, evaluation, promotion, transfers, salary, etc. Employers cannot effectively discriminate against applicants or employees in any of the above areas on the basis of gender, race, color, national origin, religion, age, or disabilities unless there is a substantial, demonstrable relationship between the trait and the job. For example, if an employer can prove that a specific gender is essential to performing a specific job, then it is legal to discriminate against the opposite gender. To reduce loss in this area, policies and procedures must be designed based on Equal Opportunity Commission guidelines, Affirmative Action, Equal Pay Act, Title VII of the Civil Rights Act, Americans With Disabilities Act, and other pertinent employment law. Employees must be aware of these policies and be required to abide by them.

Sexual harassment is another area that should be an utmost concern of facility managers ("Harassment Cases Soar," 1999). Sexual harassment is a form of sexual discrimination that violates Title VII of the Civil Rights Act of 1964 and Title IX of the Educational Amendments Act of 1972. There are two primary forms: "quid pro quo" and "hostile environment." Quid pro quo sexual harassment occurs when promotions, raises, or any other job benefits are contingent on sexual favors. The second form, hostile environment, occurs when employees or participants are subjected to a sexually offensive atmosphere that is so pervasive that it interferes with their ability to perform. If the facility employer knew, or should have known, about a sexual harassment occurrence and failed to take immediate corrective action, then the facility could be held liable. To prevent such occurrences, risk managers must implement policies and procedures to educate personnel, to investigate complaints, and to provide sanctions for violations. Sanctions may include, but are not limited to, reprimand, transfer, reassignment, removal from the complainant's area, and/or dismissal of the offending party from the organization (Achampong, 1999).

Risk Reduction in Business Operations. Strategies in this area primarily involve knowing and adhering to appropriate business practices. Specific strategies may include providing employees with an "in house" fitness program to reduce sick days, monitoring the conduct of employees to prevent fraud, and seeking legal advice periodically to insure that contracts are comprehensive and enforceable.

Risk Reduction in Property Exposures. This area involves eliminating or reducing loss related to equipment, facilities, and grounds. Strategies in this category include providing proper fencing, an adequate lock system, keycard access, and closed-circuit television (CCTV) to prevent vandalism and theft; fire prevention strategies including sprinkler system, fire extinguishers, and having the fire department inspect the premises; proper site selection (e.g., avoid flood plain, avoid high seismic areas, close to emergency facilities) and construction planning for natural disasters; and providing checklists and periodic inspections to help identify situations that may lead to property damage.

Step Five: Implement a Plan to Carry Out the Selected Method

The last step in a risk management program is to implement, monitor, and evaluate the strategies that have been selected for each risk. Implementation means integrating the selected strategies into the ongoing facility operations, training employees, and evaluating the program (IAAM, 1996).

Integration

After the strategies for dealing with risks have been identified, the director must then integrate these strategies into the ongoing facility operations. For the risks that have been deemed to be too risky to have, the risk manager must insure that these situations are either discontinued or never included in the facility operations. He or she also needs to be certain that proper insurance (e.g., type, amount, and deductibles) is purchased from a reputable company and that it is monitored on a regular basis to insure adequate coverage for the specific identified losses.

If self-insurance or "budgeting for loss" is in the risk management program, the risk manager needs to make sure that these have been addressed at the appropriate time in the budgeting cycle. If waivers, informed consent, incident reports, form contacts or any other written documents have been identified as necessary, then the risk manager should develop them and incorporate them into operational procedures through orientation and training of personnel. These documents should be reviewed on an annual basis.

For the remainder of the risk control strategies, it is most likely that the risks are addressed through safety audits (inspections) or checklists, regular maintenance schedules or standard operating procedures (SOPs). To effectively integrate these tools into the facility operations, personnel must be assigned responsibility, trained and held accountable. Communication is the key to achieving these objectives.

Assigning risk management responsibilities can be done through a job orientation interview together with a job description that provides specific risk management responsibilities. The job description should include the workers' roles in the risk management program and their responsibilities in specific emergency response procedures.

An additional tool that aids in communication and accountability is an operations manual that outlines policies and procedures for dealing with various risk situations. For this tool to be effective, management must emphasize its importance and require enough training that personnel are proficient in the cited procedures. Pre-employment and annual in-service training should be used to keep the risk management procedures current and workers proficient. The International Association of Assembly Managers (IAAM) recommends drilling of emergency procedures such as medical, fire, terrorist threats, and so on. be a part of the worker training (IAAM, 1995). Additionally, workers should be educated about pertinent codes, laws and regulations relative to safety and patron service. These include fire codes, Americans With Disabilities Act, OSHA regulations, etc.

Workers not only need to know how to perform risk management tasks, they also must know that they have the authority to perform their tasks. An organizational chart that provides clear lines of authority between the risk manager and workers should be developed and published for reference. If this is done properly, communication can be enhanced, conflicts and confusion reduced, and the program elements integrated into an ongoing approach to managing risks. Risk management must become part of the organizational culture and the risk manager should look for ways to build awareness and to educate and train personnel.

Monitoring and Evaluating

Periodic program monitoring and evaluation enable the risk manager to determine how effective the risk management program is and where improvements may be needed. IAAM (1996, pp.111-115) recommended a yearly evaluation and an evaluation

- after each training drill,
- after each emergency,
- when personnel or responsibilities change,
- when the layout or design of the facility changes, and
- when policies or procedures change.

The risk management program evaluation should also include individual performance appraisals of employees based on their job descriptions. These individual assessments compel personnel to be accountable for fulfillment of their risk management responsibilities and help insure that the risk management program is successful. Success or failure of a risk management program depends on how well individual workers perform their responsibilities; therefore, it is important that workers be held accountable.

Event Risk Management

Events that are hosted by sports and recreation facilities are frequently the lifeblood of the facility; therefore, it is imperative that participants and spectators be provided a safe, secure, and accommodating environment. Each event, whether it is a sporting event or fitness activity, has unique risk concerns that may require specific attention that cannot be addressed by a generic plan. In order to address these unique risks, a written event risk management plan for each type of event should be developed. The plan should be a part of an overall facility risk management plan.

The plan should be constructed using the risk management steps mentioned previously. Following the steps allows the planner to identify the unique needs of an event and develop a plan comprising the strategies for managing them. The following areas may need the special attention of the risk manager, depending on the size and type of event: pre-event venue preparation and safety audits, a crowd management plan (if a large crowd is expected), described as part of pre-event venue prep, event insurance, and transportation and parking.

Pre-Event Venue Preparation and Safety Audits

An important element of an event risk-management plan is insuring that the facility and its equipment are prepared for the event. This may include such activities as proper markings of fields, clearing egress and ingress passageways, or placing collapsible fencing around a playing area in addition to doing safety audits of pertinent spaces and equipment. The purpose of these inspections is to ensure a safe environment to participate in and/or observe examples of possible checks.

A thorough review of safety codes, ordinances, and laws is also important to insure compliance. Permits or special licenses, such as a temporary liquor license, may need to be secured.

In addition to the above, event planners should be prepared to accommodate individuals with special needs. If the venue has not been properly designed to accommodate persons with disabilities, then "reasonable accommodation" must be made for viewing or participation.

Event Insurance

After identifying risk exposures associated with an event (step two of the risk management process), consult with an insurance advisor to determine suitable coverages, deductibles, policy terms, and prospective carriers. Auto insurance should not be overlooked; while autos may not be used frequently, there may be increased exposure during certain events. Additional coverage may be necessary, especially if volunteers or employees are using their own vehicles in conjunction with the event.

Transportation and Parking

A comprehensive event risk management plan must include methods for handling vehicles that bring attendees to events. Parking lots should be a source of concern for risk managers in that assaults, vandalism, vehicle collisions and personal injury accidents can occur. Well-trained and supervised parking aids may be needed to direct and park vehicles. They should have bright clothing and flashlights if it is an evening event. The parking area should be well lit and maintained to avoid trips and falls. If vandalism and theft are a significant risk, then the parking area should be patrolled and possibly monitored by CCTV.

If shuttles or chauffeuring special guests from parking areas is necessary and the facility is using its own employees, then they should be screened for acceptable driving records and appropriate licenses to drive the type of vehicle that they drive.

Event Crowd Management Plan

Another important consideration of an event risk-management plan is crowd management. This is especially important if a large crowd is expected; but even in small group, some crowd control is important. If planned appropriately, it should provide facility management with a tool that will mitigate many of the event risks. Suggested components of a crowd management plan include the following: 1) trained and competent staff; 2) crisis management and emergency action plans to prevent and reduce the consequences of crises such as bomb threats, tornado or other inclement weather, fire, and medical emergency; 3) procedures for dealing with unruly or intoxicated patrons; 4) communications network; and 5) effective signage (Ammon & Unruh, 2003). The crowd management plan should be formulated based on the characteristics of the crowd (IAAM, 1996). This enables the risk manager to anticipate problems and adjust crowd management procedures accordingly.

The first, and arguably the most important, element of a crowd management plan is trained and competent personnel. Whether the workers are volunteers or paid, close attention to acquiring an adequate number of competent personnel and then training them how to respond appropriately to patron requests, to emergency situations, and to security concerns is essential to an effective crowd management plan. If a facility does not have a sufficient number of trained persons needed for a particular event, the operator may consider "outsourcing" the work to trained specialists from a reputable company.

The second component of crowd management is crisis management and emergency action plans to prevent and reduce the consequences of crises, such as bomb threats, tornado or other inclement weather, fire, and medical emergency. These plans should be in writing, and personnel should be trained in how to perform the procedures so that they are done in a proficient and timely manner.

Closely allied with crisis management is crowd security. Security is a significant element of a crowd management plan and is a term used to describe a facility's strategy for protecting patrons or property from actions of a third party during an event. Typical security risk situations that may arise during an event are riotous behavior of spectators, such as a celebratory rushing of the field, throwing objects, spectators attacking participants, officials, other event attendees, and stadium/arena vandalism and graffiti. Additionally, sporting events may be attractive targets for terrorists' activities. Without effective security, the safety of those in attendance as well as those participating in the event may be compromised.

Quality personnel, appropriate technology, and a good strategy are the keys to effective security. Good security should include a team of trained personnel such as hired police, peer security, ushers, and ticket takers. Each should understand his or her role in securing the event. If a large crowd is expected, it may be best to hire a security firm. These personnel can be very useful if it becomes necessary to escort troublemakers or intoxicated attendees from the premises. In addition to security personnel, security technology such as scanners, CCTV, cell phones or multi-channeled phones, should be incorporated into the crisis management strategy. The security strategy should begin at the time patrons enter the facility (probably a parking lot) and end when all patrons have left the venue.

A third element of a crowd management plan is having written procedures for ejecting disruptive, unruly, or intoxicated patrons. It is very important that these procedures address the rights and the safety of the ejected individual. Ejections should be documented and only trained and authorized staff should take part in an ejection. Using untrained personnel to handle these disturbances could prove disastrous (Ammon & Unruh, 2003).

An effective communications network is another element of a crowd management plan. Many aspects of a crowd management plan require communication between facility staff, the patrons, or possibly outside emergency agencies. Facility personnel should anticipate communications needs related to handling emergencies and crowd supervision and accommodate these needs with communications strategies and technology.

The last crowd management plan component suggested by Ammon and Unruh (2003) is effective signage. Signage that provides information about the facility's rules of behavior, prohibited items, and warnings and "directional" signage such as egress and ingress signage are invaluable in providing safe and enjoyable environment.

Summary

All sports and recreation facilities are subject to risk exposures that have the potential to significantly interfere with a facility's mission. To effectively reduce or eliminate the potential impact of these occurrences sports facility operators must design and implement a risk management program. Designing a risk management program involves the following steps:

- Identify applicable areas or categories of concern.
- Identify specific risk exposures in each category.
- Estimate the probable impact of the risk and classify the impact using a matrix or an educated guess.

- Select the optimum method of treating the risk from one of the following: *avoiding* or abandoning the risk; *retaining* the risk and budgeting for the consequences; *transferring* the risk through insurance, waivers, or independent contractors; *reducing* the risk through practices, policies, and standard operating procedures.
- Implement a plan to carry out the selected method, monitor and evaluate.

Since events held in sports and recreation facilities are very important, facility operators should develop a risk management plan for each unique event relative to the overall risk management plan. To develop such a plan, the above steps should be utilized with special consideration toward pre-event venue preparation and safety audits, a crowd management plan (if a large crowd is expected), event insurance, and transportation and parking.

If facility operators develop a good risk management program that includes an effective event risk management plan, losses will be significantly reduced and the achievement of the facility's mission greatly enhanced.

Planning Facilities for Safety and Risk Management

Todd L. Seidler

12

Sports and recreation facilities that are poorly planned, designed, or constructed often increase participants' exposure to hazardous conditions and not only render the facility harder to maintain, operate, and staff but can also significantly increase the organization's exposure to liability. A poorly designed facility can usually be traced to a lack of effort or expertise of the planning and design team. It is not uncommon for a sports, physical education, or recreation facility to be designed by an architect who has little or no experience in that type of building. For those without the proper background and understanding of the unique properties of sports and recreation facilities, many opportunities for mistakes exist that may lead to increased problems related to safety, operations, and staffing.

Design problems commonly seen in activity facilities include inadequate safety zones around courts and fields, poorly planned pedestrian traffic flow through activity areas, poor access control and security, lack of proper storage space, and the use of improper building materials. Often, safety problems related to design are difficult, expensive, or impossible to fix once the facility has been built. It is essential that these facilities be planned and designed by professionals with activity-related knowledge and experience.

In order to protect themselves from claims of negligence, managers of sports and recreation programs and facilities have a number of legal responsibilities they are expected to perform. In this case, negligence is the failure to act as a reasonably prudent and careful sports or facility manager would act in the same or similar circumstances. In general, facility managers are required to run their programs so as not to create an unreasonable risk of harm to participants, staff, and spectators. One of their specific legal duties is to ensure that the environment provided is free from foreseeable risks or hazards. Unsafe facilities are one of the leading claims made in negligence lawsuits related to sports and physical activity. When discussing facility liability, Page (1988, p. 138) called it "one of the largest subcategories within the broad spectrum of tort law." More specifically, managers of sports facilities are expected to provide a reasonably safe environment and at least to carry out the following five duties:

- Keep the premises in safe repair.
- Inspect the premises to discover obvious and hidden hazards.
- Remove the hazards or warn of their presence.
- Anticipate foreseeable uses and activities by invitees and take reasonable precautions to protect the invitee from foreseeable dangers.
- Conduct operations on the premises with reasonable care for the safety of the invitee.

According to van der Smissen (1990), "The design, layout, and construction of areas and facilities can provide either safe or hazardous conditions, enhancing or detracting from the activity in which one is engaged" (1990, p. 235). A facility that has been properly planned, designed, and constructed will greatly enhance the ability of the facility manager to effectively carry out these legal duties. A look at common safety problems in sports facilities has determined that they can usually be traced to two primary causes: poor facility planning and design and poor management.

When discussing safe facilities, Maloy (2001) states, "Most liability problems dealing with safe environment, however, stem from maintenance and operation of the premises, not their design and construction" (2001, p. 105). Even though this may be true, it is important to understand that there are many things that can be done during the planning process that will enhance the sports manager's ability to safely and properly maintain and operate the premises. A well-designed facility makes the management process more effective and efficient. It follows that the easier it is to maintain a facility, the more likely it is that it will be done well. According to Jewell (1992) in his book, *Public Assembly Facilities*, "Public safety begins with good architectural design . . ." (1992, p. 111). Therefore, the majority of this chapter will focus on the planning and design of safe facilities.

Learning Objectives

After reading this chapter, the student should be able to

- understand negligence and become familiar with the basic legal duties expected of facility managers;
- understand the role that good facility planning has in the design and construction of safe facilities;
- identify at least five methods of controlling access to facilities;
- describe the importance of and identify the minimal guidelines for safety or buffer zones;
- discuss the problem of traffic patterns within facilities and identify alternatives; and
- understand the need for selecting the proper materials for floors, walls, and ceilings.

Planning Safe Facilities

In order to plan and build a facility that is safe, efficient, and that optimally supports activities likely to occur in each area, a thorough understanding of those activities is required. During the planning process, each individual space within the facility must be studied in an attempt to identify every activity that will, or might, take place in that space. After this has been done, the requirements of the space necessary for each of the activities must be determined. For example, if it is determined that a multipurpose room will house classes in aerobic dance, martial arts, yoga, and gymnastics, and will also act occasionally as a small lecture set-up with portable chairs, the needs of each of these activities must be met, even though some may be in conflict with others. After the design requirements have been identified for each activity, a master list for each area should be developed. This master list is then used to plan that area in order to reduce the number of design errors as much as possible. The following are areas where errors in planning often create hazardous situations within facilities.

Security and Access Control

When designing a facility, the following two kinds of access will be addressed: controlling access (1) to the facility and (2) within the facility. Controlling access to sports, recreation, and fitness facilities is an important function of facility managers. Legal liability, deterrence of vandalism and theft, member safety and satisfaction, and maintaining exclusivity and value for those who pay for the privilege of using the facility are a few of the reasons it is necessary to deny access to those who don't belong. A properly designed and equipped facility along with the use of computerized controls and a well-trained staff can make access control relatively easy to deal with.

Many facilities, especially older spectator facilities, can be a nightmare to control. Fire regulations require many outside doors for quick evacuation. When limited access is desired, how can these doors be secured, monitored, and controlled without violating fire codes?

When designing a facility, it is often advantageous to plan for one control point through which everyone entering or leaving the building must pass. This control point is usually staffed during open hours so the appropriate fee is paid, ID card checked, or permission given to those who are eligible to enter. If a higher degree of control is desired, a door, gate, or turnstile can also be used.

Recently, many computer software programs have become available to help with access control. If patrons and staff are issued ID cards, such as in a club, school, or corporate setting, systems with magnetic strip or bar code readers can be used to quickly check a person's status. Swiping the ID card through an electronic card reader can determine if the user is eligible to enter. In systems designed for high traffic flow, the computer can be connected directly to a turnstile.

Example of an illegal control mechanism.

If, after scanning the ID, the computer determines that the person should be permitted to enter, it can send a signal to release the turnstile and allow the individual to come in. This, however, does not prevent an unauthorized person from using someone else's ID. For increased security, picture IDs are desirable to ensure that the person using the card is the legal owner. Other new systems of access control include software programs that, upon scanning an ID card, display a picture of the patron on a computer monitor. If a higher level of security is desired, some systems actually use biometric identification. These systems may scan a patron's fingerprint, palm print, or even retina and compare it to records in the computer's memory. These systems are not only used to admit members, but can also track attendance and adherence to fitness programs, determine patrons' attendance habits, help set staffing levels to provide services at the proper times of the day, and provide information for marketing efforts.

Another aspect of access control that is improving with advances in technology is the replacement of standard door locks and keys. Systems now exist that place an electronic card reader at each door. Instead of a key, each authorized person is issued a card that can be passed through, or near, any of the card readers. A central computer receives the information from the card and compares it with the information stored in memory. The computer determines if the person who was issued that card is authorized to open that particular door and either unlocks it or refuses access.

This type of system has many advantages. The computer can be programmed to allow access only to certain areas for each individual cardholder. A part-time employee may have a card that works only on certain doors, while the facility manager's card can be programmed to open them all, like a master key. Also, the computer may be programmed so that certain cards only work during specified hours.

In the case of regular locks, if someone loses a key, it is often necessary to re-key many of the locks in the building. New keys must then be issued to everyone, often at great expense. With the card system, if someone loses an access card, that card can simply be turned off on the computer and a new card issued to the owner. The old card then becomes useless.

Another feature of the card access system is that each time someone uses a card to open a door it can be recorded on the computer. For example, computer records may show not only that a certain door was opened on Tuesday night at 11:05 but also whose card was used and if the person went in or out through the door. This information can be extremely valuable for facility security. The system can also be connected to the fire alarm and programmed to automatically unlock any or all of the doors when the alarm is triggered. Though it may initially be more expensive to install the card reader system than to install standard locks, it will usually pay for itself in increased efficiency, convenience, and long-term cost.

It is often desirable to control access to certain areas within a facility. Most buildings limit access to areas such as equipment rooms, office areas, mechanical rooms, or storage, but when a multiuse facility has more than one event or activity taking place at the same time, it may also be desirable to separate different parts of the building. For example, in a college activity center, it is not uncommon to have a varsity basketball game in the main arena while the rest of the facility is kept open for recreation. With good planning, this can be accomplished by physically separating the spaces through the use of different entrances and exits; different floors; and locking doors, gates, and fences that can quickly restrict passage from one area to another. There are two basic concepts to be familiar with for controlling access within a facility: (1) horizontal and (2) vertical circulation control.

Horizontal circulation control is a common method of managing access to different parts of a facility when there is a need to separate areas on the same floor. In the above example, when the entire facility is open for recreation, an open access plan is utilized. However, when a varsity basketball game is scheduled, certain doors, gates, and fences can be opened or closed in order to restrict spectator access to the arena without having to close down the rest of the building.

Sometimes it may be most efficient to plan for managing access through vertical circulation control. For example, it may be desirable in a large arena to have limited access to the lower level. This level may include the playing floor, locker rooms, coaches' offices, training rooms, and storage areas. By limiting public access to the entire floor, it becomes much easier to secure each individual area. In some arenas and stadiums, the luxury suites are located on one floor and only certain elevators, stairways, or gates can gain access to that floor. Patrons in general seating areas cannot gain access to the suite level, thereby enhancing security and also providing a feel of exclusivity for suite holders. If vertical circulation is needed for a large number of people, providing nonskid ramps with good handrails or escalators usually provides a safer method than stairs.

Safety Zones

Some activities require a certain amount of space surrounding the court, field, or equipment to enhance the safety of the participants. An inadequate amount of space for a safety or buffer zone can present foreseeable risks of injury. A number of lawsuits have been based on claims that an injury occurred as a result of an inadequate safety or buffer zone. Whether it is to separate two adjacent courts or to provide room between the court and a wall or another object, safety zones must be considered.

Failure to provide activity space free of obstruction.

Indoor

Basketball courts should have at least 10 feet (preferred) or 6 feet (minimum) of clear space around the court that is free from walls, obstructions, or other courts (NCAA, 2001, p. 33). Anything less than 6 feet presents a foreseeable risk of collision. The area under the basket is especially important. If a full 10 feet of clear space between the end-line and the wall cannot be provided, padding should be placed on the wall to soften the impact where players are most likely to hit if they lose control while going out of bounds. It is recommended that wall padding cover from the floor to a height of 7 feet and extend the entire width of the court. When walls are padded, typically the padding begins six to 12 inches above the floor, rises only to 5 or 6 feet and extends only the width of the lane. In these facilities, players diving for a ball and sliding into the wall, those over 6 feet tall or others outside the lane receive no protection. It is also recommended that wall pads be considered even when the safety zone is greater than 10 feet. One exception to the 10-foot guideline is for competitive volleyball. In this case, it is recommended that a minimum of 15 feet of clear space beyond the end lines be provided. Another problem that is common in basketball is with the scorer's table. These are nearly always placed within 3 feet of the sideline and often go unpadded. Padded scorer's tables are available; however, there are too few in use, especially at the high school level.

Currently, there are no standards regarding padding in athletic facilities, but this may change in the near future. According to Steinbach (2004), ASTM International recently assembled a task group within ASTM's Wrestling and Gymnastics Subcommittee which has "authored a four-page draft that it hopes will establish long-overdue industry standards for wall padding."

Activity spaces and surrounding areas should also be designed to be free of obstructions such as doors, poles, columns, and supports. If any such obstruction cannot be moved or eliminated from the activity area or safety zone, it must be padded. All other protrusions that may cause a safety hazard in the gymnasium should be avoided if possible. Common examples of such protrusions include drinking fountains and fire extinguishers, which, during the planning process, can easily be recessed into a wall. Standard doorknobs located in an activity area can also present a hazard, and alternative types of knobs that are recessed in the door are available. Such handles are commonly used on racquetball courts.

Dangerous overlap of adjacent activity areas.

Another area where safety or buffer zones are important and often overlooked is in the weight room. Placing weight equipment too close together can present a serious safety hazard. Most weight equipment should be spaced a minimum of three feet apart. This measurement should be made with the movement of the machine or exercise in mind. Some exercises require a horizontal movement and the safety or buffer zone should be measured from the extremes of this movement. An example occurs with many leg extension machines. As the movement is executed, the legs straighten and extend another two feet or so out from the machine. The safety zone should be measured from the point of full extension. Some exercises require more than a three-foot safety zone. Certain free-weight exercises such as squats and power cleans require more room because of the amount of weight and relative lack of control typically encountered during such exercises.

It should be recognized that an activity area such as a gymnasium may be used occasionally for activities other than those it was designed for. It is not uncommon for outdoor activities such as softball, ultimate frisbee, or track practice to be moved indoors during inclement weather. These activities must be considered when planning a safe gym. The main point is that not all activities will use the traditional court markings for their activity area. This means that the distance from out-of-bounds to the wall is not always a safety factor for those activities that ignore the floor markings. If these activities can be identified and planned for before construction, there is an opportunity to provide a safe environment for them also. Otherwise, it becomes a management concern and a potentially hazardous aspect of the facility that must be compensated for.

Allowing more than one activity to take place in one area can be dangerous. Playing more than one basketball game on two or more courts that overlap, such as using a side basket for one game and an end basket for another, produces a situation in which an injury is foreseeable.

Outdoor

Outdoor fields and courts have many of the same problems. Overlapping fields are a common occurrence and can cause a significant safety hazard if activities are allowed to take place simultaneously. A common example is two softball fields that share a part of the outfields. If games are being played at the same time on each field, the outfielders are at risk of collision. Overlapping courts and fields should be avoided if at all possible. An alternative might be to turn the fields around.

Two activity areas adjacent to each other can be just as dangerous as those that overlap. It is not uncommon to see a baseball field located next to a track. Sometimes this can lead to joggers on the track having to dodge errant baseballs. All adjacent activity areas must be planned with the idea that activities may occur simultaneously, so that foreseeably dangerous situations can be avoided.

Another common design that can produce several hazardous conditions is the typical football field that is surrounded by a track. Very often, facilities for field events are constructed inside the track and include asphalt runways and pit areas in addition to the track and pit areas constructed with concrete curbs. In this situation, there is often little distance between the football sidelines and the inner perimeter of the track, much less the runways, pits, and the commonly used concrete pole vault box.

Ideally, two activity areas, such as a football field and a track, should not be combined in one space. Realistically, there often is not sufficient space to construct the two separately, and they must be combined. If this type of mixed-use field is necessary, it is recommended that there be no obstructions within a minimum of 15 feet of the sidelines or end zone of the football field. At the very least, the jumping and vaulting runways can be placed outside the track. If bleachers on the opposite side of the field are not adequate to accommodate crowds, removable bleachers can be temporarily installed over those runways and pit areas. The high-jump approach as well as the shot put and discus pads can be located more than 15 feet from the end zone without encroaching on the track.

Other common obstructions that can create hazardous conditions are telephone, water, and/or electrical boxes used during football games that are often placed adjacent to the inner perimeter of the track. These are typically metal boxes mounted on poles several inches above the ground. A runner (either track or football) who is bumped, stumbles, or is tackled, can fall and strike the sharp metal receptacle and be severely injured. If such boxes are essential, they should be placed underground with the top flush with the field surface. Any obstructions that are within 15 feet of the field should be padded for safety. The primary problem with padding obstructions is that, even padded, they are still a hazard. Also, the padding deteriorates over time or disappears, or people get lax about installing it prior to usage of the field. It is better to plan and construct the area without such hazards in the first place.

Many fields have been built with steel manhole covers or storm drain grates in, or next to, the playing area. Also, fences are constructed or trees planted just outside the boundary lines, typically with no thought for the safety of the people using the field. It is important to understand that not all activities take place within the playing field. Whether chasing a fly ball into foul territory or getting tackled on the sideline, obstructions that are just out-of-bounds can be significant hazards. With proper planning these can often be easily avoided.

Another common safety hazard often seen in high school baseball and softball facilities is open dugouts. All dugouts should be screened in front to protect those within from line-drive foul balls and errant throws. Providing protected access to and from the dugout is also important. Water fountains and bat racks should be placed inside or behind the dugout with players being able to gain access to them from the dugout without being directly exposed to the field.

Portable soccer goals that are left out on fields also can create a very hazardous situation. Several children are killed or severely injured each year by climbing on goals that are not anchored to the ground. These goals are often heavy, poorly balanced and tend to tip over when someone hangs on them. Injuries typically occur when a child hangs from the crossbar and is then crushed as it tips over. Either permanently anchoring soccer goals or using a chain or cable to lock them in place can prevent these incidents.

Pedestrian Traffic Flow

A common flaw in planning a facility that can cause safety problems is failure to properly plan for pedestrian traffic flow from one area to another. Requiring people to walk through an activity area in order to get to their desired destination can result in a needlessly high-risk situation. A very common example is when the main entrance to the locker room can only be reached by walking across the gym floor. The result is people entering and leaving the locker room while an activity is taking place in the same space.

Another example of poor traffic flow planning often occurs when pedestrians are forced to walk across a court or between two adjacent courts to get to another part of the facility. This also puts pedestrians in a situation where a collision with a participant is likely.

Planning pedestrian traffic flow within some activity areas is an important consideration. A weight room can be more hazardous if people do not have good, clear, open pathways to move around to different parts of the room. The design and layout of the weight room should take into account the movement of the users, especially during times of peak occupancy. Laying out the optimal pathways within the weight room that provide users with easy access to the more popular areas or machines will help prevent excess traffic between machines.

Storage

One of the most common complaints that facility managers report when asked about their facility is a lack of adequate storage space. The following is a typical example of how this often occurs. A new facility is planned with plenty of storage space in the early stages of planning. As the design is developed and the estimated cost of construction becomes clearer, it is determined that the project is over budget and something must be cut. Storage areas are often the first spaces to go.

Without proper storage space, equipment will usually be stored in a corner of the gym, in one of the hallways, or on the side of the pool deck. Besides the fact that improperly stored equipment is much more likely to be vandalized or stolen, it may also attract children (see attractive nuisance in the photo below) or others to use or play with it, usually unsupervised and not in the manner for which it was designed. Equipment such as mats and Port-a-pits, gymnastic apparatus, standards, nets, goals, chairs, hurdles, tables, ladders, maintenance equipment, and so on are often seen stacked in the corners of gyms. No longer a common sight, trampolines were often pushed into a corner and left unattended. This improper storage and poor supervision led to many catastrophic injuries and deaths and has resulted in the elimination of trampolines from most programs today. It is essential that adequate storage space be planned and constructed and that it be readily accessible and easily secured to prevent unauthorized use of the contents.

Example of lack of adequate storage space.

Lack of sufficient storage space for outdoor equipment is also often a problem. Providing a fenced, lockable storage area for items that are too large to be moved indoors for things such as blocking sleds is recommended. A fully enclosed storage area for pole vault and high-jump pits, hurdles, judge's stands, and other moveable equipment will provide protection from the weather and vandals and will prevent creating an attractive nuisance.

Proper Materials

Many factors must be considered during the selection of materials to be used in the construction of a sports or recreation facility. Among these are initial cost, functionality, durability and expected life span, ease, and cost of maintenance and aesthetics. Another often-overlooked factor is safety. Without proper consideration, building and finishing materials can play a large role in the inherent safety of the facility. The potential activities that may take place in every space must be studied thoroughly to ensure that the facility will optimally support each.

Flooring materials must be selected with great care. Poor selection of the floor surface can contribute to significant safety hazards. One of the most dangerous examples commonly occurs in wet areas such as locker rooms, shower areas, training rooms, and pool decks. The material selected for the floors in these areas should be a long-lasting, easily maintained, nonslip surface. All too often, these wet areas are constructed with a smooth finish such as smooth or polished concrete, linoleum, or terrazzo. These are excellent surfaces in the proper situation and are usually selected for cost, durability, and ease of maintenance; however, they all can become extremely slippery when wet. Many excellent nonslip surfaces are available for areas where they may get wet. One of the best surfaces for wet areas is rough-finish ceramic or quarry tile. All wet areas should be designed to slope toward a floor drain to avoid standing water.

Inappropriate use of acoustical panels.

Wall surfaces also offer opportunities for hazards to be designed into a facility. A major hazard often introduced into a facility is the use of glass in or near activity areas. Glass in doors or windows or covering fire extinguishers is a common cause of injury. Even the use of strengthened glass, such as windows with wire mesh, should be questioned in activity areas. Even though it takes greater force to break this kind of glass, it still occurs and may cause severe injuries.

Another relatively common problem has occurred with the use of glass in what most people think of as a non-activity area. The trophy case in the lobbies of most high school gyms is a good example. Planners often overlook the fact that lobby space is frequently used for activities, whether it is the wrestling team running in the halls during inclement weather, cheerleaders practicing, or just the everyday horseplay that occurs with teenagers. Safety glass of some type should be used in this area. Mirrors used in weight rooms and dance studios must be selected and located with care. They should be high-strength, shatter-proof glass designed for activity areas. Weight-room mirrors should be mounted about 18 inches above the floor to avoid contact with a barbell that may roll against the wall.

It is also important to select proper ceiling materials. Acoustic ceiling panels can be excellent for classrooms and offices but can become a maintenance headache and safety hazard when used in activity areas such as gyms. Acoustic panels are not meant to withstand abuse from balls and often break or shatter when hit.

The materials selected must be chosen with care in order to withstand the abuse likely to occur in each particular area. Lighting fixtures in activity areas must be appropriate to withstand the activities that will take place. In gyms where balls or other objects may hit the lights, each fixture must be designed to withstand potential punishment. The proper light typically has a plastic cover and a wire screen for protection. If the fixture is struck hard enough to shatter the bulb, the broken glass will be contained by the plastic cover and prevented from falling to the floor. Fixtures without this feature may shower broken glass on the participants below when struck.

Supervision

Designing a facility so that it can be supervised efficiently is a great advantage for two major reasons. First, a lack of proper supervision is one of the most common allegations made in lawsuits alleging negligence in sports and physical activity programs. The design and layout of the facility are often overlooked as a primary reason for poor supervision. Some facilities are inherently easy to supervise and some are not.

Second, a poorly designed facility may require five staff members to properly supervise activities, whereas a well-designed building of similar size and offerings may require only three. Figuring the cost of paying even one extra supervisor, using the number of hours the facility is open each year over the life of the facility, can result in a dramatic increase in operating cost.

A well-designed facility can be adequately supervised by a minimum number of staff members. Design features that enhance efficiency of supervision include activity areas that are close together and easily monitored. Instead of spreading activity areas around the perimeter of the facility, one efficient method being used is to design a long central hallway or mall off of which are placed the activity areas. With proper windows or other means of observing, a supervisor can view many different areas in a short period of time.

The locker room is another area that is often poorly designed for adequate supervision. Concrete floors and walls, steel lockers with sharp corners, and standing water all make locker rooms perhaps the single most dangerous facility in sports and recreation. In school settings, there is also a great amount of unstructured time with classes coming and going, showering, and changing clothes. It all adds up to a need for close, active supervision. Most locker rooms are laid out in rows of high lockers, which makes it difficult to supervise the activities and easy for someone to hide. All too often, the teacher/coaches' office is located in a position that does not allow an adequate view of the entire room. Providing the ability to easily and adequately supervise must be considered while planning and designing a locker room.

Another innovation that is seeing increased usage is closed-circuit television (CCTV) systems. A well-designed system can allow a supervisor in one location to visually monitor many diverse locations from both within and outside of the facility. Often the supervisor is equipped with a two-way radio in order to stay in constant communication with attendants on duty inside and outside the building. If a problem is observed on the CCTV monitor, the supervisor can direct an attendant to respond immediately. A properly planned system may allow for a smaller staff than might otherwise be required, while actually increasing supervisory coverage of the facility.

Miscellaneous Considerations

All facilities must be planned in compliance with all applicable codes. This includes all Occupational Safety and Health Administration (OSHA), Americans With Disabilities Act (ADA), fire, safety, and health codes that are appropriate for a given situation.

Emergency safety device.

Humidity must be controlled throughout the facility. Excessive humidity not only reduces the comfort level but can cause corrosion and deterioration of building materials. Under the right conditions, high humidity can also condense onto activity floors, steps, and walkways and create a dangerous condition. Lighting levels must be sufficient for the activity. Improper lighting can cause a hazardous situation, especially in areas where participants must visually track fast-moving objects such as in racquetball.

Signage can be an important part of a facility risk management program. Rules, procedures, and warning signs must be developed and posted in proper locations.

Summary

This chapter focused primarily on planning and designing facilities for safety and risk management. It is important to understand that this is only a first step in running a safe program. Once the facility is open, it is essential that a complete risk management program be established and practiced on an ongoing basis.

One of the most common claims made in negligence lawsuits related to sports and recreation is that of unsafe facilities. Managers of sports, physical education, and recreation programs have a legal and moral obligation to make their programs as free from foreseeable risks as possible. As part of this, managers must be aware of how unsafe facilities can increase potential hazards for participants, staff, and spectators alike. In our increasingly litigious society, unnecessary injuries are likely to lead to lawsuits and increased exposure of the program's financial resources to loss. Safe facilities are essential, and a well-planned facility is safer, as well as easier, to supervise, manage, and maintain.

Many of the factors that go into making a facility safe are easy to implement if they are planned from the beginning. Once the concrete has been poured and the facility is open, it is often much harder or even impossible to make changes. Planning and designing facilities with safety and risk management in mind can help prevent problems, headaches, injuries, and lawsuits in the future.

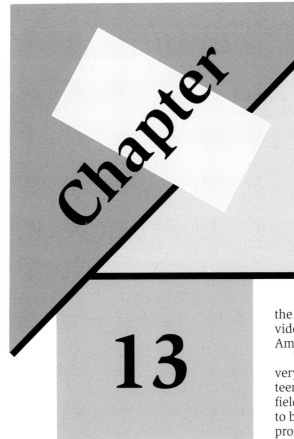

Volunteers: The Soldiers in Fund-Raising and Event Management[1]

Thomas H. Sawyer

Prior to 1970, relatively little was known about the scope and size of the volunteer sector. Since then, several major national surveys have provided information useful in drawing a profile of the volunteer corps in America. Table 13.1 outlines several characteristics of volunteers.

In youth, interscholastic, and intercollegiate sports, volunteers are very important to the successful operations of these programs. The volunteers are often ticket sellers, ticket takers, ushers, swimming and track and field officials, youth sports coaches, and fund-raisers. If volunteers failed to be involved in these programs, these programs would not exist. Not-for-profit youth organizations would never be able to employ adequate numbers of paid personnel to operate the various youth sports programs. This chapter will outline everything the sports manager will need to know about volunteers and how to manage the volunteer corps.

Learning Objectives

After reading this chapter, the student should be able to

- deal with volunteers,
- recognize and recruit volunteers,
- develop a volunteer personnel management system,
- design an orientation and training program for volunteers,
- supervise volunteers, and
- provide appropriate recognition to volunteers.

Dealing With Volunteers

Before beginning to understand what a manager should put into place regarding the management of volunteers, it is important to understand the characteristics of volunteers as outlined in Table 13.1. Further, the manager needs to consider the characteristics below when dealing with volunteers. These characteristics have been identified by Meagher (1995), Stier (1993), and Heidrich (1990) including:

- The 25% rule—25% of the volunteers will do nearly all that is asked of them.
- The 20% rule—refers to those individuals who are truly effective, who are the real producers and "result-getters.,"
- Volunteers have feelings, so make them feel valuable and wanted, treat them with respect, and provide them with special privileges to reward them for their contributions.
- Volunteers have needs and wants—satisfy them.
- Volunteers have suggestions—seek their input.
- Volunteers have specific interests; provide options and alternatives for them.
- Volunteers have specific competencies; recognize these skills and do not attempt to place square pegs in round holes.
- Volunteers are individuals working with other individuals; encourage them to work as a team, not as competing individuals.
- Volunteers are not (usually) professionals within the organization or profession; treat them with a special understanding and empathy.

---

[1]This chapter has been reprinted with modifications with permission from Sagamore Publishing . It represents Chapter 18, Volunteers: The soldiers in fund raising and event management, from Sawyer, T. H., & Smith, O. R. (2004). *Financing the sport enterprise*. Champaign, IL: Sagamore Publishing.

Table 13.1
Characteristics of Volunteers

A recent Gallup Poll outlined the following characteristics relative to volunteers:

- Nearly half of all Americans over 14 years old volunteer (approximately 89 million).
- Volunteers contribute an average of 5.3 hours per week; up from 2.6 in 1980, 3.5 in 1985, 4.4 in 1990, and 4.9 in 1995.
- Volunteer activities range from informal volunteering (e.g., helping a neighbor) to more formal volunteering (e.g., working for a nonprofit organization such as Little League, Red Cross, Salvation Army, American Heart Association, church, YMCA, YWCA, Boy Scouts, Girl Scouts, Boys and Girls Clubs of America). The major areas of volunteering have been religion (23 percent), informal volunteering (19 percent), education (13 percent), youth sports organizations (13 percent), general fund-raising (11 percent), amateur sporting events (11 percent), and recreation (10 percent).
- Most volunteers (80 percent) contribute time to charitable organizations, 17 percent contribute time to governmental organizations, and three percent reported contributing time to for-profit organizations.
- Volunteers do a variety of jobs including, but not limited to, assisting the elderly, performing caretaker duties, coaching youth sports, member and/or officer of the board of directors, financial consultant, and being an officer of an organization. The most popular form of volunteers' work was assisting older persons, people with disabilities, or social welfare recipients or working for nonprofit services agencies and youth sports organizations.
- The primary reasons given for becoming volunteers were; wanting to do something useful to help others (52 percent), having an interest in the work or activity (36 percent), or enjoying the work (32 percent).
- People who volunteer their time are much more likely than non-volunteers to donate money to charitable organizations. They are also far more likely to donate money in the area in which they volunteer.

Other characteristics associated with volunteering include:

- The prime years for volunteering are from about age 27 to 29 through retirement, with the peak being 35 to 49 years of age.
- Overall, more women than men volunteer.
- Working class ("blue collar") urban people tend to be active in their churches, unions, lodges, and sport clubs. Middle- and upper-middle-class people tend to be active in general interest areas, career-related business and professional, community-oriented, service-oriented, educational, cultural, and political or pressure groups.
- Married individuals participate more extensively in volunteering than any other marital status group. This group is followed by widows and widowers, single, divorced, and separated people.
- Having children is associated with higher rates of volunteering and having children of school age produces even greater involvement in volunteering.
- The majority of volunteers are white.

- Volunteers are not paid staff; try not to involve them in staff politics.
- Volunteers desire to be of assistance; let them know how they are doing (feedback), answer their questions, and provide good two-way communications.
- Volunteers have the potential to be excellent recruiters, especially through networking of other potentially helpful volunteers.
- Volunteers can be educated to assume a variety of roles within the fund-raising process.
- Volunteers are able to grow in professional competency with appropriate and timely training, motivation, and opportunity.

Role of Volunteers

The role of the volunteer should be examined prior to the development of a volunteer management program. Each volunteer position should have a job description with the minimum qualifications listed. Further, there should be a clear description of what the volunteer will be required to accomplish.

After a preliminary survey, appropriate roles for volunteers should be defined. If volunteer roles already exist, some of the following questions may reveal areas for improvement:

- Is there an organizational chart that shows how various components of the program relate to another?
- Are there job descriptions for each position?
- Are the job descriptions updated regularly?
- Are they useful in the guidance and supervision of volunteers?
- Do volunteer jobs provide enough challenge, authority, and responsibility to be rewarding?
- Are volunteers an integral part of the planning, implementing, and evaluating process in all programs?
- Is there a systematic approach to recruiting new volunteers that emphasizes matching the volunteer with the job?
- Are there sufficient opportunities for orientation?
- Are there regular, ongoing opportunities for training?
- What kind of supervision system is there for volunteers?
- Is there a recognition program that goes beyond annual formal recognition dinners? (Heidrich, 1999, 47)

Recruiting Volunteers

Once the organizers have determined the structure of the board, you can begin recruiting and retaining a volunteer base among employees. Many volunteers join organization boards because they enjoy serving others and would like to increase employee morale. Look for people who possess qualities such as honesty, trust, teamwork, leadership, enthusiasm, humor, responsibility, and competence. Board members should also have a business interest whether it be in marketing, coalition building, training, finance, or technology. A balanced board of directors can assist with the growth of the programs.

Recruiting volunteers to help with organizations seems to become more difficult every year. Most people's time is stretched so thin, not leaving time for an employee to volunteer. A lament of managers is that the same group of people (pre-baby boomers and baby boomers) volunteer over and over. The younger employees (Generation Xers who often ask, "What is in it for me?") rarely are seen volunteering for anything (Sawyer & Smith, 1999).

Ask yourself these questions: Why would I volunteer? How does this appeal to me? How can this be more appealing to me? (Borja, 1999b).

The event where volunteers are needed should be promoted as if it were the event of the year. Emphasize the uniqueness of the challenge, aim to achieve a new goal each time, make it competitive (offer prizes), and throw in a perk or two. It is easy to obtain employee volunteers for high-profile events. It is difficult to obtain volunteers for a simple fund-raising project. In the latter case, incentives for people to volunteer are needed, such as discounts on tickets to local events or logo merchandise or a banquet and a small gift. Recruiting must be an ongoing process. The volunteer recruiter needs to inform people that volunteering is a great networking opportunity that leads to making new friends and gaining new skills such as communication, organization, planning, time management, budgeting, negotiation, and priority setting (Beagley, 1998). Further, other methods can be used to recruit volunteers, including "(1) making the event or activity fun; (2) finding out what the employees respond to; (3) involving the employee and family; (4) making it easy, attractive, and interesting to volunteer; (5) making the employee responsible for something; (6) treating the employee (volunteer) with respect; (7) asking for referrals; (8) planning social events for the volunteers; (9) paying for a volunteer's training; and (10) placing volunteers' photographs on bulletin boards, Web sites, or in e-mail messages" (Beagley, 1998, p.36).

Successful volunteer recruiting is not an isolated activity. Recruiting actually begins with carefully written job descriptions that delineate the volunteers' responsibilities. It is nearly impossible to recruit someone for a job that is not defined.

Before recruiting begins, groundwork must be done to ensure a successful recruiting experience. Meagher (1995), Stier (1994, 1993), and Heidrich (1990) suggest that some of the topics that need to be discussed are:

- Recruiters — Who will do the recruiting? Whoever the recruiters are, they should have or be willing to develop the following characteristics: (1) knowledge of the jobs for which they are recruiting, (2) detailed knowledge of the organization and its programs, (3) knowledge of how the programs are administered, (4) understanding of the culture of the prospective volunteer, (5) ability to communicate effectively with a wide range of people, (6) commitment to the purpose and goals of the organization, (7) enjoyment in meeting and talking with people, and (8) commitment to assisting the organization and its programs to grow.

- Job descriptions.
- Prospective volunteers—A system for identifying potential volunteers.
- Match people with jobs.
- Obtain approvals—It is wise to obtain approvals from each volunteer's supervisor.
- Annual plans—Determine the volunteer needs on a year-round basis and use an annual calendar to schedule various steps in the volunteer management system. Take a moment and answer the following planning questions: (1) What times of the year are optimal for recruiting within the organization? (2) When do terms of office in clubs and associations expire? (3) What documents need to be in place before recruiting begins? (4) What methods will be used to recruit? (5) Who will serve as recruiters? (6) What training will be provided for the recruiters? (7) What orientation and training will be provided for the new volunteers? (8) What recognition events will be planned?
- Recruiting techniques—The following are some useful recruiting techniques: (1) grow your own, (2) appointment by management from within, (3) management for referrals, (4) friendship groups, (5) family involvement, (6) benefits packages, (7) peripheral groups, and (8) use of media to communicate volunteer opportunities.

Job Descriptions for Volunteers

Written job descriptions delineate volunteers' responsibilities and are a key part of a risk management plan for the organization. Although liability rules vary from state to state, it is not likely that the organization is immune from liability merely because an employee is acting as a volunteer. The simple fact is whether a person is paid or not-paid has very little bearing on the case before the bar. In the eyes of the court, if the person works for the organization, he or she is representing the organization. Therefore, the manager has developed specific job descriptions and reduced them to writing for all positions whether or not the people holding positions are paid.

Many human resources management professionals have indicated the benefits of a job description include: foundation for recruiting, comfort and security, performance, continuity, communication and teamwork, and support a risk management plan. Table 13.2 describes the common steps in developing a job description.

Table 13.2
Common Steps in Developing Volunteer Job Descriptions

There are five common steps in human resources management that should be followed in developing a job description:

- Explain the concept to the chief executive officer and board and outline its benefits to them.
- Form a committee to develop the job description and have the committee answer the following questions: Does the organization need individual position and committee leadership job descriptions? What job descriptions are needed? What will be the outline for the job description? What will be the procedure for the annual review of job descriptions so they can be updated and improved over time? Who will be responsible for writing the job descriptions? Who will review the job descriptions before they are finalized?
- Establish job clusters such as committee chairs, club or league president, trip coordinators, and project leaders.
- Evaluate job system.
- Format job description: title, function statement, reports to, staff liaison, task to be performed, time commitment, training, evaluation, benefits received, and qualifications.

Motivating Volunteers

Everyone who has time to volunteer should understand there are many reasons why they should volunteer, including involvement, reward or recognition, networking, companionship, fulfillment, "the next best thing to being there," "nothing else to do," and "it is just plain fun" (Borja, 1998). See Table 13.3 for questions a sports manager needs to ask before developing the motivation plan.

Table 13.3
Questions for the Sports Manager to Ask About
Volunteers Before Establishing the Motivation Plan

Before recruiting volunteers the sports manager should ask the following questions:

- Do you have enough time to volunteer?
- How can you help the organization?
- Will you be able to learn from the experience?
- Will you like what you will be doing for the organization?
- What are the rewards and benefits you are seeking?
- Will your time be well spent?
- Most importantly, will you have fun?

Retaining Volunteers

After recruiting volunteers, the next trick is to keep them as volunteers in the future. This can be accomplished by making (1) the event or activity attractive to belong to; (2) certain the event is well organized; (3) people feel needed and appreciated; (4) sure there is a friendly atmosphere; (5) certain volunteers understand what their responsibilities will entail, including time commitments and workload; (6) a special effort to call volunteers by their first names and know something about them or the work they do; (7) sure to encourage volunteers' input; (8) a special effort to recognize or reward their volunteer efforts for the organization; (9) the event or activity fun; and (10) certain that everyone receives an appropriate thank you (e.g., free lunch or dinner and a framed certificate).

Educating Volunteers

A volunteer is no different (except that he or she receives no monetary remuneration) than any other employee on the staff. It is important to provide training to the volunteers. The training can be simple or elaborate. The key point to consider is that the volunteer should be clearly informed about goals, procedures, schedules, expectations, responsibilities, emergency procedures, and staff rosters.

Information should be provided orally with a backup hard copy for each volunteer. This material should be placed in a neat folder with the volunteer's name imprinted on it. Personalizing the material gives the volunteer a feeling of self-worth and importance and, in turn, will motivate the volunteer to be a more valuable resource.

Orientation and Training for Volunteers

Once the volunteers are on board, it is important to provide them with a sound orientation and a continuous education program. Without good orientation and training, volunteers may not be able to do their assigned jobs well or receive the intrinsic rewards they expected. The purpose of orienting and training volunteers is to ensure the highest possible degree of satisfaction with and contribution to the portion of the program that they are to implement.

- Orientation helps volunteers become acquainted with one another and the staff, learn the organization's culture, and learn about their own volunteer role in relation to the entire organization. Orientation differs from in-service training, with orientation usually occurring at the beginning of a volunteer's commitment and in-service training at various times during a volunteer's commitment with the organization.
- Training, on the other hand, introduces new skills, knowledge, and abilities or reinforces existing ones; can be used to plan and manage program changes; and provides opportunities for self-renewal and growth.

The Orientation Program

The orientation program should be conducted by the head of the volunteer management system and key volunteers. The orientation program should be conducted more frequently than once a year if the organization is bringing in new volunteers on a monthly or weekly basis. Many organizations establish cohorts of volunteers who go through the orientation together. It is not uncommon to see an organization scheduling quarterly orientations.

Orientation can be scheduled as

- large group sessions;
- small group sessions;
- personal, one-on-one orientation sessions; or
- personal, one-on-one mentoring systems.

The agenda for an orientation session may include

- a philosophical and conceptual framework of the organization,
- content of the various programs,
- organization of the various programs,
- governance of the organization,
- history of the organization,
- policies and procedures of the organization,
- bylaws and the proper conduct of business,
- ethics issues,
- benefits of volunteering and special privileges,
- identification of key people in the organization,
- telephone numbers of key people, and
- realistic job previews.

Orientation and Training Checklist

The following set of questions should be used in guiding the final plans for an orientation or training session:

- Does every new volunteer have an opportunity to be oriented to his or her role either in a one-on-one conference, a small group, or a large group meeting?
- Are there orientation materials prepared for volunteers: job descriptions, volunteers' handbooks, policies, etc.?
- Are orientation and training meetings planned with plenty of volunteer input and participation?
- Are volunteers offered leadership roles in orientation and training of other volunteers?
- Does the organization provide books, films, tapes, trips, or other educational materials for volunteers?
- Does the organization pay for volunteers to attend appropriate training events or take courses at other institutions?
- Are all orientation and training programs evaluated?

The Volunteer Personnel Management System

The sports manager should ask a series of questions after he or she understands the environment that the volunteers will be asked to work in. I think Rudyard Kipling put it best when he said, "He kept six honest serving men (They taught me all I knew); their names are What, Why, When, How, Where, and Who." If you keep this in mind at all times, whether it be managing volunteer personnel or the budget, you will be successful in most of your efforts.

One of the most notable trends in volunteerism has been professionalization. In most organizations using the services of volunteers, there has been a gradual realization that volunteers should be recognized as the valuable staff members they are. As a result, the management of volunteers has taken on many of the characteristics of the management of paid staff. Managers in voluntary organizations perform many of the same personnel functions for volunteers as for paid staff: they design and define volunteer jobs and write job descriptions, recruit and interview volunteers aggressively, orient, train, supervise, evaluate, and reward. See Table 13.4 for reasons why to professionalize volunteer management.

Table 13.4
Reasons for Professionalizing Volunteer Management

Heidrich (1990) indicates there are several reasons for this professionalization of volunteer management, including:

- Many voluntary organizations and volunteer programs are quite large (e.g., Girl Scouts, Boy Scouts, American Red Cross, Salvation Army, United Way, and others).
- Increasing concern about liability has forced organizations to improve control of programs conducted by volunteers.
- Volunteers have become more sophisticated and discerning about the organizations to which they donate their time and energy.
- Management positions in voluntary organizations have become more professionalized.
- Managing volunteers is, in many ways, more difficult than managing paid employees; since volunteers are, by definition, not paid, the incentive structure is intrinsic rather than extrinsic.

Supervision of Volunteers

Supervision is a managerial function that helps to ensure the satisfactory completion of program objectives. The effective volunteer manager maximizes volunteers' expectations by providing support and resources. Further, the manager ensures that the volunteers possess the skills and abilities to get the job done. Finally, the supervisor must discuss problems as well as successes with volunteers and suggest constructive ways to improve.

As a process, supervision involves three elements:

- Establishing criteria of success, standards of performance, and program objectives such as the job description and annual plan of work.
- Measuring actual volunteer performance with respect to these stated criteria of success through observation, conferences, and evaluation.
- Making corrections, as needed, through managerial action.

Working With Difficult Volunteers

Working with volunteers generally is enjoyable. They want to be involved and are not motivated by compensation. However, there are volunteers who create problems and cause difficult supervisory problems. See Table 13.5 for suggestions for working with difficult volunteers.

Table 13.5
Dealing With Difficult Volunteers

When conflict arises, Heidrich (1990) suggests it can usually be traced to one or a combination of the following factors:

- Lack of agreement about the program's goals and components.
- Ill-defined and unmeasurable objectives.
- Absence of a preconceived plan.
- Exclusion from the planning process of those who will be responsible for carrying out the plan.
- Inaccessibility of leaders.
- Distortion of information accidentally or deliberately.
- Lack of trust, which induces people to withhold opinions that are negative or critical; people will play it safe rather than risk the wrath of someone else.
- Hidden agendas and other manipulations that reduce trust in the long run.
- Ineffective listening, which often represents a desire to dominate and an unwillingness to tolerate others' views.
- A belief in absolutes, which leads to a tendency to cast blame.
- A belief that only two sides of an issue exist and that one must be "right" and the other "wrong." This belief precludes compromise.
- Individual differences in race, age, culture, or status. Sometimes it is difficult to appreciate others' points of view.
- Misunderstandings about territory, policy, authority, and role expectations.

Recognition of Volunteers

Recognizing volunteers for their work is widely accepted as an important aspect of successful management. There is no single recognition event that will make everyone happy. Understanding that different volunteers are satisfied by different rewards is essential to the success of a recognition program. Recognition is not just a way of saying thank you, but it is also a response to individual interests and reasons for being involved in the program.

The common types of awards include:

- group recognition
- individual recognition
- informal recognition (e.g., get well cards, birthday cards, flowers, thank you notes, have a happy vacation note, photographs, lunch or coffee)
- public and media recognition
- formal recognition

The planning for a recognition, in many cases, is as important as the recognition itself. The first step is to appoint a recognition planning committee. The functions of the planning committee would include

- planning and conducting recognition event(s),
- evaluating recognition event(s),
- determining whether or not to establish formal awards program(s),
- researching the reasons why people have volunteered to work with the organization so that future recognition can be planned to meet their needs, and
- maintaining a record-keeping system that will provide data on volunteers' contributions to the organization.

The recognition planning committee needs to address a number of questions as it develops the format for volunteer recognition. These questions include:

- Does the organization see recognition as an event rather than a process?
- Has the organization fallen into a rut with traditional recognition events?
- Are there parts of the awards program that no one understands because the meaning is lost in the past?
- Is the awards program really fair to everyone?
- How many people are recognized as individuals?

If the recognition planning committee decides it is important to have a formal awards program, a number of items need to be considered. These items include, but are not limited to:

- Each award has a name that distinguishes it from other awards.
- Awards are incremental with some reserved for people with long tenure and distinguished service, including retirees, and others for short-term or one-time service.
- Each award has written criteria that must be met.
- Awards criteria and nominating forms are distributed to all volunteers.
- Favoritism in nomination and selection is scrupulously avoided.
- Volunteers are involved in the decision-making process.
- Award nominations are handled confidentially.
- There is an official time when formal awards are presented to recipients.
- A permanent record of award recipients is maintained, preferably on a large plaque visible to all in a prominent location.
- The formal recognition system is regularly reviewed.
- Name something after an outstanding volunteer (be cautious—this idea has long-term implications).
- Design a formal award program.
- Make a monetary gift in a volunteer's name to his or her favorite volunteer agency.
- Hold a banquet, brunch, luncheon, or party at a unique location.

Summary

No organization has enough staff to adequately raise funds through solicitation; therefore, volunteers become critical to any fund-raising effort. The volunteer plays the role of a loyal community supporter of the organization involved in raising funds for vital projects. They can easily influence colleagues, newer members, former classmates, and other community leaders regarding the importance of a project and the need for the funds. Volunteers are great ambassadors of goodwill.

Stier (1993, 1994) suggests that managers of any organization involved with volunteers must understand how to best involve them in the organization. The organization must develop a strong volunteer management system that treats volunteers as full-time paid staff. The organization must provide appropriate orientation programs, in-service training, and recognition programs. Finally, volunteers need supervision and attention just as do regular employees.

Section

II

Common Facility
Components

Universal and Accessible Design: Creating Facilities That Work for All People

Richard J. LaRue and Donald Rogers

14

This chapter presents historical, conceptual, and regulatory information as well as planning resources related to universal and accessible design. Primary to the regulatory development of accessibility planning today are the key statutes from the 1990 Americans With Disabilities Act (ADA) and information regarding the most recent accessibility guidelines as published by the Architectural and Transportation Barriers Compliance Board (Access Board). Given the nonspecific nature of the regulations, the interpretations of many ADA statutes have been tested in court. The results of this litigation have created a body of case law under each ADA title. When planning facilities where issues of accessibility are not clearly defined, it may be helpful to research the available case law. Generally, the government was unresponsive to early accessibility legislation such as the 1968 Architectural Barriers Act (ABA). Today, accessibility is not the overlooked factor that it once was in the design of public facilities. Private entities are another matter. There are still many questions about compliance and how to best meet the access needs of people with disabilities.

Even with published standards and guidelines, plus regular updates, it is possible for planners and designers to make misinterpretations and oversights. This chapter attempts to provide facilities planners and designers with accessibility standards and guidelines associated with typical design features such as parking, restrooms, entryways, ramps, and information areas. Additional resources will be provided in the form of Web sites and other references to assist in locating more detailed and specific information. It is important to realize that beyond all the supporting features associated with facilities addressed in this book, there are often specific activity space, program, and equipment accessibility features to consider.

In this chapter and in resources located on the Web and other places, differences between the terms "final rule," "guidelines," and "standards" may be difficult to understand. For example, in many of the documents found on the Access Board's Web site, the term final rule is used. This would seem to indicate that this is now an enforceable mandate but, in fact, it may not be. There is a sequence that begins with the law, and then guidelines are developed, and finally they become standards or regulations after being reviewed and approved by the necessary agency or agencies. This means that when the Access Board publishes final rules, these are only guidelines until the Office of Management and Budget (OMB) reviews them and then the entities responsible for enforcement must approve them and they then become enforceable standards or regulations. Enforcement responsibilities are explained in this chapter. A unique situation exists with the ABA that allows final rules by the Access Board to become standards as soon as the OMB approves them. This happens because the Access Board is responsible for enforcing the ABA while other entities are responsible for the ADA and its subsequent titles.

If you are thinking that this is difficult to follow, you are not alone. The hope, however, is that planners will go beyond the minimum guidelines or standards as they create spaces that meet the broadest needs of participants while making everyone feel welcome. In situations where guidelines have not been established, or standards and regulations are not in effect, the ADA is clear that all covered entities must still comply with the law which prohibits discrimination against people with disabilities. In these situations, enforcement entities expect planners to use current best practices when designing and building for accessibility. Where guidelines have been published, but have not become standards, these guidelines then would probably constitute best practices or minimum requirements. When no guidelines exist, then it is the responsibility of the planners and designers to research what is being done with regard to accessibility in the types of facilities they are creating. It will be very important to involve people with disabilities in this type of information-gathering process to get a sense of what the real needs are and whether new design ideas or adaptations will be functional.

Terminology is an important consideration when discussing, writing about, and reporting on matters that involve people with disabilities. There are a number of trendy terms used in these situations; however, most violate basic principles of acceptable terminology. A deliberate effort was made in this chapter to follow what is known as "person-first" terminology. The federal government uses this approach and scholars writing in the field prefer it, and perhaps most importantly, it is widely endorsed by the professional community of people with disabilities. Its usage is prominently seen in the ADA and the Individuals With Disabilities Education Act. This approach acknowledges the person ahead of the disability, emphasizing that the disability is a fraction of the whole person. While a person can undeniably have a disability, he or she should not be considered disabled. The term *handicapped* is often used with regard to accessibility as with handicapped parking and handicapped restroom stall. In fact, when these facilities meet code, they are actually accessible features. When they do not meet code, they present a barrier to a person with a disability, which creates a handicapping situation. Helping designers create accessible and universal facilities instead of "handicapped" facilities is the primary purpose of this chapter.

Two final topics of foundation knowledge and awareness are the concepts of accessible and universal design. Frequently, these two terms are used interchangeably when considering the access needs of people with disabilities. While they are related in some ways, each has a unique meaning. *Accessible* has a popular, or nontechnical meaning, that suggests something is made usable or available through some type of adaptation for individuals who have disabilities. It also has well-developed legal meaning in the context of the ADA and ABA. Consider the situation where a ramp does not comply with The Americans With Disabilities Act Accessibility Guidelines (ADAAG). Some would say that the ramp provides access, even in cases where it is quite steep. Others who have knowledge of the ADA might reference the ADAAG indicating the need for an "accessible" ramp to be no steeper than 1:12. In either case, the term *accessible* is referring specifically to meeting the needs of people with disabilities.

The second term, *universal design*, moves beyond the narrow concept of accessible. Accessible design juxtaposes accessible components with typical construction in order to eliminate or minimize environmental barriers for people with disabilities. Universal design creates a broadly inclusive environment that effectively blends a variety of design concepts, including accessible, into a range of meaningful options for all users. In a universally designed facility, it is not evident that modifications have been made for a specific person or group. This approach facilitates inclusion by focusing on people's abilities and emphasizing socially meaningful roles.

As you begin to explore the complexities of universal and accessible design, it can be an overwhelming prospect. There are so many codes and regulations that designers and planners are expected to follow in addition to accessibility that the process may seem restrictive to the point of stifling creativity. While codes and regulations do present boundaries of a sort, they also provide concrete beginning points that can actually stimulate creative design ideas. A helpful suggestion is to envision a comprehensive plan of accessibility that goes beyond minimum standards while taking into consideration the many potential uses of the space by people with a wide range of needs and abilities.

Learning Objectives

After reading this chapter, the student should be able to

- understand the historical development of constitutional protection and the civil rights of people with disabilities including the ADAAG, ADA of 1990, Uniform Federal Accessibility Standards (UFAS) of 1984, Sections 502 and 504 of the Rehabilitation Act of 1973, and the ABA of 1968;
- understand the concepts of accessible and universal design and further appreciate the benefits of creating accessible and usable facilities for all people;
- understand the meaning and/or intentions of ADA terminology, including: architectural barriers, undue hardship, readily achievable, and reasonable accommodation;
- understand the difference between standards and guidelines related to the ADA and other federal accessibility legislation, and;
- understand the legal advantages related to compliance, including tax incentives and the administrative responsibilities related to regulatory enforcement.

Civil Rights Legislation for Persons With Disabilities

The ABA of 1968, PL 90-480, authorized four primary agencies to issue accessibility standards in accordance with its respective statutory authority. Those agencies are the General Services Administration (GSA), the Department of Defense (DOD), the Department of Housing and Urban Development (HUD), and the U.S. Postal Service (USPS). The problem that surfaced with this approach is that guidelines were inconsistent between the agencies, resulting in much confusion. To address the issue of compliance with the ABA, "...Congress established the Architectural and Transportation Barriers Compliance Board (ATBCB) [aka. Access Board] in Section 502 of the Rehabilitation Act of 1973" (Access Board, Retrieved February 6, 2001, p. 3).

The Access Board is composed of representatives from the four initial agencies, seven other governmental agencies (Health and Human Services, Interior, Justice, Labor, and Transportation, and the Veterans Administration), and 12 members appointed from the general public by the president of the United States. A 1978 amendment to Section 502 of the Rehabilitation Act of 1973 added to the Access Board's functions. This amendment required the Access Board to issue minimum guidelines and requirements for the standards then established by the four standard-setting agencies (GSA, DOD, HUD, and USPS). The final rule establishing the guidelines now in effect was published in the *Federal Register* on August 4, 1982 (Access Board, Retrieved February 6, 2001). These guidelines are referred to as the Minimum Guidelines and Requirements for Accessible Design (MGRAD).

The four standard-setting agencies determined that the adopted uniform standards would, as much as possible, conform to the 1982 Guidelines of the Access Board and be consistent with standards published by the American National Standards Institute (ANSI). "ANSI is a non-governmental national organization that publishes a wide variety of recommended standards. ANSI's standards for barrier-free design are developed by a committee made up of 52 organizations representing associations of handicapped people, rehabilitation professionals, design professionals, builders, and manufacturers" (Access Board, Retrieved February 6, 2001, p. 5).

It is important to note that ANSI's 1961 standards, "Specifications for Making Buildings and Facilities Accessible to, and Usable by, Physically Handicapped People," formed the technical basis for the first accessibility standards adopted by the federal government and most state governments. The development of ANSI's revised standards in 1980 was based upon research funded by HUD. The 1980 ANSI standards were generally accepted by the private sector including the Council of American Building Officials (Access Board, Retrieved February 6, 2001).

In 1984, the Access Board updated the MGRAD and published the UFAS, which became the standard used by the four agencies responsible for accessibility to enforce the ABA. The UFAS followed the ANSI 1980 standards in format and, with regard to scope provisions and technical requirements, met or exceeded the comparable provisions of MGRAD (Access Board, Retrieved February 6, 2001).

The ADA of 1990 significantly expanded the role of the Access Board. Under the ADA, the Access Board became responsible for developing accessibility guidelines for entities covered by the Act and for providing technical assistance to individuals and organizations on the removal of architectural, transportation, and communication barriers.

In 1991, the Access Board published ADAAG, considered more stringent than the UFAS guidelines. The Access Board maintains responsibility for revisions of the ADAAG as well as the UFAS. In November 2000, the Access Board published a comprehensive proposal to update and merge both its ADA and ABA accessibility guidelines into the ADA-ABA Accessibility Guidelines. This will provide more consistency between the ADA and ABA while broadening the scope of what is covered. After extensive review and public comment, the Access Board approved the guidelines in final form on January 14, 2004. Once cleared by the Office of Management and Budget, the guidelines were published by the Access Board as a final rule, on July 23, 2004 (available online: http://www.access-board.gov/ada-aba/final.htm).

A final rule covering recreation facilities was published in September 2002 as a supplement to ADAAG. These guidelines cover newly constructed and altered recreation facilities in the areas of amusement rides, boating facilities, fishing piers and platforms, miniature golf courses, golf courses, exercise equipment, bowling lanes, shooting facilities, swimming pools, wading pools, and spas (available online: http://www.access-board.gov/recreation/final.htm). In addition, new guidelines, effective November 17, 2000, were adopted by ADAAG for playgrounds. "The guidelines cover the number of play components required to be accessible, accessible surfacing in play areas, ramp access and transfer system access to elevated structures, and access to soft contained play structures. They address play areas provided at schools, parks, child care facilities (except those based in the operator's home, which are exempt), and other facilities subject to the ADA" (available online: http://www.access-board.gov/play/finalrule.htm).

As of the writing of this chapter, the Access Board has generated a report that contains the guidelines for outdoor developed areas, which includes trails, beaches, picnic areas, and campgrounds. The Access Board is completing an economic feasibility study to submit with the report to the Office of Management and Budget, with the provision that the current report will serve as the final report. For further information contact the Access Board (http://www.access-board.gov) or the National Center on Accessibility (http://ww.ncaonline.org).

Presently, the only areas not covered by accessibility legislation in the United States are churches and private clubs. Exceptions include a church that rents or leases facilities to the public; then those facilities are covered. Private clubs must demonstrate sufficient cause for existing as such. They cannot just charge a fee, generate a list of "members," and then expect to be exempt from accessibility law. An area that was considered exempt by some is historically significant facilities protected by the 1966 Historic Preservation Act. It has been determined that historic preservation law does not supersede accessibility law and the reverse is also true. It is expected that accessibility law be applied sensitively to these types of facilities with thoughtful designs that do not compromise important historical features while creating the greatest degree of access possible. A more detailed discussion with illustrations to assist in making historically significant facilities accessible can be found in *Preservation Briefs 32: Making Historic Properties Accessible* available from the National Park Service, Heritage Preservation Services Office in Washington, D.C.

Other Related Legislation

Section 504 of the Rehabilitation Act of 1973, as amended, set out the functions of the Access Board and further specified that "no otherwise qualified handicapped person shall, on the basis of handicap, be excluded from participation in, be denied the benefits of, or otherwise be subjected to discrimination under any program which receives or benefits from Federal financial assistance" (Lumpkin, 1998, p. 229). This strengthened the intent of the ABA because it would be necessary to remove architectural barriers within facilities in order to provide accessible programming.

The Education Amendment Act of 1974 "mandated that all children must be placed in the least restrictive environment (LRE) or the setting in which their optimal learning and development could occur" (Lumpkin, 1998, p. 229). The All Handicapped Children Act of 1975 (Public Law 94-142) mandates that opportunity for participation in school athletic programs be provided to students with disabilities. Further recognizing the value and right of sports participation for persons with disabilities, the Amateur Sports Act of 1978 requires programs and facilities to accommodate the needs of athletes with disabilities (Lumpkin, 1998).

The Telecommunications Act of 1996 requires the Access Board to develop and maintain accessibility guidelines for telecommunications and customer premises equipment (e.g., mandated closed-captioning options on the newest models of televisions). Access standards for electronic and information technology in the Federal sector were issued under Section 508 of the Rehabilitation Act Amendments of 1998 "which requires that such technology be accessible when developed, procured, maintained, or used by a Federal agency" (Access Board, Retrieved February 4, 2001, p. 1)

The Five Titles of the ADA and Enforcement Responsibilities

Title I, Employment, prohibits discrimination against qualified individuals with disabilities in such areas as job-application procedures, hiring, discharge, promotion, job training, and other conditions of employment. Employers must make "reasonable" accommodations for an individual's disabilities, unless to do so would cause hardship for the employer. Employers must also post notices that explain the act (Miller, 1992, p. 18). The Equal Employment Opportunity Commission (EEOC) is responsible for enforcement of Title I of the ADA. The EEOC is further responsible for issuing interpretative guidance.

Title II, Public Services, prohibits exclusion of persons with disabilities from benefits, services, or activities, including transportation, offered by federal, state, and local government in accordance with the requirements of section 504 of the Rehabilitation Act of 1973. This coverage now includes all services provided by state and local governments regardless of whether they receive federal money or are privately funded. Part A covers state and local government and part B covers transportation. Part A is enforceable as designated in 28 Code of Federal Regulations (CFR) 35.190 and individuals may also file a private lawsuit. Part B enforcing agency is the Department of Transportation. The Department of the Interior will enforce new guidelines for recreation areas under Title II.

Automated handicapped entrance.

Title III, Public Accommodations, guarantees persons with disabilities access to all public businesses and the programs and services of private, commercial and not-for-profit agencies. Also covered is public transportation provided by a private entity. The Department of Justice and the Department of Transportation are the enforcing agencies and they accept individual complaints. Individuals may also file complaints with the U.S. Attorney General and file private lawsuits with local courts. The Department of the Interior will serve as the enforcement entity for recreation areas under Title III of the ADA.

Curb cut.

Title IV, Telecommunications, requires telephone companies to provide interstate and intrastate telecommunications relay service so that hearing-impaired and speech-impaired individuals can communicate with others (Miller, 1992, p. 18). Enforcement is the responsibility of the Federal Communication Commission, which does receive complaints from individuals.

Title V, Miscellaneous, refers to the administration and handling of complaints under the ADA. Administrative actions may include: awarding of reasonable attorney's fees in any proceeding under the ADA, prohibiting retaliation against, or coercion of any person who makes a charge, allowing insurers to continue to rely on actuarial procedures in underwriting risks, authorizing state governments to be sued under the ADA, providing that state laws offering greater or equal protection cannot be preempted, and, amending the Rehabilitation Act to conform its coverage of drug users to the provisions of ADA (Miller, 1992, p. 18).

As you can see, responsibility for enforcement of the ADA is shared by multiple government agencies based on each title of the law. While individuals can complain directly to federal agencies, it is preferred that they try to work through the dispute at the source of the problem. The Access Board suggests, "Where appropriate and to the extent authorized by law, the use of alternative means of dispute resolution is encouraged." Also, "The Department of Justice may not sue a party unless negotiations to settle the dispute have failed. The Department of Justice may file lawsuits in federal court to enforce the ADA, and courts may order compensatory damages and back pay to remedy discrimination if the Department prevails. Under title III, the Department of Justice may also obtain civil penalties of up to $50,000 for the first violation and $100,000 for any subsequent violation" (U.S. Department of Justice, Retrieved February 19, 2001, p.1-2).

In order to research and/or stay current with enforcement activities, the Department of Justice publishes quarterly reports that include: ADA litigation, formal settlement agreements, other settlements, and mediation activities (available online: http://www.usdoj.gov/crt/ada/enforce.htm). Additionally, the Department of Justice provides technical assistance manuals and publications for state and local governments (available online: http://www.usdoj.gov/crt/ada/publicat.htm).

It was not the intent of the legislation to create an atmosphere of conflict around the accessibility needs of people with disabilities. A thoughtful, rational, and cooperative process that involves all parties will more effectively educate an entity on the needs of people with disabilities. Improved awareness, sensitivity, and knowledge will provide a basis for understanding the guidelines and valuing accessibility. This approach has greater potential to result in accessible facility designs that are optimally functional and relationships that will promote inclusion.

Striving for Inclusion: Accessible and Universal Design

It is important to not get drawn into the "standards game" when designing facilities that are accessible to people with disabilities. The ADA is not meant to be seen simply as a set of building codes. Its primary purpose is civil rights legislation that makes it illegal to discriminate against people with disabilities because of their disability. To assist in the implementation of these efforts, there are regulations to follow, including the ADAAG, UFAS, and applicable State and Municipal Accessibility Codes and guidelines. Designers then have a choice to either apply the existing minimum standards in an effort to comply with accessibility law or to incorporate the guidelines into a universal design approach.

While the design of sports and recreation facilities strives to meet aesthetic goals, the primary purpose is usually based on some desired experience for the users. Whether the facility is designed for specific or multipurpose use, there will typically be a variety of human interactions to plan for. These interactions happen with people with disabilities during staff meetings, at the information desk, in activity/event spaces, in support areas (e.g., restrooms, water fountains, locker rooms, and concessions), and so on. Universal design provides opportunities for these interactions to happen in dignified and meaningful ways and creates a foundation for full inclusion of all participants and staff.

Universal design has its roots in accessible design beginning with the ABA. As a result of early accessible design efforts, and before the ADA, it was becoming apparent that creating accessible facilities helped more than just people with disabilities. It helped everyone at different times and in different ways. According to Salmen (1996), "Universal design uses accessibility standards as a starting point and goes further, to consider issues such as perception, social and environmental relationships, cost effectiveness and aesthetics. The very nature of these issues puts them beyond the range of what could be mandated by minimum design criteria found in the accessibility codes, and squarely within the concerns of people in their every day lives" (p.14).

In addition to accessibility, universal design embodies other important concepts that benefit all people. These concepts include:

- Providing a range of choices in how a space can be utilized or an activity can be experienced. People with and without disabilities can select from the same choices.
- Offering a range of challenge levels for everyone within those choices. Don't assume that similar individuals want similar challenge levels.
- Minimal use of signage that indicates special services or access features. By nature, universal design reduces the need for this type of signage because functional options are more apparent.
- Providing access and services in and through the same space for everyone. Do not use a design that sends different people to separate features.
- Go well beyond the minimum standards when providing accessible spaces and features such as more accessible restroom stalls, easier ramp grades, and wider doors and passageways.

Most people at some time in their lives will experience either temporary or permanent sensory impairment and/or physical disability. These range from broken bones to age-related changes in functioning. Approximately 50 million Americans live with a disability, with countless others affected by them. While there are legal mandates to create accessible facilities for all people, those of us in the leisure, recreation, and sport fields have a moral imperative to apply universal design strategies. It is during leisure time experiences that our diverse society finds merge points between different classes, races, beliefs, and abilities. All people are capable of leisure, just as we are capable of creating universal facilities that serve the leisure needs of all people.

Accessibility and Public Accommodations

Like no other previous legislation, Title III of the ADA, Public Accommodation, covers private, for-profit businesses, and not-for-profit agencies. This casts a huge net covering most sports and recreation facilities, programs, and services. There are some situations allowed by the law that permit alternative and partial methods of compliance and those will be discussed in this section. A place of public accommodation is defined as a facility, operated by a private entity, whose operations affect commerce and fall within at least one of the following 12 categories:

Handicapped parking.

- Places of lodging. (see also the Fair Housing Amendments Act. In instances where such housing is "rented" to the public, e.g. students, etc.; there are specific accessibility requirements that must be met.)
- Establishments serving food or drink.
- Places of exhibition or entertainment (stadium).
- Places of public gathering (auditorium).
- Sales or rental establishments.
- Service establishments.
- Stations used for specified public transportation.
- Places of public display or collection.
- Places of recreation (park).
- Places of education.
- Social service center establishments.
- Places of exercise or recreational sports (gymnasium, health spa, bowling alley, golf course, or other place of exercise or recreation).

Public accommodation further refers to the private entity that owns, leases or leases to, or operates a place of public accommodation. Thus, the ADA establishes responsibility for compliance not with a physical location but with the individual or group that owns or otherwise operates the physical location (Cocco & Zimmerman, 1996, p. 46).

A public accommodation shall remove architectural barriers in existing facilities where such removal is readily achievable. Examples of barrier removal include:

- installing ramps over steps or adjacent to steps
- making curb cuts that access sidewalks or accessible routes
- repositioning telephones within accessible reach ranges
- adding raised markings on elevator control buttons
- installing flashing alarm lights
- widening doors
- lowering a section of counter top that provides customer service, information, or equipment check-out
- bypassing a turnstile by providing an adjacent accessible alternative
- installing door hardware that provides accessible entry/egress
- installing grab bars in toilet stalls
- rearranging toilet partitions to increase maneuvering space
- repositioning a paper towel dispenser, soap dispenser, and mirror in a bathroom
- installing an accessible paper cup dispenser, at existing inaccessible water fountains
- removing high-pile, low-density carpeting
- lowering high doorway thresholds
- ramping indoor grade/level changes

Sample handicapped accessible ramp, Science Building, Indiana State University.

A public accommodation is urged to take measures to comply with barrier removal in accordance with the following order of priorities:

- Provide access to a place of public accommodation from public sidewalks, parking, or public transportation, which includes accessible parking spaces, accessible routes to facilities, installing an entrance ramp if necessary and widening entrances.
- Provide access within places of public accommodation where goods and services are made available to the public; including aisles that access merchandise, dressing/changing areas, ticket booths, food purchases, eating areas and checkout counters.
- Provide access to restrooms throughout the facility, including staff/employee areas.
- Take any other measures necessary to provide access to the goods, services, privileges, advantages, or accommodations of a place of public accommodation.

**Retrofitted aquatic transfer seat,
Indiana State University.**

The ADA is designed to allow an otherwise covered public accommodation to limit or "customize" its compliance using auxiliary aids and services or alternative means of providing equal goods, services, facilities, privileges, advantage, or accommodations. This is only required if those methods are readily achievable (ADA, 1990). In rare cases, due to concerns with an undue burden or a fundamental alteration in the nature of the service, program, or activity, it may be that a covered entity will not be required to provide accessible facilities and/or access to equal services. Language within the ADA that guides these decisions is explained in the following.

**Handicapped aquatic ramp,
YMCA, Murfreesboro, Tennessee.**

Though not clearly defined in the ADA, *undue burden* is understood to mean that the actions needed to comply will require significant difficulty or expense. Determination of undue burden considers a number of factors, including an employer's size, the financial resources of the entity, and/or the nature and structure of the operation (Miller, 1990).

In the process of meeting the needs of individuals with disabilities, public entities are required to make reasonable accommodations. Should it be determined that the accommodation will drastically change (i.e., fundamentally alter) the service, program, or activity, the accommodation may not be required. A formal legal procedure is required to evaluate and substantiate this defense.

Similar to the standard of undue burden is the consideration of whether or not an accommodation is readily achievable. To be *readily achievable* means the accommodation is easily accomplishable and able to be carried out without much difficulty or expense. While using identical determining factors as undue burden, the readily achievable standard is a lower standard than undue burden (Cocco & Zimmerman, 1996). In determining whether an action is readily achievable, the following factors are to be considered:

- The nature and cost of the action needed under the Act.
- The overall financial resources of the facility or facilities involved in the action, the number of persons employed at such facility, the effect on expenses and resources, or the impact otherwise of such action upon the operation of the facility.
- The overall financial resources of the covered entity; the overall size of the business or the covered entity with respect to the number of its employees; and the number, type, and location of its facilities. For example, corporations that own locally operated enterprises are responsible for complying with the ADA, and are deemed capable of affording accommodations based on the financial assets of the

corporation. This is true also for state-funded entities, such as universities.

- The type of operation or operations of the covered entity, including the composition, structure, and functions of the work force of such entity; the geographic separateness, administrative or fiscal relationship of the facility or facilities in question to the covered entity (ADA, 1990).

Short- and long-range strategic planning is an integral part of an organization's stated intention to comply with federal accessibility regulations. These plans should include specific actions and timelines for compliance. If an organization claims "undue burden" to avoid financial strife, it will only provide short-term relief. Planning to permanently discriminate against people with disabilities is not an option. It is important to note that the ADA itself is not static legislation. It will continue to evolve, increasing in scope and degrees of accessibility. Waiting to comply when it is convenient for the organization is an ill-advised strategy. It is imperative that organizations plan ahead, take advantage of federal tax incentives, and strive to at least meet, and where possible, exceed current accessibility legislation.

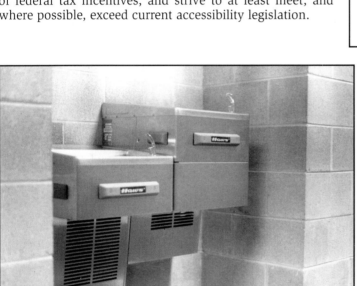

Removing architectural barriers for drinking fountains.

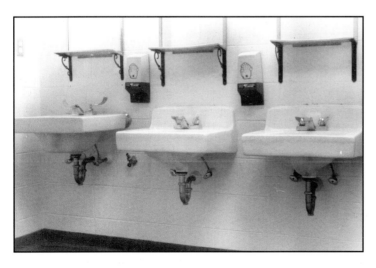

Removing architectural barriers for sinks.

Removing architectural barriers in the shower.

Compliance with public accommodation accessibility regulations is required with all new construction, with remodeling projects, and when offering programs and services to the public. All elements of new recreation and sports buildings, parking facilities, and site development must be accessible. Where specific guidelines are not available for new facilities, then the best information available should be used. All remodeling of facilities and developed areas must meet applicable standards and guidelines with consideration being given to concerns of undue burden and impact on the essential nature of the service or experience (Quarve-Peterson, 1996).

Making programs and services accessible will range from relatively simple to complicated. Modifying seating, installing a wheelchair lift on a van, widening a racquetball court door, and providing large print literature are examples of accommodations that will allow participants with disabilities access to the same program or service available to all other participants. In some cases, however, it will be necessary to create equitable alternatives in order to provide program access. Usually there will be a variety of ways to provide accessible options. In these situations it is suggested that people with disabilities and technical experts be consulted to help identify the "best and most cost-effective option" (Quarve-Peterson, 1996, p.46).

Summary

Discrimination against people based on disability is illegal. The ADA and other federal legislation mandates that all covered facilities, programs, and services be accessible to persons with disabilities. Small businesses and large corporations alike are expected to have strategies for including people with disabilities in the opportunities they provide to the general public. In cases where it is not clear how to meet the needs of people with disabilities, it is important to include them in the planning process. There are also countless organizations committed to assisting public and private entities with design solutions.

Removing architectural barriers for toilets.

Beyond implementing components that provide accessibility is the strategy of universal design. Planning facilities that offer all people meaningful choices and opportunities for dynamic social interaction creates places that benefit whole communities. As designers of sports and recreation facilities and programs, we have legal and moral responsibilities to make accessibility and inclusion a reality. Doing so in creative ways will advance a new generation of designs that merge function and form with social justice.

A good example of an accessible drinking fountain.

Notes

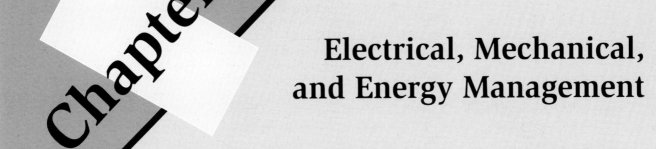

Chapter 15

Electrical, Mechanical, and Energy Management

Richard J. LaRue, Thomas H. Sawyer, and Jack Vivian

At its best, technology should conform to the way we work, the way we play, and the way we live. Through electrical and mechanical engineering, we have an opportunity to create extraordinary environments through the manipulation of basic components: lighting, sound, and other electronic technologies; heating, ventilation, and air-conditioning (HVAC); and humidity and air quality control. Advancements in engineering these technologies in both indoor and outdoor spaces require planners to understand the basics and expect unlimited potential for new technologies. Planners must avoid setting limits on how far ahead they look. Only a few years ago, the computer was a luxury. Now computers are a necessity of everyday life, operating everything from membership systems to the building automation and HVAC systems of "intelligent buildings" (Myers, 1997, p. 53). Today's engineering must be about providing for the way we will work, the way we will play, and the way we will live.

Lighting is an important factor when selecting facility surfaces. With increased efforts to address aesthetics, as well as participant and spectator satisfaction, lighting should be addressed in the planning phase of building construction. Indirect lighting is largely viewed as ideal for most competitive sports and recreational settings. Indirect lighting, however, is heavily influenced by its surroundings. Paint type (flat vs. gloss), paint color, shadows, HVAC, sprinkler pipes, and acoustic strips all impact lighting efforts (Cohen, 2002). As mentioned numerous times previously, the efforts of the architect can have a significant impact on a variety of design elements within a facility.

Learning Objectives

After reading this chapter, the student should be able to

- understand lighting and sound in terms of functionality;
- understand the challenges of implementing electronic technologies;
- understand climate control concepts in terms of efficiency;
- recognize the administrative responsibilities related to electronic technology and climate control;
- understand the challenges of sick building syndrome;
- understand both the trends and new technologies in electrical and mechanical engineering;
- understand terminology related to energy management;
- understand the design, construction, and operating considerations related to energy management;
- identify the various energy savings considerations when planning, operating, and maintaining a sports and recreational facility; and
- learn sources of energy management information and reference materials.

Electrical Engineering

A theoretical basis of electrical engineering includes an understanding of circuits, electronics, electromagnetics, energy conversion, and controls. Conceptually, when planners consider lighting and sound, they are also considering the broader areas of illumination and acoustics. Therefore, the planning basics of lighting, sound, and other electronic technologies will also include information relevant to the design of electrical systems, which goes beyond electrical engineering in its strictest sense.

Basic Considerations in Lighting

Lighting is simply a means to illuminate or further brighten an area or space. The two primary lighting options are energy-produced lighting and natural lighting. The product of lighting in combination with other variables, such as the level of darkness, the amount of reflective light (from surfaces), and the color of the lighting, results in illumination.

Illumination is measured by the foot-candle. Brightness is the luminous intensity of any surface and is measured by the foot-lambert. Glare, which is an important consideration in physical education and sports facilities, is nothing more than excessively high brightness.

The amount of light in any given area and the quality of light are of equal importance. Providing efficient illumination is complicated and challenging, and the services of an illumination engineer are recommended in order to obtain maximum lighting efficiency. Gymnasiums, classrooms, corridors, and other areas have specific and different lighting requirements. Planning for electric illumination requires that each area be considered relative to specific use.

The foot-candle is a measurement of light intensity at a given point. Light intensity, measured in foot-candles, is one vital factor in eye comfort and seeing efficiency, but intensity must be considered in relation to the brightness balance of all light sources and reflective surfaces within the visual field.

The reflection factor is the percentage of light falling on a surface that is reflected by that surface. In order to maintain a brightness balance with a quantity and quality of light for good visibility, all surfaces within a room should be relatively light, with a matte rather than a glossy finish.

The foot-lambert is the product of the illumination in foot-candles and the reflection factor of the surface. For example, 40 foot-candles striking a surface with a reflection factor of 50% would produce a brightness of 20 foot-lamberts (40 x .50 = 20). These values are necessary when computing brightness differences in order to achieve a balanced visual field. Table 15.1 gives a relative indication as to a comparison of illuminations for specific indoor spaces.

Table 15.1
Levels of Illumination Recommended for Specific Indoor Spaces

Area	Foot-Candles on Tasks
Adapted physical education gymnasium	50
Auditorium	
Assembly only	15
Exhibitions	30 to 50
Social activities	5 to 15
Classrooms	
Laboratories	100
Lecture rooms	
Audience area	70
Demonstration area	150
Study halls	70
Corridors and stairways	20
Dance studio	5 to 50[2]
Field houses	80
First-aid rooms	
General	50
Examining table	125
Gymnasiums	
Exhibitions	50[2]
General exercise and recreation	35
Dances	5 to 50[2]
Locker and shower rooms	30
Gymnastics	50
Archery	
Shooting tee	50
Target area	70
Badminton	50[1]
Basketball	80[1]
Deck tennis	50
Fencing	70[1]
Handball	70[1]
Paddle tennis	70[1]
Rifle range	

continued

Table 15.1 continued
Levels of Illumination Recommended for Specific Indoor Spaces

Area	Foot-Candles on Tasks
Point area 50	
Target area	70
Rowing practice area	50
Squash	70[1]
Tennis	70[1]
Volleyball	50
Weight-exercise room	50
Wrestling and personal defense room	50
Games room	70
Ice rink	100[2]
Library	
Study and notes	70
Ordinary reading	50 to 70
Lounges	
General	50
Reading books, magazines, and newspapers	50 to 70
Offices	
Accounting, auditing, tabulating, bookkeeping, and business-machine operation	150
Regular office work, active filing, index references, and mail sorting	100
Reading and transcribing handwriting in ink or medium pencil on good-quality paper, and intermittent filing	70
Reading high-contrast or well-printed material not involving critical or prolonged seeing, and conferring and interviewing	50
Parking areas	1
Storerooms	
Inactive	10
Active	
Rough bulky	15
Medium	30
Fine	60
Swimming pools	
General and overhead	50[3]
Underwater[3]	
Toilets and washrooms	30

These standards have been developed by a panel of experts on facilities for health, physical education, and recreation after careful consideration of the activities involved. In all instances, the standards in this table are equal to, or exceed, the standards that have been recommended by the Illumination Engineering Society, American Institute of Architects, and National Council on Schoolhouse Construction. [1]Care must be taken to achieve a brightness balance to eliminate extremes of brightness and glare. [2]Should be equipped with rheostats. [3]Must be balanced with overhead lighting and should provide 100 lamp lumens per square foot of pool surface.

Courtesy of Illuminating Engineering Society of North America.

Notes

Installation

Lights in arenas, gymnasiums, and other high-ceiling activity spaces need to be a minimum of 24 feet above the playing surface so they will not interfere with official clearance heights for indoor sports. Indoor lighting systems are generally of two types: direct and indirect lighting. Direct lighting systems face directly down at the floor. Indirect lighting systems face in some direction other than the floor, such as sidewalls or ceiling, to reflect the beaming light in an effort to reduce glare. Indirect lighting is more expensive to operate, since with each reflection light is diminished. Therefore, more energy is consumed in indirect lighting compared to direct lighting in order to obtain the same final illumination of an area. Both lighting systems should meet the required level of foot-candles without causing glare or shadows on the playing surface. The type of lighting—incandescent, fluorescent, mercury-vapor, metal halide, quartz, or sodium-vapor—will likely depend upon the type of space and the way the space will be used (see Figure 15.1). The style of fixture may have more to do with aesthetics than functionality, though the advantages and disadvantages of aesthetics versus functionality should always be considered.

Figure 15.1

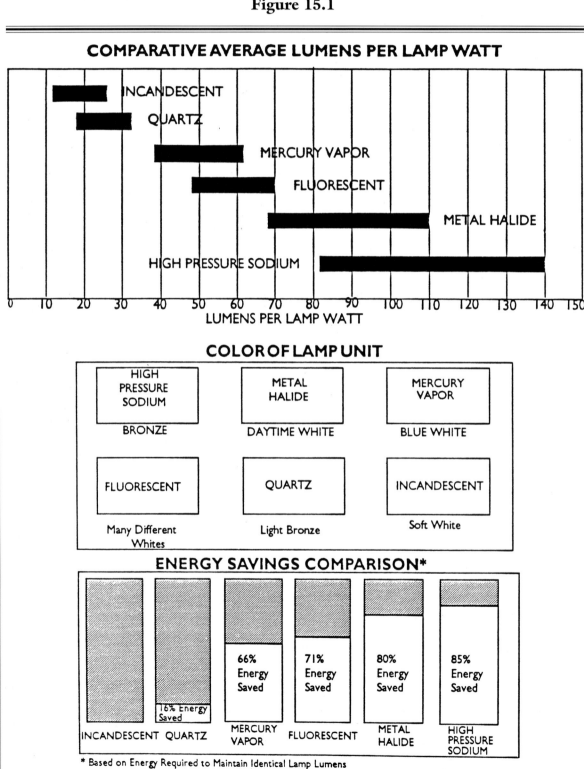

Designed for Impact

In spaces where the play may involve hitting, kicking, or throwing balls, lighting fixtures should be designed to absorb their impact. Lighting systems are available that include shock-absorbing characteristics. Perhaps more important is the additional protection these lights require in the event that they are struck and the bulb is broken. Falling shards of glass from broken lights should be avoided at all costs. Lights need to be covered with a transparent polycarbonate sheeting (a screen may not be enough) that will catch broken glass bulbs and also protect the bulbs from direct impact. The sheeting or cover should also keep softer, potentially flammable sports implements (e.g., tennis balls, shuttlecocks, and Nerf or wiffle-balls) from lodging within the fixture against a high-temperature bulb (Turner, 1993).

Lighting Types

The incandescent light is instantaneous, burns without sound, and is not affected by the number of times the light is turned on or off. Incandescent lights and fixtures are considerably cheaper in initial cost; are easier to change; and the lamp, within limits, may be varied in size within a given fixture. Incandescent fixtures, however, have excessively high spot brightness and give off considerable heat; a problem when high levels of illumination are necessary.

Fluorescent lamps have the advantage of long life and give at least two and a half times the amount of light that incandescent lamps give for the same amount of electrical current used. They frequently are used in old buildings to raise the illumination level without installing new wiring.

Mercury-vapor lighting is expensive in terms of initial installation. The overall cost of mercury-vapor lighting, however, is cheaper than incandescent lighting. The primary objection to mercury-vapor lighting is its bluish color. However, when incandescent lighting is used in addition to mercury-vapor, a highly satisfactory lighting system results. Mercury-vapor lights are being phased out in favor of metal halide lights.

Metal halide lights do not last as long as mercury-vapor lights but give a better light output and operate more efficiently. Metal halide lights do not have the bluish tint of mercury-vapor lights. Quartz lights and high-pressure sodium lights are outdoor lights. It has been only over the past few years that these lights have been utilized indoors. Quartz lights are not much different than incandescent lights, except they have a slight bronze color and are slightly more efficient. High-pressure sodium lights might well be the indoor activity light of the future. They have long life expectancy; they are highly efficient and give the best light output of all the lights mentioned. The only problem with high-pressure sodium lights is the yellow-bronze hue associated with them.

Lighting Levels

A number of systems exist that allow different levels of lighting so that special events or lighting requirements can be met. The Jack Breslin Student Events Center at Michigan State University (opened in 1989) affords such variety using an intricate Holophane lighting system.

The lighting levels are turned up or down through a computerized control system, which is preprogrammed for different lighting and uniformity levels. On another control panel, a single button designated for one of eight different preprogrammed scenes can adjust the lights. For example, facility personnel can press one button to set the lighting for televised basketball games, another for non-televised games, another for pregame setup, and so forth (Rabin, 1993, p. 6).

When the Dan and Kathleen Hogan Sports Center at Colby-Sawyer College opened in 1991, the NCAA lighting standard for swimming was 60 foot-candles at the water's surface. Today 100 foot-candles of illumination are required for U.S. swimming and collegiate championship events. Because the planners decided upon a higher-than-minimum level for lighting the natatorium at the center, the facility continues to meet required lighting standards without any modification.

Using Natural Lighting

Windows and other translucent materials allow natural light into a facility. Natural lighting can reduce operational costs and enhance the aesthetics of an indoor space. The major problem with windows is that it is very difficult to control the glare that they allow to enter. Avoid windows in any activity area where visual acuity is an important commodity for both learning activity skills and safety. However, other translucent building materials are available that do several things windows cannot:

- Provide higher values for insulation reducing both heat loss (during colder seasons) and/or heat gain (during warmer seasons).
- Diffuse the light that comes through, reducing glare.
- Provide greater resistance to breaking so they are safer to use in spaces where broken glass is a serious problem, and they are harder to break into from a security standpoint.

Translucent materials are not perfect. Translucent panels or blocks in a high-moisture area will still allow moisture to condense on the inside surface if it is colder outside, and they do not allow clear images to transfer. Windows can also have movable shades, shutters, curtains, or blinds that assist with controlling glare and can improve insulating levels. Skylights are acceptable in "slow movement areas," and vertical skylights are recommended in order to keep both glare and leakage to a minimum. Regardless of the materials used, natural light seems a worthy goal when the facility is designed and used appropriately.

Notes

Maintenance

Planning must also take into account the need to change bulbs or replace fixtures. Unless there is a catwalk or crawl space in the ceiling, the lights will need to be changed from the floor using poles, ladders, scaffolding, or hydraulic hoists. Experience informs us that changing all the lights in a space at the same time is the most cost-effective approach to maintenance. However, if your lighting fails to meet required levels whenever a single fixture is out, you will be forced to change your bulbs more frequently. Consider adding a couple of fixtures more than are required in each space (e.g., if the space/activity standard calls for 50 foot-candles on task, you may wish to exceed this standard by four fixtures, so that you can lose up to four lamps and still meet the minimum). And when four bulbs are gone, it is probably time to replace all the bulbs in the space. As you plan for the need to change bulbs and replace fixtures, remember the characteristics of the space. Even telescoping poles need minimum clearance to get inside a space. Racquetball courts with standard-sized doors may allow the use of a small hydraulic hoist rather than a giant stepladder. Finally, direct-lighting bulbs can sometimes be changed using only a pole (standing on the floor), while indirect lighting can only be changed using a catwalk, crawlspace, or more time-consuming approach. Therefore, when planning your lighting system maintenance, you should consider designs that will serve the facility without being labor intensive.

Unique Lighting Settings and Issues

Unique settings in sports and recreational facilities require either special lighting systems, special fixtures, or carefully planned designs. In spaces with a higher level of moisture (pool areas, shower and toilet areas, locker rooms, etc.), vapor-proof lighting units are recommended. Remember that broken glass in any such area is a mini-disaster. If a bulb breaks in spaces where participants are often barefooted, extensive cleanup will be required. Locker rooms and athletic training rooms are two examples of spaces where light placement will directly affect the quality of the environment. Fixtures should be placed to enhance the areas between lockers in locker rooms, to afford clear reflections at mirrors, and to brighten places where visibility is critical to the activity in athletic training rooms.

Aquatic Facilities

Lighting indoor swimming spaces has never been the easiest part of natatorium design, although frequently, and with regrettable results, it has been treated that way. With today's multipurpose aquatic centers frequently accommodating diverse programming activities in a shared environment, it has become an even greater creative challenge to get the light right. Natural light is an increasingly attractive option for indoor aquatic facilities. Large windows or open fenestration can be energy-efficient ways to supplement artificial heat and lighting, and they add interest for users and a much-appreciated connection to the outside for employees who work all day in an enclosed environment. With all its advantages, however, natural light can be accompanied by an undesirable partner—glare (Hunsaker, 1998, p.51).

If windows are used in aquatic areas, the glare trade-off must be addressed during the planning stages. Glare is not an exclusive problem of natural lighting. Glare can result from improperly located artificial lighting when the lights reflect off either the water surface or sidewalls. With safety a major consideration in aquatic facilities, every effort must be made to control for glare and/or the blind spots caused by glare. Underwater lighting can reduce some of the glare problem and can further enhance visibility in deeper water (underwater lighting is required in some jurisdictions). And in aquatic facilities, there are maintenance issues related to the location of light fixtures over the pool (the preferred location for competitive facilities). The YMCA's Walter Schroeder Aquatic Center in Milwaukee, Wisconsin, was able to locate light fixtures directly over the 50-meter indoor pool after determining that by using the two movable bulkheads, a hoist could be positioned anywhere a fixture required re-lamping. This avoided the added construction expense of a catwalk or crawl space and the labor intensiveness of using a scaffolding setup in an empty pool to replace bulbs. Finally, artificial lighting in pool areas must consider the variability of water depth.

Outdoor Lighting

Outdoor lighting for sports fields can have some very specific requirements. "Sport lighting should provide a specified quantity and quality of light on the playing surface. For a football field, the quantity (level) of light is determined by the player's skill level, the number of spectators and any television requirements" (Rogers, 1994, p. 53). Although specific considerations apply when planning illumination of a specific-use field, for the purpose of this chapter, the discussion of outdoor lighting will focus on multipurpose installations.

Multipurpose sports fields are more complicated to light than single-purpose fields, but you'll save money by combining activities on one field. Several issues need to be addressed when lighting a multipurpose field. Light levels and pole placement become big factors, and design decisions become critical. Controlling spill and glare is also very important. Lighting a multipurpose field is extremely cost-effective. By sharing poles and fixtures among several sports, initial costs can be reduced by 40% or more. At some point, making the decision to use the field for both sports increases the land's productivity, and so will the decision to give it light (Rogers, 1996, p. 51).

Planning steps include the following:

- "Determine the layout of the field and all its potential uses. The most common multipurpose fields combine football with soccer, or football or soccer with softball" (Rogers, 1996, p. 51).

- Determine the quantity (level) as well as the quality needed (Rogers, 1996). The Illuminating Engineering Society of North America (IESNA) publishes light-level guidelines for outdoor sports (see IESNA's Web site for further information: http://www.iesna.org).
- Determine the type of lamp desired (Rogers, 1996).
- Determine the number of luminaire assemblies (luminaire assemblies consist of lamp reflector, ballast mounting, crossarm and mounting hardware) and poles required to light the playing surfaces while avoiding spill and glare (Rogers, 1996).
- Decide on the type of poles to be used: wood, concrete, and steel are the standard options. Each has advantages and disadvantages.
- Consider all aspects of safety. The lighting system must comply with the National Electric Code as well as state and local codes and use luminaire assemblies that have the Underwriters Laboratory approval (Rogers, 1996).
- Establish switching controls that allow for maximum flexibility and maximum efficiency.
- Recalling that some activities require more lighting than others; switches should afford higher and lower levels of illumination. "Switching capacity becomes even more important with overlapping fields" (Rogers, 1996, p. 54).

Outdoor lighting on metal poles.

Outdoor sports lighting should be safe, simple, and efficient. Basic requirements include one transformer and a simple service entrance with a basic feeder and branch circuit. Grounding at the service center and at each pole is needed to ensure the safety of anyone who comes in contact with the pole or electrical equipment. Grounding for lighting protection should be designed and installed according to the National Fire Protection Association (NFPA) Code 780. Safety disconnects on each pole provide additional protection for service crews. Individual fusing of each fixture avoids gang failure of the lights, eliminating costly emergency repairs (Rogers, 1994, p. 56).

Finally, the planner should consider and compare the warranties offered by different manufacturers: the length of the warranty, the items included, and those not included. "Manufacturers that offer a multi-year warranty are making a strong statement of confidence in their product" (Rogers, 1994, p. 56).

Supplementary and Special Lighting Requirements

It is advisable to provide supplementary lighting on such areas as those containing goals or targets. Supplementary light sources should be shielded from the eyes of participants and spectators in order to provide the proper brightness balance. Other special lighting requirements include:

- Night lighting—lights that remain on 24 hours per day (can be the same circuit as the emergency lighting), lighting large spaces, lobbies, corridors, stairwells, and classrooms.
- Exit lighting—located at all exits (including exit-only locations), should be mounted according to local and state codes. Because these lights remain on 24 hours per day, cost savings can be realized if fluorescent bulbs are used instead of incandescent bulbs or LED (light-emitting diode) signs are used as both fluorescent bulbs or LED fixtures have much longer lives. All exit lighting should be on special circuits that will remain on, even if the power is lost.
- Emergency (white) lighting—should be provided for exits (including exterior open spaces to which exits lead). This lighting should be on a special emergency circuit (battery powered) that will power-up whenever normal power is lost.

Lighting Controls

When planning for lighting, the methods of control are also important to consider. The central light-switch box should be located at a major entrance area, and all teaching [or activity] spaces should have individual light switches. A relatively unusual approach to controlling illumination in spaces where lighting is only on as needed (e.g., individual racquetball or squash courts, rest rooms, etc.) is motion sensor or "occupancy sensors" switching. If the sensor detects no movement over a period of 10 to 15 minutes, the lights automatically switch off. The lights come back on as soon as someone enters the room. Light-level sensors are also available for use indoors as well as outdoors. These sensors adjust the lighting level in response to the amount of natural lighting. Replacing the all-or-nothing on/off switch in parking areas or skylit rooms can give just the right amount of artificial light needed as the natural light fades.

Trends in Lighting

On the horizon, if not already here, is the use of Circadian lighting systems in 24-hour operations. Circadian lights facilitate true physiological adaptation to working nights and sleeping during the day. These system installations have proven "entirely successful in providing a means in keeping the shift workers awake (industrial settings) and alert while on-shift, improving the safety of the commute home, improving the day sleep of the shift worker, and having a positive impact on family life" (Murphy, 1998, p. 1). In other words, Circadian lighting systems have proven to have a positive biological effect on users in a 24-hour, three-shift environment. More research will be needed to determine the possible use and effects of Circadian lighting in more traditional settings.

Basic Considerations in Sound and Acoustics

Sound

Sound is an important part of everyday life, and subsequently it is an important part of sports and recreation. From the public address system to the telemetric microphone, the ability to hear what is going on is almost as critical as seeing what is going on; frequently, one sense will support another in completing the act of communication. From the sound quality we need in aerobic dance studios to the sound system required for a halftime show at the Super Bowl, technology is advancing the availability of high-resolution sound (Fenton, 1997).

For the sports or recreational facility, sound design starts with creating a suitable sound environment. Beginning in the lobby, where users first enter, several approaches can be utilized:

* Design a small audio/video system that plays videos (either cable or tape), with the audio portion of the videos distributed to other areas as well.
* Building on the first approach, include a video wall in the workout area that receives the same video as the unit in the front lobby.
* Have your sound distribution originate in a workout space such as an aerobics studio, and then distribute this sound or allow it to "drift" to the lobby and/or other areas of the facility (Hall, 1993).

In strength-training spaces, the major sound considerations are: even distribution, the ability to overcome background noise, and low-fatigue factors. Correct selection and placement of appropriate speakers will provide even distribution, reduce the impact of background interference, and satisfy low-fatigue requirements. Wall-mounted speakers usually work best, although clubs that have a lot of tall equipment in rooms with low ceilings should use ceiling speakers. Whenever possible, include in your design a dedicated sound system for free-weight areas to increase your flexibility in sound sources and level control (Hall, 1993, p. 42).

In cardiovascular areas, "the most satisfactory approach for most clubs is to supply each exercise station with a headphone outlet and flexibility in source selection, along with one or more video monitors visible to several stations at once" (Hall, 1993, p. 43).

The aerobics room is the one area where facility users most expect to hear sophisticated, high-quality sound. Achieving this in a room full of hard surfaces and highly active people is difficult. A well-designed and properly operated sound system will add precision and impact to your classes, establishing a sense of timing and inspiration without fatigue, stress, or hearing damage created by distortion and excessive volume levels (Hall, 1995, pp. 42-43).

Four categories of components have a very direct effect on these various factors (Hall, 1991, p. 40):

* speakers,
* cassette decks, turntables, or CD players
* amplifier, receiver, and equalizer (soft limiter)
* wireless microphone and microphone mixer (Hall, 1991).

Selecting the correct components is easier when you understand the elements of a high-quality sound system. However, it is important to seek the advice of individuals and/or companies who are familiar with the specific needs of an aerobic studio when choosing components for your new studio or when upgrading your current system

Acoustics

Because of the amount of noise and sound that emanates from the activities in physical education and sports, acoustics and sound are of paramount importance in building design. Acoustical treatments in building design are the domain of the acoustical engineer. An acoustical engineer should be consulted when dealing with absorption and reflection qualities of all surfaces within a facility.

Acoustical treatments must both enhance sound so that we can hear easily, and absorb sound. Background noise, basically unwanted sound that originates either in the teaching station itself or intrudes from another area, must be controlled. Internal background noise might consist of "squeaking" chairs sliding on a floor, reverberation or "echoing" of sound, and reflective sound. All sound travels spherically. When a space is to be acoustically treated, walls, ceilings, floors, and other surfaces within that space must be considered for appropriate materials.

Internal Treatments

There are four common modes of internal acoustical treatment of spaces. The use of walls and other barriers is one method of controlling sound. Air space itself is an acoustical treatment. The larger the space, and therefore the farther sound travels, the more it is absorbed. The use of soft acoustical materials on various surfaces is a major means of sound control. Acoustical clouds suspended over large open arenas are yet another means of controlling sound. Extending walls beyond dropped ceilings can afford better acoustical control than stopping internal walls at the dropped ceiling height.

External Treatments

External background noise or unwanted sound from outside the teaching space also must be planned for acoustically. Unwanted sound or noise may be transmitted into the room by means of ventilating ducts, pipes, and spaces around pipe sleeves. The transmission of sound through ducts can be reduced by the use of baffles, or by lining the ducts with sound-absorbent, fire-resistant materials. The ducts also may be connected with canvas or rubberized material to interrupt the transmission through the metal in the ducts. Pipes can be covered with pipe covering, and spaces in the pipe sleeves can be filled.

Sound also can be transmitted through the walls, floors, and ceilings. This can be reduced to a desirable minimum by the proper structural design and materials. In conventional wall construction, alternate studs can support the sides of the wall in such a manner that there is no through connection from one wall surface to another. This sometimes is known as double-wall construction. The space inside the walls can be filled with sound-absorbing material to further decrease sound transmission. Sometimes three or four inches of sand inside the walls at the baseboard will cut down the transmission appreciably. Likewise, sound absorption blankets laid over the partitions in suspended ceiling construction frequently can reduce the sound from one room to another.

Machinery vibration or impact sounds can be reduced by use of the proper floor covering and/or by installing the machinery on floating or resilient mountings. "Sound locks," such as double walls or doors, are needed between noisy areas and adjoining quiet areas. Improper location of doors and windows can create noise problems. It is imperative to consider the location of the facility itself and also to consider the placement of internal areas of the facility for sound control. Placing physical education and sports facilities in a semi-isolated area of a school helps control acoustics. This same theory needs to be applied internally within the sports facility. The placement of "noisy" areas such as weight-training areas, aerobic areas, locker rooms, swimming pools, gymnasiums, and spectator areas must be planned for in relation to quiet areas such as classrooms and offices. It is not good acoustical planning to have a weight room above or next to a classroom. Care must be taken in the maintenance of acoustical materials. Oil-based paint reduces the sound-absorbent qualities of most materials. Surface treatment for different acoustical materials will vary. The most common treatment of acoustical-fiber tile is a light brush coat of water-based paint, but most acoustical materials lose their efficiency after several applications of paint.

Exterior Treatments

Sometimes the exterior of a space or building must be acoustically treated. If a gym is located on the landing flight path of a local airport, or if it is located next to a fairly steep grade on a major truck thoroughfare, exterior acoustical treatment might be needed. Utilize the same acoustical principles as inside, with an exterior twist. Keep hard surfaces such as paved areas and parking lots to a minimum. Use shrubbery, trees, and grass wherever possible. Walls, solid fences, berms, and water are all good exterior acoustical items. It is important to plan for acoustics and sound control in a variety of ways. Think spherical, think internal, think external, and think exterior in order to best acoustically treat a facility.

Whitney and Foulkes indicated that "Many acoustical problems can be avoided from the start if sound transmission concepts are kept in mind at the initial planning stage of a recreational facility. Keeping noisy spaces separated from quiet areas is easy to achieve in the initial design phase; correcting problems due to improper space adjacencies is more difficult. Even the best sound-isolating construction techniques cannot completely solve the problems created by improper adjacencies. The final results will always be more acceptable if serious acoustical issues are solved in the schematic design" (1994, p. 58).

Other Electronic Technologies

Electronic Communication

The standard communication tools in sports and recreation facilities include an intercom system and two-way audio systems to various activity and office spaces. Additionally, telecommunication has advanced tremendously, allowing for the integration of telecommunications devices for the deaf (TDDs), text typewriters (TTS) or teletypewriters (TTYs), and faxing capabilities to standard telephone installations.

Audio and visual communication needs for the 21st century require many facilities to be integrated for computerization and satellite/cable television reception. Any space that might utilize a computer or video connection should be part of this integration. Fiber optics is the current standard for such integration. However, a thorough planning process will also consider future technologies. Minimally, appropriate conduits should be installed during facility construction to afford the broadest range of future choices.

Within spaces, especially those used for instruction, the planning process should also consider the electronic technologies required for distance education, such as two-way audio and visual communication tools (I see you—you see me, I hear you—you hear me), computer links for internet and computer presentation, conference-call telephones, digital and laser disc players, LCD overhead projectors, keypads for student responses, and so forth.

Scoreboards and Electronic Timing Systems

The science and technology of scoreboard design has changed the entire sports spectator experience. A scoreboard not only provides spectators with game data, but it can be configured with a giant video screen and message system and integrated with the facility's sound system (Bradley, 1994). Large indoor sports arenas are using giant four-sided scoreboards that literally pay for themselves with sponsor advertisement. If timing is your need, recent advances in video systems allow sports races to be judged fairly, regardless of the hundredths of seconds between finish times or the failure of conventional timing equipment (Goldman, 1995).

Elevators and Other Hydraulic Lifts

Elevators and other hydraulic lifts are necessary design features of many sports and recreational facilities. Besides offering users with disabilities federally mandated access to facilities, they enhance the ability of staff to move equipment (possibly reducing the potential for worker-related injury), and they facilitate deliveries. To determine if your facility is required to provide elevators and/or hydraulic lifts, refer to Chapter 14, Designing for Inclusion.

Security

Effective facility security begins with building designs that control access to the facility through a main-desk control area and egress-only doors that do not allow re-entry. A number of electronic technologies can further affect the security of a facility, including:

- Entrance/exit (access/egress) controls and alarms such as card systems; electronically controlled doors and gates, check points with metal detectors (magnetometers), and annunciators (egress door alarms). Card access can also be used to gather enlightening and useful data on the facility's clientele (Patton, 1997, p. 64).
- Closed-circuit television monitor systems
- Motion-sensor alarms for controlled areas such as pools (sensor detects water motion).

It is important to remember that as electronic technology is applied to security, any power failure will disrupt such systems unless they are backed up by battery or emergency generator systems.

Emergency Alarms

Facility safety begins with smoke and fire and emergency alarm systems that appropriately warn building users in the event of fire and warn facility staff in the event of a life-threatening emergency. Smoke and fire alarms include those that are user-activated, smoke- or heat-activated, and water pressure-activated (usually found in wet sprinkler systems). Special alarms for the pool or other exercise area have been designed to notify facility staff in the event of a life-threatening emergency; these are staff activated. Weather or disaster notification will usually utilize an existing intercom system to warn facility users. Emergency alarms, especially those that are designed to warn users, must also be backed up by battery or emergency generator systems.

Emergency Generators

With an increasing reliance upon some of the above electronic technologies and/or the use of air-supported roofs for indoor sports spaces, power outages will require an emergency generator back-up to ensure the safety of facility users and the well-being of the facility. These generators need only provide minimum levels of power (to be determined by the specifications of the facility) to be effective tools. However, where electric energy is at a premium, it is possible that some sports or recreational facilities will plan on a bank of generators to provide unrestricted energy service.

Trends in Electronic Technologies

Illuminated game lines on sports courts and underwater pace lights in swimming pools are two of the more innovative uses of electronic technology. And, with laser technology, it is only a matter of time before distances in field events are determined using a laser rather than a tape measure.

Web-to-telephone calling combines the convenience of IP telephony (IP telephony is the use of an IP network to transmit voice, video, and data) with the flexibility of traditional calling. The Web-to-phone interface works via a Web browser plug-in that can be downloaded from a Web site. There is no software to buy. Once call center components are in place, people browsing a company's Web page can use the Web-to-phone plug-in to speak over the Internet directly with someone (Dresner, 1998, p. 42).

Finally, Cable Microcell Integrators (CMIs) are in the news, turning terrestrial television cable systems into communications networks for overcrowded cellular systems. A unique characteristic of CMI technology is the independence of signal coverage from the number of base transceiver stations. In other words, service providers need not build excess capacity to handle occasional, but regular, surges in demand. "Fans and reporters who clog a professional football stadium eight Sundays out of the year might require an additional cell tower/base station to use their telephones, but a CMI system can handle this demand surge without an additional physical plant" (Ackerman, 1997, p. 21). Facility planners may well consider checking with area wireless communication companies to see if a CMI installation is appropriate for their facility. It is fair to say that as technology continues to develop in the 21st century, new ideas will result in wonderful advances.

Basic Considerations in HVAC

Sports and recreational buildings incorporate a wide variety of HVAC systems. The principal goal of an energy management program is to maximize the efficiency of all systems. Efficiency is a term that describes the relationship between energy input and usable energy output (ASHRAE, 1994).

Air-Handling Systems

Air-handling systems consist of air-handling units and distribution equipment such as ductwork, dampers, and air diffusers. The typical air-handling unit refers to a ventilation device that, when installed in a building, may serve a number of purposes. The system should be providing an airflow with adequate pressure and speed to reach all areas served by the unit; filtering and conditioning the air with cooling, heating, and dehumidification processes; and mixing a measured quantity of fresh air with recirculated air. A typical air-handling unit may contain some or all of the following components: fan(s), filters; heating, cooling, and dehumidification coils; humidifier; dampers to control the direction of the airflow and the mixing of outside and recirculated air; and control devices to regulate temperature and humidity of the airflow.

Conditioning the Air

Conditioning of the incoming air is generally limited to dehumidification and heating. A room thermostat generally controls the amount of heat required to maintain room comfort. Desiccant systems and heat pipes dry air far more efficiently than causing condensation by super-cooling air. Using a desiccant dehumidifier dries air without cooling it, causing the water to absorb to the surface of the desiccant. The desiccant is recharged using either waste heat from the boiler, from a solar collector, or with gas heat that is returned to the space.

The components of an air-exhaust system include an exhaust fan, ductwork and grilles, and hoods to capture contaminated air as close as possible to the source. In addition, most exhaust systems incorporate a series of controls to regulate the operation of the fan and its accessories, such as a motorized damper. Energy management action for exhaust systems will depend in part on the area being exhausted. Fans that exhaust air from locker rooms normally need to operate continuously, especially when athletic equipment needs dried. If this is not the case, then these exhaust fans can be run only when the rooms are occupied.

Heat recovery potential is present in most air-handling systems. However, the use of the recovered heat by a system must be economically justifiable. Return of the recovered heat to the process from which it came should be the first priority, since such systems usually require less control and are less expensive to install.

The hot water-heating plant of a building incorporates a number of components that individually are responsible for some form of heat transfer and therefore have their own particular efficiency. Heating systems are made up of three principal components: supply equipment (e.g., boiler); distribution equipment (e.g., supply and return piping); and end-use equipment (e.g., heaters and associated controls). Boiler efficiency is indicated directly from temperature and composition of flue gases. The latter indicates the air/fuel ratio at the burner, which is the most important parameter affecting combustion efficiency. Maintaining boiler water quality is essential to maintaining high system efficiency. In the generation of steam in a boiler, certain impurities (solids) in the water must be purged from the system on a continual basis via an adjustable blow-down valve. Proper adjustment of the blow-down valve must be maintained at all times. Furthermore, ensuring the regular maintenance of distribution piping can minimize energy losses in the heating system. Regular maintenance includes an inventory of the system components and documentation of their condition.

End-use equipment in heating systems includes steam and hot water radiators, and heating coils in ventilation units. Conditions that result in excessive energy use in these components include valves that leak or are stuck open and faulty controls. These conditions are often associated with comfort problems in the space that is heated. Proper maintenance will avoid excessive energy use by end-use equipment.

Air Conditioning

All air-conditioning equipment requires regular, planned maintenance to ensure energy-efficient operation. Cooling system maintenance should include periodic inspection of cooling coils (chilled water or direct expansion) for icing or dirt accumulation on the coil. Both will reduce heat transfer rates, reduce airflow to the space, make it difficult to maintain comfort, and waste energy. Cooling system valves and controls should also be inspected periodically to ensure efficient system operation.

Ventilation Systems

Ventilation systems can be large energy users and energy wasters—both directly and indirectly (Energy Ideas, Nov. 92). Energy is used directly in operating fans. Indirect energy use takes place in heating or cooling and dehumidifying the fresh air brought in from outside. Damper condition should be checked periodically, because damper efficiency and general condition are directly affected by frequency of use. A damper assembly generally controls the damper unit. A motor mounted at one end of the assembly will control damper positioning. The damper controls how much air is brought in from the outside.

Filter Maintenance

Filter maintenance is another factor that is important in ensuring the energy-efficient operation of air-handling systems. Filter replacement or cleaning should occur on a regular basis according to the rate of the dirt buildup. Clogging of filters does not increase energy use directly. However, a pressure drop increase across a filter, due to dirt buildup, will result in an airflow reduction and fan power increase. The system cannot operate efficiently with dirty filters.

Other Considerations

Other operating and maintenance energy considerations are:

- Dehumidifier Maintenance—Improperly maintained dehumidifiers can increase energy use by maintaining a humidity level higher than required.
- Water Treatment of HVAC Systems—An effective water treatment program should maintain a clean system, free of any hard-water deposits or any corrosion products. A water distribution system that is fouled with deposits has a much lower rate of heat exchange and will reduce the energy efficiency of the entire distribution system.
- Cooling Tower Condenser Water—The most expensive part of an HVAC system to treat is the condenser cooling tower system. A cooling tower has high water losses due to evaporative cooling and requires water make-up to prevent water deposits from forming on the condenser tubes of the chiller. Proper water treatment procedures require the use of water scale control chemicals and corrosion inhibitors.
- Domestic Hot Water Systems—Domestic hot water temperatures should be closely monitored to reduce excessive scaling. Systems can be flushed and de-scaled at regularly scheduled intervals to improve heat transfer at the heat exchanger.

Environmental Climate Control

Environmental climate controls related to HVAC affect the quality of our work and play environments. Sports and recreational facilities, specifically, must provide an environment where fresh air is exchanged and effectively circulated, where air temperature and humidity are controlled in a manner that promotes good health, and where the air quality is safe.

There are four factors that, when combined, give an optimal thermal environment:

- radiant temperature where surface and air temperatures are balanced
- air temperature between 64° and 72°F
- humidity between 40 and 60%
- constant air movement of 20 to 40 linear feet per minute at a sitting height

These factors must all be considered to achieve an optimal thermal environment. However, they are only part of the planning that must go into providing indoor environments that are technically sophisticated and also enhance user effectiveness, communication, and overall user satisfaction—the best definition of an "intelligent building" (Tarricone, 1995). Intelligent buildings link such technologies as "HVAC, fire detection and alarm, access, security, elevator, and communication systems to one computer . . ." (Tarricone, 1995). Although this section deals specifically with HVAC, it is important to consider the advantages of creating the intelligent building with a single computer control. This concept has been implemented in both new designs and retrofits. The key is planning ahead.

Additionally, a number of building design characteristics directly impact the optimal thermal environment in buildings. These interior and exterior characteristics include:

- building envelopes that reduce heat loss and gain through insulation, barriers and thermal mass
- moisture control through vapor barriers and external shading devices
- properly glazed windows that have good insulating and glare reduction properties
- double- or triple-paned glazed windows that prevent condensation on windows
- adequately sized [facilities], ventilated, cooled, and designed for easy access, future growth, and reconfiguration; and passive heating, cooling, and lighting methods (Myers, 1997, p. 52)

And when considering building automation and HVAC systems, there are additional choices to make, including:

- centralized or decentralized HVAC systems; heating systems (such as boilers) and cooling systems (such as chillers and cooling towers); ventilation systems; substation sensing; humidification and dehumidification control; facility energy management programs such as Night Cycle, Night Purge . . . (Myers, 1997, p. 53)

All of this does not negate the need for design planning that includes the choice of heat or energy source: fossil fuels (coal and heating oil), and heat or energy alternatives (propane/natural gas, wood, electricity, below grade heat pumps, and solar or wind energy). Factors in these choices include geographic location and heat and energy resource availability. Additionally, the start-up or installation costs of some systems are more expensive, but cost less to operate and/or maintain over the long term, and viceversa for installation of other systems. If the facility is located in a rural area with clean extended air, make sure windows can be opened (double hung, slider, hopper, awning, or casement). In polluted environments such as urban areas, single hung windows are acceptable.

Propane/natural gas, solar, wind, heat pump, and nuclear power are all considered "clean" sources of heat or energy and are worth thinking about, considering the depletion of ozone in our atmosphere from the use of fossil fuels. These sources of heat or energy may ultimately reduce operating costs, including the "scrubbing" of exhausted air from your building. Finally, the actual selection and type of HVAC should consider the economy of operation, flexibility of control, quietness of operation, and capacity to provide desirable thermal conditions.

Air Quality

Facility ventilation is directly tied to the indoor air quality (IAQ). The IAQ is a product of the quality of the fresh air introduced into the ventilation system and the quality of the existing indoor air that is recycled.

Typically, HVAC systems recirculate as much conditioned air (warm or cooled) as is allowed by health and building codes in order to maximize energy efficiency and reduce the size of mechanical and electrical equipment. In facilities where health and indoor air-quality issues are paramount (or in facilities where no energy-recovery system exists) as much as 100% of the conditioned air may be exhausted. Such facilities in climates with significant indoor/outdoor temperature differentials in winter and summer can exhaust otherwise reclaimable energy.

Energy recovery in HVAC systems involves transferring heat from one air stream to another. In summer months, intake air at a higher temperature rejects heat to cooler exhaust air prior to being mechanically cooled by the chilled-water or direct-expansion coil (of the air-conditioning process). Conversely, during the winter, intake air is warmed by transferring heat from exhaust air. Approximately 60% to 65% of the available sensible heat may be recovered; latent heat is not recovered (Fabel, 1996, p. 36).

The air-quality issue in sports and recreational buildings has developed into a significant concern for today's building owners and operators. The public now has greater awareness of health-related concerns, and there is increased research documenting these issues. On the other hand, heating and cooling systems that use excess fresh air also require more energy. To compound this problem, there is no single, accurate method of measuring air quality, and solutions to air-quality problems tend to be building- and site-specific. The challenge for building managers is to find the optimum levels of fresh air to maintain comfort conditions. Good air quality and energy conservation should be complementary. One should not be achieved at the expense of the other.

Air quality is an evolving issue. Standards and guidelines for air quality in buildings have developed along with an evolving understanding of human requirements for fresh air to support health and of the major air-related contaminants and their effects. The American Society of Heating Refrigerating and Air-Conditioning Engineers, Inc. (ASHRAE) was one of the first organizations to establish guidelines for air quality. ASHRAE's research has led to the publication of minimum ventilation rates to maintain the indoor environment within a key range of guidelines.

Air quality is a complex issue that affects occupant comfort, health, productivity, and acceptance of energy conservation measures. Modern building materials contain many new chemicals that can give off gases or vapors such as formaldehyde and radon. Other organic and inorganic chemicals are introduced to recreation buildings through paints, solvents, and photocopiers. Allergens from airborne particles and dust are also present in these environments.

HVAC designers and building managers in existing buildings have reduced outside air ventilation rates to lower levels in keeping with energy conservation guidelines. Moreover, outside air quality has generally deteriorated in our major cities due to pollution from industrial plants, automobiles, and other combustion-type processes.

Variable air-volume systems used in many large spectator facilities often have decreased air-circulation rates compared to conventional constant-volume systems. Air-circulation rates affect the purging of local contaminants such as cigarette smoke and heat from the activity and spectator areas. Many older buildings are undergoing major retrofits to HVAC systems to reduce energy costs. Fans are being modified and generally operated for fewer hours each day. New control strategies call for the conversion from outside air systems to recirculation-type systems with less outside air delivered to the space. This is especially helpful in settings where the outside air is of poor quality.

In older or poorly designed HVAC systems that merely recirculate conditioned air without exhausting enough air and/or introducing enough fresh air, the IAQ can become compromised. Indoor air quality can be managed, even in older systems, if a proactive approach is used to address the IAQ issues. This includes controlling pollution at its source, from both indoor and outdoor sources.

One low-cost way to prevent IAQ problems is to stop potential sources of indoor air pollution where they originate. Known as source control, this process manages pollutants by removing them from the building, isolating them from people by using physical barriers, and controlling when they are used (Anonymous, 1998, p. A10).

The National Institute of Health (NIH) and ASHRAE have been busy funding research related to IAQ and controlling pollutants at the source. Specifically, the NIH recently funded a study of the

CREON2000™ Disinfection Unit. The CREON2000™ uses ultraviolet light to destroy harmful microbes causing allergy, asthma, and illness. Another such disinfecting unit, designed to be placed directly into building ventilation systems, is the Sanuvox™ UV Air Purifier. In one documented application, the Sanuvox™ UV Air Purifier reduced air contaminants by 66% in a southern California classroom. In this case the UV unit picked up where vacuuming, HVAC maintenance and fresh-air ventilation left off, stripping contaminants in the air such as mold spores, bacteria, mildew, formaldehyde, solvents and viruses (Author, 2003).

In 2003 ASHRAE approved funding for eight research projects in the areas of indoor air quality, comfort and health, energy conservation, operating and maintenance tools, and environmentally safe materials and design tools (ASHRAE, 2003).

Generally, comfort is perceived when physical, chemical, and biological stresses are at a minimum. Quality of air and the perception of air quality can be quite different. The major components influencing each are common and are listed below.

- physical—physical contaminants in the air
- chemical—chemical contaminants in the air
- biological—biological contaminants in the air
- thermal factors—air temperature and relative humidity, air velocity

Physical Contaminants

Some of the major physical contaminants are listed below.

Contaminant	Source
Dust particles	Outdoor air
Tobacco smoke (particulates & vapor)	Cigarettes
Asbestos fibers	Asbestos building products
Metallic dust	Building materials
Wood particles	Building materials

The particles of smoke, dust, pollen, and other physical contaminants enter the indoor environment either from outside by infiltration or from activities and processes in the building. The amount of material entering the building from outdoors will depend on the wind velocity and the amount of infiltration. Particles can be generated indoors by smoking, other indoor combustion processes, and existing building materials.

Chemical Contaminants

A number of chemical contaminants can be found in the indoor air of a typical sport or recreation building. These include the products of combustion, namely, carbon monoxide (CO), carbon dioxide (CO_2), oxides of nitrogen (NO_x), and sulphur dioxide (SO_2). These chemicals, in some concentrations, can be found in the indoor air whenever a combustion source is within the building. Ice resurfacers and edgers in ice arenas, carpet cleaning, and forklifts on indoor soccer and field houses, and vacuum systems for cleaning seating capacity venues can contaminate the air with carbon monoxide and nitrogen dioxide fumes. Ozone concentrations can increase due to photocopiers and other sources, such as aerosol spray cans. Cleaning agents can give off toxic fumes. Building materials such as paints and particleboards can add to formaldehyde and other hydrocarbon concentrations.

Biological Contaminants

Biological contaminants are microorganisms that can spread through a facility and be inhaled. Constant temperature levels between 60 and 120 degrees in stagnant pools of water provide ideal conditions for the growth of microorganisms. These conditions are found in humidifiers, dehumidifiers, and cooling towers, where there is sufficient moisture and appropriate temperature for the growth of bacteria algae and microorganisms. Examples of bacteria-related building epidemics, such as Legionnaires' disease and humidifier fever, have been cited in literature on air quality.

Finding the best solution to an air-quality problem in a specific facility requires knowledge of the building and its mechanical systems as well as its environment and occupancy conditions. As detailed earlier, the design and construction of the building envelope will determine the infiltration rate, that is the rate of uncontrolled air leakage into the building. In some buildings, infiltration is depended on as a source of supply for makeup air to replace air removed by exhaust appliances. Any change to the air tightness of the envelope will affect the infiltration rate and the amount of fresh air available to the building.

Thermal Factors

Thermal factors affect air quality in two ways. The human perception of air-quality control is related to factors such as air temperature, as well as the actual composition of the air. For example, too high a temperature or lack of air movement may create a sensation of "stuffiness." Secondly, the thermal characteristics of the air will affect the actions of contaminants in the environment. For example, excessive humidity will promote the growth of microorganisms. A thermally acceptable environment will minimize physical stress. Thermal comfort depends on the factors that follow.

- Air temperature—The temperature set by building operation can vary considerably due to temperature stratification within the space, and such variations can affect occupant comfort.
- Air velocity—Air-distribution systems may create the sensation of drafts or conversely of "stuffiness."
- Relative humidity—Relative humidity expressed as a percentage varies in the range of 20% to 80% for most buildings. Relative humidity below 20% will result in discomfort for some people.
- Static electricity—Static buildup can also occur with low relative humidity. Testing has shown that most people link dryness or perception of humidity level to air temperature.

Air-Quality Checklist

There is no single method for improving indoor air quality. A general checklist follows that will serve as a reference for air-quality troubleshooting. As a first step, it is always useful to check air temperatures and comfort criteria in problem areas.

Exhaust Re-intake
- Check for recirculation of exhaust air into outside air intake.
- Check outside air intakes at ground level to ensure automobile exhaust or other contaminants are not introduced into outside air intake. Since many sports teams travel by bus, it is important to park the buses away from the facility. Motor fumes can be easily sucked into the building by the air-handling systems.
- Check exhaust air systems to ensure toilet exhaust is not recirculated to return to air systems.

Avoid Exhaust Air Opening Near Outside Air Intakes
- Check proximity of cooling tower to outside air intake. Ensure biological water treatment of cooling tower, especially in summer months.
- Avoid having stagnant pools of water on roof or near outside air intakes.
- Check humidifier pans and sprayed cooling coils for biological contaminants or growths.

Ensure Proper Water Treatment of Spray Systems
- Check fan coil units for stagnant water in drip pans. Ensure drip pans drain properly.
- Check flooded carpet areas for biological contamination. Change carpet in contaminated areas.
- Check fan rooms for solvents and other chemicals to ensure chemical contamination is not spread by the air-handling system.
- Check chemicals used for rug cleaning and review concentration of cleaning agents used on rugs and floors.

Exhaust at Source
- Check for exhaust from high humidity locations, smoking rooms, kitchens, photocopy rooms, and other process applications.

Dilution
- Check minimum outside air setting and calibrate for normal occupancy.
- Check ambient air concentrations for CO_2 and other contaminants.
- Adjust fan hours of operation and schedule to suit occupancy.
- Check supply air distribution patterns to ensure adequate flushing of occupied space.
- Check for vertical temperature stratification as evidence of poor air distribution.

Planning for the Future

When planning for the future, an essential component leading to quality HVAC is the integrity of the building envelope. Integrity in a building envelope is accomplished when the designer creates a space that is protected from the outdoor elements and is free of challenges, such as roof leaks, moisture that seeps in through the walls or up through the floors, and so on. The integrity of the building envelope is then further guaranteed when building materials are used that will ensure the space's envelope will not be breached. Because facilities are generally intended to last for many years, the envelope materials should be capable of withstanding the stresses of time and/or be readily maintainable/replaceable when needed.

Experience with sick building syndrome is establishing poor envelope design, poor materials, and/or improper maintenance as the leading causes for poor IAQ. An elementary school in Saco, Maine, was recently deemed useless because of mold. Clearly, over time, this building's envelope failed to keep out moisture and undetected mold began to grow in parts of the building. Only after a period of time, when staff and students began to get sick, was the mold established as the cause of the illnesses. And, there was no doubt that the flat roof design and perhaps unforeseen/unattended maintenance issues allowed the envelope component of the building to fail!

Jim Moravek (1996) has further challenged future decision-making with the concept that technologies no longer outlast buildings:

> Designing for flexibility in buildings rather than for specific technologies is the best way to overcome obsolescence of the structure in the future. Buildings often outlast the most current technologies, and new consideration must be given to making buildings and technologies work together. Flexible design has both structural and system components. Buildings require ample space—both vertically and horizontally—so old systems can be removed and new systems installed quickly, without affecting structure, exits, or life-safety systems. Heating, ventilating, and air-conditioning (HVAC) and power-distribution systems need the capacity to service existing loads and the ability to respond to future requirements (p. 28).

However, no project can be considered without planning for HVAC. And this planning should be done by an engineering professional and based upon the technical data and procedures of ASHRAE and appropriate federal regulations.

An example of an ASHRAE standard appears in Appendix L. This standard and others are in constant review by the ASHRAE based upon various changes in technologies and government regulations. The ASHRAE also issues position statements, such as the Indoor Air Quality Position Statement (approved by ASHRAE Board of Directors, February 2, 1989). This ASHRAE document states the importance of indoor air quality and energy conservation and its impacts, with the belief that "indoor air quality should be maintained at levels expected to protect occupants from adverse effects and discomfort" (p. 1).

Challenges and Future Trends in HVAC

Sick building syndrome is the result of poor indoor air quality. The basics of IAQ seem to minimally require that potential indoor pollutants are controlled at the source and that the building's HVAC system—including all the equipment used to ventilate, heat and cool; the ductwork to deliver air; and the filters to clear air—are well maintained (Anonymous, 1998).

The challenge of HVAC is clearly to increase energy savings without compromising indoor air quality. Future trends in HVAC involve continued research in evaporation cooling and the compliance with ever-changing federal and ASHRAE standards.

Mechanical and Electrical Summary

The technologies of mechanical and electrical engineering are constantly changing. However, facility planners should become familiar with concepts related to the function of HVAC, sound, and lighting. Each of these technologies has professional organizations that support ongoing research and publish commercial and consumer information online. Before facility planners make the final decision to accept a solution and purchase and install equipment; they need to do their homework and seek out the best solutions for their situations.

Basic Considerations in Energy Management

Over the last decade, energy management has moved from being a one-time activity to an ongoing and essential part of facility planning and management. Furthermore, energy management has become a widely known applied science with new measures, technologies, and analytic approaches. The importance of energy management to facility planning cannot be overemphasized, especially in sports and recreation facilities that consume large amounts of energy.

The long-range forecasts for the world's energy supplies and prices indicate that it is wise to design systems to reduce consumption of energy during periods of shortage and rapidly escalating prices. New technologies and improved heating and air conditioning equipment show that further savings are possible, even during periods of lower fuel prices.

Next to staffing, utilities normally are the second-highest cost of operating sports and recreational facilities. This section will provide an overview of energy management and outline specific aspects of energy management in the building envelope; building operations and maintenance; heating, cooling, and air-handling systems. We will look at how domestic hot water and air quality affect energy consumption and the impact that lighting and building automation systems have on energy management opportunities. Energy management will be addressed, looking at planning and construction issues as well as maintenance and operating criteria. Finally, the chapter provides reference sources and Web sources for the further study of energy management.

In the planning and construction process for sports and recreation facilities, whether for a new building, a building addition, or major renovation, there are thousands of issues that must be resolved by the owner, the architect, and the construction contractors. Many of these issues deal with design, selection and integration of facilities energy systems (the HVAC systems, lighting, and other energy-consuming equipment). Oftentimes, these issues get very little attention in the design process and end up being serious and costly mistakes, because over the life of the facility, the energy costs will exceed the initial cost of all the energy systems.

Because many of these issues are quite technical and involve parts of the facility no one usually sees, energy questions may be mishandled in the design process. This results from design professionals designing the building envelope, HVAC, lighting, and other energy-consuming systems independently and, to protect themselves from liability or complaints, typically over-engineering these systems. Energy-efficient buildings should be designed by an integrated design approach in which all of the design professionals work together with energy efficiency as one of their goals.

A second reason energy issues are mishandled in design is the fact that almost everyone makes decisions on the basis of initial cost or first cost rather than on life cycle costs that take into account the initial cost and all of the costs associated with operating and maintaining the facility during its useful life. The most cost-effective time to incorporate energy efficiency into a sports and recreational facility is during construction, when the energy savings need only pay back the incremental cost difference between a "regular" system and a more efficient one. Unless the design team evaluates alternative options on a life cycle cost basis, sound decisions cannot be made.

Energy Management as a Process

Initially, energy management was viewed as a one-time application of conservation principles to the building envelope and mechanical systems. Experience has shown that greater savings may be obtained and sustained when energy management is considered to be an ongoing process. It is a process that involves a number of key elements such as:

- an assessment of the building and its operating systems
- a list of appropriate energy conservation measures based on the assessment
- careful, planned implementation
- regular review of actual energy savings

Once started, energy management is an ongoing process that is integrated with building maintenance and operation and with any changes in building occupancy, envelope, or mechanical equipment. Sports and recreation facilities have major changes in occupancy loads during varying periods of the day and seasons of the year, and understanding these impacts on the mechanical system is a critical step to designing systems. Moreover, these facilities are normally large spaces with big building envelopes containing glass entrances and large roofing structures. Under normal circumstances, these characteristics do not lend themselves to being energy efficient.

Energy management as a process also recognizes that buildings are not static. Occupancy changes can affect internal space allocations and patterns of building use, which affect the demands on and performance of mechanical systems. Occupancy codes require a certain number of air changes per hour to satisfy the fresh air needs of the participants as well as the spectators. These requirements directly affect the HVAC systems.

The three major steps involved in energy management are: conduct an energy audit and analysis, implementation of a strategy, and monitoring of the results.

Energy Audit and Analysis

While a simple walk-through audit will often reveal many opportunities for savings, it is recommended that a full energy audit be undertaken. This will serve as the foundation of the implementation program and as a reference point for partial studies that may be required in future years owing to major changes in building occupancy, envelope, or mechanical systems.

A full energy audit is a complete assessment of the building and its energy use patterns. The physical characteristics of the building shell (e.g., walls, windows and doors, roof, floor, etc.) and the various electrical and mechanical systems (e.g., HVAC equipment, lights, water heaters, etc.) are inspected (Energy Ideas, Feb. 93). Utility bills are reviewed to determine actual energy use. If possible, energy use is allocated to each building system separately.

The energy audit also provides the necessary information for designing an implementation program. A list of energy conservation measures is developed based on the energy analysis and target energy use. The list is usually divided into no-cost housekeeping measures, low-cost maintenance, and upgrading and major retrofit or upgrading projects involving considerable capital expenditure. Capital costs and estimated savings for each measure are summarized in the energy audit report. With the deregulation of electricity, there are numerous energy audit companies available to work with sports and recreation professionals to design conservation plans for facilities.

Implementation of Strategy

In addition to the building information and recommended measures from the building energy audit, many other practical concerns should be considered in the development of the implementation plan. These include: existing maintenance program for envelope and mechanical system, existing repair and upgrading program for envelope and mechanical system, projected plans for changes in building occupancy, projected plans for major repairs or renovations; available funds, and available staff resources for implementation and program management.

Implementation of specific energy management measures will proceed according to the implementation program. Some key steps in the program are: allocating of capital funds and staff resources, obtaining estimates and selecting consultants for measures that require professional assistance, assigning a project manager or energy manager responsibility for program implementation and monitoring results, and selecting contractors and/or internal staff to implement measures.

Monitoring of Results

Monitoring an energy management program is essential in order to measure results and to steer the program with progressive feedback. The simplest monitoring technique involves reviewing energy bills on a monthly and annual basis and comparing them to a previous reference year. However, a more complete monitoring program will include keeping records of factors that affect energy usage. A sample list of the components of a complete monitoring program is noted below:

- measuring energy/usage and costs
- logging building system performance through indicators such as supply air temperature and boiler efficiency
- logging weather conditions
- recording any additions or modifications to the building, patterns of building occupancy and use, and occupant comments on comfort
- recording any changes in occupancy patterns and use
- recording energy management measures as they are implemented
- logging maintenance of building equipment and systems

Energy Accounting

Energy accounting is defined as the systematic tracking and analysis of energy costs and consumption in order to better manage and control energy in buildings (Energy Ideas, Feb 93). In energy accounting, the information gathered through monitoring is used to report on the progress of the energy management program. It involves determining where, how much, and why energy is used.

Many factors affect building energy use. These include: weather conditions at the building site; design, quality, and condition of the building envelope; insulation value of walls and roof; number and size of windows; quality and type of windows; air leakage around windows, doors, and other openings; building mechanical systems; HVAC systems and their operation; process activities inside the building such as lighting, hot water and appliances; maintenance of building equipment and systems; efficiency of systems and components; and patterns of building occupancy and use.

A good energy accounting system can provide tangible benefits that pay for the cost of the system many times over (Goldberger & Jessop, 1994). Some of the most attractive benefits include: verifies monthly invoices, pinpoints problem areas, helps manage budgets, monitors energy management programs, justifies energy conservation investments, provides reports to senior management, and provides financing options for energy.

Energy management programs can be financed using a number of options:

- Operating Funds—Many low-cost/no-cost measures can be funded from existing operating budgets. Energy is an operating expenditure, and energy cost savings can be used to purchase energy retrofits.
- Capital Budgets—Energy management retrofit programs can be funded from capital budgets.
- Leases—Leases can be used to purchase energy management equipment. Lease payments can be designed to be less than the projected energy cost savings.
- Energy Service Agreement—An energy service agreement is a performance contract in which a private company offers to execute efficiency capital improvements in exchange for a portion of the energy cost savings that accrue. Typically, a company enters into a long-term contract and, at its expense, designs, installs, and manages or co-manages an energy efficiency system for the facility.

It is important to evaluate the cost and payback period for each measure as it relates to a particular building. What may be a low-cost measure for a large sports facility would represent a substantial investment for a smaller recreation operation. Each situation has to be looked at separately.

Building Envelope

The building envelope consists of the roof, floor, walls, windows, and doors—all parts of the building that enclose the interior building space and separate it from the outdoor climate. The envelope performs several functions. It provides shelter from the elements, lighting (windows), and in some cases, air changes through natural ventilation (windows), and infiltration. The envelope's success in performing these functions is dependent on the building design, quality of construction, and maintenance of the envelope components.

A building's shape and size will greatly affect its heating and cooling loads. Compact facilities generally require less energy than large seating capacity sports venues that ramble and sprawl all over the site. Proper choice of architectural form and orientation can often reduce energy cost. Large sports facilities should respect the path of the sun and be oriented east–west to minimize solar gain in the summer and maximize solar gain in the winter. Reduced air infiltration and proper analysis for optimum insulation is also critical to study early in the design process.

The role of the mechanical systems and purchased energy is to make up the difference between that which the envelope can provide in occupant comfort and what is required (Energy Ideas, Oct 92). The quality of the envelope, then, is a major factor in determining energy used for heating, cooling, lighting, and ventilation. Improvements to the envelope can significantly reduce energy demand.

Uncontrolled air leakage through the building envelope is often associated with moisture damage to building components. An added benefit of energy management attention to the envelope is the resolution and prevention of problems affecting the service life of envelope components. It is important to understand the causes of heat loss through the building envelope and to understand the strategies for upgrading the thermal performance of the building envelope.

Energy to heat interior spaces (in winter) or to cool interior spaces (in summer) is lost through heat transfer and infiltration/exfiltration. Heat transfer refers to the movement of heat through walls, windows, doors, roof, or floors whenever there is a difference between the exterior temperature and the interior temperature. Heat transfer occurs through three natural processes: convection, conduction, and radiation.

Convection is the transfer of heat by the movement of a fluid such as air. For example, cool air moving over a warmer surface picks up heat, carries it, and transfers it to a cooler surface. *Conduction* is the transfer of heat directly through a solid (e.g., wood, brick, drywall, etc.). *Radiation* is the transfer of heat from a surface by electromagnetic waves.

The temperature difference and thermal resistance factored against the square foot area of the envelope determines the amount of heat transferred. Poor thermal performance of the envelope puts greater demand on the mechanical systems for heating and cooling. In addition, cold surfaces or excessive solar gain can create comfort problems and decrease the efficient use of the space. Building elements with poor thermal performance such as single-glazed windows can be the site of condensation that can cause deterioration of surrounding finishes. Thermal weak points in the envelope can also contribute to the defacement and/or deterioration of building components.

During cold weather, warm air rises to upper levels, where it leaks out to colder outside air (exfiltration). The air lost at the top is replaced by cold air leaking into the building at the bottom (infiltration). The building mechanical systems can affect the pattern of infiltration/exfiltration through requirements for the combustion and draft air and by operation of ventilation systems.

There are two basic approaches to saving energy through modifications to the building shell. Infiltration/exfiltration may be reduced by air sealing cracks, air barriers, weather-stripping, or adding better-fitting windows and doors. Thermal performance may be improved by adding insulation to the roof, walls, or floor, or by adding double- or triple-glazed windows. Insulated windows, either aerogel or multiple-paned, can prevent conduction of heat through the glass. Low-emissivity (low-E) windows and window films allow windows to reflect heat rather than transmit it, keeping rooms cool in the summer and warm in the winter (Energy Ideas, 1998).

In general, air sealing and other measures that reduce air infiltration/exfiltration should be implemented before adding insulation. The major areas and extent of air leakage can be determined by means of a complete building audit. The techniques used may include: a walk-through building audit, a fan-depressurization test, an infrared thermograph scan, and a smoke pencil test. Normally, infiltration and exfiltration should be checked at building joints, windows and doors, mechanical penetration areas, and at the top of buildings where the roof structure attaches to the walls. Since sports and recreation facilities are large buildings with roofs spanning long distances, these are important areas to have sealed.

Upgrading the thermal performance of the building envelope can lower demand for heating and cooling. It can also improve occupant comfort and use of space by eliminating uncomfortable drafts and cold spots. Energy conservation measures may also provide effective solutions to serious building damage by correcting thermal weak points that can cause deterioration of building components. A complete energy audit of the building will present a "thermal picture" of the envelope. Furthermore, this will indicate areas of greatest heat loss and cooling load. A thermal picture will be determined by the size and shape of the building, its age, and type of construction. Each part of the building envelope offers unique opportunities and constraints regarding thermal upgrading. The best time to address the thermal performance of a sports facility is during the design phase.

Operation and Maintenance

Proper maintenance is essential to conserving energy in the long term. The building should be designed with future maintenance in mind. Easy access to equipment, having major components of the mechanical and electrical systems labeled and as-built drawings provided are good first steps to making maintenance easier to perform. A manual containing operating instructions and information on all of the components of the mechanical and electrical systems should be turned over to the owner when the systems are commissioned.

A thorough and well-managed maintenance program will directly contribute to reducing energy costs. Equipment that is well maintained operates more efficiently and consumes less energy. If maintenance of HVAC, or electrical systems is neglected, costs will increase in the long term. This includes the cost of equipment downtime, emergency repair costs, and the increased energy cost to operate the equipment. Energy costs will also increase, owing to poor operating efficiencies resulting from neglect.

Good operational and maintenance procedures can complement a well-designed energy management program, specifically as they relate to the following systems: heating, cooling, ventilation, water treatment, and lighting. Energy management must become part of daily operations to be effective. All operating procedures should be energy efficient. Operations logs and well-documented operating procedures are essential ingredients of energy management. Keeping operational logs is one activity that is part of the standard operating procedure for a building. Operating logs perform several functions: they provide a permanent historical record of system performance, ensure that systems are inspected frequently, identify problems by providing historical records of changes in operation and/or energy performance, and provide a base for evaluating new energy efficient measures and their cost effectiveness.

Heat Pumps

A heat pump is essentially a refrigeration cycle where the heat rejected at the condenser is used for heating purposes. The total heat delivered to the condenser is the sum of the heat extracted in the evaporator and the heat from the compressor work necessary to compress the refrigerant.

The heat pump must have a source of heat to be cooled in order to work. In residential applications, the source of heat is usually outside air, water, or the ground. In large buildings, the source of heat can be waste heat from lighting in interior building areas or heat from computers. The heating requirement must occur at the same time as the cooling requirement if the heat source is inside the building or thermal storage must be used to transfer the heat to another time period.

Domestic Hot Water

A hot water plant may include one or several hot water boilers, a heat exchanger to produce domestic hot water, circulating pumps, and control devices. A hot water distribution system, sometimes called a hydronic system, is used to circulate hot water between a boiler and the heat transfer equipment located in the various heated areas of the building. A steam distribution system is used to convey steam from a boiler to the heat transfer equipment (Energy Ideas, March 93).

Domestic hot water systems provide potable water for hand washing, showers, swimming pools, ice resurfacing, and cleaning. Most sports and recreation buildings incorporate some form of domestic hot water heating system. The domestic hot water system is similar to hot water heating systems, except that the heated water is potable and cannot be chemically treated. Cold water is supplied as make-up to this system from the local water utility.

Domestic hot water systems can be subdivided into unitary and central systems. Unitary systems are point-of-use systems with no distribution piping to serve multiple points of use. Unitary systems, or instantaneous water heaters, eliminate long pipe runs and associated line losses. Central systems are more common in sports facilities and incorporate distribution piping to serve more than one point of use. A central domestic hot water system generally includes: a hot water generator heated by steam, by natural gas, or by an electric element; a storage tank (frequently integrated with the hot water generator); piping (usually copper pipes); recirculating pump(s); plumbing fixtures such as faucets and showerheads; and control devices that regulate the water temperature and occasionally the water flow to the appliances.

The key energy management measures related to various components of the above systems include:

- Hot water consumption can be reduced through the use of restricted water flow showerheads.
- Cconsider use of separate boiler for domestic hot water heating if domestic hot water is the only summer load for a large boiler.
- Stopping circulating pumps one hour after occupied periods end can reduce piping losses. Restart the re-circulation pumps not more than one hour before occupancy periods begin. Computerized energy management systems can be programmed to accomplish these functions based on the activities scheduled in the facility.
- Reduce tank losses of the water heater when hot water will not be used for a period of 72 hours or more. Tanks and lines should be insulated to avoid unnecessary losses.

Water, like energy, is an increasingly scarce and expensive commodity whose use has enormous environmental repercussions. Unfortunately, the prices most users pay for clean water do not come close to covering the real cost (Chernushenko, 1994). Moves are afoot in a number of areas, however, to develop pricing mechanisms that transfer the real cost of water to the consumer. Since price can only go up, the sports facility that has taken steps to reduce its water consumption may be only marginally affected.

Large volumes of water are typically consumed by sports facilities for indoor pools, landscaping, and turf maintenance. Artificial snowmaking is another major water consumer. Below are some effective general steps.

Indoor Water Use

The principal areas of indoor water consumption are washrooms, showers, and laundry rooms. Steps to improve water conservation in these areas are:

- Instruct and remind washroom and shower users to shut off taps fully.
- Repair drips and leaks promptly.
- For automatic flushing systems, check that timing cycles are appropriate for the frequency of urinal use. Shut them down entirely after hours.
- Install low-flow aerators and automatic shutoff valves on tapes.
- Retrofit toilets to reduce water consumption.

Outdoor Water Use

Facilities such as golf courses and playing fields spend heavily on keeping their turf healthy and green. Watering during dry spells actually works against the health of the ecosystem as a whole by depleting water reserves elsewhere. Sports facilities can reduce demand for irrigation by helping encourage an evolution in the attitudes of users to the point where turf, which is less than forest green, is acceptable.

Steps to reduce outdoor water consumption are:

• Plant only native vegetation or species suited to the climate.
• Limit watering of turf to playing surfaces that receive heavy use.
• Water only during the evening and overnight to reduce evaporation.
• Use trickle or soaker hoses rather than aerial sprinklers.
• Design parking lots and roadways to allow rainwater to return to the soil, streams, and ground water.

Lighting

Lighting costs in sports and recreation facilities can account for 30 to 50% of total energy costs (Energy Ideas, March 93). Until recently, electrical costs were low and little thought was given in building design to the operational costs of lighting systems. Rather, the selection and design of lighting systems were often based on minimizing capital cost. As a result, there exists a wide range of opportunities to reduce lighting energy use in most buildings.

Lighting systems in sports and recreation facilities serve five distinct purposes: to provide sufficient illumination to enable occupants to see and play in a safe manner; to illuminate safe pathways for the movement of persons in and out of the building; to complement the architectural and interior design by providing a comfortable and pleasant environment; to deter vandalism (outside lighting); and, to enhance or highlight a product or display. A lighting system with higher levels than necessary results in higher first cost and operating expenses.

A well-designed lighting system should provide adequate and safe levels of light for the activities carried out in a space. Often, when a system is designed, the quantity (illuminance) of light is used as the only criterion for providing suitable lighting. However, recent studies have now found that the quality of light installed is also a very important factor to consider when designing or upgrading a lighting system.

Occupant visual comfort and productivity are directly related to the amount of lighting and the way it is provided. Opportunities for reducing lighting energy usage should also be looked upon as opportunities to improve the quality of lighting. Please refer to Chapter 15 for information related to other considerations related to lighting for sports and recreational facilities.

Before developing an energy management plan or program for a building's lighting system, an analysis of the existing facilities should be undertaken. Information should be collected that relates to: the amount of light provided in each area; the type of fixtures and their energy consumption; and the occupant activity for specific lighting areas, including the time period in use.

Once this information is collected, lighting levels can be compared to recommended levels for the activities involved. Opportunities for energy savings can then be identified. They may include: reducing power consumption of fixtures through modification or replacement of fixtures or through reduced lighting levels and reducing the operating period of fixtures based on occupant activity. The quality of lighting depends on the following factors as well as the actual level of illumination: geometry of the space to be illuminated; mounting height of lighting fixtures; light-reflecting properties of the ceiling, walls and floor; and color rendering of the particular light type under consideration.

Maintaining adequate illumination levels requires effective lighting system maintenance. An effective maintenance program comprises not only lamp replacement but also routine, planned cleaning of lighting fixtures and room surfaces. A regular cleaning and relamping program has definite long-term benefits: more light is delivered per unit cost of electricity, lower-wattage lamps can be installed, fewer luminaries can be installed, and overall labor costs are reduced.

A final factor to be considered before embarking on a lighting energy management program, particularly for large sports and recreation buildings, is the effect of lighting on the HVAC systems. The lighting–HVAC effect refers to the impact of lighting on the heating and cooling load of a building.

Effectively, all of the energy consumed for lighting ultimately ends up as heat. This heat can become a significant part of the cooling load of an air-conditioned space. The energy required to air-condition an interior space includes the energy used by the refrigerating equipment (central chiller or rooftop air conditioners). It may also include pump energy to deliver chilled water to the space, and fan energy to deliver cool air. All of these components can be reduced in size if heat output from lights is reduced. Conversely, reducing the energy use of lights increases the heating load of a space in winter, since the heating effect of lights is reduced. This lighting–HVAC effect in heating and cooling must be calculated when planning lighting measures.

Building Automation Systems

Building automation systems can be included in energy management plans both in the planning and design phases of new facilities and with the renovation of older facilities with operating problems, owing to antiquated control systems. Installing a building automation system not only saves money by reducing unnecessary energy consumption, but it can also increase comfort significantly.

The features of an automated control system that can be utilized in conjunction with an energy management program are: sensors to measure the environment, controllers to regulate equipment, and operating equipment. An example of a sensor is a temperature sensor that sends a pneumatic or electronic signal proportional to the temperature back to a controller. Controllers are designed to received sensor inputs, compare the input to a set-point, and send a signal output to a controlled device. The operating equipment is any device connected to and operated by the controller.

Building automation systems include systems that control energy-management functions as well as systems that control other building-management functions, such as security (Cohen, 2000). Building automation systems can be classified by: the number of control points, the means of control, and the type of data communication used between the controller and the control points.

There are a number of reasons why a building operator or manager might want to incorporate an automated control system into a building: to improve building operation and comfort; to increase building safety or security; to reduce operating costs, including energy costs; or to provide more efficient building management. Below is a brief description of the various control options that can be incorporated into a computer-controlled, automated system:

- Programmed Start/Stop—Programmed start/stop is a software-based function that permits the user to schedule starting and stopping of equipment according to a predetermined schedule. In sports facilities when specific occupancy scenarios are known, air-handling equipment can be programmed to increase air volumes when spectators are scheduled in the facility and reduce the volumes during non-use periods. Furthermore, hot water circulating pumps can be programmed to deliver hot water when users are expected to take showers and be turned off otherwise.
- Alarms/Monitoring—This type of software-based function signals an alarm or initiates a particular action when an upper or lower limit has been exceeded. Sports and recreation facilities have many entry and exit doors to monitor and control. This type of system can be used to signal an unauthorized entry into a space.
- Energy Monitoring—This function allows the recording and accumulation of fuel and electricity consumption data, allowing for improved analysis of the consumption rate of fuel and electricity.
- Demand Control—This software feature reduces electrical power demand by stopping or delaying the operation of certain pieces of nonessential electrical equipment during peak demand periods. Utilities charge a premium to users who consume a lot of electricity at peak periods of time. Staying below this demand level will cut electrical costs all year long, since one high-use period sets the rate for the entire year.
- Duty Cycling—This software executes the stop/start cycles for equipment. One can therefore avoid the simultaneous operation of several loads that do not require continuous operation and limit the energy consumption of all the controlled equipment.
- Optimized Stop/Start—This type of program function calculates the best time to initiate preheating or precooling of the building.
- Optimized Ventilation—This software is used to optimize the blending of outside air and return air based on the enthalpy of the two air streams.
- Optimization of Supply Air Temperature—This software allows the adjustment of supply air temperature as a function of the heating and cooling loads of the building.
- Chiller/Boiler Optimization—When the cooling system comprises several chillers, this type of function operates the minimum chilling capacity to satisfy the load.
- Supply Water Temperature Optimization—This type of control can regulate the chilled water and hot water supply temperatures of the cooling/heating systems as a function of the actual demand of the building.
- Temperature Setback/Setup—Temperature setback/setup type of controls provide scheduling of building space temperatures during unoccupied periods.

Other control options available with building automation systems include: controls for exterior and/or interior lighting and security; domestic hot water optimization; cistern flow optimization that modulates water flow to cistern-operated urinals; and options for specialized applications, such as swimming pools and ice arenas. As the technology improves, these systems will change to reflect the additional energy and cost savings available.

Summary

During the design and operation of a sports and recreation facility, one of the most important factors for the management to understand and address is the energy use of the facility. Faced with a future of ever-increasing utility costs, managers must take a fresh look at old operating procedures and install new technologies designed to reduce the amount of energy needed to operate. Building components like the envelope and the infiltration and exfiltration of air through the envelope, the amount and quality of air and the type of HVAC systems greatly impact energy use. Heating and use of hot water, and the type and amount of lighting to accommodate sports and recreational activities further compound energy consumption. While the computer and its use has automated some of these systems and enabled the operator to study and control energy use, establishing operating procedures that consider energy consumption along with user comfort will be the final ingredient in a total management program.

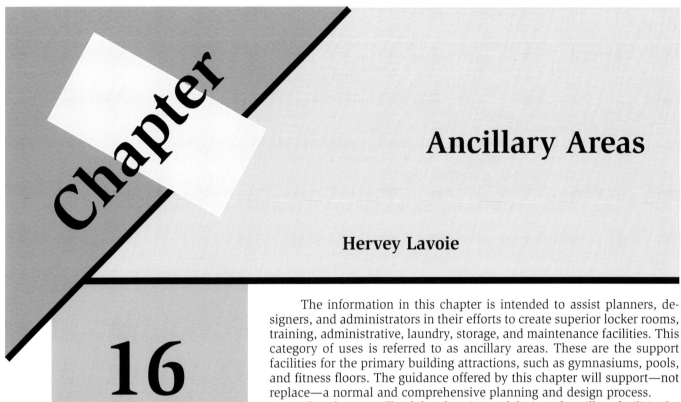

Ancillary Areas

Hervey Lavoie

The information in this chapter is intended to assist planners, designers, and administrators in their efforts to create superior locker rooms, training, administrative, laundry, storage, and maintenance facilities. This category of uses is referred to as ancillary areas. These are the support facilities for the primary building attractions, such as gymnasiums, pools, and fitness floors. The guidance offered by this chapter will support—not replace—a normal and comprehensive planning and design process.

This chapter will aid the planning and design of ancillary facilities by identifying many of the questions that must be asked, along with the variables that should be considered as the project development team responds to the unique circumstances of each project mission, each site, and each community of users.

Actual design recommendations for specific solutions will not be presented here, because the professional planning/design team that follows the analytical guidelines and considerations brought out in this chapter will be well prepared to reach its own conclusions. Asking the right questions is an essential part of recognizing the best answers.

Learning Objectives

After reading this chapter, the student should be able to

- identify the types of ancillary area specialists to be included on the development team,
- describe design considerations for locker room facilities,
- explain the concepts of wet and dry areas,
- describe the various amenities to be included in ancillary areas,
- identify the major factors to consider in planning a training room,
- understand the design variables that influence the programming and function of ancillary areas, and
- gain the ability to critique planning and design work.

The Development Team

Design of ancillary areas will require input from the following specialists who are commonly represented on a facility development team:

- Owner's Project Manager—The individual (in-house) or company (out-sourced) who is assigned responsibility to represent the interest of the owner and manage the diverse parties of the development team for the duration of the project.
- Facility Planner/Programmer/Business Planner—The individual or company responsible for analyzing the needs of the project owner and producing recommendations as to the mix and magnitude of uses, revenue projections, expense estimates, and so forth.
- Architect—This is the individual or company responsible for taking the work of the facility planner/programmer and creating a building to accommodate the functional requirements and to express the image and style of the building.
- Cost Authority/Construction Provider—This is the individual or company responsible for predicting the cost required to create the desired building and site improvements. The same party is often engaged to provide the actual construction of the building.
- Operational Consultant—The individual or company responsible for managing the facility, operating the business, hiring staff, creating programs, and providing financial controls. The operational consultant will provide input related to staffing, management, maintenance, marketing, specialized FF&E (fixtures, furnishings and equipment), and other operational issues that impact the design of ancillary areas.

- Component Suppliers—Providers of facility components (lockers, washing machines, basketball hoops, etc.) are the manufacturers of the special products and equipment that will be included in the facility. They are an essential source of information regarding proper application of their products.

Design Variables

For each ancillary area, the following design variables will be examined and discussed:

- Issues of size, quantity, and dimension.
- Issues of location and relationship (adjacent/proximate, remote).
- Access and circulation considerations for all users—staff, guests, users with disabilities.
- Matters of style, image, and color.
- Issues of materials, finishes, and function.
- Engineering issues regarding lighting; heating, ventilation, and air-conditioning (HVAC); plumbing; and communication systems.
- Gender-specific requirements and other user needs.
- Requirements for expansion and adaptability.

Facility Types

The most significant variable affecting ancillary areas is that of facility type. As the title of this book suggests, there are many types (and sub-types), including athletics (sub-types for different sports), physical education (sub-types for different age groups: elementary, junior high, high school, and college), and recreation/fitness (sub-types for university, municipal, and private).

In addition, many facilities try to wear two or three hats; that is, their mission is to serve the programming needs of a variety of users, such as varsity athletics, intramural athletics, and physical education. Proper design for ancillary areas will be driven by the particular needs of the overall facility type. For example, the next section will discuss locker rooms in general and then distinguish between the design of locker rooms for specific types of facilities.

Clearly, planning and design of locker rooms should vary according to facility type. Similarly, other kinds of ancillary areas will vary in use and function for different facility types. The planning and design of training rooms, administrative offices, laundry facilities, storage rooms, and maintenance areas must be viewed in light of their fit to the overall facility mission.

Ancillary, by definition, refers to those functions that are necessary to support the destination program activities for which the facility is created. Users don't come to a facility to use the locker rooms. Rather, they come to use the swimming pool, and the locker room enables them to do so.

Locker Rooms

The term *locker room* encompasses a multitude of components and facilities. More than a room of lockers, the modern locker room accommodates a broad range of functions related to dressing, storage, grooming, personal hygiene, therapy, social exchange, information handling, aesthetics, comfort, safety, and privacy.

Many aspects of locker room planning and design must be considered in light of the overall facility type. However, there are some basic principles that apply to all types of locker rooms, regardless of the facility type. These principles are the planning and design considerations that must be addressed in defining the basic components common to all locker rooms: lockers, toilets, showers, amenities, and grooming stations.

Essential to the accommodation of these functions is the proper location of the locker room within the overall facility and the proper relationship of these components within the locker room itself. Figure 16.1 illustrates the primary relationship that must be considered in properly locating the locker room within the overall facility. Whenever possible, the locker room should be on the same floor level as the aquatic facilities.

One wall of the locker room block is often designed to be a removable wall, located so future expansion also can be accommodated by means of internal conversion of "soft" use spaces that are intentionally located next to the locker room. "Soft" space refers to uses that require little or no special provisions (such as plumbing or expensive finishes), and therefore is space that is easily vacated and converted to locker-room expansion. Examples of "soft" uses include storage rooms, offices, and meeting rooms.

Another approach to expanding existing locker rooms is to convert the existing women's locker room into an expansion of the men's locker room concurrent with the construction of an entirely new women's locker room as part of a new building addition.

All but the most primitive locker rooms will have lockers, showers, grooming stations, amenities, and toilet facilities. Figure 16.2 provides a conceptual illustration of the proper relationship of these components. Conventional design wisdom has held that consolidation of plumbing facilities to minimize piping runs is a primary consideration in the layout of locker rooms. In truth, the actual economics of clustered plumbing are not significant. The consolidation of plumbing can be quite contrary to the principles of user-friendly design. Toilet facilities backed up to showers will save minor quantities of piping, but can result in a mix of wet bare feet from shower traffic with soiled street shoes from toilet room users.

Figure 16.1
The Relationship of Locker Rooms to the Facilty

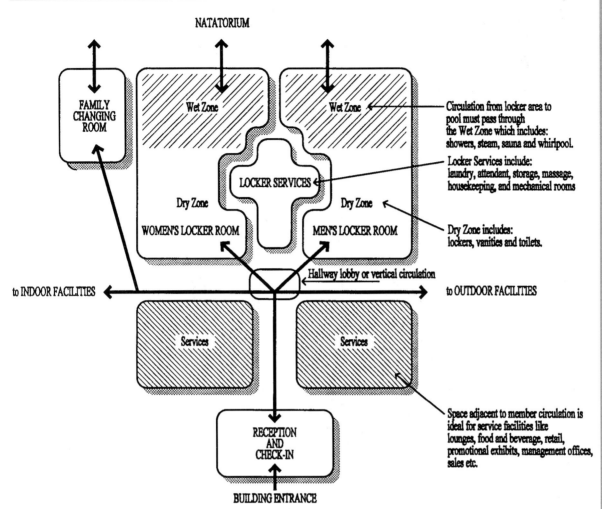

NATATORIUM

FAMILY CHANGING ROOM

Wet Zone

Wet Zone

Circulation from locker area to pool must pass through the Wet Zone which includes: showers, steam, sauna and whirlpool.

LOCKER SERVICES

Locker Services include: laundry, attendant, storage, massage, housekeeping, and mechanical rooms

Dry Zone

Dry Zone

Dry Zone includes: lockers, vanities and toilets.

WOMEN'S LOCKER ROOM

MEN'S LOCKER ROOM

Hallway lobby or vertical circulation

to INDOOR FACILITIES

to OUTDOOR FACILITIES

Services

Services

Space adjacent to member circulation is ideal for service facilities like lounges, food and beverage, retail, promotional exhibits, management offices, sales etc.

RECEPTION AND CHECK-IN

BUILDING ENTRANCE

Locker Location

The location of the locker rooms within the facility is important. After going through the reception area, users pass through retail areas, promotional exhibits, and lounges, which help guide them to the locker rooms.

Lavatory grooming counters near toilets and urinals again will save minor amount of piping, but may result in a loss of privacy for toilet users and a compromised atmosphere for personal grooming functions.

Locker Room Size

The number and size of lockers required will help determine the size of the overall changing room, as will the inclusion of special amenities, such as steam rooms, saunas, massage pools, baths, lounges, or massage rooms. A range of 7 to 15 square feet per locker is possible, depending on locker size and other variables. The best way to accurately program the locker-room size that is appropriate for a given facility is to calculate the user capacity of destination attractions (such as gyms, courts, fitness floors, etc.) during peak usage periods. Total occupancy factors are listed next:

- Group Exercise Rooms: one person per 45 square feet
- Gymnasium: 12 persons per game court
- Racquet Courts: two persons per court (four for tennis)
- Lap Pools: four persons per lane
- Exercise Pools: one person per 50 square feet
- Fitness Floors: one person per 65 square feet
- Walk/Jog Tracks: one person per 25 linear feet

When an allowance is made for those who are waiting to participate and those who are finished and showering (an additional 25% to 45% of user occupancy), the total demand for lockers can be predicted. Estimates of the gender ratio of users will allow the total locker count to be distributed be-

Figure 16.2
Layout of the Chicago Athletic Club's Locker Area

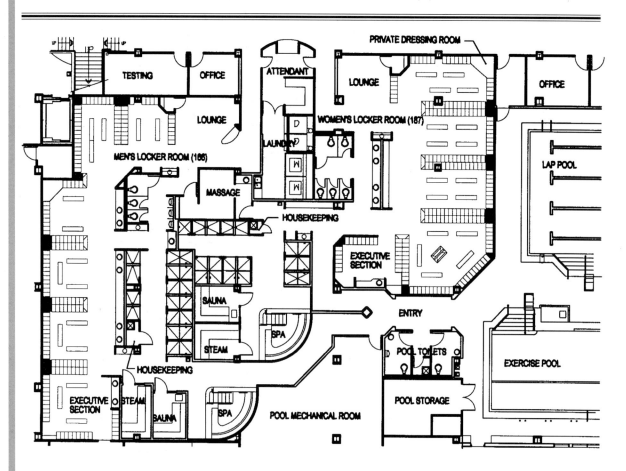

Example of Locker Room Layout
In this Chicago athletic club, the coordination of lockers, wet areas, dry areas and support facilities can be seen. Maintaining separation between men's and women's facilities while entering and exiting through common gateways and promoting user-friendly flow patterns is key to good locker-room layout.

---

tween men's and women's locker rooms. Unless special circumstances dictate otherwise, the size of locker rooms for men and women should be the same and each locker count equal to 60% of the total predicted demand. This will account for use patterns that may occasionally result in unequal participation according to gender. On a case-by-case basis, special-use patterns may allow for reasonable reduction of locker count. A university recreation facility that is surrounded by student dormitories may, for example, have many users who shower and change in their dorms. This will cause reduced demand for lockers, showers, and vanities.

The planning objective is to provide a balance between locker-room capacity and the total floor capacity of primary facility attractions, such as fitness equipment, aerobic rooms, and gymnasiums. An imbalance in this ratio will result in unused capacity or dysfunctional congestion in either the locker rooms or the primary attraction areas. Application of the formula outlined above will ensure properly sized facilities.

Locker Area
The locker area must provide more than securable storage compartments. A good locker layout will allow for a multitude of functional considerations, including:

- Seated dressing space removed from main circulation paths.
- At least one private dressing cubicle for users with special privacy needs.
- At least one dressing/locker cubicle equipped for use by persons with disabilities.
- Size and quantities of lockers determined by analysis of anticipated user groups. In most cases, it is appropriate and sometimes required to provide facilities of equal size for men and women, boys and girls.

- Odor control achieved by means of natural or induced locker ventilation. Management procedures that encourage proper care of locker contents by users also will be beneficial. Provision of swimsuit dryers can help prevent odors and locker damage caused by storing wet suits. Swimsuit dryers are compact, self-operated devices that use centrifugal force to "spin" a suit dry in less than one minute.
- Efficiency of locker count can be improved by increasing the height of locker tiers, but caution must be exercised to avoid having lockers so high that they are out of reach of the expected user. It is also problematic to have small lockers located low to the floor where they will be difficult to use without kneeling down.

Figure 16.3 illustrates a range of possible locker and bench configurations with recommended dimensions. When possible, avoid vast and deep maze-like arrays of lockers. Shallow perimeter layouts

Figure 16.3
Variations of Alcove-Type Locker Arrangements

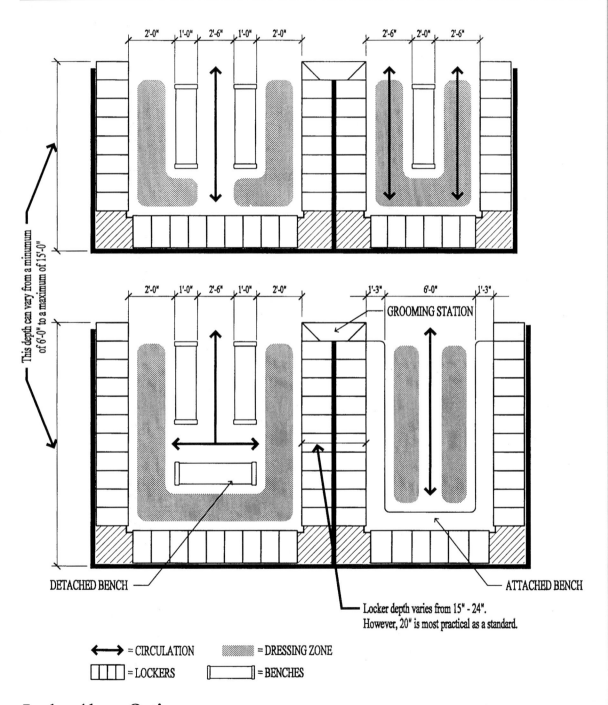

← → = CIRCULATION   ▨ = DRESSING ZONE

▥ = LOCKERS   ▭ = BENCHES

Locker Alcove Options

To maximize the space available for lockers, alcoves are created as a way to maximize locker count while separating circulation from dressing.

around two or three sides of a wet core are more user friendly. This will allow shorter walking distances between locker and shower as well as improved way-finding. Supervision of locker areas may be an important consideration for some facility types where vandalism or victimizing behavior can be expected. Avoid hidden alcoves where unobserved activities can take place.

The main locker-room access will need to accommodate heavy two-way traffic from users carrying bags or equipment. Therefore, locker-room doors should be avoided, and if required for code or security reasons, may be held open with code-approved electro-magnetic devices connected to the fire alarm system. Doorless entries are a commonplace answer to the need for unobstructed two-way circulation in high-volume uses such as stadiums and airports. The necessary visual screening of locker-room interiors can be provided easily by blocking sight lines with corners or wing-walls (see Figure 16.4). These visual baffles should be provided even if doors are installed.

Figure 16.4
Functional and Attractive Locker Area

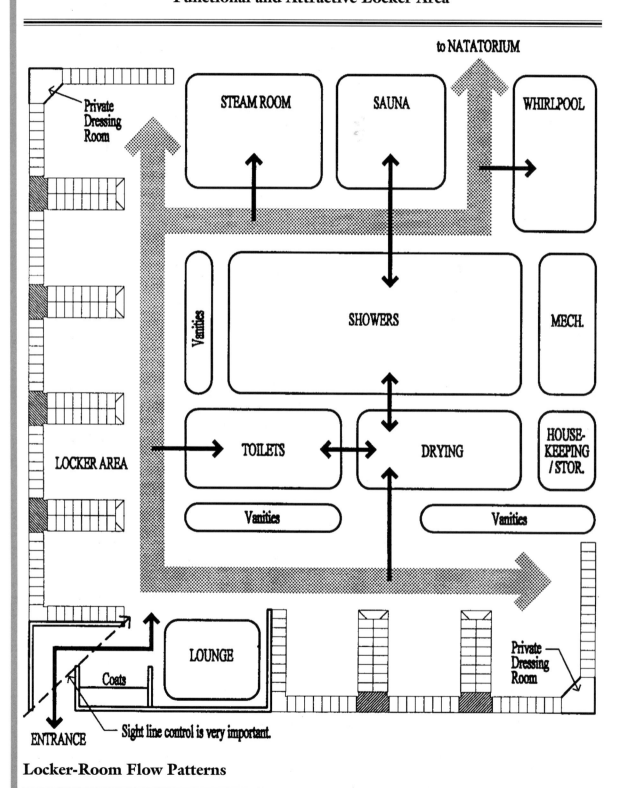

Locker-Room Flow Patterns

Materials and finishes for wet area floors should be selected with maintenance in mind. A variety of impervious floor surfaces are available—ceramic tile, etched terrazzo, vinyl, and synthetics. Considerations should be given to slip coefficients, cleaning techniques, color selection, grout maintenance, aesthetics, and cost. If the daily maintenance program will consist of a hosing down or pressure wash, the best choice of flooring for wet areas is a 1" x 1" ceramic tile or a liquid-applied synthetic. Such materials should be detailed with coved base.

Floor material options for locker-room dressing areas include wood and carpet. Wood floors have been used successfully as an accent in upscale club locker rooms. Carpet is a good choice for locker-room dressing areas when a proper maintenance program can be assured. The benefits of carpet (quiet, soil-hiding, colorful, durable) will be lost if it is not vacuumed twice daily and steam cleaned at least four times annually. Odor control of carpet can be enhanced by specifying a factory-applied anti-microbial treatment and taking care in planning of wet area circulation to prevent excessive tracking of water to the carpet.

Ceilings should provide for good light diffusion and acoustic absorption. Moisture resistance is also important. If a lay-in grid ceiling is to be specified, an aluminum grid will resist moisture-induced corrosion. Lay-in panels must have sufficient stiffness to resist "pillowing." The aesthetic impact of ceiling treatment should not be overlooked. Consider the possibility of lighting the locker room indirectly by mounting strip light fixtures on top of lockers. Emergency lighting must be provided. Natural day lighting by means of skylights, glass block, or obscure glazing will enhance the locker-room environment.

Lockers

Locker systems are available in a variety of materials: painted steel, mesh steel, wood panel, and plastic laminate-faced particle board or fiber-resin board. The selection of locker material and construction is a function of several factors. Considerations include:

- cost
- appearance requirements
- resistance to abuse
- resistance to corrosion
- availability of desired size, accessories, and locking system
- installation requirements

Wood may be most suitable in applications where a traditional or luxury image is desired, and the risk of vandalism is small. A variety of wood stains and door designs is available.

Painted steel may be most suitable in noncorrosive environments where the desire for an upscale ambiance does not exist and the risk of abusive behavior is present. A variety of standard and custom paint colors are available. Choice of door styles is somewhat limited, but painted steel lockers have been the standard choice for applications where economy, utility, security, and durability are the prime concerns.

Plastic laminate-faced particle board may be the most suitable choice where economy and upscale design image are both important. A rich variety of colors, textures, and finishes is readily available for door faces. This type of locker is also a good choice for moisture resistance. Many optional accessories, such as shelves, hooks, rods, and mirrors are available. The choice of locking systems must consider the operational challenges and security issues associated with keys, padlocks, cards, and combinations. A new generation of keyless locking systems is becoming available and can offer unique benefits to both users and facility managers. These locks employ a keypad for the user to enter a self-selected code to lock and unlock the device. No key or padlock is required.

Toilets

Careful consideration must be given to location of locker-room toilets. Will they be used under wet or dry conditions? Are the locker-room toilets intended to serve the nearby aquatic facilities? If so, users will be wet, and toilets must be located in the locker-room wet area. In this case, other toilet facilities should be provided for "dry" users in the dry zone of the locker room or in a location outside of the locker room. In any case, mixing of dry and wet toilet room traffic should be avoided. Street shoes on wet slippery floors are a hazard, and the presence of bare feet on wet floors that have been soiled by street shoes is unsanitary and unpleasant. Possible solutions are:

- "Dry" toilets near the locker-room entry and "wet" toilets near the shower area.
- "Dry" toilets near the entry (for convenience of use from outside of locker room) and wet toilets within the natatorium.
- "Dry" toilets outside of the locker room and "wet" toilets near the shower area.

Other considerations for planning and designing locker room toilets include:

- Sufficient quantities of fixtures (water closets and urinals) should be provided to meet peak user demand. The unique circumstances of each project must be evaluated in making this determination. Rules of thumb suggest that a ratio of one water closet per 60 lockers is sufficient, but this ratio should be modified to account for special circumstances such as large group use or schedule-driven programs that result in surging use patterns.

- Careful attention should be paid to toilet partition materials and construction. Problems with rusting, delamination, warping, and vandalism are common. This is not the place to cut quality for the purpose of reducing cost.
- Lighting of toilet stalls should be placed toward the back of the stall in the form of downlight, wall scone or valance light. This location will provide the best lighting for cleanliness inspections of the water closet.
- Maintenance access to piping and valves must be provided. Access panels in plumbing walls are a common solution to this need. Water-conserving fixtures are often required by code. Auto-activated fittings can also be beneficial for sanitation and user consequence.

Showers

The quantity of showers and the corresponding capacity of hot water-generating equipment together are the most critical components of an athletic facility's ancillary areas. Shortcomings in any other design features can be adapted to or in some way tolerated. Cold showers and/or long lines of people waiting for too few showers will create an extremely negative experience for the facility user.

Unfortunately, rules of thumb for shower count are not always reliable. One shower per 20 lockers is a ratio that sometimes is applicable. However, there will be cases when that ratio will result in too many or too few showers. The best approach is for the project planner to conduct an analysis of anticipated overall user capacity (similar to that process suggested for estimating locker quantities) in the facility as the basis for predicting the peak shower-taking population at any given time. This projection will, in turn, form the basis of the mechanical engineers' calculation of flow rate and duration of hot water that must be supplied for showers.

The selection of a control valve and showerhead should be considered carefully to arrive at the balance of shower quality, water economy, and scald safety that is most appropriate for a given facility and the users it serves. Control valves can be specified for automatic shut-off, automatic temperature control, variable or fixed volume, and vandal resistance. It is desirable that shower piping and valves be accessible for maintenance and repair without destruction of the enclosing wall and finishes. Access panels can be provided and detailed to coordinate with the overall decor.

Shower rooms must be ventilated and exhausted to prevent odors and moisture accumulation. Air supply points must be arranged to minimize drafts. In general, ventilation systems must be designed to promote the migration of air from dry areas to wet areas.

A variety of shower types and layouts is possible and is illustrated in Figure 16.5.

Other general guidelines for shower planning and design include:

- Provide a drying area adjacent to the showering facility.
- Provide flush-type recessed hose bibs for cleaning purposes.
- Walls and floors of the shower enclosure must be completely waterproof (see Figure 16.6).
- Showerheads should be self-cleaning and water-conserving. Adjustability of spray and angle should be considered on a case-by-case basis. Locate the showerhead where the user can turn on the water and test the temperature without having to stand in the water stream.
- Shower finishes must be impervious to water and easily cleaned. Ceramic tile, stone, or etched terrazzo are good choices for floors and walls.
- Ceilings can be finished with ceramic tile or epoxy paint.
- Minimum spacing for gang showers is 30 inches. Showerhead heights should be set according to anticipated size of users. A variety of heights can be provided if a mix of users is anticipated. Recommended mounting heights for showerheads depend on pipe configuration. The actual height of the pipe coming out of the wall will be 4 to 8 inches higher than the head:
  —Men: 6'-8" to 7'-0" (from floor to shower head)
  —Women: 6'-2" to 6'-6" (from floor to shower head)
  —Children: 5'-6" (or adjustable)

Other design issues affecting wet area finishes are:

- Evaluate nonslip characteristics of a floor material when wet. Most manufacturers can provide a slip coefficient for their products. Avoid use of step-over shower curbs, as they can be a safety problem and an access barrier.
- Substrate—a finish material will perform only as well as its underlying support. Of the many options for wet area wall substrate, gypsum board is the least reliable. Concrete masonry and cement boards are preferred, and will stand up to the moisture that will inevitably penetrate the finish material.
- Floor construction of showers and drying areas must be sloped to perimeter or center drains in order to avoid birdbath-like puddles of water on the floor.

Shower planning also must address the inclusion or exclusion of clean towel distribution; towel hooks; foot rests; amenity shelving; consumable dispensers; used towel collection; and provision, if any, of consumables such as soap and shampoo. Inclusion of a drying zone between showers and lockers is important. This area can be equipped with floor mats and drains to prevent tracking of water onto dry

Figure 16.5
Shower Layouts and Typical Dimensions

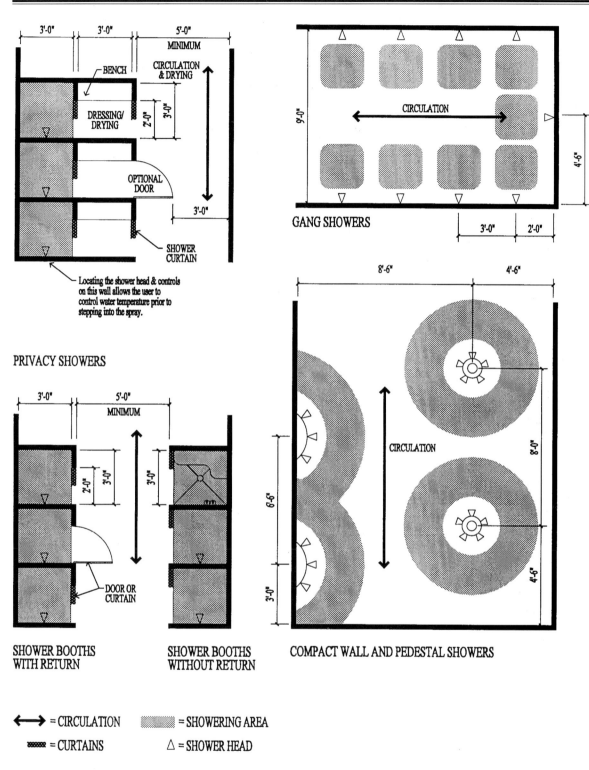

PRIVACY SHOWERS

GANG SHOWERS

SHOWER BOOTHS
WITH RETURN

SHOWER BOOTHS
WITHOUT RETURN

COMPACT WALL AND PEDESTAL SHOWERS

←→ = CIRCULATION   ▨▨▨ = SHOWERING AREA

〰 = CURTAINS   △ = SHOWER HEAD

Shower Variations

area finishes. The shower area often is positioned to serve users of indoor and outdoor aquatic facilities as well as locker room amenities such as steam room, sauna, and whirlpool bath. Users of these amenities should be encouraged by the layout and flow to shower prior to use. In many jurisdictions, health codes require that all access to pools pass through a showering area.

Amenities

Steam, sauna, whirlpool bath, and grooming stations are the amenities most often considered for inclusion in an upscale locker room facility. Each of these features requires careful attention to a host of planning and design considerations.

Figure 16.6
Individual Showers

Steam Rooms

Steam rooms are the most maintenance-intensive of all ancillary facilities and will readily self-destruct if not properly constructed.

- As a guideline, sizing should be based on a capacity factor of one person per 12 square feet or 2.2 linear feet of bench. Steam generators are sized by the manufacturer according to the volume of the room.
- Entrance doors to steam rooms will release large quantities of steam when opened, and should always swing out and be located where this vapor-laden air will not damage nearby fittings and finishes, particularly on the ceiling.
- Walls, floor, and ceiling of steam rooms must be completely waterproof and finished with nonslip ceramic tile or stone.
- Provision of a glazed door and sidelight will improve supervision and make a more pleasant and open experience for the steam room user.
- Slope the steam room ceiling at 1:12 to a side wall or uninhabited drip point in order to prevent condensation from dripping on users.
- All components of steam rooms (lights, hinges, frames, fire sprinklers, fasteners, etc.) must be corrosion resistant. Plastic and aluminum usually are satisfactory. Stainless steel is not a reliable choice and will likely rust. Avoid painted steel or black iron at all costs.
- Most steam room failures are related to failure of the substrate or wall structures to resist the corrosive effects of the vapor-laden air. Proven steam room construction details are published by the ceramic tile industry and should be followed carefully. Compatibility of components (substrates, membranes, bonding agents, adhesives and finishes) cannot be taken for granted. Any substitutions must be thoroughly researched.
- Maintenance access to the steam generator room should be available from a mixed gender corridor so that servicing of steam equipment can occur without closing the locker room. Even the best steam-generating equipment will require frequent maintenance. Steam-room controls, other than a thermostatic sensor, should be located in a staff-only area to prevent tampering.

The decision to include a steam room must be based on consideration of the operating and maintenance expense, as well as the initial construction cost. Periodic staff supervision also is necessary to prevent misuse. Location of steam jets and sensor must be planned and detailed to minimize risk of burns from steam and metallic fittings and ensure proper temperature control and heat distribution.

Accessories usually include thermometer, hose bib, hose, and clock. An overhead shower-head sometimes is included. Depending on characteristics of local water supply, a water softener may be required to prevent mineral deposits on the steam heating elements.

Sauna

Saunas (Figure 16.7) are designed to provide dry heat at extremely high temperatures. They are less costly to install than steam rooms but will still require a diligent maintenance program. Planning and design considerations follow:

Figure 16.7
Sauna

- Wood-lined walls, floors, and seats are the usual choice; however, tile-surfaced accent walls may be included for ease of maintenance. The high temperatures involved (in excess of 180° F) require that users be protected from contact with metal and other highly conductive materials which could cause burns. Wood hardware, plastic mats, or towels can provide this protection.
- The main problem with wood surface sauna seats is the staining that occurs from accumulated soaked-in sweat and the odors that result. Use of a light-colored wood will reduce the unsightliness of the staining problem. The best approach to odor control is to require use of individual towels for seating, along with daily pressure cleaning and application of disinfectant. For these reasons, a sauna may not be suitable for many types of public facilities where towels and multiple daily cleanings cannot be provided.
- Glazed doors and sidelights will create a more pleasant and more easily supervised sauna.
- As a guideline, sizing decisions can be based on a capacity factor of one person per 12 square feet.
- Adequate lighting is particularly important for sanitation and maintenance operations.
- Commonly specified accessories are clock, thermometer, and water supply.
- A floor drain can be provided for ease of cleaning, but it may need to be a self-priming type to prevent the sauna heat from drying out the trap and releasing sewer gases into the room.

Whirlpool Bath

This amenity (see Figure 16.8) is a communal body of water (100 to 104° F) equipped with air and water jets to create a turbulent massage effect for the immersed user. Pre-packaged molded fiberglass

Figure 16.8
Whirlpool Bath

units generally are unsuitable for the applications addressed in this book and should be avoided. Water quality control is the single most important issue impacting the planning and design of these facilities. Local health regulations will control many aspects of the water purification system, as well as pool and deck materials and configuration.

Other considerations:

- Capacity factors are in the range of 10 to 15 square feet per person.
- Equipment rooms should be located for easy access by maintenance or repair personnel of either gender.
- It is important to encourage users to shower before using the whirlpool bath by locating showers convenient to the whirlpool bath.
- Pool basins should be completely tile lined to allow for the frequent draining and cleaning that is necessary to keep a sanitary and attractive body of water. Plaster-lined pools will be more difficult to clean.
- The vapor-laden air of the whirlpool bath area will be made more corrosive by the presence of chlorine. Certain grades of stainless steel eventually will succumb to corrosion in this atmosphere. Aluminum, stone, plastic, glass, and ceramic tile are acceptable materials for use in a whirlpool bath environment.
- It is essential that air-handling systems for the whirlpool bath area be designed to produce a negative air pressure relative to surrounding uses. This will prevent the migration of corrosive vapors and disagreeable odors to other parts of the building.
- Buried piping (which requires jack hammers and shovels to access) is the most economical choice for grade supported pools. However, access points must be provided for cleanouts, valves, and stub-outs.
- For safety reasons it is necessary for the whirlpool bath to be surrounded on at least two sides by a non-slip deck at least four feet wide.

Grooming Stations
Sometimes called a vanity, a grooming station is a place in the locker room where users brush teeth, comb hair, wash hands, shave, apply makeup, and so forth. The fit out for a wet grooming station includes a sink with hot and cold water, a mirror, and a ground fault-protected power source. Minimal facilities for a dry grooming station are a mirror, a power source, and a small shelf. Optional enhancements of grooming provisions can include such niceties as hand-held hair dryers, wall-mounted hand/hair dryers, makeup mirrors, stools, soap or lotion dispensers, face towels, paper towels, waste recep-

tacles, and disposable grooming aids, such as razors and combs. The management of each facility must develop its own policy regarding provision of these optional services. Will they be supplied by building management or by each individual user?

General considerations for user-friendly planning and design of grooming stations follow:

- The required number of wet and dry grooming stations needed must be analyzed according to the unique circumstances of each project and gender-specific grooming practices. As a rule of thumb, total grooming stations should be approximately the same or slightly less than the shower count. A 20-80 split between wet and dry grooming stations may be varied by some planners to provide more wet stations for men (shaving) and more dry stations for women (makeup).
- Lighting at grooming mirrors should be arranged to illuminate both sides of a person's face. Provide a color of light that enhances flesh tones, such as incandescent or warm white fluorescent (Figure 16.9).
- Avoid locating grooming facilities with toilets or placing them too deeply into wet areas. For convenience of use, they should be located on the seam between the locker dry zone and the shower wet zone. Users will find it very inconvenient to have long distances to walk between their locker and the grooming station.
- Vanity tops must be designed for standing (36" +/-), stool-height (42" +/-) seating, or chair-height seating (30" +/-), depending on user preference.
- The design image of grooming stations can be used to convey the intended character of a facility. Upscale club environments should have luxurious grooming facilities. Public recreation facilities may want to convey a more modest but functional character.
- A full-length wall-mounted mirror should be provided for use somewhere along the locker room exit path.

Locker Room Auxiliary Spaces

Special uses are sometimes incorporated into locker-room plans to meet particular user needs. The specific requirements of each must be identified. Examples including social lounges, attendant services, shoe shine, laundry service, workout clothing service, massage, tanning, private telephone cubicles, and personal storage lockers of various sizes. The planning team should consider the arguments for inclusion or exclusion of each amenity.

Locker-room Accessories

Considerations for a well-equipped locker room include an electric water cooler, clock, scale, automatic swimsuit dryer, telephone, emergency call system, plastic bag dispenser, waste containers, hair dryers, television sets, and vending machines for personal grooming items or beverages.

Figure 16.9
Wet and Dry Grooming Stations

Special Types of Locker Rooms

Family Locker Room: This is a handy name for an arrangement of changing facilities designed to serve cross-gender couples with special needs, for example:

- Mother and a young son who is too old to join her in the women's locker room and too young to venture into the men's locker room alone.
- Father and a young daughter who is too old to join him in the men's locker room and too young to venture into the women's locker room alone.
- An elderly couple, one of whom needs assistance from the other in dressing for a rehab session or senior exercise program.
- An individual man or woman with a special privacy need due to a surgical scar, deformity, or personal preference. Family locker rooms can be used for patient changing rooms in facilities that offer integrated clinical services, such as physical therapy or cardiac rehab.

The family locker room (see Figure 16.10) is an array of individual changing rooms, each one equipped with a shower, toilet, sink, and changing space. As many as five or six such changing rooms can be provided. An arrangement of storage lockers and benches is provided in a spacious coed common area adjacent to the changing rooms. Grooming, showering, toilet, and dressing functions take place in the privacy of the changing rooms. Storage of clothing and final stages of dressing and grooming take place in the coed locker area. These rooms should be fully accessible to persons with disabilities and could in itself satisfy the legal requirement for a handicap-accessible locker facility. Other amenities that can be included in the family locker common area are an electric water cooler, swimsuit dryer, wet vanity, dry vanity, towel station, full-length mirror, scale, diaper-changing platform, coat rack, wet bag dispenser, telephone, waste container, and janitor closet. A selection of full-size and half-size storage lockers works well. Provide at least eight lockers for each changing room. The family locker room generally works best with direct access to aquatic attractions (Figure 16.10).

Express Lockers: It is true for any athletic/fitness facility that some members prefer to arrive wearing their workout/sports attire. They have no desire to use the changing, shower, or grooming facilities. They prefer to return to their homes for that purpose after working out. These users need only a secure place for their purse/wallet, hat, car keys, gloves, coat, and so forth. There is no need to force these members into a gender-specific locker room and add to the potential congestion.

Express lockers can be provided in an area convenient to the ingress/egress circulation of members. This is a coed environment and should include a variety of locker sizes (and a coat rack in four-season climates) and comfortable benches for those users who need to change shoes. Express lockers have proven in practice to be a very cost-effective way of diverting unnecessary traffic from overcrowded men's and women's locker rooms. An express locker count equal to 10% of the total gender-specific locker rooms will usually be adequate.

Figure 16.10
Family Changing Rooms

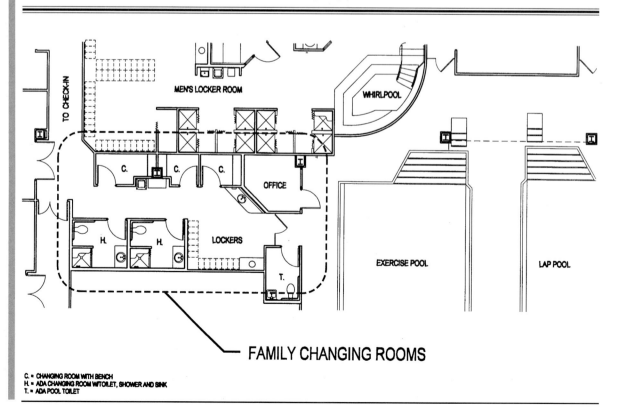

FAMILY CHANGING ROOMS

C. = CHANGING ROOM WITH BENCH
H. = ADA CHANGING ROOM W/TOILET, SHOWER AND SINK
T. = ADA POOL TOILET

Staff Locker Room: The question of staff changing facilities is important. If staff use the main locker rooms, they may, in effect, displace a paying customer. Yet providing a separate dedicated staff locker room can be space-consuming and costly. Certainly, there is a legitimate need in an athletic facility for staff changing, showering, and grooming functions, as well as a secure holding area for their personal effects.

Many facilities have found it effective to provide a coed staff lounge with a mini-kitchen, basic furnishings such as tables and chairs, and an arrangement of storage lockers for clothing and personal effects. A pair of private unisex changing and shower compartments can be included to allow staff to freshen up after work without competing with the membership for limited locker and shower availability. A wet vanity/grooming station can also be included. Some management systems will prefer to have the staff mingling with the membership and thus doing an ongoing quality check as they use the same locker facilities that the members do. Once again, a case-by-case determination must be made in order to fit the facility design concept to the management concept.

Officials Locker Room: Facilities designed for competitive team sports activities will require locker room accommodation for umpires, referees and visiting teams. These facilities are gender specific and require a secure location away from contestant and spectator areas.

Administrative Offices

Staff offices must be barrier free to job candidates with disabilities and equally accessible to men and women. Staff offices generally fall into two categories of space.

Back office space is required for staff who have little or no regular contact with active facility users. Examples include: accounting, human resources, marketing staff and copy/fax/print functions. Front office space is required for staff with supervisory responsibilities and regular contact with active users. Examples include management staff, sales personnel, program directors, and counselors. Other administrative functions that require a mainstream location include:

- reception, access control, and check-in for the facility at large
- supervisory stations for natatorium, fitness floor, gymnasium, racquet sports
- faculty/coaches/instructors' offices

The size, quantity, and furnishings required by each of these staff offices must be determined by the planner in dialogue with department heads and user representatives. Questions to be considered include:

- What are the expected number of full- and part-time staff? What are their titles and work descriptions?
- Which staff members require enclosed private offices? Open but private work stations? Shared work stations (concurrently or alternately)? In-office conference capability?
- Which staff members require frequent contact with each other? With certain activity areas? With certain users?

With answers to these questions in hand, the designer can begin preparation of a space plan for administrative offices. Design considerations include:

- anticipated circulation patterns for users and staff
- type of partition and extent of glass, if any, in walls and doors
- need for acoustic privacy
- lighting system for both ambient and task lighting
- provision of adequate power, communication, and computer hook-ups
- provision of year-round heating/cooling and temperature control zones
- need for natural daylight or outside view
- computer terminals, computer desks, or computer tables and wiring for main frame and internet access

Office uses require supplemental spaces that can accommodate the functions necessary to support the working station. The design process should bring these questions to the table for discussion by all appropriate parties. Such spaces include:

- Utility area for facsimile machines, copiers, printers, office supplies, and storage.
- Employee kitchen area with coffee maker, microwave, refrigerator, dishwasher, and storage (sometimes included as part of a lunch room or staff lounge)
- Conference rooms
- Coat closets or employee security lockers
- Designated and specially ventilated smokers' room if operating policies will allow staff smoking on premises
- Staff-only restrooms and shower/locker rooms may be desired to maintain separation from customers/users
- Location and type of central telephone reception and distribution must be determined. Many multi-feature phone systems are available

- Mail and message-handling system should be planned into the administrative component, voice-mail phone systems are now an expected and widely accepted productivity tool for administrative staff.

Laundry

Planning and design of laundry facilities is predicated upon the workload. Just as kitchen design is based on the menu, so laundry design is based on quantity and type of articles to be processed. Towels and athletic clothing are the most common articles needing to be laundered in a recreation facility. The unit of measure applicable to laundry equipment is the pound. Therefore, it is necessary to translate the laundry workload from quantity of articles to their weight in pounds, which must be processed per hour. This is a measure of the actual dry weight of articles to be washed. Without reliable information on weight, quantity, and use rates of laundered articles, the planning of laundry facilities is pure guesswork.

Most equipment cycles allow two loads per hour. Thus, it is possible to arrive at a calculation of required laundry capacity by establishing with the facility operator how many hours per day the laundry will be staffed and running. Certainly a double-shift operation will get more production from a given quantity of equipment than a single 8-hour work shift, but a double shift may not be practical for other reasons. Once the workload is determined, the size and quantity of washers and dryers can be set. It generally is advisable to select machine sizes that allow at least two washing units and two drying units. In this way, a malfunction in one machine will not completely shut down the laundry operation.

The location of laundry facilities is of great importance. The best locations are close to the storage/ distribution place for cleaned articles or the collection point for soiled articles. A ground level, grade-supported floor slab is preferred for ease of plumbing and control of vibrations from the equipment. Commercial washer extractors work at very high revolutions per minute (RPM), which can generate destructive vibrations. Most units must be bolted securely to a 24-inch-thick grade-supported concrete slab in order to control vibration. If an on-grade location is not possible, it will be necessary to specify an extraction washing machine with a built-in vibration dampening system. Most manufacturers offer such a unit as an option. Other factors to consider in selecting a laundry location are:

- The need for an outside combustion air supply for gas-fired dryers may suggest a location along an outside wall.
- The need for an exhaust flue for both gas and electric dryers may suggest a single-story location with a roof surface immediately overhead. A booster fan may be required if the length of exhaust duct exceeds manufacturer limits. Lint build-up in the exhaust ductwork requires that maintenance access be planned for and used regularly.
- The high volume of waste water discharge for most commercial washers requires a high-capacity trench drain recessed into the floor.
- Consideration should be given to how equipment can be moved into and out of the laundry space. Washer and dryer sizes should be researched carefully prior to sizing and locating access doorways.
- Accessibility by both male and female staff is needed.

The laundry planner must consider how and by what route both soiled and cleaned articles will arrive at their proper destinations. If carts are used, space must be allocated for storage or holding of extra carts at points of collection, cleaning, and distribution. Folding and sorting of laundered articles is a very labor-intensive process. However, the location of the laundry facility can be planned to allow towel-handling personnel to cover other staff functions such as locker attendant or housekeeping. Other planning and design considerations for laundry facilities are:

- Confirm that adequate utility capacities exist for electric power, water supply, water temperature, sanitary waste, and gas.
- Domestic washers and dryers will prove unsuitable for all but the most incidental, low-volume laundry operation.
- Placement of washers and dryers should be conducive to a logical and efficient work flow.
- Extractor-type washers use centrifugal force to wring maximum moisture from wet articles prior to drying. This will conserve dryer energy and save time in the drying process.
- Laundry room floors, walls, and ceilings should be finished with a smooth, easily cleaned impervious coating that will not trap dust and lint.
- Dryers typically have a greater weight capacity than a corresponding washer. A 35-pound washer normally will be paired with a 50-pound dryer.
- The laundry room must include space for chemical storage, carts, folding counters, a two-compartment sink, and adequate service access space around the equipment.
- The final pieces of the laundry puzzle are the washer and dryer themselves. Numerous manufacturers offer commercial units varying in size, power, quality, durability, design, and cost. Selection of the best manufacturers (washers and dryers are not necessarily made by the same company) requires diligent comparisons of actual cylinder sizes, types of motor control capabilities, automatic detergent injection systems, control cycles, physical construction, warranties, energy efficiency, and maintenance schedules.

Storage Facilities

Of course, storage rooms should be sized, shaped, and furnished with racks, shelves, bins, and so forth as required to accommodate the items to be stored. However, it is not always possible to predict, over the life of a facility, how much and what kinds of things will need to be stored. Therefore, when it comes to sizing storage rooms, it is best to err on the side of accommodation and provide at least 20% more storage space than can be justified by actual measurement of the volume of articles to be stored.

Designers frequently assign the storage function to odd-shaped, leftover spaces that are not necessarily conducive to efficient storage. There are a few simple planning and design guidelines for storage rooms:

- Within the storage room, allow for a double-loaded circulation way between actual storage space on either side. The depth of the storage space must be appropriate to the item stored so that it may be retrieved without repositioning of intervening stored items.
- Storage room doors should open out from the room and swing flat against adjacent walls. Double-door openings should be considered wherever bulky items will be stored.
- Access to certain storage rooms should be configured so that large, long articles such as ladders can be maneuvered in and out of the room.
- Adequate, utilitarian lighting is a must.
- All storage rooms should be mechanically ventilated.
- Provisions must be made for storage of outside field equipment so that access to storage does not result in unnecessary soiling of interior walkways.
- Code restrictions may impose limits on storage room locations. Many codes, for example, do not allow the dead space under a stairway enclosure to be used for storage.

In general, storage rooms should be located close to the point of use for items being stored. The matter of maintaining storage security and limiting access to authorized persons deserves careful consideration by the design team. Proper door hardware and a well thought-out keying schedule will enhance storage security. The use of motion detection alarms or video surveillance may be appropriate for storage of high-cost items such as audiovisual equipment.

Customizing Ancillary Facilities

The remainder of this chapter will examine the ways in which ancillary facilities in general should be customized to meet the unique requirements of each project type: athletic facilities, physical education facilities, and recreation/fitness clubs.

Athletic Facilities

These are the buildings and fields used by educational institutions to conduct competitive, interschool athletic programs and include facilities for both training and performance. It normally is only at the collegiate level that designated facilities are provided for the exclusive use of the intercollegiate athletic program. High school athletic facilities are generally shared with physical education uses.

Requirements for the ancillary areas of intercollegiate athletic facilities include recognition of the important role such facilities play in recruiting top-level athletes and coaches and the creation of a successful competitive record.

Locker Rooms

Size, quantity, type, and location of team locker rooms will be determined by the number and size of active sports teams, the timing of practice and competitive seasons, the timing of daily practice sessions, and the location of practice and competition facilities. Other design and planning considerations for team locker rooms include:

- Visiting team locker rooms must be provided for competitive events. Planners must analyze scheduling patterns for all sports with overlapping seasons to determine the number of visiting team locker rooms needed. Security for this area is of utmost importance.
- Locker sizes for athletics will be determined by the equipment required for a given sport. Of course, football and hockey lockers will be larger than basketball and track lockers. The amount of dressing space allowed should also increase as locker sizes increase to accommodate the handling of larger equipment. Sports with nonoverlapping practice and competition seasons can share the same locker space.
- Direct outside access to practice and/or game fields may be desirable for sports such as football, soccer, lacrosse, and baseball. The soiling of interior hallways thus can be minimized.
- Planning efforts must ensure that locker room facilities provide equal opportunities for both men and women and persons with disabilities.
- Game day locker facilities also should be provided for coaches and officials.
- Proper locker ventilation for drying stored articles is extremely important in preventing the build-up of unpleasant odors.

Competitive sports will require team meetings and "chalk talks," which can be conducted in one or more lecture rooms ideally located close to the locker rooms. Such rooms should be equipped with chalkboards and audiovisual equipment. Video replay and analysis is a key component of most coaching programs and planning for the location and networking of the hardware for this function is essential.

Administrative Offices

The need for staff work stations for athletic team programs can be quite extensive. This is particularly true for the high-profile competitive sports programs found in Division I universities. Each program must be analyzed for its own unique set of requirements, but it is not unusual for multisport programs to require defined working quarters for such staff positions as athletic director and assistants, head coaches and assistants, public relations and media coordinators, sports psychologists, fund-raising and alumni relations director(s), facilities manager, ticket sales staff, recruiting and scholarship coordinator, accounting staff, student advisors, chaplain, transportation coordinator, equipment and supply manager, director of security, secretarial and clerical aides, audiovisual personnel, and part-time or seasonal employees. Allowances should be made for anticipated growth in the scale of the athletic program and the staff to support it.

The planning process must identify all positions requiring a workstation, and itemize the needs of each in a written document that will be approved by the controlling authority prior to the start of the facility design work. In developing a layout of staff offices, the designer will confront the issue of centralized versus decentralized administrative offices. This matter is best resolved with input from user groups.

Laundry

Requirements for laundry services to athletic team programs go beyond the provision of clean towels. The laundry service for a team sport facility must deal with the program's need for clean and sanitary towels; practice and game uniforms; protective equipment (shoulder pads, headgear, etc.); personal wear; and miscellaneous items such as floor mats, foul weather gear, equipment bags, footwear, and utility items. Competitive travel schedules require shipping and receiving facilities not unlike a commercial warehouse operation, complete with loading docks and truck berths. The laundry is best located at the distribution/collection point for all materials to be supplied by the institution. If the laundry is to be a large central plant shared with other institutional users, a remote location may be required. However, a convenient and secure distribution center should then be created for the team sport facility.

The use of individual mesh laundry bags is an effective way to simplify handling of personal items. Each bag carries an identification tag and can be filled with soiled personal wear, turned in, washed, dried, and held for later retrieval by the user. A numbered storage rack will be helpful in keeping the bags arranged for speedy retrieval.

Storage and Maintenance

Off-season handling of reusable sports equipment must be provided. Planning and design considerations include:

- Adequate space for storage includes shelving and/or racks appropriate for the items being stored. Helmets and shoulder pads, for example, will have a longer useful life if properly racked instead of being dumped into a bulk storage bin. Provide for receiving incoming equipment and issuing outgoing equipment.
- Adequate space for repair of items before being stored is important. This procedure will allow non-repairable inventory to be identified, discarded, and reordered prior to the next season. Allow cabinet space for tools and spare parts.
- For team sports, the security of stored items is particularly important. Designers must address the issue of lock keying and access control in coordination with the equipment manager.
- Storage areas should be kept ventilated and dry to prevent mildew, mold, and odor buildup.

Physical Education Facilities

These are the buildings and fields used by institutions of learning in the conduct of physical education programs for all ages. Such programs commonly are provided for students of elementary, middle, junior high, and high schools, as well as the university undergraduate level. Programming of physical education generally is organized in a class format with one or more instructors. A wide variety of skill development activities must be accommodated. Special considerations for the planning and design of the ancillary facilities that support the physical education program follow.

Locker Rooms

Because of the scheduled class format, physical education locker rooms must be able to accommodate large influxes of user groups occupying and quickly vacating lockers, toilets, showers, and grooming facilities. Planners must analyze these use patterns in terms of class size, class duration, age, gender mix, duration of changeover time between classes, and types of activities being conducted. Not all classes will require use of locker rooms. This analysis will guide determinations such as number and size of lockers; number of toilets, showers, and lavatories; types of locker room accessories provided; and types of finishes to be used throughout. Designers will reference the same analysis as they create and select provisions for towels, soap handling, energy conservation, grooming aids, handling of refuse, and control of vandalism. The design strategy for dealing with each of these issues should be developed from the dialogue among planners, designers, manager, faculty, and users. Other planning and design considerations unique to physical education locker rooms include:

- Height of locker benches, lockers, and locker security devises should be studied carefully, relative to the average height, reach, and eye level of the typical user. This also applies to heights of water coolers, lavatories, toilets, urinals, and countertops. In case of a wide mix of users, the design orientation should favor the least able user or provide a mix of accommodations.
- Many schools have after-hours programs for community meetings. If the overall facility is going to offer such programs, the toilet facilities portion of the locker room can be positioned to permit access for community users without allowing them access to the remainder of the locker room.

Locker systems must be customized to meet the special needs of the physical education program being served. The dressing locker and box storage system frequently is used. In this system, a series of small storage lockers is located near a large dressing locker. Security of the storage locker is accomplished with a combination padlock, which is transferred to the dressing locker along with all the contents of the storage locker when the student is in class. Many variations of locker systems have been developed to meet the special needs of physical education facilities. The designer must analyze the unique circumstances of each application before selecting the most appropriate system for a given project.

Because these locker rooms may play host to large groups of unsupervised adolescents, the design of all components and finishes should be as abuse-resistant as practical. Plastic laminate and glass and wood veneer, for example, are not considered to be abuse resistant. Avoid creating hidden alcoves where unsupervised behavior could lead to facility damage or personal safety problems.

The need for visual inspection by facility managers of locker contents may exist. If this is the case, the use of an expanded mesh locker construction may be the best choice. Otherwise, a means of overriding locker security devices must be planned for.

Staff Offices

The need for physical education staff work stations is limited primarily to faculty office space. The relationship of these offices to those of the athletic teams and administration is the subject of much discussion in schools with both programs. In general, administrative units requiring little or no contact with students may not benefit from close proximity to those with regular involvement with large numbers of students. However, in some cases, interaction and good communication between these groups of staff may produce beneficial results. This is another planning question that defies universal resolution. It must be resolved as a matter of policy, on a case-by-case basis, for each institution.

Laundry

Options for handling the laundry needs of physical education students are:

- Students are responsible for personal laundry needs, including towels and/or gym uniforms.
- School maintains a laundry facility on the premises for towels and/or gym uniforms.
- School contracts to an outside service for towel laundry and/or gym uniforms.

Potential benefits of a school laundry are improved health, reduction of odors, and cleaner uniforms. The feasibility of an on-site laundry must be demonstrated on a case-by-case basis by analysis of all factors of cost such as staff, equipment, floor space, maintenance, utility connections, operating costs, and supplies.

Recreation/Fitness Clubs

This section addresses those buildings and fields created by universities, hospitals, municipalities, and a variety of private entrepreneurs to serve the recreational/fitness needs of their respective constituencies. These constituencies include: student intramural programs, public recreation programs, and individual fee-paying users/members. The basic motivation underlying the purpose of these facilities is enjoyment of sporting activities and/or desire for self-improvements and health maintenance through fitness. To be successful, this type of facility must serve the needs of its users/members who are not obligated to participate or who can elect to take their business elsewhere. This customer service orientation can exist on many levels of quality, image, and cost, but it is clearly an orientation that must be reflected in the substance and style of a facility's ancillary areas. The following summary of special planning and design considerations is directed toward the ancillary areas of recreation/fitness clubs.

Locker Rooms

Comfort, style, and service are matters of concern in recreation/fitness locker rooms. However, these concerns do not override the basic functional requirements of locker rooms discussed earlier. Depending on the target market of the facility and the operational economics, which are driven by price and volume of users/members, the level of comfort, style, and service must be set by the planning/design team in collaboration with the management group.

The level of comfort is affected by number, size, and spacing of lockers, lavatories, and showers. It also is affected by spaciousness and the kind of seating provided in dressing areas, the lighting, the quality of the heating and cooling systems, and the acoustical ambiance of the space. For a space such as this, where users are in various states of undress, all circulation paths should be a minimum of five feet in width.

Color, texture, finish materials, and furnishings influence the style and image of the locker room. These must be selected to ensure compatibility with the overall facility mission and maintain the consistency of the aesthetic statement being made throughout the building. Whether this statement is spartan and utilitarian, luxurious and rich, or high-tech and polished, the choices made send a message to the user/member. The designer's challenge is to fit that message to the target market.

The service level of the recreation/fitness locker room is conveyed by the choices made regarding the means of providing locker security; the system for collecting and distributing towels; the availability of soap, shampoo, lotions and grooming aids; the means of drying hair; and the availability of such amenities as steam, sauna and whirlpool bath, telephone, and shoe shine.

Attention to the details of providing comfort, style, and service at a level appropriate to the target market is the key to creating a successful recreation/fitness locker room. Other planning and design considerations unique to locker rooms of this facility type follow:

- Private shower booths with doors, curtains, or a private changing chamber may be provided.
- It generally is impractical to offer a permanent, full-size private locker to each member. Many facilities of this type have up to 5,000 members, which could require locker rooms of 18,000 to 24,000 square feet if a private locker is provided to each member. Consider offering a mix of small-sized private rental lockers as an extra-cost option and providing a full-size dressing locker to each member for day use.
- A ratio of one full-size day locker per 10 members will be sufficient for facilities with average rates of utilization by its members. Adjustment of this ratio up or down can be made by planning on a case-by-case basis to respond to higher or lower frequency of use.

Administrative Offices

In general, the administrative departments of a recreation/fitness club may include the following units: membership sales, management, recreation/fitness programming, accounting, maintenance/housekeeping, personnel, food/beverage, and front desk/check-in. There is little benefit to consolidating these offices into a single administrative block. Management and sales offices should be located near the front desk check-in point. Recreation/fitness programming staff should be located close to the activity areas they serve. Accounting, maintenance/housekeeping, and personnel can be placed in a more remote back office location, because they have little need for direct member contact. The food and beverage office should be included within the restaurant/bar area if provided. The front desk reception station must be equipped to confirm validity of arriving members, control access to the facility, handle telephone reception and routing, confirm activity programming and court reservations, and handle all public inquiries and member service requests. The front desk also may be the best place from which to control lighting throughout the facility and to conduct announcements over the public address system. It is essential that the front desk be positioned to provide clear control of the line separating the public/free access zone of the facility from the member-only zones. This control of access will preserve the value of membership by preventing guests and nonmembers from using the facilities without proper payment and signing of liability release forms.

Multipurpose Facilities

It is not uncommon for a sports facility to be an intercollegiate athletic team center serving student athletics, a physical education center serving all students, and a center for recreation and fitness serving dues-paying alumni and faculty, as well as the student intramural sports system.

Facilities that attempt to accommodate a variety of uses must be planned accordingly. With so many diverse groups competing for space and time, conflicts are inevitable. The economic benefits are obvious. Multipurpose facilities are utilized more fully by avoiding duplication of facilities that may sit idle during large parts of the day. However, scheduling compromises may reduce access by certain user groups to unacceptably low levels. Institutions without the financial resources to fund independent facilities for athletics, physical education, and recreation/fitness may elect to undertake the planning challenges of a multipurpose facility. These challenges involve facility planning, curriculum planning, and schedule planning to accommodate as effectively as possible the needs of each constituency. The Loyola University Medical Center in Chicago, Illinois, is one example of a multipurpose recreation/fitness facility that serves the medical school student body, hospital faculty and staff, and outside community members.

Summary

In general, the key to creating superior ancillary facilities is found in a design process that invites input from users, managers, staff, design specialists, and component providers. Such a process will always examine comparable design solutions with a critical eye in a diligent effort to avoid repeating past mistakes and to learn from past successes. It is the mix of solid experience, careful listening, and open-minded inventiveness that allows an architect to produce successful design solutions.

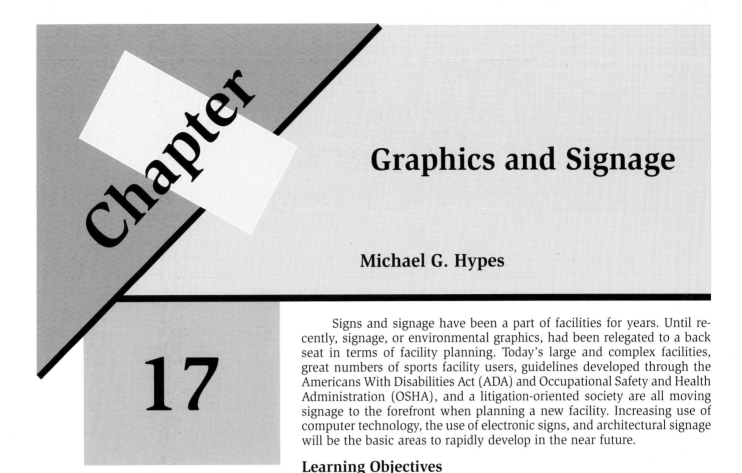

Graphics and Signage

Michael G. Hypes

Signs and signage have been a part of facilities for years. Until recently, signage, or environmental graphics, had been relegated to a back seat in terms of facility planning. Today's large and complex facilities, great numbers of sports facility users, guidelines developed through the Americans With Disabilities Act (ADA) and Occupational Safety and Health Administration (OSHA), and a litigation-oriented society are all moving signage to the forefront when planning a new facility. Increasing use of computer technology, the use of electronic signs, and architectural signage will be the basic areas to rapidly develop in the near future.

Learning Objectives

After reading this chapter, the student should be able to

- understand the importance of signage,
- know how to design effective signage,
- know the type of sign needed for a given situation,
- understand the cost and maintenance factors of signage, and
- understand the place of graphics in facility architecture.

Planning for Signs and Graphics

Have you ever visited an arena, stadium, or convention center for the first time and found that the signs were too small, hard to read, lacking, or obstructed from view? People in that situation experience a high level of frustration, become lost, and eventually stop looking for their destination.

Clear, informative graphics and signs are essential for conveying directional, instructional, or general information to the public. This is especially true in arenas, stadiums, or convention centers that house a wide range of events and attract large crowds.

Townsend (2004) suggests, when thinking through graphics and signs for a facility, the planners should consider the following key questions during the design phase:

- What will the sign be used for?
- How long will it be used?
- What image is the graphic or sign to depict?
- What is the target audience for the graphic or sign?
- What is the viewing distance for the graphic or sign and the length of time it will take for viewers to read it?
- Where will the graphic or sign be placed and how will it be installed?
- What is the budget for the graphic or sign project?
- Are there permits required or restrictions imposed on the sign?
- What other graphics or signs does the facility need?
- When is the graphic or sign needed?

Importance of Signs

Signs are an essential part of a facility and should be an integral part of the planning process in a new facility. Signs have come a long way in the last decade. New materials, colors, and graphics have changed the signage world. Many architectural firms now refer to a signage system as the environmental graphics of a facility. All sports and recreation facilities include a wide variety of signs. It is important to identify facility entrances and to direct individuals to concourse levels and seating sections. Restrooms, concession areas, first aid stations, information centers, locker areas, security areas, and exits must be clearly designated. Information concerning parking area locations must be located near the exits.

Traffic-flow information must be imparted by external facility signage. The parking area, if large, will need to be sectioned off by effective signs.

Elevator and room designation signs must have raised-letter markings for users with visual impairments. The centers of these signs should be placed 60 inches above the floor. Other facility signs should also have raised letters, even though at this time this is not an ADA requirement (see Figure 17.1). Where diverse populations exist, signs must be designed in multiple languages. The use of international graphics (or pictograms) can also help in designing signage for multiple languages.

Figure 17.1
Guidelines for ADA Signage

- Pictograms must be placed on a background with a height of at least 6 inches. Pictograms must have a text counterpart.
- Raised characters must be at a minimum of 5/8 inch and a maximum of 2 inches.
- There are character proportions as well. Letters and numbers must have a ratio of width to height of between 3:5 and 1:1, and a stroke width-to-height ratio of between 1:5 and 1:10.
- Braille and raised characters have to be raised 1/32 inch, and the font must be either upper-case sans serif or simple sans serif. The font must be accompanied with Braille grade 2.
- There are requirements for the finish and contrast of the characters. The contrast must be at least 70%, and the colors of the background and characters must either be matte, eggshell, or some other nonglare finish.
- Signage must be mounted at least 60 inches above the floor to the center line of the sign.
- Signage must be mounted and installed on a wall that is adjacent to the door's latch side. But, if there is no space for that, then the signage needs to be installed on the nearest adjacent wall. Individuals must be able to approach the signage within 3 inches without any protrusions, such as the door swinging or any nearby objects.

Many sports facilities are large, sprawling, one- or two-floor facilities. If the facilities have been around for a number of years, there is a good chance additions have enhanced them. Add-ons can create logistic nightmares and signs become paramount to direct individuals through a facility. It is not uncommon to find sports facilities with interiors of more than 200,000 square feet. Sports facilities are also among the most heavily used facilities on campuses and related sites. Large sports facilities, such as arenas and stadiums with large numbers of users, call for a well-planned signage system.

Types of Signs

The basic purpose of any sign is to impart information. This information varies with the type of sign used. Five categories of signs are identified for use in facilities. These categories are:

- warning, danger, caution, and emergency signs
- notice and standard operational signs
- directional signs
- rules and regulations
- sign graphics

Even though signage is divided into five distinct categories, the groups overlap. A sign could fall into just one category or it might fall into two or three categories depending on its purpose and the type of information it is conveying.

When developing signage for a facility or a specific area within the facility, special consideration should be given to the purpose of the signage and the eventual audience for the information. OSHA identified the following issues regarding the communication of hazardous conditions:

- comprehensibility
- readability
- standard phrases

Comprehensibility refers to the ability of the individual reading a sign to understand the information sufficiently to take the desired action. Comprehensibility is different from *readability* in that the latter is simply a measure of the grade level of the written information while the former is a measure of how well the receiver of the information understood it.

Standard phrases refers to the use of "signal words" in signage. The use of the word *danger* indicates an imminently hazardous situation, which, if not avoided, may result in death or serious injury. This signal word should be limited to the most extreme situations. *Warning* indicates a potentially hazardous situation, which, if not avoided, could result in death or serious injury. *Caution* indicates a potentially hazardous situation, which, if not avoided, may result in minor or moderate injury. It may also be used to alert against unsafe practices.

The population at large may not share the importance that professionals attach to signal words. Many organizations (e.g., American National Standards Institute, U.S. Military) have guidelines for the determination of what signal words are to be used with specific hazards, and these are usually unknown to the public. The arousal effects of signal words and accepted organizational guidelines need to be incorporated into the design of effective signage.

Designing Signs

If at all possible, design your signs during the planning process of your building and its surroundings. If you are renovating or making additions to an existing facility, this is a prime time to plan for all new environmental graphics in your complex. Make your signs an aesthetically pleasing part of your facility.

Signs need to be simple and understandable and they need to attract the facility user's attention. Placement, size, shape, repetitiveness, color, and graphics are all important in designing simple, understandable signs that attract user attention.

Placement

Signs must attract the facility user's attention. A well-placed sign maximizes its effect on the facility user. Signs need to be placed in the appropriate area and need to be placed at the appropriate place and height to have the greatest impact on the user. For instance, a sign stating "No Skateboards Allowed in the Building" will not make its point in the interior of the building. This sign needs to be placed at all building entrances so that it can be seen before one enters the building with a skateboard. On the other hand, the sign "No Food or Drink in the Weight Area" needs to be posted outside the weight area as well as inside the weight area.

It is also important to place signs in normal sight lines. Placing signs too high, too low, or off to the side makes them less visible. It is important to remember that sight lines vary according to the user's height. Signs for young users, six to eight years of age, should be placed lower than signs for adults. Individuals in wheelchairs need signs placed in their sight lines.

Signs may be on a wall, a ceiling, a floor, suspended, freestanding, on columns, or on doors. In some instances, a sign may be on two or more surfaces. It may be partially on a wall and continue onto an adjacent wall or floor. The effect of a sign on multiple surfaces is eye-catching, thus attracting attention to it.

At times, signs must be repetitive within a facility. An example of repetitive signage is in an indoor racquet court battery. If there are eight courts, some signs will need to be repeated eight times, once at each court. An example of repetitive signage is: "Eye Guards Are Mandatory!"

Materials

Signs may be an integral part of the facility as a permanent part of the structure (painted on walls or other surfaces or tiles of different colors that make a sign) or they can be attached to surfaces by a frame or brackets. Architectural or permanent signs are recommended whenever possible. These signs not only impart information but they are also an aesthetically pleasing part of the structure of your facility. If architectural signage is used,

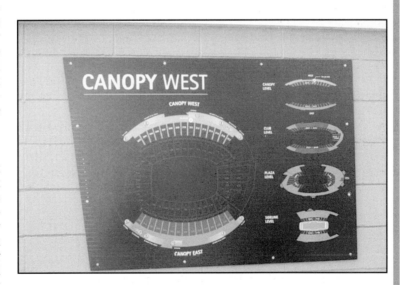

**Stadium seating signage,
Paul Brown Stadium.**

and planned for carefully, few signs will need to be added to your facility. It is paramount to plan in advance for successful architectural signage. If mistakes are made in the planning process, they become permanent mistakes, or, at the least, costly mistakes to overcome. Even with the greatest of planning of architectural signage, some signs will have to be non-permanent and some signs will have to be later

Notes

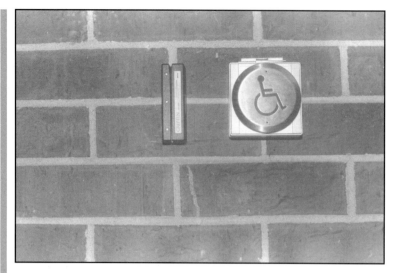

Handicap-accessible signage.

must be in a secured location since they are easily broken and are expensive to repair. If electrical signs are to be used, one must plan carefully for electrical outlets or electrical hookups directly in relation to sign placement.

Extension cords running from signs to an electrical power source are unaesthetic, unsafe, and unacceptable.

Shape, Color, Size, and Graphics

Signs do not have to be rectangular in shape. Rectangular signs do afford maximum use of space if the signs contain only words. Other sign shapes have the ability to be eye-catching and/or informational. Take the eight-sided red sign at the end of the street, attached to a metal post, located on the right hand side of the street. This does not need to

additions. As time and facility use change, signs need to be changed and updated even though some architectural signage will never need to be changed. Architectural signs are usually made of "like" building material. For instance, a painted wall has a painted sign or an asphalt tile floor has different size, texture, or color inset tiles to form a sign.

Signs may be made of wood, metal, tile, paper, glass, paint, and plastic or any combination of the aforementioned items. Signs may be electrified such as lighted signs, billboards, scoreboards, or "running" sign boards. Electrical signs are more expensive than nonelectrical signs. An electrified sign, on the other hand, stands out and attracts attention to it. Electrical signs

Directional signage.

An example of repetitive signage.

be read—the octagonal shape, location, and color indicate *stop*. Explicitly shaped signs, for specific information, can be used in facilities to impart information by using sign shape. Example: all pentagonal signs indicate classrooms, all circular signs indicate laboratories, and all diamond-shaped signs indicate offices.

An X-shaped sign in facilities immediately signals not to do something ("No Diving," "Do Not Run") just by the shape of the sign itself. The idea of effective sign shapes follows a recent international trend toward standard pictorial signs. Facility signs now must take on and convey a universal message to many ethnic populations. A sign featuring graphics will not alienate a facility's foreign users as much as a sign in English might.

Color, as the red in stop signs, can also be an important aspect of signage design. All signs of one color can indicate storage and housekeeping areas. Color in signs can be used to attract the attention of facility users. Bright-colored signs on a bland wall surface, in most instances, attract attention. A colored sign will attract a user's attention better than a black and white sign. Incorporate color in your signage theme.

Signs vary in size. The size of a sign, in itself, is a method of drawing the attention of facility users. A very small sign indicating *exit* is easily seen suspended from the ceiling or wall. Sometimes a large sign is needed to house important infor-

Scoreboard signage, Paul Brown Stadium.

mation and to draw the facility user's attention. "No Lifeguard on Duty—Swim at Your Own Risk" is effective as a large sign. Vary the size of your signs depending upon the information to be imparted and make use of sign size to attract attention.

The size of a sign's images and print also are instrumental in how the information is relayed. Words and graphics that are too small make the reader work harder and can result in the sign being ignored.

Just as some signs can be too wordy or hard to comprehend, too many signs posted in a small area also create problems. An overabundance of signs may cause the reader to miss a certain sign that has been

Example of signage found in swimming areas.

lumped together in the busy array of other signs. Separating and isolating signs is important to their overall effectiveness (Turner, 1994).

The content and message of a sign must be designed for the educational level(s) of the individuals using the facility. Content of a sign for a university will read differently than the content of the same sign for an elementary school. In all cases, it is important to keep signs as simple as possible. The simpler a sign, the easier it is to read and understand its content, thus making the sign more effective.

The old adage that a picture or graphic is worth a thousand words is still accurate for sign design. Using a clown figure to enhance a "No Clowning" sign in a weight area attracts attention to the sign. A facility user's attention is drawn to attractive signs and adding graphics to signs makes them more attractive. A little humor about a serious matter can help to impart important information to facility users.

Signage and the Three Groups It Serves

Though most signage will be directed at facility users, there are two other groups for whom signage is vital: facility employees and emergency personnel. The litigious society that we live in has placed an increased importance on proper and effective signage in our facilities. Effective signage may prevent an injury from occurring or it may be important in one's defense during a trial. Think of effective signage as both a money and stress saver when it comes to litigation.

Information contained in signage is important not only to the facility users but also to the facility staff. Signs help facility staff acclimate quicker and more safely to their jobs. Good location, direction, and rules signs help new employees adapt more quickly to a new environment.

Hazardous materials are found in many facility laboratories and swimming pools. Staff must handle biohazardous waste, toxic chemicals and gases, and nuclear contaminants routinely. Signage is paramount in these areas. Signs should first indicate the hazard and secondly inform the employee how to work safely with the hazard. Containers for hazardous material and waste need effective signage in the form of visible labels. Signage should also be placed in break room and workroom areas to inform employees of various performance and safety requirements.

When there are too many signs they will not be read.

Emergency personnel are the third group of individuals for whom signage must be well planned. Signs must be planned so that emergency personnel can find their way easily in a complex facility to save lives or deter additional injuries to facility occupants. Emergency personnel should not have to wander around a building before they can complete their jobs. Clear and effective signage in laboratories and pools indicating specifically what hazardous materials were present when an injury occurred can save a life.

Signage Maintenance

Signs placed throughout the facility need to be maintained. If you have electrical signs, you will have to replace bulbs and other electronic components. Plan for this in sign placement. Most of these signs can be maintained from the front; however, there are some electrical signs that need to be maintained from the rear or from the top. If the electrical signs are small, they are easy to remove and repair. If the electrical signs are large, heavy, and cumbersome, one needs to plan for this in sign placement. A large rear-entry sign can be placed over a planned opening in a wall so that there is easy access for repair work to the rear of the sign without having to remove the sign.

Signs can break. Breakage of signs may be accidental or intentional. Signs in sports complexes take much abuse. Balls hit them, rackets and bats hit them, and for this reason, they need to be protected. If possible, place signs out of abuse range. Placing signs higher and in areas away from projectiles and hitting devices will help to prolong sign life and reduce maintenance costs. Some signs must be placed in "harm's way." Polycarbonate sheeting works best for signs that need to be encased or covered with a clear material. Be careful, though, because the glossy finish of the sign or its covering can create glare problems and take away from the effectiveness of the sign, as well as provide an unwelcome distraction. Wire mesh (the kind that sometimes covers clocks in school gymnasiums) works as an effective cover on signs whose faces would not be sufficiently protected by plastic sheeting, such as signs that are in the path of balls and other flying objects. If a sign must be covered with a mesh cage, make sure it can still be seen well enough to convey its message (Turner, 1994).

Signs can also be defaced. By placing signs out of reach, one can avoid some defacing. Use materials in the construction and covering of signs that deter defacing. The use of polycarbonate sheeting and other slick surfaces will help keep sign defacing at a minimum.

Signs need to be cleaned on a regular basis. Fingerprints, smudges, dust, and other airborne particles need to be removed from signage as a regular routine. Electronic signs need special attention and regular cleaning to ensure that they function at an optimal level. Soiled signage of any type can curtail the amount of information imparted by the sign. Set up a regular cleaning schedule for signage.

Miscellaneous Considerations

Signage cost will vary with materials, size, number of signs, and whether or not the sign is electrical. It is suggested to figure your signage cost as a part of your facility construction cost. In some cases, parts of construction costs are bid separately and signage may be bid after the facility is built. This is not recommended. Repetitive signs will reduce costs since more of the same product reduces the cost per sign. The geographic location of your facility will also be a factor in signage cost. It is suggested to purchase high-quality products even though initially these products

Using humor to relay information.

may be more costly than low-quality products. Over the lifetime of facility signage, quality products cost less.

The geographic location of the sports complex will dictate which and how many languages will be used in signs. Locations of multiple ethnic populations will dictate signage languages.

Signs can be affixed to surfaces either permanently or semi-permanently. The method of affixing will depend on the philosophy of the design and use of the facility. It will also depend on the longevity of the signage. "Exit" signs, for example, are rather permanent, whereas rules and regulation signs may change over time. Signs may

Bengal seating, Paul Brown Stadium.

Example of static and dynamic signage.

be attached flat onto a surface or they may extend out perpendicularly or horizontally from a surface. Protruding signs are sometimes needed for visibility and code adherence. One of the problems with protruding signs is that they are more susceptible to breakage than flush-mounted signs.

Keep in mind that the size and shape of some signs might be dictated by local, state, and federal regulations. Check local fire and building codes to be certain that a particular facility includes all the required signs. Additionally, check with state and national offices for signage needed to meet ADA and OSHA requirements.

In some instances, a one-sided, flush-mounted sign is not sufficient. Signs suspended from the ceiling may impart information on two, three, or four sides. Protruding signs usually give information on two or three sides. As signage is designed, always consider using signs with multiple sides. Some signs will need to be freestanding in order to be moved from one area to another area of the facility. An example of a freestanding sign would be, "Caution: Wet Floor." Freestanding signs can take any shape or form; however, the most common is a two-sided pyramid shape.

Sponsorship in sports complexes is common. Sharing a sign with a sponsor is common in athletics (e.g., rolling sponsorship signs). Scoreboards and other signs are either purchased by the sponsor or rented by the sponsor so they

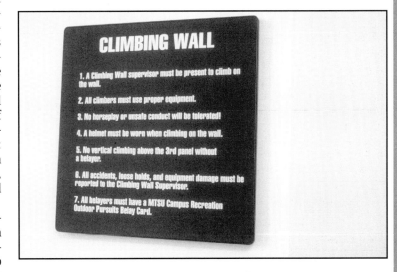

Information signage.

can advertise on the sign. This concept of sponsorship can be used for signage in other areas—not just for athletics. Sponsorship or sharing of signage is an important concept and should be studied carefully for all signage in a facility. In any case, sign sponsors and sports complex directors can both obtain mutual benefits by this partnership (Turner, 1994).

A good example of an entrance sign leading into a universally accessible playground.

A rather new area in signage design is the use of art graphics in a sports complex. These art graphics or permanently painted or inset materials are designed as integral parts of the facility. Various images can be placed on surfaces in the form of sports art, murals, or basic signage. These images are color coordinated with the color scheme of the facility. The images can bring life, motion, brightness, and attractiveness to an otherwise plain and dull facility. Currently, there are a number of companies that do art graphic work for sports complexes. Computer imagery is now enhancing the appearance of sports art, graphics and murals.

Summary

Effective signage in a sports complex must be well planned. Signage should be an integral part of facility design. There are various types of signs that will be used in any given sports complex. Well-planned, easily maintained, well-designed, cost effective signs can help prevent injury and related problems.

Examples of use of graphics (above and below).

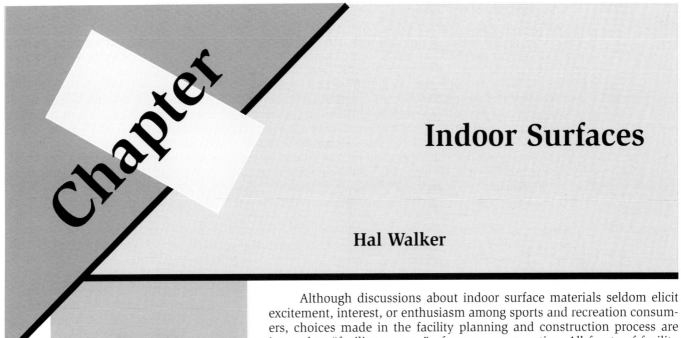

Indoor Surfaces

Hal Walker

18

Although discussions about indoor surface materials seldom elicit excitement, interest, or enthusiasm among sports and recreation consumers, choices made in the facility planning and construction process are integral to "facility success"—from any perspective. All facets of facility appearance, utility, maintenance, cost, safety, and functionality are influenced by the flooring surfaces. Three main categories of indoor surfacing include floors, walls, and ceilings. These surfaces have far-reaching and profound effects on numerous aspects of facility utilization and care. This chapter will provide useful information to assist in the process of outlining the types of materials available for these surfaces along with some advantages and disadvantages based on use in specific areas. The importance of planning in the selection of surface materials along with a consideration of individual needs, cost, maintenance, safety, acoustics and aesthetics will be addressed in this chapter.

Indoor facility surfaces are generally divided into three distinct areas. These areas are the service/ancillary areas, the main floor, and the office/administrative areas. Planning for, and the selection of, appropriate indoor surface materials, along with proper installation and maintenance over the facility's lifespan, can profoundly impact facility use and costs. Making informed surface choices allows for optimal facility's use, enhanced user satisfaction, and reduced incidence of injuries. Surface options, however, provide a vast and confusing array of choices and numerous companies tout state of the art textures, materials, colors, and performance characteristics. Yet, of the hundreds of products currently offered on the market, few surfaces are ideal for all activities a typical facility plans to offer. This situation leads to countless errors in the decision-making process as it is rare that facility planning takes place with equal participation among all "players" impacted by this process: owner/funding source, facility manager, maintenance staff, and the end users. There really is no perfect surface, as the needs and desires of each of these groups can be vastly different. Communication, however, is critical to the selection of facility surfaces that effectively meet the demands of the various planning constituents. Available budget, planned activity offerings, life expectancy, maintenance costs, risk management, foundation, and climate are but a few of the factors that must be considered when making informed facility surface choices.

Learning Objectives

After reading this chapter, the student should be able to

- demonstrate knowledge of the primary surface design areas of a facility;
- demonstrate knowledge of the types of materials available for these surfaces and their characteristics;
- understand the nature of various surface materials, use characteristics, safety issues, aesthetics, and acoustics;
- identify various advantages and disadvantages of surface materials that should be taken into consideration for flooring, wall, and ceiling materials;
- demonstrate awareness of facility surface options and relative cost factors;
- understand the impact of equipment and pedestrian traffic and the impact this has on facility surface life;
- explain recommended maintenance and upkeep practices for various surface materials;
- explain the concept of hardness and how it is measured;
- demonstrate an understanding of an appropriate selection process for facility flooring options; and
- understand the role of a facility manager in the selection of appropriate surface materials for sports facilities.

Selection of Indoor Surface Materials

Indoor surface materials must be carefully selected by considering the nature of the facility and the activities that are planned. As mentioned above, the primary surfaces addressed in this section are floors, walls, and ceilings. "When viewed as an essential piece of equipment in a sports facility, the sports floor is the point where the athlete and the activity merge" (Cooper, 2004, p. 4). The following text will outline the types of materials available for these surfaces and their characteristics along with factors to consider when going through the planning and decision making process.

Notes

Generally speaking, the planned activity in a given area should dictate the type of flooring surface utilized. Many, if not all surfaces, however, are utilized for more than a single purpose. There are three distinct areas of consideration in facilities currently being built. The first of these areas are the service/ancillary areas such as locker rooms, shower rooms and bathrooms. These areas require surfaces that take into account heavy moisture content as well as "slip and fall" concerns. The second area is the main arena or activity center of the facility. This area tends to receive the majority of time spent on the decision-making process; however, each area should warrant considerable thought and planning. These central activity areas typically require either a hardwood floor or a resilient synthetic material. Offices, administrative areas, and classrooms account for the third facility location (Flynn, 1993). Special areas require different materials, layouts, and treatments. For example, basketball courts should be made out of a nonslip surface material while a dance area should have a finished treatment that allows individuals to slide across the floor (Flynn, 1993). Safety, hardness, absorption, resilience, and lateral foot support are each critical in the selection of surfaces for dance floors (see also http://www.stagestep.com/).

Durability, flexibility, and cost are three considerations that have allowed synthetic floors to challenge traditional hardwood flooring. Synthetic surfaces take the form of grass or non-grass surfaces. The two most popular synthetic surfacing materials are polyvinyl chlorides (PVCs) and polyurethane. Polyurethane is either poured in place or produced in prefabricated sheets, which are adhered on the site, while PVCs are typically prefabricated. The general perception is that polyurethane possesses most of the desirable characteristics sought in a multipurpose facility surface (Flynn, 1993).

Multipurpose approaches are common for many facilities, as a variety of activities takes place on the same court. Multipurpose courts often "include hardwood, synthetic sheet goods, poured urethane products and suspended interlocking plastic tiles" (Popke, 2001, p. 47). No surface meets the specific needs of each activity; however, finding the right surface that meets a majority of user needs is the goal of most facility managers.

It is essential to understand that there are countless types of wooden floors and many floor manufacturers and that the costs can vary dramatically. Costs also vary extensively among other surface alternatives such as synthetics and carpets. Varying costs often depend on the materials used, the thickness of the surface selected, and the condition of the existing surface. Thicker synthetic surfaces for example, although they may absorb more shock and offer greater resilience, are generally more expensive (Flynn, 1993). Once again, the planned use should be the central factor directing all facility surface decisions.

In the past, the third area—administrative offices and classrooms—has been satisfactorily covered with some type of tile that may include vinyl, vinyl asbestos, asphalt, rubber, or linoleum. Many believe consideration should be given to using carpet in some of these spaces. Hard maple floors are generally the most expensive when looking at initial installation; however, over a long period of time these flooring options become more than competitive when compared with most synthetic surfaces. Unfortunately, many decisions are made based on available finances during initial facility construction rather than the best and most economical surface for the long term. The cheapest flooring surface option is generally viewed as indoor-outdoor carpeting (Flynn, 1993).

Floors

Flooring choices are influenced by many factors. Initial cost, maintenance, performance features, aesthetics, and longevity are examples. According to Kroll (2002), flooring choices should be made on the basis of "a facility's design, function and budget." With ever advancing technology and a variety of factors that contribute to flooring decisions, the large number of options only tends to make this decision more complicated (Piper, 2003; Steinbach, 2002). According to Piper (2000), flooring choices tend to be made by individuals responsible for design and construction aspects of a project rather than those ensuring that the surface meets the needs of the end users. Maintenance and operational costs, although frequently the most significant overall facility expenses, are often overlooked by concerns over the initial financial outlay (Piper, 2003; Piper, 2000).

Before analyzing factors related to flooring choices, various issues need to be considered. Sports flooring surfaces, according to Viklund (1995), are categorized as point-elastic or area-elastic. Point-elastic surfaces maintain impact effects at the immediate point of contact on the floor with the ball, object, or individual. Area-elastic surfaces allow for dispersion of impact, where a bouncing object, or an individual jumping, can be felt approximately 20 inches around the point of impact. Hardness is another term that is utilized to describe the nature of a flooring surface and its ability to react to surface contact. The term hardness is defined readily in the fields of mineralogy, metallurgy, and engineering. In mineralogy, hardness is defined as the ability of the surface to resist scratching, with a softer surface obviously scratching more easily. This is measured by the Mohs scale, after Friedrich Mohs, a German mineralogist. In metallurgy and engineering, hardness is determined by pressing a hard material on a given surface and the size of the indentation made is measured to report the "hardness" of a substance. This is called the Brinnel test, named after Swedish engineer Johann Brinell.

Another internationally recognized standard for sports flooring surfaces is known as Deutsches Institut für Normans (DIN). (See Appendix C.2) This standard was developed by a testing lab in Germany establishing minimum standards for flooring (Cohen, 1998). DIN standards are available for minimum levels of shock absorption, ball bounce, deflection, surface friction and rolling load. These standards suggest a floor must meet the following: 1) shock absorption—flooring needs to absorb at least 53% of an object's impact; 2) ball bounce—balls must maintain 90% of their bounce if on concrete;

3) deflection—the point of impact must be a minimum of 3/32 inch, and 20 inches from the point of floor impact, the floor must measure 15% or less than the original point of impact; 4) surface friction—these standards vary depending on the nature of the activity; and 5) rolling load—floors need to withstand 367.7 pounds (Cohen, 1998).

Viklund (1995) discusses the concept of resilience when analyzing performance characteristics of various flooring options. Resilience is the shock absorption ability of a floor based on the amount of force applied to the surface area. For comparison, concrete is a base value with no resiliency (0%). Point-elastic surfaces (synthetics) have a low absorption level (10 to 50%) with most in the 25- to 35-% range. Resilience is influenced by both the thickness and the hardness of the floor material as well as the subfloor (Viklund, 1995). When considering carpeting as a surface choice, the quality of the underlay also has a significant impact on the carpet performance as well as the carpet life. According to Driscoll (2000), "The use of a quality underlay can prolong the life of a carpet from 50 to 75%" (p. 54).

Facility surface choices must also consider the influence of the subfloor material. Flooring characteristics on porous or "floating" surfaces will react very differently than others placed on concrete. Flooring choices, in fact, should be carefully considered based on the subfloor material that is present. The condition of this subfloor can also influence the cost of the project—as this surface may need special preparation for the chosen surface materials to be placed on top. According to Dahlgren (2000), shock absorption characteristics of wood floors may be more heavily influenced by the subfloor than the actual surface material itself.

Area-elastic floors also need to be evaluated based on activities planned for the space. *Area of deflection* must be considered with regard to the primary use of the facility surface. Area deflection is the amount of impact that is felt in the vicinity of the point of contact. With area-elastic flooring, it must be decided that the area of deflection will not adversely impact the activities of other individuals concurrently on the surface. Cooper (2004) states ". . .with the possible exception of the famed Boston Garden parquet floor, as notorious for its dead spots as it is for its beauty and mystical winning tradition, sports floors just haven't received a lot of attention" (p. 1). According to Viklund (1995), area of deflection is not a major concern for recreational use; however, it could be a major consideration for competitive or varsity play.

Another important consideration for most organizations in making flooring choices is a concept known as the "rolling load." Rolling load is the capacity of a floor to withstand damage from external forces such as bleacher movement, equipment transport, or similar activities (Viklund, 1995). Any surface utilized for multipurpose activities must be able to withstand the movement of equipment or materials over the surface area during transition from one activity to another. Related to this concept are the "walk-off" areas that experience heavy use. Even the most durable surfaces will undergo rapid deterioration under heavy pedestrian or equipment traffic. Mats, padding, or varied traffic patterns can be established by the careful planning of equipment storage areas to extend the life of most facility surfaces. The choices made for the planning of tare space or areas that are not developed for primary activities may also influence the wear and tear on a floor over the life of the facility surface. Decisions for the storage and transport of equipment should not be viewed as unimportant in the facility surface decision process as this can directly influence the deterioration of a surface with heavy equipment and pedestrian traffic.

Life-cycle costs of a surface are also important to consider when making various flooring choices. Piper (2000) suggests that hardwood flooring is rated for 25 years, as is terrazzo, followed by 15 years for vinyl tile, and approximately 10 years for most carpets. It is stressed; however, that these suggested guidelines may not necessarily match individual expectations. A product's life cycle may describe how long a product will withstand expected use; however, the aesthetic appearance is also valued by most organizations. For this concept, a product's attractive life describes how long a surface will remain acceptable based on the product's appearance, not its functionality. As a result, organizations should consider the amount of churn, which describes the general wear and tear on a particular surface, given the expectations for a specific location (Piper, 2000). If extensive churn is predicted for a given area, it may not be sensible to place a long-term, high-quality surface that will not remain aesthetic for the life cycle of the product when compared with its attractive life.

There are a variety of floor surface options that can be used successfully as a main gym floor. Once again, this important surface choice is normally dictated by the primary activity planned for this area. Options are generally broken down into three surfaces: hardwood, vinyl, and synthetics. Each surface option has strengths and weaknesses. Many existing athletic facilities have selected either a hardwood or a standard vinyl tile. According to Bishop (1997), wood flooring with proper maintenance can last 50 years compared with 20 years for a synthetic surface and 15 years for a vinyl tile. Table 18.1 illustrates initial cost, life expectancy, and annual maintenance cost for vinyl tile, synthetic surface, and wood flooring for a 5,000 square foot gymnasium (Bishop, 1997).

Vinyl tile floors have a life expectancy of approximately 10 to 15 years but begin to show their wear after the first few years (Bishop, 1997). Recent technology, however, has significantly improved the quality of sheet vinyl and vinyl composition tile, making this flooring choice both more aesthetic as well as more durable (Hasenkamp & Lutz, 2001). Vinyl floors, however, tend to be very hard and have poor absorption qualities. These characteristics can also lead to athletic injuries if high humidity levels are prevalent or if water spills are not managed properly. Unlike other sports surfaces, which require only washing and damp mopping, a vinyl tile floor must be stripped, sealed, and waxed at least three times annually. In contrast, synthetic floors also require regular cleaning but may require line repainting or a touch-up every 5 years (Bishop, 1997).

Table 18.1
Costs for Various Floor Surfaces

Type of Flooring	Life Expectancy	Initial Cost
Vinyl Tile	15 years	$15,000
Synthetic Surface	20 years	$40,000
Wood Flooring	50 years	$65,000

Initial Cost/Life Expectancy	Maintenance Cost Annually	Total Cost Annually
$1,000/yr (vinyl)	$1,210	$2,210
$2,000/yr (synthetic)	$2,000	$4,000
$1,300/yr (wood)	$2,666	$3,966

Hardwood floors are generally designed with intricate subfloors to provide shock absorption and can be expected to last the life of the school. Wooden floors must always be kept clean to provide proper traction. They must also have the lines repainted or touched up and should be sanded down and refinished every three years. Synthetic floors do not allow for as much sliding as hardwood floors. As a result, if the activities on the floor involve sliding actions, a wood floor is the better choice. Wood floors can also be designed in a number of ways including subfloor systems, cushioned systems, and spring systems (Flynn, 1993).

As mentioned above, the nature of the subfloor can often be a more significant factor than the actual surface material selected for a floor (Dahlgren, 2000; Holzrichter, 2001). Kroll (2002) suggests that cost-cutting processes during the planning phase of building development often alter the subfloor preparation intended for a given flooring option. This in turn may extensively alter the actual performance and longevity characteristics of the chosen surface.

Generally, there are three types of recommended subfloor constructions. The first is a suspension floor, which is made out of plywood, foam rubber, or some other type of synthetic material, available in a variety of patterns. The finished floor rests on top of the subfloor material. The second type of subfloor construction is a spring floor. This involves coiled metal springs, covered by a plywood subfloor, with the finished floor resting on the plywood. The third type is referred to as a padded floor. Padded materials such as foam or other synthetic or porous materials are laid over concrete or plywood and then covered with the finished floor (Stoll & Beller, 1989). As technology and testing procedures for various flooring options continue to develop, manufacturers pay increasing attention to various floor performance characteristics (Steinbach, 2002). Steinbach describes an approach where "strips of foam, as opposed to one solid sheet, can effectively soften a floor" (p. 82). Any number of variables can be altered to result in subtle or profound changes in the ultimate performance of the floor. Naturally, the more materials needed, along with the cost of these materials, impact the cost of the flooring choice. Safety is yet another consideration that should also be considered throughout the decision-making process. In any instance, it is important to be familiar with all of these issues so that everyone is aware of the factors involved and their subsequent impact on performance, cost, appearance, and life-expectancy of the surface selected.

Synthetic floors remain a popular choice and they tend to be much softer than wood floors and perform much better acoustically. Wood floors, depending on the effectiveness of their suspension systems, can also have "dead spots." Dead spots are areas on the floor that can cause objects impacting the floor surface to perform inconsistently. An example would be a basketball that would have a variable bounce due to a change in the characteristics of the floor. Synthetic floors are evenly laid and are less likely to have "dead spots," although inconsistent ball performance can still occur. Quality installation will maximize optimal surface performance with any surface choice. Upkeep of all gym floors calls for constant maintenance. Rubberized synthetic floors, although popular, tend to have higher maintenance costs when compared with wooden floors.

There are many different floor-covering options related to sports and recreational activities in today's market. Some examples include ceramic tile, cushioned wood flooring, and rubber compound flooring. The selection criteria for certain flooring materials should include:

- Economic feasibility with initial outlay and life-cycle costs. Floor covering choices entail much more than the initial up-front cost. Many now realize that the initial cost for materials and installation is only a small component of the total investment needed. Life-cycle cost considerations not only include the initial expense and installation but the number of years the flooring is expected to last, cost for removal or disposal of the floor, lost revenues during remodeling or replacement periods, and maintenance costs over the course of the surface's life (Hard Questions, Critical Answers, 1998).

- Ease of maintenance and replacement.
- Potential performance capabilities for both intended and possible use.
- Overall compatibility in appearance according to surrounding surfaces and equipment in the facility (Barkley, 1997; & Dahlgren, 2000).

An important factor that is often overlooked when considering floor options concerns the planned events within the facility. Access to electrical outlets, placement of equipment securing devices (floor plates for volleyball uprights), and tare space necessary for intended spectator traffic and equipment movement are each important considerations. If floor plates are to be utilized, they should be taken into consideration early in the process, as well as covered for ease of maintenance, access, and safety factors. In particular, electrical outlets should be installed in the floor, covered, and made flush with the floor's surface, as they are commonly associated with safety issues related to traffic flow. Also to be taken into consideration is the time spent in preparing a facility for various activities. Greater planning for both functional and safety factors, can save time (equipment set up and tear down), reduce costs (tape and mats to cover electrical and media system cords), and reduce accidents (tripping over exposed wires and cords).

When selecting a surface, it is a wise choice to consult other facilities that have similar need and use patterns to explore all flooring options based on performance characteristics. It is also important to consult with individuals who work with and maintain these facilities (e.g., maintenance personnel, students, athletes, publics, etc.) since they will likely have a different perspective regarding the suitability of various facility surfaces. The planning team makes the ultimate choice; however, all factors should be considered to make optimal surface decisions.

Although cost tends to be perceived as the overriding factor that drives a facility surface choice, aesthetic factors are being increasingly considered in the decision-making process. Wood flooring, for example, tends to be selected based on the quality, or "grade," of the actual wood. Quality is categorized into first, second and third grades. First-grade wood has the fewest number of defects and deficiencies when inspected prior to sale. "First grade allows for a very modern, clean and, in some minds, sterile look because it is fairly defect-free. You don't see dark blemishes or a lot of graining" (Dahlgren, 2000, p. 78).

Wood flooring choices are also made based on color, which once again is influenced by visual appeal. Maple tends to be the industry standard and offers good durability due to a "tight grain and density"; however, the light color also supports its popularity (Dahlgren, 2000). Second- and third-grade woods tend to offer a darker, more grainy, and "warmer" appearance; however, this choice once again boils down to personal or committee preference. Also a consideration that should not be overlooked is the impact of the floor color or aesthetics on the participant as well as the spectator. A dark or grainy floor, although more appealing to the eye, may be a distraction to the participant. As far as performance is concerned, according to the president of the Maple Flooring Manufacturers Association, "You could blindfold a person and have them dribble a ball on a first-grade floor, a second-grade floor and a third-grade floor, and he or she would never know the difference" (Hamar, 2000, p. 84).

A final consideration in the quest for enhancing the visual appeal of a floor surface is achieved by creative efforts with paint, patterns, colors, and contrast. Tiled flooring can easily be created in various patterns and designs that are very appealing to the eye; however, during the reconditioning process of a wood floor, alterations in surface applications can create a "new" look with the same "old" floor. Once again, all these issues need to be addressed by communicating with other facility management personnel and discovering the strengths and weaknesses of the numerous options available—before an ultimate decision is made for any facility.

Flooring Selection Process

As stated earlier, selecting the appropriate flooring surface is a major decision in either the initial design or the renovation process. Floor materials and maintenance patterns can greatly impact athletic performance, determine how well multiple uses are served, and influence the incidence of sports injuries. Floor surfaces come in innumerable materials, textures, colors, and performance characteristics. Yet, of the hundreds of products on the market, no one surface is perfect for all uses and there is plenty of opportunity to make the wrong choice (Viklund, 1995).

A logical and systematic approach should be followed in conducting a search for the appropriate surface. These guidelines will assist in the decision-making process. According to Viklund (1995), the steps in the following "flooring checklist" are recommended:

- Select the room or space to be considered.
- Prioritize the sports/activities that will occur within the space.
- Decide whether the preferred floor should be area-elastic or point-elastic.
- Review the performance criteria for the selected floor type.
- Test flooring options by reviewing samples and comparing costs.
- Compare life-cycle costs for flooring options.
- Play on the different surfaces.
- Check the manufacturers' referenced projects.
- Make the final decision. (p. 46)

Flynn (1993) recommends the following steps in the surface selection process:

- Definition: Define the characteristics required to meet specified needs (e.g., bounce characteristics, sunlight effects, etc.). Manufacturers in their literature address many of these questions.
- Solicitation: Cost should not be a limitation for one's initial research and review of possible flooring systems. One should request as much information from as many manufacturers as deemed reasonable. The review of this information will allow for a broader knowledge of different systems and a basis for comparison. Material estimates and project costs should be obtained from various manufacturers. Manufacturers should also provide references, a list of installers, and the location of like facilities for comparative analysis.
- Comparison: After reviewing manufacturer materials and comparing all possible systems, a categorization of all materials should be performed. Categorize information by type and desirable qualities (i.e., natural vs. synthetic, resiliency, initial cost, longevity, safety, aesthetics, and any additional factors significant to your decision-making process). A table that compares the various positive and negative attributes of each surface option is generally deemed helpful in making the right surface choice for your facility (see Figure 18.1).
- Visitation: After the field of choices has been narrowed down based on established criteria, a site visit for each of the considered facility surfaces should be performed. A closer inspection and discussion with personnel at each facility is likely to be helpful in making the best choice for your facility. Performance as well as maintenance factors must be explored as initial cost and utility are only two of numerous factors in making a wise surface choice.
- Selection: At this point, select a system based on all research efforts. Take into consideration all performance criteria and always keep in mind that surface choices are a significant factor in the overall success of a facility.
- Quality: A specific surface may be selected from numerous quality levels, among many surface options. Once more, take into consideration the quality of the materials, workmanship, guarantees, facility use factors, and any other significant considerations when making this important decision.
- Manufacturer: Selecting a manufacturer is also important. How long have they been in business? Have their surfaces withstood the test of time to explore wear factors? What type of technical support do they provide? What are their methods of quality control, both in the manufacturing process and in the field? What is their reputation? How soon can they provide you with the requested materials? What guarantees do they provide? Many questions should be compiled and asked of each company being considered. Always remember that references are important to obtain; however, be careful to do your homework in the inquiry process. One should never rely too heavily on references provided by the company being considered, as they will obviously be more than willing to provide positive references for their own work history. Unsolicited references should be sought for all finalists in the bidding process. It is common in the industry that manufacturers will provide products to clients in exchange for positive reviews.
- Installer: An installer should be recommended by the manufacturer to help insure that they are familiar with installation of the manufacturer's product. The installer should be asked questions similar to those asked of the manufacturer. Another key piece of information is the time frame required for completing the installation. Many jobs are started on time; however, seek guarantees for job completion, or factor this item into a reduction in cost for jobs not finished when promised. Facility visits and communication with other clients will once again be helpful in deciding upon an installation company.
- Maintenance: Maintenance is a considerable portion of the operating budget and it is important to define exactly what is involved. What type of maintenance is required? How often will the surface need to be refinished, covered, lacquered, replaced, and so on? Can this maintenance work be performed in-house or will you need to seek outside contracts for planned care? Facility planners should not underestimate the expense of properly maintaining facility surfaces and should figure this expense into the overall surface cost and flooring choice process.
- Kennedy (2000) recommends that maintenance staff should have a thorough knowledge of the various floor surfaces they are maintaining. Maintenance and cleaning costs can "typically account for more than 50% of the total cost of ownership" (Piper, August 2000, p. 4). Cleaning approaches can also vary based on the intended use of the surface. Recent research by Agron (2001) describes an overall reduction in expenditures for both maintenance and operations in elementary and secondary schools in recent years. This same author, however, reports an increase in spending for maintenance and operations budgets in higher-education facilities. In either case, this concept needs to be factored into the flooring decision process. A less expensive floor may have a very limited life span without proper care. The same can be stated for more expensive flooring that requires more specialized care to attain maximal life-cycle utilization.
- Moussatche, Languell-Urquhart, and Woodson (2000) provide information that relates life-cycle costs with operations and maintenance considerations for hard flooring, resilient flooring, and soft flooring

Figure 18.1
Attributes of Various Floor Surfaces

Legend:
- ● = Above Average
- ▶ = Average
- ○ = Below Average
- V = Variable
- D = Daily
- W = Weekly
- M = Monthly
- Y = Yearly
- P = Periodically
- S = Semiannually in high traffic areas or yearly in average traffic areas

Material	Strength	Durability	Thermal Insulation	Moisture, oil, chemical resistance	Stain Resistance	Abrasion Resistance/Wearability	Mildew Resistance	Heat Absorption	Limited Application Locations	Sweeping or dust mopping	Vacuuming	Damp mopping	Wet mopping	Scrubbing	Stripping	Dry cleaning (chemicals)	Hot water extraction	Waxing	Buffing	Resealing	Regrouting	Sanding & refinishing	Overall Maintenance Ranking
Hard — Ceramic Tile (6"x6"x1/2") Mortar & Grout	●	●	●	V	▶	●	●	○	x	D	x	D	x	S	S	x	x	M	M	x	x	x	High
Ceramic Tile (6"x6"x1/2") Mastic & Grout	●	▶	●	V	▶	●	●	○	x	D	x	D	x	Y	Y	x	x	M	M	x	x	x	High
Quarry Tile Mortar & Grout	●	●	●	●	●	●	●	○	x	D	x	D	x	x	x	x	x	Y	Y	x	x	x	Medium
Exposed Concrete Sealant (2 coats)	●	●	○	○	▶	●	▶	●	✓	D	x	W	Y	x	x	x	x	Y	x	x	x	x	Medium
Terrazzo (1 3/4") Cast in place	●	●	▶	●	●	●	●	●	▶	x	D	x	W	x	Y	x	x	x	x	x	x	P	x	Low
Epoxy resin	▶	○	●	●	●	▶	●	○	x	D	x	W	x	Y	x	x	x	x	x	x	P	x	Low
Laminated wood (synthetic core) vapor barrier & Adhesive	▶	▶	●	▶	▶	▶	●	▶	x	D	x	W	x	Y	x	x	x	x	x	x	P	x	Low
Wood plank (2 1/4") vapor barrier & urethane	●	▶	●	▶	▶	▶	●	▶	x	x	D	x	x	x	x	S	S	x	x	x	x	x	Medium
Resilient — Bamboo flooring vapor barrier & adhesive	●	▶	●	○	▶	●	●	▶	x	x	D	x	x	x	x	S	S	x	x	x	x	x	Medium
Linoleum (.125") - Adhesive	▶	●	●	▶	▶	●	●	○	x	x	D	x	x	x	x	S	S	x	x	x	x	x	Medium
Vinyl Composition Tile (VCT) Vapor barrier and Adhesive	▶	▶	●	○	V	▶	○	○	x	D	x	D	x	x	x	x	x	x	x	Y	x	x	Low
Vinyl Sheet Vapor barrier and Adhesive	▶	▶	●	○	V	▶	○	○	x	D	x	W	x	M	x	x	x	x	x	x	P	x	Medium
Rubber Sheet (1/8") - Adhesive	●	○	●	●	▶	●	▶	▶	x	D	x	W	x	M	x	x	x	Y	Y	x	x	x	Medium
Cork (1/8") - Adhesive	○	○	●	▶	○	○	▶	○	x	D	x	W	x	M	x	x	x	x	x	x	x	x	Low
Soft — Carpet tile (18"x18", 20oz/syd) Hard back	▶	▶	●	▶	●	▶	▶	●	✓	D	x	D	x	x	x	x	x	x	x	P	x	P	Low
Carpet tile (18"x18", 20 oz/syd) Cushion back	▶	●	●	▶	●	▶	▶	●	✓	D	x	D	x	x	x	x	x	x	x	x	x	x	Low
Carpet (Nylon loop pile 40oz/syd) Adhesive	▶	▶	●	▶	●	▶	▶	●	✓	D	x	D	x	x	x	x	x	x	x	x	x	P	Low

Moussatche, Languell-Urquhart, & Woodson. (September 2000). Life cycle costs in education: Operations & maintenance considered. Facilities Design & Management (p. 22).

options. As mentioned earlier, the actual cost of the initial flooring is only a portion of the life-cycle flooring expense. "Life-cycle cost analysis allows the evaluator to fully examine each alternative and the true service-life cost of the material" (p. 20).

- Initial Cost: What is the "total" initial cost of the system? Be certain there are no hidden costs that will arise later. If two systems are considered similar, yet one is more costly than the other—why? Is it the quality of the system, materials, or both? Sometimes a product name or reputation is a reason for cost inflation.
- Life-Cycle Cost: This comparative analysis considers the initial cost, operational costs, maintenance costs, and, if necessary, replacement costs during the estimated life-cycle. These figures will generate the anticipated total costs. Generally, a higher initial cost system will be comparable in the long run with less expensive systems when all factors are considered.
- Bidding: When bidding is required, attention should be directed toward written specifications to ensure the product and installation methods are accurately described to avoid misunderstandings.
- Installation: It is in the owner's interest to require the manufacturer to perform periodic on-site supervision of the installer. This will help insure compliance with the manufacturer's specifications (p. 77).

Risk Management and Safety Considerations

Flooring surface choices clearly need to be assessed based on facility use expectations; however, with liability concerns, surface choices need to be made with extensive consideration of various safety factors. Resiliency, slip, traction, absorption, foot support, activities planned for the space, age, and ability of the intended users are some of the considerations when deciding upon a flooring choice. Literature supports the notion that a lack of effective communication exists within the process of deciding upon a flooring choice; however, all parties should be concerned about the impact of this choice on risk management outcomes. "Health considerations and their accordant legal and financial liabilities are influencing the selection of sports surfacing" (Cooper, 2004, p. 2). Another author states "the distance between the recreation and maintenance professions" is a key factor (Cohen, 2002, p. 106). In this article, the author discusses the fact that recreation management professionals often have little input into maintenance functions. Longtime city employees, refugees from other businesses, volunteers, and seasonal and part-time workers state maintenance functions (Cohen, 2002). Piper (2003) states that flooring choices are frequently chosen based on aesthetic appearance when new as compared with how they will last through their service-life as well as their resistance to gouging, indentations, stains, rolling loads, acoustics, and slip-resistance characteristics.

Wood floor protective coverings.

A device recognized by the American Society of Testing and Materials (ASTM), called a tribometer, establishes the "slip resistance" of various flooring surfaces and footwear (Di Pilla, 2001). Knowing exactly how slippery each floor surface is enables a determination of appropriate activities for this space, possible shoe requirements, and cleaning schedules. A simple change in cleaning materials or application method can impact how slippery the surface will be. Although a comprehensive risk management program can address some of these factors, this issue needs to be considered in the planning process to avoid the resultant risks from slips and falls.

Repairs to surface materials also need to consider the impact on end users, as well as the effect on initial manufacturing warranties. Although some repairs may be made by custodial and maintenance staff, surface repairs may need to be made by industry flooring professionals to maintain the initial integrity of the surface. Facility surface repairs tend not to be repairs that can go on a list of "things to do later" as the utilization of the facility is dependent on a quick solution. According to Cohen (2000), "... each player . . . is just one misstep from finding that hole, breaking an ankle and suing you for negligence" (p. 46).

Walls and Ceilings

Walls can serve a much greater function than simply providing a divider or an area perimeter for specific activity areas. Walls can function as barriers to sound, heat, light, and moisture. Depending on the location and intended use within a facility, the selection of wall surfaces should be extended careful consideration for a number of functional properties. Generally speaking, moisture-resistant walls with sound acoustical properties are ideal.

Perhaps one of the most common characteristics of a typical gym is the inability of the various surfaces to absorb sound (Holzrichter, 2001). The acoustical treatments utilized on walls or within the overhead structures should be high enough so they will not impede the utilization of wall space and the pathway of objects and will not be easily damaged by users. As mentioned previously with flooring, there remains a trend toward greater aesthetic pursuits on walls and ceilings in the utilization of colors, pictures, and graphics on these surfaces. Banners, sound panels, and other porous materials can be utilized to improve acoustical sound properties of a typical gymnasium. Tasteful color schemes can also have a positive psychological value for the participant or spectator along with making the environment more aesthetically pleasing (Flynn, 1993; Hasenkamp & Lutz, 2001).

Another consideration that has evolved tremendously in recent years is that of wall padding. How much, how high, how thick, and what material should be utilized? With various facility-related lawsuits remaining a concern, the presence and performance of wall padding has earned considerable attention from facility architects, planners, and managers alike. Not only is wall padding necessary in specific facility locations, but also its effectiveness can prevent serious injury upon contact. An additional factor is how extensive should efforts be to pad all possible contact zones? Steinbach (2004) describes a 1997 accident where an eighth-grade student collided with a padded gym wall during a basketball tryout and eventually died from the sustained injuries. Steinbach (2004) elaborates on this topic describing ongoing efforts to establish recognizable standards for wall padding—thickness, material, and location.

Walls in the main gym or activity area should have a minimum height of 8 feet and should always be padded for safety reasons. Electrical outlets should be provided every 50 feet and should also be protected by padding (Flynn, 1993). Small inserts can be cut out of the padding and affixed with fasteners for easy removal and replacement and for easy access to electrical outlets. All padding should be checked with regularity, as it can wear and harden with age and contribute to significant injury upon contact. Keep in mind that some unobstructed flat wall space may still be desirable as appropriate for teaching purposes. In some cases all walls should be kept entirely unobstructed; however, this would be based solely on the specific activities planned for the space (e.g., indoor soccer).

Roof design, local building codes, and the nature of the planned activities should determine ceiling construction. Ceilings should be insulated to prevent condensation and be the appropriate height to accommodate all planned and future activities whenever possible. Painted ceilings can also improve the physical look of the facility as well as enhance light reflection properties. Bright white ceilings are strongly advised against in areas where light-colored objects are utilized (e.g., shuttlecocks and volleyballs). It is difficult to visually follow these objects against a bright white ceiling background. A light color is still recommended for ceilings, however, and most facilities find an off-white color to work best. A 24-foot minimum distance (lowest suspended object) is required in any teaching station designed for a variety of activities (Flynn, 1993). Cohen (2003), suggests 25 feet; however, he also states that volleyball has a minimum ceiling requirement of 12.5 meters (37.5 feet), as well as the impact of other planned facility uses, which may force planners to greater ceiling heights to accommodate activities such as commencements and concerts. Whenever possible, facility planners should attempt to exceed minimum ceiling heights, as minimum heights can still contribute to game interference, equipment lodging (e.g., shuttlecocks), and greater ceiling fixture expenses as a result of occasional contact with equipment (e.g., volleyballs).

Ceiling height may also impact factors not initially considered when making such choices. Planning for high ceilings may result in alterations of original equipment plans, as "high ceilings might render ceiling-hung basketball standards impractical, necessitating greater storage to accommodate portable backstops" (Cohen, 2003, p. 72).

Acoustical ceiling materials are needed in instructional spaces and areas with many planned activities. Dropped ceiling panels will require considerable maintenance since they are susceptible to damage by objects or individuals. Since most acoustical instruments are not necessarily made out of the hardest materials, they need to be placed out of range of flying objects. In some cases where there are low ceiling activity areas, dropped ceilings may be equipped with spring-loaded clips that will return the acoustical panel back into place after contact. It should be noted that false ceilings with catwalks above them have been effectively constructed to allow for easier maintenance and the repair of lighting and ventilation arrangements (Flynn, 1993).

As mentioned earlier, the ceiling should have a minimum height of 24 feet to the lowest obstacle with an off-white color usually being appropriate. A clear-span ceiling design without minimum support pillars and substructure girders should be investigated for safety, viewing, aesthetics, and more open and usable space. If one chooses to mount or store equipment in the ceiling area, structural reinforcement may become necessary at these sites (Flynn, 1993). It is very important to consider all necessary factors when constructing or remodeling the primary features of a facility.

Once again, the planned use of a given area should guide all planning and material requirements. "The ceiling is the primary acoustical treatment in the office" (Moeller, 2002). According to Roberts (2000) and Kroll (2003), Noise Reduction Coefficient (NRC) is the capability of a ceiling to absorb noise. An additional consideration is the Sound Transmission Class (STC). This concept measures the effectiveness of a wall or ceiling in blocking sound between offices. Kroll (2003) elaborates on the increased demand for sound reduction within many facilities based on privacy concerns. With the passage of the Health Insurance Portability and Accountability Act (HIPAA), health care providers must make reasonable efforts to respect the privacy of clients. This is particularly true within medical facilities where sensitive material is shared and the ability of a surface to minimize sound deflection is important.

Figure 18.2 provides a guide for floor, wall, and ceiling choices for a variety of rooms within your facility.

Windows

The use and aesthetic value of windows are often overlooked in the planning of indoor facilities as well as within the process of making surface choices. Windows can provide durable and attractive enclosures as well as divisions of space within a facility. Facility planners must keep in mind, however, that windows may face daily exposure to the elements, along with frequent contact with objects utilized by the activities planned for the space (Johnson & Patterson, 1997). Climate is also a consideration when deciding on window placement and use, as it can enhance warming features due to sunlight—which can obviously be a benefit or a detriment—depending on the facility's geographical location. Windows can also create glare problems; however, appropriate placement (northern exposure) can greatly enhance the aesthetic quality and appeal of indoor surfaces (Holzrichter, 2001). Fenestration is the technical term utilized to describe natural lighting created by windows.

The selection process for windows according to Piper (1998), is based on a number of factors, some of which include: 1) lighting—the three most common ways for controlling the light passing through windows are tinted glazing, heat absorbing glazing, and low-emissivity coatings; 2) keeping the elements out; 3) heat loss; 4) aesthetics; 5) security; and 6) view. Windows are often overlooked when making wall surface decisions; however, they should be incorporated into the building's overall aesthetic

Figure 18.2
Suggested Indoor Surface Materials

ROOMS	FLOORS							LOWER WALLS								UPPER WALLS						CEILINGS			
	Carpeting	Synthetics	Tile, asphalt, rubber, linoleum	Cement, abrasive, non-abrasive	Maple, hard	Terrazzo, abrasive	Tile, ceramic	Brick	Brick, glazed	Cinder Block	Concrete	Plaster	Tile, ceramic	Wood Panel	Moistureproof	Brick	Brick, glazed	Cinder Block	Plaster	Acoustic	Moisture-resistant	Concrete or Structure Tile	Plaster	Tile, acoustic	Moisture-resistant
Apparatus Storage Room			1	2				1				2	1	C											
Classrooms		2	1								2	1		2				2	1			C	C	1	
Clubroom		2	1								2	1		2				2	1			C	C	1	
Corrective Room		1			2					2	1	2						2	2	1	2			1	
Custodial Supply Room				1			2																		
Dance Studio					1																	C	C	1	
Drying Room (equip.)				1				2	2	1	2	1	1					1	1						
Gymnasium		1			1						2	1					2	2	1	2	*	C	C	1	
Health-Service Unit		1			1						2	1		2					2	1				1	
Laundry Room				2				1	2	1	2	2	1	C	*						*			*	*
Locker Rooms		3	3			2	1		1	2	2	3	1		*		1	1	2				C	1	
Natatorium							2	1	2	1	3	2	1		*		2	2	1	*	*	C	C	1	*
Offices	1	3	2								2	1		1					2					1	
Recreation Room		2			1					2	2	1		1				2	1	2	*		C	1	
Shower Rooms			3			2	1		1		2		1		*		2	1	2	2	*			1	*
Special-activity Room		2	1								2	1		1				1	1	1			C	1	
Team Room	1	3				2	1		2	1	2	2	3		1	*	1	1	2				C	1	
Toilet Room			3			2	1		1	2	2	2	1		*			1	1						1
Toweling-Drying Room			3			2	1		1		2		1		*		2	1	2	2		*		1	*

Note: The numbers in the table indicate first, second, and third choices. "C" indicates the material as being contrary to good practice. An * indicates desirable quality.

plan, the regional location of the facility, as well as the planned activities within the facility. Windows also add to the construction costs; however, apart from the impact they may have on the activities planned for the space, they can add extensively to the aesthetic appeal of most facilities.

Additional Floor, Wall, and Ceiling Considerations
Floor considerations include:

- An adequate number of floor drains in the proper locations.
- Proper floor sloping for adequate drainage (if necessary).
- Water-resistant, rounded base, where the flooring and wall meet in any locker or shower area.
- Floor plates are flush-mounted and placed where they are needed.
- Provision of nonskid, slip resistant flooring in all wet areas (e.g., pool, shower, etc.).
- Lines painted as appropriate, prior to any sealers being applied. (Patton et al., 1989)

Wall considerations include:
- An adequate number of drinking fountains, fully recessed into the walls.
- A minimum of one wall of any exercise room with full-length mirrors.
- All "corners" in the shower and locker room areas are rounded.

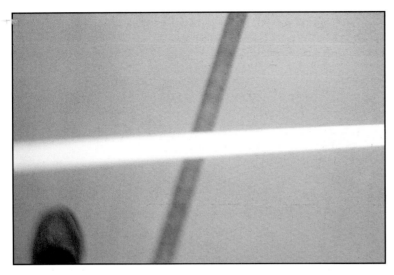

Intersecting lines.

Overlapping and broken lines.

Solid and broken contrasting lines.

- All wall coverings should be aesthetically pleasing, as well as matching the decor and color scheme of the facility.
- Electrical outlets placed strategically within the wall (or floor), firmly attached, and accessible, if the wall is protected with padding.
- In wet or humid areas, materials should be easy to clean and impervious to moisture. (Patton et al., 1989)

Ceiling considerations include:
- Ensure that ceiling support beams are engineered and designed to withstand stress.
- Ensure the provision of adequate ceiling heights for all planned facility activities.
- All ceilings, except storage areas, are acoustically treated with sound-absorbent materials.
- Ceilings and access areas are easily accessible for purposes of routine repair and maintenance.
- Use acoustical materials that are impervious to moisture when they will be used in moisture-dense areas. (Patton et al., 1989)

Service and Ancillary Areas

Locker Rooms

Locker area surfaces should possess a combination of maintenance ease along with a strong consideration for hygiene properties. All surfaces should be durable and able to withstand excessive moisture and humidity as well as the accumulation of dirt. Aesthetic appeal once again remains a central issue in facility design within locker room areas, as many participants base their attitudes and opinions about the facility, as a whole, on their likes and dislikes of the locker-room environment. This idea is espoused by Huddleston (2001): "Careful attention to the design and maintenance of locker rooms can greatly enhance a facility's image—and contain its odor" (p. 63).

Locker-room areas should contain hot and humid/wet areas as well as dry dressing areas that are typically within close proximity. Floors in wet areas should always be designed with safety, aesthetics, and maintenance in mind. For obvious reasons, nonslip tile is the best surface for these floors. Since soap and dirt often have a tendency to build up, a beige or brown-colored grout is recommended to keep the tile looking clean. Some facilities have stopped providing soap, as the resultant slips and falls can create legal problems. Frequently wet areas, such as locker rooms, require greater risk management efforts to readily notice problem areas and reduce potential risks for patrons (Di Pilla, 2001).

All wet-area floors within locker rooms should be pitched away from the dry areas and directed towards a drain. Some alternative sources include epoxy sealants over waterproof sheet rock or concrete block. These surfaces have proven in the past to work satisfactorily in the dressing room, sink, and common areas. It should also be noted that all corners of these areas should be rounded so moisture cannot penetrate the seams (Patton et al., 1989). Although many facilities make decisions to avoid carpeted surfaces within locker rooms, the right carpeting is better equipped to handle moisture than people think, particularly in changing areas (Huddleston, 2001). Carpeting is not particularly advised in heavy water areas near showers; however, flow-through flooring has been known to handle heavy water areas. Flow-through flooring allows excessive water to pass through the surface area to the subfloor below before it passes to the floor drains. As long as this process allows for air circulation and drying of the subfloor system, this helps maintain a dry surface and can reduce slip and fall occurrences (Huddleston, 2001).

Moisture is clearly the enemy in any building and even more so where humid or wet areas exist. Precautions during the design process as well as the lifespan of the facility are important to minimize negative outcomes resulting from humidity, moisture, and microbial growth. Migration of moisture into contiguous areas must also be controlled. Measures must also be taken during the construction process to ensure that all building materials are not moisture damaged prior to installation. An effective and efficient heating, ventilation, and air (HVAC) system must maintain a balance between humidity control and energy savings (Straus & Kirihara, 1996).

Prevention is the key in controlling microbiological gardens from growing in your building. Clearly, the most imminent hazard is moisture. Moisture can range from large pools of water from roof leaks or broken water pipes to invisible rain that is absorbed into building materials, to moisture that condenses on facility surfaces. Dust also serves as a nutrient source for microbial growth. Although chemicals are a common method to combat these problems, moisture is the real culprit and should be the primary focus of effective and routine maintenance procedures (Straus & Kirihara, 1996).

In drier areas of the locker room, the floor is a major concern for interior decorators and designers. Mildew and mold are constant problems and the materials should be able to withstand long periods of moist conditions and show little or no signs of delaminating. A 100% nylon carpet is recommended for flooring material in a health and fitness setting. The carpeting provides an aesthetically pleasing appearance and is easily maintained with daily vacuuming and periodic shampooing. It should also be noted that the nylon carpets will have a longer life and will be more easily maintained if they are mildew resistant and protected by a stain-resistant application. (Patton et al., 1989). Wear tests have also concluded that appropriate cushioning beneath the carpet surface can greatly enhance carpet life, as well as comfort for the participant (Goodman, 2000).

Wall coverings in locker room areas usually consist of epoxy-coated paint, vinyl, or wallpaper. The selected material should be strong and not show dirt. There should also be consideration given to the corners and wall-to-wall moldings to reduce the amount of black marks and cuts that often appear, typically with heavy use. Ceilings are usually finished with moisture-proof, hand-finished paint. As mentioned earlier, acoustical materials should also be used in conjunction with paint to reduce the noise levels that also occur in locker room areas (Patton et al., 1989).

Steam Rooms

Steam rooms require specialized knowledge for construction and care. Building materials utilized and the planned methods of application are critical to minimizing the maintenance efforts in steam rooms. It is highly recommended to hire a contractor with previous experience in the construction of wet areas when considering steam room construction. The floor surface of a steam room should be covered with a liquid rubber material and applied over a concrete slab. A layer of fiberglass fabric is laid over the rubber material followed with an additional coat of liquid rubber. The floor should also slope toward the drain for proper water drainage. This system both protects against water leaks and expands with floor movement (Patton et al., 1989).

Steam room walls and ceilings should be covered with a cement building board and fiberglass tape. This wall surface should also be placed on galvanized metal studs or Wolmanized® lumber. It is important to remember to slope ceilings as well, enabling moisture to run-off rather than drip-off. This system has proven to be durable and helps to prevent against rot and mildew. As with other wet areas, the selected tile should be both attractive and durable. A textured nonslip tile should be used on the floors, whereas many prefer glazed ceramic tile for the walls and ceilings (Patton et al., 1989).

Aerobic Exercise Facilities

As aerobic exercise and other impact activities remain popular in fitness, recreational, and athletic centers across the nation, the effort to reduce impact-related injuries continues. Spring-loaded or "floating" hardwood floors are the most popular surfaces, followed closely by heavily padded carpeting that is sealed and plastic-laminate-bonded to inhibit moisture leaks into the pile textures. This type of flooring allows for regular steam cleaning and avoids the hygiene problems from accumulated perspiration as with a carpeted and/or padded area. Important considerations are compliance (shock absorption), foot stability, surface traction, and resiliency (energy return). Furthermore, there are synthetic and specially made floors that may be used as alternatives (Patton et al., 1989). Research on various flooring types should be available from most manufacturers that address the specific needs and demands of the activity planned for a given location.

Finding a balance between all facility surface areas is a considerable challenge for the facility planning team. For example, one of the best shock-absorbing floorings is any type of thick sponge pad. Regular foam may develop dips after prolonged use; however, some new synthetics have been specially developed to hold their shape. One such surface is micro-cell foam, which is available at one-fourth the cost of wood; however, it should be noted some difficulties may arise with the interlocking sections. These types of synthetic floors are usually soft enough that individual mats are not needed for floor exercises. It should be noted that cleaning may also present unique problems with these floor types. Bacteria growth may also be a problem, in particular if the surface is textured or not properly maintained (Walker & Stotlar, 1997).

Although the quality of polyurethane surfaces continues to improve, these surfaces are not considered resilient enough by some because they are simply poured directly over concrete. The testing results of a surface may meet all the necessary industry standards; however, the surface hardness may still be inappropriate for many activities—again due to the nature of the subfloor material. This point was made earlier; however, it is imperative to consider the subfloor material just as vital to the qualities and characteristics of use as the visible surface that is applied, laid, or poured on top. Maintenance issues remain a significant factor as these surfaces are often plagued with cracking and peeling over time. The life cycles of these surfaces also tend to be much shorter than wood.

Carpeting is relatively easy to install and newer sports varieties contain special shock-absorption properties. These should always be used with foam cushioning and never be applied directly over concrete surfaces. Carpet is versatile, inexpensive, and works well, especially in multipurpose areas. It should be noted, however, that carpets are highly susceptible to staining, can be easily discolored or stretched, and retain odors. The expected life span of most carpets is 2 to 4 years depending on the use, cleaning methods, and quality of the materials.

Historically, wood floors remain a popular choice. Wood is aesthetically pleasing and provides a high degree of flexibility within most multipurpose activity areas. Wood floors however, depending on the subfloor utilized, are often extremely hard and not resilient enough for high-energy exercise and excessive humidity can cause the wood to warp (Walker & Stotlar, 1997).

Strength Training Areas

Another area of continued popularity is dedicated spaces for strength training. The dark and dingy weight rooms of the past are being replaced with colorful new flooring options and light, airy, and open spaces (Steinbach, 2002). The type of flooring sought for these spaces depends largely on the nature of the equipment selected; however, the aesthetic appeal is increasingly becoming important in this decision-making process. If a weight area is primarily equipped with machines (e.g., Nautilus, Universal, etc.), an easily maintained durable carpet is sufficient. If the room is dominated by free weights, a resilient rubber surface is recommended—tiled, poured, or pre-fabricated. Pre-fabricated options come in the form of sheets or tiles and are simply glued on top of the existing surface or concrete slab.

The desired appearance of the strength training room is an important consideration when selecting a flooring material. The level of supervision over these areas is also a factor as observed participants tend to be less likely to treat equipment roughly and purposely damage equipment or flooring surfaces. Once again, aesthetic appeal remains important and creative and attractive options are not necessarily more expensive; yet they do tend to require additional planning (Hasenkamp & Lutz, 2001). The color schemes of the walls, equipment, upholstery, and flooring must all be coordinated to appeal to the user. Consultants or interior designers can provide assistance in this area, and seeking the assistance of these individuals is becoming more popular (Steinbach, January 2002; Patton et al., 1989).

Handball/Racquetball/Squash Courts

The overall playing surface for a court requires 800 square feet for handball and racquetball courts and 700 square feet for singles and 900 square feet for doubles in squash courts. Traditionally, courts are covered with a wood floor surface unless they are outdoor courts (i.e., asphalt or concrete). Maple floors are attractive, provide a favorable bounce, and absorb shock to the feet; however, there is one major disadvantage. When moisture enters the wood, it will buckle the system and cause swelling in the floor. This becomes an important factor to note if the courts are built in a subterranean area with porous floors. A minor disadvantage found when using wood floors is that they will shrink and expand depending on the moisture in the air. As the wood floor shrinks, gaps develop and collect dust balls.

The only other viable system is a synthetic one. New polyurethane materials have been implemented with satisfactory results. These floors are poured and trawled over a concrete slab (Patton et al., 1989).

The most popular wall systems to choose from are reinforced fiberglass, concrete, plaster, poured-in-place cement slab, and shatterproof glass. Before deciding on a wall system, one should consider the following: material cost, land considerations (e.g., moisture and stability), overall appearance, maintenance, and ball action. Plaster is often viewed as a mainstay, as it has been around years, but maintenance costs usually prove to be expensive. Pour-in-place concrete slabs have not been used very often. The cost is prohibitive, and obtaining a straight wall from a slab that is poured on the ground and then erected is difficult to accomplish. Reinforced fiberglass concrete has a promising future but many applications have proven inconsistent. Walls made from acrylic plastic sheets provide an aesthetic appeal but are too costly for some facilities. Lastly, the floor system with perhaps the best reputation is a panel system designed of compressed wood. The quality of panel systems varies widely, so facility planning members must be careful in selecting a system with a satisfactory quality-to-price ratio (Patton et al., 1989).

The court ceiling is often constructed from the same materials used for the walls. A popular alternative involves combination of the wall material for the front half of the ceiling and acoustical tile has been found to be successful, as has the use of sheet rock covered by paint or a glazed material (Patton et al., 1989).

Offices and Teaching Areas

Most offices and teaching stations employ a smooth-surfaced glazed block or similar smooth surface on walls ranging from 8 to 10 feet. Smoother walls are easier to maintain and clean, more durable, and safer. As mentioned earlier, walls are important aspects of many teaching stations and must be planned appropriately. Many walls are utilized as rebound areas, barriers for equipment storage, sound barriers, and areas for fitness testing and measurement (Flynn, 1993). Many varieties of wall barriers are available and must be considered based on facility needs and area utilization.

Summary

Facility surfaces are an integral facet of any athletic or recreational complex—public or private. Activities planned for each area of the facility should dictate all surface selection decisions. These decisions should include some of the following topics: available budget, life expectancy, function, climate, safety, foundation, and perhaps most important—maintenance and operational costs. There are three distinct areas or divisions within facilities. The first of these areas is the service/ancillary areas such as locker rooms, bathrooms, exercise rooms, and so forth. These areas require surfaces that are able to withstand heavy moisture content. The second area is the main arena or activity focus within the facility. The third component represents the office and administrative areas within the facility.

Flooring surfaces are categorized into three areas: wood, vinyl, and synthetics. The two most popular forms of synthetic flooring are polyvinyl chlorides (PVCs) and polyurethane. It is important to note that there are countless types of wood flooring, and the costs vary depending on the system that is utilized, (the manufacturer), and the installer. Facility walls do more than simply act as dividers between given areas. Walls serve as barriers to sound, heat, light, and moisture. Walls also influence the aesthetic appeal of a facility. When selecting wall surfaces, consideration should be given to the acoustical properties of the material and, of course, the planned activities within this space. Moisture-resistant walls with acoustical properties are usually favored. There are also several issues to consider when selecting materials for ceiling construction. The activities planned for the area, roof design, and local building codes should all be taken into account. Ceilings should possess materials that allow for acceptable acoustical standards, be high enough for all planned activities, and be insulated to prevent condensation.

Facility surfaces are available in many colors, textures, and materials, and also with varying degrees of performance characteristics. When trying to find the correct fit for your facility, please keep in mind the following concepts in the decision-making process:

- economic feasibility of the initial and life-cycle costs
- maintenance and replacement ease
- performance capabilities for intended use and possible future use
- overall compatibility in appearance with other surrounding materials within facility
- safety and risk management factors.

Landscape Design, Sports Turf, and Parking Lots

Richard J. LaRue, David A. LaRue, and Thomas H. Sawyer

19

When planning the outdoor spaces of sports and recreation facilities, adjacent "transitional" space, and/or sports fields, the process must include individuals who can lend their understanding and expertise to the process. From a design standpoint, a licensed landscape architect or experienced landscape designer should be employed. If a sports field is the focus of, or is included in, the plan, then an experienced sports turf manager is important to the process. Finally, as all outdoor facilities and spaces will require maintenance, a logical planning resource will be the maintenance director and/or an experienced representative of the maintenance staff.

Perhaps the most important individual in the early stages of the planning process is the landscape professional. This person will be invaluable when making decisions related to site selection for the facility and utilization of all adjacent outdoor spaces.

More than any of the other major environmental design professions, landscape architecture is a profession on the move. It is comprehensive by definition—no less than the art and science of analysis, planning design, management, preservation and rehabilitation of the land. In providing well-managed design and development plans, landscape architects offer an essential array of services and expertise that reduce costs and add long-term value to a project. A landscape architect has a working knowledge of architecture, civil engineering, and urban planning and takes elements from each of these fields to design aesthetic and practical relationships with the land. Members of the profession have a special commitment to improving the quality of life through the best design of places for people and other living things (ASLA, 1998, on-line).

Sports fields are truly special facilities. When natural turf is selected, a sports turf specialist is needed to oversee the development of a total field management program (Lewis, 1994). Lewis suggests a comprehensive program should include the following:

> 1) selecting an adapted grass for the locality; 2) mowing this selected grass at proper height and frequency; 3) fertilizing at the proper time and rate according to the turfgrass growth; 4) irrigating as needed to encourage establishment and to reduce stress periods; 5) aerifying to relieve compaction or dethatching according to the turf and the amount of play; and 6) using the appropriate preemergence and postemergence herbicides. The goal is to first produce a vigorous turf that will be competitive to the weeds. (p. 28)

Such a program will be served by the design of the field, including irrigation and drainage, the choice of grass, and so on. Careful consideration involves knowing the grass and soil makeup, need for aeration, fertilization, top dressing, seeding, and later, weed control (Mazzola, 1998).

Parking lot design is a related part of the planning process. A successful parking facility can present an important and positive first image to visitors to the recreation or sports facility.

Finally, as the ultimate success of the facility planning process is often measured years later, it is important to consider those aspects of groundskeeping and parking that will be predetermined in the design of the fields and other outdoor spaces. Specifically, the labor and equipment required to maintain these spaces can be controlled with a carefully prepared design. Additionally, the life expectancy of the green and hard goods is directly related to the level of quality afforded. Management of money and resources (capital expenditures, debt load, salaries and wages, existing equipment vs. new equipment, etc.) begins with the planning process and the investment decisions made prior to plan implementation (Hughes Jr., 1996).

In summary, the planning process must include consideration of both the facility and the adjacent outside or transitional space. Further, the planning process will benefit from the expertise of a certified landscape architect or experienced landscape designer, an experienced sports turf specialist (if planning a formal play space), an experienced parking lot consultant, and a representative of the facilities maintenance staff. The quality of the planning process will be measured against the ability of the facility and all aspects of the plan to meet the goals described in the facility's case statement or building program document.

Learning Objectives

After reading this chapter, the student should be able to

- understand landscape design concepts in terms of aesthetics, function, and safety;
- recognize the planning responsibilities related to groundskeeping management, maintenance, and equipment;
- understand the design and operation concepts of surface and subsurface irrigation and drainage;
- understand the concepts related to parking design for aesthetics, function, and safety;
- understand the difference between standards and guidelines related to chemical handling and storage;
- understand both the trends and new technologies in landscape design and groundskeeping; and
- understand the planning of a parking area for a sports or recreation venue.

Landscape Design: Aesthetics, Function, and Safety

Photo by Meghan Rosselli

Sample use of lighting, bench, and garbage can.

Frequently, when money is tight and/or the facility costs are exceeding expectations, careful development of the adjacent outdoor space is readily ignored. Experience has demonstrated that this is shortsighted as there are essential components that must be considered exclusive of the site selection of a facility. The design of this transitional space, whether for an indoor or outdoor facility, should consider the following characteristics:

- the aesthetics of the space relative to all adjacent facilities
- the functional characteristics of the space relative to adjacent facilities
- the safety of users (including accessibility) within the space and relative to adjacent facilities

Aesthetics

The basics of aesthetics in landscape design are sight lines that bring focus to important features of a facility or space, the use of space (especially spatial relationships), and the ability of the finished product to enhance the quality of the experience for all users.

Annuals Commonly Used in Landscaping

A good landscape needs anchor plants: trees, shrubs, and perennials that keep providing color year after year. However, to keep the landscape lively, you need to mix in new, different annuals each season. The annuals need to be selected for sun or shade, cool or hot weather, and humid dry conditions. The top 10 annuals for landscaping are (Atchison, 2003):

- impatiens (shade)
- petunia (sunny)
- angelonia or summer snapdragon (full sun)
- geranium (sunny)
- vinca (sunny)
- pentas or star cluster (sunny)
- viola (sunny, cool)
- begonia (shade)
- ornamental millet (sunny)
- marigold (sunny)

Function

There are critical components to a comprehensive design related to function. The way the implemented design reacts to natural and man-made stresses is indicative of the time and resources invested in the planning process. Further, the long-term demand for maintenance will be affected by the design. And the way the design serves the facility program and user needs is a direct result of the planning process.

In addition to the characteristics described above, site selection is an important part of function for an outdoor facility and should also include consideration of

- the orientation of play spaces with respect to the sun angle and predominant wind direction,
- the topography of the developed and undeveloped outdoor space,
- the existing and necessary surface and subsurface irrigation and drainage,
- the appropriate use of natural and man-made barriers,
- environmental concerns, and
- the minimization of normal wear and vandalism (Macomber, 1993).

Safety

It is critical that the planning process for safety results in a landscape design that manages the risk of all adjacent outdoor spaces so that all foreseeable user accidents or injuries can be avoided. This planning for safety and security should include

- signage in large lettering that clearly identifies pedestrian and vehicular paths, facilities, right-of-way, accessible parking, no parking and fire zones, and any other user-friendly restrictions or expectations;
- perimeter fencing or appropriate use of natural barriers;
- programmable and/or light-sensitive night lighting;
- pedestrian and vehicular circulation that is easy to maintain and has reasonable and unobstructed views of cross traffic at every intersection;
- smooth (yet skid resistant) pavements and other path or road surfaces;
- bollards (permanent and removable barriers) restricting vehicular travel on pedestrian paths; and
- surveillance.

Photo by Meghan Rosselli

Tree-lined sidewalks (above and below).

Photo by Meghan Rosselli

Surface and Subsurface Irrigation and Drainage

An effective landscape design will consider the operation of surface and subsurface irrigation and drainage. Not having enough moisture can be deadly to your grass and plants. Too much moisture and no way for the water to drain can also drown your plants and fields. When rain does not come, appropriate irrigation must be available. Irrigation planning is both an art and a science. There are extraordinary examples of how, after large amounts of rain and subsequent flooding, the drainage of a sports field has allowed a contest to be held in an amazingly short time (Smith, 1998; Tracinski, 1998).

Irrigation

The principle of "deep and infrequent" watering remains the norm. This practice over the years has proven to be effective. The physical properties of the soil must be considered in planning any watering program. For example, a clay soil will not accept as much water as a sandy soil and will require lighter, more frequent irrigation.

Most turfgrasses need as much as 1 to 1.5 inches of water per week during the growing season to support turf growth (Puhalla et al., 1999, p. 82). The best time to irrigate turf is in the early morning hours, just prior to or after sunrise. This eliminates interference with use, reduces disease incidence, and increases the amount of water placed in the soil for plant use.

There are two basic types of irrigation systems available for use—portable and installed irrigation. Portable irrigation systems include traveling irrigators (i.e., rotating sprinkler attached to a hose, propelling itself along a wire), quick coupler systems (i.e., systems are comprised of a series of underground pipes with quick couplers permanently installed flush with the ground), and rain guns (i.e., a huge impact-type sprinkler that is used to irrigate a large turf area).

The price for installed systems is decreasing, while the reliability of operation is increasing. Automatic systems save maintenance labor costs when compared to portable systems and the even distribution of water is improved.

Drainage

Whether designing a drainage system for a new field or for an existing field, certain questions need to be answered, including:

- How quickly should the field be returned to playable condition after a rainstorm?
- In what climate is the field located?
- Is the field designed for amateur or professional use?
- What kind of flexibility will there be in rescheduling?
- Will the field have a crown or will it be flat but sloped?
- Will the field have a dense clay-like soil or a sand soil?
- Will the collection system be shallow or deep?
- Will there be a single- or multi-layered filter system?

Photo by Tom Sawyer

Example of a culvert.

Most landscape architects will use the following rule of thumb relative to drainage: whether designing a single field or a multifield complex, keep in mind that each field should be designed and constructed as an individual drainage unit. A well-designed drainage plan will install interceptor drains to isolate water, cuts and fills, catch basins, swales, and French drains.

Further, Puhalla et al. (1999) suggest field designs for surface drainage fall into one of two categories—crowned or flat. The typical percentage of slope for a sports field runs between 1% and 1.75%.

Photo by Tom Sawyer

Example of a drainage ditch.

The most common type of crowned field has been a football field. However, now that many football fields are also used for soccer, they have become flat fields because the soccer field overlaps the football field. Most soccer fields are often designed using a lower percentage of slope and installed drain systems are usually added.

Most flat fields need an installed parallel or grid drainage pattern while crowned fields typically have a herringbone pattern (Breems, 2001). In either case the drainage pattern should extend at least 15 feet beyond the playing surface on all sides. Be certain that the field records indicate it is a flat, sloped, or a crowned field. Otherwise, 10 years after initial construction, some well-meaning person might try to "recrown" the field, causing a real mess.

The collection system should be located near the surface of the field. The deeper the collectors are located, the slower the drainage will be. The system that is submerged 6 inches with sand located above and around the collectors is fast and efficient (Breems, 2001).

Finally, a multi-layered filter system protects the collectors from failure due to binding and guarantees a long life. A fabric filter prevents the core from filling with fine sand and silt. A 3.5- to 4-ounce needle punched geo-synthetic fabric does a fine job. An inch or two of very course sand surrounding the

Photo by Tom Sawyer

Example of French drain.

fabric will prevent the fabric from blocking. As the water passes through, the sand particles of clay and silt are arrested before they reach the fabric filter (Breems, 2001).

Trends and New Technologies in Landscape Design

Finally, the planning process will consider new trends or cutting-edge technologies when designing outdoor spaces. Consider making a significant investment in all aspects of the planning process to reduce short- and long-term mistakes. Once the plan is implemented, the success of the planning process will be easily measured in its ability to meet the needs of the facility program. Include the right people in the planning process. The experts are easy to remember. However, user input is also critical to promote inclusion and a sense of ownership in the process. Users include the people who will manage the facility and outdoor spaces as well as those who will participate in facility programs. An appropriate number of such people will help build goodwill and, more importantly, should serve the planning process effectively because of their unique "user" viewpoint. The long-term reality of maintenance and the cost of labor, materials, and equipment demand that landscape designs provide for minimal maintenance. A landscape architect or experienced landscape designer as well as a representative member of the groundskeeping staff should provide the expertise to design minimal maintenance into the outdoor spaces. Finally, the planning process should consider future implementation of the design when it comes to the level of quality selected in green and hard goods. Experience tells us that when purchasing such goods, the better the quality, the better the satisfaction.

Trends and new technologies in turf management are often made available by academics who are committed to this aspect of venue design and management. An excellent source of such information can be found at http://turfgrass.hort.iastate.edu/extension. Some of the articles specific to athletic fields made available by Dr. David Minner of Iowa State University at this internet site include:

- Infield Skin Testing
- Athletic Field Generic Football Field Maintenance
- Athletic Field Procedure for Selecting a Sand Rootzone
- Athletic Field Coring and Topdressing
- Athletic Field Safety and Maintenance Checklist
- Athletic Field Evaluation and Traffic Survey
- Athletic Field Construction, Renovation, and Maintenance Costs
- Athletic Field Management-Tips for a Limited Budget
- Athletic Field Liability Signage
- Athletic Field End of Season Practices

Sports Grasses and Turfs

Characteristics of Turfgrasses Commonly Used for Sports Turfs

Puhalla, Krans, and Goatley (1999) suggest there are 11 grasses commonly used as turfgrasses. However, of these species, only five are widely used in sports turf situations: Bermuda grass, Kentucky bluegrass, tall fescue, perennial ryegrass, and creeping bentgrass. There are two other grasses that are sometimes used: buffalo grass and zoysiagrass.

Further, Puhalla et al. (1999) indicate Bermuda grass (monostand) is planted and maintained alone except when overseeded with perennial and annual ryegrass for winter play. Tall fescue, perennial ryegrass, and Kentucky bluegrass are planted and maintained as either monostands or in combination with other cultivars (polystands). Creeping bentgrass is usually planted as a monostand.

Turfgrass selection is usually based upon weather zones (i.e., warm, transitional, or cool). In warm weather zones (Southern states across the United States), sports turf is generally dominated by Bermuda grass because it flourishes in the hot summers and mild winters and can withstand occasional summer dryness without damage. In the transitional zone, fields are dominated by tall fescues and specifically developed Bermuda grass. Finally, in cold zones (Northern states across the United States), Kentucky bluegrass and perennial ryegrass predominate and a mixture of those species is probably the most popular sports turf (Puhalla et al., 1999). "Both types tolerate the cold northern winters adequately, and the mixture allows for the aggressive spreading and recovery characteristic of Kentucky bluegrass, along with the stability and wear resistance of perennial ryegrass" (p.8).

The National Turfgrass Evaluation Program (NTEP) tests hundreds of commercially available cultivars and experimental entries of turfgrass annually. Researchers conduct these tests at universities in 40 states and a few Canadian provinces. Data from each year are summarized and published on a Web site (http://www.ntep.org) and also in CD-ROM format. Go to the Web site and read the disclaimer at the bottom of that page, then click enter. This will take you to the main page (http:www.ntep.org/contents2.shtml). To find a grass species, simply click on the link in the yellow box "All NTEP Reports—Select a Turfgrass Species."

Portable Grass

During the '90s, Popke (2000) indicated a number of natural-grass suppliers (e.g., GreenTech® Inc-ITM turf modules, Hummer Turfgrass Systems Inc.-Grasstiles™, the Motz Group-TS-II™, Desso DLW Sports International-DD GrassMaster, SportGrass® Inc-SportGrass system, Southern Turf Nurseries-STN 2000, Thomas Brothers Grass, a division of Turf-Grass America Co-SquAyers, Southwest Recreational Industries Inc.-AstroGrass® became responsive to facilities' needs for a more durable natural grass product. The suppliers began to use (1) portable grass that unrolls as a cover for concrete floors and parking lots, (2) grass tiles with roots that are reinforced and stabilized with synthetic fibers, and (3) systems that mix grass with synthetic fibers woven or stitched into a backing. These renewed processes allow sections of worn surface (e.g., golf tee-boxes, areas in front of a soccer goal, middle sections of football fields) to be replaced without tearing up the entire area and the entire surface can usually be removed or installed in less than 24 hours. All of the systems claim to be able to better reinforce the root zone and extend usage.

Often, with these portable systems, grass is grown in trays that allow for drainage and air movement. Synthetic reinforcements play a role in several portable grass surfaces and are considered 100 percent natural by their suppliers. This can be said because the majority of the additional synthetic material is inserted below the grass surface for root reinforcement and additional wear resistance. However, a better term might be *hybrid*.

Some of the hybrid systems are a combination of sand-filled, fibrillated synthetic tufts and a dual-component backing of biodegradable fibers and plastic mesh. The matrix shelters the vegetative parts of the grass plant that are essential to rapid growth and recuperation while the grass roots intertwine with the tufts and grow down through the plastic mesh. If the turf canopy wears away, the sand-filled synthetic matrix continues to provide a consistent playing surface. There are a few systems that do not use a cloth backing. Instead, they train the roots to grow on top of a plastic barrier, similar to roots in a potted plant.

A Kinder, Gentler Synthetic Turf

Popke (2000) describes three new kinder, gentler synthetic turfs—Astroplay®, Fieldturf™, and Sofsport™. These synthetic surfaces have been designed to reduce injuries to players. The new synthetic surfaces blend and tuft polyethylene and polypropylene fibers into a permeable surface backing. Each synthetic grass fiber is placed so as to create a pattern of natural grass. The fill is made from sand and ground rubber, which surround each fiber much like soil holds a blade of grass. One supplier does not use sand, but rather uses a combination of rubber and nylon fibers mixed with longer polyolefin strands. This combination enhances drainage, reduces compaction, and adds resilence.

Groundskeeping: Management, Maintenance, and Equipment Planning Responsibilities

Appropriate to the review of groundskeeping management, maintenance, and equipment are three concepts related to success in these areas: time management, money and resource management, and machinery and equipment management (Hughes, 1996, pp. 2-3). The responsibility for planning related to groundskeeping should be shared by a seasoned member of the groundskeeping staff. Efficient use of staff time can be facilitated in a properly planned landscape design. A significant aspect of the plan will be the reduction of labor as it relates to maintenance. If, by design, you reduce the employee labor required, you are managing time more efficiently. Secondly, if you demand quality green goods when installing your landscape design, then the money and resources for your project will be managed more efficiently. Finally, if your planning process includes a design that can be maintained with existing equipment, you are taking responsibility for the future without ignoring the reality of the present. Groundskeeping management must be considered when designing your landscape. And few people can better assist you with this planning than a knowledgeable representative of your groundskeeping staff.

Topdressing a Baseball Softball Field

Topdressing describes the application of a structural material to the top layer of turf. According to Wilkinson (2002), a structural material is one that is not solubilized rapidly in water (e.g., soil conditioners, sand, and soil). Topdressing benefits the field in three ways: 1) improves the quality of the turf surface, 2) protects the turf crowns, and 3) improves the soil's porosity and reduces the organic thatch. Most baseball and softball fields can be improved by topdressing. Both the skinned and turf areas can benefit.

The skinned area of a baseball or softball field is often built using heavy-textured clay and then a soil clay amendment is worked into the top few inches to achieve a desired surface (Wilkinson, 2002). The surface of the skinned area should be almost 100 percent soil clay amendment. The surface should be topdressed once or twice a month depending on usage. The soil amendment should be spread uniformly and raked into the top inch of the soil. The use of ceramic conditioners will dry out the skinned area and cause it to harden and crack. A great deal of water will need to be used to achieve a great playing surface.

Topdressing a baseball or softball turf can help the turf and produce a great playing surface. A turf area should not be topdressed with a structural material containing more than 40% ceramic conditioner (Wilkinson, 2002). The more clay soil amendment added, the greater the chance of stressing the turf. The recommended mixture for a topdressing is 30% or less ceramic conditioner to 70% or more the natural soil the turf is growing in. If the field was built with sand, then add 30% soil amendment to the same kind of sand. For single application of topdressing, add enough to achieve a layer 1/8 inch thick or less (Wilkinson, 2002).

How to Select a Field Cover

Field covers keep fields dry, reduce the risk of rainouts, increase turf enhancement, and lend themselves to great advertising and sponsorship arrangements. The advertising dollars should be spent on the cover for the tarp when it is rolled up. More people will see the advertisement and it is easier to place logos on the cover for the rolled-up tarp than it is to place logos on the actual tarp material.

The color of covers can play an important role in turf management. Tests conducted by several turf specialists found that certain colors of covers can have a positive effect on turf development. For example:

- White/silver combination with white side exposed to the sun, on average, has 14° F less heat build up under the cover than other color combinations. This color combination would be appropriate for southern climates.
- Black/silver combination with black side exposed to the sun draws more heat to the turf surface. This combination would work well in northern climates.
- Orange/white combination allows light penetration and enhances turf development. This combination would be appropriate for northern and southern climates.

Both woven polyethylene and vinyl provide a good cover. The common differences between polyethylene and vinyl are outlined in Table 19.1.

Table 19.1
Comparison of Polyethylene and Vinyl Covers

Characteristic	Polyethylene	Vinyl
Weight	1/3 lighter	1/3 heavier
Price	1/2 less in cost	1/2 more in cost
Color	fewer choices	greater choices
Snow removal	not as durable	more durable
Wind	less effective	more effective
Joining sections	Velcro®	plastic zipper

Field Traffic

A frequent concern for turf managers relates to field traffic (number of events per field, per year). Minner (2004) has been collecting field-use data (by hours and user group) over the past four years, relating field use to field performance.

> On average an individual field is receiving 125 events per year. A field receiving over 79 events should not be able to recover to an acceptable level. Most turf managers feel they could maintain an acceptable field if the annual event schedule were less than 64 events. (p. 38).

However, this is not a definite maximum. Some programs cannot even tolerate 64 events, while others because of proper management have tolerated many more. There are a number of variables regarding field tolerance, including: "warm/cool season climate, soil type, grass selection, irrigation, cultivation, seeding/sodding renovation, etc." (p. 38).

Minner (2004) recommends that turf managers begin collecting their own data (specific information reflecting field activity and performance) to use when making important field-use and planning decisions. "Without this type of data, it will be difficult to limit field-use or to plan the appropriate number of fields when building for future growth" (p. 38). You can review Minner's *Athletic Field Traffic Survey and Quality Assessment* at http://turfgrass.hort.iastate.edu/extension/Egtrafficsurvey.pdf

Combining field performance information with accurate field use records on a person/hour or field/hour basis will give the turf manager the best decision-making data from which to work.

When organizations do not allow for reasonable field usage, Minner (2004) suggests that,

> an appropriate amount of funding must be channeled to grounds management to offset field damages from high use. In cases of extreme field activity there may be no level of funding that will keep the fields from wearing out and your only recourse is to close the fields for revegetation (p. 38).

Rotational Field: A New Concept

As the interest in team sports, such as soccer, continues to grow at all levels, the demand for time on traditional playing fields has escalated. Daily team practices, 8- to 10-game weekend schedules, and pick-up games when the fields are not in use are becoming quite common. Bob Stienhaus, president of Pioneer Fields (Pittsburgh) and fellow founder Matthew Butch have come up with a practical solution for preserving natural turf fields that requires less maintenance and provides for safer, year-round play. The concept is a rotational athletic field.

The design concept incorporates a rectangular athletic playing field fitted within a substantially circular turf area. The uniquely graded circular area can essentially be scaled to fit any size rectangular playing field (e.g., football, field hockey, lacrosse, or soccer) with some buffer space. The playing field rotates at select times throughout the season of play to limit the amount of play in high traffic areas or to avoid damage or unsafe turf. The rotation schedule can range from daily, such as following a rough game in heavy rains, to just three times a year for seasonal play and seasonal turf repairs (Saunders, 2001).

Chemical Handling and Storage, Legal Aspects, and Recommendations

Besides the Chemical Hazards Act managed under the Occupational Safety and Health Administration (OSHA), both state and federal regulations govern the handling of many of the chemicals used in weed control, insect management, and fertilization. The Chemical Hazards Act requires the employer to properly warn and protect employees using such chemicals. All chemical manufacturers must ship hazardous chemicals with Material Safety Data Sheets (MSDS), which should be kept on file for employees and specifically outline the guidelines for proper use of their products. Other government regulations require groundskeeping staff to be certified in the proper application and handling of chemicals. It is the responsibility of the groundskeeping staff to be knowledgeable in the use and handling of these chemicals and associated equipment. With a knowledgeable resource on the planning committee, the facility can provide for proper storage of chemicals and clean up of chemical application equipment used in groundskeeping.

Lining Athletic Fields

Steinbach (2000) suggests the primary concern when marking grass fields is to keep the turf in good growing condition. Water-based paints are the preferred choice. Chalk (e.g., limestone or marble) is less friendly to turf due to the accumulated build-up that blocks water's movement to the grass root system. The best paint contains a higher concentration (one to two pounds per gallon) of titanium oxide (TiO_2) which brightens the paint. The other common ingredient is calcium carbonate ($CaCO_2$), a paint filler. Colored paints will have a higher amount of calcium carbonate. White paint can be diluted up to 9:1, but colored paints can only be diluted to 1:1 ratio. Too much calcium carbonate makes playing fields abrasive, and it can kill the turf grass.

The following are a few painting tips provided by Mike Hebrard, owner, Athletic Field Design:

- Grid method—make an enlargement of the logo to be painted, then draw a series of lines in a graph format on the logo at a workable uniform spacing. Lay out the size of the logo, converting inches to feet, and mark dots on the grass at the edges of the design. Use an inverted spray chalk or blue to do the initial layout. Repeat the graph, using string and long nails, going back and forth until the graph is completed. By looking at the drawing, note where each line crosses a grid and duplicate it on the grass by painting a line, gradually connecting the shape of the logo. Use inverted aerosol cans to differentiate colors and features. Once the logo has been completed, you can brighten it using an airless sprayer.
- The most popular method of painting on athletic turf is the stencil on a heavy plastic sheet or tarp. These are readily available from most athletic paint suppliers. After use, fold up the stencil and put into a marked duffle bag to store and identify its contents.
- The key to painting dirt is to have it moist enough to take the paint, much like staining wood. If it is too wet, the paint will bleed into the other colors. If it is too dry, the paint will not be very bright and will wear off quickly.

Parking Lot Design

Facilities managers are being challenged to 1) develop fair and customer-focused parking strategies, 2) prioritize the use of decreasing parking resources, 3) understand the explosion in parking technology, 4) provide cost-effective parking solutions while catching up with deferred maintenance, and 5) address the widely held perception that safe and convenient parking can only be provided next to the front door. The traditional parking paradigm must be expanded in order to meet the planning challenge. In the past, planning focused on the number of vehicles within given parking parameters. However, as the number of available sites decreases and the cost to develop and operate parking facilities increases, communities are demanding more cost-effective solutions.

Ideally, the parking design should be incorporated into the overall landscape and building design, especially in terms of aesthetics, function, and safety. However, there are some additional design options to be considered including function, aesthetics, and safety.

Function

Will parking discriminate against users who arrive later in the day? Do plans include large and visible signage in order that users understand all allowances and restrictions? Is there adequate parking? Will the facility require a parking garage? Can users exit the parking areas in a timely fashion?

In the past, planning focused on the number of vehicles within given parking parameters. The new focus should be on consumer needs. Planners and facilities managers should move away from the traditional parking paradigm to one that is consumer oriented.

The Traditional Parking Paradigm

Considerable energy has been focused on the management of vehicles and pedestrians within the boundaries of parking areas. Traditional parking technology contributed to this planning focus, with the "pay-on-foot" approach in parking structures, central pay stations in surface lots, "smart cards," debit cards, proximity cards, and so on. Planners are bombarded with issues, concerns, and solutions within the parking space boundaries. Traditional master planning guidelines for sports and recreation venues have also contributed to this planning focus.

Kirkpatrick (1997) suggests that,

> many planners have successfully implemented a pedestrian orientation to the recreation and sport environment, resulting in parking located at perimeter or off-site locations. Typically with this approach, the need for transportation has correspondingly increased. (p. 950)

Yet, the planning focus has remained within the boundaries of the parking areas as planners have attempted to match and manage the vehicle demand to the space available. Over the years, many strategies have been developed to manage the increasing demand for limited parking space.

Parking planners have matched various forms and combinations of reserved parking, zoned parking, and open parking to the specific community culture. But the planning focus remained directed at single-occupant vehicles within designated parking boundaries. Regardless of the system that is used to manage vehicles within designated parking boundaries at perimeter locations, customer dissatisfaction with parking systems increased dramatically. Customers lamented that convenient parking space was not available and that the cost of parking was rising. At the same time, many facility managers were faced with deferred maintenance, escalating costs to operate and maintain a parking system, and increasing customer demand for a decreasing supply of parking.

The following factors contribute to the increasing customer and administration dissatisfaction with parking systems that traditionally were perceived as successful:

- New parking structures are costly to build.
- Costs to maintain structures are escalating.
- Surface lots are costly to build.
- Costs to maintain core area surface lots are escalating.
- Deferred maintenance is adding up for many older structures and surface lots where security, aesthetics, and quality construction may not have been a priority in the past.

Thus, it can be seen that costs to build, repair, and maintain parking structures and surface parking lots are escalating. At the same time, customers are not willing to absorb these additional costs by paying higher parking rates, especially when a perceived value may not be present.

A Parking Paradigm Shift: Customer-Oriented Parking

Planning that traditionally started once a vehicle reached a parking area now encompasses options for getting from home to the sports and recreation venue. This has become necessary because

- many sports and recreation venues cannot cost effectively operate and maintain the traditional expansion of surface lot and structure parking,
- the customer or participant is typically not willing to pay the increasing cost, and
- the traditional parking planning focus of one vehicle per person no longer meets the diverse needs of all customers.

The customer-oriented parking paradigm requires that planners understand and know the customers so as to meet their needs and provide a better service. The parking menu should reflect choices in terms of cost to convenience. For example, the following parking options may be included:

- Reserved space or parking area.
- Core area parking.
- Perimeter area parking.
- Designated motorcycle parking in the preceding four areas if demand requires.
- Carpool/vanpool parking in the first four areas above if demand requires it.
- Bicycle parking, which might include bicycle storage lockers and the traditional hoop.
- Shared parking resources with the surrounding community, such as with park-and-ride programs.
- Economic incentives provided to promote shared bus services with the surrounding community.
- Walking may be a parking option that needs only to be promoted. Typically, the implementation of many sports and recreation venue master plans has resulted in a pedestrian orientation to the venue where special attention has been focused on providing appropriately placed sidewalks (seven- or eight-feet wide for snow removal, which is also a good width for group walking) with excellent lighting, an effective emergency telephone system, and beautiful grounds.

Kirkpatrick (1997) indicates that

> The key to implementing a successful menu of parking options, based on the match of cost to convenience, is an understanding of customers' needs and their perceptions of solutions, as well as a willingness by all involved to be receptive to trying new ideas. (p. 953)

Another key to success is the flexibility of a parking system to provide multiple options to fit diverse life-styles.

Parking Systems

Parking administrators have matched various forms and combinations of reserved parking, zoned parking, and open parking to their specific recreation and sports and cultures. The following are advantages and disadvantages of each form:

- Reserved parking is typically the most expensive, with the lowest occupancy. As space constraints continue to grow with the projected decrease in core area parking, it may be increasingly difficult to provide reserved parking for large numbers of people.
- Zoned parking typically restricts parkers to an area close to their work site. The occupancy rate is generally higher than that for reserved parking. As core area parking space continues to decline, the demand will typically exceed the supply.
- Open parking, commonly referred to as "hunting license" parking, provides a system of parking on a first-come basis and has the highest occupancy rate. However, as the demand for parking increases, the level of frustration grows as customers perceive wasted time in hunting for a parking space.

Parking Options

The following menu of seven parking options is listed, in order, from the most expensive to the least expensive:

- Reserved space or area. This option is usually the most expensive and has the lowest occupancy rate. If the demand exceeds the supply, the challenge may be to develop criteria for eligibility that customers perceive to be fair.

- Core area parking. This option typically provides parking within a reasonably short walking distance to most recreation or sports activities.

- Perimeter parking. This option generally provides parking that requires a longer walk or a short bus ride to most recreation or sports activities.

- Motorcycle programs. Space that typically cannot be used for vehicle parking may be promoted for motorcycle parking. Because less space is required for motorcycles than for cars, a lower rate could be charged, whether in a reserved area, core area, or perimeter area parking location.

- Carpool/vanpool programs. This is a cost-effective approach for those who are willing to contend with the perceived inconvenience of organizing. Payment choices could be offered depending on whether reserved, core area, or perimeter parking is used.

- Bicycle parking. A choice of bicycle parking could be offered, from the traditional hoops to bicycle lockers. Because many bicycles are expensive, the provision of lockers may promote the use of bicycles over vehicles. Attended bike corrals are also becoming more available.

- Park-and-ride parking. This option may provide an opportunity to share resources with the surrounding community, to reduce operating costs, to take advantage of parking space that may be underused, and to address a unique need of commuting participants.

Notes

Photo by Meghan Rosselli

Parking lot security monitors.

Finally, flexibility must be built into the parking system to provide customers with easy access to multiple parking options based on their own unique needs.

Parking Technology

Like many fields of endeavor, the parking industry is experiencing an explosion in technology. Extensive amounts of data may be tracked and monitored. However, implementation of such technology may be costly. The initial task is to identify the information that is essential to manage a successful parking system. The typical challenge is to fund only the hardware and software that are actually needed but with expansion capabilities for future growth. Effective strategic planning, together with a total quality management approach, will help to identify the likely future direction for use of emerging parking technologies.

The following are examples of parking technologies that are available.

- Equipment to monitor parking structure activity. Typically this involves a chip in a card or on a permit or sensors installed in the pavement. For enforcement purposes, gate equipment may be used. Types of information that may be monitored are as follows:
  —Number and time of entry/ exit.
  —Occupancy trends.
  —Use by permit type such as student, client with disability, or guest.
  —Amount of parking used per parker.
  —Identification of mainte nance needs such as a gate remaining open.
  —The system may include a "Parking Available/Full" sign at the entrance for customers' convenience. If the system operates close to full occupancy on a daily basis, all structures may be net worked so that if a particular structure is full, a message sign will direct customers to the next closest structures that have parking available.

Photo by Meghan Rosselli

Toll parking entrance and exit.

Photo by Meghan Rosselli

Parking garage.

- Central pay stations may be used in structures or surface lots. Individual parking meters are eliminated and customers are directed to a central location to pay. Advantages for the customer are that a parking receipt is provided and dollar bills may be used, eliminating the need to carry a large number of coins. Advantages operationally are that 1) enforcement will pull a tape at the central pay station to quickly identify vehicles whose time has expired, 2) collection time is saved because collection occurs at one location, and 3) audit control is simplified because a tape is provided that identifies the amount of revenue being collected. If multiple locations are added, central pay stations may be networked to an administrative location for on-time identification of all activity in total or per lot. For example, data could include occupancy, percentage of illegal parkers, and/or revenue collected.

- Debit card systems. These systems allow the parker to add value to a card from a central location or multiple locations and pay only for actual time parked. Debit card capability may be added to many systems such as central pay stations or individual parking meters. The key advantage to the customer is convenience (i.e., not having to carry change). Advantages operationally are that revenue is collected up front, collection costs are reduced, and audit control is simplified.

Referencing the above examples, astute questions must be asked to determine the minimal level of hardware and software needed to operate an effective parking system; however, there must be an understanding of future directions to ensure that the system can be expanded.

For example, in monitoring structure activity, is it necessary to know parking use per customer or is overall occupancy and identification of peak use enough information to operate a parking system successfully? Networking parking structures with a message sign may be costly. Is the cost worth the customer service? Networking multiple central pay station locations provides extensive information at a glance. Does the need for quick information justify the cost of networking and staff time to track and monitor data? Debit cards are a customer convenience. Careful planning must be done to determine whether one solution is better than other options.

Aesthetics

The first experience people have at the facility will likely come when they park their vehicle and approach the facility on foot. What are the sight lines, the use of space, and the placement of parking to the facility that make this experience inviting? Can parking be distributed in a way that avoids a large "car lot" look? Are there natural and man-made barriers that can enhance the aesthetics of the parking space(s) without compromising safety?

Image of the Parking Facility

The parking environment can influence a visitor's first impression of the facility. Many factors will contribute to a positive image. Key factors are the level of maintenance, lighting, signage, and the perception of safety.

Level of Maintenance

An appropriate level of maintenance must be established in the following areas:

- landscape care
- striping
- miscellaneous painting such as pavement arrows, objects of caution, structure railing, stairwells, and lobby areas
- sweeping
- pavement cleaning such as of oil spills
- relamping and cleaning of light fixtures
- pavement care such as repair of potholes and cracks
- replacement of faded, damaged, or missing signs
- structure window washing
- trash removal
- snow removal

Ideally, maintenance should be scheduled during times of low occupancy. However, when this is not possible, prior notification of any closure should be provided for good public relations.

Lighting

Many customers associate safety with lighting level. Incorrect lighting, particularly in parking structures, can create a variety of problems including shadow zones, sense of insecurity, reduced visibility, loss of direction, and even a sense of claustrophobia. Planners have to be sensitive to the correct illumination, uniformity, color of light, surface colors, and reflectance.

Signage

Most successful signage systems are those that provide as little overall signage as possible. The following 10 guidelines will contribute to a successful system:

- Letter size and wording should be standardized throughout the system.
- "Warm, fuzzy" wording will contribute to a friendly image. For example, "Please Drive Slowly," rather than "Drive Slowly," may go a long way toward achieving customer cooperation.
- Sign locations should be standardized as much as possible. Customers typically learn where to look for directional signage.

- Signage should be coordinated with lighting locations to further enhance signage visibility.
- High-pressure sodium lighting will distort many colors. If color coding is used as a level indicator, colors should be selected that will not be distorted. For example, red will appear brown, but yellow will not change in appearance.
- Typically, a successful directional system will incorporate multiple approaches. For example, some customers will remember colors better than the printed word. A level or area indicator sign may include the number "2" above the written word "TWO" against a blue background. Such a sign includes numerical and written identifiers as well as color coding.
- Traditional colors such as red, brown, yellow, and blue will probably have a higher recognition level than trendy colors such as mauve, taupe, coral, and cinnamon. Some customers may not know the name of such colors to use when asking for directions.
- Signage located around the perimeter of a surface lot rather than within the parking lot will provide ease of snow removal and sweeping.
- Information panels, campus directories, and "you-are-here" maps should be clustered in pedestrian areas such as structure elevator lobbies and bus pullouts.
- Standardizing signage, maintaining an inventory, and fabricating and installing in-house typically will provide faster service and a more cost-effective approach.

Funding of the Parking System

Ideally, a parking system should be self-supporting. Typical funding sources are as follows:

- permits
- metered parking
- designated visitor parking
- parking for special events
- parking tickets

Budget for the Parking System

Assuming that the parking system is self-supporting, rates should be set to fund the following components annually:

- administration
- maintenance
- repair and renovation
- deferred maintenance
- new construction
- a reserve for new construction
- alternate transportation options

As the annual budget is itemized for projected expenses and revenue, it is helpful to attach an explanation for each item. For example, why is permit revenue expected to increase/decrease or why are utility costs expected to increase/decrease? This information may be invaluable in the future for projecting trends.

Safety

The safety and security of users are the most important characteristics of parking design. Will facility users circulate between the facility and parking areas secure in the knowledge that they will be safe and their vehicle will remain intact? Will the location of the parking areas mandate use of perimeter fencing? Can pedestrian paths be designed that allow users to avoid walking in vehicular areas in the parking lot? Are permanent or removable bollards required to manage vehicular traffic on pedestrian paths? Is lighting adequate for user safety and security at night? How will surveillance in the parking areas be managed: using closed-circuit cameras or parking attendant(s)? Will the parking areas have emergency telephone towers or "call stations"? And, if the lot is gated, will the entrance use pedestrian-safe, one-way traffic controllers with below-grade spikes?

The parking area should be controlled and monitored for safety. This will require a number of important decisions to be made, including:

- type of parking systems (e.g., ticket and ticketless—magnetic stripe, microwave, etc.)
- type of dispensers (e.g., machines, meters, cards or tags)
- using a van or shuttle system

Additional action may be needed to combat a past stereotype that parking structures or areas are not safe. The following strategies may have to be considered:

- installing an emergency telephone system, highly visible, in standard locations
- adding of glass panels in stairwells to increase visibility

- installing video cameras
- adding parking attendants during evening hours
- providing security personnel walking or driving through the structure
- increasing lighting level
- publishing procedures to enhance safety awareness
- establishing safety programs such as escort services

Summary

When planning a sports or recreational facility, it is imperative that the process include the expertise of a licensed landscape architect or experienced landscape planner. The facility manager should have a significant role in the planning process. Other people who may lend their expertise and/or experience include those responsible for facility maintenance and safety, facility users, and program staff.

Parking areas should be designed to be multipurpose (e.g., unused parking space as additional recreation space). Provided that vehicular controls are in operation, it is entirely possible to use flat, well-maintained parking surfaces as additional outdoor recreation space or sports courts. However, the best recreation or sports spaces are designed specifically as such a space and regular use of a parking lot as a play space probably indicates a flaw in the outdoor space planning. Yet planners must be sensitive to planning for multipurpose uses and maintain flexibility in their plans.

Section

III

Field and Court Specifications

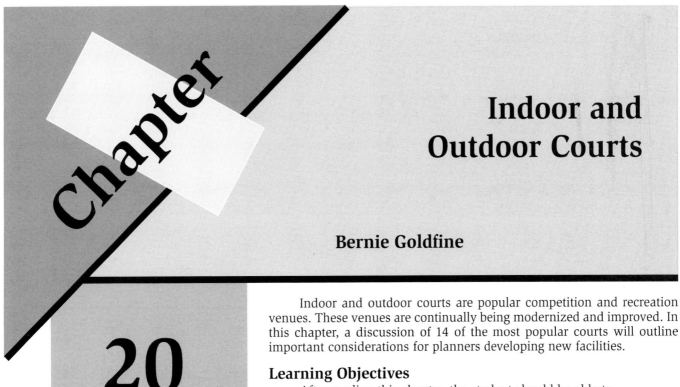

Indoor and Outdoor Courts

Bernie Goldfine

20

Indoor and outdoor courts are popular competition and recreation venues. These venues are continually being modernized and improved. In this chapter, a discussion of 14 of the most popular courts will outline important considerations for planners developing new facilities.

Learning Objectives

After reading this chapter, the student should be able to

- identify and describe layout, dimensions, and orientations;
- describe and identify various materials used in construction; and
- identify and describe a variety of important specifications and information (e.g., surfacing and lighting) for the courts described in this chapter.

Tennis Courts

Layout, Orientation, Dimensions, and Fencing

Tennis was first played in the United States during the mid-1870s. At that time, the game was slow-paced and played on the grass lawns of houses and parks. The game has now changed to a fast-paced athletic sport. As tennis has changed, so too have the courts on which it is played. Today's outdoor courts are laid out in a manner that minimizes the effects of wind, sun, background vision, and the lay of the land. Tennis courts are constructed of grass, clay, soft and hard composition, asphalt, concrete, and various synthetic materials. Many other features such as accessibility, storage, parking, lighting, and fencing need to be carefully planned for indoor tennis court construction.

In constructing outdoor tennis courts, prevailing winds must be taken into account in the planning process. If prevailing winds exist, courts should be placed near natural barriers such as woods or hills that act as a windbreak. If no existing barriers are in the area of court construction, a thick stand of staggered trees can be planted to serve as a barrier. Alternatively, if existing buildings are near the construction site, they may be used as a wind barrier.

Visual background must be planned for in the layout of tennis courts. The background at both ends of the courts should be natural grass, shrubs, woods, or other natural landscaping. Roads, parking areas, and pedestrian high-traffic areas are not acceptable at the ends of tennis courts. Too many objects moving in front of the tennis player causes lapses in concentration and makes play more difficult. If the busy areas must coexist with tennis courts, they should be at the sides of the courts. Furthermore, tennis complexes should not be placed too far from the remainder of the sports complex or center campus. The more removed the courts are, the more difficult user access will be. Court layout must also meet Americans With Disabilities Act (ADA) requirements for all users with disabilities.

The contour of the land for proposed tennis court construction also needs careful thought. It is much cheaper to construct tennis courts on flat land than on rolling terrain; it is less expensive in terms of both earth-moving and drainage concerns. If courts must be on rolling terrain, they should be laid out with the minimum of cost for earth moving and drainage. Also, hills should serve as natural barriers whenever possible.

Outdoor tennis court planning must also include the sun, which can create visual problems for the tennis player. If tennis courts are to be used mostly between April and October, they should be aligned north to south on the long axis of the court. If courts are to be used year round, the long axis should be northwest to southeast at 22° off true north. These orientations minimize the amount of sun-related visual problems for tennis players (USTA, 1997).

If courts are nonporous, provisions must be made for the drainage of water off the courts. Courts may be sloped from 0.5% to 1.5% depending on the type of surface. Any slope greater than 1.5% can be visually detected by the players and is not acceptable. Courts may be sloped side-to-side, end-to-end, center-to-end, or end-to-center. If only one individual court is constructed, either a side-to-side or an end-to-end slope works well. If a battery of courts is being constructed, the slope should be dictated by the fastest way to drain the most courts as quickly as possible. For example, if five courts were built side by side, an end-to-end slope would be best, since all courts would drain and dry simultaneously. If a side-to-side slope were used, the courts on the upper end of the slope would dry quickly but the last few courts would retain water for a much longer period of time since the water from the upper end-slope courts would have to drain across the courts at the lower end of the slope (USTA, 1997).

Center-to-end and end-to-center slopes are least desirable. When these types of slopes are used, the water remains on the court and court perimeter-playing surface much longer than when side-to-side or end-to-end slopes are used. Additionally, an end-to-center slope requires drains at or near the net. Drains on the court itself are not desirable.

When planning to use slope, natural drainage basins should be used whenever possible. Thus, if a small creek basin or lower land is adjacent to the court area, it is worthwhile to slope courts to these areas to limit artificial drainage and minimize drainage costs.

As outdoor tennis courts are planned, the size of the courts as well as the perimeter space around the court need careful attention. A singles court is 78 feet long and 36 feet wide. Including perimeter space, the minimum size for one doubles court would be 122 feet by 66 feet. These dimensions give minimum safety between the court and the fencing on both the sides and the ends of the court (USTA, 1997).

The minimum distance between side-by-side courts is 12 feet. The minimum distance between the court sideline and the side fence is 15 feet. Finally, the minimum distance between the court baseline and the end fence is 24 feet (USTA, 1997). The shortest distance is between courts since a player has open space (the adjacent court) to run to in order to retrieve a ball. There is more distance between the sideline and the side fence since players can run into the fence. Finally, the baseline distance is the greatest since this area is essentially a part of the playing area even though it is not a part of the actual court. Figure 20.1 illustrates these minimum distances as well as the dimensions of a tennis court.

Tennis courts should be enclosed with chain-link fence. The fence can be either 10 or 12 feet high.

Figure 20.1
Tennis Court Diagram and Dimensions

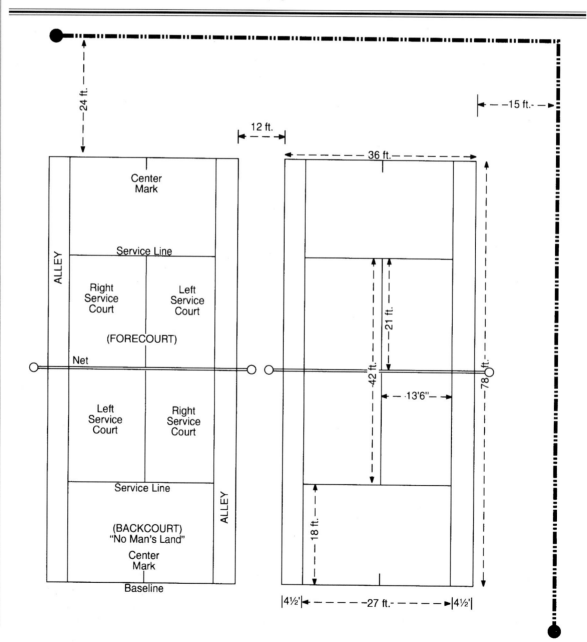

The 12-foot-high fence is more expensive than the 10-foot-high fence; however, those additional 2 feet of fencing keep in a significantly greater percentage of balls (USTA, 1997).

Chain-link fence comes in a No. 6 or No. 9 gauge. The No. 6 gauge is thicker and thus more costly. Either gauge is acceptable. Fence is also available with a polyvinyl chloride (PVC) plastic coating (most often green). Coated fencing is more expensive; however, in addition to its aesthetic qualities, it does not rust as will galvanized fencing.

Line posts that hold the fencing must be no farther than 10 feet apart and all corner and gateposts should be stabilized by cross braces. All line posts should be embedded at least 3 feet into the ground. If a wind/visual screen is attached to the fence, all line posts should be embedded in a concrete footer.

Adequate gates should be placed throughout the tennis court complex. These gates need to meet the needs of both instructors and players. Each set of courts in a complex must have an external gate and internal gates. Gates are expensive; but compromising on the number of gates will compromise accessibility to the courts, both internally and externally.

Types of Courts

Courts are classified as either porous (those that allow water to filter and drain through the court surface itself) or nonporous (those that do not allow water to penetrate the surface). The sloping as previously mentioned is for nonporous courts but is sometimes used in porous courts to carry penetrated water into the subsurface drainage system. Clay, grass, soft composition (fast dry), porous concrete, and various synthetics are porous courts. Concrete, asphalt (cushioned and non-cushioned), hard composition (liquid applied synthetic), and various synthetics are nonporous courts. As a group, asphalt courts are composed of (1) asphalt plant mix, (2) emulsified asphalt mix, (3) plant and emulsified mix, (4) asphalt penetration mix, and (5) asphalt bound system (cushioned) (USTA, 1997).

Numerous items must be considered when selecting the appropriate type of court. Initial cost, cost of upkeep, amount of use, area of country, maintenance personnel needed, type of players, level of competition, and age of players must be factored in when determining the type of court to be selected.

Clay, grass, and soft composition courts are much easier on the legs of players and allow for a much slower ball bounce than other courts. These courts are superior for young players, beginning players, and older players. However, they need a high level of maintenance, which is costly in both materials and personnel. Clay courts must be leveled, must have clay added periodically, require watering, and must be kept free of vegetation. Soft composition courts must be rolled, require watering, and need to have screen and base components added often. Grass courts are similar to golf greens and need daily maintenance. Additionally, grass courts that receive heavy use should be alternated daily. That is, a court used on Monday should not be used again until Wednesday. Consequently, more court space is necessary for heavily used grass courts. Grass courts give a skidding ball bounce, and sometimes an erratic bounce, because of small divots, excessive wear, and taped lines. Overall, clay, grass, and soft composition courts are recommended for commercial clubs where the cost of upkeep can be packaged into member fees. They are not recommended for schools and recreation programs because of upkeep costs.

Asphalt, concrete, and hard composition courts need less maintenance but provide a faster ball bounce and cause more stress on the legs of players. Of the three types, asphalt courts are the most inexpensive to construct and hard composition courts are most costly. Hard composition courts take a few months to cure and harden and they should not be used until they cure completely. Hard composition courts can be constructed with multiple layers of cushioning material. The more layers in the courts, the greater the resiliency of the surface will be; however, each additional layer of cushioning increases the cost. Hard composition courts are smoother than concrete or asphalt, therefore they cause less wear and tear on balls, shoes, and rackets. Asphalt, concrete, and hard composition courts are recommended for schools and recreation programs. Hard composition is the optimum choice of the three.

Numerous synthetic court surfaces are available. If synthetic outdoor courts are to be constructed, users should be consulted to determine the advantages and disadvantages of such courts for both players and owners. Also, product descriptions of the material should be studied carefully to help determine which synthetic surface best meets the specific needs of the court under construction.

Regardless of the type of court surface, it is paramount that a tennis court construction firm be employed to build the court(s). A local construction firm with no tennis court-building experience should not be permitted to construct the courts. Typically, a builder inexperienced in tennis court construction does not have the expertise to properly build tennis courts. This lack of expertise results in the use of poor construction techniques; more importantly, it ultimately results in premature (and costly) repairs and renovations.

Costs for an outdoor court surface and base vary depending upon the number of courts being built, the geographic location, and the amount of grading and drainage required, ranging from $25,000 to $50,000 for an asphalt court (Lavallee and Westervelt, 2004). Clay courts usually run about $10,000, whereas synthetic courts range from $40,000 to $50,000. These costs do not include fencing ($5,000 to $10,000 per court) or lighting ($5,000 to $10,000 per court). Without a doubt, tennis courts are expensive (USTA, 1997).

Miscellaneous Considerations

All tennis courts should have sufficient secured storage areas constructed on a concrete base adjacent to the court complex. The size of the storage area is dictated by the amount and type of equipment to be stored in it. Consider ball hoppers, tennis rackets, fanny packs, ball-throwing machines, and other teaching equipment. The storage area must be waterproof and include shelving, bins, racks, and hooks.

If maintenance equipment is needed at the courts, a separate storage area must be built for appropriate machines, rakes, hoses, screens, and materials.

Parking areas need to be built in close proximity to the court complex. The size of the parking area is dictated by the maximum number of user vehicles for the complex in addition to sufficient space for spectator parking. If the tennis complex is lighted, the parking area should be illuminated with high-pressure sodium lights.

Night outdoor tennis is popular in many areas of the country. The recommended surface lighting level for recreational tennis is 38 foot-candles and 63 foot-candles for tournament tennis. Lighting tennis courts is a necessity in some areas. Information as to the number of light standards and how much light will be needed for the complex can be obtained by consulting the local electric company and a manufacturer (e.g., General Electric). A number of outdoor sports lighting companies install quality tennis court lighting systems. If the cost of ongoing high electric use is of concern, coin-operated light boxes can be installed to defray the electricity cost (USTA, 1997).

Although lighting may be optional, water must be provided at each court complex. One water fountain (refrigerated) and one hose connector are recommended for each set of four courts. Electrical outlets must be provided for each court and for any electrical maintenance equipment. All outlets should be located in the fence area and at the storage areas.

Benches need to be provided outside the fencing for those awaiting an empty court. Unobstructed spectator seating should be provided as close to the courts as possible if tournaments or instruction are to be provided on the courts. Courts used for tournaments and high-level competition also require scoring equipment, officials' seating, tables, benches, concession areas, and a protected area for videotaping.

Finally, court surfaces can be a variety of colors. Synthetics can be found in any color whereas most nonporous tennis courts use a contrasting red and green color scheme. Several factors should be considered when deciding on court colors including the effect of a color on perception of the ball, how well a color scheme masks or highlights wear and stains, and the color's compatibility with its surroundings (Jones, 1990). Considering ball perspective, single-colored courts are easiest on participants' eyes due to the fact that multicolored courts promote eye fatigue as one's vision changes focus from light to dark areas. A subtle difference between actual court coloring (within the lines) and surrounding court coloring (e.g., light green inside the lines, surrounded by dark green) allows for similar reflectivity level and subsequently less eye fatigue. As far as a court's ability to hide stains or wear marks, darker colors are advantageous. It should be noted that a variety of colors are available for tennis courts from traditional green to the much-publicized purple courts the Association of Tennis Professionals (ATP) experimented with during the Men's Tour of 2000. Choosing a color that is in harmony with the surrounding vegetation (e.g., green courts in an area surrounding by lush green vegetation) provides a nice aesthetic appeal (Jones, 1990).

Indoor Tennis Courts

Indoor courts can be practical for tennis. Since the weather can affect the ability to play, tennis is a seasonal sport in many parts of the country. Consequently, indoor courts meet a specific need in certain regions.

The number of courts to be enclosed depends on the number of users and the amount of money available for construction. The type of enclosure varies greatly from complex to complex. Prefabricated steel buildings, air structures, tension membrane structures, and standard brick-and-mortar buildings have all been employed successfully. The use of combination structures has some advantages. A translucent tension membrane that allows light onto the courts combined with a turnkey or one standard structure can save roofing costs as well as electricity costs during the day. The following is a cost comparison of three four-court structures (USTA, 1997):

- sports frame metal building—$561,000 ($140,250 per court)
- tension structure—$422,495 ($105,624 per court)
- air structure—$366,000 ($91,500 per court)

Lighting should be indirect, so that the tennis ball is not lost in the glare of lights. The background at the end of the courts should be plain. Traffic patterns need careful planning to ensure they do not conflict with play on the courts. Netting must be used between courts, since fencing does not exist, and the ceiling height needs to be a minimum of 30 feet. Most indoor court surfaces are synthetic. As with outdoor courts, planning should include storage, parking, water fountains, electrical outlets, seating, concessions, officials' needs, videotaping, and locker and shower facilities.

Paddle Tennis

Dimensions

Paddle tennis courts are 50 feet long by 20 feet wide. The safety space or unobstructed area should be a minimum of 15 feet behind each baseline and 10 feet from each sideline or between each adjacent court. As Figure 20.2 shows, service lines for each side of the court run the entire width of the court, parallel to and three feet inside each baseline. The center service line extends from the service end line, down the middle of the court. The service boxes, therefore, are 22 feet long by 10 feet wide (USPTA, 1996).

Figure 20.2
Paddle Tennis Court Dimensions With Restraint Line

Paddle Tennis Web

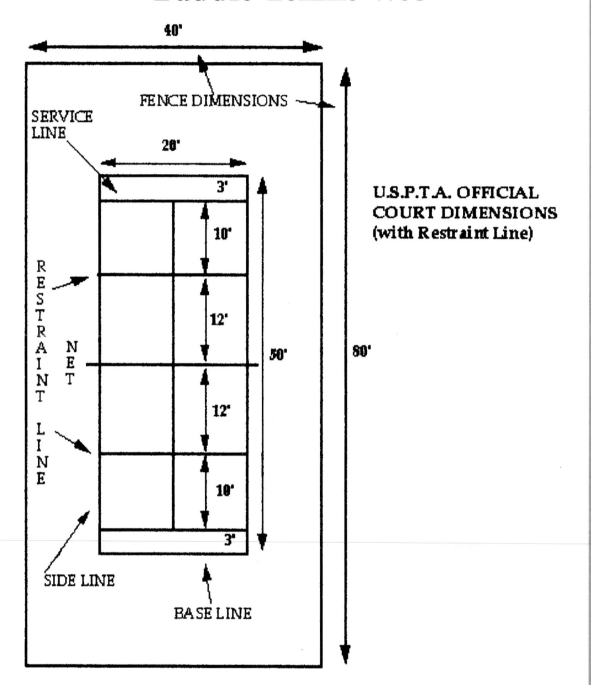

U.S.P.T.A. OFFICIAL
COURT DIMENSIONS
(with Restraint Line)

An optional restraint line extends the width of the court, 12 feet from the net. These restraint lines are used in doubles play only. All dimensions for paddle tennis court markings are to the outside of the lines with the exception of the center service line, which is divided equally between service courts.

Miscellaneous Considerations

Paddle tennis net posts are located 18 inches outside of each sideline and are 31 inches in height. Unlike tennis courts, the net is strung taut so that the height measures the same (31 inches) at each post and in the middle of the court. Court surfaces are concrete or asphalt, although competition can also take place on hard-packed sand (USPTA, 1996).

If construction of stand-alone paddle tennis courts is not an option, paddle tennis court markings can be superimposed on a regulation tennis court by using chalk or tape or by painting lighter colored lines and the net can be lowered to the proper height.

Paddle

Dimensions

The sport of paddle has recently been introduced in the United States and is played in approximately 15 countries. A paddle court is 65 feet, 7 7/16 inches (20 meters) long by 32 feet, 9 3/4 inches (10 meters) wide with a plus or minus 1% tolerance level. The net which divides the court in half extends to the perimeter fence where it is anchored to the two center posts of this fencing or to an independent anchoring system. Regardless of the anchoring system, the net must coincide with the perimeter fence. The net measures 37 7/16 inches (0.95 meters) at the posts and is 2 inches lower at the center of the court (35 7/16 inches or 0.90 meters) where it is held down at the center by a central belt that is 2 inches wide (APA, 1996).

The service lines for each side of the court run parallel to the net and are placed 22 feet, 9 1/2 inches (6.95 meters) from the net. A central service line, 2 inches wide, runs perpendicular to the net. This line bisects the court, dividing it into equal service zones on both sides of the net. Each service zone measures 22 feet, 9 1/2 inches long by 16 feet, 4 7/8 inches wide. All measurements for the court markings are made from the net or center of the central, perpendicular service line (APA, 1996).

The paddle court (Figure 20.3) is completely enclosed by back walls, sidewalls, and fencing on the remaining sideline areas. The back walls at the end of each court, measure the width of the court (32 feet, 9 3/4 inches) and are between 9 feet, 10 1/8 inches (3 meters) and 13 feet, 1 1/2 inches (4 meters) in height. The partial side or "wing walls" extend 13 feet, 1 1/2 inches (4 meters) from the back walls. The wing walls decrease in height from 9 feet, 10 1/8 inches (3 meters) to 5 feet (1.5 meters) beginning at the wing wall's midpoint (6 feet, 6 3/4 inches, that is, two meters from the junction of the back and wing walls) to the end of the wall. This decrease in height on the wing wall should be at approximately a 38-degree angle. The remainder of the court perimeter is enclosed with a wire fence measuring 13 feet, 1 1/2 inches (4 meters) in height from the court surface (APA, 1996).

Figure 20.3
Paddle Court

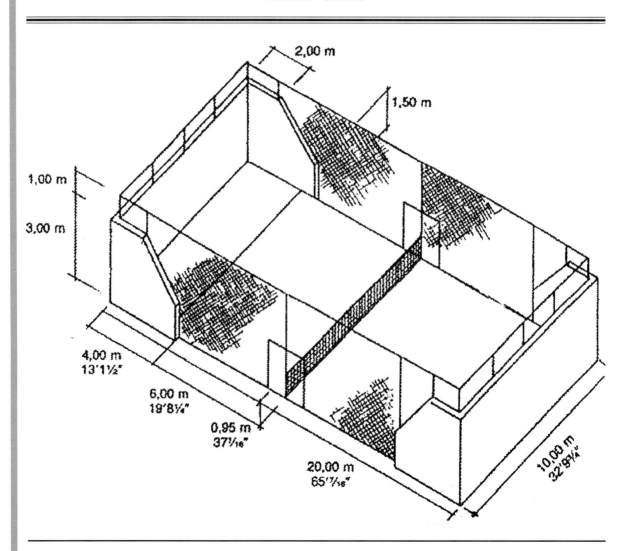

Miscellaneous Considerations

Paddle court surfaces vary from hard courts to artificial grass. The sport can be played on outdoor as well as indoor courts. If played indoors, however, courts must have a minimum ceiling clearance of 25 feet.

Back walls and partial sidewalls consist of stucco, concrete, or glass and/or a blindex material that provides for optimum spectator viewing of the court from all surrounding areas.

Portable courts (not inclusive of surfacing) are available for purchase for approximately $25,000.

Platform Tennis

Dimensions

A platform tennis court is 44 feet long by 20 feet wide. The entire platform surface is 60 feet by 30 feet, which allows for 8 feet of space beyond each baseline and 5 feet of space between each doubles sideline and the fencing. All court markings are two inches wide and measurements are to the outside of the lines except for the center service line, which is equally divided between the right and left service courts. Service lines running parallel to the net are 12 feet from the net, and doubles alleys are 2 feet wide (Flynn, 1985).

Net posts are located 18 inches outside of the doubles sidelines and the net height is 37 inches at the posts and 34 inches at the center of the court. Fencing, which measures 12 feet in height, is 16-gauge hexagonal, galvanized, one-inch flat wire mesh fabric.

Miscellaneous Considerations

The total area needed for construction of a platform tennis court is 2,584 square feet (68 feet by 38 feet). This allows for the foundation beams at the corners and at the locations of the uprights (Figure 20.4). Specifications for a platform tennis court typically call for 4-inch-by-6-inch foundation beams across the base of the platform. It is recommended that wood beams be waterproofed with creosote. Each beam rests on four evenly spaced concrete blocks; the blocks should be placed such that the beams rest 4 feet apart (measured from center to center). The foundation beams at the corners and at the locations of the uprights must project far enough to afford a base for the outer support of the uprights. The deck surface should be constructed of Douglas fir planks measuring 2 feet by 6 feet. The planks should be laid 1/8 inch to 1/4 inch apart to allow for drainage. The corner uprights and the intermediate uprights must measure 12 feet from their base (i.e., the deck surface) to their top. The corner uprights should be constructed of 4-inch-by-4-inch beams; the intermediate uprights should measure 2 inches by 4 inches (Flynn, 1985).

Figure 20.4
Platform Tennis Court

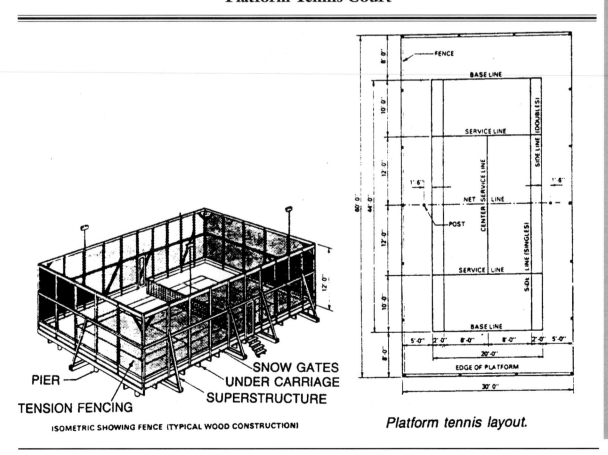

PIER

TENSION FENCING

ISOMETRIC SHOWING FENCE (TYPICAL WOOD CONSTRUCTION)

SNOW GATES
UNDER CARRIAGE
SUPERSTRUCTURE

Platform tennis layout.

The construction of the backstop is a detailed procedure. Top rails are bolted horizontally to the insides of the tops of the uprights and measure two inches by four inches along the sides. Therefore, the rails to which the wire fabric is attached project inside the uprights by four inches at the ends and two inches at the sides. All of the space around the platform is covered by wire except 12-foot openings in the center of each side, at least one of which is closed with either netting. This closure is for containing errant balls. All wiring should be attached vertically on the insides of the uprights and stretched in six-foot widths from the top down to the tension rail below (Flynn, 1985).

Badminton

Dimensions

A badminton doubles court (Figure 20.5) is 44 feet in length by 20 feet wide; a singles court is the same length (44 feet), but 3 feet narrower (17 feet). All court markings including the center service line, short service lines, and doubles long service lines are marked in yellow or white and measure 1.5 inches in width. All dimensions are measured from the outside of the court lines except for the center service line, which is equally divided between service courts.

A net that is exactly five feet above the ground at the center of the court and five feet, one inch at the net posts bisects the court laterally. The net posts are placed directly on the doubles sidelines. However, when it is not possible to have the posts over the sidelines, this boundary should be marked with a thin post or strips of material attached to the sideline and rising to the net cord.

The safety distance or unobstructed space behind the back boundary line should measure eight feet behind and four to five feet outside of each sideline or between courts.

Miscellaneous Considerations

Ideally, ceiling clearance for indoor badminton should be no less than 30 feet over the entire full-court area. This is the standard for international play. However, a 25-foot clearance is the recommended minimum and is sufficient for other levels of play.

Figure 20.5
Badminton Court

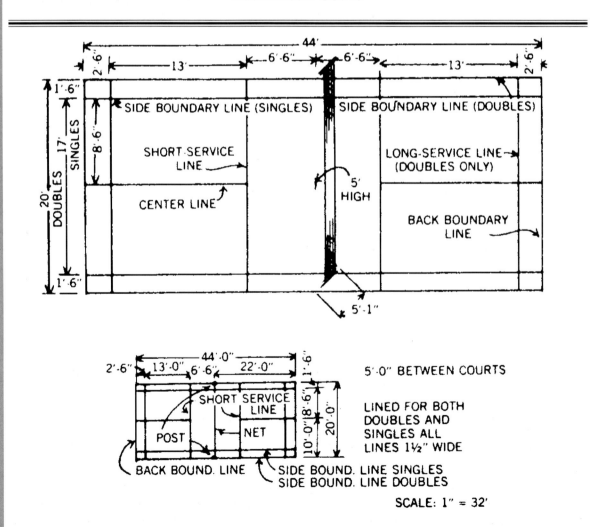

Basketball

Dimensions

Indoor and outdoor basketball courts vary in size depending upon the level of competitive play. It is recommended that courts for junior high, high school, and recreational play be 50 feet wide by 84 feet long. Competitive collegiate and professional basketball requires a 50-foot-by-94-foot court. Regardless of the level of play, a 10-foot unobstructed or safety space is highly recommended, especially considering today's game and the increased size of the players. However, if a court is constructed with less than 10 feet of safety space (8 feet is a minimum at the end lines and 6 feet on the sidelines), wall padding should be installed the entire distance of the wall that parallels the side or end line. Another important safety consideration concerns any glass or windows that are part of the surrounding basketball gymnasium. All glass and windows should be shatterproof safety glass. Finally, in a gymnasium setting, especially where other sports can be played, a height clearance of 30 feet is strongly recommended, but a minimum clearance of 23 feet is imperative. Appendix A provides a detailed display of basketball court markings (NCAA, 2000).

Concerning the size and colors of the lines, several guidelines should be kept in mind:

- All lines must be two inches wide, except for the neutral zones.
- The color of the boundary lines should match the midcourt markings.
- The color of the lane space and neutral zone markings should contrast with the color of the boundary lines (NCAA, 2000).

Note: The three-point arch measures 19 feet, 9 inches from the center of the basket for both high school and collegiate competition.

Miscellaneous Considerations

Collegiate competition requires backboards that are transparent and measure 6 feet horizontally by 4 feet vertically. The backboard should have a 2-inch white-lined target centered behind the goal. This target should measure 24 inches horizontally by 18 inches vertically. The backboard should also have two-inch-thick gray padding on the bottom and up the sides for the players' protection (Head-Summit & Jennings, 1996). Attached to the backboard is an 18-inch (inner diameter) bright orange ring mounted parallel to and 10 feet above the floor. Although the standard height for a basketball goal (from rim to floor) is 10 feet, adjustable standards that allow the rim to be set at the standard height or lower (i.e., as low as 8 feet) provide opportunities for young children to practice shooting at a goal that is more age-appropriate (NCAA, 2000).

The gymnasium flooring is an important consideration. It is imperative that the flooring provides sliding characteristics (the surface friction of a finished floor) and shock absorption that conform to criteria established by the Deutches Institute für Normung (DIN) standards (see Appendix C.2) to help minimize the possibility of participant injury. Also, the flooring should provide adequate ball bounce or deflection as prescribed under the DIN standards. A final consideration is the placement of padding in appropriate areas, such as the wall directly behind each basketball backboard, especially if the distance between the backboard and wall is less than 10 feet.

Outdoor basketball courts should run lengthwise in approximately a north-south direction. Proper drainage can be insured by slanting courts from one side to the other allowing "one inch of slant. . .for every 10 feet of court." If a backboard is mounted on an in-ground pole, the pole should be padded. Additionally, the pole should be off the playing court and the backboard should be extended at least 4 feet onto the court. Fencing is not a necessity; however, if finances allow, anodized aluminum chain-link should be used. The fence height should be a minimum of 10 feet. The fence posts should be placed 6 inches to 1 foot inside the hard surface and the fence fabric should be affixed on the inside of these supporting posts. Posts should be mounted in concrete such that 35% to 40% of the length of the pole is above the surface. Gates or fences should be constructed large enough to allow maintenance equipment to be brought into the court areas (Flynn, 1985).

Volleyball

Dimensions

Although volleyball courts within the United States traditionally measure 30 feet in width by 60 feet in length, the United States Volleyball Rules (which are those of the International Volleyball Federation) call for the court to measure 59 feet by 29.5 feet (18 meters by 9 meters) (Figure 20.6). Notably, all court dimensions are measured from the outside edge of the lines and all court lines should be two inches (five centimeters) wide (Sanford, 1997).

A minimum of 6 feet, 6-inches of safety or unobstructed space should surround an indoor court; however, the ideal situation is to provide at least 10 feet from the sidelines and 13 feet from the end lines (NCAA, 1997).

Ceiling clearance is a critical issue. Although United States Volleyball Rules call for "a minimum or 23 feet (seven meters) of unobstructed space as measured from the floor, 30 feet of overhead clearance is highly recommended" (Neville, 1994, p. 6). Figure 20.6 provides a detailed display of volleyball floor markings. Notably, in recent years, the service zone has been extended the full width of the court as a result of a rule change permitting players to serve anywhere behind the end line.

Figure 20.6
Volleyball Court Dimensions

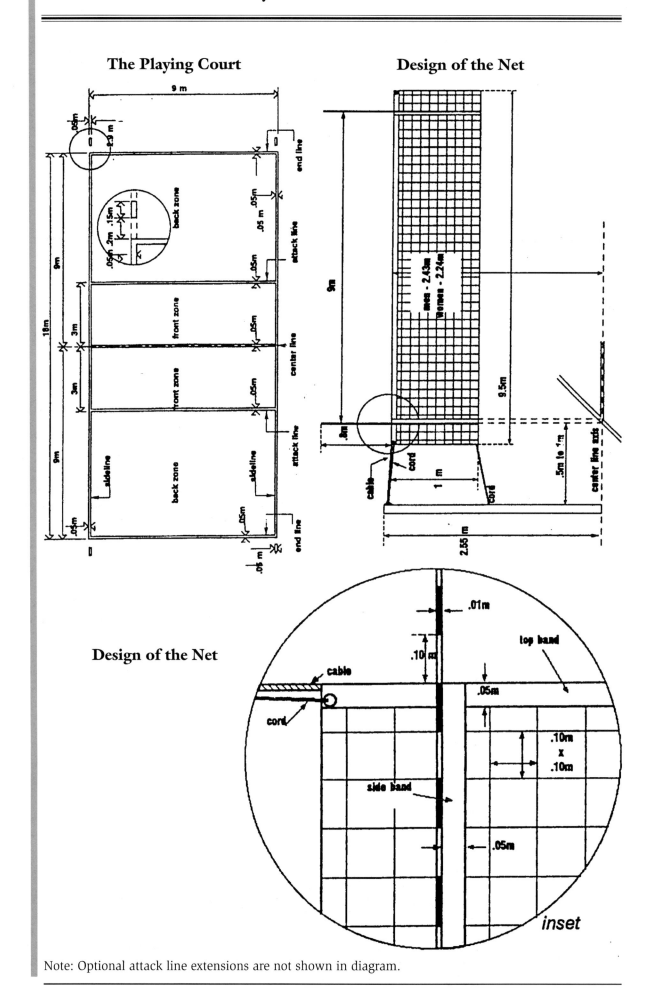

Note: Optional attack line extensions are not shown in diagram.

Net Height

The volleyball net height is 7 feet, 11 5/8 inches (2.43 meters) for men's competition and 7 feet, 4 1/8 inches (2.24 meters) for women's competition, as measured at the center of the playing court. The two ends of the net, directly over the sidelines, must be the same height from the playing surface and may not exceed the official height by 3/4 inch (although a constant height is far more desirable). The net height may be varied for specific age groups in the following ways (USVA Rule Book, 1997-98, p.14):

Age Groups	Females/ Reverse Mixed 6	Males/ Mixed 6
55 years and above		7"11 5/8" (2.38m)
45 years and above	7' 2 1/8" (2.19m)	
15 to 18 years of age	7' 4 1/8" (2.24m)	7' 11 5/8" (2.43m)
16 years and under	7' 4 1/8" (2.24m)	7' 11 5/8" (2.43m)
14 years and under	7' 4 1/8" (2.24m)	7' 4 1/8" (2.24m)
12 years and under	7' 0" (2.13m)	7' 0" (2.13m)
10 years and under	6' 6" (1.98m)	7' 0" (2.13m)

The net itself is 39 inches wide and a minimum of 32 feet long. The posts (supporting standards) are fixed to the playing surface at least 19 1/2 inches to 39 inches from each sideline. Two white side bands, 2 inches wide and 39 inches long, are fastened around the net vertically and placed perpendicularly over each sideline. Six-foot-long antennas are attached at the outer edge of each side band and extend 32 inches above the height of the net (USVA, 1997).

Miscellaneous Considerations

One of the most important safety factors is to provide poles that are sunk directly below floor level in sleeves or that telescope up from below the floor. Volleyball standards/poles that are on mounted or weighted bases are extremely hazardous. Likewise, volleyball net systems that rely on guy wires are not desirable. If wires are part of an existing volleyball net system, they should be clearly identified and padded. Furthermore, volleyball posts should be padded to a minimum height of six feet and all official stands should be padded.

Ideally, in a facility built primarily for volleyball, the walls (particularly those behind each end line) should be painted a color that provides some contrast to the color of volleyballs, which are generally white. This contrast in color allows participants to more easily track the flight of the ball during play. Additionally, the ceiling color should be off-white or another light color that provides a contrasting background for players attempting to follow the flight path of the volleyball.

Light fixtures need to be placed at least as high as the lowest ceiling obstructions to avoid any shadowing effects. Also, lighting needs to be bright (a minimum of 27.9 foot-candles, measured at one meter above the playing surface). The lights, however, should not be closely grouped such that they would create a blinding effect for participants (USVA, 1997).

Outdoor Sand Volleyball Court Guidelines

The dimensions for an outdoor sand court are identical to indoor volleyball court dimensions (i.e., 59 feet [18 meters] long by 29 feet, 6 inches [9 meters] wide, as measured from the outer edge of the boundary lines). It should be noted that the Federation Internationale de Volleyball (FIVB), the world governing body, approved the reduction of the dimensions of the two-person outdoor sand volleyball court from 16 meters in length to 8 meters in width. In nonmetric measurements, this particular professional court is 6 feet shorter and 3 feet narrower than the traditional measurements.

Ideally, the court should be constructed with the net running in an east-west direction so that the morning and evening sun does not face directly into the eyes of one team. Outdoor courts should provide a minimum of 9 feet, 10 inches or 3 meters of free space, composed of sand, surrounding the court area. In other words, the complete sand area should measure a minimum of 80 feet long by 50 feet wide. For professional competitions, the court should be centered on an area 93 feet long by 57 feet wide. Standard net heights are the same as for the indoor game: 7 feet, 11 5/8 inches (2.43 meters) for men's and coed play and 7 feet, 4 1/8 inches for women's and reverse coed play. Children ages 10 to 16 may have the net height adjusted according to the standards listed above regarding indoor volleyball net adjustments (Sandorfi, 1995).

Boundary lines are brightly colored 1/4-inch rope or 1 1/2-inch webbing tied to the four corners with buried deadpan anchors. No centerline is required for outdoor play but approximately 14 feet of rope will be needed, beyond the 177 feet total necessary for court lines, to anchor the corners (Sandorfi, 1995).

Net supports should be made of metal, wood, or other material that will withstand tension. The supports should be about 14 feet long and should be buried 5 feet deep using a concrete footing unless the soil is solid, in which case packing in and washing the soil should suffice. These support standards should be set 39 inches (one meter) from the boundary of the court. Any less space will leave insufficient room for the full net and adjusting cables (Sandorfi, 1995).

Suggested specifications for different net supports are as follows. Metal net supports should be four-inch, diameter schedule 40, galvanized steel pipes. Round wood poles should measure eight inches in diameter and should be made of treated, weather-resistant wood. Square wood supports are not recommended, because of the potential for participant injury on corner edges. In all instances, padding the support poles is an important safety measure. If the support does not have equal sides, the narrower side should be the net anchor side (facing the court) (Sandorfi, 1995).

Hooks, hook-and-eye hardware, and any winch hardware (padded) are necessary to attach the net to the standards. One way to provide for total adjustability of net height is to have four metal collars made that have loops for attaching the net (i.e., the top and the bottom of the net on both sides) that can slide up and down the poles. Holes can be drilled into the collars and set screws inserted which can be tightened with an Allen wrench. Finally, the net should be 10 meters in length with a cable top, although strong rope such as Kevlar also works well. However, the effort of fashioning this system can be avoided by purchasing outdoor standards now available from a variety of vendors.

Actual sand court construction should start with the excavation of the area with a front-end loader. The court area should be excavated between two and three feet in depth. In low-lying areas, such as the shoreline areas of Florida, the court should be excavated only six to eight inches. This will yield an elevated court rather than one that is flush with the ground. Also, the dirt that is excavated should be used to create a slight slope up to the court.

The court perimeter edges can be contained to keep dirt and grass from leaking into the court. Lawn edging material or rubber handrail material from escalator companies seated atop two-inch-by-six-inch wooden boundaries is a good method of providing perimeter boundaries. If railroad ties or similar materials are used, the top edges should be padded to minimize injury potential (Sandorfi, 1995).

Drainage of the court under the sand is important. The installation of leaching pipe on the standards with a slant of 14 degrees is highly recommended for a good permanent court. Perforated pipe (approximately two rolls of 250 feet) can be laid perforated side down with the open end at the low point of the court. Each section of the pipe should be wrapped with a flex wrap or "handicap wrap" which can be purchased at plumbing supply houses. This wrap prevents sand from filling up the pipes. Finally, the drainage points should lead away from the court at the lowest point (Sandorfi, 1995).

The next step is to set the standards in concrete. Poles should be set at a slight angle outward from the court to allow for any bending caused by eventual net tension. To allow for ease of maintenance or replacement, steel poles should be seated in steel sleeves so that they can be easily removed.

Small pea-sized gravel used for drainage (#56, #57, #2, or #3) should then be placed over the drainage pipe to a depth of about one foot. Approximately 2,600 cubic feet (110 tons) of this gravel is necessary. Plastic landscaping or ground stabilization filter fabric (a woven polyblend that will not deteriorate easily) is placed over the gravel to prevent the sand from washing through (Sandorfi, 1995).

The final step in sand court construction is depositing the sand. A good court requires an investment in good sand. Sand comes in a variety of grades; some types are very "dirty" and unsuitable for a court. Washed beach (dune), washed plaster, washed masonry, or washed river sand are the most desirable types of court sand. The most highly recommended sand is silica sand regionally available by contacting Best Sand at 1-800-237-4986. This sand should be deposited and raked level around the court; it should measure one to two feet in depth. The minimum recommended depth of the sand is 19 1/2 inches. In essence, a sand court requires approximately 5,200 cubic feet (205 tons of washed sand). The final price tag for the construction of a good sand volleyball court will range anywhere from $6,000 to $10,000 (Sandorfi, 1995).

Racquetball, Handball, and Squash Courts

Dimensions and Design Considerations

Four-wall courts for squash and handball have been in sports facilities for over three-quarters of a century. Originally, these courts were made from Portland cement with smaller than normal doors. Paddleball and racquetball were first played on these courts in the late 1950s and early 1960s. Today's courts are designed for racquetball, handball, and squash, even though other activities may also be played in these enclosed four-wall courts (such as walleyball and Bi-Rakits). Today's state-of-the-art courts are constructed of laminated panels and/or tempered glass. In the planning of four-wall courts, teaching, competition, accessibility, and amenities need to be considered (AARA, 1997).

The recommended four-wall racquetball/handball court is 40 feet long and 20 feet wide with a front wall and ceiling height of 20 feet and a back wall at least 14 feet high (Figure 20.7). The lower back wall provides a space for a viewing or for an instructional gallery, which may be open with a three- to four-foot-high railing. Clear polycarbonate sheeting should be placed under the railing for seated viewing purposes and safety. The gallery may be totally enclosed with clear polycarbonate sheeting and a small four-foot-square open window. An open gallery is recommended for communication purposes between instructors/officials and the players. However, an open gallery poses the risk of spectators being hit by a ball, therefore appropriate signage should be posted to indicate this hazard.

Squash is becoming very popular in some regions of the United States. The international singles squash court is 21 feet wide and 32 feet long (Figure 20.9). The old North American standard of an 18 foot, 6 inches-wide singles squash court is no longer acceptable and should be avoided (Figure 20.10). North American doubles squash is played on a larger court measuring 25 feet wide and 45 feet long (Figure 20.8). Squash court wall heights vary compared to the standard 20-foot racquetball/handball wall heights (USSRA, 1997).

When more than a single battery of courts is to be constructed, the batteries should be arranged so a corridor approximately 10 feet wide and 12 feet high separates the back walls of each. Courts should be located in the same area of the facility rather than being spread out. Courts should be placed on adjacent walls rather than on opposite walls in order to achieve close proximity, thereby aiding in quality instruc-

Figure 20.7
Four-Wall Handball and Racquetball Courts and Dimensions

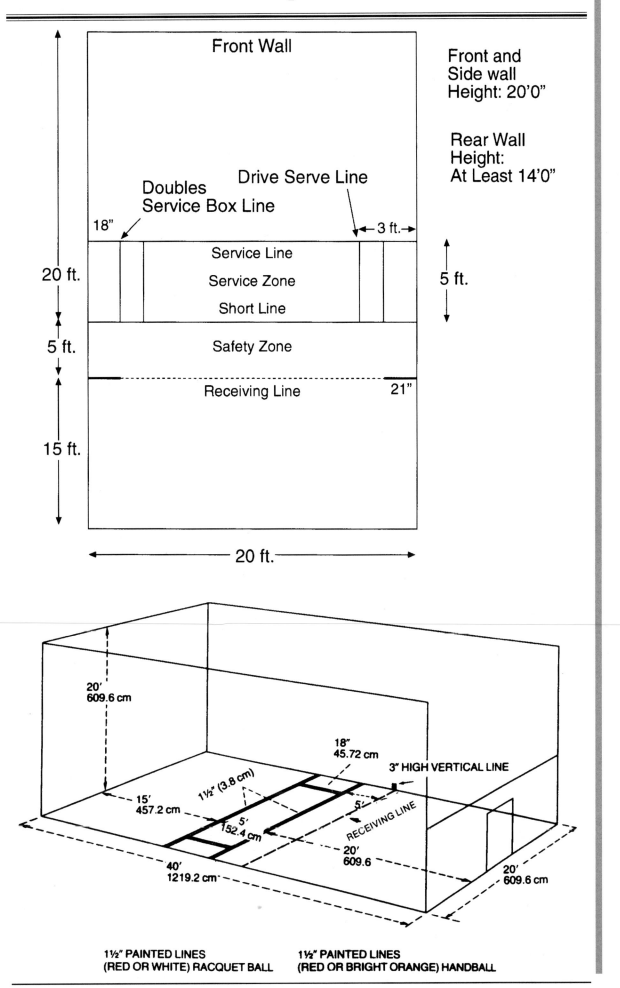

1½" PAINTED LINES   1½" PAINTED LINES
(RED OR WHITE) RACQUET BALL   (RED OR BRIGHT ORANGE) HANDBALL

**Figure 20.8a
North American Doubles Squash Court**

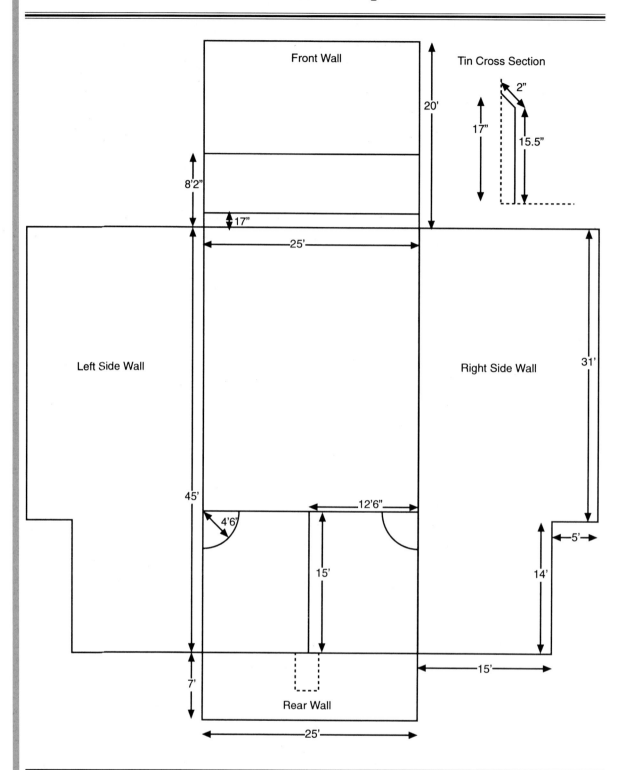

tional time. Corridors and galleries should be illuminated with indirect light. The minimum number of courts for schools should be dictated by maximum class size and total student enrollment. Normally, no fewer than six to eight courts are recommended, which can adequately handle 15 to 20 students at a time. The number of courts for clubs and private usage is determined by the number of users and by the popularity of racquetball, handball, and squash in any given area.

Walls may be constructed of hard plaster, Portland cement, wood, laminated panels, or tempered glass. Laminated panels and tempered glass are recommended. The panels are four-by-eight-foot particleboard or resin-impregnated Kraft papers covered with a melamine sheet. The panels come in different thicknesses, from 13/16 to 1 1/8 inches. The thicker the panel is, the truer the rebound action of the ball will be; however, the thicker panel is also more expensive. Panels are mounted on aluminum channels or metal studs. Screws that hold them to the wall superstructure are inset and covered with a plug. This creates a monolithic surface for the walls. The panels have a high life expectancy and are easily maintained. Glass walls of 0.5-inch-thick tempered, heat-soaked glass is ideal but expensive. All courts

Figure 20.9
International Singles Squash Court

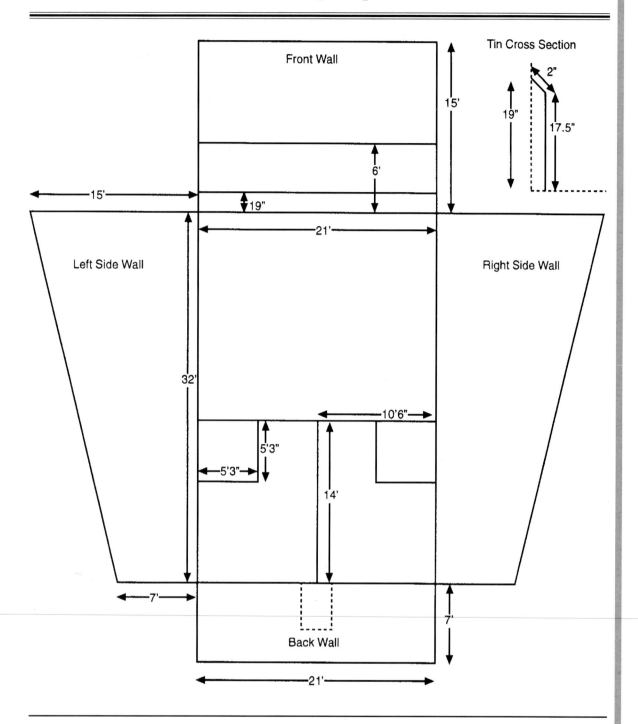

are recommended to have the minimum of glass back walls, and one court should have an additional glass sidewall. This will offer good instructional and spectator viewing (Figure 20.11). Finally, one-way glass, which provides spectator viewing but appears to be a solid surface to participants within the court, is a relatively new innovation.

If glass walls are utilized, spectator and instructional viewing areas should be planned for carefully. These areas usually are stepped with carpeted risers along the sidewall or back wall of the court. A built-in, two-way audio system should be utilized for this court. Carpet color should not be totally dark and definitely should not be blue or green, since ball visibility through the glass walls is obscured with dark colors as a background. Courts with two glass sidewalls, those with glass sidewalls and a glass back wall, and all glass-wall courts are superior to other courts; however, their cost is prohibitive in most facilities.

Doors are standard size and are placed in the middle of the back wall, not in the corners of the court. The corners are crucial real estate in intermediate and advanced racquet sports, so doors that can cause "untrue" bounces should not be placed there. Door handles should be small and recessed, and all door framing should be flush on the inside of the court. Doors should open into the court and there should be no thresholds under the doors.

Figure 20.10

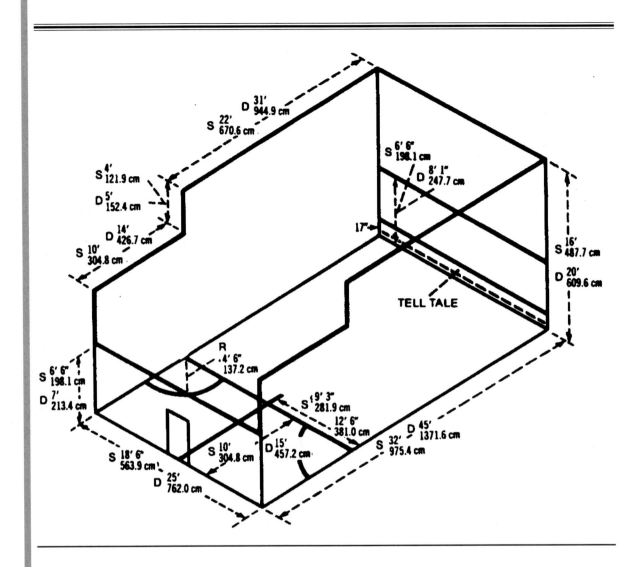

Figure 20.11
Racquetball Teaching Court

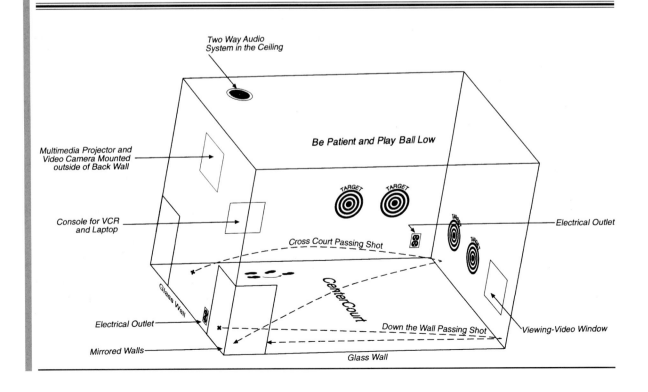

Floors should be hardwood, as in standard gymnasium construction. The more sophisticated the floor system is, the more costly it will be. Resilient wood floors play differently than more rigid system wood floors but they are more expensive. Any good hard maple floor system is acceptable. Floors should be flush with sidewalls so that no joint is evident. Joints collect dirt, dust, and debris and are a maintenance nightmare. Floors should be resurfaced as needed with a high-grade finish. When floors need refinishing, they become slippery and can be very dangerous. The amount of use, the types of shoes worn during play, and the amount of dirt and grit brought into the courts on shoes will dictate how often refinishing is needed. Floors should be cleaned with a treated mop daily or as needed. Synthetic floors should not be used in racquet courts because they create too much friction and do not allow feet to slide, which is needed for effective and safe racquet sports.

Court line markings should be a lighter color, rather than a dark color like blue or black, which helps the participants' visual acuity in following a dark ball across lighter lines. Off-white, light pastel yellow, or light gray lines are best. Squash lines are red.

For racquetball and handball courts, the first 12 feet of the ceiling from the front wall should be devoid of any heat or ventilating ducts. This portion of the ceiling must be hard and compatible to the wall surfaces for ball rebounding. Lighting and any other fixtures in the ceiling must be totally flush. The rear 8 feet of the ceiling is not as crucial since this part of the ceiling is used very seldom in play.

The ceiling is not used in squash but it should still be made of an impact-resistant material in case errant balls hit it. Panels or Portland cement would be good for the front 12 feet of the ceiling.

If wallyball is to be played in the court, the ceiling must be strong enough to absorb the impact of the volleyball. Panels, but not Portland cement, work well in wallyball courts.

Lighting, Acoustics, and Ventilation

All lighting must be flush with the ceiling. Lights should illuminate all portions of the court equally; therefore, they should be spread throughout the ceiling. Shadows and low-light areas are not acceptable in these courts. Light accessibility for changing bulbs must be planned carefully. Since there is normally a battery of courts, the chore of changing light bulbs is magnified by the number of courts needing a bulb-changing system. The best light bulb-changing method for courts is to have a crawl space above the ceiling. This enables maintenance personnel to change bulbs from above. This system eliminates the need to use cumbersome hydraulic lifts and/or A-frame ladders (AARA, 1997).

A metal halide system of lighting is recommended. Metal halide lights give the most light at the least cost. Metal halide bulbs also have a long life expectancy. However, to garner cost savings and longevity, the court lights must be on at all times. Turning these lights off and on causes a delay (about 6 to 8 minutes) for the bulbs to obtain full brightness. Turning halide lights off and on also increases the cost of lighting and decreases bulb life expectancy. Metal halide lights should be controlled from a central console, not at each court.

If single courts are not used often, a recommended method of turning the lights on and off is to install switches that are activated by opening or closing the door to the court. This method requires a metal halide lighting system. When the door is closed, lights in the court will turn on. When the door is opened, the lights will turn off automatically, leaving only the night light to burn continuously. Usually, a 2- to 3-minute delay occurs before the lights go off after the door has been opened preventing a disruption of lighting during the brief time it takes for players to exit or exchange the court.

A relatively new concept utilizes an annunciator (an electrically controlled signal board) to indicate to the building reservation/control center which courts are occupied at any time. Lights on the signal board are activated by the trip switch on each door as it opens or closes. When lights are to be continually turned off and on, incandescent bulbs work fairly well. Fluorescent lights should not be used in racquet courts, because they tend to flicker and can cause visual acuity problems during play. If wallyball is to be played in the court, stronger light shields and light fixtures will be needed to absorb the impact of a volleyball.

Court walls and floors are hard surfaces, and much sound reverberates in the courts. For non-glass court surfaces, acoustical treatment is important within the surfaces. Insulation in the walls and ceiling will help to buffer sound within a court and also between courts. The rear eight feet of the ceiling should be constructed of acoustical tiles, because this area is seldom used in racquetball and handball and never used in squash. Although these tiles provide minimal acoustical treatment, it is very important to attempt to control sound and they should be considered in each court. If walleyball is played in a court, soft acoustical treatment cannot be installed on the ceiling.

Ventilation should be provided by air-conditioning. The ventilation of each court is very important so that moisture does not build on wall surfaces and make the courts unplayable. Ample air-circulation and air dehumidification are major concerns in the ventilation of the courts. Only air-conditioning can provide circulation, cooling, and dehumidification. To minimize the potential for moisture, courts should not be built underground with walls exposed to external moisture. Moisture and/or condensation can easily intrude to the interior wall surfaces of the courts. If courts must be built underground, extra waterproofing needs to be completed in this portion of the facility.

All vents for air circulation should be located in the back eight feet of the ceiling for racquetball and handball (Turner, 1992), but squash courts may have vents anywhere in the ceiling. The temperature of each court should be controlled by an individual, jar-proof, flush thermostat that is preset and tamper-proof.

Miscellaneous Considerations

Small storage boxes should be built flush with wall surfaces into sidewalls near the back wall of each court to house valuables and extra balls. The door to this storage box should be constructed of clear polycarbonate sheeting. Storage areas for students' coats, books, and other gear should be provided in an area near the courts. Extra storage must be provided for rain gear and winter gear where applicable. Secured storage for racquetball rackets, handball gloves, squash rackets, eye guards, and balls should be provided near the court area.

All courts should have joints, seams, doors, vents, lights, and corners flush with the surrounding surface. Any unevenness in a court will cause untrue ball rebounds, which are unacceptable in court games. Each court should be equipped with a two-way audio system. Access to this system should be housed in the central console. This audio system can be used to make announcements, provide music, and facilitate instructional purposes between the court user and the instructor.

Effective external signage is important for all courts. Signs for court rules need to be posted near each court entrance. Rule signs such as "Eye guards are mandatory" and "Only non-marking athletic shoes may be worn in courts" are typical for racquet courts. Other signage includes the designation of a challenge court(s) with rules and a daily sign-up sheet. Courts also must be numbered and a visible wall clock near the courts is important.

Courts and galleries should be accessible to individuals with disabilities. Doors should be wide enough for wheelchair passage and have no barriers such as thresholds or steps at access points. Additionally, the court's location within the sports facility and a route from adjacent parking areas must be free of barriers.

University courts should be built at a location with easy access from all points on campus and ample parking in close proximity of the courts should be carefully planned. Within the sports complex, the courts should be located near the console control area.

In any facility, all courts need to be situated near refrigerated water fountains. In a commercial court complex, an area close to the courts must be designated for a pro shop. This area needs to be large enough to accommodate the types of equipment and apparel to be sold. The pro shop area must also be able to be secured by either lockable doors or a metal mesh gate, since it will not be staffed during all operation hours of the court area.

If there is a hallway access to courts and/or galleries, the hallway must have a ceiling height of 12 feet. A lower ceiling height lends itself to damage from individuals jumping up and hitting it with their rackets. Light shields in these hallways should be flush with the ceiling to deter breakage. Skylights above the court ceiling height, in gallery areas only, add a nice aesthetic touch. The use of a translucent glass or polycarbonate sheeting in skylights will alleviate glare problems.

Movable metal "telltales" can be installed across the front of handball and racquetball courts for use in squash instruction. However, the courts are racquetball size, not squash size. The floors, walls, ceilings, lighting, heating, and ventilation of squash courts are similar to those of four-wall racquetball and handball courts.

One court at any instructional facility should be a permanent teaching court. There should be a three-foot-by-three-foot front wall viewing and videotaping square. This "window" should be covered with a single sheet of clear polycarbonate sheeting. The window should be three or four feet high from the floor and closer to one side or the other of the front wall. Access to this window from outside the court must be provided. There should be a small lockable area behind the viewing window, preferably five feet by five feet with a ceiling height of eight feet. An adjustable-height table and chair need to be in this small room and a small area for storage of a portable video camera, videotapes, and speed gun should be provided there as well.

The teaching court also needs two flush, covered, electrical outlets for power sources. A multi media projector and a video camera should be mounted within the back wall. Both projector and camera need to be protected with a clear polycarbonate sheet. A lockable, flush console should be built into a sidewall to house a laptop computer and VCR. This setup allows for slides, videotapes, television, and computer viewing. None of this high-tech equipment ever needs to be moved into or around the courts.

Polycarbonate mirrors, each section measuring six feet long by six feet high, should be placed flush on two adjacent walls. The back wall and a sidewall work best for the mirrors. Mirrors are great instructional tools, because they allow the students to view themselves.

Foot templates for various movement patterns should be permanently placed on the floor. Different colors may be utilized along with arrows to indicate foot movement direction. Ball flight path patterns should be painted on the floor and flight paths for a down-the-wall passing shot and/or a cross-court passing shot should actually be templated onto the floor. Again, different colors should be used for different ball paths. An elliptical circle six feet wide and four feet deep should be painted and labeled "center court" in the center area of the court. An area three feet square also needs to be painted and labeled in each back corner. The back corners and center court are the two most important areas in racquet courts.

Targets of varying size and height should be placed on both the front wall and sidewalls to serve as aiming points for various shots. A few targets also need to be placed on the ceiling near the front wall as ceiling shot templates for racquetball and handball. Skill templates such as "Be Patient and Play the Ball Low" and "Culminate All Sources of Power at Ball-Racquet Impact" should be placed in a few selected areas of the court. These become constant visual educational reminders for students.

Ideally, the teaching court should have one glass sidewall and a glass back wall. A glass back wall alone will suffice. A two-way communication system must be in place for the instructor when in the court to be able to talk to students out of the court and vice-versa (see Figure 20.11).

Good court construction is paramount for teaching, competition, safety, and maintenance. All court surfaces must be flush. The activity that is played in the court will be a determining factor in both the size of the court and the materials used in court construction.

Shuffleboard

Dimensions

The actual playing area of a shuffleboard court is 39 feet long and 6 feet wide (Figure 20.12). However, the area outside the court markings includes a 6-foot, 6-inch standing area at both ends of the court and a 2-foot area adjacent to the sideline boundaries. Thus, the entire area for a shuffleboard court should measure 52 feet in length and 10 feet in width (Flynn, 1985).

Lines painted with a black dye, white road paint, or white acrylic stain mark off the shuffleboard court. The lines measure from 3/4 to 1 inch in width. The base lines are extended to adjoining courts or two feet beyond the sides of the court (Flynn, 1985).

The separation triangle in the 10/off area measures 3 inches at the base and extends to form a point in the direction of the scoring area. The outline of the legs of this triangle is 1/4-inch wide, with a clearance of 1/2 inch at both the point and base. Finally, the base of the separation triangle is not marked (Flynn, 1985).

Figure 20.12
Shuffleboard Court

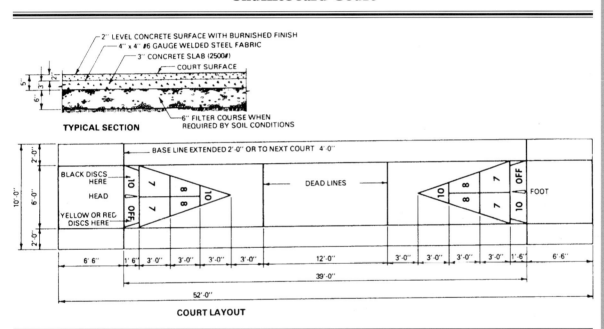

Miscellaneous Considerations

Outdoor shuffleboard courts should be oriented north-south and must be constructed on a level area. A smooth playing surface is essential; therefore, the surface of an outdoor court is typically concrete or asphalt. Furthermore, the courts should be developed over a well-drained area. For proper drainage, a depressed alley should be installed between and at the sides of all courts. The alley must be 24 inches wide and must slope from both baselines toward the center of the court. To ensure proper flow of rainwater, the alley should descend one inch in depth during the first 6 inches in length (moving along the alley from each baseline toward the center of the court) and gradually increase in depth to at least 4 inches at mid-court where a suitable drain should be installed. The court can be lit using a 20-inch hinged pole with a 1,500-watt quartzite floodlight. This pole should be erected outside the courts next to the scoreboard or benches at the base of the courts. Overhead lighting is also an option in recreational areas. Frequently, 2-inch-by-2-inch backstops are installed (in a loose fashion) to prevent discs from rebounding back onto the court (Flynn, 1985).

Indoor shuffleboard courts must also be constructed in a level area. Reinforced concrete or any reasonably smooth surface is sufficient. Also, portable courts are available from vendors.

Croquet

Dimensions

The two most common forms of American croquet are six-wicket croquet (Figure 20.13) and nine-wicket croquet (Figure 20.14). Dimensions, configurations, and layouts are different for each game and are described separately.

Notes

The standard croquet court for American six-wicket croquet is a rectangle measuring 105 feet (35 yards) long by 84 feet (28 yards) wide. Boundary lines should be clearly marked, the inside edge of this border being the actual court boundary. If the area is too small to accommodate a standard court, a modified court may be laid out in accordance with the same proportions as a standard court (i.e., five units long by four units wide; for example, a court could be 50 feet long by 40 feet wide). In fact, in instances where the grass is cut high or beginners are competing, a smaller court such as a 50-foot-by-40-foot court is more desirable (USCA, 1997).

The stake is set in the center of the court (see Figure 20.13). On a standard full court, the wickets are set parallel to the north and south boundaries, the centers of the two inner wickets are set 21 feet to the north and south of the stake, and the centers of the four outer wickets are set 21 feet from their adjacent boundaries. On a smaller modified 50-foot-by-40-foot court, the corner wickets are 10 feet from their adjacent boundaries, and the center wickets are 10 feet in each direction from the stake (USCA, 1997).

American nine-wicket croquet is played on a rectangular court that is 100 feet long by 50 feet wide with boundaries, although marked boundaries are optional. However, a court may be reduced to fit the size and shape of the available play space. If the court is reduced, a six-foot separation should be maintained between the starting/turning stake and the adjacent wickets (USCA, 1997).

Miscellaneous Considerations

For further information regarding the construction of courts, rules, or equipment, contact the United States Croquet Association. Their contact information can be found at http://www.croquetamerica.com.

Figure 20.13
Six-Wicket Croquet Layout

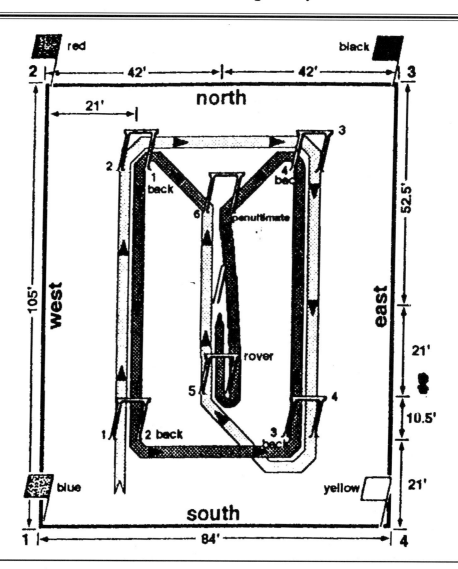

Figure 20.14
Nine-Wicket Croquet Layout

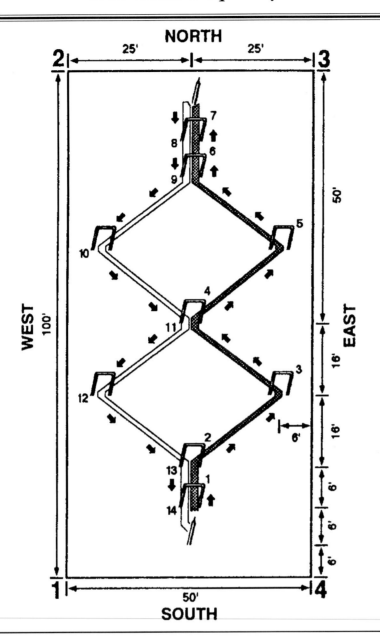

Fencing

Dimensions

The fencing court (Figure 20.15) is referred to as the foil strip or piste and is constructed of wood, rubber, cork, linoleum, or synthetic material such as plastic. The strip is from 5 feet, 10 inches (1.8 meters) wide to 6 feet, 7 inches (2 meters) wide and 45 feet, 11 inches (14 meters) long. The strip markings include seven lines which cross the width of the entire strip: one center line; two on-guard lines, one drawn 6 feet, 7 inches (2 meters) from each side of the center line; two end lines at the rear limit of the strip; and two warning lines marked 3 feet, 3 inches (1 meter) in front of the end lines (Bower, 1980). Portable strips are also an option for those wishing to avoid permanent floor markings. Finally, ceiling clearance should be a minimum of 12 feet.

Miscellaneous Considerations

For electric foil and epee, a metallic piste must cover the entire length of the strip, including the extension areas. Electrical outlets and jacks should be located at the ends of the strips to provide power for electrical equipment. For safety, any rackets for mounting fencing targets should be either recessed flush with the wall or fastened to the wall at least as high as seven feet.

Figure 20.15
Fencing Court Layout

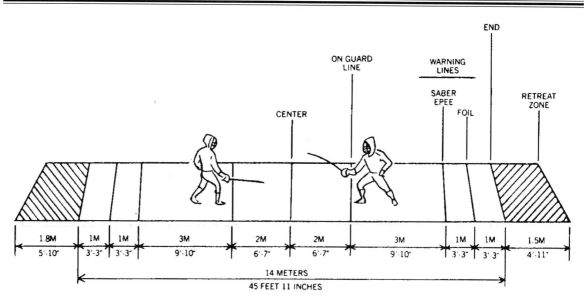

NOTE: The width of the strip shall be a minimum of 1.8 meters (5'10")
and a maximum of 2 meters (6'7"). The length of the retreat zone shall
be a minimum of 1.5 meters (4'11") and a maximum of 2 meters (6'7").
For Foil and Epee, the metallic surface of the strip shall cover the entire retreat zone.

Summary

Courts, whether they are inside or out, need special planning in relation to playing surfaces, safety
issues, playing dimensions, and access. Additionally, planners need to consider storage areas, electrical
outlets, lighting, and water fountains.

Field Spaces and Bleachers

Thomas H. Sawyer, Michael G. Hypes, and Arthur H. Mittlestaedt Jr.

21

Sports fields generally require the largest amount of space in an outdoor complex. The activities that can be conducted are varied and require a variety of sizes. Additional acreage is required for spectators, officials, service personnel, and service areas (e.g., concessions, restrooms, equipment storage, score boards, and press box).

The usability of the areas, particularly at night and after inclement weather, often requires substantial support utilities, such as communication, drainage, irrigation, lighting, security, and sewer systems. Further, the surface material, synthetic or natural, and its substructure systems are also critical.

The various sports field venues that will be highlighted in this chapter include baseball and softball, boccie, cricket, croquet, field hockey, football, lacrosse, lawn badminton, lawn bowling, lawn volleyball, rugby, soccer, and team handball. The beginning of the chapter will highlight common planning challenges for all fields, and the latter portion will cover specific needs for the various fields.

All fields must have adequate seating for spectators. Numerous types of seating are available, from concrete stands to steel or wood bleachers of various heights, to portable aluminum bleachers. The seating has changed from 18 inches wide to 20 inches to accommodate the spectators' larger backsides. Many of the seats are fiberglass rather than wood, and some are aluminum. The seats are contoured for greater comfort and some areas have soft theater seating. The choice comes down to the size of the purchaser's pocketbook.

The planners need to consider the following safety suggestions when developing seating for spectators for outdoor events: 1) conforming to Americans With Disabilities Act (ADA) guidelines (see Chapter 14); 2) conforming to Consumer Product Safety Commission guidelines to providing railings for each side and the top row to prevent falls; 3) closing areas under each row of seats to prevent children from falling through or climbing; 4) enclosing the structure to gain space for storage, concessions, or restrooms and at the same time preventing children from playing under the bleachers; and 5) providing aisles with railings for ease of accessing seating.

Learning Objectives

After reading this chapter, the student should be able to

- design a safe outdoor sports field complex,
- identify the different types of bleachers,
- understand the basic components of a bleacher system,
- discuss ways to improve safety in bleachers, and
- understand the place of bleachers in facility architecture.

Safety and Fields

The owner of a potential sports field property must apply the sound and proven guidelines for planning a facility that are outlined in this textbook to reduce the athletes' exposure to risks (see Chapter 12). The planning process should include an analysis of the causation of injuries.

The size of the field area is critical. Neither athletes nor spectators should be exposed to any of the following hazards, and planners need to consider each concern when selecting a location for a field:

- Streets should not be located any closer than 100 yards to a facility and should be fenced off.
- Railroad tracks, like streets, should not be any closer than 100 yards to a facility and should be fenced off.
- Watercourses, man-made culverts, or natural stream ways can contain deep, fast-moving water that can trap or entangle people who slip, walk, or slide into them. They should not be any closer than 100 yards to a facility and should be fenced off.

- Trenches or gulleys can be hazards that hold deep muck, hidden snakes, other reptiles, or rodents or that contain wires, quicksand, or reinforcing rods that can pierce or entrap a person. They should not be any closer than 100 yards to a facility and should be fenced off.
- Settlement ponds or basins can contain toxic liquids, silt, or flammable materials and should not be any closer than 100 yards to a facility and should be fenced off.
- Storage yards, with old concrete or other culvert pipes that can roll and crush; junk cars and machinery that can cut or pierce; old wood and metal junk piles; and hazardous drums of liquids (e.g., lead paint, paints, sealants) or acids that can explode or burn should not be any closer than 100 yards to a facility and should be fenced off.
- Climatic noise, odors, smoke, and dust should be avoided.
- The protective perimeter of the area should consist of fencing to keep spectators away from the area of play and to keep players within the play area.
- The area must not consist of soils that are toxic, poor draining, decaying, or of poor structure. They should be free of debris and glass.
- The field space should be located in an area that has no other activity spaces in close proximity in order to protect the athletes and spectators.
- The visibility of the entire area should accommodate foot and vehicle security.
- The area should be illuminated at critical times to facilitate supervision and security.
- The multipurpose fields that are used for baseball or softball as well as soccer, field hockey, or football should not have ruts that create dangerous high-speed bounces of the ball on the playing surface.
- The games of baseball and softball have three major concerns for spectators and parking areas—foul balls, home runs, and overthrows as well as overruns which are likely in all field sports.
- The participants' age, gender, skill levels and/or experience must be considered in creating facilities for all participants.
- The area must be accessible to participants and spectators with disabilities.
- Concealment areas caused by shrubbery or tree canopy or adjacent structures should be eliminated to deter improper activity.
- The public comfort for players and spectators must include restroom facilities close to supervised areas, properly designed and positioned litter containers, benches, drinking fountains, and walkways.
- The safety or buffer zone around the field and its appurtenance and equipment must be large enough to keep players from hitting stationary objects along its perimeter and if existing, such objects should be padded.
- The padding or other accepted, proven safety precautions, such as releasable or yieldable devices for outfield fences, stanchions, barriers, and other perimeter containments must be used and/or sufficient buffered perimeter areas should be used.
- The safety glazing of nearby windows, observation panels, and doors is a necessity.
- The relationship of fields and appurtenance among facilities should be harmonious and complementary in encouraging and facilitating play.
- The traffic flow of users from one field or appurtenance to another should be designed to be safe.
- The durability and maintainability of the types of appurtenances within and adjacent to the field must be considered.
- The pedestrian, player, and spectator traffic around the activity field is important. The field must be located so that there is no interference with the traffic of people, buses, automobiles, service vehicles, vendors, and bicycles. Pedestrian traffic should be routed to have easy access to comfort stations, security, refreshments, lockers, and other related facilities.
- The automotive and service (e.g., lawn mowers, maintenance vehicles) driveways should not bisect or parallel open play or human access areas.
- Immovable barriers should be installed to separate any automotive traffic routes from all activity areas.
- Maintenance vehicle access to fields should have the correct subbase and surface materials installed so as to limit wear and irregular surfaces.
- The utility lines, above, on, or below ground should be positioned so as not interfere with players, the game, or spectators, or to be accessible to contact with any person.
- Storm drains are frequent hazards, often within the field limits or directly adjacent to them. Players can have their feet entrapped by such street-sized drains. They should be located at least five yards from the play line.
- Irrigation heads for pop-up or quick-couple sprinklers can cause tripping if not designed properly. They should be recessed as per manufacturers' guidelines.
- Relocatable aluminum irrigation pipes and sports equipment left on the field are also hazardous and should be properly stored and secured.
- Power lines, poles, transformers and control panels must not be in proximity to playing and/or spectator areas. They should be in remote and inaccessible, secure locations.
- Fire hydrants, hose bibs, and drinking fountains must not be placed in the vicinity of the area of play.
- The buffer/safety zone for outdoor fields should be 10 yards. When there are multiple fields in a field complex the distance between parallel fields should not be less than 10 yards on each side of the field. Bleachers should not be any closer than 10 yards from the sideline or end zone.

Field Turf

The types of turf that are used on sports fields are synthetic and natural turf. (See Chapter 19 for a complete discussion on natural turf.) In the 1960s to the late 1980s many natural turf fields were converted to synthetic turf fields. The conversions were intended to reduce the cost of maintenance and to provide flexibility to sports schedules without concern about the wear and tear that occurred on natural-turf fields being used by numerous sports teams. Conversions back to natural turf through the 1980s and 1990s were prompted by the increase in athletic injury related to synthetic turf. In 1988 the next generation of synthetic turfs, which replicate a natural grass surface began to appear. This product is durable, cost efficient, and consists of a sand and rubber infield system that has reduced sports injuries related to synthetic fields.

Type of Surfaces

Bioengineered Surface

Synthetic materials can be soft or firm. They can be piled, turfed, graveled, or smoothed. They can be rolled or poured, paneled, or sprayed. The ingredients of the turf can be rubber, polymer, pigment, polyvinyl chloride (PVC), thermoset, thermoplastic, and a host of other new high-tech materials. Synthetic products have substrates that are also of varied ingredients.

Synthetic turf is attractive to players for a number of reasons, including that the surface and footwear interact well for better footing, the surface stays in place, it is resilient, balls bounce well, the surface dries rapidly, and it has a cooling effect. It also has distractions for players, including that the surface has little resiliency, balls respond inconsistently, the surface affects the speed of the ball (making it faster), and the surface is very hot on hot days.

Attractions for operators include that the surface is repairable, picturesque, portable, durable, stable, and paintable and it drains rapidly. However, the greatest detraction of synthetic surfaces for the operator is life of the surface, which is approximately 15 years.

Photo by Tom Sawyer

Portable bleachers, Indiana State University.

Bleachers

Bleachers and grandstands are part of almost every sports facility. It has been estimated that there are approximately 60,000 facilities with bleachers in the United States. This number includes school facilities, sports facilities, state and local parks, and fitness and recreation centers. Providing safe bleachers and grandstands has prompted the passage of the Minnesota Bleacher Safety Act and the development of the Consumer Product Safety Commission's (CPSC) Guidelines for Retrofitting Bleachers.

Type of Bleachers

Bleachers are structures designed to provide tiered or stepped seating and are available in various sizes and configurations. The bleacher system normally consists of a series of seat boards and footboards, generally without any type of backrest. A grandstand is nothing more than a bleacher with a roof attached. The type and number of bleacher components are dependent upon the activity, space requirements, number of spectators, and available financial resources.

Bleachers can be classified into one of four basic categories:

- permanent or stationary bleachers
- portable or movable bleachers

Photo by Tom Sawyer

Permanent bleachers, Rose Hulman Institute of Technology.

Notes

- telescopic or folding bleachers
- temporary bleachers

Permanent or stationary bleachers are typically large units that will remain in the same location for the life of the facility. Permanent bleachers can be made of metal or concrete and are usually secured to the ground by an anchor. If they are made of metal, exposure to the sun can create extremely hot conditions, which could cause burns.

Portable bleachers are usually smaller units and are constructed of lightweight materials. Such bleachers will have skids or a wheel system that makes them easy to relocate from one site to another.

Photo by Tom Sawyer

Aisle railing.

Photo by Tom Sawyer

Examples of bleacher seating (above and below), Rose Hulman Institute of Technology.

Telescopic bleachers are typically found in gymnasiums where space is at a minimum. These bleachers can either be pushed in or pulled out for spectator seating. When closed, this type of system takes up relatively little space and can function as a divider.

Temporary bleachers are typically stored in pieces or sections and then constructed together for use during special events (e.g., golf tournaments, parades, circuses, inaugurations). After the event, the bleachers are then disassembled and stored until needed the next time.

Bleacher Components

As mentioned above, a bleacher system has some common elements. These common elements include

- footboards
- seat boards
- risers
- guardrails railings

Rails are used as a safety feature. They provide security while entering or exiting the bleachers. There are a variety of styles that will minimize the exposure to injury. Folding rails are ideal for recessed areas and other obstacles. Rails should be lightweight for easy setup and takedown, yet strong enough to provide adequate support. Guardrails should extend 42 inches above the lowest surface of the leading edge of the bleacher component (i.e., footboard, seat board, or aisle).

Risers and footboards are typically aluminum and should be weather resistant for outdoor use. Seat boards can be aluminum or vinyl-covered metal. Indoor bleachers may have risers, footboards, and seat boards made of wood. It is desirable to mark the edges of treads so that they can be distinguished.

Photo by Tom Sawyer

When planning bleachers, it is important to consider any gaps or openings that will be in the final product. Any opening between the components in the seating, such as between the footboard, seat board, and riser, should prevent passage of a 4-inch sphere where the footboard is 30 inches or more above the ground and where the opening would permit a fall of 30 inches or more.

Bleachers usually come in 4- to 52-row systems. Local and state building codes should be consulted when planning bleachers. Figure 21.1 provides generalized seating capacity for various types of bleachers.

Telescopic or pull-out bleachers should have a wheel or channel system to prevent damage to the floor surface. In addition, these systems are best utilized if they are automated. Electrical systems allow the telescopic bleachers to open or close with the turn of a key. This type of system allows the user to open entirely or partially a section of bleachers without having the section get out of line or damaged. With any mechanical system, a manual override is suggested. For bleachers already installed that do not have an automated system, there is equipment (such as a portable power system) that is easily handled for convenient movement of bleachers.

Photo by Tom Sawyer

Figure 21.1
Sample Number of Bleacher Seats Based on Length and Number of Rows

Length in Feet	4 Rows	7 Rows	10 Rows	13 Rows	16 Rows
18	48	84	120	156	192
36	96	168	240	312	384
54	104	252	360	468	676
72	192	336	480	624	768
90	240	420	600	780	960
108	288	504	720	936	1,152
126	336	588	840	1,092	1,344
144	384	672	960	1,248	1,536
162	432	756	1,080	1,404	1,728
180	480	840	1,200	1,560	1,920
198	528	924	1,320	1,716	2,112
216	576	1,008	1,440	1,872	2,304
234	624	1,092	1,560	2,028	2,496
252	672	1,176	1,680	2,184	2,688
270	720	1,260	1,800	2,340	2,880
288	768	1,344	1,920	2,496	3,072
306	816	1,428	2,040	2,652	3,264

Length in Feet	19 Rows	22 Rows	25 Rows	28 Rows	31 Rows
18	228				
36	456				
54	684	792	900	1,008	
72	912	1,056	1,200	1,344	1,488
90	1,140	1,320	1,500	1,680	1,860
108	1,386	1,584	1,800	2,016	2,232
126	1,596	1,848	2,100	2,352	2,604
144	1,824	2,112	2,400	2,688	2,976
162	2,052	2,376	2,700	3,024	3,348
180	2,280	2,649	3,000	3,360	3,720
198	2,508	2,904	3,300	3,696	4,092
216	2,736	3,168	3,600	4,032	4,464
234	2,964	3,432	3,900	4,368	4,836
252	3,192	3,696	4,200	4,704	5,208
270	3,420	3,960	4,500	5,040	5,580
288	3,648	4,224	4,800	5,376	5,952
306	3,876	4,488	5,100	5,712	6,324

The power or automated system:

- provides the ability to open and close bleacher systems quickly and correctly,
- omits and/or reduces maintenance costs,
- solves the problem of broken board ends from manual operation,
- adds stability to the gym bleachers by attaching all sections together to operate as one system,
- omits manual operation by unauthorized personnel, and
- reduces liability exposure on your gym bleacher equipment.

Codes and Regulations

There are several agencies/organizations that have developed codes and/or standards for the construction of bleachers. These organizations include:

- International Building Code (IBC) of the International Code Council (ICC)
- National Building Code (NBC) of the Building Officials and Code Administrators (BOCA)
- Standard Building Code (SBC) of the Southern Building Code Congress International (SBCCI)
- Uniform Building Code (UBC) of the International Conference of Building Officials (ICBO)
- National Fire Protection Association (NFPA)

Figure 21.2 provides a summary of current industry codes and standard requirements for guardrails and openings in bleachers. In addition, state and local codes adopt and modify these codes to develop policy for constructing new bleachers. The local building inspector should be consulted early in the planning phase to avoid expensive and time-consuming errors in the construction of a bleacher system.

2001 Minnesota Building Codes and Standards Division Requirements

States (such as Minnesota) develop their own policies regarding construction. The Minnesota Building Codes and Standards Division reviewed the Uniform Building Code, International Building Code, and the National Fire Protection Association Life Safety Code in developing Policy PR-04 (3/00).

Under Minnesota law, reviewing stands, grandstands, bleachers and folding/telescopic seating, whether indoors or out, must be designed, constructed, and installed in accordance with the applicable provisions contained in the Minnesota State Building Code. (Minnesota, 2001)

This policy addresses the following areas of concern with regard to bleachers and grandstands:

- press box construction
- number of seats to an aisle
- required plumbing fixtures
- aisle width
- accessibility
- foundations
- use of space below bleachers/grandstands

Press Box Construction

According to UBC Section 303.2.2.3, combustible non-rated A-4 occupancies are limited to a height of 20 feet above grade. Except for the press box located on top of most school grandstands serving ball fields, most grandstands are built of noncombustible construction. These noncombustible bleacher structures are permitted to be at least 40 feet in height. However, press boxes are typically built with combustible construction materials (wood framing). This results in classifying the entire structure as combustible, and, therefore, severely limiting the maximum permitted height of noncombustible grandstands with combustible press boxes to 20 feet (Minnesota, 2001).

Minnesota derived the following alternative to part of UBC Section 303.2.2.3. Press boxes located atop open-air bleachers may be built of combustible construction as long as other components of the bleacher system are of noncombustible construction.

Number of Seats to an Aisle

Prior to the 1997 edition of the Uniform Building Code, the number of seats without backrests between any seat and an aisle could not be greater than 20, for a total of 42 seats in a row with aisles at each end. In general, this is what the bleacher seating industry has used as a standard for the manufacture of their products for years. Now both the 1997 UBC and 2000 IBC only permit a maximum of 14 seats per row with the typical 12-inch wide aisle accessway. In contrast, for indoor bleachers the 1997 UBC permits nine seats between any seat and an aisle, for a total of 20 seats in a row. This is less restrictive than that permitted outdoors. The maximum number of seats permitted between furthest seat and an aisle in bleachers is 20 in outdoor bleacher seating. (Minnesota, 2001).

Figure 21.2
Overview of Code and Standard Requirements

2000 International Building Code (IBC) of the International Code Council (ICC)
Guardrails
- Required on open sides more than 30 inches above grade.
- Guardrails must be at least 42 inches high, vertically measured from leading edge.
- Guardrails shall have balusters to prevent passage of 4-inch sphere through any opening up to a height of 34 inches.
- From a height of 34 to 42 inches, should prevent passage of an 8-inch sphere.

Openings
- Where footboards are more than 30 inches above grade, openings between seat and footboard shall not allow passage of a sphere greater than 4 inches.
- Horizontal gaps shall not exceed .25 inch between footboards and seatboards.
- At aisles, horizontal gaps shall not exceed .25 inch between footboards.

1999 National Building Code (NBC) of the Building Officials and Code Administrators (BOCA)
Guardrails
- Required along open-sided surfaces located more than 15.5 inches above grade.
- Guardrails should be at least 42 inches in height measured vertically above leading edge.
- Open guardrails shall have balusters of solid material that prevents passage of 4-inch sphere through any opening.
- Guardrails shall not have an ornamental pattern that would have a ladder effect.

Openings
- Openings between footboards and seat boards should prevent passage of 4-inch sphere when openings are located more than 30 inches above grade.
- Horizontal gaps between footboards and seat boards shall not exceed .25 inches.

1997 Standard Building Code (SBC) of the Southern Building Code Congress International (SBCCI)
Guardrails
- Located along open-sided walking surfaces and elevated seating facilities which are located more than 30 inches above grade.
- Guardrails shall not be less than 42 inches vertically from leading edge.
- Open guardrails shall have intermediate rails or ornamental pattern to prevent passage of 4-inch sphere through any opening.

Openings
- There shall be no horizontal gaps exceeding .25 inch between footboards and seat boards.
- At aisles, no horizontal gaps should exceed .25 inch between footboards.

1997 Uniform Building Code (UBC) of the International Conference of Building Officials (ICBO)
Guardrails
- Perimeter guardrails shall be provided for all portions of elevated seating more than 30 inches above grade.
- Guardrails shall be 42 inches above the rear of a seatboard or 42 inches above the rear of the steps in an aisle.
- Open guardrails shall have intermediate rails or ornamental pattern to prevent passage of a 4-inch sphere.

Openings
- The open vertical space between footboards and seats shall not exceed 9 inches when footboards are more than 30 inches above grade.

2000 National Fire Protection Association (NFPA) 101 Life Safety Code
Guardrails (applies to both new construction and existing installations)
- Guardrails are required on open sides more than 48 inches above adjacent ground.
- Guardrails must be at least 42 inches above the aisle or footboard or at least 36 inches above the seat board.

continued

Figure 21.2 continued
Overview of Code and Standard Requirements

- Guardrail is exempted where an adjacent wall or fence affords an equivalent safeguard.
- Openings in guardrails cannot allow passage of 4-inch diameter sphere.

Openings (applies to both new construction and existing installations)
- Vertical openings between footboards and seat boards cannot allow passage of 4-inch diameter sphere where footboards are more than 30 inches above grade.
- Openings in footboards cannot allow passage of .5-inch diameter sphere.

Inspections (existing installations)
- Annual inspection and maintenance of bleacher/grandstand or folding/telescopic seating required to be provided by owner to ensure safe conditions.
- Biennially, the inspection is to be performed by a professional engineer, registered architect, or individual certified by the manufacturer.
- Owner required to provide certification that such inspection has been performed as required by authority having jurisdiction.

Modified from U.S. Consumer Product Safety Commission, Guidelines for Retrofitting Bleachers.

Required Plumbing Fixtures

Minimum numbers of water closets and lavatories are to be provided for all buildings and structures including exterior assembly areas, such as bleachers and grandstands. The Standards Division recognizes either of the following to satisfy this requirement:

- permanent fixtures located either on site or available in an adjacent building
- portable temporary fixtures that are available on site when the bleachers are in use

The use of portable fixtures as acceptable modifications is based on the concept that outdoor bleachers are seasonal in nature. Lastly, the ratio of water closets for women to the total of water closets and urinals provided for men must be at least 3:2 in accordance with the Minnesota Building Code (1300.3900).

Aisle Width

The Standards Division identified two methods for determining aisle width. Method A identifies that aisles are not required to be more than 66 inches in width, nor does one have to be considered a dead-end aisle when the following are satisfied:

- The seating is composed entirely of bleachers.
- The row-to-row dimension is 28 inches or less.
- Front egress is not limited.

Method B is based on IBC Section 1008.5.3. The clear width in inches of aisles shall be not less than the total occupant load served by the egress element multiplied by 0.08 where egress is by aisles and/or stairs. The multiplier is 0.06 where egress is by ramps, tunnels, corridors or vomitories (Minnesota, 2001).

Accessibility

Bleacher seating structures complying with the Minnesota Accessibility Code require:

- Access—Exterior access to elevated seating areas in exterior bleachers must be accessible by a route having a slope not exceeding 1 in 20 and a width not less than 48 inches.
- Wheelchair locations are to be provided in the number and location required.
- Alterations to an existing area containing a primary function will not apply if alterations to existing bleacher seating facilities only address compliance with the Minnesota Bleacher Safety Act (Minnesota, 2001).

Foundations

"A foundation plan must be prepared by a Minnesota Licensed Engineer for all open-air bleacher and grandstand facilities. This does not apply to 'portable' bleachers of five rows or less" (Minnesota, 2001).

Use of Space Below Bleachers or Grandstands

Spaces under a grandstand or bleacher shall be kept free of flammable or combustible material. Storage is permitted under bleachers, provided it is separated with fire-resistive construction (Minnesota, 2001).

Figure 21.3
Summary of Retrofit Recommendations

- Guardrails should be present on the backs and portions of the open ends of bleachers where the footboard, seat board, or aisle is 30 inches or more above the floor or ground below.
- The top surface of the guardrail should be at least 42 inches above the leading edge of the footboard, seat board, or aisle, whichever is adjacent.
- When bleachers are used adjacent to a wall that is as high as the recommended guardrail height, the guardrail is not needed if a 4-inch diameter sphere fails to pass between the bleachers and the wall.
- Any opening between components of the guardrail should prevent passage of a 4-inch sphere.
- Any opening between the components in the seating should prevent passage of a 4-inch sphere where the footboard is 30 inches or more above the ground.
- The preferable guardrail design uses only vertical members as in-fill between the top and bottom rails. Openings in the in-fill should be limited to a maximum of 1.75 inches. If chain-link fencing is used on guardrails, it should have a mesh size of 1.25-inch square or less.
- Aisles, handrails, nonskid surfaces, and other items that assist in access and egress on bleachers should be incorporated into any retrofit project where feasible.
- The option of replacing as opposed to retrofitting should be considered.
- Retrofitting materials and methods should prevent the introduction of new hazards, such as bleacher tip-over, bleacher collapse, guardrail collapse, or contact/tripping hazards.
- Bleachers should be thoroughly inspected at least quarterly by trained personnel and problems should be corrected immediately. Maintain records of these actions.
- Bleachers should be inspected at least every two years and written certification should be obtained that the bleachers are fit for use. A licensed professional engineer, registered architect, or company that is qualified to provide bleacher products and services should conduct inspections.
- Keep records of all incidents and injuries.

Modified from U.S. Consumer Product Safety Commission, Guidelines for Retrofitting Bleachers.

U.S. Consumer Product Safety Commission Guidelines
The U.S. Consumer Product Safety Commission (CPSC) has developed Guidelines for Retrofitting Bleachers as a result of a petition by Representatives Luther and Ramstad of Minnesota in 1999. This petition led to the adoption of the first bleacher safety law at the state level. A summary of the CPSC's retrofit recommendations is found in Figure 21.3.

Sports Field Lighting
Lighting (illumination) is critical to safety and revenue generation (see Chapter 7 for detailed information). The illumination level for baseball and softball is 20 foot-candles for the outfield and 30 for the infield. The lighting for other team sport fields (e.g., field hockey, football, lacrosse, rugby, and soccer) requires a minimum of 30 foot-candles. If sporting events are to be televised, the lighting requirement will be much different. However, if this happens only occasionally, portable lighting companies can be hired to provide additional lighting requirements. The air should be monitored for contaminants that can cause the reflector surface to change by increasing diffusion and decreasing total reflection. This results in less total light energy leaving the face of the light, with less lumens. There should be no shadows on the field that create unsafe catching, nor should there be any glare or irregular bright patches. All stanchions or poles must be outside the field of play.

Sports Field Orientation
There are various thoughts as to the orientation of baseball and softball fields. It depends on where the field is and the time games are to be held. One school of thought is that the back of home plate should be set to point south to southwest or have the baseline from home plate to first base run in an easterly direction. The theory is for the batter to look into the sun, which implies the catcher as well. Another

Photo by Tom Sawyer

thought is for the batter to look away from the sun. Presently, the orientation is probably the least of the safety problems. However, since batter and catcher or pitcher are in the most hazardous positions, they still require consideration. A line through these positions would be the axis for orientation for either position. After locating the axis, locate the sun's position at sunrise, early morning, late afternoon, and sunset. Establish an orientation for the field that avoids the batter and catcher or pitcher from facing directly into the early morning or late afternoon sun.

All other fields should run north to south to avoid the direct movement of the sun from east to west. However, if all contests are played in the evening after sundown, the sun does not become a factor.

Sports Field Fencing

Generally speaking, fields should be fenced to protect the field, athletes, and spectators. The height of the fence ranges from four feet for youth fields to eight feet for interscholastic, intercollegiate, and professional fields. A number of fields have six-foot fences, which is acceptable but not ideal. All fences less than eight feet high should be covered with a brightly colored vinyl protector with or without padding. The fence should be sturdy enough to withstand an athlete's weight as well as serve as a windscreen.

Photo by Tom Sawyer

Baseball and Softball Fields

The fence height should start at eight feet as it leaves the backstop around the circumference of the field, including in front of the dugouts. The fencing should be attached on the field side of the poles, with all attachments and prongs on the outside of the fence. The fence should be stretched down from the top to the tension rail on the bottom. The fence is meant to protect players as well as spectators. It should be no closer than 30 feet to the sidelines or foul lines but preferably will be 50 to 75 feet away.

Photo by Tom Sawyer

French drain.

Sports Field Drainage and Irrigation

A properly constructed sports field has a good drainage system (see Chapter 19), so that play can resume after a short waiting period, and the turf is not destroyed when played upon in a wet condition. Turf that is too wet or too dry will be compromised. The subsoil of the field should be composed of sand (80 to 90% sand base) to improve the speed of drainage. The playing field should be crowned to allow the heavy rainwater that cannot be absorbed to drain to the sidelines. The slope on either side of the crown should not exceed 1/4 inch per foot toward the sideline drainage area. The sideline drainage area should be at least 5 yards from the playing field, contoured and, sloped to catch the runoff to direct it to large drains that are approximately 20 yards apart along the sidelines. These drains should be approximately 15 to 20 feet deep with a 3- to 5-foot diameter filled with gravel and covered with a metal grate. Marketers always say the key to sales is "location, location, location." The key to a great field is drainage, drainage, drainage.

The irrigation of a field is very important in dry climates. There are basically three types of irrigation systems available for fields, including underground with sprinkler heads throughout the field space, underground with sprinkler heads on the perimeter of the field, and above ground with portable piping and sprinkler heads or hoses. The latter option is very labor intensive and requires a lot of equipment storage. The other options are the most convenient and least labor intensive.

The planners of the irrigation system need to consider the following: 1) the safety of the participants (i.e., perimeter or within-field sprinkler layout), 2) type of sprinkler heads, 3) the watering pattern layout (i.e., the number of overlapping zones needed, based on the available water pressure, to reach all areas of the field evenly), 4) the source of water (i.e., wells with a pumping system or government or private water company), 5) a timing system, 6) a plan for winterizing in climates that have temperatures below freezing, 7) tie-ins for drinking fountains and hose bibs, and 8) the possibility of a liquid fertilization option.

Photos by Tom Sawyer

Sports Field Service Areas

Sports field service areas include concessions areas, press box, restrooms, scoreboards, and storage. These areas are very important to spectators and support staff. If the service areas are well designed and maintained, they will increase fan loyalty.

Photo by Tom Sawyer

Concessions Area

The concessions area should be centralized ideally behind home plate, especially in multi-field complexes as shown in Figure 21.4. The area can be constructed from wood or concrete block. It should have plenty of counter space for preparation of products and to service the patrons. The floor should be concrete with numerous drains. There should be at least one double sink and ample cabinet space for storage. The area should have numerous electrical outlets and ground fault interruption (GFI) outlets near water sources. The lighting should be florescent. The equipment in the area should include refrigerator, freezer, stove top with at least four cooking elements, microwave, popcorn popper, hot dog cooker/warmer, coffee maker, soda fountain, ceiling fans, shelving for merchandise, sign board for advertising, and cash register.

Press Box

The press box is important for the press, scouts, scoreboard operator, and those filming games. The press box should be located higher than the highest part of the bleachers. The size will be dependent upon the number of users. It should have an unobstructed view of the playing field. The following should be available for the press: 1) table to write on or broadcast from; 2) comfortable chairs; 3) phone hookups; 4) computer hook-ups; 5) electrical outlets; 6) refrigerator; 7) coffee maker; 8) separate areas for press, radio announcers, scorekeeper, public address (PA) announcer, coaches, and scouts; and 9) an area above the press area exclusively for filming games. These facilities are generally constructed of wood with fluorescent lighting.

Figure 21.4
Diagram of a Multi-Field Arrangement

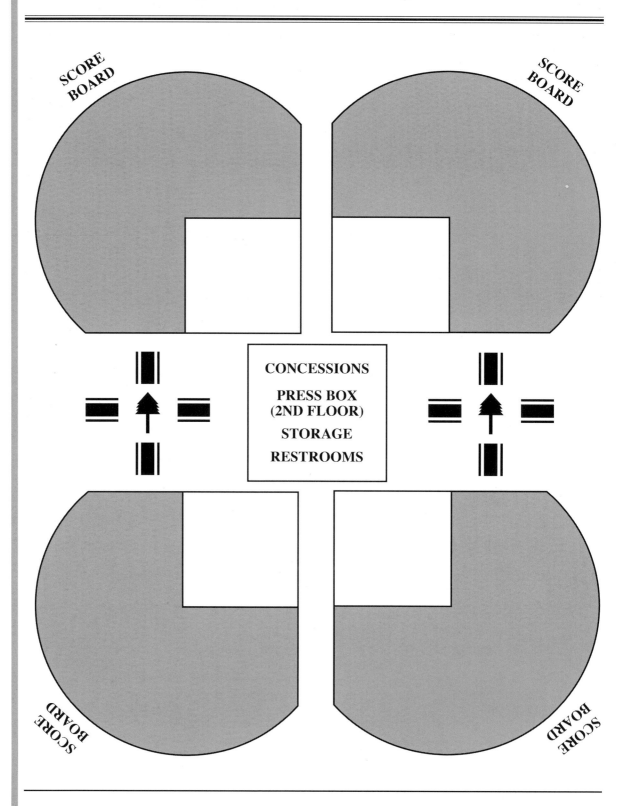

Restrooms

There need to be numerous restrooms provided, preferably not portable. The number of facilities for women should be twice as many as that provided for men. Each restroom should provide changing areas for babies, with adjacent waste disposal units. Each restroom area should be handicapped-accessible, or at least an appropriate number of restrooms need to be handicapped-accessible and so labeled. These facilities are generally constructed of concrete block with concrete floors with drains for cleaning. The lighting should be fluorescent. The rooms should be adequately ventilated.

Scoreboards

There are a number of reliable scoreboard companies. The planners need to consider first what the function of the scoreboard will be—to depict score and time remaining only or to provide entertainment and information as well. Scoreboards can be simple or very complex in nature. The planners need to consider what they want the scoreboard to depict before determining the type of scoreboard to be purchased. The choices include

Photo by Tom Sawyer

1) score; 2) periods or innings; 3) injury time or penalty time remaining; 4) times and places by lanes; 5) diving score by judge, degree of difficulty, total points scored, ranking after "x" number of dives; 6) balls, strikes, outs; 7) roster; 8) players vital statistics; 9) advertising; 10) PA system; 11) multiple functions for various sports using the field complex; 12) close-ups of players and spectators; 13) time of day; 14) scores from other games; and much more depending on the planner's imagination.

Storage

Photo by Tom Sawyer

As is true with indoor facilities, there is never enough storage. The planners need to consider what items need to be stored. These include, but are not limited to: 1) various types of riding lawn mowers; 2) push mowers; 3) tillers; 4) weed eaters; 5) shovels, rakes, and hoes; 6) utility vehicles; 7) irrigation pipes; 8) hoses and sprinkler heads; 9) field liners; 10) goals; 11) field flags; 12) benches; 13) waste containers; 14) protection screens; 15) pitching machines; 16) tarps; 17) fertilizers, insecticides, and talc; 18) paint; 19) chains, yard markers, and padding for goal post for football; and much more.

Storage areas generally are constructed out of concrete blocks with concrete floors and an appropriate number of drains for cleaning. The space should have fluorescent lighting with an adequate number of electrical outlets. There should be a separate work area with a workbench and adequate amount of storage with shelving. The entrance should be an automatic roll-up door at least eight feet high. The ceiling height should be at least 10 feet. The voids under bleachers should be enclosed (these spaces make inexpensive storage areas). The space for chemical storage must meet OSHA guidelines.

Baseball and Softball Fields

Baseball and softball facilities are important aspects of sport in public schools (grades 5 to 12), colleges and universities (varsity competition as well as recreation), community recreation programs, Babe Ruth Leagues, Little Leagues, Miss Softball Leagues, corporate recreation programs, and military recreation programs. Due to the alarming number of injuries reported to the CPSC, safety is a principal concern. This concern places pressure on field operators, turf managers, maintenance managers, and others to have a safe playing field. A "field of dreams" is created from a consistent set of proven guidelines and safety standards to ensure consistency around the country. It is important for the planners to be aware of the field specifications described in the various rules books that govern these two sports (e.g.,

National Federation of High School Activities Association, National Collegiate Athletic Association, National Intercollegiate Athletic Association, National Junior College Athletic Association, Softball USA, International Softball Federation, National Association for Girls and Women's Sports, Little League Association, etc.). These rulebooks are the "gospel" in regard to the specific dimensions for the fields, and most rulebooks are revised annually.

Bases

The base areas must be level, with all irregularities eliminated. The type of base used in either baseball or softball varies, and the rulebooks stipulate what types are permissible. The planner should contact the American Society of Testing and Materials (ASTM) for detailed information regarding the appropriate standards for bases. Presently, the ASTM F-8 Committee on Sports Equipment and Facilities is establishing standards and classifications for bases.

Bases are intended to be a reference point on a baseball or softball field. They are an integral part of the game. There are four types of base designs used, including permanent or stationary bases, modified stationary bases, release-type bases, and throw-down bases. The type of base usually refers to how the base is secured to the playing field, or its function.

Stationary Base

This base uses a ground anchor permanently installed in the playing field. The anchor measures either 1 or 1 1/2 inches, installed a minimum of 1 inch below the playing surface. The base is designed with a stem that fits into or over the ground anchor and holds the base securely in place.

The base should be constructed of permanently white material, which can be rubber, polyvinyl, polyurethane, or other synthetic material to increase service life. The base top should have a molded tread pattern to increase player traction and reduce slippage. Base size and color should conform to individual governing organizations. Permanent or stationary bases can be used on fields by players with more advanced or higher skill levels only after 1) the players have been thoroughly warned that they can be seriously injured for life if they make a mistake in judgment or miscalculation, and 2) they have been made thoroughly aware of other options (e.g., the tapered side base or low silhouette which tapers to the ground eliminating impact of a sliding player against a vertical surface and uses that momentum to slide over the base). Bases are the number-one cause of injuries to ankles and other body parts, especially stationary, modified-stationary, and poorly designed release-type bases.

Modified Stationary Bases

The flexible base is a one-piece base that uses a fixed anchor system for secure placement. It is constructed with interdependent ribs that allow the base to compress and absorb energy generated by a sliding player. The cover flexes inward and downward but does not release.

The strap-down base or tie-down base must be held in place by four spikes inserted into the ground. Straps attached to the base are inserted through loops in the spike head and tightened down. The base is constructed of vinyl-coated nylon or canvas filled with a foam or other resilient material. If installed properly, a portion of the base will remain somewhat stable. However, it has a tendency during play to loosen and move. This style is low cost relative to other base styles, which accounts for its popularity.

Release-Type Base

The release-type base is designed to reduce the chance of injury to a sliding player by releasing from its anchor system on the impact of a hard lateral slide. The release base must use a permanent ground anchor securely positioned below ground for installation. There are two-piece and three-piece designs. The release-type must not expose hidden secondary hazards after the primary aboveground base portion releases.

Throw-Down Base

This base is a thin square, sometimes using a waffle design on the bottom, usually constructed of canvas or synthetic material with little or no padding. It is not physically attached to the playing surface, and therefore is dangerously subject to moving when a player steps on or rounds a base. Throw-down bases are not recommended for teaching basic skills in a gym, such as in a physical education class.

Specialized Bases

The flush or recessed base (except home plate, which is mounted flush with the playing field) is usually not considered for the following reasons: 1) difficulty in keeping the base visible and clean, 2) difficulty for umpire in making a call at the base when the base is not visible, 3) the change in the nature of the game, and 4) the fact that it is not widely used.

Double First Base

The double first base uses a securely positioned ground anchor system. The base is designed to reduce or eliminate the contact between the first baseman and base runner. It is a unit equal in size to two bases side by side, one-half white and mounted in the normal first base position, and one-half colored, and mounted in foul territory.

Home Plate

The home plate, batter's box, and catcher box and their correct dimensional size and positioning must conform to the game and the rules of the appropriate governing body. The area should be well compacted, properly tapered, and level, with no irregularities. The plate must be firmly anchored and any undermining or ruts corrected before play begins.

The home plate is a reference point on the playing field. It establishes the horizontal limits of the strike zone used by the umpire in calling balls and strikes. It is imperative that all home plates have a white surface that measures 17 by 8 1/2 by 8 1/2 by 12 by 12 inches flush with the surrounding playing surface. Further, all home plates must have a peripheral black bevel that does not exceed 35 degrees. The outermost edge of the bevel must be sufficiently below the playing surface. It does not matter how the plates are field mounted as long as they remain flat and flush with surrounding playing surfaces with no sharp corners or sharp nails exposed.

There are four styles of home plate, including buried, staked, anchored, and throw down.

Buried. A rubber or synthetic plate 2 inches or more thick is buried, and the uppermost white surface is installed flush with the playing surface. It can be mounted in a concrete subbase to provide greater leveling stability.

Staked. A rubber or synthetic plate 3/4 to 1 inch thick has an installed white surface flush to the playing surface. It can be mounted in a concrete subbase for better anchoring.

Anchored. A rubber or synthetic plate has a stem built into the bottom that fits into a permanent ground anchor. The uppermost white surface must be installed flush with the playing surface.

Throw down. A rubber or synthetic thin mat sometimes using a waffle design on the bottom is laid down on the playing surface and is not mechanically held in place. Throw-down home plates are not recommended for teaching basic skills in a gym, such as in a physical education class.

Skinned Infield

With an eye to player safety, begin the outfield slope 20 feet back into the outfield, lessening the transition from the infield to outfield (this is for both synthetic and natural fields). The infield slope should be established at 0.5%, and the outfield slope at 1.3% all the way around to further speed drainage. The infield should be a 80:20 premixed sand to clay material at a depth of three inches. The demarcation between skinned area and turf must be smooth and firm. The skinned areas must maintain the proper pitch to eliminate puddling and erosion. Irregular clumps of turf, uneven edges, and undermining of skinned materials are among some of the causes of ankle and leg injuries in the game.

Skinned areas could be just cutouts around the bases, home plate, and pitchers mound or include baselines or the entire infield area. In all cases, the skinned areas must be continuously inspected and groomed. All irregularities must be eliminated, particularly around bases where sliding groves the area.

Clay is most often used for a skinned area; however, other materials and mix of materials have been used depending upon local sources and preference. Most fields should be designed to be playable within 15 to 20 minutes after rain. A higher percentage of sand may be needed to achieve that without underground drainage.

Turf Infield and Outfield

Chapter 19 contains a discussion regarding natural turf as well as irrigation concerns. However, it needs to be noted here that natural turf in the infield and outfield should be Tifway™ Bermuda grass. It should be overseeded (see Base Paths) with Topflite™ perennial ryegrass.

Pitchers Mound

The pitchers mound and its plate must meet the requirements of the game's governing body. The height of the plate, the pitch of the slope within the circle toward home plate, the radius of the circle, the level plate length and width size are all critical to safety in any type of designated and designed fields and must be checked and maintained before any game.

Base Paths

A regular maintenance concern is the rutting of the base path. Like the infield, the base path should be free of ruts and irregularities in the surface. Periodically hand rake the base paths between first and second and second and third to identify any low spots. The base paths between home and first and first and third can be composed of clay and sand like the infield, or natural turf or synthetic material. If the base path is composed of natural turf, it should be overseeded with Topflight™ perennial ryegrass prior to the season, periodically during the season, and at the conclusion of the season, as well as in early fall. Prior to overseeding in the early spring and early fall the area should be aerated, then de-thatched to provide good seed-to-soil contact. The seeded area should be fertilized first with 10-10-10 fertilizer, and one month later with a slow-release 30-16-10.

Warning Track

The warning track should encircle the entire playing field and provide noticeable surface variations in feel and sound to provide ample warning to players chasing a fly ball who are unaware of the perimeter and any obstacles. The track can be made of clay or crushed (M-10) granite or brick. The crushed brick will add color for enhanced TV coverage. The warning track and/or buffer zone should be equal in width to 5% of the distance from home plate to the deepest part of the playing field and completely encircle the field. Care should be taken that any edge between the track and the turf be smooth and even.

Backstop

The backstop is a key element of a field for safeguarding the players and spectators. The basic purposes of backstop include 1) keeping the ball within the playing area, 2) protecting the spectator, 3) safeguarding others involved in the game (e.g., batters in the on-deck circle, bat persons), and 4) protecting nearby activities from conflict with pop-ups (e.g., adjacent ball fields, concessions areas, rest-rooms, parking areas).

When designing the backstop, the planners should consider the following: 1) using small mesh to discourage people from climbing the structure; 2) ensuring the parking and traffic areas are not close; 3) installing a double mesh to prevent fingers, faces, and other body parts of spectators from being crushed by errant balls or thrown bats; 4) keeping the mesh free from any barbs or penetrating parts to ensure safety for players and spectators; 5) ensuring the distance between home plate and the backstop is not less than 25 feet but preferably 60 feet to ensure player safety; 6) using ground materials of either turf with an appropriate warning track composed of clay or crushed granite (M-10) or crushed brick, or no turf with either clay or crushed granite (M-10) or crushed brick; and 7) ensuring the height of the backstop is at least 18 feet, preferably 20 feet, with a 4- to 6-foot overhang at the top with a 45-degree angle.

The most frequently used backstop consists of three 12-feet wide panels that are 18 to 20 feet high covered with a 1 1/2-inch galvanized wire mesh material. These panels can be made of steel, aluminum, or wood. One panel is placed directly behind home plate and the other two on each side flaring at 30 degrees with the center panel. The fencing on either side of the side panels should gradually taper down to 8 feet behind the players' bench area to provide greater protection for the spectators in bleachers on the other side of the fence. The top of the backstop will have three panels, 4 to 6 feet by 12 feet, attached to the upright panels and positioned at a 45-degree angle to contain errant balls. This overhang will be covered with the same material as the uprights.

Players' Bench Area

There are two types of player' bench areas commonly constructed for baseball and softball. These areas are the dugouts and field-level shelters. The safer of the two is the dugout, but it is also the most expensive to construct. The dugout is usually four feet deep, constructed of poured concrete and concrete blocks with drains to remove water quickly. It has an elevated players' bench area, entrance to locker rooms (if in a stadium complex), drinking fountain, communication system, bat rack, other storage space, lights, and electrical outlets. Recently, to better safeguard the players, either shatter-proof plastic or wire mesh has been installed to repel errant balls and bats. The roof is constructed so as to discourage people from sitting or climbing on it.

The field-level shelter is at field level with a poured concrete floor and concrete block walls. It has a wire mesh fence at least six feet high to repel errant balls or bats. The space should have a bat rack, communication system, a drinking fountain, additional storage, lights, and electrical outlets. The roof should be constructed to discourage sitting and climbing.

Batting Cage

The batting cage should be located outside the fenced playing field. It should be constructed of steel, aluminum, or wood. The minimum size for one batter should be 10 feet wide, 100 feet long, and 10 feet high. If more than one batter is going to be hitting, then the cage needs to be wider (i.e., 10 feet wider for each batter) with a separating mesh curtain. The space must be completely covered by mesh netting to protect other players and spectators. There needs to be a source of electricity and numerous GFI electrical outlets. The floor surface should be similar to home plate for the batters and natural mounds for the pitchers.

Bullpen

The bullpens should be located either down the first- and third-base lines into the outfield area or in right and left center fields. These areas should be protected from errant balls and the spectators. The area behind the catcher should have a protective fence to protect the spectators. The pitching mounds should be exact replicas of the actual playing field mound. There should also be a home plate area. Finally, there should be benches available for the players.

Field Size

The area required for a baseball or softball field will vary from 260 to 460 feet, depending on the level of play anticipated. Since baseball and softball are now often scheduled on the same fields, the age group and type of activity govern the field size. It is recommended that if multiple age groups are to play on a field, it should be sized for the optimum use. Many fields have been planned for a size for high school play, only to have young adults scheduled for the same field. This creates numerous incidents with players colliding with obstacles or other players. Ideally, if funding is available, there should be separate facilities for the various age groups.

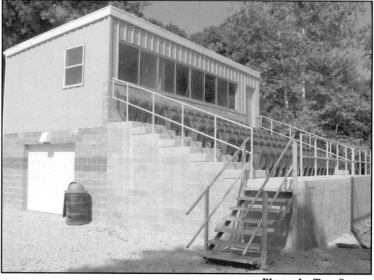

Photos by Tom Sawyer

Multi-Field Complex

It is common to see multi-field complexes for baseball, softball, and combination baseball and softball. The most common multi-field complex contains four fields. If one were to view the complex

Photo by Tom Sawyer

from an airplane, it would resemble a wheel with four spokes coming from a central hub.

The central hub (See Figure 21.4) would contain a two-story building with each side facing a different backstop and field. The first floor would contain a concession area, restrooms, storage for game and maintenance equipment, and a first-aid space. The second floor would have four large screened windows, four scorer tables, four scoreboard controls, a communication center, and field light controls. The pathways leading to the various fields would contain either crushed granite (M-10) or crushed brick. The parking area would be located at least 100 yards from the nearest outfield fence. All fields would be lighted.

Field Hockey, Football, Lacrosse, Rugby, and Soccer Fields

Fields for field hockey, football, lacrosse, rugby, and soccer have a number of common requirements. For example, a drinking fountain should be available for each team to use near the team benches. A utility structure should be placed at midfield, set back from the field 25 feet, to store equipment and house the scorer and controls for the field lights and score board. Shade must be available for the teams at halftime, preferably from a deciduous tree grove at either end or side of the field and about 25 yards away from the playing field.

Field Hockey

This sport needs sleeves in the ground for corner flags and goal posts. The actual field dimensions are similar to those in Appendix A. Official rule books can be purchased from the NCAA or National Association for Girls and Women in Sport (NAGWS); rules are revised annually.

Football

There should be sleeves in the ground for the end zone flags. The goal posts (usually a single pole with uprights) need to be centered and secured at the end line. Actual field dimensions are similar to the ones in Appendix A. Official rule books can be purchased from the NCAA; rules are revised annually. Planners should review carefully the ASTM publication Safety in Football.

Lacrosse

There should be sleeves in the ground to hold the goals. Actual field dimensions are similar to the ones in Appendix A. Official rule books can be purchased from the NCAA or NAGWS; rules are revised annually.

Rugby

There should be sleeves in the ground for the end flags and the goal posts. Actual field dimensions are similar to the ones in Appendix A. Official rule books can be purchased from the United States Rugby Association; rules are revised annually.

Soccer

Sleeves in the ground are needed for the flags for the corner kick area, substitute area, and the goal posts on the end line. Tie down hooks should be inserted at least one foot into the ground for securing the nets to the ground. There should be a drinking fountain available for each team to use near the team benches. Actual field dimensions are similar to the ones in Appendix A. Official rule books can be purchased from the NCAA; rules are revised annually.

Planning Checklist for Fields

The following is a checklist to be used by field planners when designing field spaces:

- Define the use of the field complex (i.e., single- or multiple-sport users; youth, adolescent, or adult; amateur or professional).

- Pay careful attention to slope on fields to encourage proper and adequate pitch for drainage.
- Ensure sub-drainage requirements are met, the type as well as placement of drainage outlets is well out of the playing area, and swales are beyond safety or buffer zones.
- Make sure fences on the perimeter are offset beyond safety or buffer zones. The height of the fence should be consistent with the ASTM standard (i.e., at least eight feet) for the type of activity. Fences should be flexible, resilient, and padded. Further, ensure that fences are placed in front of players (i.e., dugouts and field-level shelters) and spectators. The fence should be sturdy enough to attach a wind-screen or sunscreen. Finally, the mesh on the fences should be of a size to discourage climbing and the top should have knuckled mesh.

Photo by Tom Sawyer

- Provide gates for security and for service of different practice areas and game areas.
- Design warning tracks to provide advanced warning of perimeter barriers and ensure they are wide enough and of appropriate material to meet ASTM standards.
- Ensure that light poles, fence poles, and foul poles are not in the field of play and are padded.
- Plan that mowing or maintenance strips along fences are provided so they are not hazardous.
- Place all shrubs and tree plantings well outside the playing area.
- Ensure that the turf (artificial or natural) is suitable for different weather conditions (i.e., hot, cold, dry, or wet).
- Install the scoreboard well outside the playing area and its fence line.
- Design the irrigation system so that it will not interfere with play and that all valves, distribution boxes, and other fixtures are well outside the field of play.

Photo by Tom Sawyer

- Make sure that vehicular and pedestrian traffic-flow patterns prevent conflict and interference, and that bike and vehicle parking is marked and controlled.
- Ensure that emergency call stations are placed at strategic locations and emergency vehicle access is available for immediate response to all areas.
- Plan the field area so that hazards are not nearby (e.g., major highways, railroad tracks, waterways, culverts, ravines, industries, woods, uncut roughs, and utility lines).
- Create the field area so that security vehicles have easy access and surveillance during game time as well as other times.
- Understand the importance of field orientation relative to the movement of the sun and prevailing wind patterns.
- Configure spectator seating to ensure the best viewing of the game as well as easy access and exit.
- Ensure each activity space has the appropriate safety or buffer zones.
- Review the plan to ensure that the field dimensions are accurate and meet the specified association rules for the level of play.
- Configure all field spaces to include metal sleeves for goalpost, goals, and flags.

- Encourage the owners to ensure that regular maintenance and inspections are done to eliminate ruts, ridges, and depressions in the fields after use; remove debris and rocks from the playing area as well as safety zones; ensure all hooks on goalposts, foul line posts, and fencing are recessed; eliminate all sharp edges on posts, rails, and welds; and make sure benches, seats, and bleachers are protected by screening or barriers.
- Create backstops that protect players, spectators, and other game personnel from injury from errant balls or bats.

Summary

Designing safe sports fields is important to athletes of all ages, genders, and skill and experience levels, as well as to spectators and parents. The number of sports fields being built each year has increased dramatically. Sports field complexes with multiple fields will become the norm rather than the oddity.

Bleachers are a part of almost every sports facility. The type and number are dependent upon the activity, space requirements, number of spectators, and available financial resources. The construction of bleachers is an integral part of the overall facility-planning process. Making bleachers safer for spectators should be a priority for anyone involved in planning or managing a facility.

Track and Field, and Cross-Country Facilities

John McNichols, John Gartland, and Thomas H. Sawyer

22

A track and field competition complex is complicated at best when compared to other outdoor or indoor sports spaces such as an indoor basketball or volleyball court or a baseball, football, or soccer field. The track and field complex includes areas such as throwing, jumping, running, relaxation and warmup, spectator, timing and recording, storage, and officials' dressing room. The areas are basically the same for an indoor facility.

A cross-country course (see Appendix J) requires appropriate planning to service girls, women, boys, and men. The distances differ for genders and level of competition (e.g., interscholastic and intercollegiate).

This chapter will describe the facilities needed for indoor and outdoor track and field and cross country. Further, it will describe various pieces of equipment needed to assist and protect the athletes. The text in this chapter is based on the NCAA Track and Field/Cross Country Men and Women rules.

Learning Objectives

After reading this chapter, the student should be able to

- select an appropriate site for a track and field complex as well as a cross-country course, and
- properly design a track and field complex and cross-country facility.

Site Selection and Planning the Track

Building a running track can be a formidable task since few athletic facilities are as complex and yet have so many acceptable building options. With so many choices, no two track projects are the same. Each is a product of site constraints, owner preferences, location, budget, and availability of materials and expertise.

Faced with the task of building a track, an owner or facility manager can become overwhelmed by the choices and concerned about the possibility of costly mistakes. The first step, then, is identifying all decisions that must be made in planning a track facility and learning what to expect from the construction project. The success of the project will depend on proper site analysis, quality design and engineering, expert construction including construction of proper drainage; a stable, well-built base and a quality synthetic surface; and accurate marking.

The first stage in the construction of a running track is selecting a site and designing a track to fit the site. In calculating the accuracy of a finished 400-meter track, no minus tolerance is acceptable, and a plus tolerance must be no more than 1/2 inch in any lane. These very small tolerances and the numerous design and site factors to be considered make track design extremely complex and demanding. Owners should begin by deciding what size and shape of track is needed. A 400-meter, 6- or 8-lane track is the standard for high school and college competition, although a few high school tracks and many large college tracks are 10 lanes wide.

There are two basic shapes. An equal-quadrant track has two 100-meter straightaways and two 100-meter curves, while a non-equal quadrant track has two straightaways of one length and two curves of another length totaling 400 meters. In the latter case, the result is a track with either a slightly stretched or compressed oval shape.

Recently, a third design—the so-called broken-back track—has come into use. This design features a more square track with shorter straightaways and rounded ends made of double curves. This design creates a larger infield that is large enough for an NCAA soccer field (which neither of the two more common designs can accommodate) and is useful for sites where one of the more common track designs will not work. Generally, an equal quadrant track is desirable, but site factors will determine which design is most feasible.

Will the track have a curb? Most high school tracks are built without curbs; however, curbs are required on tracks where NCAA record events will be conducted. The curb will require additional area on the inside perimeter of the track.

How large a site is available? A track will require a site of no less than five acres, a minimum of 600 feet long by 300 feet wide. Additional area must be allowed for grading, curbs, and drainage and for amenities such as grandstands, bleachers, lighting, walkways, and fencing.

Will the track be built around playing fields? Many tracks are built around football or soccer fields. In addition to allowing space for the field itself, space must be allowed for player seating, walkways, and other associated facilities. Artificial turf fields require additional space for anchoring detail at the perimeter.

Will the construction project include field events? Most track projects built today include construction of a high-jump pad, long-jump runway and pit, pole-vault runway and landing area, shot put, discus, and hammer-throwing pads and landing areas, and sometimes a javelin runway and a triple-jump runway and landing pit. It is more economical to construct field event areas at the same time as the track.

It is during the design phase that the design team must consider where the field events will be located. Placing the field events in the infield of the track may facilitate spectator viewing but may mean more traffic over the runways. Wind must also be considered. Straightaways should be parallel to prevailing winds, which is especially important for dashes and hurdle races. For athlete safety, jumping events should also take place with the wind since crosswinds are particularly dangerous. Multiple-jump runways should be considered because of the addition of the women's pole vault and time constraints during competition when there is only one runway for men and women for the long jump and triple jump.

Throwing events should be located so that participants are throwing into the wind. Likewise, for safety reasons, it is essential that high-jump and pole-vault runways be located so that the athlete does not have to look into the sun or artificial lighting.

There are a number of other important considerations in site selection:

- Does a potential site allow for proper drainage and storm water management? Water should drain away from the track. It is best to locate a track on a relatively level plain, higher than surrounding areas. Additional filling or drainage work required by a low site may add substantially to construction costs. Even under the best site conditions, tracks should be constructed with a perimeter drain on the inside of the track to remove storm water that has drained from the track and playing field. Note: No expense should be spared in developing a good, solid base for the running surface.
- Is the site reasonably level? While the track will be sloped slightly for drainage, for all practical purposes, the track must be level in the running direction.
- What type of soil exists at the site? Poor soil conditions often lead to excessive settling, heaving caused by freeze/thaw action, and drainage problems. The best soil is hard, well-drained, and non-heaving. Locations with peat, clay, topsoil, shear sand, or other organic materials at a depth of 8 to 12 inches should be avoided.
- Where are underground utilities located? While the finished facility will require utility service, it is better to avoid constructing the track over underground utilities.

Many track projects are reconstruction or renovation projects. These projects can be even more complex to design than a new facility because of existing constraints.

Track and Field Facilities

Measuring Distances

The distance to be run in any race is measured from start to finish between two theoretical hairlines. All distances not run in lanes are measured 30 centimeters (11.81 inches) outward from the inner edge of the track if a regulation curb is in place. If no curb is used, lane 1 is measured 20 centimeters (7.87 inches) from the left lane as in other lanes. For all races in lanes around one or more curves, the distance to be run in each lane is measured 20 centimeters (7.87 inches) from the outer edge of the lane that is on the runner's left except that the distance for the lane next to the curb is measured 30 centimeters (11.81 inches) from the curb. If no curb is used, lane 1 is measured 20 centimeters (7.87 inches) from the left-hand line as in other lanes (NCAA, 2004).

Visible Starting Line and Finish Line

The visible starting line, 5.08 centimeters (two inches) wide, is marked on the track just within the measured distance so that its near edge is identical with the exactly measured and true starting line. The starting line for all races not run in lanes (except the 800 meters) is curved so that all competitors run the same distance going into the curve (Figure 22.1).

The visible finish line, 5.08 centimeters (two inches) wide, is marked on the track just outside the measured distance so that its edge nearer that start is identical with the exactly measured and true finish line. Lane numbers of reasonable size should be placed at least 15.24 centimeters (six inches) beyond the common finish line and positioned to face the timing device. The intersection of each lane line and the finish line is painted black in accordance with Figure 22.2. Finally, a common finish line is recommended for all races. Lines in the finish area should be kept to a minimum. If additional lines are necessary, they should be of a less conspicuous color than the finish line so as not to cause confusion.

Except where their use may interfere with fully automatic timing devices, two white posts may denote the finish line and be placed at least 30 centimeters (11.81 inches) from the edge of the track. The finish posts should be of rigid construction approximately 1.4 meters (4.59 inches) high, 80 millimeters (3.15 inches) wide, and 20 millimeters (0.79 inches) thick (NCAA, 2004).

Note: The white posts have been deleted from new facilities and should be removed from older facilities because virtually every track has installed automatic timing devices.

The General Track Area

Outdoor

In constructing track and field facilities, metric measurements must be used. The construction of track and field areas will follow the International Amateur Athletic Federation rules with respect to grade or slope: "The maximum inclination permitted for tracks, runways, circles, and landing areas for throwing events shall not exceed 1:100 in a lateral direction and 1:1000 in the running and throwing direction."

Figure 22.1
Track Measurements

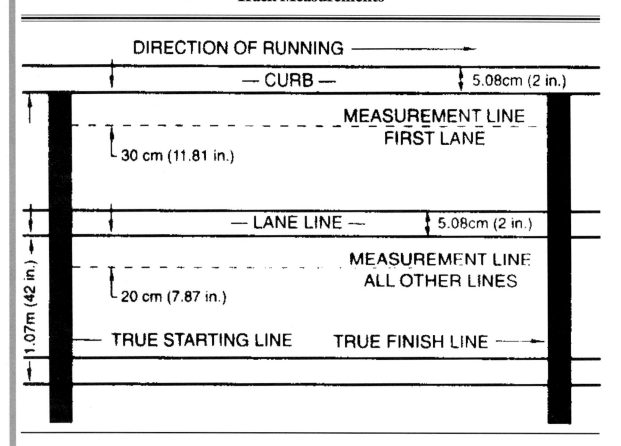

Figure 22.2
Finish-Line Intersections

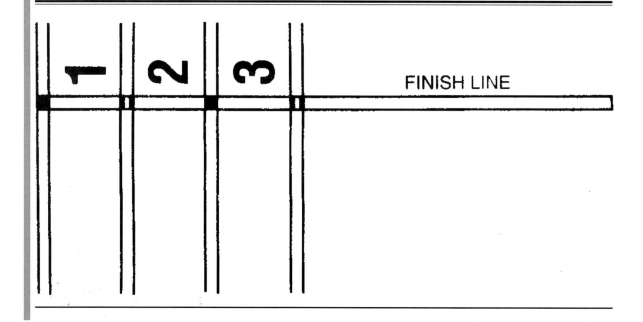

In the high jump, the maximum inclination of the approach and takeoff area not exceed 1:250 in the direction of the center of the crossbar. Prevailing wind conditions should be considered when constructing field-event areas (NCAA, 2004).

Indoor

Tracks, runways, and takeoff areas should be covered with synthetic material or have a wooden surface. These surfaces should be able to accept six millimeter (0.25 inch) spikes for synthetic surfaces and three millimeter spikes (0.13 inch) for wood (NCAA, 2004).

Running Track

Outdoor

The running track should not be less than 400 meters in length nor less than 6.40 meters (21 feet) in width, which allows six hurdle lanes of 1.07 meters (42 inches) each. It may be bordered on the inside by a curb of concrete, wood, or other suitable material a minimum of 5.08 centimeters (2 inches) in height and a maximum of 10.16 centimeters (4 inches) in width. The edges of the curb should be rounded (NCAA, 2004).

Indoor

- Straightaways—Maximum lateral inclination in the running direction should not exceed 1:250 at any point and 1:100 overall. Lanes should all have the same width with a recommended minimum of 1.07 meters (42 inches) and a maximum of 1.25 meters (48 inches) including the white line to the right. There should be a minimum of three meters (9 feet, 10 inches) behind the start line and 10 meters (32 feet, 9.75 inches) beyond the finish line free of any obstruction. It is recommended that clearance beyond the finish line be at least 20 meters (65 feet, 7.5 inches) (NCAA, 2004).
- Oval Track and Lanes—Indoor tracks may vary in size with 200 meters as the preferable distance. The track consists of two horizontal straights and two curves with consistent radii, which should be banked. The curves should be bordered with a curb of suitable material approximately 5.08 centimeters (two inches) in height (NCAA, 2004).

Where the inside edge of the track is bordered with a white line, it should be marked additionally with cones at least 20 centimeters (7.87 inches) high. The cones should be placed on the track so that the outward face of the cone coincides with the edge of the white line closest to the track. The cones should be placed at distances not exceeding 2 meters (6.56 feet) on the curves and 10 meters (32.81 feet) on the straightaways (NCAA, 2004).

The track should have a minimum of six lanes. Lanes should have a recommended minimum of 91.44 centimeters (36 inches) including the lane line to the right. Lines should mark lanes 5.08 centimeters (2 inches) wide (NCAA, 2004).

It is recommended that a maximum angle of banking should not be more than 18 degrees for a 200-meter track. This angle may vary based upon the size of a track. The angle of banking in all lanes should be the same at any cross section. Further, it is recommended that the inside radius of the curves on a 200-meter track should not be less than 18 meters (59 feet, 0.75 inches) and not more than 21 meters (68 feet, 10.75 inches) (NCAA, 2004).

Track Markings

Outdoor

It is recommended that the following color code be used when marking the track (NCAA, 2004):

- Starting line (white): 55 meters, 55-meter hurdles, 100 meters, 100-meter hurdles, 110-meter hurdles, 200 meters, 300 meters, 400 meters, 1,500 meters, mile, 3,000 meters, steeplechase, 5,000 meters, 10,000 meters;
- Starting line (green): 800 meters;
- Starting line (red): 800-meter relay;
- Starting line (blue): 1,600-meter relay;
- Finish line (white): all (A common finish line is recommended for all races.) Except where their use may interfere with fully automatic timing devices, two white posts may denote the finish line and be placed at least 30 centimeters (11.81 inches) from the edge of the track. The finish posts should be of rigid construction approximately 1.4 meters (4.59 feet) high, 80 millimeters (3.15 inches) wide, and 20 millimeters (0.79 inch) thick;
- Relay exchange zones: 400-meter relay (yellow), 800-meter relay (red), 1,600-meter relay (blue), 3,200-meter relay (green);
- Hurdle locations: 100 (yellow), 110 (blue), 300 (red), 400 (green), steeplechase (white), break line (green);
- Lanes shall be marked on both sides by lines 5.08 centimeters (two inches) wide;
- The lanes shall be numbered with lane 1 on the left when facing the finish line;
- Relay zones: in all relays around the track, the baton exchange must be made within a 20-meter (65.62 feet) zone formed by lines drawn 10 meters (32.81 feet) on each side of the measured centerline. All lines and/or boxes or triangles should be inclusive within the zone (NCAA, 2004).

Hurdles

Hurdle lanes should be at least 1.07 meters (42 inches) in width. If no hurdle lanes are marked on the track, they should be judged as equivalent to 2.54 centimeters (1 inch) wider than the total width of the hurdles (NCAA, 2004).

Steeplechase

The standard distance for the steeplechase is 3,000 meters with 28 hurdle jumps and seven water jumps. The water jump should be the fourth jump in each lap. If necessary, the finish line should be moved to accommodate this rule. The following measurements are given as a guide and lengthening or shortening the distance at the starting point of the race shall make any adjustments necessary. The chart below assumes that a lap of 400 meters or 440 yards has been shortened 10 meters (32.81 feet) by constructing the water jump inside the track. If possible, the approach to and exit from the water-jump hurdle should be straight for approximately 7 meters (NCAA, 2004).

Placement of Hurdles on Track

The hurdles, including the water jump, should be placed on the track so that 30 centimeters (11.81 inches) of the top bar measured from the inside edge of the track will be inside the track (see Figure 22.3). It is recommended that the first hurdle be at least five meters (16 feet, 4.75 inches) in width, and that all hurdles weigh at least 80 kilograms (176.4 pounds) (NCAA, 2004).

Water-Jump Construction

The water jump should be 3.66 meters (12 feet) in length and width. The water should be a minimum of 70 meters (2.29 feet) in depth immediately after the hurdle and the pit should have a constant upward slope from a point 30 centimeters (11.81 inches) past the water-jump hurdle to the level of the track at the far end. It is recommended that the water jump be placed on the inside of the track. The landing surface inside the water jump should be composed of a nonskid, shock-absorbent material. The area between the vertical uprights of the water-jump hurdle should be sealed with a solid, rigid material or lattice work to provide safety and to aid the athlete with depth perception. A water source needs to be installed to fill the water jump and a drain installed to drain the water jump after use (NCAA, 2004).

Figure 22.3
Hurdle Measurements

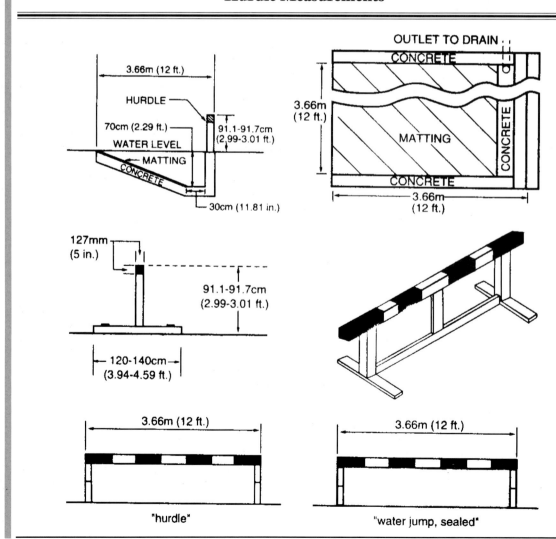

The hurdle at the water jump should be firmly fixed in front of the water and be of the same height as the other hurdles in the competition.

Jumping Areas (Indoor and Outdoor)

High Jump

It is recommended that the approach be an octagon or square with a surface of at least 21 meters (68.909 feet). The minimum length provided should be 15 meters (49.219 feet). The length of the approach run is limited.

The takeoff area is the semicircle enclosed by a three-meter (9.84-foot) radius whose centerpoint is directly under the center of the crossbar. For a record to be approved officially, no point within this area may be higher than the tolerances (NCAA, 2004).

Pole Vault

The vaulting box in which the vaulting pole is planted should be constructed of wood, metal, or other suitable materials. Its dimensions and shape should be those shown in Figure 22.4. The box should be painted white and immovably fixed in the ground so that all of its upper edges are flush with the takeoff area. The angle between the bottom of the box and the stopboard (see Figure 22.4) should be 105 degrees. The vaulting runway needs a minimum length of 38.1 meters (125 feet). It is recommended that the width of the runway be 1.22 meters (4 feet) (NCAA, 2004).

Photos by Meghan Rosselli

Water jump, Indiana State University.

Long Jump and Triple Jump

The minimum length of the runway for the long jump and triple jump should be 39.62 meters (130 feet) from the edge nearest the pit of each event's takeoff board. It is recommended that the width of the runway be 1.22 meters (4 feet). The construction and material of the runway should be extended beyond the takeoff board to the nearer edge of the landing pit. When the runway is not distinguishable from the adjacent surface, it is recommended that it be bordered by lines 5.08 centimeters (two inches) in width from the start of the nearer edge of the landing pit (NCAA, 2004).

The landing area should be not less than 2.74 meters (nine feet) in width and identical in elevation with the takeoff board. The area should be filled with sand. Figure 22.5 shows an approved device for ensuring proper sand level (NCAA, 2004).

In the long jump, the distance between the takeoff board and the nearer edge of the landing area should not be less than 1 meter (3.28 feet) or greater than 3.66 meters (12 feet). The distance between the foul line and the farther edge of the landing area should be at least 10 meters (32.81 feet).

In the men's triple jump, the nearer edge of the landing area should be at least 10.97 meters (36 feet) (12.5 meters or 41 feet is recommended) from the foul line.

In the women's triple jump, the nearer edge of the landing area should be at least 8.53 meters (28 feet) (10.36 meters or 34 feet is recommended) from the foul line.

The takeoff should be a board made of wood or other suitable rigid material 19.8 to 20.32 centimeters (7.8 to 8 inches) wide, at least 1.22 meters (four feet) long, and not more than 10 centimeters (3.94 inches) thick. The upper surface of the board must be level with the runway surface. This board should be painted white and be firmly fixed in the runway. The edge of the takeoff board nearest the landing pit should be the foul line. For the purpose of aiding the calling of fouls, the area immediately beyond the foul line may be prepared as shown in Figure 22.6. A tray 10.2 centimeters (4 inches) wide filled with plasticene or other suitable material may be used. The plasticene or other material should be of a contrasting color to, and level with, the takeoff board (NCAA, 2004).

Surfaces for Track and Runways

Once the basic design work is completed, a track surface must be selected. Natural-material track systems such as cinder and clay used to be common. These tracks were relatively inexpensive to construct, but they required constant maintenance and were rendered soggy by rains, which often caused postponement or cancellation of meets. In recent years, the growing cost of transporting the materials used in these tracks has increased their price to a point where they are nearly as expensive as more modern systems.

Figure 22.4
Pole Vault Box

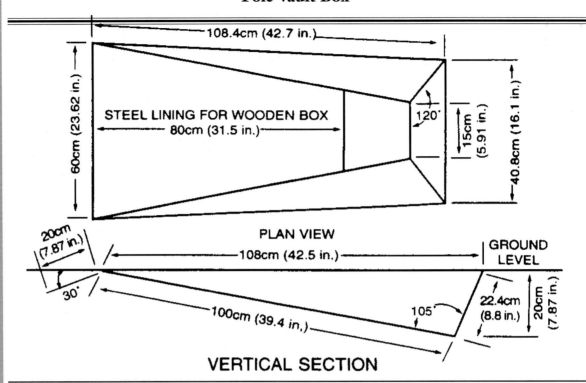

PLAN VIEW

VERTICAL SECTION

Figure 22.5
Control of Sand Level in Long Jump and Triple Jump

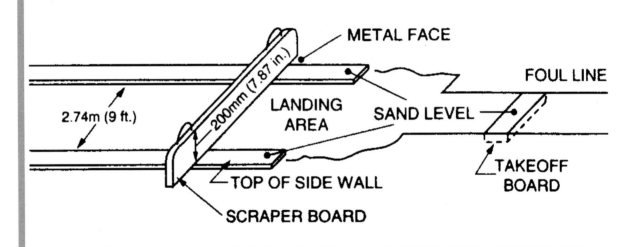

All-weather surfaces, the first modern track surfacing systems, became popular in the late 1960s. Their development meant that systems were now available that were relatively durable and unaffected by ordinary weather. Called asphalt-bound, these systems consisted of a combination of rubber with asphalt emulsion, sand and asphalt, or roofing asphalt.

Although many asphalt-bound tracks are still in use, these tracks (like cinder tracks) are no longer being constructed in large numbers because a significant cost savings no longer balances their disadvantages. Asphalt-bound tracks are affected by temperature—they become quite soft in the summer and hard in the winter. More importantly, asphalt becomes harder as it ages, so that, despite its rubber content, an older asphalt-bound track is no more resilient for runners than an ordinary street.

At the same time, the cost of an asphalt-bound track has increased because it has become increasingly difficult to find an asphalt plant willing to manufacture the special mix required at an affordable price. Existing asphalt-bound tracks in good condition are often sealed to prolong their life. An asphalt-bound track in good condition can be used as a base for a more modern all-weather surface.

Today, most tracks are constructed of rubber particles bound with latex or polyurethane. The latex or polyurethane surface is installed to a depth of 3/8 to 1/2 inch on top of an asphalt or concrete base. The rubber used may be black or colored. Black rubber particles may be granular or stranded and they may be made from natural rubber, styrene-butadiene rubber (SBR), or ethylene-propylene-diene-mono-

Figure 22.6
Long Jump and Triple Jump Takeoff Board and Foul Marker

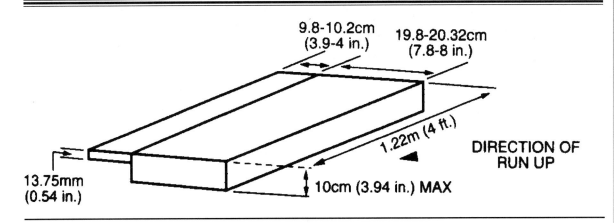

mer rubber (EPDM), virgin or recycled. Colored rubber particles are almost always made of virgin EPDM rubber and come in granular form only. The relative costs and performance characteristics of the rubber types used are beyond the scope of this book. In general, though, virgin rubber is more expensive than recycled rubber, and colored rubber is more expensive than black rubber (Bardeen et al., 1992).

Latex-bound tracks provide good performance and durability at an affordable cost. Depending on the specific type of system, color, and location, latex tracks cost from $8 to $25 per square yard (Bardeen et al., 1992). They can be installed in multiple layers or in a single layer, creating a permeable, resilient surface. In some systems, the rubber is spread over the track surface, which is then sprayed with the latex binder. In other systems, the rubber particles and binder are premixed and then spread. Virtually all latex systems are permeable to some degree.

The basic, and least expensive, system is black, but three types of colored systems are available including colored binder with black rubber, color sandwich, which has colored rubber and colored binder in the top layers over black rubber/black binder or black rubber/colored binder, or full-depth color, where both the rubber and latex binder are colored throughout the surface.

Polyurethane systems are more expensive than latex systems, costing from $14 to $55 per square yard, but they are considered to be more durable. In addition, their resilient but slightly firmer surface is often preferred by track athletes, so they are often used for world-class competitive tracks. Polyurethane surfaces can be either permeable or impermeable. They are most often mixed and installed on site, though premanufactured systems are available for locations where on-site mixing and spraying is not feasible (Bardeen et al., 1992).

Polyurethane surfaces may be colored or black. There are four types. The basic polyurethane-bound system consists of rubber particles bound with polyurethane to form a base mat. The base mat may be used alone or it may be enhanced by the addition of a structural spray consisting of a mixture of polyurethane and rubber sprayed on top of the mat, which creates a textured surface. Alternatively, the base mat may be coated with a flood coat of polyurethane and rubber to create an impermeable, textured surface. Or a full-pour system may be used where each layer is mixed and poured in place. Full-pour systems are impermeable and textured.

With so many systems available, it is important to consider initial cost, maintenance cost over the expected life of the surface, life expectancy, surface wear, repairability, and performance characteristics of the surface.

In the first step of the construction phase, the track is staked out on the site and all measurements are carefully checked. Elevations and grades are set. Next, excavation begins. The sod and topsoil are removed and the track area is excavated to a depth of 8 to 12 inches. The area of excavation is wider than the finished track will be. The asphalt courses and synthetic surfacing also will extend beyond the actual dimensions of the track lanes. This pavement extension serves several purposes—it allows for drainage of the track and infield and serves as a control point for leveling, grading, and establishing the correct length and width of the track (Bardeen et al., 1992).

In some locations, subsoil must be sterilized after excavation and prior to base construction. If weed growth under or through asphalt surfaces is a problem, herbicides should be considered.

Once excavation is completed, a grader is used to establish the appropriate slope and pitch. Normally tracks are pitched to the inside, with a slope of not more than 1% or 1/8 inch in one foot. (A slope of 2%—1/4 inch in one foot—is acceptable for a high school track.) Finally, a heavy vibratory roller is used to tightly compact the subbase, which prevents settling that may cause cracking in the finished surface (Bardeen et al., 1992).

After completion of the preliminary site work, the measurements must be rechecked. The allowable tolerances of the finished track are so small that measurements should be checked at each stage of construction to prevent problems at a later stage.

A base course is then laid. The base course is usually aggregate, but asphalt or penetration macadam also is used. The base course should be no less than four inches thick, more in colder climates. Once spread to uniform thickness, aggregate should be compacted with a tandem roller. After compaction, the grade of the base course must again be verified.

Next are the leveling and finish courses. Asphalt is commonly used for these layers, although concrete can be used. A recent development in track design is the dynamic base track, which uses a rubber, stone, and polyurethane binder mix in place of the solid asphalt or concrete track structure.

A leveling course of hot plant-mix asphalt is applied to the aggregate base to build an asphalt track. This leveling—or binding—layer contains fairly coarse aggregate to provide stability to the finished track. It is rolled and compacted to a thickness of not less than one inch. On top of the leveling course, a surface or finish course of finer asphalt is applied. Like the leveling course, the finish course is compacted to a thickness of not less than one inch. The proper type of asphalt will vary from location to location. State highway department standards can provide some guidance in selecting an asphalt mix.

The finish course is rolled and compacted to complete base construction. Once completed, the asphalt or concrete base must be cured prior to application of the surfacing system. Asphalt is usually allowed to cure for 14 days, while concrete normally cures for 28 to 30 days.

The cured surface is then inspected one last time. The finished surface must not deviate more than 1/8 inch in 10 feet from the specified grade. Its surface may be flooded to check for low areas, called bird baths, to complete the inspection of the base. The base is then cleaned to remove loose particles, dirt, or oil and, for most surfacing systems, primed.

Next, the synthetic surface is installed. The track surface must be installed in strict compliance with the specifications for that particular type of surface and, for layered systems, each layer must be properly cured prior to the installation of the next one.

The last step in constructing a track is calibration and marking. Various options—such as color code, and design or markings—must be considered in light of the type of competition that will be held on the track. The governing bodies of high school, college, national, and international amateur track have all agreed that the 200-meter race should be marked in such a way that all racers start on a turn; however, for some events, the governing bodies differ, so the markings will differ. Once such decisions are made, a track-marking specialist should perform all necessary computations and measurements to mark the required distances on the track. Today, track calibration and marking is frequently computer-assisted to ensure its accuracy.

Permanent markings are then painted on the track to indicate the various distances, start and finish areas, exchange zones, lane numbers, photo timing marks, and similar symbols. The track striper then certifies that the marking and striping meet the specifications agreed to by the owner and designer and the requirements of the appropriate governing body. For most high school tracks, certification by the striper is considered sufficient. If the track is to be used for high-level competition, it must be measured and certified as accurate by a professional engineer or licensed land surveyor.

From start to finish, a track project involves many steps. The planning phase of the project can take several months while actual construction will take at least 8 to 12 weeks, without delays caused by weather or other factors. Do your homework—the investment of time and energy now will yield a quality facility in the future.

Throwing Areas (Indoor and Outdoor)

Throwing Circles

The circles in throwing events should be made of a band of metal or suitable rigid material, the top of which should be flush with the concrete outside the circle. The interior surface should be of concrete or similar material and should be 20 millimeters (0.79 inches), plus or minus 6 millimeters (0.24 inch), lower than the surface outside the circle (NCAA, 2004).

The following is the procedure used for determining a 40-degree sector: The level of the surface within the landing area should be the same as the level of the surface of the throwing circle.

The inside diameters of the shot-put and hammer-throw circles should be 2.135 meters (7 feet), plus or minus five millimeters (0.20 inch), and the diameter of the discus circle should be 2.5 meters (8.20 feet), plus or minus five millimeters (NCAA, 2004).

The circle should be made of metal or suitable rigid material 6 millimeters (0.24 inch) in thickness and 19.05 millimeters (0.75 inch) in height, plus or minus 6 millimeters, and be firmly secured flush with the throwing surface.

The insert should be made of metal or suitable rigid material (rubber is not suitable). The top of the insert must be flush with the concrete outside the circle.

All circles should be divided in half by a 5.08 centimeter (two-inch) line extending from the outer edge of the circle to the end of the throwing pad and measured at right angles to the imaginary center of the throwing sector. There should be no lines painted within any throwing circle.

Shot-Put Area

The circle should be constructed in accordance with Figure 22.7. The stepboard is an arc of wood or other suitable material painted white and firmly fixed so that its inner edge coincides with the inner edge of the shot-put circle. It should measure 1.22 meters (four feet) in length along its inside edge, 112 to 116 millimeters (4.41 to 4.57 inches) in width and 98 to 102 millimeters (3.86 to 4.02 inches) in height (see Figure 22.7) (NCAA, 2004).

Radial lines 5.08 centimeters (two inches) wide should form a 40-degree angle extended from the center of the circle. The inside edges of these lines should mark the sector. The surface within the landing area should be on the same level as the throwing surface. Sector flags should mark the ends of the lines (NCAA, 2004).

Figure 22.7
Shot-Put Circle

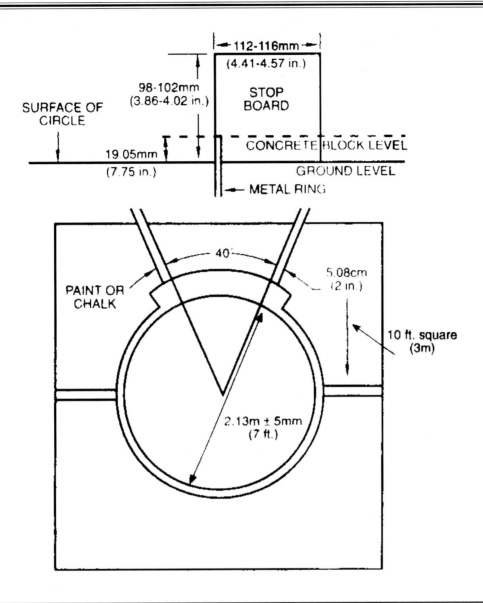

Discus Area

All discus throws should be made from an enclosure or cage centered on the circle to ensure safety of spectators, officials, and competitors (see Figure 22.8). The height of the discus cage should be at least four meters (13 feet, 1.5 inches). A discus cage (see Figure 22.9) is designed to provide limited protection for spectators, officials, and competitors. It does not ensure their safety due to the nature of the event (NCAA, 2004).

The circle should be constructed in accordance with Figure 22.8. The throwing sector for the discus should be marked by two radial lines 5.08 centimeters (two inches) wide that form a 40-degree angle extended from the center of the circle and the inside edges of these lines should mark the sector. The surface within the landing area should be on the same level as the throwing surface. Sector flags should mark the ends of the lines. The sector should be centered within the enclosure.

Hammer Area

All hammer throws should be made from an enclosure or cage centered according to the dimensions in Figure 22.10 to ensure the safety of spectators, officials, and competitors. The cage should be constructed as follows (NCAA, 2004):

- There should be two movable panels at the front of the screen at least 4.20 meters (13.78 feet) but not more than 4.35 meters (14.27 feet) in width.
- These panels should be attached to a fixed vertical support that is 2.85 meters (9.35 feet) away from the sector line and 6.086 meters (20.08 feet) out from the center of the circle. The height of the movable panels should be 6.15 meters (20.18 feet).

Figure 22.8
Discus Circle

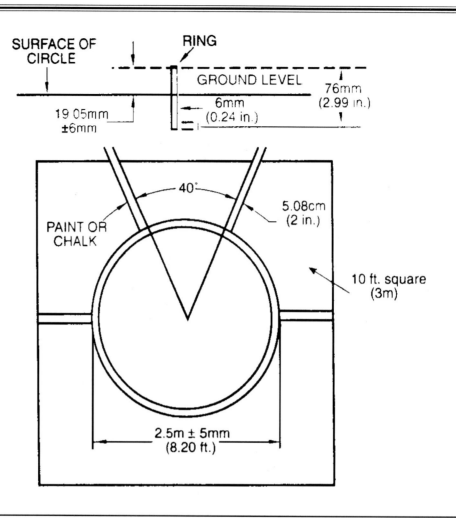

SURFACE OF CIRCLE

RING

GROUND LEVEL

76mm (2.99 in.)

6mm (0.24 in.)

19 05mm ±6mm

40°

5.08cm (2 in.)

PAINT OR CHALK

10 ft. square (3m)

2.5m ± 5mm (8.20 ft.)

Figure 22.9
Construction for Discus Cage

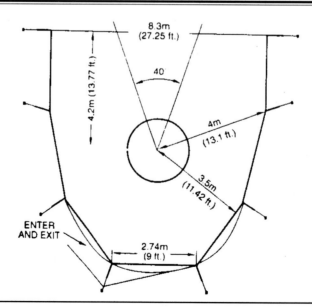

8.3m (27.25 ft.)

4.2m (13.77 ft.)

40°

4m (13.1 ft.)

3.5m (11.42 ft.)

ENTER AND EXIT

2.74m (9 ft.)

The circle should be constructed in accordance with Figure 22.11. The throwing sector for the hammer should be marked by two radial lines 5.08 centimeters (two inches) wide that form a 40-degree angle extended from the center of the circle. The inside edges of these lines should mark the sector. The surface within the landing area should be on the same level as the throwing surface. Sector flags should mark the ends of the lines. The sector should be centered within the enclosure.

Figure 22.10
Construction of Hammer Cage

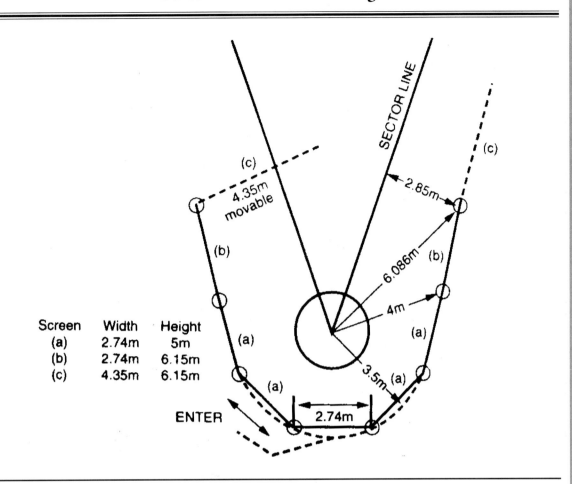

Screen	Width	Height
(a)	2.74m	5m
(b)	2.74m	6.15m
(c)	4.35m	6.15m

Figure 22.11
Hammer-Throw Circle

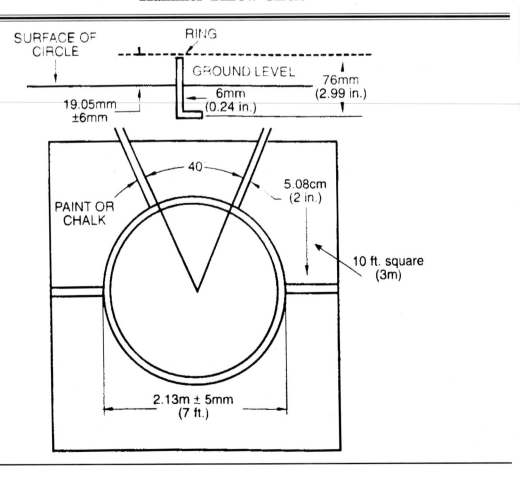

Javelin Area

It is recommended that the runway be constructed of an artificial surface for a width of four meters (13.12 feet) for the entire length of the runway. The minimum length of the runway for the javelin should be 36.58 meters (120 feet). If an artificial surface is used, it is recommended that the runway be extended 1 meter (3.28 feet) beyond the foul line for safety reasons. The runway should be marked by two parallel lines 5.08 centimeters (two inches) in width and a minimum of 1.22 meters (4 feet) apart for 21.34 meters (70.01 feet), widening to 4 meters (13.12 feet) apart for the 15.24 meters (50 feet) before the foul line (NCAA, 2004).

The foul line should be seven centimeters (2.76 inches) wide and painted white in the shape of an arc with a radius of eight meters (26.25 feet). The distance between its extremities should be four meters (13.12 feet) measured straight across from end to end (see Figure 22.12) (NCAA, 2004).

Radius lines 5.08 centimeters (two inches) wide should be extended from the center of the circle of which the arc of the foul board is a part through the extremities of the arc. The inside edges of these lines should mark the sector. The surface within the landing area should be on the same level as the throwing surface. Sector flags should mark the ends of the lines (NCAA, 2004).

Figure 22.12
Javelin Throwing Area

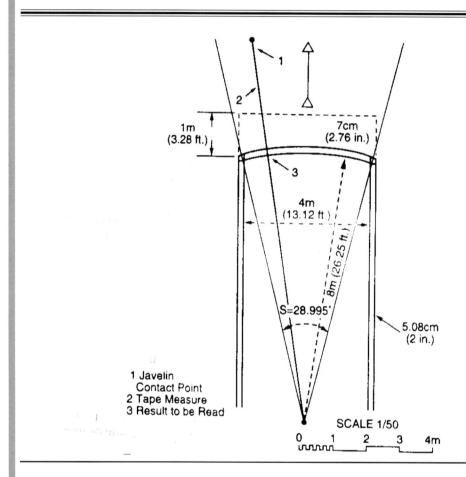

1 Javelin Contact Point
2 Tape Measure
3 Result to be Read

SCALE 1/50

Other Structures/Facilities: Finish Line Towers/Press Box

Towers

The finish line is the control center for running events. The finish line tower should be directly across from the finish line. There could be up to three towers on a track, one at either end of the straightaway, and another diagonally across from the main tower at the 200-meter start position.

Tower A should be a two-story enclosed structure, 20 feet by 40 feet square with eight-foot ceilings and a roof designed as a deck with railings. The first-floor area will contain space for restrooms, a storage area (for hurdles, etc.) with a small roll-up door, and concessions. The second floor will have picture windows facing the finish line. The second floor area will have space for the press, announcer, and the automatic timer, computers, and cameras.

Tower B will be a duplicate of Tower A except the first floor will be dedicated to the storage of hurdles, implements, and pads. The first-floor storage area will have a large roll-up door to accommodate the large landing pads.

Both towers should have hot and cold water, sewer connection, communications lines (i.e., telephone, computer, and television), electricity, and appropriate ventilation.

Lighting

The track and field area should be lighted for security at a minimum, but serious consideration should be given to lighting the area for evening competition.

Fencing

The entire facility should be fenced so it can be secured when not in use. The fence should be at least eight feet high, plastic or vinyl coated, and painted to match the surrounding paint patterns. The fence should have gates in appropriate locations for entrance of athletes, officials, spectators, and maintenance vehicles.

Fences need to be installed to protect athletes and officials from throwing areas (e.g., discus, hammer, and javelin). These fences need to be at least six feet high. They should also be constructed with plastic- or vinyl-coated material.

Spectator Seating

Spectator seating is a necessity. The planners should design seating for both sides of the track. The running track will have two finish lines going in opposite directions. Depending on the prevailing wind, a decision will be made as to which direction the races will be run. Therefore, it is necessary to provide seating on both sides of the track for spectators. (See Chapter 21 for standards relative to new bleachers or retrofitting old bleachers.)

The total number of seats should be based on historical data regarding spectator involvement over the past five years. The seating can either be permanent; constructed of metal, wood, or other appropriate materials; or be portable aluminum bleachers. The higher the bleachers, the greater the liability concerns. If money is not a problem, construct concrete seating large enough to incorporate storage areas underneath the seats and a press box on the upper level (Flynn, 1993).

Starting System

Modern timing systems are connected to the starter's gun. Therefore, the hard wiring that is required should be placed underground and junction boxes made available at the various starting lines for the races. These junction boxes should be at least four feet off the ground with a storage container for cable to be used by the starter crew.

Landscaping

There should be an irrigation system designed to provide water to all grass areas, shrubbery, and flowers. When planning the irrigation system, careful consideration needs to be given to providing additional water to drinking fountains throughout the complex and water for the water jump. The track and field area should be large enough to provide at least a half-acre of shaded area for athletes between events spread around the facility. The areas at the ends of the straightaways should have trees to provide a wind break for the athletes.

Track and Field Equipment

Starting Blocks

Starting blocks must be made without devices that could provide artificial aid in starting. They may be adjustable but must be constructed entirely of rigid materials.

Hurdles

Hurdles should be constructed of metal, wood, or other suitable material. The hurdles should consist of two bases and two uprights supporting a rectangular frame reinforced by one or more crossbars. The top crossbar should be wood or other suitable material with beveled edges and a height of 70 millimeters (2.76 inches). The center of the crossbar should be directly over the end of the base. The surface facing the starting line should be white in color with two vertical or diagonal stripes. A center chevron should be added to help contestants determine the center of the lane (see Figure 22.13) (NCAA, 2004).

Pull-over force refers to the 3.6 kilograms (eight pounds) of steady pulling force required to overturn a hurdle when applied to the center of the uppermost edge of the top crossbar and in the direction of the finish line. If the weights cannot be adjusted to the required overturning force, it is recommended that the next greater setting be used, since records will not be allowed when the overturning force or the weight of the hurdle is less than the required minimum (NCAA, 2004).

When no definite counterweight setting for intermediate hurdles has been made by the manufacturer, it is sometimes possible to attain the correct adjustment by setting one weight as for the 106.7-centimeter (42-inch) height and the other weight as for 76.2-centimeter (30-inch) height. A difference of three millimeters (0.12 inch) above or below the required height will be tolerated (NCAA, 2004).

Steeplechase Hurdles

Hurdles should be constructed of metal, wood, or other suitable material. The hurdles shall consist of a base and two uprights supporting a rectangular frame with a single crossbar. The crossbar shall be of wood or other suitable material without sharp edges or with a 6.35 millimeter (0.25 inch) bevel and have a height of 127 millimeters (5 inch) square. The crossbar shall be white in color with stripes of one distinctive contrasting color.

Figure 22.13
Hurdle Measurements

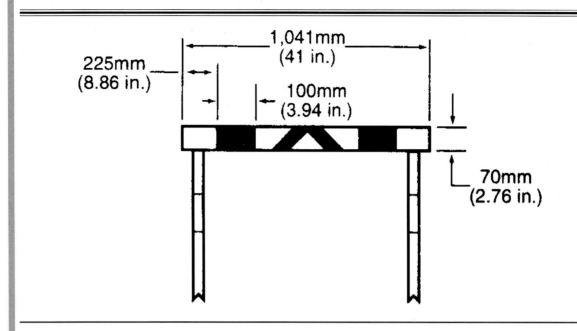

Steeplechase and water-jump hurdles for men should not be less than 91.1 centimeters (2.99 feet) nor more than 91.7 centimeters (3.01 feet) high and should be at least 3.66 meters (12 feet) in width; and for women the hurdles should be not less than 75.9 centimeters (2.49 feet) nor more than 76.5 centimeters (2.51 feet) high and should be at least 3.66 meters (12 feet) in width. It is recommended that the first hurdle be at least five meters (16 feet, 4.75 inches) in width. The section of the top bar of the hurdles and the hurdle at the water jump should be 127 millimeters (5 inches) square without sharp edges or with a 6.35-millimeter (0.25-inch) bevel. The weight of each hurdle should be at least 80 kilograms (176.4 pounds). Each hurdle should have on either side a base between 1.2 meters (3.94 feet) and 1.4 meters (4.59 feet) long (NCAA, 2004).

High Jump

The high jump pad should be a minimum of 4.88 meters wide by 2.44 meters deep (16 feet by 8 feet). It should be high enough and of a composition that will provide a safe and comfortable landing. A minimum height of 66.04 centimeters (26 inches), including the top pad unit, is preferred (NCAA, 2004).

The horizontal supports of the crossbar should be flat and rectangular, 4 centimeters (1.6 inches) wide and 6 centimeters (2.4 inches) long, and friction-free. Each support should point toward the opposite upright so that the crossbar will rest between the uprights along the narrow dimension (3.81 centimeters [1.5 inches]) of the support (NCAA, 2004).

The uprights should extend at least 100 millimeters (3.94 inches) above the support of the crossbar. The crossbar should be circular and be made of suitable material. The ends of the crossbar should be smooth and not be covered with rubber or any other material that has the effect of increasing the friction between the surface of the crossbar and the supports. The diameter of the bar must be at least 25 millimeters but not more than 30 millimeters (0.98 to 1.18 inches). The crossbar should be constructed in such a way that a flat surface of 25 to 30 millimeters (0.98 to 1.18 inches) by 150 to 200 millimeters (5.91 to 7.87 inches) is designed for the purpose of placing the bar on the supports of the uprights (NCAA, 2004).

Pole Vault

The pole vault pad measurement beyond the vertical plane of the stopboard should be a minimum of 4.88 meters wide by 3.66 meters deep (16 feet by 12 feet). It is recommended that the front portion of the pad be the same width as the back units, 4.88 meters (16 feet), extending 91.44 centimeters (36 inches) from the back edge of the stopboard to the front edge of the vaulting box measured across the bottom of the cutout. The back of the cutout should be placed no farther than 36 millimeters (14.17 inches) from the vertical plane of the stopboard. A height of 81.28 centimeters (32 inches), including the top pad unit, is required. Suitable padding should be placed around the base of the standards (NCAA, 2004).

Any style upright or posts may be used for the pole vault, provided the style is rigid and supported by a base not to exceed 10.16 centimeters (four inches) in height above the ground. Cantilevered uprights are recommended. The distance between the vertical uprights or between the extension arms where such are used should be 4.32 meters (14.7 feet) (NCAA, 2004).

The crossbar should rest on round metal pins that project not more than 75 millimeters (2.95 inches) at right angles from the uprights and have diameters of not more than 13 millimeters (0.512 inches). The upper surfaces of these pins should be smooth without indentations or aids of any kind that might help to hold the crossbar in place. The crossbar should be circular and made of suitable material.

The ends of the crossbar shall be smooth and not be covered with rubber or any other material that has the effect of increasing the friction between the surface of the crossbar and the supports. The diameter of the crossbar must be at least 29 millimeters but not more than 31 millimeters (1.14 to 1.22 inches). The crossbar should be between 4.48 and 4.52 meters (14.7 to 14.83 feet) in length. The maximum weight shall be 2.25 kilograms (4.96 pounds). For the purpose of placing the bar on the supports of the uprights, the ends of the crossbar should be constructed in such a way that a flat surface of 29 to 35 millimeters (1.14 to 1.38 inches) by 200 millimeters (7.87 inches) is provided (NCAA, 2004).

Other Accessory Equipment

The following pieces of equipment will be very useful for both indoor and outdoor track and field facilities (NCAA, 2004):

- pole vault standards base protection pads
- countdown timer
- wind gauge—now required for all collegiate 100, 200, 110, 110 hurdles, long jump, and high jump
- implement certification unit
- aluminum water jump
- foundation tray
- blanking lid
- take-off board with plasticine insert
- long jump/triple jump aluminum pit covers
- throwing rings
- toe boards
- concentric circles
- stainless steel or aluminum pole-vault box
- pole-vault covers
- finish post
- aluminum track curbing
- rotating track gate
- hammer cage
- discus cage
- indoor throwing event cage
- lane markers
- distance marker boxes
- long jump/triple jump distance indicator
- performance boards
- lap counter
- wind display
- awards stand
- judge's stand
- starter's rostrum
- hurdle carts
- platform cart
- starting block caddy
- implement carts—shotput cart, hammer cart, javelin cart, discus cart, combo cart

Cross-Country Facility

The Course

The length of the cross-country course varies as follows:

- Men—The length of a cross-country race should be from 8,000 to 10,000 meters, unless otherwise mutually agreed upon by coaches or determined by the games committee.
- High school—5,000-meter standard, some variations are found between state associations.
- Women—5,000 meters, high school—3,000 to 5,000 meters.

Course Layout

The course should be confined to fields, woods, and grasslands. Parks, golf courses, or specially designed courses (see Figure 22.14) are recommended. There should be a control facility constructed at or near the finish line with elevated seating. The turf should be a quality to promote safety and freedom from injury to the runners, keeping the following in mind:

- Dangerous ascents or descents; undergrowth; deep ditches; and, in general, any hindrance detrimental to the contestants must be avoided.

- Narrow gaps must be no less than 2 and preferably 5 meters in width for non-championship courses. Obstacles and other hindrances should be avoided for the first 600 to 800 meters as well as the last 200 to 300 meters of the race. Note: Championship courses must be at least 10 meters wide at all points.
- Continuous traversing of roadways should be avoided.
- The direction and path of the course should be defined clearly for the runners.
- All turns must be gradual.

Course Markings

The course should be properly measured along the shortest possible route that a runner may take and it must be marked clearly by at least two of the following methods presented in order of preference:

- Sign posts not less than seven feet high with large directional arrows on boards fastened to the tops of the posts so that the arrows will be visible plainly at a distance to competitors approaching the posts. The posts must be placed at every point where the course turns, on the side of the direction of the turn, and wherever there is any doubt as to the direction of travel.
- A single white or colored line for directional purposes only—not to be assumed as the measured line— or two lines that mark the outside borders of the course, one on the measured course marking its shortest perimeter and the second such that runners cannot vary from the proper course. In addition, these two lines serve as restraining lines for spectators. Lines on the turns must vary in color from the color of lines approaching the turn.
- Flags, sign posts, or stakes that meet the following conditions:
  —markers at least seven feet above the ground level
  —a turn to the left marked by a red flag or arrow of direction on a sign post or stake
  —a turn to the right marked by a yellow flag or arrow of direction on a sign post or stake
  —a course continuing straight marked by a blue flag or arrow of direction on a sign post or stake
  —all flags, sign posts, or stakes marking the shortest perimeter of the course

Finally, all of the above course-marking devices must be placed on the edge of the measured line when lines and flags, sign posts, or stakes are used to mark the course.

Starting Area

The starting area for a championship course should be wide enough for at least 50 teams (see Figure 22.14). The area should be flat and well drained. At either side of the starting line there should be permanent elevated (8 to 10 feet high) recall starter stands with steps to the platform and a roof over the platform to protect the recall starter during inclement weather. The lower portion of the platform should be enclosed and used as a storage area. Two more stands should be constructed across from each other

Figure 22.14
LaVern Gibson Championship Cross-Country Course

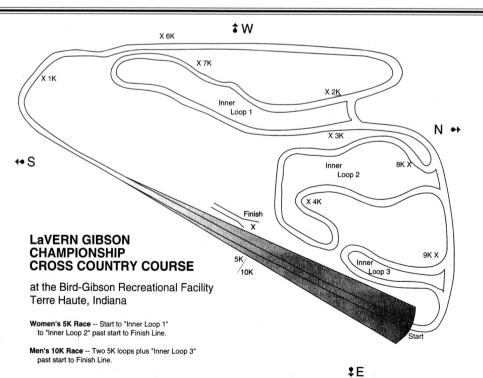

at the 100 yard mark for the second set of recall starters.

There should be a fence (six to eight feet high) at the end of the starting area to separate the runners from the spectators. Behind the fence would be the official staging area for the athletes and portable toilets.

An elevated permanent starter stand should be located in the center of the course. The tower should be equipped with a public address system and communications to the finish line. The stand platform should be at least eight feet high with a ladder for the starter to climb to reach the platform.

Photo by Meghan Rosselli

Track press box and control center, Indiana State University.

Finish Area

The finish area for a championship course should have an arched entrance with a digital clock

Photo by Meghan Rosselli

Cross-country control center (above and below), Indiana State University.

embedded into the arch. The finish area should be 15 to 20 feet wide with a fence (6 feet) along each side (see Figure 22.14). The fenced area should extend for at least 30 yards. The actual finish line should be a concrete pad (20 by 20 feet) on which the timing pads can be placed. Directly adjacent the concrete pad would be a timing booth to house the timing equipment and personnel. This booth should be covered to protect the equipment from inclement weather conditions. The booth area should have communication linkages to the starter tower and electricity.

The final 300 meters of the course should have fencing (six feet) along both sides to keep spectators off the course as the athletes finish. This fencing may stretch from the starting area to the finish area if the course overlaps these two areas.

Control Center Building

The control center building for a championship course is used as a press box and for spectator seating. The building will be a two-story structure near the finish line. The lower portion of the building should be enclosed and used for storage of equipment, mowing vehicles, and utility vehicles. The second story will be the press box area. Above the press box will be spectator seating. The press box will have electricity, heating, and communication linkages to the finish and starting lines.

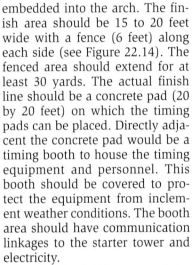

Photo by Meghan Rosselli

Summary

A track and field competition complex is complicated at best when compared to other outdoor or indoor sports spaces, such as an indoor basketball and volleyball court or a baseball, football, or soccer field.

Section

IV

Recreational Spaces

Chapter

23

Aquatic Facilities

Tom Griffiths, Michael W. Edwards, and Richard T. Scott

The major growth in aquatic facilities took place in this country shortly after World War II. With a stronger economy and a new interest in aquatics generated by successful swimming training programs in the military, a significant increase in swimming pools occurred in schools, universities, and agencies throughout the United States. Most pools designed and constructed during the 1950s through the 1970s were built to competitive swimming and diving standards. Those wishing to take lessons or engage in aquatics recreation simply did their thing in these rectangular, deep pools. However, with the advent of the water slide and water parks in the 1980s, a whole new thought process evolved for those designing and building pools. The leisure pool concept or family aquatic centers that originated in Europe and then migrated to Canada and other countries before coming to the United States called for a great amount of shallow water, much of it moving with currents, waves and slides. This continues to be a positive and popular trend because while the traditional, competitive rectangular pool may recover 20 to 40% of its operating expenses, leisure pool designs usually can recover more than 50% of their operating costs with many recovering up to 85%.

This chapter will cover both competitive and recreational aquatic facilities; however, the emphasis will specifically be on aquatic design planning rather than some of the ancillary topics (e.g., locker rooms, spectator areas, mechanicals, etc.) already discussed in this text. The chapter will progress from the older, more traditional public pools to the newer aquatic facilities including the family aquatic centers. Also, special attention will be given to particularly troublesome areas like nonslip flooring and ventilation.

The overall planning process for a facility can be found in Chapters 3 and 4. Linked to planning process for an aquatic facility, as well as other facilities, is a market analysis. This is an excellent tool to have in place when planning a project. The market analysis will determine if there is a demand for a new aquatic facility. Some considerations for market analysis should be, but are not necessarily limited to, organizational support, geography, demographic survey, customer profile, economy, any dominant industries, and the competition.

Further, a successful project rests upon how well an architect and operator initially reach an understanding of the most important issues, including the building program, a definition of multipurpose use, the operational design for the facility, space utilization, and a design that will accommodate new trends in aquatics. The operator must decide which activities can be combined and which activities must be separated. The operator must foresee who will use, how many different uses will be included, and how many users are anticipated. The program is based on these projections. The architect can help provide a reality check for what the operator envisions. The best possible result of the program phase is producing a program where budget, quality, and size are not compromised.

Furthermore, with any financial analysis, a total understanding of the operational costs is needed. This is sometimes not factored into a project and will affect the end result. Raising the money to build the project is much easier than funding the building operation over the expected lifetime of the building. Operational costs to be considered are utilities, maintenance, additional staffing, and repair and replacement. Before developing an operational cost analysis, the organization should consider the future as it pertains to growth in staffing and programming. Many times these important areas are overlooked. Neglecting these areas will cost more to the organization in the future than if they are planned for in the present. It is sometimes better to have help in this area from an outside consultant who is able to ask the hard questions and provide guidance.

Finally, the programming phase of a project is very important. This is the phase that will determine what spaces will go into your building and their relationship to each other and the overall operation of the building itself. The entire project will be based on this phase, design, cost, and construction. If it does not appear in the program, it will not be designed or constructed. If additional items or changes to the program in the latter stages of design or construction are requested, it will cost extra.

Children enjoying leisure pool activities.

Before starting the program phase, a firm understanding of the current operation and future growth is imperative. Visiting as many facilities around the country as possible to obtain ideas for the new facility is of paramount importance. Before going on these tours, a list of questions should be developed beforehand to ask the operators of these facilities. Pictures and videos are beneficial and developing a catalog of these images helps demonstrate the specific desires in an aquatic facility to the architect.

Learning Objectives

After reading this chapter, the student should be able to

- identify the latest trends in aquatic facilities,
- describe typical design problems associated with aquatic facilities, and
- list safety considerations when planning aquatic facilities.

Planning Issues

Priority User Groups

Prior to planning any type of aquatic facility, perhaps the first and most important task is to itemize priority user groups that will frequent the facility. If most of the patrons will be serious competitive swimmers and divers then a more traditional pool may be appropriate. If most of the pool patrons tend to be recreational, instructional, and therapeutic users, undoubtedly a more diverse type of aquatic facility should be designed. If all types of users will be using the pools, including competitive swimmers as well as younger and older persons and individuals with disabilities, it is possible to have it all under one roof by designing both competitive and recreational vessels in close proximity to one another.

Outdoor Versus Indoor Aquatic Facilities

Comparatively speaking, outdoor aquatic facilities are much easier to plan and build than indoor facilities and, of course are much less expensive. Perhaps the biggest problem to overcome in indoor aquatic facilities is poor air quality caused by recirculating chloramines produced in the pool. Outdoor pools do not have this problem because the outside environment rids the pool area of chloramine odors. Likewise, lighting is an expensive and comprehensive task to tackle indoors; however, it is not required outdoors. Several light fixtures on high poles can be added at a modest cost to extend outdoor pool usage beyond 8:30 p.m. Windows, heating, and dehumidification are just a few areas not considered in outdoor environments.

Regardless of the warmth provided by the geography, outdoor pools tend to be open only three months a year. Even in our warmer climates in the United States, many swimmers only swim outdoors "in-season" that is, between Memorial Day and Labor Day.

Lawns or sun turf areas are both aesthetically pleasing and user friendly, they often are maintenance headaches for the pool managers/operators and are attractive to Canadian geese. Today's outdoor aquatic facilities do require more shaded areas because of the heightened awareness of skin cancer caused by exposure to the sun.

A variety of large, colorful shade structures are now available. Skin damage is not the only disadvantage of an outdoor pool, however. With the sunlight comes algae growth at outdoor facilities, which is typically not the case indoors. Higher levels of chlorine, algaecides, and daily brushing are all recommended for outdoor aquatic facilities to combat algae growth, particularly for those below the Mason-Dixon Line. The sunlight also dissipates chlorine rapidly. For this reason, stabilized chlorines are often used outdoors because they are resistant to the ultraviolet rays of the sun and last longer in the water.

Stabilized chlorines do save significant sums of money compared to the traditional, non-stabilized chlorines used in indoor pools. Stabilized chlorines do come with some disadvantages however, and the cyanuric acid they contain must be kept below 100 parts per million (PPM) in pool water.

Vacuums and housekeeping equipment is a more vital consideration outdoors because more debris finds its way into the pool as opposed to indoor facilities. Pool furniture, shade structures, and food concessions are just a few of the considerations for outdoor facilities that are not considered for indoor facilities.

Security is another important factor when planning outdoor

aquatic facilities. When darkness comes and the facility is locked for the evening, trespassers are often tempted to sneak in. Although chain-link fence may be the most popular and least expensive to install around the perimeter of an aquatic facility, it is perhaps the easiest to climb. Fencing with electronic security systems and security personnel may be required at the outdoor aquatic facility, depending on the demographics surrounding the pool. Finally, for a myriad of safety and maintenance reasons, outdoor pools should not be emptied during the off-season, winter months. The following discussions will focus on indoor aquatic facilities.

Traditional Public Pool Configurations

The predominant type of swimming pools constructed in the 1950s through the 1970s was more competitive and rectangular in nature. These pools continue to be constructed today in facilities that have competitive swimming and diving as their priority. It is possible, however, to construct a pool that caters to both the competitive and recreational interests of the pool patrons. Traditional, competitive pools are somewhat easier to plan because so many have already been constructed over decades and rule books with specifications are provided by the governing sports bodies such as YMCA, NCAA (see Figures 23.2 and 23.3), USA Swimming, and Federal Internationale de Natation (FINA).

The traditional eight-lane, 25-yard competitive pool with the starting blocks located at the shallow end and diving boards placed at the opposite, deep end are currently being challenged by more creative and innovative designs catering to a wider population. First and foremost, springboard diving and competitive swimming should not be planned for the same vessel; too many programming conflicts quickly result when both venues are placed in the same pool. It is best to have a separate diving well for springboard diving, SCUBA, synchronized swimming, water polo and deep water walking, but if this is not possible, a T- or L-shaped pool is a good compromise with the deep portion located away and out of the racing course.

A "Stretch 25-meter" or "Stretch 50-meter" pool is a good alternative to T- or L-shaped pools. They consist of 25 yards or meters or 50 yards or meters swim course with a movable bulkhead that can adjust distances. While competitive swimming takes place in the racing course, other activities such as springboard diving or water aerobics can take place in the stretched portion of the pool beyond the swimming course. If diving boards do remain in the racing course, numerous visual and tactile cues must be developed so that novice recreational swimmers do not unwittingly slip from the shallow portion of the pool down the traditional slope and into the deeper diving well. Unless the competition pool will host Olympic trials or perhaps NCAA championships, most competitive swimming pools do not need more than five to six feet of water. This saves considerable construction and operating costs while increasing programming and attendance; and besides, most people prefer shallow water. The trend continues today for large, Stretch 25-meter and 50-meter pools with movable bulkheads.

The use of movable bulkheads (see Figure 23.4) allows for maximum flexibility and simultaneous programming. All movable bulkheads are not equal, so a great deal of research should be conducted in this area to find the bulkhead that meets your needs. Bulkheads generally come in two different materials, stainless steel and fiberglass. Both are excellent materials, providing both strength and durability. When researching bulkheads, you should take into consideration the movement of them. How easy or difficult is it to move them into the position needed? How many times will you have to move them in your operation and who will be moving them? What will be the position needed in your various situations? Will starting blocks be mounted on them? Will touch pads or automatic timing systems be mounted on them? And how will they need to be mounted? Answers to these questions will help you decide on the type of bulkhead to use. Remember, a bulkhead is going to stretch across your 50-meter pool and may be 45, 50, 75, or 82 feet in length, so moving them will be time and labor intensive. Most bulkheads come with some type of inflatable chamber for variable buoyancy. Typically, the pool operator inflates a large air chamber inside the bulkhead, which floats the bulkhead to allow relatively easy movement. Bulkheads are posi-

tioned (stored) in different ways around the country; the most common is constructing the pool length to allow for the positioning on the either end and still have a 50-meter competition course. There are pools, however, that store the bulkheads in the ceiling by hoisting them up with cables (University of Texas) or pulling them down into the floor (U.S. Military Academy); however, this is rare. Another consideration is the anchoring device used once the bulkhead is in place. This anchor device must be able to withstand the torque that 6, 8, or 10 lane lines will place on it. If used in a competition setting, the bulkhead must maintain its position during the competition with no movement so that no swimmer is given an advantage during the competition.

Figure 23.1
Longitudinal Section of a Pool

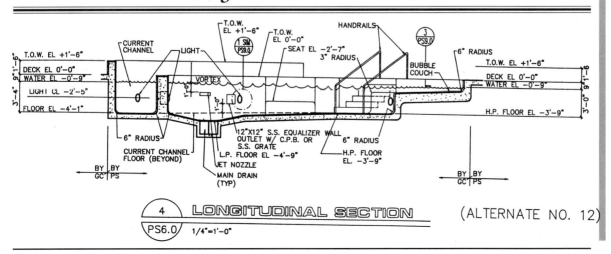

Figure 23.2
NCAA Pool Diagram, Dimensions, and Equipment Requirements

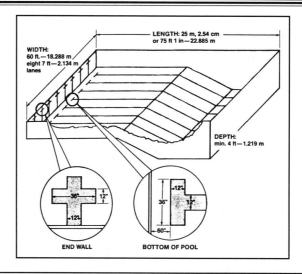

While one large swimming vessel to support many aquatic activities is both a popular and economical approach, all aquatic activities in the same pool are subject to the same water temperature which no doubt will be detrimental to some. The beauty of having completely separate pools under the same roof is that significantly different water temperatures can be maintained for each vessel. While this is a tremendous bonus for participants, it is a more costly approach, because separate heating, filtering, and circulation systems are required for each pool. While the filter area required will not change, a second set of piping manifolds on the filters will increase the cost as well as require additional pump(s) and heater(s). The greatest increase in cost comes from the building enclosure that must be expanded to cover the decks that separates the pools. A common approach to the separate pool concept is to have separate competitive swimming pools; a separate deep, warm-water diving well; and a shallow water warm-up, cool-down, and instructional pool. Most aquatic facility managers consider the appropriate temperatures provided by specialized pools vital to their pool programming. Temperatures used for different aquatic activities include:

- Race Swimming and Water Polo = 78 to 80° F.
- Swim Team Practice = 81° F, plus or minus 1°.
- Multi-purpose pool for many user groups = 82 to 84° F.
- Leisure Pool = 84 to 86° F.
- Therapy Pool = 88 to 90° F.
- Whirlpool Spa = 102 to 104° F.

Specific Elements of Facilities

Springboard Diving

Contrary to popular belief, springboard diving is an extremely safe sport and, statistically speaking, safer than most other sports. Having said that, three-meter diving boards have been disappearing for decades in existing aquatic facilities. This is not because of injuries occurring in the water or on the bottom of the pool, but rather from falls onto the deck from the board, more often from the ladder. For these reasons, when installing diving boards, regardless of the height of the board, rails should be extended further out over the water and additional railings should be installed to minimize the gaps on either side of the board. Finally, for diving boards and towers three-meters in height or greater, stairways with landings should be installed instead of vertical ladders.

Figure 23.3
NCAA Pool Dimensions and Equipment Requirements

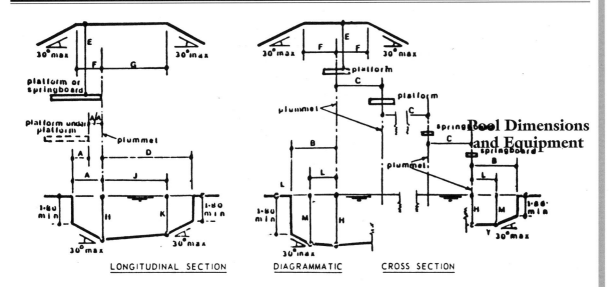

LONGITUDINAL SECTION   DIAGRAMMATIC   CROSS SECTION

NCAA Dimensions for Diving Facilities		Dimensions are in Feet	SPRINGBOARD		PLATFORM		
			1 Metre	3 Metres	5 Metres	7.5 Metres	10 Metres
		LENGTH	16'	16'	20'	20'	20'
		WIDTH	1'8"	1'8"	5'	5'	6'7"
		HEIGHT	3'4"	10'	16'5"	24'8"	32'10"
Revised to 1st Jan. 1987			Horiz. Vert.	Horiz. Vert.	Horiz. Vert.	Horiz. Vert.	Horiz. Vert.
A	From plummet BACK TO POOL WALL	Designation	A-1	A-3	A-5	A-7.5	A-10
		Minimum	6'	6'	4'2"	5'	5'
AA	From plummet BACK TO PLATFORM plummet directly below	Designation			AA5/1	AA7.5/3/1	AA10/5/3/1
		Minimum			5'	5'	5'
B	From plummet to POOL WALL AT SIDE	Designation	B-1	B-3	B-5	B-7.5	B-10
		Minimum	8'3"	11'6"	14'	14'10"	17'3"
C	From plummet to ADJACENT PLUMMET	Designation	C-1/1	C-3/3/1	C-5/3/1	C-7.5/5/3/1	C-10/7.5/5/3/1
		Minimum	8'	8'6"	8'6"	8'6"	9'
D	From plummet to POOL WALL AHEAD	Designation	D-1	D-3	D-5	D-7.5	D-10
		Minimum	29'	34'	34'	36'	45'
E	On plummet, from BOARD TO CEILING	Designation	E-1	E-3	E-5	E-7.5	E-10
		Minimum	16'5"	16'5"	11'6"	11'6"	16'5"
F	CLEAR OVERHEAD behind and each side of plummet	Designation	F-1 E-1	F-3 E-3	F-5 E-5	F-7.5 E-7.5	F-10 E-10
		Minimum	8'3" 16'6"	8'3" 16'6"	9' 11'6"	9' 11'6"	9' 16'6"
G	CLEAR OVERHEAD ahead of plummet	Designation	G-1 E-1	G-3 E-3	G-5 E-5	G-7.5 E-7.5	G-10 E-10
		Minimum	16'5" 16'5"	16'5" 16'5"	16'5" 11'6"	16'5" 11'6"	19'8" 16'5"
H	DEPTH OF WATER at plummet	Designation	H-1	H-3	H-5	H-7.5	H-10
		Minimum	11'	12'	14'2"	15'	16'
J-K	DISTANCE AND DEPTH ahead of plummet	Designation	J-1 K-1	J-3 K-3	J-5 K-5	J-7.5 K-7.5	J-10 K-10
		Minimum	16'5" 11'8"	20' 12'2"	20' 12'10"	26'3" 14'6"	36'2" 15'6"
L-M	DISTANCE AND DEPTH each side of plummet	Designation	L-1 M-1	L-3 M-3	L-5 M-5	L-7.5 M-7.5	L-10 M-10
		Minimum	5' 11'2"	6'7" 12'2"	14' 12'10"	14'10" 14'6"	17'2" 15'6"
N	MAXIMUM SLOPE TO REDUCE DIMENSIONS beyond full requirements	Pool depth	30 degrees		NOTE: Dimensions C (plummet to adjacent plummet) apply for Platforms with widths as detailed. For wider Platform increase C by half the additional width(s).		
		Ceiling Ht	30 degrees				

Vertical ladders, whether used to climb onto a diving board or into a lifeguard chair, have no place in the wet environment found in aquatic facilities. Of course, the diving section of the pool vessel should meet all depth and distance requirements by the governing competitive body (e.g., NCAA, YMCA, U.S. Diving, etc.). More on safe sport diving can be found in the U.S. Diving position paper.

Pool Decks

Perhaps more than any other feature, the spaciousness of the pool deck makes the facility user-friendly; the larger the pool deck, the more comfortable the user groups are in the facility. As one might expect, the larger the pool deck, the more costly construction is, because the footprint of the entire building is necessarily enlarged as the width of the deck grows. However, a large deck provides smooth pedestrian traffic flow for large events such as swimming meets and reduces conflicts. A large swimming pool deck would be one approximately 20 feet in width or greater. A deck width of 10 feet or less would be considered too narrow and anywhere within 10 feet of the swimming pool walls should be considered the "wet zone."

Notes

Of course, all swimming pool decks must be nonslip, and with tile decks, the size of the tile often determines the slipperiness of the deck; the smaller the tile, the more nonslip the surface should be. The grout between the tiles makes the tile nonslip by removing water off the surface of the tile so that the foot cannot hydroplane. One-by-one inch tiles provide the best nonslip surface followed by two-by-two inch tiles. Both of these mosaic tile sizes come with 7.5 abrasiveness for greater nonslip surface. As the tiles of the surface become larger, the likelihood of slippage is increased. Larger European tiles that have patterned and textured surfaces may also be used successfully.

Coefficients of friction that rate nonslip surfaces can be very misleading in swimming pool environments. Tiled decks are perhaps the most desirous deck surface at indoor aquatic facilities but, not surprisingly, they are by far the most expensive.

Other pool deck materials include: brick, brushed concrete, pebble finish, stone, pavers, wood, painted decks, and epoxy-coated decks. All of these finishes have potential problems and should be

Figure 23.4
Bulkhead Diagram

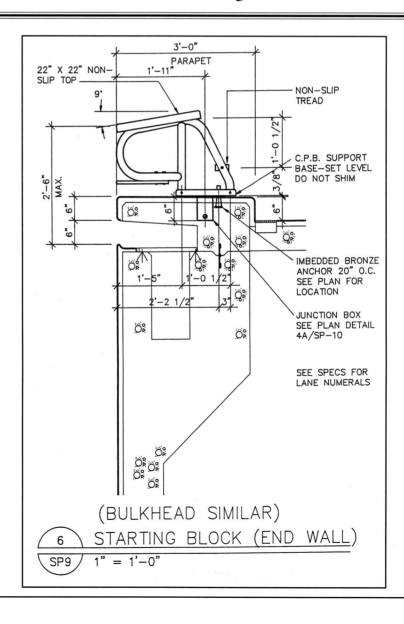

analyzed by an expert before purchasing. Whenever considering alternatives to tile, inspecting other deck surfaces already in place at other aquatic facilities is a must. Do not use carpeting or other fabric floor finishes in wet areas of aquatic facilities; they harbor moisture and thus produce mold, mildew, bacteria, and other undesirables. Large, tile depth markers and "No Diving" warnings embedded into the pool deck must also be non-slip but often, are not.

Efficient deck drainage and properly placed drains can make or break the cleanliness, upkeep, and slipperiness of a swimming pool deck. A growing trend is to install a continuous trench deck drain that completely encircles the pool perimeter. This typically provides better drainage than intermittent drains placed at various locations; however, the trench must be sufficiently wide (four to six inches) to collect water efficiently and allow for easy cleaning. Plus, the deck itself must be sufficiently sloped to the drain. Too many perimeter trench trains are too narrow to function properly. Slot deck drains placed too close to the side of the pool will allow dirty deck water to wash into the pool gutters and end up in the swimming pool water during cleaning operations and may contaminate the clean pool water. Area drains with the decks sloping to the intermittent drains are still used and may be more economical than slot drains for low budget projects; however, the deck must be warped four ways rather than two for good drainage. Widely varying deck widths may require area drains or multiple trench drains.

Lighting

A crucial consideration for indoor aquatic facilities is lighting. When it comes to illumination, competitive facilities have stricter lighting requirements than recreational facilities. For highly competitive facilities (those holding large championship meets), the NCAA and USA Swimming national governing bodies require 125 to 150- foot candles at water level for their televised events.

These levels provide good uniform lighting and color-value illumination at the deck and water surface. For mixed-use facilities, that are competitive/recreational facilities, a minimum average of 60-foot candles at water level is highly

recommended. To conserve energy, the ability to change from recreational to competitive levels is also recommended. For purely recreational facilities, 30-foot candles may be sufficient. It should be emphasized that the brightness of bulbs diminishes quickly (around 20%); therefore, regular maintenance and re-lamping should be established and scheduled. Changing from competitive to recreational levels may be accomplished easily and economically through separate circuiting or using dimmers.

When researching lighting requirements for aquatic facilities it may be best to contact the lighting experts with experience in your

lighting requirements, such as the Engineering Electrical Society of North America located in New York. The NCAA, USA Swimming, and U.S. Diving have written specifications for lighting for hosting events. It would be wise to contact them as well.

Lamp replacement in an indoor aquatic facility can be challenging to say the least, particularly if not properly planned for in the design phase. Although lighting fixtures are usually placed above the pool deck rather than the over the water in the pool, there is a good reason for that. Lighting fixtures strategically placed above the pool deck allow for a high-reach bucket to drive around the deck to change the lamps. When the lights are located directly over the water, catwalks suspended from the ceiling are expensive but make the changing of bulbs easy. Lowering the lights on cables also works well, but even stainless steel cables will need to be replaced every 10 years due to corrosion. Unfortunately, there have been too many aquatic facilities constructed in North America without a practical or affordable way of changing light bulbs. All light bulbs lose their brilliance quickly and should be changed at least once a year, if not sooner.

Although architects and swimmers alike love windows and skylights that allow ambient light to enter the facilities and liven up the facility, this concept is nearly taboo in serious competitive pools. If windows are a must, every precaution must be made not to allow direct sunlight and glare to hit the competition portion of the pools.

Windows in competitive pools also promotes glare on the water, creating difficulties for competitive swimmers, spectators, and lifeguards. To the contrary, even competitive swimmers like lots of bright, natural light, which seems to keep them happier and thereby working longer and harder. Further, recreational type leisure pool facilities successfully use an abundance of glass and windows not only to allow sunlight in, but also to give views of the surrounding areas.

Whenever windows are plan- ned for an indoor aquatic facility, algae growth is more likely to occur; glare on the surface of the water could become a safety problem for lifeguards. With the use of video cameras and computers, drowning detection systems can now be affordably purchased and installed. This technology allows lifeguards to see the bottom clearly and automatically detect near-drowning victims quickly. This, of course, helps to minimize any surface glare issues.

Skylights are generally advantageous. They provide light from above with little glare if manufactured and installed properly.

Underwater lights are another issue. When there is surface glare on the water many architects recommend underwater lighting to illuminate the bottom of the pool. For safety reasons, it is also thought that these lights will illuminate any objects or humans that may be located underwater but obscured by glare adversely affecting the lifeguard's vision of the bottom. Others suggest underwater lighting simply for aesthetics. The truth is, when underwater lights are installed in a new aquatic facility, they are rarely if ever used and, to make matters worse, often leak and malfunction as well. Conversely, some high-end facilities that use underwater cameras may need underwater lights to enhance the quality of the underwater video. While underwater lights may sound like a good idea, it would be wise to consider whether the benefits outweigh the cost and maintenance problems.

Interior Finishes

Like deck surfaces, the most versatile interior finish for the pool vessel is tile, but plaster is the most popular pool finish, particularly when it comes to concrete pools. Not surprisingly, tile is also the most expensive. Plastered pools are often referred to as marbledust, Marcite®, and Marblelite®. Unlike a tiled pool, which lasts indefinitely, plaster pools are often replastered every 8 to 10 years. A good combination is to tile gutter edges at the water lines and racing lanes with contrasting colored tiles, usually blue or black tiles, while the majority of the interior surface is plastered white. This is one compromise that saves a significant sum of money.

Regardless of the type of finish used in the aquatic facility, it should be white or light in color to help surveillance of the bottom, particularly by lifeguards. White floors are preferable in competition and leisure pools but diving pools need a darker floor like navy blue. This is important for diver safety, allowing the diver to find the water better with a darker finish. The navy bottom should be contrasted with a white ceiling and white walls so the diver can tell the difference while spinning at a high rate of speed. Other finishes include epoxy and chlorinated rubber-based paints, vinyl-lined, and stainless steel coated with epoxy.

A relatively new trend in pool construction, especially for those interested in traditional competitive pools, is pre-engineered modular swimming pools that combine stainless steel construction with polyvinyl chloride (PVC) membranes to construct on-ground competitive pools that do not require extensive excavation and may cost less for temporary uses. Another advantage of stainless steel pools is that the pool walls may also be buried in the ground or have basement spaces around them like concrete pools. These types of pools have even been constructed for the major aquatic events such as World Championships and Olympic Games and then have been sold and moved afterwards.

Movable Floors

Competitive swimming and diving facilities require fast water, which means deeper water. Recreational and therapeutic activities require shallow water. This conflict can be rectified with the design and installation of a movable floor. Movable or "false" floors allow for maximum flexibility in aquatic programming. The floors are capable of moving from seven to nine feet deep for competition to zero depth and anywhere in between for other aquatic activities such as therapy, aquacize, shallow water jogging, and even for dry-land activities like aerobics or yoga. There are different types of movable floor designs in both the material the floor is made of and the system that adjusts the floor depth. Floors are generally made of concrete, metal, or polymer type material coming in various sizes. Movement of the floor is accomplished in a number of ways but most common are hydraulically powered with one or more hydraulic lifts located underneath the floor. Another method uses scissor jacks located beneath the floor with the motors located outside the pool wall. Other methods include externally mounted motors or hydraulic arms with pulleys and cables moving the floor.

Air Quality Considerations

One of the greatest challenges when planning an indoor aquatic facility is handling and providing healthy air. Even the best managed pools can produce chloramines and when this does happen, as it often does particularly in heavily used pools, a good air-handling system needs to rid the building quickly of the noxious odors. While good water chemistry, frequent filter turnovers, volcanic ash in the filters, ozone, ultraviolet (UV) light, granulated activated carbon filters, and regular shocking and super-chlorination can all be used to help rid an aquatic facility of chloramines, there is no substitute for good ventilation. Energy efficient air handling systems that became popular in the mid-1970s and continue to be installed today, while saving significant sums of money due to conservation, recycle bad air and contribute to asthma.

Regardless of what ventilation system is selected for indoor aquatic facilities, it is imperative that the system be able to deliver 100% fresh air whenever necessary to purge the facility of bad, chloramine-laden air. A good air-handling system is even more important for indoor leisure pools where the patron load is higher. Although there are numerous recommended ventilation rates varying from two cubic feet per minute (cfm) per square foot of total natatorium floor area in a modestly used traditional pool to 10 cfm per square foot in a heavily used leisure pool, often these figures are simply too conservative, and poor air quality is the result. Likewise, fresh air requirements like 25 to 35 cfm fresh outside air per person may again be insufficient for good air quality. The important message here for those planning new indoor aquatic facilities is to hire a good, reputable heating, ventilating, and air-conditioning (HVAC) consultant who specializes in indoor pool ventilation.

HVAC systems are essential elements that are vitally important to the success of the facility. Higher water temperatures (85 to 90° F) also mean higher evaporation rates, higher bacteriological activity, higher heat loss, and, if not properly exhausted, poor air quality, leading to adverse health affects to both staff and patrons. For heavily used indoor aquatic facilities, the American Society of Heating, Refrigerating and Air-Conditioning Engineers, Inc. (ASHRAE) standards may not be adequate and should be surpassed whenever possible. Indoor aquatic facilities should also be designed to keep a negative pressure inside the building by exhausting slightly more air than is supplied. When this is done, moisture and odor migration to other portions of the building will be kept to a minimum.

The lowest initial cost systems are designed with 100% outside air using rooftop units. Typically, this type of design does not have good energy performance, because the units must operate on 100% outside air all the time. No air can be returned through the units because they have little or no protection against the natatorium environment. This system provides high indoor air quality at low initial cost with higher operating costs. For projects in some climates, this type of design may be reasonable.

Higher cost units with stainless steel construction or coated steel have been used successfully on some projects. In this case, a portion of the air is exhausted and a portion returned through the unit, approximately 50%. The outside air is used to reduce humidity, so large volumes for ventilation and outside air are required. In most climates, air conditioning is also required. These units must also have the capability to provide 100% outside air when superchlorination is being performed or when high swimmer loads occur, such as large swim meets. These units provide excellent air quality, low initial cost, and higher operating cost.

While expensive, the use of mechanical dehumidification systems is an efficient way to manage humidity and contribute to better air quality and potentially may be an energy-saving tactic. These systems also afford great opportunities for heating pool water with waste heat extracted in the dehumidification process. Airside economizer HVAC equipment is often used. This allows cool outside air to be brought into the building, when temperatures allow, rather than mechanically conditioning the air.

These units are built to withstand the natatorium air but are costly, complex and have more frequent maintenance problems than the simpler units. The manufacturers usually recommend four or five air changes per hour and 15 to 25% outside air. We know from experience that they have taken care of the humidity and condensation problems very well, especially in lap or competition pool installations. However, their record is imperfect in leisure pool projects.

What should be the first priority in any indoor aquatic facility, indoor air quality, has often been neglected.

Using the criteria of six air changes per hour and 30 percent minimum outside air, these units will work in the natatorium but are expensive. If this is the design approach taken by the mechanical engineer, a minimum of two units is recommended. When one unit is disabled, the natatorium may keep operating with partial HVAC capability. Many operators who have had units down for replacement of circuit boards or compressors were thankful they could keep operating because they had two units.

There are two main approaches to supply and return air ducts: supply low and return high or supply high and return low. Both systems have their advantages and will work. Most projects use a design that supplies high and returns or exhausts low because the chlorinated air just above the water surface has the worst air quality of anywhere in the natatorium. Taking a large portion of the exhaust or return air from this level ensures that the poor air quality at this level will be diluted. Other approaches will work. Ducts set part way up the walls is a variation of the high supply approach. It is critical that the circulation of air through the space is complete and not short-circuited as happens when the supply and return are both high. Unfortunately, to have good air quality in a heavily used, highly competitive pool, large volumes of air must be moved across the surface of the water at the expense of swimmer comfort.

When it comes to air-handling ducts, aluminum spiral ducts are recommended. Galvanized ducts will work but run the risk of rust stains at screw holes where the galvanizing is compromised. Stainless steel and fiberglass ducts cost a premium and may not be as desirable as aluminum. All metallic ducts should be coated with Tnemec's high build epoxy coatings. Stainless steel will pit and corrode if not coated. Another cost-saving alternative is fabric ducts. Fabric ducts reduce the risk of rust or corrosion without the cost premium.

In the design of the air supply ducts, caution needs to be exercised to avoid blowing air at a velocity that would chill bathers on the pool deck. Usually the velocity of the air across the deck should be below 25 feet per minute. Although conventional wisdom avoids directing air flow on the water to reduce evaporation, it improves air quality to direct air onto the water to move the poorer quality air on the surface into the return air stream.

Too often during the recent past, many natatoriums have been designed with inadequate heating and ventilating systems. If the designs for these systems are based on code minimums or other industry guidelines like ASHRAE standards, indoor pools are almost guaranteed to have air quality problems. The solution to these problems is to provide supplemental water treatment and to increase the amounts of outside air into the facility. A variety of equipment can work successfully at different levels of project budgets.

Filtration

Recently, there have been advances in swimming pool filtration that improve not only water clarity but air quality as well. While sand has been the most popular swimming pool filtration medium for decades, diatomaceous earth, recycled glass, volcanic ash (zeolite), and other filter media are now becoming more common. Regardless of the type of filter medium, both the size of the filter bed and the flow of water through the medium are extremely important. Basically, the larger the filter bed and the slower the water flow through it, the better the entrapment of particular matter, therefore, the cleaner and clearer the water.

While there are many types of swimming pool filtration systems available, basically there are variations of three filter media: sand, diatomaceous earth (DE), and cartridge. In summary, sand is the most popular because it is the easiest to maintain and operate while producing good water clarity. By way of comparison, DE offers excellent water clarity but is more labor intensive to run. Finally, cartridge filtration saves much water during the filter cleaning process and offers outstanding water clarity, but the cartridges need to be replaced often. Cartridge filtration is perhaps best suited for small volume pools and spas. For more in-depth analysis of the advantages and disadvantages of specific filter types and applications, refer to any Aquatic Facility Operator (AFO) Manual, the Certified Park Operator (CPO) Manual, or the *Complete Swimming Pool Reference* also published by Sagamore Publishing.

The turnover rater is the time it takes the entire volume of water in the pool to circulate through the filters and return back to the pool vessel. Turnover rates are also improving (getting faster). While the recommended turnover rates for traditional pools during the '50s, '60s, and '70s was eight hours, facilities are now turning over in six hours or less. Leisure pools, flumes,

and slides have incredibly fast turnovers of one to two hours. In essence, the more heavily used a vessel will be, the faster the turnovers, and smaller volume vessels typically need faster turnovers than larger vessels.

Returning the water from the pool vessel back to filters can be accomplished through a variety of surface skimmers and gutters and bottom outlets. First and foremost, every vessel recirculating water must have a minimum of two bottom outlets that are protected with anti-vortex covers and have a flow rate of six feet per second or less. Some jurisdictions now require flow rates of five feet per second.

Single bottom outlets and covers that can come off or are not protected by anti-vortex covers can entrap unsuspecting victims at the bottom. Worse yet, children sitting on unprotected drains in shallow water pools can be quickly eviscerated. Lawsuits in this regard can approach $35 million dollar settlements. It pays to do the research to ensure that every swimming or soaking vessel has a minimum of two protected bottom outlets.

Surface collection systems are also important. When designing an aquatic facility, choosing between skimmers, recessed gutter, and deck level gutter can appear to be a daunting task. Skimmers work fairly well in collecting surface water and are relatively inexpensive to install.

On the other hand, gutters are much better collectors of surface water and make for much faster competitive pools but, naturally, are more expensive to install. When building highly competitive pools, the choice becomes whether to choose a recessed gutter below deck level or a deck level gutter system. Most very fast competitive pools side with big, deep recessed gutters while pools that have recreational aspects in addition to competitive venues often consider deck level gutters for easier and safer ingress and egress.

Water Chemistry

Although chlorine has been the standard for pool water treatment in the United States, alternative sanitizers used in Europe and Canada are now challenging the use of chlorine in this country. Before considering alternatives to chlorines, readers should consider why chlorine has been so popular in the United States. Although it does have some disadvantages, chlorine is perhaps the only swimming pool sanitizer that 1) provides excellent oxidation, 2) sanitizes well, and 3) has residual properties, meaning it lasts for longer periods of time in the water. Among the challengers to chlorine, perhaps of most importance, is ozone. Ozone is a particularly strong oxidizer that oxidizes pool water better than chlorine without the bleaching and smell that characterizes many chlorinated pools. In order to provide sufficient levels of ozone for pool use, very large and expensive ozone generator plants are required on site and the corona discharge method of producing ozone is much preferred in large aquatic facilities rather than other methods such as UV light production. Ozone does not have residual properties however, so in this country, a residual chemical like bromine or chlorine must be added in low levels.

Especially in large aquatic facilities, other alternatives to chlorine have not been as successful as ozone or chlorine. UV light also shows great promise in supplementing traditional chlorination in swimming pools. UV light has been used successfully in Europe and is just recently becoming more popular in the United States. When anticipating large numbers in the pool and chloramines may be a problem, the use of UV light should also be researched.

Chlorine generation that produces chlorine at the aquatic facility with a combination of salt water and electrolytic cells also shows potential without purchasing and transporting hazardous pool chemicals to the site. It should also be mentioned here with worldwide terrorism on the rise, safe purchasing, transporting, handling, and storing pool chemicals is becoming more of a concern.

Automation

Automation of pool chemical applications and filtration is no longer a concept for future consideration. Automation saves time, money, and keeps the pool water in a much better condition and is a requirement for today's pools. Pool water is sampled and analyzed electronically by a microprocessor.

Once the pool operator has established two set points (pH & chlorine), the electronic analysis is compared to those base levels. When the analyzer samples the pool water from a sample stream that bypasses much of the recirculation system, it compares the result of the set point for the desired level. When the pH or chlorine reads low, the analyzer prompts the feed pumps to add the appropriate chemical to raise it to the appropriate level. Modern automatic water chemistry analyzers can provide for remote readouts, meaning that the pool operator can read the chemical levels in his office or even while at home through computer modem or even by telephone. The analyzers also keep wonderful records of chemical readings with dates and time to help better maintain the water as well as defend in lawsuits.

Heating

A major cost and consideration for all pools, but particularly outdoor pools subjected to winds, is heating the pool water. While the conventional way to heat both indoor and outdoor pools has been with natural or propane gas, the growing trend for larger facilities is combining energy saving solar heating systems with traditional gas heating systems used to supplement the solar. The traditional gas heating system is desirable when environmental conditions (clouds) do not allow for adequate production of solar heat. The challenge of this combination heating system is to optimize the solar system while relying on the gas system only when absolutely necessary.

Dual gas/solar heating systems will save energy costs as well as extend the season for outdoor pools. The solar source is clean, renewable, and free. Another challenge is the placement of solar panels, which should be a reasonable distance from the equipment room but should not require an overabundance of space. For an outdoor pool, the total area of the solar collectors should equal the approximate pool surface area. When designed correctly, solar/gas systems can save 30 to 50% in heating costs.

Planning the Leisure Pool Facility

The advent of leisure aquatics in the United States originated in the late 1980s as European-inspired pools were built in Western Canada and Oregon. From there they have spread to all parts of North America. The leisure pool differs from traditional American pools in its free-form shape, shallow water, warmer temperature, and water features. American pools were rectangular, deeper, cooler, and usually devoid of recreational features to suit competitive swimming and aquatic instruction.

When planning indoor leisure pools, the primary focus is on the social aspects of recreational swimming. There should be benches and games areas in the water, beach, or zero depth entries, waterfalls, lazy rivers, vortexes, whirlpool spas, and seating areas around the pool. In municipal aquatic centers, there are interactive water features, water slides, kid's slides, floating water features, and other possible attractions. These are not usually present in university leisure pools.

Outdoor Leisure Pools

The first outdoor leisure pools in the United States were pools designed by Carl Fuerst and Claude Rogers that were similar to wave pools without the wave action. Over time, these pools evolved to include many more features as listed above. When planning a municipal facility, aquatic consultants have developed proprietary formulas to determine a recommended size of bather capacity for communities of different sizes.

In broad terms, smaller communities of up to 5,000 people build outdoor leisure pools of a size based more on cost than on the popula-

tion to be served. Often the limits of construction cost are in the $1 to $2 million range with pools of 5,000 to 8,000 square feet. Pools for communities of up to 15,000 people often are in the $2 to 3.5 million range with areas of 7,000 to 13,000 square feet. Larger communities often build similar-sized pools at multiple locations; however, cost recovery will usually be better if a larger single facility is built rather than multiple smaller facilities. Pools of 15,000 to 24,000 square feet with budgets of $4.5 to $9.5 million usually achieve a positive cash flow if the population is sufficient in size and the facility is designed for market conditions and managed properly.

Every community does not have the goal of 100% cost recovery or positive cash flow. For those that do have these goals, it is important to do a market analysis, design for the market, advertise and market the facility aggressively, and manage the facility as a business enterprise with service-oriented staff. Even the best-managed and marketed aquatic facilities have a difficult time turning a profit.

Elements of facility planning include the following: changing facility, swimming pool, pool deck with drainage, sun turf and landscaping, parking, security fencing, and mechanical building.

The changing facility combines the functions of admission, bather changing, food service, facility administration, storage, and program registration. It may also include maintenance and pool equipment operations, which are often located in a separate building on the site. The building usually requires 4,000 to 5,000 square feet to include all of the above functions, including pool equipment. For larger pools, the bathhouse may have a space requirement of 5,500 to 6,500 square feet. Architects for this type of building have designed many different layouts. Some utilize an open area for admissions between bather changing rooms; others use an enclosed area with changing rooms on one side and program registration on the other; still others utilize a multiple pod approach to the buildings.

Particular attention should be paid to concessions spaces so that short travel to food and beverage equipment allows efficiency in operations. A consultant who specializes in selecting menu items and planning food service areas is a valuable member of the design team in addition to the architect and aquatics consultant. Including an area for temporary trash bag storage behind a low exterior wall allows staff to wait until a more convenient time for a trip to the trash disposal unit.

While the importance of the design of the swimming pool cannot be minimized, the deck areas, sun turf, concessions seating area, sand play areas, shade pavilions, and landscaping areas are also very important to the success of the facility. These amenities create highly aesthetic areas that attract bathers and reduce congestion in the swimming pool.

The swimming pool deck is usually constructed of concrete. In high heat southern regions, coating systems may be required to lower deck temperatures. These require maintenance and recoating and, therefore, should be avoided unless absolutely necessary. The drainage of the deck-to-deck drains is very important.

Planning the location of decks for the best solar orientation through the morning, afternoon, and evening is very important. Bathers will often move or locate their chaise lounges for a more perpendicular angle to the sun. For this reason, a circular deck pattern centered on the shallow end of the pool or zero depth area is a beneficial design. Locating the changing facility north of the zero depth area is the best solar orientation.

A lap area of six to eight lanes for competitive swimming, instruction, fitness lap swimming, open recreation, and games should be considered for most facilities. Where other pools of this type exist nearby, it is not always necessary to duplicate lanes.

A waterslide of 150 to 160 linear feet of flume should be provided for most leisure pools. For large facilities over 12,000 square feet, longer flume runs and multiple flumes should be considered. A body slide should usually be provided for the first slide. After that basic type of slide, an enclosed flume or tube slide may be considered. Tube slides will serve a larger capacity of bathers per hour. The aquatic consultant will therefore recommend the types of slides for different areas of the pool. For example, a long lazy river may include one or two tube slides that have a plunge pool feeding the tubes into the river.

Lazy rivers are recommended to be at least 1,000 linear feet in length and 15 feet in width. These may be reduced to 10 to 12 feet in width to meet budget limitations; however, they are not an ideal size.

Notes

Lazy rivers may vary from 500 to 1,500 or more linear feet. For facilities that cannot afford to build a lazy river in their initial development, they offer an option for expansion that can double the capacity of the facility.

Water features are important for the leisure pool in adding excitement, interactivity and theming. There are trends in municipal pools toward increasing use of theming, "dumping buckets," and expandable water features.

Parking requirements for outdoor swimming pools may be dictated by local ordinances. Where these are not specific, the facility designers may be able to negotiate a parking requirement equal to one car for every four bathers. This number recognizes that families come in groups to this type of swimming pool and that other bathers arrive by bicycle or are dropped off.

Indoor Leisure Pools

Indoor leisure pools in the United States are more directly descended from European and Canadian leisure pools than American outdoor leisure pools. They are usually 3,000 square feet to 8,000 square feet in size in municipal facilities. University leisure pools are usually smaller than their municipal counterparts.

For indoor facilities, budgets more frequently determine the size of the pool than does programming or community population. For large community recreation centers of 70,000 to 130,000 square feet, the leisure pool should be 5,500 to 8,500 square feet with an eight lane

by 25 yard lap pool and a whirlpool. This would require a natatorium of 15,000 to 25,000 square feet. Because of the need for other recreational facilities other than aquatics, it usually is necessary to restrict the aquatics in some way for a better-balanced center. This may require the lap pool to be a six lane by 25 yard pool and the leisure pool to be 4,000 to 4,800 square feet with a total natatorium area of 14,000 to 17,000 square feet. This is unfortunate since the pools will be overcrowded.

Smaller recreation centers and private facilities (e.g., YMCAs, JCCs, and health clubs) may be built in the 50,000 to 80,000 square feet size. These may increase attendance and membership with smaller leisure pools in the 3,000 to 4,500 square feet size. Their natatoria often include a six-lane lap pool and whirlpool with a total area of 12,000 to 15,000 square feet.

The use of separation walls between lap pools and leisure pools is beneficial to allow swim meets with little inconvenience to recreational swimmers. The wall will increase the deck area required and cost a significant amount in construction dollars; therefore, communities need to consider the costs and benefits very seriously before deciding to include this feature.

Trends for indoor leisure pools include theming, lazy rivers, "dumping buckets", expandability of water features, multiple pools based on water temperatures (i.e., lap, leisure, and spa), waterslide flumes running outside of buildings, and the use of UV light to eliminate chloramines.

Leisure pools have specific core components of zero depth or beach areas, interactive water features, lazy rivers, and waterslides. Other optional components include lap areas for water walking, games, warm water aerobics, and instruction; vortex area that spins bathers in a circle; bubble benches; drop slides; lily pad walks; kid's slides; and rope swings.

The aesthetic environment of leisure pools can be greatly enhanced by designing vertical elements into the space such as trees, decorative fencing, and light poles.

Safety Considerations

Whenever constructing a new aquatic facility or renovating an old one, planners must consider the latest safety technology. First and foremost, it is important to understand that we now have highly sophisticated drowning detection systems that not only save lives, but defend facilities against lawsuits. While we have depended on lifeguards solely for nearly the past century, the sad fact is that hundreds of guests drown in guarded facilities each year. We can no longer afford to rely upon lifeguards alone to protect the swimming public; computerized video systems are now available to alert the staff when a victim ends up on the bottom within 10 seconds. These computerized video systems help to overcome

traditional problems of poor supervision such as lack of vigilance; distractions; and seeing through surface reflections, refractions, and glare. In addition, the latest research in the area of perceptual blindness (change blindness, inattentional blindness) explains why lifeguards, pilots, and car drivers often miss the obvious leading to catastrophic accidents and injuries. The latest technology is so sophisticated it can alert lifeguards of suspicious situations under the surface of the water and detect potential drownees, thereby saving lives as well as reducing liability. Having a real-time video recording of an actual near-drowning situation goes a long way in defending against a lawsuit. Although some aquatic professionals consider these systems expensive, compared to the total cost of a facility, they are actually very affordable. Plus, if they save one life, they become extremely cost effective and they are inexpensive compared to the cost of a lawsuit.

Lifeguard Stations

Another new trend in lifeguarding is the replacing of tall, narrow, permanent lifeguard chairs installed in the pool deck with wider, lower, portable lifeguard stations that promote standing and patrolling while on duty. These stations are not only portable, but because they have eliminated the ladder on the back of the chair, the lifeguard station has been made safer. It also encourages movement, thereby increasing attention and concentration while reducing boredom. Older, traditional pools have tall, permanent lifeguard chairs installed right into the pool deck which cannot be removed and often create a climbing hazard for lifeguards.

5/30 Model of Aquatic Accountability

In order to keep lifeguards vigilant and focused on-task while on-duty, the 5/30 model of accountability comes highly recommended. The "five" in this formula represents the Five-Minute Scanning Strategy for the lifeguards, meaning that they are required to move and make an accounting statement or safety check every five minutes while on duty to increase attention, concentration, and safety. The "30" refers to a management check of the lifeguards and the facility every half hour by someone in a management position at the facility. Actually walking through the facility rather

Griffs Guard Stations.

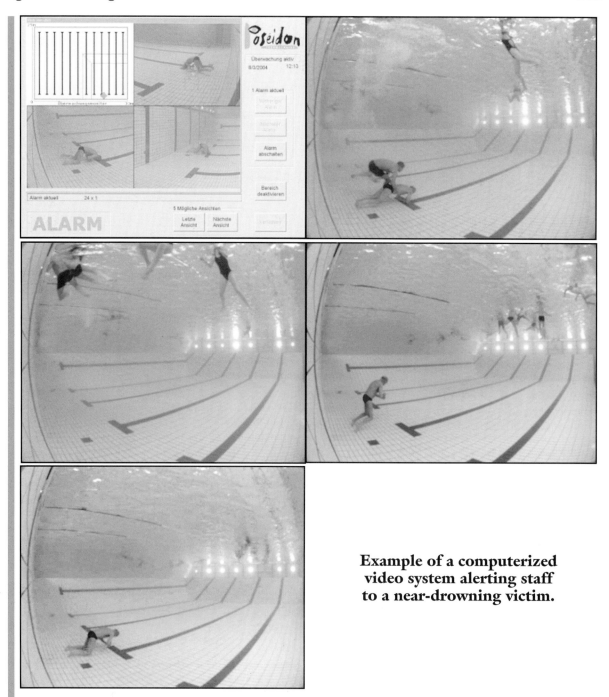

Example of a computerized video system alerting staff to a near-drowning victim.

than supervising from afar best accomplishes the management check. Some claim that when the 5/30 model is mandated at the facility, it reduces actual water rescues by 50% or more.

Automated External Defibrillators and Oxygen

Automated external defibrillators (AEDs) are now considered the standard of care in recreational and athletic facilities including aquatic facilities. The use of AEDs requires so much more than simply purchasing the machines. Comprehensive training is also required of the staff along with appropriate signage and usage protocols in the facility. The administration of oxygen should also be available at all aquatic facilities. Likewise, oxygen not only requires additional equipment but additional training for the lifeguard staff. The use of both AEDs and oxygen can significantly aid in the favorable resuscitation of near drowning victims.

Summary

It is hoped that this short chapter has stimulated the reader to try to investigate the possibilities that exist with today's new technologies in swimming pool design and construction. It should be remembered that many of the swimming pools we learned to swim in are now antiquated and would not be as inviting to today's swimming public. The new trends in aquatic facility planning today will make your facility both safer and more user-friendly. Lastly, visiting as many new aquatic facilities as possible with a note-pad and video camera will greatly enhance the planning of your facility.

Playgrounds

Donna Thompson and Susan Hudson

Playgrounds are an essential part of children's play. These play sites can be found in a variety of settings, including public parks, schools, child care centers, apartment complexes, churches, and commercial establishments. Whatever their settings, all playgrounds should have certain things in common. These include

- the fostering of a child's physical, emotional, social, and intellectual development; and
- the provision of age-appropriate equipment to meet children's needs.

The use of the word *playgrounds* for this chapter refers to designated areas where stationary and manipulative play equipment is located to facilitate a child's physical, emotional, social, and intellectual development. These areas employ

- the use of proper surfacing under and around equipment,
- the placement of equipment that allows for easy supervision by adults, and
- the regular maintenance of the equipment and the environment.

This chapter will review trends in playground design; general planning considerations; specific planning steps; installation of the equipment and the surfacing; and ongoing maintenance, repair, and inspection procedures.

Learning Objectives

After reading this chapter, the student should be able to

- identify key terms in relation to playground design,
- recognize the national guidelines and standards in playground design,
- understand general planning considerations for playground design,
- identify specific planning steps in a planning a playground,
- understand the procedures for installing playground equipment and surfacing, and
- recognize procedures for maintaining, repairing, and inspecting playground equipment and surfacing.

General Planning Considerations

Playground Guidelines and Standards

During the 1970s, in response to consumer interest and complaints, the United States Consumer Product Safety Commission (CPSC) initiated a process to develop safety guidelines for playgrounds. The first guidelines were produced in 1981. The guidelines came in two handbooks—one designed to give general information to the public, the other to give technical assistance to the manufacturers of playground equipment. These guidelines were revised in 1991 and merged into one handbook for use by the public. In 1988, the American Society for Testing and Materials (ASTM) accepted responsibility for creating a standard based on the refinement of the technical specifications for playground equipment. The CPSC has maintained its involvement with the technical standards for public use by assisting the ASTM with further development and refinement of these specifications. As a result of these efforts, the first voluntary standard for the playground industry was developed in 1993. This standard, known as F-1487-93 (Standard Consumer Safety Performance Specification for Playground Equipment for Public Use), provided technical specifications for playground equipment, use zones, prevention of entrapments, and maintenance. The standard was revised in 1995, 1997, and 2001. A surfacing standard was created in 1991 (F-1292-91). This standard provides for the testing of the impact attenuation of playground surfacing. Specifically, it provides the methodology to assess the amount of surfacing necessary under and around playground equipment to prevent fatal head injuries of children who may fall to the surface off the equipment. This standard has been revised four times (1993, 1995, 1996, and 2004).

Both the ASTM standards and the CPSC guidelines (which were revised again in 1994 and 1997) have been instrumental in creating safer play environments for children by providing design criteria for surfacing and equipment. Together, they are essential documents needed for designing playgrounds.

A third guideline now influencing the playground design comes from the United States Access Board. In November 2000, the U.S. Justice Department published the Access Board's guidelines regarding the interpretation of the Americans With Disabilities Act (ADA) and public playgrounds. These guidelines address issues of accessibility to and from play equipment as well as the use of the play equipment by children with disabilities. All new public playgrounds, including those found in schools and community parks, should conform to these guidelines. If major renovation is done on existing playgrounds, then they also need to comply with the guidelines. In addition, whether new or old, all public use playgrounds need to provide access to and from the play equipment as mandated in the ADA regulations passed in 1991.

In order to design safe playgrounds, four major elements must be considered

- the placement of equipment and support structures (e.g., benches), which facilitate the supervision of children in the play area
- the proper positioning of age-appropriate equipment to promote positive play behavior
- the selection of appropriate surfacing that will absorb the impact of children falling from the equipment
- the consideration of equipment and surface maintenance issues that contribute to the development of safe playground environments

Supervision Design Considerations

Supervision requires individuals to be able to see and move through the playground area; therefore, design considerations for supervision include age separation of equipment, use of signs, open sight lines, and zones for play.

Age Separation

It is important to divide the playground area into sections appropriate for different ages of the users. Play equipment for children ages 2 to 5 is developmentally different from equipment designed for children ages 5 to 12. Mixing the two types of equipment means that the supervisor will have a difficult time guiding children to use the equipment appropriate for their developmental age level. (A more complete discussion of this can be found in Age-Appropriate Design Considerations on next page).

Use of Signs

Signs can provide information to adults concerning both the age separation of equipment and the need for supervision. The use of signs provides adults with a clear indication as to which age group should be on the equipment. It also reminds adults that the equipment will not supervise the children. This is an important consideration for schools whose playgrounds are used before and after the organized school day and in public parks where no formalized supervision is in place. It provides a "good faith" attempt by a sponsoring agency to promote safe supervision practices.

Open Sight Lines

Open sight lines refer to several angles of visual access for the supervisor. Sight lines must occur through equipment and through natural vegetation. Further, sight lines for play structures should allow visual access to all points of the structure from at least two directions at any one point of observation on the play site (Bowers, 1988, p. 42). Essentially, the ability to respond

Age appropriate design—older elementary children using the overhead ladder.

Falls to surfaces—children replacing appropriate surfacing so the depth is proper for the next class.

to emergencies is dependent upon ". . . the ability of the supervisor to approach the structure and get to all the events to provide assistance" using the routes implied by the sight lines (Bruya & Wood, 1997).

Zones for Play

Play sites should also be divided into zones for different activity types. Two types of zones that the designer should pay attention to are activity zones and use zones. Activity zones describe the type of play behavior that children might engage in given the space and equipment that is present. Examples of activity zones include areas for social/dramatic play, fine-motor play, gross-motor play, and quiet play.

Use zones refer to the safe areas around equipment that need appropriate surfacing. Use zones will be further discussed in Considerations for Proper Surfacing on next page.

Age-Appropriate Design Considerations

Playgrounds should be designed according to the characteristics of the intended user. Therefore, age-appropriate design considerations include selection of the correct size of equipment for children, developmental needs of children, and the physical layout of equipment to support positive play activities.

Correct Size of Equipment

Size of equipment refers to its height, width, and bulk. The *height* of the equipment includes the overall distance from the top of the equipment piece to the surface. It also includes the space between various components, such as steps and platforms. Since 70% of reported playground injuries involve falls to surfaces, the height of the equipment becomes a critical factor in designing a safe playground. Experts suggest that equipment for preschool children be no taller than children can reach. Maximum height for most equipment for school-age children should be eight feet (Thompson & Hudson, 1996).

Width of platforms should also allow children to make decisions about how to get on and off equipment safely. A child standing on top of a six-foot slide should have sufficient room to turn around and climb back down the ladder if that child decides not to slide down.

Bulk is the relationship between the thickness of the material and the grip size of a child's hand. All handrails, rungs, and other components that children grasp should be between 1 and 1 1/2 inches in diameter.

Developmental Needs

Developmental needs of children are also a factor in age-appropriate design. Children grow and develop by stages. The thinking ability of a three-year-old is much different from a seven-year-old. Preschoolers are physically smaller than school-aged children. It is important to consider the developmental needs and abilities of children in planning and designing age-appropriate playgrounds. These needs and abilities include:

- physical (i.e., strength, grip, height, and weight)
- emotional (i.e., risk-taking and exploration)
- social (i.e., cooperation, sharing, and accepting)
- intellectual (i.e., decision-making, inquisitiveness, and creativity)
- accessibility (i.e., mobility)

These needs and abilities apply to all children. As previously mentioned, even children with limited physical, emotional, social, and intellectual capacities, and/or mobility have the legal right to use public play areas. Thus, the designer needs to design for the composite "typical/atypical" child if the playground is to be one where all children can interact successfully.

Physical Layout of Equipment

The physical layout of the playground pieces can limit or enhance the play value and safety for children. An interconnected play area is one in which easy movement throughout the play structure is developed through the inclusion of alternate routes of travel (Bowers, 1998). Shaw (1976) investigated interconnection between parts of the structure, which he came to call the "unified play structure." As a result of the Creative Learning Project, he determined that overall use patterns decreased for separate play modules when compared to the "unified" play space. Thus, by unifying or interconnecting play elements in a play space, overall complexity was increased. In a recent study by the National Program for Playground Safety (2004), it was found that over 95% of all school and park playgrounds now have composite structures.

While composite structures help to increase the complexity of the play space, it also can cause a safety problem if not carefully thought out. Over 84% of park playgrounds now have composite structures that they claim are appropriate for ages 2 to 12 (Hudson, Olsen, & Thompson, 2004). What this means is that the interconnections of these structures are allowing two-year-olds up to heights and on equipment not designed for their developmental abilities. Planners need to understand that one size does not fit all. If composite structures are used, they should be clearly labeled for the age group that they are designed for—either 2 to 5 or 5 to 12. Having a composite structure for ages 2 to 12 is inappropriate and goes against the ASTM standards and CPSC guidelines.

Considerations for Proper Surfacing

Surfacing is the third important general design element. Factors that need to be considered include how much fall protection is required, accessibility, maintenance, management requirements, and costs.

Adequate Fall Protection?

For the prevention of life-threatening injuries, adequate fall protection needs to be present. The National Program for Playground Safety (NPPS) has developed a safe surface decision-making model to help individuals determine whether or not a playground surface will meet the criteria of adequate fall protection. As can be seen in the model outlined in Figure 24.1, there are four decisions that are involved in the selection of surfaces that will provide adequate fall protection. These include the selection of suitable materials, the height of the equipment, the depth of the materials, and adequate coverage in the use zone.

Selection of Suitable Materials

According to the Consumer Product Safety Commission (CPSC, 1997), there are a number of materials that help to reduce the risk of life-threatening injuries. Acceptable materials include sand, gravel, wood chips, engineered wood fibers, shredded rubber, and synthetic surfaces. Hard materials such as asphalt and concrete are unacceptable surfaces under playground equipment. Similarly, earth surfaces such as dirt, soil, grass, and turf are unacceptable, because their shock-absorbing properties vary depending on wear and climatic conditions (CPSC, p. 4).

Height of the Equipment

Equipment height affects the choice of shock-absorbent surfacing in two ways. First, some surfaces, such as pea gravel, provide shock absorbency protection for limited heights (e.g., six feet in the case of pea gravel). Second, currently no surface over 12 feet has been laboratory tested. Thus, to date, no one can guarantee the shock-absorbency characteristics for equipment over the height of 12 feet. Because research studies indicate that equipment over 6 feet in height has doubled the injury rate of equipment under 6 feet, the NPPS recommends that the height of playground equipment should not exceed 8 feet for school-age children and 5 feet for preschool children.

The CPSC recommendations for the fall heights for various pieces of playground equipment are as follows:

- Climbers and horizontal ladders—the maximum height of the structure.
- Elevated platforms including slide platforms—the height of the platform.
- Merry-go-rounds—the height above the ground of any part at the perimeter on which a child may sit or stand.
- Seesaws—the maximum height attainable by any part of the seesaw.
- Spring rockers—the maximum height above the ground of the seat or designated play surface.
- Swings—since children may fall from a swing seat at its maximum attainable angle (assumed to be 90 degrees from "at rest" position), the fall height of a swing structure is the height of the pivot point where the swing's suspending elements connect to the supporting structure.
- Slides—CPSC has no recommendations concerning slide height. Research has shown that equipment higher than six feet has double the injury rate than equipment at lower heights.

It should be noted that equipment that requires a child to be standing or sitting at ground level during play is not expected to follow the recommendations for resilient surfacing. Examples of such equipment are sandboxes, activity walls, playhouses, or any other equipment that has no elevated designated playing surface.

Figure 24.1
Safe Surfacing Decision-Making Model

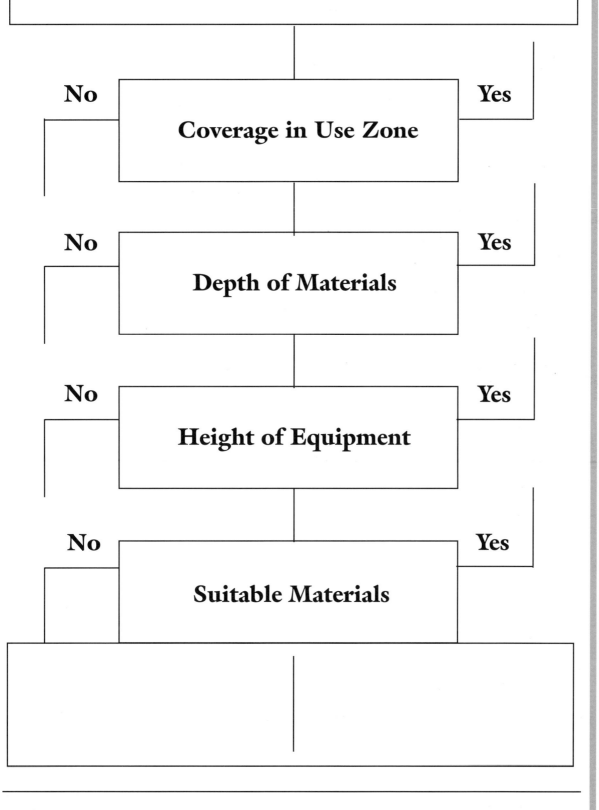

Depth of the Materials

If the surface does not meet minimum standards for shock absorbency, then it should not be used. Minimum standards are determined through testing procedures as stated in the ASTM F-1292 standard for Playground Surfacing. However, because of time and cost constraints, many consumers cannot afford to perform this testing. Consequently, as a public surface the NPPS conducted testing of five common loose-fill materials: pea gravel, sand, wood chips, shredded rubber, and engineered wood fiber. The results are provided in Table 24.1. The chart reports the heights at which a life-threatening head injury would not be expected to occur for compressed loose fill materials at three different depths. As can be seen in Table 24.1, 12 inches of compressed sand, wood chips, shredded rubber, and engineered wood fiber can provide shock absorbency for equipment up to eight feet in height. In contrast, the maximum height for 12 inches of pea gravel is six feet. The depth of any loose-fill material could be reduced during use, resulting in different shock-absorbing properties. For this reason, a margin of safety should be considered in selecting a type and depth of material for a specific use. When loose-fill materials are used, it is recommended that there be sections of containment around the perimeter of the use zone (CPSC, 1997) (See Table 24.1).

Table 24.1
Playground Surface Materials

Height of Equipment	Pea gravel			Sand			Wood Chips			Shredded Rubber			Engineered Wood Fiber		
	6"	9"	12"	6"	9"	12"	6"	9"	12"	6"	9"	12"	6"	9"	12'
1'	Y	Y	Y	Y	Y	Y	Y	Y	Y	Y	Y	Y	Y	Y	Y
2'	Y	Y	Y	Y	Y	Y	Y	Y	Y	Y	Y	Y	Y	Y	Y
3'	Y	Y	Y	Y	Y	Y	Y	Y	Y	Y	Y	Y	Y	Y	Y
4'	Y	Y	Y	Y	Y	Y	Y	Y	Y	Y	Y	Y	Y	Y	Y
5'	N	Y	Y	Y	Y	Y	Y	Y	Y	Y	Y	Y	Y	Y	Y
6'	N	N	Y	Y	Y	Y	Y	Y	Y	Y	Y	Y	Y	Y	Y
7'	N	N	N	Y	Y	Y	N	Y	Y	Y	Y	Y	Y	Y	Y
8'	N	N	N	Y	Y	Y	N	Y	Y	Y	Y	Y	N	Y	Y

*Based on depth test results conducted by NPPS or manufacturers' literature.
Note that the loose-fill results are based on materials tested in a compressed state.

Y = Yes, it did meet CPSC recommendations for this critical height.
N = No, it did not meet CPSC recommendations for this critical height.

Coverage in the Use Zone

The final element that helps decide if the appropriate surface is present is the determination of the placement of the surfacing under and around playground equipment. The Consumer Products and Safety Commission Handbook for Public Playground Safety defines these areas as use zones. Table 24.2 presents the requirements for use zones as outlined in the CSPC handbook.

The basic use zone is 6 feet. However, because children move off swings and slides in different ways than onto another piece of equipment, the use zone is expanded to provide a larger safety zone. For instance, if a swing beam is 8 feet high, then the use zone extends 16 feet in front and 16 feet in back of the swing beam to accommodate children who might jump out of the swing seat while in motion.

Table 24.2
Use Zones for Equipment

Equipment	Use Zone Requirement
Stationary equipment	Six feet on all sides of the equipment.
Slides	Six feet on all sides. Four feet plus the height of slide in front of slide chute.
Swings	Six feet on each side. Twice the height of the swing beam in front and back of swing.

Accessibility

The second characteristic that needs to be considered in the selection of surfacing is that of accessibility. According to the previously mentioned Americans With Disabilities Act of 1991, discrimination on the basis of disability in public accommodations is prohibited. While the entire playground area does not have to be accessible, there must be an accessible pathway to accessible playground equipment. Therefore, a pathway made of an accessible surface material must be provided. At this time, the testing of loose fill materials for accessibility is still in process. However, it is well accepted that sand and pea gravel are not accessible surfaces. Until more testing is done, the only materials that are generally considered accessible under certain conditions are wood fibers and unitary materials, all of which are commercially available. According to a U.S. Department of the Interior advisory, uniform wood fibers tend to knit together to form an accessible surface while other wood materials (e.g., wood chips, bark, mulch, etc.) do not (McCroy, 1994).

Maintenance

The third characteristic, which is often ignored during the selection process, is the maintenance requirements that various surfaces need in order that the shock absorbency characteristics are properly retained. Three elements that should be considered in this area include environmental conditions, soil conditions, and management requirements.

Environmental Conditions

Environmental conditions such as strong winds, rainy weather, high humidity, freezing temperatures, and so forth may influence the appropriateness of the type of surfacing selected. For example, strong winds can erode organic loose-fill materials and sand so that they must be replenished often. Wind and dirt tend to form a hard pan or crust in pea gravel that needs to be broken up periodically. When wet, sand tends to stick together and become almost rigid. Some types of unitary materials are susceptible to frost damage. Thus, the climatic conditions of the playground must be considered when selecting a surface material (Mack, Hudson, & Thompson, 1997).

A piece of playground equipment that needs maintenance.

Soil Conditions

Playgrounds located over poor soil will not drain well, causing pooling of water under equipment. In some areas of the country, the shrink/swell characteristics of clay soil can loosen the foundation of play equipment. Shrink/swell conditions can also cause sinkholes under playground surfaces. This problem can easily destroy a poured-in-place or other unitary surface. One should check with the local soil conservation district or a county extension agent to check the suitability of the soil for playground development.

Finally, the designer must pay attention to the drainage of the site. Normally, one would want water to run down away from the playground. This might mean that the area around the equipment will need to be slightly raised. Since drainage is also dependent on soil type, as mentioned above, the soil composition should be checked prior to the installation of equipment. One should also be aware of what might drain into the playground area. For instance, if a parking lot is located above the play area, grease, oils, and even gasoline may be washed into the play area during a rainstorm. Be certain that there is good drainage at and around the site to avoid problems.

Management Requirements

Consideration must be given to how the area will be managed. A site that will have high traffic use will require a surface that will be durable without frequent maintenance. Rubber tiles or poured-in-place surfaces, although initially high in cost, may be more appropriate for these types of areas. Loose-fill materials would be more easily displaced, which would have an impact on the overall safety of the site. However, in areas that have controlled use, loose-fill materials may be appropriate.

Maintenance costs and the needs of surfacing materials vary greatly, with loose-fill materials tending to have much higher maintenance needs. In high-use areas, loose materials may need to be raked daily to replace materials that have been pushed or kicked away. Loose-fill materials need to be regularly inspected for protruding and sharp objects such as glass, pop tops, sharp rocks, and metal objects. These surface materials may also have to be tilled periodically to loosen compaction. Sand should periodically be turned over, loosened, and cleaned. Additionally, loads of loose material may need to be added on an annual or semiannual basis to keep the surface at an appropriate depth.

While not as time-consuming, unitary materials such as rubber mats, tiles, and poured-in-place surfaces also have maintenance needs. Repairs may need to be made to gouges, burns, and loose areas. Unitary materials may also need to be swept frequently to prevent sand, dirt, rocks, or other loose materials from becoming a slip hazard. Finally, rubber surfaces must be washed occasionally to remove spilled beverages, animal excrement, and other foreign matter.

Costs

Cost factors of the surfacing material should be prorated over the life expectancy of the playground. Materials with low initial cost include sand, pea gravel, wood chips, and bark mulch. However, one should also consider the replenishment costs of these materials along with the initial purchase price. In addition, some method of containment is needed and the materials cannot be installed over existing hard surfaces such as concrete and asphalt.

Materials with medium initial cost include wood fiber and shredded rubber. Some of these materials are easily installed while others require professional installation. They may also require a drainage system. Like other loose-fill materials, some type of containment is required, and they cannot be installed over concrete or asphalt.

Unitary materials such as poured-in-place surfaces, rubber tiles, and rubber mats have a high initial cost when compared to low-cost loose-fill materials. Poured-in-place surfaces are usually the most expensive with a cost 10 to 15 times higher than common loose-fill surfaces. Rubber mats and tiles typically cost 6 to 12 times that of the cheaper materials. Installation and site preparation costs should also be considered, because these materials must be professionally installed. Unitary materials also require a hard base. If the existing surface is not concrete or asphalt, then a subsurface must be installed prior to the rubber surface. However, if the current surface is concrete or asphalt, installing a rubber surface will avoid the costs of excavating and removing the existing surface.

Equipment and Maintenance Considerations

Considerations about maintenance have to be part of the initial planning process. A poorly built playground is difficult to maintain. Providing good upkeep for a safe play environment begins with planning the playground site. Factors that need to be considered regarding this area include preplanning, materials, inspection, maintenance, and environment.

Prior to any installation of equipment and surfaces, a proper site analysis needs to be conducted. A site analysis addresses natural, manufactured, and aesthetic elements that may affect playgrounds. All of these items will be discussed in greater detail in the next section.

Materials

There is no perfect material for playground equipment. Without good maintenance, wood will splinter, metal will rust, and plastic will crack. Any good maintenance plan should be based on

- instructions received from the designer/manufacturer,
- materials used for equipment and surfaces,
- age of the equipment and surfaces,
- given frequency of use on the equipment and surfaces, and
- environmental factors at a specific location.

Be certain that all instructions from the designer/manufacturer are retained in a file and that the schedule of maintenance is followed. Remember, any modification, deviation, or change from these instructions means that liability issues will reside with the agency, not the designer/manufacturer.

Inspection

Inspect all materials prior to installation. Wood products are aesthetically pleasing but will weather faster than metal or plastic. Plastic materials may not be appropriate in areas of great temperature extremes. Metal materials also tend to absorb heat and cold, which can cause problems in hot and cold climates.

Even newly installed playgrounds should be inspected for hazards. Just because a playground is new does not mean that problems cannot occur. This is especially true if the equipment was installed improperly or the overall design and placement of equipment is faulty. On the other hand, older playgrounds do need more regular inspections simply because parts may wear out due to age.

Maintenance Schedule

A well-used playground will need more frequent maintenance than one that is used less often. This is especially true with playgrounds that have loose-fill materials as the surface under and around playground equipment. An agency that schedules only one refilling of these materials a year may find that over half its playgrounds are unsafe due to the high usage. Each play area may have its own use cycle and the maintenance schedule should reflect this.

Environmental Factors

Finally, the environmental factors at a specific location are going to determine the required frequency of maintenance. A playground that is located near a shady grove of trees may need to be inspected more frequently because of materials left on the surfacing (e.g., leaves) or other hazards (e.g., overhanging limbs). A playground that is in a wide-open area and exposed to the elements may also experience greater maintenance needs.

It is evident that to maintain a safe playground environment, maintenance practices and procedures need to be thought about at the beginning of the design process. It is also important that these practices and procedures be continually revised and improved.

Specific Planning Steps

The actual planning and design of a playground is accomplished in four distinct phases. They are: site analysis, preliminary design, equipment and material selection, and final design.

Site Analysis

Site analysis involves the gathering of information and data about the playground site and adjacent properties. "The purpose of site analysis is to find a place for a particular use or find a use for a particular place" (Molnar & Rutledge, 1986). One of the first steps that should be taken during the site analysis is an on-site visitation. Personal site visits enable one to see how the area is used and how it relates to surrounding land uses (IPRA, 1995). It allows the planner to mentally visualize the space available for the project. During the site analysis, step information about environmental elements, manufactured elements, and hazardous conditions is gathered and analyzed.

Environmental Characteristics

Environmental characteristics that should be considered during the site analysis includes soils and geology, drainage, topography, vegetation, and any other physical characteristics that may have an impact on the development process.

Soils and Geology

Soil type is important because it is directly related to drainage. The playground should be constructed on well-drained soils. A playground constructed on poor soil will be subject to water pooling or standing. It will also tend to erode the foundations of the equipment and cause other problems of equipment stability.

Drainage

In general, water should drain away from the playground. As mentioned earlier, the play area may need to be slightly elevated to accomplish this. One needs to remember that construction of the playground and/or surrounding areas may alter the water movement patterns on the site. If there are questions about preventing or solving water problems, a good source is the local office of the Soil Conservation Service (SCS).

Topography is concerned with the general lay of the land. Playground developments work best within a range of slopes. As a general rule, slopes around and beneath playgrounds should conform to the following guidelines (IPRA, 1995):

- Slopes between 1% and 4% are most suitable for playgrounds (a 1% slope falls one foot for every 100 linear feet).
- Slopes less than 1% may result in drainage problems.
- Slopes greater than 4% may require site modifications to install and level the equipment.

In addition, slope is an important consideration in providing equal access into the playground for everyone regardless of physical capabilities. The accessible route into the playground must have a maximum slope of 5% (one foot of fall for every 20 linear feet) and a maximum cross slope of 2%.

Vegetation

Vegetation is another environmental consideration in playground design. Shade should be an essential ingredient for every playground. If trees are not present, it may be necessary to provide man-made shade, such as the placement of shelters. While trees planted along a western and southern exposure may provide the necessary shade, caution must be taken to ensure that overhanging limbs do not interfere with play activities. "In particular, trees planted inside the playground must be carefully located because they may be used for climbing" (IPSA, p.13). In addition, one should avoid planting trees and shrubs, which are messy or likely to attract stinging insects such as bees.

Other Considerations

Other environmental considerations include sun orientation, wind patterns, climate, and animal control. Slide surfaces that tend to absorb heat should avoid being placed on a western exposure. The best orientation is north. However, if this is not possible, then natural or manufactured shade needs to be provided.

The direction of the prevailing winds should also be determined. If at all possible, the playground should be located downwind from open fields, farms, or areas like unpaved roads where dust from these sites will blow directly into the play area. In addition, if an area is susceptible to strong winds on a routine basis, some type of windbreak should be created.

Climatic conditions that affect playground equipment and surfaces include heat and cold, humidity, and precipitation. As mentioned earlier, temperature extremes have a direct influence on different materials used for equipment and surfacing. In addition, humidity may affect certain loose-fill surfaces, as well as cause the surfaces of equipment to become slippery and hazardous. An area that has constant precipitation may need to have a cover over the equipment as well as excellent drainage.

Manufactured Elements

The second factor to consider in the site analysis is manufactured elements. These include utilities, roads, buildings, adjacent land use, accessibility, and anything else that could affect or be affected by the playground.

Utilities

As a general rule, playgrounds should not be constructed under utility lines. One needs also to pay attention to unused utility easements. There might be a temptation to use these seemingly open areas, but nothing can stop a utility from using the easement at a later date for power lines. Another utility consideration is the support structures that may be found near the playground site. Power poles and towers can constitute an attractive nuisance in the play area. In addition, guidewires or other supporting cables on these utility structures can create a hazard for children in the area.

Roads

The playground should be located far enough away from roads and parking lots that moving vehicles do not pose a hazard for children. A barrier surrounding the playground is recommended if children may inadvertently run into a street. If fences are used for such barriers, it is recommended that they conform to applicable local building codes (CSPC, 1997). In addition, ASTM has developed a specific standard for fencing around playgrounds (ASTM 300).

Buildings

Proper use zones need to be maintained in relation to any buildings or structures that may be present on the site. For example, a school playground should be located far enough away from the school buildings so that a child on a climbing structure would be in no danger of falling off the play equipment into the building. In addition, close proximity of the playground to windows may encourage vandalism problems.

Adjacent Land Use

Neighboring land uses need to be considered because they may affect or be affected by the playground (IPRA, 1995). Railroads, freeways, landfills, streams, and rivers may all contribute to a hazardous environment for children. The long-term effects of some of these items (e.g., waste dumps) may not be determined for years. On the other hand, the location of the playground itself may be seen as a less-than-desirable element within the neighborhood environment. Some people may be upset by the perceived increase of noise, vandalism, and traffic they assume a playground will attract.

Accessibility

Accessibility to and from the site is also a consideration. How will project users get to the playground site? Will it involve children arriving on bicycles, walking, or being brought by cars? The answers to these questions will determine the need for bicycle racks, pathways, and parking lots.

Other Considerations

Other considerations may include sources of noise such as airports, railroad lines, roadways, heavy machinery, and factories that can detract from the recreational experiences of playground users. Odors from factories, sewage treatment facilities, and stagnant ponds can have the same effect. Locating a playground adjacent to such detractors should be avoided (IRPA, 1995, p.15).

Hazardous Conditions

A variety of hazardous conditions must be considered before determining the site location of the playground. These include visibility and security, crossings, water, and mixed recreation use zones.

Visibility and Security

Visibility and security are primary considerations. Large shrubs (above four feet in height) should not be planted around a playground since they inhibit the ability to observe children at play. In addition, as already mentioned, low tree branches (below a height of seven feet) should be removed to prevent climbing. Any trees that will be seriously affected by the development of the playground should also be removed before they create a hazardous situation.

Crossings

Children should not be required to use unprotected crossings to reach playgrounds. Railroad tracks are a similar hazard. Fencing or natural barriers may be necessary if alternative solutions are not feasible (IPRA, 1995). Another traffic consideration can occur around schools and child care centers where delivery truck routes may pose a potential hazard for children going to and from the play area. Special care should be given to be certain that these routes do not intersect the play area and are not located nearby.

Water

Water is another site element that may pose a hazardous situation. Children are attracted to ponds, streams, and drainage ditches. Cement culverts or ditches are especially dangerous, since their smooth sides may not allow a child easy escape in case of a flash flood. Signage alone will not stop children from trying to incorporate these areas into their play behavior.

Mixed Recreation Use Zones

Mixed recreation use zones can also produce hazardous situations. A soccer field or baseball diamond located too close to a playground is a safety concern because of the chance that errant balls may enter the play area and injure playground users. Locating a playground adjacent to basketball courts, tennis courts, and other similar recreation facilities can also create conflicting access patterns and users.

Preliminary Design

The preliminary design phase is where information about the activity, user, site, and necessary support factors are analyzed and alternative solutions evaluated. At the end of this step, the actual schematic plans will be developed.

Activity Information

What is the purpose of the playground? This fundamental question needs to be answered in terms of performance objectives rather than physical objectives. For instance, if one answers this question by saying the purpose of the playground is to provide slides, swings, and climbing apparatus, then one will limit the possibilities of the play behavior of children. On the other hand, if one answers this question by looking at what children should be able to do, then a different design may result. The philosophical basis for the existence of the play areas must be reflected in the answer to this question. For example, in a school setting, the purpose of the playground should be tied to the educational goals of the total curriculum. Thus, the playground may be designed so that it contributes to a child's understanding of math, language arts, science, and physical education. In a park setting, the playground may reflect the extension of school goals as well as emphasize the physical, emotional, social, and intellectual development of a child. In a child care setting, the play areas should reflect the growth and development of the different ages of young children.

Once the philosophical question about the purpose of the playground is answered, the next step is to decide what experience opportunities should be provided. Experience opportunities are ways that the child will participate in the playground experience. Four different experience opportunities are usually present in the playground environment:

- basic ability level
- skill improvement
- program participation
- unstructured participation

Basic Ability

This is especially important in planning play environments for young children. Children do develop in different stages. For instance, in terms of access on play equipment, ramps provide the easiest way for a small child to get onto equipment, followed by stairways, stepladders, rung ladders, and climbers. Thus, if one wanted to provide basic skill level opportunities, the design of the play structures would incorporate a variety of ramps and small stairways as well as be built fairly low to the ground.

Skill Improvement

This allows for children to develop their abilities in incremental steps. For instance, at the age of 6, children don't automatically have the upper-body strength to control their bodies on overhead ladders. Some intermediate type of equipment is needed between a 6-foot-long and a 20-foot-long overhead ladder where a child can build up the muscle strength and endurance needed to master the higher and longer apparatus without the fear of falling.

Program Participation

A playground developed on a school site should be designed to complement the academic offerings of the curriculum. Thus, the design of this playground should have specific equipment pieces and shapes that would supplement the academic program (math, science, art, etc.).

Unstructured Participation

This means an area where children are free to roam, explore, discover, and play. Again, this type of experience opportunity demands some specific design considerations including placement of equipment, open sight lines, and easy access.

Not all playgrounds have to emphasize the same experience opportunities. However, if the designer/planner fails to recognize which opportunities should be present, the playground may become only an area where equipment is randomly placed.

User Information

A brief profile of the intended users is an important aspect of the planning process. Such a profile should include the age distribution of the intended users, developmental and skill levels, known disabilities, and participation time patterns. In addition, information about participation rates per activity period is necessary to determine the design load of the area in terms of needed equipment units, support areas, and services. Seasonal, monthly, and weekly peak participation periods may be additional planning factors in terms of maintenance and operational considerations.

Site Factors

A third consideration in this preliminary design stage is the resource and facility factors that are directly related to the site development. Special requirements, such as the spatial size for the playground area, need to be noted. Preliminary layout of equipment on a grid will allow the planner to visualize traffic flow on and off equipment, relationships of equipment pieces with one another, and space requirements for use zones. Other special requirements may be the location of items such as tree limbs, power lines, and telephone wires that can infringe on air space and cause a hazardous situation.

The solar orientation of the space in relation to the placement of equipment is also an important factor. The primary consideration should be to minimize glare and sun blindness during play and avoid hot surfaces on the equipment.

Necessary Support Factors

Items that are auxiliary to the playground but support the area also need to be considered during this preliminary design stage. These items help enhance the overall aesthetic appearance of the area, contribute to the safety of the children, and provide amenities that create an overall positive experience. Trees, bushes, and other vegetation may need to be planted to help provide shade and/or avoid a stark appearance of the playground site. Fencing may be added to keep children safe during play and keep out unwanted animals and others during other times of the day. Benches, water fountains, and shelter areas may provide children and adults with areas to relax and refresh during their visit to the playground. These support factors and others such as bicycle racks, trash and recycling cans, and security lighting will not suddenly appear unless they are planned for in the preliminary design stage. Furthermore, if they are added later, their placement may not be in congruence with the overall design of the area.

Equipment and Material Selection

Equipment for playgrounds should be designed for public use; be durable; and meet requirements for insurance, standards, warranty, age appropriateness, and use. Any equipment purchased should conform to both CPSC guidelines and ASTM Standard F-1487.

Product Compliance

Always require a certificate of compliance with the CPSC guidelines and ASTM Standard from the manufacturer prior to the purchase of the equipment. The same type of compliance with ASTM F-1292 should be secured for any surfacing material. If a manufacturer is unable to produce such documentation or will only provide oral assurances as to compliance, purchase equipment elsewhere. In addition, be certain that any equipment purchased for public-use playgrounds is designed for that purpose. Many times, people with good intentions but limited funds will purchase equipment intended for home use and place it in a public setting. This equipment is neither durable nor strong enough to withstand the constant, heavy use that is found in public sites. In addition, the standard for home-use equipment is quite different from that for public-use equipment.

Product Materials

Playground equipment is usually made out of one of four types of materials: wood, steel, aluminum, or plastic. Each material has its own advantages and disadvantages.

Wood must be treated to prevent rotting by weather or insects. This is especially true when wood is in direct contact with the ground. Any chemical wood preservative used must be approved for contact with humans. Wood is also subject to splitting and checking, which may eventually weaken the structure. Watch out for evidence of splitting in new wood, especially pieces used as support beams and poles. Sanding and other treatments may be required to avoid injuries from splinters. Although aesthetically pleasing, wooden pieces usually have a life span of only 10 years.

Steel equipment pieces should be galvanized and have a protective coating that inhibits rust such as powder coating and painting. Any paint used should not have lead as a component. It should also be noted that scratches and construction defects are subject to rust. Steel also can heat up to dangerous levels with direct exposure to sunlight. On the other hand, steel equipment pieces are very durable and have a long life span.

Aluminum components are rust resistant and offer lightweight installation. Aluminum is sometimes more costly at purchase; however, the reduced maintenance is often worth the extra cost. Shipping charges will be reduced because of the lighter weight. Like steel, aluminum can heat up with direct exposure to sunlight.

Plastic can be molded, cut, or formed into a wide variety of shapes for playground use. Because of this, it is a favorite material that is used by many playground manufacturers. However, most plastics do not have the strength of natural lumbers and metals and can sag and bend. It is recommended that ultraviolet (UV) light inhibitors be added to the plastic to extend the life expectancy and color. Plastic components must meet safety standards (IPRA, 1995).

Purchase Factors

One should consider at least five factors prior to purchasing any equipment or surface materials. These include product liability insurance, compliance with standards, product warranty, age appropriateness, and public-use equipment.

Product liability insurance protects the buyer against any accident caused by the design of the equipment. However, if the buyer makes any alteration or modification or fails to maintain the equipment properly, the insurance will not cover the agency. The equipment vendor should furnish the agency with certificates of insurance and original endorsements affecting the coverage. As with all documentation, be certain the insurance coverage is in writing and on file.

Compliance with standards should also be documented and on file. Do not buy equipment that does not meet CPSC guidelines and ASTM standards F-1292 for surfacing and F-1487 for equipment. In addition, a certification of proper installation should be obtained from the manufacturer or his or her representative following the final inspection. Once the manufacturer agrees that the playground is in conformance with its installation recommendations, ask for a sign-off letter stating the date of inspection. Make sure that you keep this document on file. It is extremely important should an injury occur due to improper design or installation.

Product warranty simply provides the buyer with the length of time for which any products are protected against defects. Many times, the product warranty is a good indication of the product's life expectancy. Again, any modification or repair made without conformance to the manufacturer's guidelines will nullify most warranties.

Age appropriateness of the equipment has already been covered. However, you should notify the manufacturer in writing what the ages of the intended users are to ensure that they have provided you with age-appropriate equipment at the time of purchase.

Public-use equipment is the last item to consider. Not all pieces of equipment are recommended for use in a public playground. The following is a list of equipment to avoid primarily because it fails to meet safety guidelines:

- spinning equipment without speed governors
- tire swings that do not meet requirements for clearance
- seesaws that do not meet current safety standards
- heavy swings (metal, wood, animal-type)
- ropes/cables that are not attached at both ends
- swinging exercise rings and trapeze bars
- multiple occupancy swings
- trampolines
- homemade equipment

Final Design

At this stage, one is ready to put all the components together in a scaled schematic drawing that shows layout, use zones, site amenities, access points, and other construction details. Also, one needs to insure that accessible routes to the equipment are present.

The easiest way to begin this process is to use cutouts or round bubbles to represent the actual equipment and place these items on a scale grid plan. In this way, one can visualize how the equipment pieces fit together and where potential conflicts of use may arise. Any moving equipment, including swings, should be located away from other structures, preferably at the edge or corner of anticipated traffic patterns. In addition, be certain to separate preschool (ages 2 to 5) from school-age (5 to 12) equipment.

All equipment has space requirements. By moving the cutouts or squares around, one can make sure that the use zones of the various equipment pieces do not overlap. Remember that these use zones are minimum guidelines. The authors have seen several instances where slide exits were placed directly in front of swing sets. Although the proper use zone was in place, exuberant children who jumped out of the swings landed directly in front or to the side of the slide. Of course, the best way to avoid this situation is not to place these two activities across from one another in the first place.

As mentioned earlier, site amenities should be part of the planning stage. Make sure that the scaled drawings include the placement of benches, bicycle racks, trash cans, and so forth. If these items are not in the drawings, they will be haphazardly provided later, perhaps at inappropriate spots.

Before finalizing the drawings, be certain that you have considered traffic flow patterns on and off equipment and general access to the area. Every playground should have at least one accessible route to the equipment that will permit children with disabilities the opportunity to be in the playground area and interact with others. Although the final ADA regulations have not been finalized, it is important to understand that just getting to the equipment will not be enough to satisfy the law. Once at the equipment, some type of accommodation should be made to allow children on at least some of the equipment as well as to interact with their nondisabled counterparts. Consult the U.S. Access Board for further information on this subject.

Installation

Installation of equipment is an important part of the overall planning process. If equipment and surfacing are installed improperly, the safety of the total play environment will be jeopardized. When dealing with the installation of equipment and surfacing, there are three factors to consider:

- planning of the installation
- actual installation of the equipment and surfacing
- liability issues related to the installation

Planning of the Installation

Five items need to be considered during the planning of the installation process:

- the manufacturer of the equipment
- the manufacturer of the surfacing
- the materials needed
- who will perform the installation
- budgetary factors

The Manufacturer of the Equipment

This business must be selected carefully. The decision about which manufacturer to use should be made on the basis of the planning committee's criteria. It is critical that the manufacturer decided upon produces equipment that meets the ASTM F-1487 current standard and the CPSC Handbook for Public Playground Safety guidelines. After the tentative selection of the manufacturer has been made, the planning committee should talk with others who have purchased equipment from the potential vendor and check the company's competency. The committee should also find out whether the equipment installation process was understandable and reasonable, and most importantly, how the equipment held up after being installed.

The Manufacturer of the Surfacing

As with the equipment manufacturer, the surfacing manufacturer should also be selected with care. Again, any decision should be based on the criteria established by the planning committee. The surfacing manufacturer must be able to provide testing data from an independent laboratory to show the depth of the product needed proportionate to the height of the equipment purchased. The testing procedure used must be based on the ASTM F-1292 current standard. In addition, it is a good idea to talk with others who have dealt with the prospective manufacturer to determine the company's competency and service record.

Materials Needed

A third item that needs to be considered in the planning process for installation is the materials needed. It is easier to obtain materials in some areas of the country than in others. This will affect their costs. Weather factors have been previously discussed; however, the time of year that installation will occur also needs to be considered. This is especially critical in relation to surfacing and the setting of cement for footings. It also is a consideration for the drying time of preservatives on wood products.

Installer(s)

The determination of the actual installer(s) is the fourth factor. It is possible to use an installer recommended by the company. If that is the decision, the installer should be trained by the company or be a certified installer recommended by the company. A trained installer adds to the overall cost of the equipment. Thus, many times, in an effort to reduce cost, the purchaser will decide to use in-house agency personnel to install the equipment and surface. If this method of installation is selected, it is important for liability protection to have a company representative observe the actual installation process or direct the process. Either way, an agency should have the company sign off that the installation process has met the company's specifications.

Budgetary Factors

The budget for installation is the last item that needs attention. The budget will be determined by the cost factors associated with who does the installation, the materials needed, and the time it takes to perform the installation. Cutting costs on installation is many times a shortsighted cost savings. As mentioned before, if the equipment is not properly installed or poor materials are used, the playground will cost the agency more money due to increased maintenance and liability issues.

Installing the Equipment and Surfacing

Four factors should be considered in relation to the actual installation of the equipment and surfacing:

- manufacturer's instructions
- coordination of the installation
- time needed for the installation
- sign-off by the manufacturer

The Manufacturer's Instructions

According to ASTM F-1487, the manufacturer or designer must provide clear and concise instructions and procedures for the installation of each structure provided and a complete parts list (ASTM-F-1487-95, 1995). It is important that these procedures be followed during the installation process. In addition, these instructions should be filed in case any liability issues arise concerning the proper installation of equipment.

Coordination of the Installation

The next step is to coordinate the installation process. Four potential groups need to interact with one another during installation. These groups include the manufacturer, the owner of the site, the organizer for the personnel who will perform the installation, and the vendors from whom products will be purchased.

Time Needed for Installation

Time is also an important issue that needs to be considered. In particular, the amount of time needed for the installation will influence the number of people involved in the actual installation process. One needs to determine whether or not the community will tolerate weekend installation, or if the work must be done during usual work hours or in the evenings. If installation takes a period of time, protecting children from using partially built structures is a priority.

Manufacturer Sign-Off

After the installation is completed, the agency should have the manufacturer of the equipment and surfacing sign off that both items were installed according to specifications. This ensures that the structures and the surfacing are safe for children to use.

Liability Issues

Since we live in a litigious society, it is important to protect the agency from being sued. Following appropriate procedures will not prevent lawsuits, but it may reduce the amount of financial responsibility that is imposed if a suit is upheld. However, the most important item to remember about following proper installation instructions is not the liability issue, but the safety issue. By following manufacturer's instructions, the agency is being proactive in trying to reduce the potential for children being injured on the playgrounds.

An agency should be concerned with four liability issues regarding the installation of equipment. According to Clement (1988) these are

- manufacturer's specifications,
- manufacturer's recommendations,
- the posting of manufacturer's warnings, and
- the importance of following manufacturer's instructions.

Manufacturer's Specifications

It is critical that the agency is certain that the installer has followed the manufacturer's specifications for installation. The responsibility for this falls on the manufacturer, if the company performs the installation. If the agency does the actual installation, it assumes the liability and the burden of proof regarding the following of proper procedures.

Manufacturer's Recommendations

Any recommendations by the manufacturer must also be followed. For example, in order to properly deal with the impact attenuation of a surface, it may be recommended that pea gravel be separated from a wood product by use of a fabric. Once installed, it is the agency's responsibility to see that such a separation is continued. Other recommendations may include that bushings on swings be checked annually for wear or that wood products be covered with a preservative on an annual basis. In each of these cases, it is imperative that the agency follow the recommendations of the manufacturer.

Posting of Manufacturer's Warnings

The agency must post any manufacturer's warnings that are included with materials. Many manufacturers now place labels on equipment that suggest ages for which the equipment is designed or the proper depth for loose-fill surface materials. In cases where warnings accompany playground equipment, the agency is responsible for replacing the warnings if they become illegible, destroyed, or removed. Diligence on the part of the agency in regard to the posting of the warning label will inform adults about ways to prevent a child from being injured.

Following Manufacturer's Instructions

Last, following manufacturer's instructions is extremely important in the installation of equipment. These instructions should include the proper use-zone placement of equipment, the installation of the equipment at the proper depths, the correct method of mixing adhesives for surfacing materials, mixing cement in correct proportions with water, and the use of proper tools to lock joints of structures. The agency may need to be able to provide evidence that such procedures were followed.

As adults work with installation, they can conclude that they are dealing literally with the dirt of responsibility, the grit of reality, and the grind of responsibility.

Ongoing Maintenance, Repair, and Inspections

The playground area should be perceived as an environment for play that contains many elements including playground equipment (Hendy, 1997). Parking lots, sidewalks, field areas, seating, shelters, and restroom facilities are only a few of the amenities that complement many playground areas. These amenities require maintenance as well. To insure proper long-term maintenance, a comprehensive program must include the total playground environment, not just the equipment.

The basic function of maintenance is to ensure the safety of users by keeping the playground area and equipment in a safe condition. Maintenance also keeps the equipment functioning efficiently and effectively. A track ride is not much fun if the bearings are worn and the mechanism won't glide easily. Maintenance is also performed to keep the area hygienically clean. By keeping an area well maintained, it remains aesthetically pleasing.

A safety audit should be performed when new equipment is purchased and installed to verify that the equipment and installation are consistent with the Standard of Care set forth by the agency and the manufacturer. The audit will not need to be repeated unless the Standard of Care changes, the equipment is heavily vandalized, or a natural disaster impacts the equipment.

Inspections

There are basically two types of maintenance inspections that are performed on playground equipment: seasonal (periodic) and daily (high frequency). A seasonal or periodic inspection is one performed two to three times a year. This is an in-depth type of inspection to evaluate the general wear and tear on the equipment. A daily or high frequency inspection is done routinely to identify rapidly changing conditions due to weather, vandalism, and sudden breakage. It also identifies surfacing problems typically associated with loose-fill surfacing materials.

There is no magic formula for determining the frequency necessary to perform each type of maintenance inspection. How often the playground is used and by what age group are two of the common considerations that will determine frequency of inspection. The vandalism rate in an area will also dictate the timetable chosen to inspect the playground.

The nature of the area and the environment will influence the need for playground maintenance. The soil type and drainage conditions as well as other geographic and climatic conditions will also influence inspection frequency.

Record Keeping

Documentation of inspections, repairs, and maintenance should be recorded regularly. In addition, the agency must establish a system of work requests that will enable maintenance staff to expedite the ordering of replacement parts and repair services. As part of the overall comprehensive program of playground maintenance, it is important to document all inspections and maintenance procedures. A fail-proof system of follow-up must be established that enables a supervisor to review the inspection forms, noting

- who performed the inspection;
- items that were corrected on site at the time of inspection;
- hazards that need to be corrected;
- work orders that were issued;
- purchase orders for equipment services or replacement parts;
- when equipment, parts, or services were supplied or rendered;
- when repair work was completed;
- who performed the repair work and
- final approval from the supervisor.

Summary

Playgrounds should be an important facility consideration for inclusion in schools, child care centers, parks, and other recreation facilities. By following the systematic design process outlined in this chapter, playgrounds can be safe as well as foster children's physical, emotional, social, and intellectual development. By paying attention to age-appropriate equipment, proper surfacing under and around equipment, the placement of equipment for easy supervision, and the regular maintenance of the equipment and the environment, HPERD professionals will be able to design a play environment that allows children to be playful. It will also provide a setting in which children can increase their ability to take appropriate challenges without fear of taking inappropriate risks.

Chapter 25

Designing Facilities for Parks and Recreation

Thomas H. Sawyer, Michael G. Hypes,
Daniel D. McLean, Kimberly J. Bodey, and Steven Smidley

Park and recreation facilities are experiencing a multitude of trends that are impacting the planning process. Planning principles are not typically subject to change. However, inputs to the process are undergoing substantial change.

The late 1990s were characterized by a variety of trends:

- Changing participation rates in existing recreation and leisure activities.
- Expanding new recreation activities, especially in adventure recreation.
- Changes in the stability of employment and in the workplace as the baby boomer generation begins to retire and new generations enter the workforce.
- A greater recognition of how cultural and ethnic background impacts the type of recreation and recreation facilities.
- A greater understanding and recognition of women's needs in recreation.
- A changing population and household composition.
- Marked advances in medical care.
- Dramatic innovations in leisure equipment technology.
- Impact of computers, electronic media, and burgeoning electronic marketplace.
- Changes in world energy.
- Changes in regional economies.
- Unstable political environments.
- The slowdown of the economy and resultant impact on recreation facility development and construction.

Facilities and open spaces must clearly be conceptualized and designed to accommodate the dramatic changes occurring in America. The planning process will continue to need the involvement of the varied public to be served.

Learning Objectives

After reading this chapter, the student should be able to

- understand the components of indoor and outdoor recreation facilities, and
- assist architects and planners in designing functional facilities.

General Planning Issues

A Master Plan Concept

The planning process, regardless of the size of the community involved, typically occurs at three levels. First, there must be a master plan conceptualized at the policy-making level. Second, there is a concept plan which concerns physical matters in that it is site-specific and incorporates factors associated with landscaping, layout, facility mix, and construction. Third is the planning stage, which has a focus on operation and maintenance for facilities, parks, and open spaces. All three levels are critical to sound planning (see Chapters 3 and 4); however, the master plan level is the most important since it is at the policy-making level where critical initial decisions are made that guide and control all future decisions at the second and third levels of planning.

Community Involvement

In developing plans for new recreation, park, and open spaces and in proposing improvements to existing facilities and areas, all planning, as suggested within the master plan concept, must reflect the wants and needs of the community.

Public cooperation and involvement in the initial planning stages will serve to strengthen community interest, both actively and financially.

There are many ways to involve the public in the planning process. One is the public meeting. Although time-consuming, a series of well-organized public meetings is an effective means of presenting proposed plans. While the public meeting has been a marginally successful method in the past and should not be discarded, it cannot be the only method. Public meetings are effective in bringing large groups of people together although even the best planned meetings cannot bring large crowds out. In many communities, large crowds are brought about by controversy over proposed planning. Other methods of involving the public are also effective and may provide more detailed and useful information. These include focus groups (small groups of 8 to 12 people), individual interviews, presentations to service clubs and special interest groups, and the like.

A survey of leisure behavior and attitudes can be useful in determining the needs and desires of the people within the planning area. Surveys can be conducted by mail, telephone, internet, or through the newspaper. Conducting a successful survey requires a carefully constructed process, and even then many people have become wary of responding. Surveys can be costly and, if not well constructed, might not provide effective information for the agency. Use of consultants or universities in the process is strongly encouraged.

Today, in most of America, far more taxpayers do not have children in public school than do have children in public schools. It is important to engage this large tax-paying population in any recreation and park project. They need to see that the project will benefit them as well as the rest of the community. One of the methods used to strengthen proposals is through interagency agreements for shared use and funding of facilities. Also, cooperation between community agencies and organized groups facilitates planning, promotes financial considerations, and assures community involvement.

Planning Considerations for Urban Areas

Rapidly growing urban population centers have placed open space at a premium This has led to a growing public concern about recreational facilities and services. The following factors must be considered when planning recreational facilities within congested urban areas:

- Declining availability of open space and limited economic resources make it essential that multi-jurisdiction government agencies cooperate in planning facilities areas. Recreation use of public housing facilities, the presence of social and health care programs in recreation centers, and parks and trails crossing multiple jurisdictions and jointly administered are a few examples of ways in which the public can maximize facility use.
- Multiple and not necessarily compatible uses of facilities, both public and private, should be considered. For example, the parking lot of an industrial plant can be used for recreation activities on evenings and weekends with little or no additional cost if properly planned.
- The mobility of people in dense urban areas is often restricted. Therefore, facilities must be easily accessible to the people.
- All facilities need to meet the requirements of the Americans With Disabilities Act.

Multiple Use

Planning facilities for multiple use is a major consideration in the establishment of parks and recreation areas. Multiple-use facilities require space that can accommodate varied activities for all age groups during various times of the day, week, month, season, or year. The traditions of seasonal activities are lessening as technology allows most weather dependent activities to be conducted year-round and single sports have developed year-round training programs and participation. Facilities that are planned to accommodate a single use become an expensive investment if allowed to stand idle much of the year. Changing recreation preferences requires that indoor and outdoor areas not be restricted with permanent spatial and architectural fixtures designed for specific activities in a set period of time. There must be flexibility built into indoor and outdoor facilities.

The character and location of the population are constantly changing. The ethnic, socioeconomic, and demographic features such as age and family size can vary within neighborhoods. With today's mobile population, a community facility that is planned on the basis of a static population soon has many obsolete features. And yet, failing to plan for a neighborhood's ethnic and cultural foundations also means the use for the facilities may be nonexistent. Only in recent years have recreation and park planners come to a realization that recreation patterns are strongly affected by ethnic background and culture. Understanding these cultural impacts allows planners to develop facilities that meet specific ethnic needs and can be adapted for differing populations.

Eliminating Architectural Barriers

It is essential that all recreation facilities be designed to serve people with disabilities. Therapeutic recreation services for people with disabilities need to be considered in the planning process to ensure that activities and facilities will serve them. Guidelines for the elimination of architectural barriers are detailed in Chapter 14.

Indoor Recreation and Community Centers

Neighborhoods, quadrants, communities, and cities form the basic units for planning programs, activities, and facilities. The park and recreation agency, in order to plan and manage its services properly, establishes its activities and facilities on the demands of its designated service populations. The larger the planning and managing agency, the broader the population groups with which it will be concerned.

Recreation and Community Center Types

There are different types of recreation centers based on community needs. Traditionally, the two main types have been neighborhood recreation centers and community recreation centers. Neighborhood recreation centers focus on serving neighborhood needs and are discussed in more detail below. Neighborhood recreation centers are more common in large communities (500,000 or more) but are sometimes present in smaller cities. Community recreation centers serve a larger population base. Community centers are common in cities of various sizes. In smaller cities and communities they may be the only recreation centers available. In larger cities they supplement neighborhood centers and provide specialized services and programs.

There is a new type of recreation center, frequently referred to as a supercenter, which has a minimum of 80,000 square feet in size. Super-centers are a reflection of commercial trends of creating large, one-stop shopping super stores. The supercenter reflects an expectation by consumers to meet all of their recreational needs in one location. These supercenters can cost in excess of $20 million.

Authors and organizations have historically provided classifications for types of recreation facilities based on service areas. Some larger communities have created their own standards for recreation facilities. Yet there remains no commonly accepted standard for the number of people a recreation center should serve or what should be contained in a recreation center. Recreation planners have learned that communities have different expectations for services, and the cookie-cutter approach of the 1960s and 1970s has given way to unique facilities designed to meet community member desires. Even with this knowledge, some common terminologies for recreation centers can be suggested. Table 25.1 shows what types of facilities may be found based on community size.

Table 25.1
Recreation Center Type and Frequency Based on Size

Type of Recreation Center	Large City (250,000 or More)	Medium City (100,000 to 250,000)	Small City (50,000 to 100,000)	Small Community (Less Than 50,000)
Neighborhood recreation center				
Community recreation center				
Supercenter				
Specialized facilities				

Recreation centers should be planned to meet the needs and interests of all people in the neighborhood or community. They should provide a safe, healthful, and attractive atmosphere in which every person in the community or neighborhood may enjoy his or her leisure by participating in activities of a social, inspirational, cultural, or physical nature.

Recreation centers range from the simple picnic shelter to a multipurpose community recreation center with a variety of common and special service facilities. They vary in design from the rustic to the contemporary. Present-day buildings provide for adaptability and multiple uses. This change from the simple to the complex has stimulated the development of a variety of recreation centers. These are classified by function and then categorized by size. The size of a recreation center is usually based on the population to be served and the program to be conducted.

The Neighborhood Center

The facility which is, perhaps, closest to the grassroots service level is the neighborhood center. A neighborhood recreation center is designed to service a specific area of the city. Such a building encloses 15,000 to 30,000 square feet. The size will depend also on whether the building is a separate entity or part of a park-school complex where facilities are available in the school.

The neighborhood center usually includes the following facilities:

- multipurpose room or rooms
- gymnasium (if not available in neighborhood school [see Chapter 30])
- shower and locker rooms when a gymnasium is provided (see Chapter 16)
- arts and crafts room
- fitness and aerobics room
- dance and aerobics room
- child care area
- kitchen
- restrooms
- lounge and lobby
- office
- large storage areas

The Community Center

The community recreation center functions beyond the primary purpose of serving a neighborhood. It is designed to meet the complete recreation needs of all the people in the community. The size of the building depends on (1) the number of people to be served, (2) the projected program plan, and (3) whether it is a part of a park-school site or a separate building. This building usually contains 20,000 to 75,000 square feet of space and is usually located in a major recreation area such as a park-school site or community park.

The community center usually includes the following facilities:

- multipurpose rooms that can be organized into one large room and multiple smaller rooms
- gymnasium (see Chapter 21)
- shower and locker rooms (see Chapter 16)
- stage and auditorium (sometimes combined with gymnasium)
- rooms for programs in the arts (art, dance, music, drama)
- game room
- kitchen
- restrooms
- lounge and lobby
- office
- large storage areas
- clubs or classrooms
- seniors area
- fitness area
- dance and aerobics room
- child care area
- video room
- computer/technology room
- teen area
- possible specialized areas as program dictates (racquet courts, gymnastics, weight and exercise room, photography workshop

The Supercenter

The supercenter represents the newest trend in the development of recreation centers. As previously mentioned, it ranges in size from 80,000 to well over 100,000 square feet and is designed to be a true one-stop recreation center. It serves a large metropolitan area or may serve several communities. It is usually not linked to a school park. The size of the facility allows for both indoor and outdoor facilities. It might, for example, include a water park rather than a traditional swimming pool and have water play equipment, slides, a lazy river, and the like. It almost always has a large fitness, aerobics, and gymnasium area and an indoor track. It usually has many classrooms and specialized rooms such as preschools, arts and crafts rooms, teen areas, or a photography room. Most rooms are designed to be multiple use. The use of folding walls allows rooms to be configured in different sizes so groups as small as 10 or 15 can be accommodated as well as groups of several hundred. The child care area allows the family to come to the center and leave their toddlers in a licensed day-care setting while the parents work out and the school age children attend classes such as fitness, martial arts, arts and crafts, or computers, or they have fun in the indoor water park. Many of the supercenters are supported with outdoor facilities such as golf courses, outdoor water parks, large park pavilions, and so forth. There is no single common design for a supercenter; however, the use of computers to track facility use, conduct registration, manage the facility, and track maintenance operations is mandatory. Many of the buildings are also wireless, encouraging residents to bring their laptops for use in the open spaces. Open space that is inviting and comfortable is essential. There is usually a single entry that has a front-desk monitored by knowledgeable staff who help patrons find where they need to go, check for membership, take registration for classes, and monitor building use.

Specialized Rooms

Multipurpose Room

The multipurpose room should be designed to accommodate such activities as general meetings, social recreation, active table games, dancing, dramatics, music, concerts, banquets, and the like. The area of this room should be approximately 2,000 to 3,000 square feet. It should be rectangular in shape, with a minimum width of 40 feet. The minimum ceiling height should be 16 feet.

There are many types of flooring surfaces available. Wood flooring, usually maple, is always a favorite but it requires considerable upkeep and does not respond well to some uses. Composite flooring such as a Mondo® type of floor is as costly as a wood floor but is highly versatile. Participants can play basketball on it in the morning and it can be the shot put area in the afternoon, then used for indoor soccer in the evening. The floor should have a nonskid surface to prevent many common accidents. It is recommended that the floor also be level to permit multiple use for meetings, dancing, dramatic presentations, and so on.

Gymnasium

If only a single court is constructed then the structure should be at least 90 feet by 100 feet with a minimum height of 24 feet. This size will permit a basketball court of 50 feet by 84 feet with additional room for telescopic bleachers seating approximately 325 spectators on one side of the gymnasium (see also Chapter 30). Community centers and super-centers will have multiple courts side by side, typically with 12 feet between the courts and vinyl walls with netting that descends from the ceiling when desired. Multiple court gymnasiums will usually have seating for just one court and it is retractable.

Provision should be made for a mechanical ventilating system with air-conditioning considered where climate dictates. It is preferable to have no windows in the gymnasium. However, if desired, windows should be placed at right angles to the sun at a height of 12 feet or more and they should be equipped with protective guards. The wainscotting, or tile, in the gymnasium should provide clear, unobstructed wall space from the floor to a height of 12 feet. Many recreation centers are moving to portable basketball standards, thus removing the basketball areas from multiple use structures.

Floors with synthetic surfaces have become predominant in recreation gymnasiums. Maple flooring continues to be selected as a preferred alternative to a synthetic surface, usually when the floor will have limited conflicting use. If maple flooring is used, the cork spring clip or other type of expansion joint should be installed on all four sides. If suspended apparatus requiring wall attachments is used in the gymnasium, these attachments should be at least seven feet above floor level.

Recessed drinking fountains should be located where they will cause a minimum of interference. Fountains should be hand- or hand-and-foot operated with up-front spouts and controls. Protective floor covering or drainage at the base of the fountain should be considered to avoid floor damage.

Locker and Shower Rooms

Locker and shower rooms should be provided for physical activities, athletics, faculty, and the like (see Chapter 16).

Stage and Auditorium

A stage and related facilities were traditionally built in conjunction with the gymnasium or multipurpose room. Contemporary facilities are building separate stages or working with community groups that provide auditorium space. The stage proper should be about 20 feet in depth and the proscenium opening should be at least two-thirds the width of the crafts area.

The approach to the stage from the floor of the main room should be by inclined ramp with a nonskid surface to accommodate older persons and persons with disabilities and to facilitate movement of equipment.

The room should be equipped with a modern public address system, permanently installed with matched speakers and outlets for additional microphones and audiovisual equipment. Consideration should be given to a master control from the office of the building. All stage lighting should be modern and should be controlled from a dimmer-control cabinet equipped with a rheostat or professional lighting console.

The base and wall of the room should be equipped with electrical outlets to accommodate floor and table lamps, motion picture equipment, floodlights, and other electrical apparatus. A heavy-voltage line may be necessary. Computer cabling, video projection equipment built into the ceiling, and an area where computer equipment can be accessed and used are also desirable.

The entrance should contain double doors. Stage doors should be of sufficient width and height to facilitate the movement of scenery. It is desirable to have a door at the rear of the stage area to permit the handling of stage properties and scenery. Adequate exit doors should be provided and should be equipped with panic hardware. Door frames and thresholds should be flush.

Space should be provided for the storage of chairs, tables, and portable staging. This space can be under the stage or in an adjacent storage room provided with dollies that have swivel ballbearing fiber or rubber-covered casters.

Acoustics are an important factor in an auditorium and should be kept in mind in the selection of materials for walls and ceilings. Rigid acoustical materials for ceilings are more economical and discourage vandalism better than suspended acoustical tile.

The entrance should contain double doors and should be at the end opposite the stage. Each door should have a minimum unobstructed opening of at least 32 inches with a removable mullion.

Game Room

The game room, approximately 30 feet by 64 feet in size, is designed for a variety of games including pool, table tennis, foosball, video games, and computer games. In planning this room, sufficient storage space should be provided for the various items of game equipment and supplies.

This room should be close to office supervision and should be acoustically treated. The choice of floor material should be carefully considered because of the heavy traffic anticipated in this room. Windows should be placed high in the walls to reduce glass breakage. A chair rail or wainscotting to prevent the marring of walls should be installed to a height of three feet above the floor. Whenever possible, noncontact (nonmarring) furniture should be used.

The game room should include tables for billiards, table tennis, and other popular table-top games.

Kitchen

A kitchen is desirable for most community and neighborhood recreation centers. There is a choice between having a warming kitchen where the food is prepared elsewhere and taken on-site and served or having a full-service kitchen. Warming kitchens have become very popular with food preparation done either by a vendor or in a centralized kitchen. All kitchens must meet the local and state health board requirements and are subject to regular inspections. The kitchen should be located near the multipurpose rooms and the gymnasium. The kitchen is sometimes placed between two multipurpose rooms and made available to both rooms by the use of aluminum roll-up doors.

Adequate storage space, cabinet space, and electrical outlets for such appliances as the refrigerator, range, dishwasher, and can openers should be provided. Exhaust fans should also be installed.

Arts and Crafts Room

A separate room for arts should conform to local health regulations and have an open floor space at least 54 inches wide. Ample storage cabinets, closets, or lockers should be included for the safe storage of craft materials, unfinished projects, and exhibit materials. Base and wall outlets should be provided in all club rooms for the operation of electric irons, sewing machines, power tools, movie projectors, and other equipment. If a kiln is used, it should be equipped with a heavy-duty 220-volt electrical outlet. Bulletin boards and exhibit cases may be used to display completed projects.

Computer Room

Many recreation centers have computer rooms. A computer room may have few or many computers and is open to the general public. The room is networked and ideally linked to a T1 line for fast internet access. It is best to work with information technology (IT) experts to design and manage the network. Issues of security and keeping pornography off the computers is a major concern for most IT managers and recreation staff. Many recreation centers are now organized for wireless access from anywhere in the building.

Information Desk and Lobby, and Community Area

The information desk and lobby is located at the entrance of the recreation center. The information desk is the first contact point for all recreation center users. It should have a counter that can be accessed by individuals with disabilities as well as the able-bodied. It has a computer and is networked. It provides space for information and registration. Depending on the size of the center it may be staffed by one to five individuals. Staffing is dependent upon the time of day and season of the year. The adjacent lobby is spacious, so when a number of people are present it does not feel crowded. It provides access to the remainder of the building. The community area should open off the lobby and, if possible, should be close to the central office and to other recreation center features. The community area and lobby are often combined into one room.

This facility should be attractively lighted and should contain a wall-mounted, and recessed drinking fountain, comfortable seating, possibly a television, and other amenities. Adequate space, preferably recessed, and electrical and water connections for automatic vending machines should be included.

Carpet floor-covering is desirable for the lounge and lobby areas. However, terrazzo, quarry tile, and patio tile are preferred when cigarette damage is a possibility.

Office

The community center and super-center provide offices for administrative, supervisory, and building staff. Each office area has a different function and should be so designed. The administrative area may be the primary office for the recreation and park department and should be separate from the entrance to the building. It will be in the same building but, because of the function, should not be in the main flow of traffic. Supervisory and building staff should be closer to the action. Building staff should be located so they can see the day-to-day operations of the facility. This places them in the flow of activities so that they are available to handle day-to-day challenges and needs. However, provision must be made to ensure privacy when dealing with disciplinary problems, small meetings, and the like. Secretarial and program offices should be adjacent to the director's office.

Storage Areas

One of the most common errors in planning recreation centers is lack of sufficient storage space for equipment, maintenance, and custodial purposes. An area adjacent to the gymnasium should be provided for such storage. It should have a eight-foot-wide roll-up door opening with flush, louvered doors and a flush threshold to permit passage of the most bulky equipment. The minimum size of the storage room should be approximately 800 to 1,200 square feet. Provision should be made for storage of inflated balls, bats, softballs, and other supplies, either in separate cabinets or a special closet. Appropriate bins, shelves, and racks are suggested. In addition, a recessed alcove for the storage of a piano is desirable. Storage rooms should be located strategically throughout the building to support specialized needs as well as to reduce the amount of time to move equipment into rooms.

The maintenance storage room varies in size depending on the adjacent outdoor space and the size of the building. The room is ordinarily located on the ground level adjacent to the outdoor areas. An outside entrance should be provided by means of a burglar-resistant door large enough to permit the passage of motorized maintenance equipment. Recessed wall shelving and cabinet storage should be provided for tools, supplies, and equipment. This space should contain hot and cold water, a slop sink, a lavatory, a water closet, and a clothes closet. The floor should be concrete and pitched to a central drain. The junction of the floor and wall should be covered.

A supply closet equipped with a slop sink and space for mops, pails, brooms, and cleaning supplies should be centrally located on each floor level.

Meeting and Multipurpose Classrooms

Experience indicates the desirability of providing a minimum of 1,000 square feet of floor space per meeting room. For community recreation centers, at least three to five rooms should be provided for multiple use. At least one large club room should be located adjoining a kitchen or warming room. The rooms may use moveable walls to increase or decrease classroom size.

When windows in clubrooms and lounges are placed high in a wall, they are not broken as often as low windows and they also allow more space for furniture, bulletin boards, pegboards, chalkboards, and exhibits. Since broken window glass is a major problem, a nonbreakable type of pane is preferred. Windows may be omitted and sky domes and vent domes used, thus eliminating the need for draperies, venetian blinds, and curtains—all items subject to vandalism.

A chair rail or wainscotting to prevent the marring of walls should be installed to a height of three feet above the floor. Whenever possible, noncontact (nonmarring) furniture should be used. Floor-level radiant heat in rooms where programs for small children will be conducted should be considered.

Photography Room

A special room can be equipped as a darkroom. Ventilation should be provided through light-proof ventilators. Hot and cold running water, special light outlets (both wall and base), and photographic sinks for developing and washing prints should also be provided. A mixer is desirable to control the water temperatures accurately. A filter should also be provided if the water quality is not good. Doors must be light-proof.

Music Room

The size of the music room should be determined by the potential number in the choral or instrumental group using this facility at any given time. A guide commonly used is to allow 20 square feet for each participant. Provision should be made for the storage of music, instruments, band uniforms, and supplies. Shelves are commonly used for storage of music equipment.

Auxiliary Gymnasium

The auxiliary gymnasium (see also Chapter 30) is for such activities as wrestling, weight lifting, tumbling, gymnastics (see Figure 25.1), fencing, and apparatus work. Acoustical treatment for this room is desirable. The size of the room and height of the ceiling will depend on the various activities for which this facility will be used. The floor should be treated with material that will withstand the use of such equipment as heavy weights.

At least one well-ventilated storage room will be needed for equipment and supplies used in the auxiliary gymnasium. If the apparatus is to be cleared from this room, an additional apparatus storage room should be provided.

Specialized Recreation Centers

Many cities and communities provide recreation programs that require specialized facilities. While the construction of these facilities can be justified in the majority of cases, care must be taken to provide for maximum year-round use. The specialized centers should be centrally located to serve all the public.

Figure 25.1
Free-standing Gymnastics Area

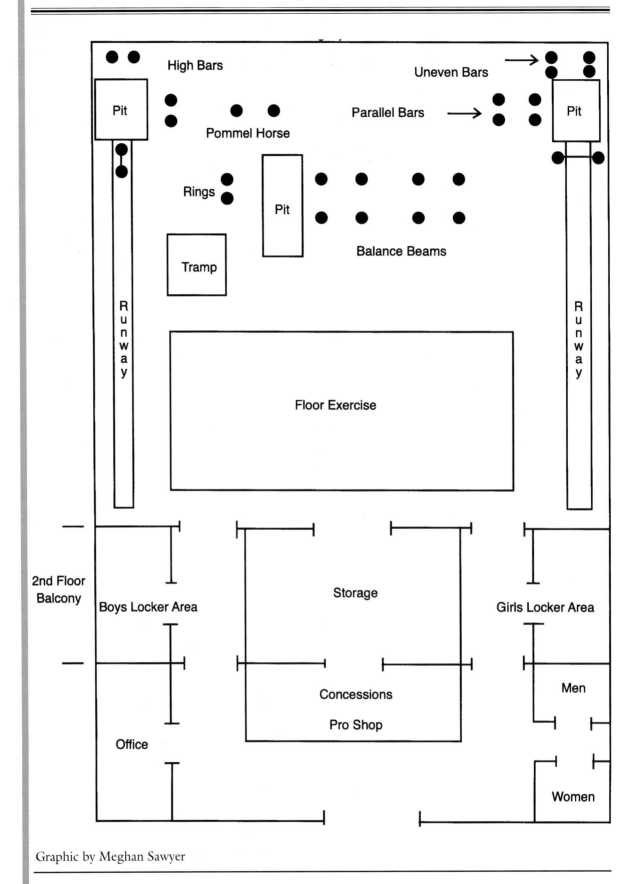

Graphic by Meghan Sawyer

Art Center

In recent years, many cities have constructed community art centers to satisfy the public demand for programs in the arts. The size of the facility will be determined by the number of people to be served and type of art programs to be conducted. Generally, art centers will include work areas for ceramics, sculpture, painting, and sketching. Depending on the interests in the community, a center may also include facilities for woodworking, lapidary, stonecutting, and other arts and crafts. Some art centers include facilities for dance, music, and drama classes and programs as well.

Preschool Center

Preschool centers for day care, Head Start, and nursery school programs are being built in some communities with the aid of grants or federal funds. These buildings are smaller than neighborhood center buildings, and the design scale is geared to preschool children. Generally, the centers include a large multipurpose room, small rooms for small-group activities, an office, possibly a kitchen and eating facilities, and ample storage space. Special care should be taken to ensure good acoustic treatment in the center.

Senior Citizen Centers

Senior citizen centers are similar in design to neighborhood recreation centers. However, more emphasis is placed on facilities for the arts, areas for discussion, and rooms for passive games than for large-scale physical activities. While a gymnasium is seldom found in a senior citizen area, a large multipurpose room is needed for square dancing, shuffleboard, and similar activities. The senior citizen center should be a single-floor building and special care should be taken to eliminate all hazards such as steps and protrusions on walls.

Aquatic Center (Natatorium)

Many neighborhoods and communities have a considerable interest in swimming and demand that an aquatic center (see also Chapter 23) be included as part of the recreation center. A combination of learn-to-swim spaces, lap swim, and a water playground are becoming more common. Mixing the types of aquatic attractions makes more effective use of available space and serves a larger clientele.

Teen Centers

While teen centers have been very popular and continue to be built, the trend today is to construct multiuse centers that will provide opportunities for teen programs along with other activities. For example, a teen office and lounge are provided in many community recreation centers.

When a separate teen center is desired, it could include:

- multipurpose meeting rooms
- gymnasium
- shower and locker rooms
- game room
- computer room
- music room
- rooms for programs in the arts
- restrooms
- game room
- lounge and lobby
- office

Other Specialized Spaces or Facilities

The planning of any specialized recreation center demands a precise and logical approach. Since a recreation center reflects the unique needs and interests of a neighborhood or community, the specific design will vary, but the preliminary considerations of planning objectives will be the same. Types of spaces include fitness rooms, weight rooms, running tracks, child care, aerobics, and a computer center.

The successful incorporation of accepted planning objectives will ensure maximum use of the building. The initial functional/spatial specification and the continuous reevaluation of the architectural specifications of the building prior to its construction should be considered in terms of the following checklist for indoor recreation facilities:

- Has the most effective use of the entire structure been determined?
- Does the preliminary sketch include all the essential facilities necessary to fulfill the program objectives?
- Does the layout provide for flexibility in use and for future expansion?
- Does the floor plan permit convenient access to and facilitate circulation within the building?
- Does the floor plan provide for ease of supervision and administration of the building?
- Have individual rooms been located to encourage multiple use within safety limits?
- Has the building been designed to ensure opportunity for its use by all members of the community, including older persons and individuals with disabilities?

- Does the design encompass accepted aesthetic qualities that relate harmoniously to the surroundings?
- Is the building designed to ensure cooperative use with other public or private agencies?
- Is the building designed to permit economy in construction and subsequent maintenance?

Outdoor Facilities and Open Spaces

Population growth projections suggest that few metropolitan areas in the United States have sufficient open space to meet the demands of the future. Based on these projections, it is imperative that planning boards and commissions on all levels of government review previous planning philosophies with the intent of revision or, when necessary, the development of new master plans.

As open space becomes more expensive and less available, greater consideration must be given to multiple use of available lands and every measure taken to use them both efficiently and consistent with good environmental management. Municipal and school authorities should acquire, plan, and develop areas for joint use. This process calls for professional guidance in the fields of planning, designing, and engineering and for the advice and counsel of professionals in the fields of education, recreation, and park planning.

The most efficient and successful planning is accomplished when everyone in the organization, particularly those who will be identified with the finished product, have an opportunity to participate in the planning. Those who are to be served also should have a voice in the planning through community meetings.

Standards

Various standards for the size, location, and number of educational and recreation areas and facilities (See Appendix CC) have been proposed over the years by persons with a great deal of experience in the operation of such areas and facilities. These standards are formulated to make possible a program to serve the basic needs of people for physical education and recreation. However, they are not valid in prescribing specific activities or facilities for every neighborhood. While they are a useful guide in the acquisition and construction of a property, standards can seldom, if ever, be applied completely or without modification, because a typical or common situation is seldom found. Standards are formulated to indicate a basis for the intelligent development of local plans. Therefore, the standards for areas and facilities should be reviewed and appraised for each planning unit and modified whenever changing conditions warrant their revision.

Standards for areas and facilities developed by private planning firms, public agencies, and service organizations at the local, state, and national levels have been widely endorsed throughout the United States and have provided the basis for recommendations in scores of long-range plans for school, park, and recreation systems. The proposal that at least one acre of recreation and park space be set aside by urban areas for every 100 members of the present and estimated future population has been more widely accepted than any other space standard. However, this standard does not relate to the demographic or physiographic character of particular locales and is becoming obsolete. Professional and governmental authorities, including the National Recreation and Park Association and the National Park Service, have previously suggested the desirability of providing an even higher ratio of land-to-population in towns and small cities.

Modification of this general standard has been suggested for all planning entities based upon local requirements for populated cities. Some municipal planning officials believe the development of large outlying properties owned by the municipality will help meet the recognized deficiency in the inner municipality. However, this proposal should be considered as a practicable substitute indicative not just of necessity, but also of feasibility.

Previous number standards related to the number of tennis courts or swimming pools per thousands of people and so forth. Such numbers do not take into consideration the land or people and the climatic and geographic locale of the planning entity. The specification and allocation of facilities per thousand are arbitrary. They neither reflect the requirements of the community or neighborhood nor are universally applicable. A planning process of interaction and participation by the public should determine the number of facilities from one end of town to the other.

Recreation acreage should be based on potential usage. Basing acreage and number of facilities on potential usage has some serious deficiencies but remains the best possible approach. Marketing demand studies can suggest levels of use but do not account for changing recreation patterns, changes in the economy, unanticipated competition, and the like. Guidelines for acreage allocations for different park types are only illustrative. Every activity has a public demand. The demand for some activities is often met by the commercial, nonprofit, or volunteer sector. Ski lodges, tennis centers, and other corporations all conduct market studies to ascertain the leisure needs of and probable use by their clientele. Public agencies must conduct comparable studies to analyze demand. If the municipality can ascertain the probable use, turnover, capacity, and low/peak load for each activity, it can compute the number of activity stations and facilities for each activity group. The park acreage is then computed for actual facilities, for circulating paths and roads, for landscaping, and for other features.

Park and Recreation Areas

The types of outdoor recreation areas described here represent a variety of service units that may be used in programs of athletics, sports, physical education, and recreation. Local conditions will dictate to

Photo by Meghan Rosselli

Play apparatus.

a large extent which types are to be used in any given locality. Hence, different combinations of areas and facilities will emerge as the solution to the problem of meeting the needs and interests of a particular locality.

There is some controversy over parkland aesthetics as measured by the terms active and passive recreation. Many individuals with inherent interest in recreation or leisure pursuits associated with nature denounce the intrusion into parklands by activities that alter the natural environment. Battles have been fought over ball diamond location, loss of wetlands, and elimination of native species. Obviously, these two groups have different attitudes about the character and purpose of parklands. Parklands can be designed for active or passive use, or both, without destroying their aesthetic values. The use of parklands should reflect the greatest good for the greatest number and the protection of the health, well-being, and safety of all. Parklands may be of multiple use in many cases, but there are also strong cases for maintaining natural areas. The balance between the two is often difficult to agree upon, but there should be a commitment for both. Community involvement is essential in helping to make these determinations. In some instances, state and federal environmental standards may determine what can and cannot be accomplished.

If a community is split over use of parklands, a cost-benefit analysis should be made to ascertain the feasibility and costs of trade-offs. There is no sense in preserving a swamp that was created artificially and lacks any ecological value, but a natural swamp might be found elsewhere and preserved to meet specific needs and interests. There are alternatives in every planning process and they should be considered. The aesthetic values of a parkland, whether oriented toward play apparatus or floral displays, do not have to be sacrificed because they are termed passive or active.

Abandoned industrial sites such as strip mines, waste disposal areas, and sand and gravel pits offer unique possibilities for park and recreation development. In many cases, recreation use is not only the most beneficial but the most economic use of such sites. The cost of development of the sites can sometimes be born by the owner, by state or federal reclamation funds, or through previous court settlements. Brownfields, waste

Photo by Meghan Rosselli

Celebration station.

disposal sites, and other areas that have been adversely affected by previous use should be carefully assessed and tested before being accepted for recreation and park use. The cost of environmental cleanup can easily run into the millions of dollars. The recreation planner must not overlook the possibility of obtaining these sites for public use. If possible, cooperative planning should be started while the site is still being used by industry so landscape features can be developed to make it more appealing for recreation use.

Playlot/Mini-Parks: Location, Size, and Features

A playlot/mini-park is a small recreational area designed for the safe play of preschool children. As an independent unit, the playlot/mini-park is most frequently developed in large housing projects or in other densely populated urban areas with high concentrations of preschool children. More often, it is incorporated as a feature of a larger recreation area. If a community is able to operate a neighborhood park within a one-quarter-mile zone of every home, playlots should be located at the playground sites. A

Notes

location near a playground entrance close to restrooms and away from active game areas is best.

The playlot/mini-park should be enclosed with a low fence or solid planting to assist mothers or guardians in safeguarding their children. Thought should be given to placement of benches, with and without shade, for ease of supervision and comfort for parents and guardians. A drinking fountain with a step for tots will serve both children and adults. Playground equipment geared to the preschool child should combine attractive traditional play apparatus with creative, imaginative alternatives. Playground equipment should be marked with signs to designate the age group for which it is designed.

Photo by Meghan Rosselli

Additional examples of play equipment.

The Neighborhood Park

The neighborhood park is land set aside primarily for both active and passive recreation. Ideally, it gives the impression of being rural, sylvan, or national in its character. It emphasizes horticultural features with spacious turf areas bordered by trees, shrubs, and, sometimes, floral arrangements. It is essential in densely populated areas but not required where there is ample yard space at individual home sites.

Photo by Meghan Rosselli

Fountain.

A neighborhood park should be provided for each neighborhood. In many neighborhoods, it will be incorporated in the park-school site. A separate location is required if this combination is not feasible.

A separately located neighborhood park normally requires three to five acres. As a measure of expediency, however, an isolated area as small as one or two acres may be used. Sometimes the functions of a neighborhood park can be satisfactorily included in a community or citywide park.

The neighborhood park plays an important role in setting standards for community aesthetics. Therefore, it should include open lawn areas, plantings, and walks. Sculpture forms, pools, and fountains should also be considered for ornamentation. Creative planning will employ contouring, contrasting surfaces, masonry, and other modern techniques to provide both eye appeal and utility.

Community Parks

The community park, like the neighborhood park, is designed primarily to provide facilities for a variety of types of organized recreation activities but it should also have the characteristics of a landscaped park. It should include passive recreation areas, provide vis-

Photo by Meghan Rosselli

Example of an outdoor court.

Photo by Meghan Rosselli

A good example of park lighting.

ibility for security purposes, and have adequate lighting for night-time security. It usually serves as the playground for the children living in the immediate neighborhood but its primary service is to a much wider age group. Thus, it supplies a greater variety of facilities and more extensive service than can be justified at the neighborhood park. The school child, teenager, young adult, hobbyist, senior citizen, and family group all find attractive facilities at the well-developed community park and playfield. Because there is no school building at this area, some type of indoor facility is needed. In many cases, a multipurpose recreation center is provided to meet this need.

Citywide or District Parks

The citywide or district park serves a district of a large city or an entire smaller city. It should serve a population of 50,000 to 100,000 with a wide variety of activities. The ideal location for this area is in combination with a high school as a park-school complex. Where this is not feasible, consideration should be given to placing the park as close as possible to the center of the population to be served. The land available will be a determining factor in site selection. While the service zone will vary according to population density, a normal use zone is two to four miles. The size may range from 50 to 100 acres but is generally recommended to be in excess of 100 acres.

Depending on available acreage, topography, and natural features, the city-wide or district park will contain a large number of different components. These would include, but not be limited to, the following:

- fields for baseball, football, soccer, and softball (see Chapter 21)
- tennis center (see Chapter 20)
- winter sports facilities (see Chapter 29)
- day-camp center
- picnic areas (group and family)
- cycling paths or tracks
- swimming pool (see Chapter 23)
- water sports lake
- golf course (which requires considerably more acreage)
- recreation center
- nature trails
- skate parks
- multiple playgrounds for different age groups
- parking areas
- outdoor theater.

The above facilities should be separated by large turf and landscaped areas. Natural areas and perimeter buffers should be provided.

Special-Use Areas and Facilities

Trails

Trails used by walkers and joggers have become very popular. In many locations in the United States, old, abandoned rail lines have been secured from the railroad companies. In some cases the companies have salvaged the rails and cross ties. In other cases they have donated the land, rails, and

Photo by Meghan Rosselli

Pagoda.

ties to the government. Once a trail has been established, it should easily blend into the environment. The planners need to consider the climate, flora and fauna, topography, local history, and available materials for the infrastructure.

The width of a walking trail should be between three and six feet. When developing a walking trail, the following points should be considered: 1) local community input, 2) initial cost and long-term maintenance costs, 3) interesting attractions featured along the trail, 4) access to public transportation, 5) appropriate signage (e.g., names of plants and trees, distances, grades or elevations, direction of trail, trail layout and map, warnings of hazards, etc.), 6) surface preparation (e.g., asphalt, dirt, gravel, wood chips, saw dust, etc.), 7) fitness equipment along trail, and 8) loops and networks to provide options for the walkers. Many communities are developing city-wide trail systems that link together walking and bicycle paths with the park trails being the anchor for the system.

Photo by Meghan Rosselli
Covered bridge.

A walking trail requires some basic infrastructure: 1) handicapped accessibility (e.g., ramps, handrails); 2) adequate parking at the beginning of the trail and at select entry points along the trail; 3) rest stops with benches, drinking water, rest rooms, shelters, and picnic areas; and 4) a trail design to eliminate water drainage problems.

Bicycle Facilities and Pathways

Most of the recommended bicycle programs and facilities will require considerable investments of time and money to bring them to fruition. An alternative program might be considered. This program would develop bicycle touring routes in and across the country using rural and low volume vehicular routes. The only expenses involved in the creation of this system are for initial system planning, printing bikeway maps, and marking intersections. County and city governments together with schools and universities have implemented touring systems.

The steps in the development of bicycling facilities are:

* Appoint a committee from interested groups of individuals, including representatives of the school or university and the recreation department.
* Make a survey of county road maps and mark a conceptual bicycle system on a work map. One of the objectives is to create a roughly circular route. "Spoke" routes would radiate from the campus to the peripheral route. Select the safest possible routes. High-volume roads and intersections should be avoided. After the road map is finished, the committee should find that it has the framework for an adequate bicycling touring system.
* The next step involves field reconnaissance of the roads marked on the working map. Alternate routes may be selected if the original roads are not appropriate for bicycling. Actual travel by bicycle is recommended for the reconnaissance.
* Following the completion of the field reconnaissance, the next step is the drafting of the final bikeway map. Titles and safety information are also placed on the map. The back of the map may be filled with a variety of information. The bikeway should be marked, especially the abrupt turns. Paint distinctive symbols and arrows on the pavement of the road. Standard highway marking paint may be used and stencils for the symbols may be cut from heavy gauge linoleum.

Cycle trails require some additional planning beyond that needed for a walking or jogging trail. The planners need to include the following additional factors in the design: 1) minimum width of dual path should be 12 feet, 2) the path should have a safety zone on either side extending 5 feet clear of all vegetation, 3) the ideal surface material is asphalt for the path and small gravel or brick chips for the safety buffer, 4) appropriate sight lines will need to be determined for cyclists to avoid hitting walkers on corners, and 5) the cyclists may require bike racks at rest stops.

Bridle Paths and Rings

Horseback riding is popular with all age groups but is generally restricted to the larger park areas because of space requirements. Riding trails are usually a minimum of 10 feet wide to permit riders going in opposite directions to pass in safety. Except on very steep terrain, very little is required in the way of construction. Clearing, a small amount of leveling, removal of large rocks and boulders, and trimming or removal of low-hanging tree limbs constitute the major items. Most small streams can be forded but an occasional bridge may be required as well as cross drainage on steep gradients. No special surfacing is required except that a gravel base may be needed in wet or boggy areas that cannot be avoided. Tanbark, cinders, and other materials are also used frequently on heavily used trails and in areas of concentrated use around hitching racks and in riding rings.

Stables and adjoining facilities such as feed racks, holding corrals, riding rings, and hitching racks should be located at least 500 feet from the nearest public-use area because of the fly and odor problem. The size of these facilities will depend on the number of horses. However, the stable will ordinarily contain a limited number of horse stalls, a feed storage room, a tack room, a small office, and toilet facilities for men and women. A fenced enclosure commonly called a holding corral or paddock into which the horses can be turned at the end of the day is required. A surfaced riding ring, sometimes encircled with a rail fence, is frequently provided for training novices in the fundamentals of riding.

Finally, horse riding trails (sometimes called bridle paths) are not compatible with walkers or cyclists. The horse trail cannot be of hard surface (e.g., asphalt or concrete) but rather a softer topsoil and clay mixture. The trail needs a good base in order to reduce maintenance costs. The tree limbs need to be cut close to the trunk. It is also necessary to provide good horizontal vegetation clearance (over 6 feet) and vertical vegetation clearance (over 10 feet). The width of the trail should be between 2 and 6 feet.

Golf Courses

The design, construction, operation, and maintenance of golf courses is too vast a subject to be covered in detail in this publication. For general information and guidance, write the National Golf Foundation at 1150 South US Highway One, Suite 401, Jupiter, FL 33477 or The American Society of Golf Course Architects, 125 North Executive Drive, Suite 106, Brookfield, WI 53005.

The creation of new golf course facilities throughout the nation continued at a very healthy pace in the '90s despite periodic economic slowdowns and shows no decline throughout the first decade of the new century. As the popularity of the game continues to grow, there is an obvious need to increase the number of golf courses to keep up with demand. Currently, there are over 25 million golfers playing more than 500 million rounds of golf annually on nearly 15,000 courses. Should new player development continue in the same statistical trends as the past 10 years, the number of golfers and rounds played could increase by 35% between now and the year 2010.

Golf course construction costs vary greatly, but generally planners can count on spending at least $2.5 million. This does not include the cost of the land. A golf course construction budget might look like this:

- Construction of 18-hole course $2.5 to $4.5 million*
- Maintenance equipment $300,000 to $500,000
- Maintenance building $125,000 to $450,000
- Clubhouse $750,000 to $1.5 million
- Total $3.9 to $6.95 million
- * Includes basic golf course construction, clearing, grading, drainage, construction of tees, fairway and fairway features, greens, sand bunkers, irrigation system, seeding and grassing, shelters, bridges, and cart paths.

It must be emphasized that these cost figures are intended only as a rough guideline and do not include the cost of land, entry road, parking lot, other support facilities (e.g., restrooms, chemical storage areas, fuel storage, sand and topsoil storage areas, golf cart storage space, practice putting green, driving range, and tree nursery), golf course architect, and other necessary professional consulting fees. In addition, maintenance costs usually run between $250,000 and $650,000 annually, plus club operations and golf cart fleets.

Assuming the land is suitable for construction of a golf course, the following space requirements must be taken into consideration:

- For a standard 18-hole course—145 to 200 acres.
- For shorter executive courses—75 to 120 acres.
- For a standard 9-hole course—70 to 90 acres.
- For a 9-hole par three course (including a couple of par four holes)—45 to 60 acres.

Some of the most desirable features of the land to be used include rolling hills, interesting landscaping, ravines, creeks and ponds or lake sites, and irrigation resources. The more of these features that can be found on a piece of land, the less the overall construction cost will be. The planners need to also be concerned about environmental issues (e.g., wetlands), drainage, and quality of the soil. Other key components for site selection are the ease of utility connections and accessibility to the new project.

Marinas and Boat Ramps

America abounds in waterways. The myriad of inland lakes, the rivers and streams, the vast Great Lakes, and the thousands of miles of coastline invite America's citizens to take advantage of this natural resource. Today, boating commands more of the recreation dollar than baseball, fishing, golf, or any

Photo by Meghan Rosselli

Fishing deck.

other single activity. There is a need for efficient, realistic, and functional planning for facilities to accommodate the present needs and the future growth that this recreation interest will precipitate. The launching, mooring, and storage of yachts and rowboats are the function of a marina that will serve the needs of the recreation boat owner. It is suggested that knowledgeable and experienced personnel be engaged to study the number, types, and sizes of existing boats in the area, the number and size of existing berthing facilities, and the condition of such existing facilities. The survey should also include the potential population growth in the community and surrounding area to determine the future boat ownership. An accurate and comprehensive evaluation of such a study is the first step in planning a marina.

The study will determine the next important consideration in laying out a marina: selecting the correct number of slips of each size that will be required. Based on the needs of the community to be served, planners will determine the necessary number of slips to accommodate boats of various sizes.

Because marinas vary so greatly in their design, function, location, and capacity, it is virtually impossible to arrive at standard conclusions and judgments concerning a model marina. Each planner will be able to apply the general principles to his unique circumstances. From that point, however, he must adapt his marina to the peculiar needs and characteristics of a community.

A marina, since it is a parking lot for boats, will most likely be surrounded by a repair shop, fuel station, dry dock area, and general marine supply shop. Key planning issues include, but are not limited to: 1) environmental impact, 2) local politics, 3) waste management, 4) conservation, 5) quality of construction and compatibility with the environment, 6) financing (i.e., initial cost and long-term maintenance costs), 7) management and safety, 8) size of the project, and 9) monitoring of environmental problems.

A boat ramp is necessary for launching boats into a waterway. The initial task is to locate adequate, safe launching and retrieval facilities. Contrary to popular opinion, suitable locations for boat ramps are hard to find. Planners should consider the following when selecting a suitable location for a boat ramp: 1) protection from severe weather; 2) minimal impact on the surrounding environment; 3) large enough space to accommodate the ramp and trailer and vehicle parking as well as rigging and maneuvering of trailers; 4) accessibility to the proposed site by an all-weather road; 5) ancillary facilities such as restrooms, water supply, night lighting, telephone accessibility, wash down area, and waste disposal facility; 6) legal requirements (e.g., requirement for environmental impact study, zoning requirements, etc.); 7) local community input; 8) initial cost and long-term maintenance costs; and 9) water conditions (e.g., wave patterns and currents).

Curling

Curling is an ice sport popular in Canada and the northern United States. Sponsored by clubs and leagues, it is played with hand-propelled 42.5 pound stones, referred to as rocks. There are four members on a team, each shooting two rocks. The object is to slide one team's rocks nearest the center of a circle, called the house, at the far end of the rink. The advent of artificial ice has broadened the popularity of curling and extended its geographical interest zone.

Performing Arts Areas

In the past few years there has been increased demand for suitable indoor and outdoor facilities for operas, plays, band and orchestral concerts, pageants, festivals, holiday programs, and civic celebrations. When performed outdoors, such activities usually require a stage or band shell with adjoining amphitheater capable of accommodating large numbers of spectators.

Selection of the proper site for an outdoor theater is of primary importance. It should have good acoustical properties and be located in a quiet place away from the noise of traffic or of groups at play. A natural bowl or depression on a hillside with a slope of 10 to 20 degrees, preferably bordered by slopes or densely wooded areas, provides a fine location.

At some theaters, people sit on the slope of the amphitheater. At others, permanent seats are installed. Terraces with a turf surface are not recommended because they are too difficult to maintain. Sufficient level space should be provided at the rear of the seating area for the circulation of spectators, and aisles should be wide enough to facilitate the seating of large numbers in a short period of time. Public comfort stations and refreshment facilities are usually provided near the entrance to the amphitheater. Provision for the nearby parking of automobiles is essential, but parking areas must be located where noises and car lights do not disturb the stage action.

The dimensions of the stage are determined by the proposed uses but rarely should a stage be less than 50 feet in width or 30 feet in depth. The rear of the stage may be a wall or high hedge, or even a planting of trees, and the wings may be formed by natural plant materials. The band or music shell, however, is more satisfactory for projecting voices and sound free from echoes and interference. A vertical rear wall with an inclined ceiling is not only the simplest and most economical to construct but affords excellent acoustical qualities.

The band shell usually contains dressing rooms, toilets, storage space, and control centers for amplifying and lighting equipment, although sometimes these facilities are provided in separate structures near the back of the stage. An orchestra pit is generally located between the auditorium and the stage.

Mobile storage units with self-contained lighting and acoustical systems are becoming very popular, because they can be used in many parks instead of restricting programs to one permanent location. Equipped to serve as a band shell, stage, puppet theater, or platform for other performing arts, these mobile units can bring productions to audiences never exposed to such activities. Excellent units can be obtained at a cost less than that required for a permanent band shell.

Archery Range

This sport appeals to a sizable group in most communities. Sufficient space is needed to ensure the safety and enjoyment of the participants. An earth bunker or bales of hay and straw piled up to the top of the target may protect this space.

An archery range (see Chapter 33) should be fairly level. Orientation should be north and south so the archers will not be facing the sun. A fence enclosure is desirable, but not essential. The public should be controlled in some manner, however, so they do not walk through the range.

Boccie Ball

A boccie court is 91 feet by 13 feet. Many boccie courts are sunken, with retaining walls constructed out of pressure-treated landscaping timbers. When built above ground, a boccie court needs side and back walls. These can be constructed of wood, lattice, landscape stones, brick, or cinder block.

The boccie court area should include

- shade trees,
- flowers,
- storage area for equipment,
- lawn chairs and tables, and
- possibly lights for evening play.

Areas for Outdoor Education and Recreation

Outdoor education is a term that refers to learning activities in, and for, the outdoors. Such activities can be provided in the curriculums of schools, colleges, and universities as well as in the programs of recreation; camping; and federal, state, and community agencies. Outdoor education is a means of curriculum extension and enrichment through outdoor experiences. It is not a separate discipline with prescribed objectives, like science and mathematics; it is simply a learning climate that offers opportunities for direct laboratory experiences in identifying and resolving real-life problems, for acquiring skills with which to enjoy a lifetime of creative living, for building concepts and developing concern about humankind and our natural environment, and for getting us back in touch with those aspects of living where our roots were once firm and deep.

Outdoor education and outdoor recreation encompass a great variety of activities, many of which

Photo by Meghan Rosselli

Picnic shelter.

can be conducted on a single, large tract of land. With careful planning, facilities, some in or near an urban area and others in more distant places, can be used. An outdoor-education complex on one piece of land or on several plots in close proximity has many advantages in the areas of administration, leadership, equipment, and transportation. Such a site lends itself to wide community use with responsibilities for leadership and finances shared by several agencies. Obviously, the size and physical characteristics of an outdoor-education complex will depend on the geographic location and the topography of the land.

Some of the facilities and types of site treatment for a complex that would accommodate a broad program of outdoor education and outdoor recreation, and which would constitute an outdoor laboratory or field campus, are briefly described below. It is assumed that there will be many areas and facilities, public and private, that can also be used in a comprehensive program.

Considerations in Selecting and Developing Sites

Size

The type of program planned should determine the size of the site. Size alone does not necessarily mean much except that it does affect the numbers of certain species of wildlife that might live in the area. A large area does not necessarily have a diversity of physical features. It may just be level land, harboring only a few species of trees, with no particularly outstanding features. Nevertheless, such an area could be made interesting from an educational point of view, provided good leadership is available.

Many schools, recreation departments, and community agencies already have school sites, parks, and recreation areas that could be developed for outdoor programs. Schools, as well as other agencies, in some sections of the country, also have forest lands that could be developed and used in a broad educational and recreation program.

Site Characteristics

The type of program planned also determines the characteristics of the site. If plans call for a resident camp, many more requirements must be met than if the site will be used only on a daily basis. If the land and facilities are to contribute to all aspects of the educational curriculum, or if there is to be special emphasis on science, conservation, and outdoor skills, many characteristics will need to be considered, such as the following:

Photo by Meghan Rosselli

Picnic pavilion.

- A location to give some privacy and solitude.
- Year-round accessibility by road.
- A minimum of natural and man-made hazards.
- Interesting geologic features, such as rock outcroppings, open field, flat terrain, and a variety of soil types.
- A variety of native vegetation including woods.
- Wildlife that can be maintained with good management.
- A pond, stream, seashore, or large body of water.
- Demonstration areas for conservation practices.
- Woods for practicing outdoor skills and use of native materials.
- Sanitary facilities including good drainage and good drinking water.
- Simple shelters in the event of inclement weather.
- Proximity to adequate medical and hospital services.

Special Features

Many kinds of developments are found in various types of outdoor education areas. Some of these are appropriate for camps, some for outdoor laboratories or nature centers, and some for outdoor recreation and sports centers. An outdoor education and outdoor recreation complex would include many site plans and facilities not possible in more limited areas. The adaptability of the area to the proposed program, the cost of construction, maintenance problems, aesthetic considerations, and available leadership are all factors in determining what facilities might be developed in a particular land area or cluster of acreages.

Listed below are some of the special developments that might be included in appropriate sites. Some of the features listed are discussed elsewhere in this text and are merely mentioned here. Others, not mentioned in other places, are discussed in more detail.

Grass, shrubs, and trees. They provide shade, prevent soil erosion, provide food and cover for wildlife, serve as windbreaks, mark the boundary of the property, act as a buffer zone to ensure privacy against an adjacent (presently or potentially) populated area, demonstrate principles of plant growth, serve as a resource for ecological studies, and give practice in forest management. A school forest offers many popular activities.

A vegetable garden or a bog garden.

Soil-erosion demonstration areas. Such an area should be rich in vegetation, feature good conservation practices, be situated on inclined terrain, and be located next to a piece of land denuded of its vegetation and also located on an incline. Comparisons can then be made over a period of time to determine what happens to the quantity and quality of soil in both areas.

Wildlife sanctuary. Provide mixed plantings and construct birdhouses, feeders, and bird baths to attract a variety of birds.

Weather station. This is for the study of meteorology and should be located in an area that can be fenced off and locked.

Campfire ring. This facility provides a place for campfires, for conducting orientations before field trips, and for other special programs. The campfire ring should be located in a wooded area to ensure a feeling of isolation. Use logs for seats.

Nature trails. Develop, if space permits, a variety of trails with individual or multiple purposes. The use of trail markers, brochures, and naturalist-conducted programs can focus the trail use. One may be a geology trail winding its way through an area rich in geologic features. Another trail may emphasize the study of erosion while still another may lead to a historic spot.

Pioneer living area. Social studies lessons are vividly illustrated in such an area. Dramatize the life of the pioneer, including such activities as making dyes from plants, cooking outdoors, constructing shelters, learning to identify edible plants, and learning other survival practices.

Observation platform. This platform can be used for observing birds and for studying astronomy. It should be located on the highest point of the property.

Miniature gardens. Each garden features a particular grouping of native plants found in the typical setting in which they normally grow.

Plant grafting. A demonstration area that provides interesting studies in genetics.

Animal-baiting area. Place a salt lick and some meat in a cleared area. Spread loose dirt around the baited spot, press it down with your feet, and smooth it out. Animals attracted to the area will leave their footprints, which can then be observed and studied.

Photo by Meghan Rosselli

Horseshoe pit.

Natural preserve. An area could be set aside in which no developments would be made. It would be given complete protection and would provide a spot for the observation of ecological aspects.

Orienteering courses. The development of several courses for map and compass use would stimulate educational and recreation use of the area (see Appendix U).

Greenhouse. A place for the propagation of plants, some of which may be used for area improvement, is important. A greenhouse would make possible an acquaintance with plants and would be a means of providing projects for study during the off-season.

Winter sports area. Places for skating, skiing, and coasting would be desirable in those parts of the country that have sufficient snow and cold weather to make these sports feasible.

Natural play area. An area set aside for children, containing such elements as climbing logs, ropes for swinging across low areas, sandbanks, and hide-and-seek areas, can provide play opportunities different from those found in the city.

Turtle pond. An attractive pond with water and plantings would make possible the study and observation of turtles and other amphibians.

Rifle and skeet ranges. Such an area will provide opportunities for instruction in gun safety as well as for participation in rifle and skeet shooting. These areas should be located away from high use areas and should have controls to monitor potential safety issues.

Casting and angling area. Developments for casting and angling would serve both instructional and recreation uses.

Amphitheater. For large-group programs, an amphitheater would be important. It could be used for lectures, drama, music, and a variety of demonstrations.

Astronomy area. A special area for astronomy may be developed on a large open area, waterfront, dock, or even a roof. Seating facilities are desirable and often a telescope is permanently mounted to facilitate observations.

Bird feeding station.

Historical markers. Sites of old farms, early settlers' homes, Native American trails and village sites, and pioneer roads are illustrations of the kinds of historical sites that might be used for student projects.

Shelters. Adirondack or picnic shelters can serve day-camp and day-use groups during inclement weather.

Tree stump. Locate a fairly well-preserved tree stump. Make a sloping cut, smooth the top by sanding, and treat it with clear waterproofing material such as fiberglass resin. Much can be learned about tree growth from carefully studying a tree stump.

Herb garden. This garden features food seasoning and medicinal plants and serves as a useful teaching aid for a home economics class.

Photographic blind. Construct a blind near a bird-feeding station for taking pictures of wild birds.

Evergreen tree nursery. Trees can later be transplanted to desired areas.

Field archery. Targets are set up in wooded areas or fields to simulate actual hunting conditions.

Natural areas. Such areas are left relatively undisturbed and man-made modifications should be avoided as much as possible. These places serve as excellent resources for scientific studies of natural phenomena.

Picnic site. It is desirable to locate the picnic site on the periphery of the property.

Seashore areas. Communities adjacent to seashores may have areas set aside for study and observation. Developments might include ramps or walks to facilitate observation. Walkways through tidelands may be developed as nature trails. One of the national parks has an underwater nature trail.

Outdoor Laboratories

The term "outdoor laboratory" is used for a piece of land (including wetlands, lakes, and seashores) set aside by a school for learning experiences directly related to land and its resources. It may be located close to an individual school or it may serve a group of schools. It may be a part of the school grounds or a section of a park-school development. It may consist of only a few acres nearby or of several hundred acres nearby or many miles away. It may serve individual elementary schools, high schools, or universities or all of them jointly. Because outdoor laboratories are extremely varied in their site possibilities and their purposes, no rigid format for their development is possible.

The term "land for learning" has been applied to the school laboratory. It implies the opportunity of school groups to study, explore, and experiment with land and its resources. Outdoor study, field trips, and experiments with water, soil, plants, and animals constitute its major functions.

Developments may range from nothing more than a few trails, with the area left natural, to nature trails, class and museum buildings, horticultural plots, developed ponds, forest plantations, gardens, and small-farm operations. The creativity of the teacher or outdoor education specialist, the potential of the available site, and funds available may be the only limiting factors in the development of program facilities.

If a laboratory is heavily used, water and toilet facilities might be essential. A storage building for tools and supplies might also be desirable.

Nature Centers

The term "nature center" is used to designate a particular type of development that will facilitate learning in the outdoors and the growth of recreation interests. The establishment of nature centers is being promoted extensively by several science- and nature-related organizations. Many centers exist across the United States. Children's museums may be considered a part of this development although some of these museums lack adjacent lands for outdoor education.

Principally three types of financing and management have developed nature centers: schools, private associations, and public park and recreation departments.

The Site

Some of the suggestions for the school outdoor education laboratory are applicable here. Nature trails, ponds, bogs, gardens, forest plantings, and the like may provide the variety essential for a rich outdoor education program.

The Building

The building should be designed in order to permit expansion as the program grows and as more funds become available. In its initial stage, the building should contain a minimum space of 2,500 square feet, which is large enough to contain one class adequately. The building should be designed according to the needs set by the program. The following general facilities are recommended:

- Office for staff.
- Restrooms. Access should be provided to the outside as well as to the interior of the building.
- Large meeting room. The wall space can be utilized for exhibits. Low cabinets along the walls should be provided for storage of educational aids. A long counter providing work and display space should be constructed on top of the cabinets.
- Classrooms. Two classrooms should be provided so that a class may be broken up into smaller groups if necessary.
- Workroom. This room would be used for constructing displays and for arts and crafts.
- Science laboratory. A room should be equipped with microscopes, soil- and mineral-testing equipment, and other materials necessary for scientific studies. Inclusion of GPS and GIS technology is becoming more common.

- Library. The large meeting room can contain the library, which would occupy one section of the room. The library should contain reference material, field guides, magazines, and novels concerned with the outdoors.
- Storage room. Adequate space should be provided for storage of the many pieces of instructional and janitorial equipment that will accumulate over the years.

It should be emphasized again that it is not essential for one center to have most of the facilities described here. Dynamic leadership is, to a large degree, more important and not even the ultimate in good facilities can ever satisfactorily replace the need for effective leadership.

Interpretive Centers

Although the name "interpretive centers" might well be applied to the outdoor laboratories and the nature centers mentioned earlier, it has a specific use in describing certain facilities of public parks offered as a service to the general public and, in some cases, to school groups. The National Park Service has the most extensive development of such centers. The United States Forest Service, Corps of Engineers, and Bureau of Land Management as well as other federal land managing agencies provide interpretive facilities. State parks and larger metropolitan parks have also developed interpretive centers.

The primary purpose of interpretive centers is to help visitors understand and appreciate the natural, historical, cultural, or archeological features of the areas in which the centers are located. Interpretation is tailored for each area. Facility developments are likewise varied and often unique to the site being interpreted.

Interpretive centers frequently contain a trailside museum or interpretive-center building. This may vary in size from 10 feet by 20 feet to a large, multifocused structure. The size depends on the groups to be accommodated, the interpretive materials available, and the types of programs to be presented. A large building may contain some or all of the following:

- Museum quality display rooms depicting cultural, historic, wildlife, and other exhibits.
- Office space for staff members.
- A laboratory for research and the preparation of display materials.
- Meeting rooms for lectures, video, or computer presentations.
- Lavatories and toilets.
- Theater.
- A counter for the sale of books and the distribution of pamphlets.
- An outdoor amphitheater or campfire area for lectures and movies.
- Trails to points of interest (often self-guiding nature trails).
- Parapets or other special observation points, often including mounted telescopes and pointers indicating places of interest.
- Interpretive devices at points of interest.

School and Community Gardens, Farms, and Forests

Gardens, farms, and forests provide direct experiences with growing plants and, in some cases, with domestic animals. Schools, park and recreation agencies, and a few private agencies have been responsible for the development of facilities. Even when facilities are developed and operated by park and recreation departments or private agencies, some direct relationship with schools is often provided through an instructional program in which the school children are enrolled.

Display Gardens

Gardens of various kinds should be developed to provide for visual, cultural, and educational equipment.

A formal garden may be composed entirely of one type of plant (such as roses), of various types of assorted plant materials, or of a series of individual gardens comprised of single types of plant units. Features such as a water fountain and statuary can be incorporated into the design.

Informal gardens should have long, sweeping lawn areas to serve as a setting for plants and flower beds. Plants may include large specimen trees, flowering trees, shrubs, and vines. The flower borders can be of varied plants. All the plants should be of interest to the average homeowner and should be useful in helping him or her select plants for his or her own yard. Attempts should be made to keep abreast of the latest introductions and to display those types of plants that are hardy to the particular region in which the garden is located. This aspect of planting for the homeowner should be stressed in both formal and informal gardens, and demonstrations of plant cultural practice should be provided.

Naturalistic and native, or wildflower, gardens are established in a wilderness location where the plants native to the region can be assembled in one area so they are easily accessible to the citizens. Developers will probably need an area of varied topography—lowlands, highlands, and prairies—and an area with varied soil conditions—from alkaline to acid—to accommodate the various types of plants.

Tract Gardens

In a tract garden, which is the most common type of school or community garden, a piece of property ranging in size from 1 to 10 acres is divided into small tracts for the use of individuals. A typical plot size may be 10 feet by 20 feet but adults and families can use larger gardens. A garden program with

25 plots can be set up on 1/4 acre of land although more space is desirable. Four acres of land can hold 100 gardeners with plots of varied size and community crops. This size allows space for a service building and activity area. It should be on rich, well-drained soil with water available.

Garden programs may involve instruction, environmental projects, field trips, and science activities. Community projects may include novelty crops such as a pumpkin patch, gourds, Indian corn, and a Christmas tree farm. Gardening appeals to all ages and is an excellent program for families.

Some of the necessary or desirable features of the tract garden are the following:

- Garden building—either a small building for the storage of tools and equipment or a building large enough for class meetings and indoor activities during bad weather.
- Toilet facilities adequate to care for the maximum number of participants expected on the garden plot at one time.
- Greenhouse for plant propagation.
- Ready access to water, with spigots and hoses available for limited irrigation.
- Fencing for protection of the garden.
- Pathways and walkways to provide easy access to all plots.
- A demonstration home yard, with grass, flowers, and shrubs.
- Good landscaping.

Preferably, the tract garden should be located within walking distance of the homes of the participants. In many cases, gardens are developed on or adjacent to school grounds.

Tract gardens for adults and families have been established in some communities. They are usually intended for people living in crowded urban centers or apartments who would not otherwise be able to garden. In some communities, these gardens are located some distance from homes, and transportation is left up to the individuals concerned.

Farms

Community or school farms are becoming increasingly important, especially near metropolitan centers, and offer opportunities for a rich and varied program. Farm programs include animal care and training and traditional rural activities such as hay rides, picnics, and nature activities. Families who just want to walk through to see and pet the animals heavily use model farms.

Simple barns and pens contain horses, cows, pigs, chickens, sheep, and other domestic animals, which children can help care for and feed. In an urban setting, it is essential that the facility be attractive and well maintained. There must be water, feed storage, and adequate exercise space for the animals. An office, restrooms, drinking fountain, indoor and outdoor activity areas, and storage space are needed for the people.

In addition to the buildings that are generally found on a diversified farm, there are meeting places and exhibits that make it possible to carry on indoor instruction. Picnic areas, farm ponds, day-camp facilities, campfire circles, and hiking trails are often developed also.

Working farms are sometimes adapted for recreational purposes. This type of facility actually produces while city residents visit to learn, observe, take part in, and enjoy farming activities. Groups may use the farm on a day basis and overnight accommodations can be provided. In either case, a large room and open outdoor space are needed for activity and instruction.

Farm camps offer opportunities for a farm-oriented camping experience. The farm camp is a farm not worked for production but set up for resident programs in environmental education, farm activities, natural history, science, and other outdoor recreation. There may be a large farmhouse converted to a program building and farm buildings converted to cabins. Facilities needed are a kitchen, dining area, sleeping quarters, restrooms, large activity room, and ample storage space. Additionally, barns, farm equipment, and other facilities will be needed. These facilities and animals will be required dependent on program direction.

Forests

Numerous school and community forests can be found throughout the United States. Many of these were acquired from tax-delinquent land, through gifts, or through protection programs for community watersheds. Their use has followed diverse patterns. Some schools have carried on field trips, forest improvement projects, and other outdoor education activities. In general, however, schools have not made the maximum use of such areas.

Many of these forests could be developed as outdoor educational laboratories. Some might be suitable sites for nature centers, day camps, or even resident camps.

School and community forests may serve valuable purposes even without extensive development. Water, trails, and toilets may be all the developments need to provide useful educational facilities. Such areas may serve their best functions as places in which to study the ecological changes taking place over a period of years.

Outdoor Skills and Sports Areas

Outdoor skills or sports areas should be included in the outdoor education and recreation complex; however, it may be necessary to acquire special sites depending on the topography of the land. These areas should provide opportunities to learn and practice skills but they may also be used as outdoor laboratories.

The following are some of the specialized program facilities that might be included in the outdoor skills and sports area:

- Casting and angling—platforms and open, level spaces.
- Outdoor shooting range.
- Archery range—target field course, archery, golf, and other games.
- Campcraft skills area.
- Overnight camping area.
- Outpost camping—Adirondack shelters.
- Facilities for water sports including swimming, canoeing, boating, sailing, skin diving, and water skiing.
- Area for crafts with native materials—carving, lapidary, weaving, and ceramics—with a simple structure to provide shelter in inclement weather and to house equipment.
- Water sports—ski slopes and tow, ski shelter, tobogganing, and ice-skating rinks.

Natural Areas

Natural areas are generally thought of as representative of native plants and animals of a locale. They may encompass a variety of habitats such as woodlands, deserts, swamps, bogs, wetlands, shorelines, or sand dunes.

It is almost impossible today, even in the wilderness, to find undisturbed areas. Most places categorized as natural areas are protected lands that indicate the least disturbance and that, through protection, planting, and development, approximate the original characteristics.

It is characteristic of natural areas that they are protected from inharmonious developments and activities. Simple access trails, protective fencing, and simple interpretive developments such as entrance bulletin boards are usually acceptable. In designated natural areas, the enjoyment and study of the natural features are encouraged and uses that detract from the natural features are discouraged.

Schools, parks, and camps are often the agencies that develop, maintain, and protect natural areas. Such areas are valuable assets in environmental education.

Camps and Camping

Historically, the word *camping* signified simple living outdoors and engaging in activities related primarily to the outdoors. Today, the term has broadened tremendously and encompasses a wide spectrum of developments for families and children. Resident centers, day camps, group camps, family camps, and wilderness camps are the common designations used for the various types of camps.

Camps have been developed by public agencies at all levels of government and by many voluntary youth-serving organizations. The rapidly increasing participation of children and adults in camping necessitates careful consideration of desirable areas and facilities.

Although most organized camping takes place on agency-owned or private property, public land is becoming increasingly involved. Public land is one of the major resources for school outdoor educational programs, and many resident centers have been constructed on public property or by public funds. Schools use the facilities during the school year and park and recreation agencies use them during the summer. The purposes of outdoor education, whether sponsored by park and recreation departments or by schools, are similar in many respects, and cooperative planning is not only necessary in order to get the most from the community dollar but imperative if suitable lands and sites are to be obtained. If adequate facilities are to be provided to meet the needs of both organized camping groups and schools, the facilities must be designed for year-round use.

Program Facilities—What to Expect

Following are some of the facilities used for various camp programs. Specifications and construction details for most are found elsewhere in this book.

Water-related activities are among the most popular in summer camps. During the fall and spring, school groups and other groups may use developments for fishing, canoeing, and boating.

Lakes, ponds, streams, bays, and inlets offer many recreational opportunities. All should be studied in detail with regard to currents, eddies, depth, slope, shoreline, debris, and other factors.

Canoeing, boating, and sailing are activities that may be conducted on a lake, pond, river, reservoir, bay, or other body of water. The water area should have accessory facilities such as floats, docks, markers, or buoys. Various sizes of water bodies are required for different activities and events. For instance, canoe racing courses are 100, 200, 440, and 880 yards, as well as one mile. Sailing requires a wider body of water because the boats usually finish to windward. The different classes of sailboats such as Sunfish and Sailfish, require different courses.

Casting is simulated rod-and-reel fishing. Practice casting on a playing field or in a gymnasium is possible year round. If a pond or lake is nearby, a beach or dock affords an excellent facility for the casting program.

In order to teach all phases of the activity, an area 300 by 100 feet is desirable. A football, soccer, hockey, or lacrosse field is ideal for class instruction.

Casting targets, which are 30 inches in diameter are easily constructed and can be an excellent project for any woodshop program. It is recommended that at least 10 targets be made. Others can be added as the program expands. Targets for use on the water are also 30 inches in diameter and are made of hollow metal tubing. They float and can be easily anchored.

Other program facilities include campfire circles and council rings for which most camps develop centers for meetings and evening programs and craft centers, which can range from canvas-covered areas with provisions for storing tools to extensive and well-equipped craft shops.

Day Camps

A day camp is an area and facility intended to provide a program similar to that of the resident camp except that campers sleep at home. Many of the considerations of planning for resident camps apply to day camps. However, facility problems are simpler because day campers sleep at home and usually eat two of the day's meals at home. Provisions, however simple, must nonetheless be made for water, toilets, rainy-day shelters, eating and cooking, refrigeration, first-aid and health, and program supplies. The focus of this section is that of selecting an appropriate day camp facility.

Abundant land for programs is extremely desirable, particularly when the emphasis is on outdoor-related activities. Reasonable isolation and a varied topography with outdoor program possibilities are essential. Natural parks, park-school areas, and community forests often lend themselves for use as day-camp sites. Some communities have developed special day-camp areas; others make appropriate picnic areas available for this special use.

Buses are often used to transport campers to the day camp. If more than half an hour is consumed in daily travel each way, the effectiveness of the program is reduced.

Day-camp groups are divided into units or counselor groups ranging from 8 to 20 campers. Most day camps provide simple facilities for each unit including a fireplace for cooking, storage cabinets, and tables. Some day camps serve a daily meal in a central dining hall to reduce or eliminate the need for unit cooking facilities.

Storage is needed for equipment, food, and program supplies. Some day camps use trailers or trucks for storage, hauling them back and forth each day. Also, a well-equipped first-aid station and a rest-area facility are necessary.

Group Camps

Many public agencies today provide special campsites for small groups such as scouts, church groups, and school classes. These sites generally accommodate from 10 to 40 persons. In most cases, the groups stay from one to five days. Small units in decentralized resident camps sometimes have facilities that can be used for group camping. Simple fireplaces for cooking, picnic shelters for use in bad weather, toilets, and safe drinking water are necessities.

The great increase in winter camping by small groups often necessitates special developments. Some winter campers live completely outdoors in the cold, even in snow. Usually, however, winterized buildings are used for cooking, sleeping, and evening activities.

Campgrounds

Campgrounds are found in many types of settings and in many formats. Tent camping is the traditional form of camping, but the increase in motor homes, trailers, and pop-up trailers has changed the camping mix. Public campgrounds such as those found in federal, state, county, and municipal park systems have had to accommodate the changing camper. Traditional amenities have included water somewhere in the campground, restrooms, and maybe showers. In today's marketplace these are called primitive conditions. Campgrounds desiring to attract motor homes and trailers now provide electrical (usually 110 and 220 volts), sewer, and water. Additional services can include cable television and telephone lines.

Campgrounds should be segregated, or at least partitioned. Motor homes, trailers, and pop-up trailers should be located in one section and tent camping in another. A natural segregation occurs by the designation of campgrounds as 3 hook-up, 2 hook-up, 1 hook-up, or primitive. The more hook-ups a section has, the more likely the higher end campers will use it.

Roads need to be wide enough to handle a single motor home and most often are one way. Parking areas need to be hard stand, asphalt, or concrete and ideally long enough so a motor home can drive through the site, entering from one side and exiting from the other. This prevents potential problems with motor homes backing up and into other campers. Turns need to be casual enough to allow longer motor homes to make full turns without striking obstructions. The campground, unless it is free, should include a fee-taking station at or near the entrance. Honor systems are available, but still require a ranger to check the site.

Family Camps

Family resident camps offer complete meal and living accommodations for families or for adults only. The facilities may be similar to those of resident camps except that some of the sleeping quarters may be adapted to families.

Most of the campgrounds in state or federal areas are destination camps. Campers generally stay more than one night and often for several weeks. In recent years, a great many resort camps have sprung up. These resorts, generally privately developed, are more or less complete vacationlands in themselves offering, frequently under leadership, a recreation program and facilities including swimming pools, recreation centers, children's playgrounds, special game courts, marinas, and horseback riding trails to cite a few examples.

Waterfronts

The use of waterfronts varies with the program offered. The type of program will determine the nature of the waterfront, and yet the environmental situation, such as ocean, stream, or lake, may influence the type and design of the facility. The following categories of use identify the specific areas of the aquatic program:

- Familiarization—Familiarization involves programs for acquainting the user with the water.
- Instruction—Instruction involves programs of teaching the user basic activities related to aquatics.
- Recreation—Recreation involves programs that are largely unstructured, for relaxing and refreshing the user, including participating in or watching special events such as synchronized swimming, water shows, and competitive swimming.
- Competition—Competition involves programs of training and competing in swimming and other aquatic activities. The user of a waterfront should be able to participate in a variety of aquatic activities in order to attain the desired objectives. This is especially true in the camp setting where the camper participates in the constructive fulfillment of inherent attitudes and aptitudes.

Waterfronts for the conduct of aquatic activities are found in children's camps, parks, resorts, marinas, clubs, hotels, residential developments, and other recreational areas. The waterfront, whether it is a beach, floating crib, dock, pond, lake shore, pool deck, or some other area where aquatic programs take place, must be properly located and constructed to insure the health and safety of the public using this facility. The post-World War II years have seen a tremendous development in children's camps in the United States, particularly day camps. Although many of the aspects of this chapter deal primarily with camps, most of the criteria may be applied to beachfront developments as well. In planning the location and construction of natural and artificial waterfront facilities, definite criteria should be established. These criteria should reflect not only the camp program, but also the health and safety requirements.

Criteria for Natural Waterfronts

The natural waterfront site should have certain characteristics to make it desirable for aquatic-program use. The recommended criteria for the selection of waterfront or beach sites are discussed below and helpful checklists have been provided for the planners.

Water Characteristics

The water content should be of a sanitary quality affording safe usage. The health conditions of a site are primarily judged by a careful examination of both its surrounding environs and its water content. The first is accomplished by a careful field analysis, the second by a laboratory analysis. Both examinations can indicate the bacterial quality and physical clarity of the water.

Checklist:

- Surrounding water source
- Water quality (bacterial content)
- Water clarity (visibility test)

Water-Condition Characteristics

The circulation of the water through the potential waterfront site should be examined. Slow-moving water can produce swampy or built-up mud conditions while fast-moving water can produce undercurrents and erosive conditions.

The ideal water temperature for swimming ranges from 72° to 78° F depending upon the air temperature. The American Public Health Association indicates that less than 500 gallons of additional water per bather per day is too small a diluting volume unless there is sufficient application of disinfection.

Checklist:

- rate of water flow
- rate of water turnover
- water-level fluctuation
- water constancy
- availability of water
- types of currents and undertow
- outlet for water
- eddies, floods, waves, or wash
- weeds, fungi, mold, or slime
- parasites, fish, animals
- debris, broken glass, and so on
- oil slick
- odor, color, taste

Bottom Characteristics

The waterfront bottom should be unobstructed and clear of debris, rock, muck, mulch, peat, and mud. The waterfront should not be in an area where the channel shifts or silt builds up. The most desirable bottom is white sand with a gradual pitch sloping from the shallow to the deep end. The bottom should not be precipitous or too shallow nor have holes, pots, channels, bars, or islands.

The bottom should be of gravel, sand, or stable hard ground to afford firm and secure footing. An investigation by taking soundings in a boat and by making an actual underwater survey should be undertaken before a final decision is made on the location of the waterfront.

Checklist:

- bottom movement
- amount of holes, debris
- slope of subsurface
- amount of area
- condition of soil
- porosity of bottom
- average depth and various depths
- bottom color

Climatic Characteristics

Continuous dry spells or numerous rainy seasons will cause the site to have water-retention problems. Dangerous storms including tornadoes, lightning, hurricanes, and northeasters create extremely dangerous waterfront conditions. The severity of the winter can also affect the waterfront. Ice and ice movement can cause damage to waterfront facilities and bottom. A south-southeast exposure is ideal so that maximum benefit is derived from the sun and there is least exposure to the wind.

Checklist:

- number of storms and type
- prevailing winds
- amount of ice
- change of air temperature
- amount of precipitation
- fluctuation of temperature
- sun exposure

Environmental Characteristics

The locale of the waterfront should be carefully examined for all influences on its construction and utilization. Zoning regulations, building codes, insurance restrictions, health ordinances, title covenants, and a multitude of other legal restrictions by the Coast Guard, Conservation Department, Water Resources Commission, public works agencies, and Fire Department should be studied. The arrangement of land uses and their compatibility to the project, transportation, utilities, community facilities, population, and area economics should also be considered.

Checklist:

- ownership and riparian rights
- availability of water supply
- zoning and deed restrictions
- local, state, and federal regulations
- adjacent ownerships
- water patrol and a control agency

Program Characteristics

The waterfront should be so situated that it can be protected by a fence or other controlled access, particularly in a camp, marina, or other small area. It should also be internally segregated (e.g., bathing from boating, boating from fishing, and so on). The site should also have storage room for waterfront equipment, adequate spectator area for use during special events, a safety area near the lifeguard station or post, and ready access to a road.

Checklist:

- distance of waterfront from other areas
- access road
- separation of waterfront activities
- area for unity of controls
- space available for adjunct activities

Access Characteristics

The waterfront facility must be accessible by transportation available to the user. There should always be a means of vehicular access for emergency or maintenance use. The site around the waterfront and along its approach should be free of poison ivy, sumac, poison oak, burdock thistle, and other irritating plants.

Check list:

- location for access road
- area free of poisonous plants
- area accessible yet controllable

Area Characteristics

The waterfront bathing area should allow for at least 50 square feet for each user. There should be areas for instruction, recreation, and competition. The depth of the area to be used primarily for the instruction of non-swimmers should not exceed three feet. The area to be used for intermediate swimmers should not exceed 5 1/2 feet (primarily for competition). Smaller or larger swimming areas may be designed if users are divided differently.

The minimum recommended size for a camp swimming area is 60 feet by 30 feet and the desirable size is 75 feet by 45 feet providing a 25-yard short course.

Checklist:

- space for bathing
- capacity of waterfront
- water depths
- division of bathing area into stations
- size of boating area
- size of fishing area

Shore Characteristics

The shoreline for the waterfront facility should be free of irregular rocks, stumps, debris, or obstruction. It should be a minimum of 100 feet long for bathing in a camp area and can be many miles long in a park beach.

There should be trees adjacent to waterfront areas to provide shade and wind protection. Large, high trees should be eliminated because they attract lightning and moldy trees have many decayed overhanging branches. Too many trees of a deciduous nature create mucky shores and water bottoms because of their autumn leaves. There are fewer problems with coniferous trees.

Checklist:

- surrounding vegetation
- slope of the shore
- existing beach
- extent of clearing
- amount of debris

Criteria for Artificial Waterfronts

In locating and considering an artificial waterfront, most of the same characteristics as described for natural areas should be examined. Additional criteria that should be considered are outlined below.

Environmental Characteristics

If all available bodies of water are being utilized, then artificial waterfront facilities must be developed. In some cases, waterfront locations are unsatisfactory or unavailable for new camps or resorts. Thus, consideration must be given to utilizing undeveloped sites with sufficient watershed (runoff water), water table (underground water), and water bodies (surface water) for lakes, pools, or impondments.

Water Characteristics

Before any site is selected, the perculation rate and, in particular, the permeability of the soil should be carefully checked in order to be sure that water will be retained. The stability and structure of the soil must also be determined (from test borings and/or test pits) because of the various types of dams, pump houses, dikes, pools, berms, spillways, and other structures that must be built.

Water-Content Characteristics

Unlike natural bodies of water, the content of artificial bodies can be controlled by chlorination and filtration. Runoff water obtained from storms, and contained in a pond or lake, should be collected by diversion ditches and fed to a reservoir and chlorination plant. This water can then be recirculated until potable water is obtained.

Underground water that is obtained from wells or springs can also be contained in a pond. This type of artificial water body usually would have a continuous flow and thus would need only a simple filtration system plus chlorination.

Surface water that is obtained from running streams is usually contained in a bypass pond or in a pond in the stream itself. Both methods require the construction of a dam. These artificial water bodies have continuous running water. However, gate valves and floodgates are required, especially during storms when there is a large flow of water to control. Unless there is a constant turnover or supply of clean water, these impondments will require a filtration and chlorination system.

Climatic Characteristics

Climatic considerations are very important in developing artificial bodies of water and waterfronts. In most cases, natural bodies of water will fluctuate very little because of weather conditions. On the other hand, artificial bodies are solely dependent upon the climate because the water table, runoff, and stream flow depend on the amount and time of rainfall. All other climatic considerations mentioned for natural waterfronts generally apply to artificial waterfronts as well.

Drainage Characteristics

A low-lying area, regardless of its appeal, is not a good location for a pool or pond. Adequate drainage is essential so the surface and deck water will drain away from the water body and so the water body itself can be emptied without pumping. Groundwater and frost action resulting from improper drainage can undermine a foundation by causing it to heave and settle.

Construction Criteria for Natural Waterfronts

The natural waterfront facility should have features that make it both safe and usable. The following criteria are suggested as a basis for the construction of such a facility.

Bottom Characteristics

Most swimming facilities around natural bodies of water require the dragging and grading of the bottom subsurfaces to eliminate hazards. In many cases, where definite improvement of the bottom is required, feed mat, mesh, or plastic sheets have to be laid down on top of muck and staked down. Once these sheets have been laid, sand must be spread over the mat surface. When the bottom is firm, sand can be spread six inches thick on top of ice in the crib area during winter. As the ice melts, the sand will fall fairly evenly over the bottom. This can only be accomplished, however, when the ice does not shift or break and float away.

Shore Characteristics

When a beach is constructed, a gentle slope of from 6 to 12 feet in 100 feet should be maintained. Where the waterfront requires a great deal of construction, a dock shoreline is recommended, rather than trying to maintain an unstable beach. The ground above the water can then be developed with turf, terraces, decks, and boardwalks, depending upon the nature of the project. When the bottom drops off very quickly, the shore can be dug out to the grade desired underwater. This forms a crescent-shaped waterfront with an excellent beach.

Access Characteristics

The owner should acquire access roads and streets around waterfront areas, if possible, to keep the area buffered from conflicting uses. These roads should be durable and be attractively maintained. Access roads should have clear horizontal and vertical vision so that pedestrian and vehicular conflict can be prevented.

Program Characteristics

The waterfront in small recreational areas such as camps or resorts should be completely enclosed by planting or fencing. There should be a central control for ingress and exit. Many facilities require the use of check in-out boards, tickets, and other similar devices for controlling the use of the area. The waterfront bathing, boating, and fishing facilities should be separated, each with its own control.

Construction Criteria for Artificial Waterfronts

Both artificial and natural waterfronts should have certain features that make them safe and usable. In improving and developing an artificial waterfront, most of the same considerations should be rendered as illustrated for the natural waterfront. The following criteria should be carefully considered in providing an artificial waterfront.

Bottom Characteristics

When constructing an artificial beach, the grade should be the same as that recommended for natural shores—6 feet to 12 feet in 100 feet. For reservoirs and ponds, there should be a minimum of nine inches of large, crushed stone, then four inches of well-graded smooth gravel to fill in the voids, and then nine inches of washed medium sand. Where the sand beach terminates at a depth of approximately 7 feet of water, it is recommended that rip-rapping be established to resist the tendency of the beach sand to move down the slope. The area above the beach should also be ditched where the natural slope of the ground exceeds that of the beach. Thus, the slopes of the beach should be approximately 6% percent below the water and 10% above. For areas in tidal waters, a maximum slope of five for 15 feet can be established for the bottom below-water line.

Shore Characteristics

In creating the shoreline for artificial bodies of water, there should be either a berm or dike if the water is to be confined. A steep slope to eliminate shallow areas is usually required to prevent weeds and other plant materials from growing in the water. If the soil conditions will not allow a steep slope under-water three feet deep to retard water-plant growth, then bulkheads or docks will be required, or only a limited beach can be provided.

Design and Construction of Camp Waterfronts

The camp waterfront is usually composed of either permanent docks or floats to provide safe swimming and boating areas.

Docks and Floats

Permanent structures are usually set on concrete, wood, or steel foundations, or pier piles. The decks should be made in sections of 10 to 20 feet for ease in removing for repairs or winter storage. The dock should be constructed with at least a one-foot air space between the deck and water. Underwater braces and other cross beams should be limited to prevent swimmers from becoming entangled in them. When water levels change, allowances should be made for the piers to be outside the deck limits so the deck can move up and down on sleeves or brackets. Walkways or decks should be a minimum of 6 feet wide, preferably 8 or 10 feet. They should be cross-planked so swimmers will avoid splinters. The planking should not be less than two inches thick by four to six inches wide. Boards should be spaced a maximum of 1/4 inch apart to prevent toe-stubbing. The deck should be treated with a non-creosote-based preservative, since creosote will burn feet, plus a plastic, non-lead paint that is not heat-absorbing. The paint should be white with a blue or green tint to reduce the glare and aid in reflection.

Flotation structures may be made of drums, balsa wood, cork, rigid polystyrene plastic, steel tanks, or other forms of flotation material. There are many innovations that have carried over from war days. Pontoon decks, for example, are sometimes made from surplus bridge parts, airplane fuel tanks, or fuel-oil tanks. All such materials should be treated with red lead after scraping, sanding, and repairing. A frame should be constructed of 2 inch by 8 inch boards to fit over and contain the supporting units. The frame should fit securely, yet be removable at the close of the season. Some flotation materials or devices are just placed in the framing under the floats without any type of anchorage to the frame. Galvanized steel or aluminum straps of 1/8 inches by 1 1/2 inches under the floating units will save time and effort to prevent sinking when these units acquire a leak and fill with water.

The various types of designs employed in waterfronts are shown in Figure 25.4. A typical camp waterfront is shown in Figure 25.5.

Figure 25.4
Sample Waterfront Configurations

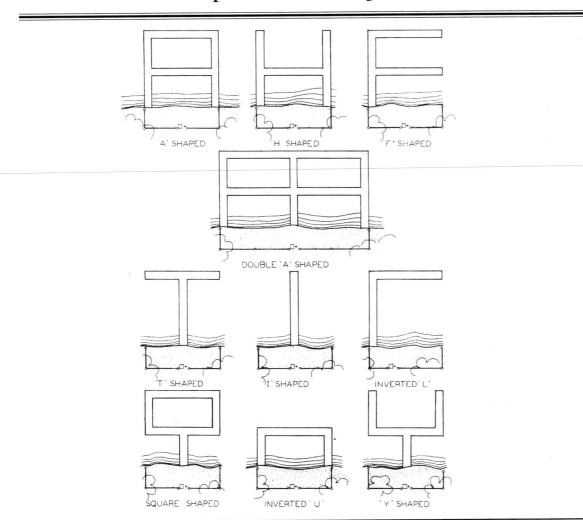

Figure 25.5
Sample Waterfront

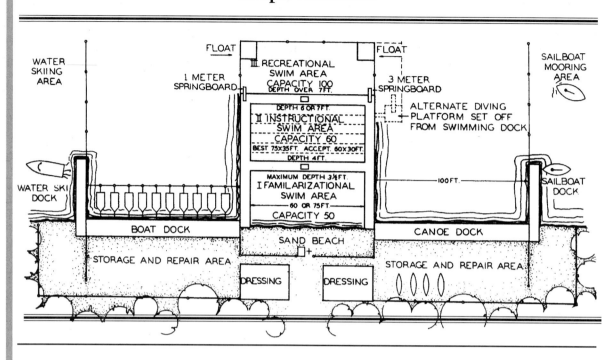

Waterfront Equipment

It is important to plan initially for all needed accessory equipment. The amount of equipment required will vary with the size of the waterfront. All necessary safety equipment must be located so as to afford immediate emergency use.

Lifeguard Station

Lifeguard chairs should be placed at a point where the location of beach equipment and sunbathing limit lines do not interfere with the guards' vision of the water areas. Chairs should be a minimum of 6 feet to a maximum of 10 feet above grade. Usually lifeguard chairs are made of galvanized pipe or wood.

Ladders

In all swimming cribs, there should be a ladder at least two feet in width placed at the sides in order not to interfere with persons swimming the length of the simulated pool.

Log Booms

Logs fastened end to end can form a continuous lifeline around bathing limits in rustic settings and, at the same time, provide the safety to swimmers so necessary at a waterfront.

Lemmon Lines

Lemmon lines are small floats attached by a nylon or plastic rope or cable outlining and restricting swimming areas. They can be made of rounded wood, cork, or plastic.

Markers and Buoys

These are floats indicating the limits of areas or channels or for marking underwater obstructions, divers, moorings, and fishing nets. They are usually hollow cans or drums. They can also be flag buoys, a six-inch-square wood block with attached flag, a wooden cross of two inches by four inches with can on top, or a metal ballast with flag.

Rescue Craft

Boats should be of the round-bottom or dory type between 12 and 14 feet long. There should be lifesaving equipment in the boat at all times. The seats should be removable, and oarlocks should be of a permanent type. A catamaran, surfboards, and, in large beach waterfront facilities, helicopters supplement the lifeboat as a means of patrol.

Kick Rails

A rail for practicing and teaching swimming should be placed at water level. This can be made of galvanized pipe, wood rods, or rope.

Towel Racks

Racks for drying towels and bathing suits should be installed at or near the waterfront.

Miscellaneous Equipment

Life ring buoys should be spaced strategically around the waterfront on racks. These racks are usually in the form of a cross, with the ring suspended from the center and the rope wrapped around the ring from pegs protruding from each end of the cross. Torpedo buoys, bamboo poles, grappling irons, lifelines, shepherd's crooks, stretchers, blankets, microphones, and other such devices should be available to the lifeguards. Numbers indicating depths and the capacities of the crib and other swimming areas should be clearly visible. Kickboards should be available for practice as well as emergency use.

Summary

Park and recreation facilities are diverse, specialized, and require expertise and involvement in the planning phase. Well designed park and recreation facilities can be expected to last for decades and provide thousands of hours of opportunity for community members to enjoy recreation, leisure, and relaxation.

Campus Recreational Sports Centers

Thomas H. Sawyer and John K. Lentz

26

Over the past 20 years, a number of recreational sports centers have been constructed on campuses to meet the needs of the student body. These centers have been built for recreational purposes, not instructional or athletic ones. However, recently a number have been built with large aquatic areas (e.g., University of Toledo, Miami University of Ohio, University of Texas, Georgia Tech, University of Michigan, University of Minnesota, and Indiana University) to be used for both recreational and athletic purposes. These centers have been financed primarily with student fees and state and private funds. Most of the facilities include aquatic centers, entrance/lobby area, lounge areas, racquetball/wallyball courts, indoor and outdoor tennis courts, basketball courts, dance exercise areas, indoor running/jogging tracks, strength and cardiovascular training areas, climbing wall, locker rooms, indoor/outdoor in-line skating hockey court, indoor soccer area, administration area, pro shops, concessions, and an area for equipment rental.

This chapter has been designed to provide the planner with an overview of the needs for a campus recreational sports center. The specifics relating to many of the spaces are found in other chapters in this book.

Learning Objectives

After reading this chapter, the student should be able to

- begin planning a new recreational sports center,
- describe indoor activities and facility needs,
- outline outdoor activities and facility needs, and
- describe the security needs for a recreational sports center.

Planning for a New Recreational Sports Center

A common problem is how to secure these new facilities. The following can form the basis from which to justify requests for additional facilities. The initial step in the process of securing any new facility is defining the space requirements. This planning process uses three different types of space used in recreational, intramural, and informal sports programs. The three types, according to Mull, Bayless, Ross, and Jamieson (1977), are described below:

Type A space includes the following areas:

- Indoor teaching stations—space requirements: 8.5 to 9.5 square feet per student (total undergraduate enrollment) including 1) gym floors, mat areas, swimming pools, court areas, and so on; and 2) location adjacent to lockers and showers and within a 10-minute walking distance of academic classrooms (Mull et al., 1997).
- Uses—Recreational, intramural, and informal sports participation for student and faculty recreation.
- Al—Large gymnasium area with relatively high ceiling (22 feet minimum) for basketball, badminton, volleyball, and so on. (approximately 55% of Type A space).
- A2—Activity areas with relatively low ceiling (12 feet minimum) for combatives, therapeutic exercises, dancing, weight lifting, and so on. (approximately 30% of Type A space).
- A3—Indoor swimming and diving pools (approximately 15% of Type A space) (Mull et al., 1997).

Type B space includes the following areas:

- Outdoor teaching stations—space requirements including 1) sports fields of all types; and 2) location adjacent to locker and showers, and within a 10-minute walking distance of academic classrooms.
- Uses—Recreational, intramural, and informal sports participation for student and faculty recreation.

- B1—Sodded areas for soccer, touch football, softball, and so on (approximately 60% of Type B space).
- B2—Court type areas for tennis, volleyball, and so forth (approximately 15% of Type B space).
- B3—Specialized athletic areas for track and field, baseball, archery, varsity football, golf, camping demonstrations, and the like (approximately 25% of Type B space).
- B4—Swimming pools (included in B3 approximation) (Mull et al., 1997).

Type C spaces include the following:

- Sports fields and buildings, intramural and general outdoor recreation areas—space requirements, 120 to 140 square feet per student (total undergraduate enrollment) including playing fields and athletic buildings of all types, softball diamonds, tennis courts, field houses, and so on. Too far removed from student lockers, showers, living quarters and academic buildings for use as teaching stations.
- Uses—Recreation, intramural, and informal sports for student and faculty recreation.
- C1—Sodded areas for soccer, touch football, softball, and so on (approximately 40% of Type C space).
- C2—Court type areas for tennis, volleyball, and the like (approximately 10% of Type C space).
- C3—Specialized athletic area for track and field, baseball, archery, varsity football, golf, camping demonstrations, and so forth (approximately 45% of Type C space).
- C4—Swimming pools (included in C3 approximation).
- C5—Sports and intramural buildings providing lockers, showers, play space, office space, lounge rooms, and so on (approximately 5% of Type C space) (Mull et al., 1997).

Photo by Balthazar Korab, Ltd. courtesy of
TMP Associates, Inc.

**Multipurpose gym with rounded
corners, Central Michigan University.**

Photo by Balthazar Korab, Ltd. courtesy of
TMP Associates, Inc.

**Main Street, Student Recreation
Center, Central Michigan
University.**

In order to compare a campus with the accepted standards, five steps should be followed: The first step involves the location of existing and potential areas within the boundaries of the campus. This is achieved by physically canvassing the campus and envisioning the potential of all areas. The initial phase of Step 1 should be the location and identification of all areas that are currently used by recreational, intramural, and informal sports.

The second phase is more difficult and requires more effort and imagination on the part of the observer. Potential areas of expansion are spaces (outdoor and indoor) that can be converted from whatever they are currently being used for to usable recreation areas. Costs of converting each area should be kept at a minimum to further enhance the attractiveness of securing new facilities (Mull et al., 1997). For example, the cost of converting a relatively small (50 feet by 100 feet) grassy area to an outdoor volleyball area would only include the installation of two poles and a net. If further funds were available and the sport popular, this area could be converted to a sand or beach volleyball court at a small additional cost. Providing alternatives or options also enhances the acceptability of the proposal.

Space for conversion should meet the general criteria for Type A, B, or C space before being considered for alteration (Mull et al., 1997). For example, an indoor area with an eight-foot ceiling should not be considered for conversion to gymnasium space; however, it could be converted to a dance studio or a karate practice room with the addition of mirrors and mats.

After all available and potential areas have been located, the next step requires computations of the area in square feet. For indoor areas, a tape measure is used; however, for large outdoor areas, a cross-country measuring wheel is most effective.

When measuring any area, precautions should be taken to allow for a buffer zone of safety around any proposed playing area. An outdoor grassy area measuring 100 yards by 40 yards could theoretically accommodate an intramural football field, but if the boundaries are close to hazards such as chainlink fence poles, trees, or buildings, this area should be considered for some other recreational purpose.

The same precautions apply to indoor space. Most areas considered will be fairly easy to measure. Normally, spaces are either rectangular or square in shape. Odd-shaped areas should not be ignored and their areas should be estimated to the best of the measurer's ability while still allowing for the safety buffer zone. Odd-shaped areas are also sometimes ignored, because they do not fit the shape of a standard playing field. These areas may, however, accommodate a combination of two or more sports in that area. Any particular space should not be viewed as usable only for football or basketball, but leftover spaces could easily be used for a frisbee golf course or a single table tennis table.

The square footage for all areas considered should next be classified and totaled under one of the three types of spaces. This total figure of space classified according to type can now be compared with the recommended amount of space. Recommended space is computed by taking current enrollment figures and multiplying them by the median figure in the range of each type of space (Mull et al., 1997). For example, a university with an enrollment of 15,000 students should have a recommended space requirement for Type A space of 135,000 square feet. The total amount of each type space is then compared with the actual amount to arrive at a figure illustrating the amount above or below recommended standards.

A further breakdown of space within each type into the 12 subclassifications is required to determine the correct "mix" of facilities. This subclassification of space enables the director to specifically locate areas of deficiency.

When standards in terms of square feet per student are used as guides in college or university planning, it is natural to ask where the cut-off begins. Obviously, for a college of 200 students, nine square feet per student of indoor area for sports and athletics would be inadequate. It would not even provide one basketball court. A university or college meeting the space standards for 1,500 students represents the minimum physical recreation space needs of any college institution. As a college or university increases in size, these standards are applicable regardless of enrollment. Also, a ceiling effect applies to some subclassifications of space.

In the beginning phases of planning for recreational facilities, area standards must be developed. A variety of standards relative to size, location, and development of school and recreation areas and facilities has been developed.

The standards provide a useful guide; however, standards can seldom, if ever, be applied completely or without modification. Because a typical or ideal situation is seldom found, standards simply indicate a basis for the intelligent development of local plans.

The third step involves a description of current and potential uses of each area. A description of current uses should be done first. It should include uses by physical education, recreation, intramural sports, and "outside" departments. If a particular area is not being used for any specific purpose, it should be so listed.

Potential uses (see figures 26.1 and 26.2 for examples) should be as closely linked to the subclassifications as possible. It is in this phase of the process where the director must make responsible choices as to the development of any given area. A single area must have the potential to be developed into several different types of space. The director must refer to individual program needs and areas of deficiency to make informed decisions as to the development of that particular area. Again, it is important to provide campus planners with options. However, the director should limit the flexibility of the proposal to stay within the most urgent needs of his particular program.

The next step is to determine the cost of converting an area from its current use to its potential use. In some cases, the cost of conversion will be zero. This type of space should be accentuated in presenting the proposal before any board involved with campus planning. Often, cooperation between two departments regarding scheduling can vastly increase facilities available for recreational use at no cost to either program.

Obtaining other costs of conversion generally involves requesting estimates from the physical plant operations staff on campus or from outside contractors. These estimates should be obtained prior to presenting any proposal. Also, the estimates should enhance the flexibility built into the proposal. That is to say, each option should have its own separate estimate. This allows campus planning boards to examine all suggestions in the proposal independently of other suggestions in the proposal.

Finally, the last step involves defining the availability for use by the major users. If two or more users share facilities, the priority schedule for usage should also be listed. After all, a program may have access to a facility 40% of the total time available, but if those times are at undesirable hours, the facility is not meeting the needs of the program. If no consideration is given to the prime-time needs of students for recreational use, the percentage of availability may be misleading.

After information has been gathered, supporting documents for requesting new facilities must be prepared. The proposal should contain five major parts.

The first part should state clearly the objectives of the study. It should also list all areas and departments of the campus involved in conducting the study. Finally, it should include limitations or qualifications specific to the institution.

Figure 26.1
Indoor Recreational, Intramural, and Informal Sports Activities

The following is a partial listing of indoor recreational, intramural, and informal sports activities:

Single Function   **Specialized or Multipurpose Function**

Single Function	Specialized or Multipurpose Function	
Archery range	**Country club**	**Gymnasium**
Badminton court	Golf	Gymnastics
Basketball court	Swimming	Combatives
Billiards	Table sports	Basketball
Bowling alley	Strength training	Volleyball
Combatives room	Tennis	Badminton
Curling rink		Table tennis
Cardiovascular room		
Dance exercise room		
Diving pool		
Electronic games arcade	**Fieldhouse**	**Racquetball club**
Fencing salle	Basketball	Strength training
Gymnastics room	Track	Jogging
Handball	Soccer	
Ice rink	Lacrosse	**Recreation center**
In-line skating hockey rink	Jogging	Billards
Racquetball court	Archery	Table sports
Rifle-pistol range		Table tennis
Roller skating rink	**Fitness center**	Swimming
Shuffleboard course	Swimming	Gymnasium
Squash court	Strength training	
Swimming pool	Cardiovascular training	
Table sports room	Jogging	
Table tennis room	Combatives	
Tennis court	Dance exercise	
Strength training room		
Wrestling room		
Volleyball court		

Figure 26.2
Outdoor Recreational, Intramural, and Informal Sports Activities

The following are common outdoor recreational, intramural, and sports activities:

Airfield	Hydro-slide
Baseball field	Ice rink
Basketball court	In-line skating hockey rink
Beach volleyball	Lacrosse field
Bike trail	Marina
Bicycle track	Miniature golf course
Boat launching ramp	Motocross course
Boccie ball course	Riding paddock
Bowling green	Rifle/pistol range
Cross-country course	Roller skating rink
Curling rink	Shuffleboard
Deck tennis	Skateboard/rollerblade course and ramp
Diving pool	Skeet and trap range
Field hockey field	Skiing course
Fishing pond/lake	Soccer field
Fitness trail (Par course)	Softball field
Football field	Speedball
Frisbee golf course	Swimming pool
Go-cart track	Speedball field
Golf course	Team handball field
Golf driving range	Tennis court
Handball court	Toboggan slope
Horseshoe pit	Volleyball

Indoor soccer/roller hockey.

The second part should include brief historical developments of the sponsoring program from both a national and campus viewpoint.

The third section is a statement of the problem. In this section, all forces generating the study should be explained. All major problems affected by changing facility structures should be included, as well as the majority of the information gathered in the aforementioned steps. Listing the standards with the organizations using them will lend national support to the proposal. The relationship between the standard and enrollment is explained next. And, finally, the standards are applied to the specific campus in question. The comparison should emphasize those areas in which critical deficiencies exist, because the largest deficiencies are not always the most critical ones. Section three should conclude with a summary of the work completed on the study and a restatement of those problem areas.

Section four contains recommendations for immediate action and long-term improvements. Flexibility (options) within the overall goals of the organization should be the guiding principle when preparing this section.

Finally, appendixes should be prepared to support the proposal. Participation figures may be used in this section; however, the major part of this section should contain a map of the campus with all areas clearly marked. The map should be accompanied by a list of all buildings and rooms investigated. The most precise way of presenting existing and potential areas is to list and explain each one according to the following seven-point formula:

- location
- area (structure footage)
- type of space
- current uses
- potential uses
- cost of conversion
- percentage of use

Indoor Facilities

In planning new facilities, it should be remembered that substandard facilities usually result in a substandard program. For this reason, official court and field dimensions should be used whenever possible. The following list identifies the types of areas that should be considered in planning indoor facilities for a campus recreational sports center:

- Main gymnasium—regulation basketball, badminton, tennis, and volleyball courts with mechanical divider nets. The divider nets should be constructed of solid vinyl for the first eight feet and the remainder of a mesh material.
- Auxiliary gymnasiums—regulation basketball, badminton, tennis, and volleyball courts, gymnastics area, in-line skating hockey rink, indoor soccer area, suspended track, fencing, batting cages, and dance exercise. The dance exercise area should have hidden mirrors to protect them when the space is used for other activities (e.g., basketball or volleyball), and a retractable instructor's platform. The planners might consider the possibility of locating two gymnasiums side by side with a storage area between to store equipment, an audio system, and retractable instructor's platforms. The storage area should be at least eight feet wide.
- Swimming pools—50-meter pool, diving pool, and/or instruction pool.
- Combative room—boxing, martial arts, and judo.
- Strength training area—progressive resistance-training equipment, free-weight equipment, and stretching area.
- Cardiovascular area.
- Handball/racquetball/walleyball courts.
- Golf room—sand trap, putting area, and driving nets.
- Archery/rifle/pistol range.
- Games room—billiards, table tennis, table games, shuffleboard.
- Administrative area—offices, storage, conference rooms, and audiovisual room.

- Lounge and lobby area—bulletin boards, trophy cases, control center, and art work.
- Concessions, rental, and merchandise area—concession stand, seating area, rental shop, and pro shop.
- Training room—treatment area only.
- Locker rooms—student and faculty, gender specific, shower rooms, drying areas, locker space, and common spa area (i.e., hydro-tube, sauna, and steam room).
- Equipment and storerooms.
- Climbing wall.

Indoor track.

Outdoor Facilities

The following list identifies the types of areas that should be considered in planning outdoor facilities for a campus recreational sports center:

- Lighted fields—touch/flag football, soccer, field hockey, softball, baseball, handball, and rugby.
- Lighted courts—basketball, badminton, tennis, volleyball, handball/racquetball, and horseshoes.
- Lighted in-line skating hockey court.
- Lighted jogging/running/walking trails and/or track.
- Golf course and lighted driving range and practice green.
- Lighted skating rink.
- Swimming and diving pools.
- Boccie field and horseshoe pits.
- Storage building(s).
- Tennis practice boards and soccer kicking wall.
- Picnic areas with shelters.

Security Issues

The campus recreational sports center will quickly become the focus of campus interest. The center will be used heavily throughout the day and evening. The prime times will be 6 to 8 a.m., 11 a.m. to 1 p.m., 4 to 6 p.m., and 7 p.m. to midnight. The planners need to consider providing adequate security, including appropriate outside lighting at all sites, security cameras, alarmed doors (silent and audible), pool alarms, spa alarms, valuable lockers, fire alarms, sprinkling systems, and appropriate signage.

Summary

Recreational sports centers on campuses have become very strong recruiting tools for colleges and universities. Students want to be involved with recreational sports, to relax and play with fellow students. Many colleges and universities are adding new recreational sports centers to their campuses to meet student needs for recreation.

Photo by Anthony Brentlinger

**Outdoor recreation field at
Indiana State University.**

Chapter 27

Strength and Cardiovascular Training Facilities

Thomas H. Sawyer and David A.P. Stowe

Cardiovascular and strength training venues (commonly referred to as the fitness floor) are the lifeblood of any existing or future facility. When facilities inspire their members by capturing their imagination and promoting their safety, they will sustain their existence even with the growing number of competing exercise facilities. Strength and cardiovascular facility coordinators must embrace the advances in technology and recognize the value of incorporating entertainment mediums as they embark upon developing or refining existing programs, refurbishing existing facilities, or planning for the expansion or construction of new facilities. The responsibilities of coordinators are demanding; however, when collectively engaging others in defining program outcomes, establishing services, evaluating facility needs, and planning facility enhancements, the personal rewards are many.

As a strength and cardiovascular facility coordinator, you are responsible for not only knowing how to organize participants for strength and cardiovascular training, but also for knowing how to arrange equipment safely in order to meet the challenge. In some cases, you might be responsible for developing a facility. Planning the facility takes many hours of creating and reviewing floor plans and deciding what equipment will be needed, how space may be best utilized, what surfaces are needed in various areas, and other factors. It is worthwhile to contact professionals in other programs who have built a facility and to compile information on specific needs. A committee of people who represent various areas of expertise may be organized to help in the planning of the facility. Such a committee may consist of an administrator, contractor, lawyer, student-athlete, sport coach, instructors who would use the facility, various experts in the field of sport conditioning, and any other people who could give valuable input on design.

This chapter will focus on a discussion of current trends, existing facilities and how you might improve and reorganize them to best suit the needs of the philosophy (the ideals and values shaping the program), goals (the desired outcome), and objectives (the individual steps toward a goal) of a program, and what would be needed in a new facility.

Learning Objectives

After reading this chapter, the student should be able to

- assess the needs of an existing or new facility,
- identify the industry standards for strength and cardiovascular facilities,
- understand the design concepts and philosophies for revitalizing existing facilities and the construction of new recreational facilities,
- plan and organize an existing or new facility for maximum usage, and
- understand the environmental factors affecting facility development.

Strength and Cardiovascular Training Facility Planning

Assessing the Needs of an Existing or New Facility

After defining the program goals and objectives, the facility coordinator should assess existing equipment and the needs of the various sports groups that plan to use the facility. As the coordinator, you will need to answer these questions:

- What are the specific training goals of each group?
- What types of training does each require (e.g., circuits, machines, free weights, platform lifts, plyometrics)?
- What are the seasonal priorities of each group?
- What are the training ages (training experience) of the athletes in the groups?

- When will weight training fit into each group's schedule?
- What repairs, adaptations, and modifications must be made to meet the athletes' needs?
- How should the equipment be placed to best utilize the space in a safe and efficient manner?

Defining the Programmatic Objectives

Before evaluating and/or constructing a facility, it is important that one has a clear understanding of the programmatic objectives and the vision of the facility design. Listed below are suggestions for program assessment.

The planners of a strength and cardiovascular facility should answer a number of questions prior to initiating planning for the facility. The questions include:

- What specific activities or training functions will take place in the space?
- Will the spaces be used for team instruction, group programs, new member equipment orientations, and the like?
- Will the activities cater to individuals or small or large groups?
- What will be the size of classes?
- What is the demographic composition of clientele served: Children, teens, middle-aged persons, senior citizens?
- What is their gender?
- What are the deficiencies of the present programs?
- What equipment is needed to support the respective activities?

Desired Facility Outcomes

It is important for the planners to consider the desired outcomes of the completed facility. These outcomes should focus upon, but not be limited to: maximizing the use of existing or future space, assuring the safety of participants, achieving program objectives successfully, and increasing user satisfaction.

Existing Facility Assessment

In chapters 3 and 4, we have discussed generally the planning process that should be employed. Appendix B provides a number of facility checklists to assist the planner in designing spaces for new and existing facilities under renovation.

Facility Design Concepts and Philosophy

The visual appeal of a facility significantly impacts the ability to attract and engage participants. It is important to design visually pleasing facilities that are easily maintained. The desired outcome is to create energy and to make the visit to the facility an "experience." If facility coordinators do not have a thorough understanding of the impact of interior design, the utilization of a professional interior designer to maximize the visual ambience is highly recommended. Color is a significant dimension that contributes to the psychological, emotional, and physical response of participants. The coordination of equipment frame colors, upholstery colors, wall colors and textures, flooring patterns, use of lighting, ceiling heights, and window treatments are all factors that contribute to the overall visual appeal of the exercise experience. Facility enhancements may be as simple as painting accent colors on white walls for the purposes of creating a space that not only is visually appealing but also makes one feel good.

Safety in facility design is primarily achieved by providing sufficient walking space to keep members from inadvertently bumping into each other or when too many pieces of equipment are placed in a space that is inadequate. Meeting only minimum space standards does not allow for potential membership growth and facility expansion. When designing new facilities, attention should always focus upon how the facility can be expanded with some structural modifications such as removal of interior walls or exterior walls. Strategic facility design includes preparing for future growth.

Planning the Facility Layout

Prepare a floor plan to 1) visualize the present and potential locations of equipment; 2) organize for safety and the most efficient use of space, exits, and entrances; 3) identify areas of frequent travel; 4) develop facility flow (pathways in the facility); and 5) select supervisor station locations for maximum supervision of the whole facility, especially areas of increased risk (such as the platform area). Safety should always be a priority and the planners should make sure that adequate safety buffer zones are used between pieces of equipment and that all entrance and exit pathways are clear and easily recognizable to the participants.

Station all high-risk activities, including platform lifts, squats, overhead presses, bench and incline presses, and exercises that require spotters, away from windows, mirrors, exits, and entrances to avoid breakage of glass, distraction, or collision with the bar or lifter. Place the equipment for these activities in areas that are readily supervised to ensure safety and the execution of proper technique. Supervision is effective only if all areas of the facility can be observed at any given time. Therefore, locate supervisor stations in places with full visibility of all areas of the facility to allow quick access to participants in need of spotters or immediate assistance.

Arrange the tallest machines or pieces of equipment along the walls with the shorter, smaller pieces in the middle to improve visibility (as well as appearance) and maximize use of space. Place weight racks enough distance away from bar ends and spotter areas for ease of movement without obstruction. Tall pieces of equipment, such as squat racks, may need to be bolted to the walls or floors for increased stability.

The following are guidelines suggested by a panel of safety experts at the National Strength and Conditioning Association (NSCA) and the American College of Sports Medicine (ACSM) for the safe and efficient use of equipment (Baechle, 1994; Peterson & Tharrett, 1997):

- All weight machines and apparatus must be spaced at least 2 feet (61 cm) from one another and preferably 3 feet (91 cm) apart.
- Platform areas should have sufficient overhead space (at least 12 feet [3.7 m]) which should be free of such low-hanging items as beams, pipes, lighting, and signs.
- The proper spacing of Olympic bars is 3 feet (91 cm) between ends (12 feet [3.7 m] X 8 feet [2.4 m] = 1 platform lifting area).

Maintain a clear pathway, three feet (91 cm) wide in the facility at all times, as stipulated by federal, state, and local laws. Machines and equipment must not be allowed to block or obstruct this flow. Place equipment at least 6 inches (15 cm) from mirrors and mirrors 20 inches (51 cm) above the floor. Place free-weight equipment well away from exits and entrances to avoid obstruction, give participants ample room for passage, and guarantee safety to the pedestrian and lifter. Organize equipment into "priority sections" such as free-weight areas, machine areas, power training areas, and cardiovascular/aerobic areas. This allows the supervisor to identify and focus on the higher risk areas and keep equipment orderly in the facility.

A strength and cardiovascular training area should provide areas for cardiovascular training, resistance training (divided into free weights and machine weights), and stretching. The design and layout of a facility should provide at least 20 to 40 square feet for each piece of exercise equipment (Peterson & Tharrett, 1997). The exact amount of space is determined by the size of each particular piece of equipment and the recommendations of the manufacturer. Further, "a facility should allow for 20 to 25 sf of space for each person expected to be using the facility at any one time" (Foster & Sol, 1997, p. 51). This is not in addition to the space allocation for equipment previously mentioned.

The planners need to define the use of the space. Responding to the following questions does this:

- What programs will be offered, for example, circuit training, free weights, cardiovascular training?
- What is the size of the total membership or the membership registered to use the strength training area?
- What is the approximate peak demand for the area?
- What is the equipment preference (i.e., a mixture of free weights and machines, free weights only, machines only)?
- Is there a high demand for separate or coed areas?
- What type of flooring would be most appropriate?
- Has the equipment been chosen? If yes, who is the vendor, what are the specific dimensions of the equipment, and what is the proposed layout?

Organizing the Facility for Maximum Usage

When organizing groups of participants, you should consider the size of the facility and assess the needs of each group in terms of the following:

- Specific training needs (e.g., strength, endurance, circuits, and power).
- Seasonal priority (i.e., when sports occur, such as football in the fall and baseball in the spring).
- group size and equipment availability (i.e., a football team with 150 members may not be able to use a facility efficiently and safely without being split into groups; other sports groups may have to be scheduled at times other than football groups to ensure sufficient use of the equipment).
- The participant-staff ratio (1:10 to 1:30, depending upon the training group).
- A minimum space requirement per lifter of 30 feet (2.8 m) and a maximum of 60 feet (5.6 m) (Baechle, 1994).

Schedule facility usage so that different groups of participants train in the facility at more or less constant "density" throughout the day; avoid large, congested groups which increase the potential for injury and inefficient use of equipment. If the facility is designed for high school athletes, groups may be organized through physical education classes that offer beginning, intermediate, and advanced strength and conditioning to the students. Teams may organize facility usage time before or after practice according to seasonal priority.

Planning Specific Facility Features

Flooring

The correct selection of flooring minimizes the potential of slips, falls, and other injuries to occur. The Deutsche Institut für Normung (DIN) standards (see Appendix C.2) are ideally suited in the selection of the appropriate flooring for cardiovascular and strength training centers. The following DIN standards should be considered:

- *Shock absorption.* Without appropriate shock absorption, the potential for accruing an injury increases, specifically for ankle and knee joints. This is an essential component for aerobic and other group exercise spaces.
- *Standard vertical deformation/resilience.* Insufficient energy return in a floor causes sore ankles if a surface is too hard. Excessive energy return creates a trampoline effect.
- *Sliding characteristics/surface friction.* Side to side lateral, rotating, and pivoting movements create strain on joints without the proper friction coefficient to minimize stress. "On a friction scale of 0.1 (ice) to 0.9 (fly paper), 0.5 to 0.7 is the DIN standard" (McPherson, 2004, p. 43).
- *Rolling load.* A floor's ability to withstand heavy weight without breaking or sustaining permanent damage.

Flooring can be composed of such materials as wood, tile, rubber, interlocking mats, and carpet. The planner should carefully review the surfaces for the following concerns.

Wooden Flooring

Wooden flooring on platforms must be kept free of splinters, holes, protruding nails, uneven boards, and screws. The boards should run in the direction of the bar so that lifters do not catch their feet against the grain of the wood when widening their stance. This is the safest flooring for Olympic-style lifters.

The use of wood flooring is the most common surface found in group exercise areas. However, the maintenance of wood is a challenge, because it contracts as well as expands depending upon humidity and moisture. This can lead to the floor buckling and can be an expensive repair. A growing trend is the use of synthetic wood-look floors made of polyvinyl chloride (PVC) that has rubber padding underneath and comes in modular plastic tiles. The challenges with this type of material are that it scuffs easily, and the joints are not tight enough.

Tile

Tile flooring and antistatic floor should be treated with antifungal, antibacterial agents in the aerobic machine area. The tile should also be resistant to slipping and moisture accumulation and free from chalk accumulation.

Resilent Rubber Flooring

The use of rubberized flooring is becoming more predominant in the fitness industry because of the low maintenance requirements, durability, color options, and length of warranty. Coloring that is added to rubberized flooring is commonly referred to as fleck and comes in 10, 20, and 30% grades of color. The thicknesses and applications of rubberized flooring range from area rubber mats found under exercise equipment to entire rooms being completed in rubber flooring. The thickness of the flooring ranges from 3/8 to 1 inch, with the thicker style being suitable for free weight areas. Rubber flooring is available in rolls 48 inches wide, square tiles, or interlocking applications. With interlocking flooring the number of seams increases raising the potential for the matting to lose its initial integrity and pull apart if not permanently installed. The maximum thickness for rolled rubber flooring is 3/8 inch, with thicker matting coming in 4 feet x 8 feet rectangle sheets. Professional installers should be used with permanent rubber flooring installations and the use of rolled rubber flooring and where many cuts will be required to accommodate the facility's walls, columns, and other structural features. An organization's logo as well as geometric shapes and patterns can also be used as inlays in the rubber flooring to increase the ambience as well as brand identity of the organization.

In preparation of placing selectorized weight equipment on the rubber flooring, it is recommended to place large sheets of plywood on the floor so that pallet jackets and four wheel moving carts that are used to move the heavy equipment do not damage the floor. This precautionary measure should specifically be at the point of entrance where the continuous traffic pattern will occur.

Finally, resilient rubber flooring in the free-weight and machine areas should be similar to aerobic flooring. It must be kept free of large gaps between pieces, cuts, and worn spots.

Interlocking Mats

Interlocking mats must be secure and arranged so as not to pull apart or become deformed (with protruding tabs). The stretching area must be kept free of accumulated dust. Mats or carpets should be nonabsorbent and contain antifungal and antibacterial agents.

Carpet

Commercial grade carpet within an exercise facility has four primary applications. It is appropriate when used in an office setting, selectorized weight equipment center, general traffic areas, and in cardiovascular machines areas as long as exercise mats can be placed between the machine and the carpet to protect from oil and other elements. The use of carpet for group aerobics areas is not advisable because of the friction that can occur with movements. Carpet is not ideally suited for free weight areas because of the nature of the activity and the fabric will break down with weights being dropped. The installation of carpet may be in the form of squares or rolls. Each of these selections has its benefits as well as limitations. Carpet squares are more easily replaced than rolled flooring.

Carpet must be free of tears. High-use areas should be protected with throw mats. All areas must be swept and vacuumed or mopped on a regular basis. Flooring must be kept glued and fastened down properly. Fixed equipment must be attached securely to the floor.

Walls

The selection of materials for new wall construction or remodeling areas should be durable and have some acoustical value. Mounting sound absorption panels on the walls or other materials is highly desirable to absorb the clanging plates in the strength training areas, noise generated from cardiovascular equipment, and from normal conversations of patrons in these respective venues. Mirrors should be mounted at least 20 inches above the floor. Mirrors provide a sense of openness to the space as well as a means for checking for appropriate form; however, the overuse of mirrors can be unwelcoming to the selfconscious or deconditioned individuals. The ambience of a designated space is enhanced with the use of graphics and other artwork. Periodic painting of facilities and new and enhanced graphics should be considered. All appropriate Americans With Disabilities Act (ADA) signage (see Chapters 14 and 17) and emergency exits must be appropriately mounted. Wall-mounted apparatus and light fixtures should not be mounted in high traffic areas or walkways. Patterned galvanized steel could be mounted on the walls for protection as well as aesthetic value in high traffic areas such as in free weight areas where the numerous benches, bars, and Olympic plates may come in contact with the wall surfaces.

Ceilings

The minimum ceiling height for free weight areas is 12 feet (3.7 m) with 13 feet (3.9 m) desirable. Olympic lifts or pull-up stations require significant overhead clearance. All apparatus, ceiling fans, fire emergency sprinkler devices, and light fixtures should not be within arm's reach of the membership. Financial savings can be achieved as a result of not incorporating a drop ceiling. The expense of replacing broken or aging tiles is also eliminated. The exposed roof grid work is painted; however, a suspended ceiling may provide more interior design options and also camouflage pipes and provide some sound absorption with the ceiling tiles. The higher the ceiling is, the greater sense of openness will be.

Lighting/Electrical Requirements

Proper lighting of the exercise floor is important for the general safety of all participants. The number of foot-candles designates lighting. Optimal lighting is considered 50 to 100 foot-candles. A designated exercise facility should be void of any dark spots and equipment should be well illuminated. Lighting fixtures should be energy efficient and compliant with Green Seal Environmental Standards. Exit signs and hearing impaired signage should be illuminated and periodically inspected for burned out bulbs.

Electrical requirements for most commercial treadmills require a minimum of 120volt/20amps and designated breakers with National Electrical Manufacturers Association (NEMA) 5-20 receptacles. All electrical outlets that need modifications to accommodate these types of plugs need to be done by a qualified electrician.

Environmental Factors

Environmental factors that should be considered in helping make the facility safe and effective include noise control, temperature, ventilation, humidity, and posted signs. Music can be a form of motivation for many, but it can also pose a problem if the stereo system is not properly managed. Volume should be low enough to allow for clear communication between spotters or instructors and lifters at all times. The stereo system should be controlled by the facility coordinator and qualified supervisors only.

Air temperature should be kept constant at 68° to 72°F (22° to 26°C) to offer a reasonable training environment. If the room is too cold, athletes may become chilled after they finish warming up; if too hot, participants may become overheated or lose motivation to continue. Proper ventilation is important to maintaining air quality and keeping humidity to a minimum (relative humidity should be less than 60 percent). The ventilation system should provide at least 8 to 10 air exchanges per hour and optimally 12 to 15 air exchanges. The result should be no detectable strong odors in the room and equipment free of slickness or rust due to high humidity (Peterson & Tharrett, 1997).

All safety, regulation, and policy signs should be posted in clear view, in two or three central places within the facility; more postings may be needed in a large facility.

Acoustical Considerations

A significant amount of noise is generated with an exercise facility. Impact noise and vibrations occur from dropping of weights, members moving simultaneously during an aerobics class, and members' use of treadmills and other equipment, combined with high-volume music. Strategic placement of group exercise activities within the context of the actual center along with the inclusion of built in acoustical controls will prevent these venues from negatively impacting other programs such as yoga classes. The strategies for addressing these issues ultimately depends upon whether a group is planning a new construction or trying to remedy an existing acoustical problem.

Additional structural modification for new or existing venues is to provide multiple layers of drywall on both sides of studs when activities are going to be placed next to each other. Constructing floating wooden platform floors to support cardiovascular equipment is also another solution. Strength training acoustical issues can be enhanced with the use of rubber flooring and rubber bumpers between weight plates on selectorized weight equipment. Addressing acoustical issues with the architect, engineer, and acoustical experts should be discussed early in the design phase of a new exercise facility. When having to remedy existing acoustical problems, they should be discussed before it negatively impacts the operation.

Entrances

The entranceway to the facility should be double wide to allow for the moving of oversized exercise equipment into and out of the facility. An entrance with a removable middle door jam is advisable. Further, since the entrance to the facility is the first area seen by the participant, it should be pleasing to the eye as well as the nose.

Accommodation of Membership

The program objectives of the organization, type and availability of exercise equipment, and size of the facility ultimately impact the clientele served.

Team Related

Facilities that focus upon conditioning of students for sports teams must devise strategic time schedules for them to use facilities. The size of the respective team, the instructor-to-student ratio, and program objectives also impact accommodation. Instructor ratios of 1:30 are acceptable; however, lower ratios are advisable for team sports that involve free weight and plyometric training.

General Population

Facilities that accommodate the general public from teens to senior citizens also have strategic issues of accommodation to be addressed. Many women are intimidated to use weight training facilities because of the predominant number of men using the facilities. Providing cardiovascular and strength training facilities strictly for women and seniors is highly recommended. Doing so will increase member satisfaction and will reflect positively upon the organization in the desire to meet the unique needs of these populations.

Security

All spaces should have provisions for emergency and night lighting. Further, each space should have a system to alert staff to medical emergencies. Finally, spaces other than locker rooms should be provided with video monitoring cameras. The security monitors should be located in a central location for staff to monitor.

Special Considerations

The following are special considerations planners should include in the planning process for new strength and cardiovascular training spaces:

- There should be at least two, 220-volt electrical outlets to service heavy-duty cleaning equipment.
- There should be a provision for a large (40 to 50 inch) TV with VCR in the cardio-respiratory area.
- Commercial structures typically have a 60-pound-per-square-foot load-bearing capacity, but exercise areas need at least 100-pound-per-square-foot capacity.
- The appearance of the room is important. The right ambience entices members to exercise while enjoying their surroundings. Special consideration should be given to the use of mirrors, lighting, carpeting, rubberized flooring, graphics, and skylights.
- Carpeting that extends on the side to wainscoting height serves as an excellent acoustical buffer as a well as protective surface for the free-weight area.
- The color schemes of walls, equipment upholstery, flooring, and ceiling must all be coordinated to appeal to users.

Signage

Signage is very important to participants' safety in a strength and cardiovascular area. See Chapter 17 for detailed information about signage. However, there are some specific signs that should be found in this area. They include, but are not limited to, the following:

- Vendor Signage: All signage provided from manufacturers pertaining to the warnings of using the equipment must be posted.
- Weight Facility Signage: To increase safety and to reduce liability, the following signage should be displayed:
  —Replace weights in their designated racks.
  —Do not drop the weights.
  —The use of a spotter is advisable.
  —When in doubt on how to use a respective piece of equipment, ask for assistance.

—Children under the age of 14 must be accompanied by an adult.
—Please accommodate others in the use of equipment.
—Failure to comply with these rules and regulations may result in membership privileges being re-voked.
• Cardiovascular Center Signage: Signage for the cardiovascular area should address the following:
—Clean off consoles, seats, or handrails of equipment after use.
—Cease to use equipment if one feels light-headed, dizzy and notify a staff member immediately.
—Report any malfunctioning problems with a piece of equipment to the designated staff member on duty.
—When in doubt on how to use equipment, consult with staff member on duty.

Cardiovascular Areas and Equipment

The challenge for any facility is having an adequate amount of cardiovascular equipment to accommodate a respective organization's membership during peak hours of operation. Every effort should be made to meet this objective. Failure to do so can contribute to members' dissatisfaction if an extended waiting period for equipment is required before they can have access to the machines. Normal peak hours of use are 3:00 p.m. to 7:00 p.m. on a daily basis—after school and work hours. The popularity of the cardio center is directly influenced by the ambience of the facility as well as the availability of multiple entertainment sources. These include mounted televisions on walls or hung from the ceiling, sound systems, and the capability to connect to fitness networks whereby a member can retrieve their individual workout histories and statistics. If a respective facility has the capability of establishing multiple cardiovascular centers, this provides the opportunity to create a variety of experiences. One cardio center may be separate from the strength training area or overlook another significant activity or outdoor landscaped courtyard. These scenarios enhance the overall experience by making it more intimate as opposed to having a large room with row after row of cardiovascular equipment which is often threatening to the deconditioned and inexperienced member frequenting the cardio center. Spacing between equipment should be at least two feet with a three-foot allowance behind treadmills and any walls. All equipment power cords should be covered with a protective cover which should be glued or otherwise fastened to the floor.

Equipment for Cardiovascular Training Area

The International Health, Racquet, and Sportclub Association (IHRSA), NSCA, and the ACSM recommend that strength and cardiovascular training area planners should consider providing

• a variety of types of equipment for the cardiovascular area including treadmills, mechanical stair-climbing machines, bicycle ergometers, computerized cycles, rowing ergometers, upper-body ergometers, and total body-conditioning machines;
• at least one circuit of progressive resistance-training equipment (other than free weights) that includes either a machine or workout station for each of the following muscle groups: gluteus, quadriceps, hamstrings, calves, chest, upper back, lower back, shoulders, triceps, biceps, and abdomen; and
• a circuit for resistance training in a fashion that allows users to train the largest muscle groups first and then proceed to the smaller muscle groups. All compound movement machines should be placed in the circuit before isolated movement machines involving the same muscle(s).

The following considerations should be taken under advisement when making cardiovascular equipment selections:

• age and condition of clientele served
• available space in cardiovascular area
• sufficient electrical supply to support equipment
• budgetary considerations
• maintenance requirements of selected equipment
• proximity of equipment repair technicians to fitness facility
• length of warranty (e.g., two years for most common equipment)

Some vendors will provide on-site demonstrations of their cardiovascular equipment and can be trailed by the membership for usually a two-week period. This is an ideal time to acquire feedback from the members pertaining to the likes and dislikes of equipment. Only consider on-site demonstration of equipment if you are seriously considering the purchase of equipment. Teasing the membership with the possibility of making a purchase and not following through will only upset them. It is also inappropriate to give a respective vendor the impression you are going to make a purchase and actually have no intentions of doing so.

Indoor Cycling Studios

The facility requirements of the indoor cycling studio should complement the objectives associated with the activity, which is to enhance mental imagery of an outdoor riding experience. To a certain extent, this activity should be perceived as a theater production where the instructor can control the lighting and sound with dimmer controls, which contribute to the ambience and visual effect. The inclusion of DVD projection is also desirable. The group facilitator's bike should be placed on a platform for participants to observe the cadence, form, and technique of the instructor, as well as for the instructor to observe the participants. Self-contained heating, ventilating, and air-conditioning (HVAC) systems separate from the main facility are desirable considering the intensity of the activity and the perspiration and heat that accrues. Ceiling fans should also be installed to circulate the air and keep the participants comfortable. The total space requirements are ultimately dependent upon the number of bikes to be included in the indoor cycling studio.

Group Exercise Areas

With the growing popularity and variety of group exercise programs, the accessories associated with these activities are also expanding. For these reasons, storage of equipment is a significant priority when evaluating existing and planning future group exercise facilities. Avoiding the appearance of clutter and potential hazards can be eliminated with the installation of tiered shelving that can be rolled out and put into a storage closet after a respective activity is completed. Mirrors serve as a functional need in this area in order for the instructor to observe the participants' form and technique; however, the overuse of mirrors on all walls can be disturbing for deconditioned individuals because of their perception that everyone is staring at them.

Stretching and Core Body Training Areas

The designated space for stretching and core body training is ultimately dependent upon the scope and extent to which the following accessories are made available: stability balls, speed and agility training accessories, medicine balls, bands/tubing, plyometric training boxes, power wheels, functional training grids, balance and stabilization boards, and pads. Establishing systems to support the use and storage of accessories is essential. Will the area be used on an individual or formal group instructional basis? A minimum of at least 175 to 300 square feet is suggested for this space.

Strength Training Space Requirements and Equipment

When determining facility space requirements, the programmatic objectives, number of potential users at peak time of use, the number of pieces of exercise equipment, and requirements for space allowances between pieces of equipment and walkway areas must be taken into consideration. The facility planner, when determining overall space requirements, should use two formulas:

- For each piece of equipment: 20 to 40 square feet should be provided. The exact amount of space should adhere to the equipment manufacturer's recommendations.
- For each participant: 20 to 25 square feet allowance should be allocated for each person using the facility at peak times of use. (This square footage requirement is not in addition to the space allocation for equipment).

Having adequate space ultimately provides a means to avoid compromising the safety of the participants. The space requirements for the most common free weight activities are as follows:

- bench Press = 90 square feet (18.36 sq m)
- standing exercise (standing arm curl, shoulder press, etc.) = 40 square feet (3.7 sq m)
- standing exercises from power racks = 130 square feet (12.07 sq m)
- olympic lifting platform (power clean) = 144 square feet (13.37 sq m)

At least two feet of space should be provided between exercise equipment/stations with three feet being optimal. It is also advisable to strategically design the strength training area into zones. Activities with greater risk, such as free-weight usage, should be a separate area away from the selectorized weight machines. The strength facility supervisor or monitor's station must be in close proximity or have direct visibility of the free-weight zone.

This area will be one of the most popular spaces in the facility. You should expect a mixture of dedicated bodybuilders, recreational weight lifters, dedicated fitness and body tone people, and novices who are just becoming interested in strength training. There will be an equal number of men and women involved in strength training programs. Further, this area needs to include space for free weights, strength training machines, and cardiovascular and stretching equipment. The designer must consider all these variables and create a room that will fit the needs of all groups.

Size

The strength training area will include coed free-weight, strength-training, cardiovascular, and stretching areas. A minimum of 9,000 square feet is needed; however, 12,000 square feet is preferred for this space with at least a 10-foot ceiling. Many new strength and cardiovascular training areas are inadequate when they open, because the designer did not perceive the popularity of the activity during the design stage (Baechle, 1994).

Walls

Three of the walls should be solidly covered with materials that will reduce sound internally as well as externally. The walls should be painted with an epoxy for ease of cleaning. There should be graphics provided to make the walls come alive. Further, numerous mirrors should be placed around the walls. The fourth wall should be constructed of durable glass and face into the lobby/lounge area (with drapes) to further encourage greater use of the area. Each area should have at least one bulletin board (i.e., cardiovascular, weight machines, free weights, and stretching).

Floor

The facility should provide the following types of floor coverings for the strength and cardiovascular training area (Peterson & Tharrett, 1997):

* Cardiovascular area: Antistatic commercial carpet treated with antifungal and antibacterial agents.
* Resistance-training area: A rubber-based resilient floor.
* Stretching area: Nonabsorbent mats or antistatic commercial carpet with antifungal and antibacterial agents.

New construction should involve the establishment of a 4 to 6 inch concrete floor being constructed on top of the building slab with a two-inch air space between the floor and the building slab. The springs will provide vibration isolation and ultimately prevent transition of sound from the building slab. The free-weight area should be at least one platform, 10 feet by 10 feet by 6 inches, constructed of sturdy materials and covered with a rubberized flooring material to be used for heavy weight activities. This platform should be recessed into the concrete slab. Depending on the number of participants, multiple platforms may be needed.

Ceiling

The ceiling clearance needs to be at least 10 feet. The ceiling should be constructed with acoustical ceiling materials. A drop ceiling can be installed for these spaces; however, ceiling panels are more susceptible to damage by objects or individuals and require considerable maintenance. Therefore, it is recommended that a permanent ceiling be considered rather than a drop ceiling.

Electrical

The electrical needs of equipment (e.g., treadmills, stair climbers, computerized bicycles, etc.) in the facility must be considered as well as the equipment layout. There should be numerous receptacles around the perimeter of the room. The designer will need to provide for audio and video needs in the room as well as for computer access.

The lighting in the area should provide at least 50 foot-candles of illumination at the floor level. The ideal lighting system has both an indirect and a direct component, throwing surface light on the ceiling to give it about the same brightness as the lighting unit itself. It is recommended that fluorescent lamps be installed, since they have the advantage of long life and produce at least two and one-half times the amount of light of incandescent lamps for the same amount of current used.

Sound

The strength and cardiovascular training space by its nature and equipment is a noisy place. Therefore, it is necessary to design the room to accommodate the noise generated. Materials in the walls, on the floor, and in the ceiling should have good acoustical qualities. The sound system should provide equal sound distribution to all areas, not exceeding 90 decibels.

Climate Control

When people use weights, they generate a great amount of perspiration and odor. The designer must consider these problems when designing the mechanical aspects of the room. The three most critical concerns are heating and cooling (68 to 72° F [22 to 26° C]), humidity control (55%), and ventilation (8 to 12 exchanges per hour with a 40 to 60 mix outside to inside air). Unfortunately, designers and/or owners neglect these concerns and are extremely disappointed after the facility opens. Climate control can make or break a strength training program.

Strength Training Equipment

A comprehensive strength training facility will include: Olympic benches, bars, and plates; weight trees; power racks which include adjustable spotter's bar for squats or bench press purposes; adjustable benches for dumbbell activities; cable crossover and handle accessories; smith machine; assisted dip; hyperextension; and abdominal boards.

The number of Olympic benches and power racks is ultimately dependent upon the projected number of participants using the facility during peak hours of operation. The selection of the appropriate Olympic bars is determined by the tensile strength. Bars used for squatting, Olympic lifts and bench press ultimately require 1,500-pound test. The types of Olympic plates available are steel, rubber, or polyurethane-coated. The selected style is ultimately influenced by the budget and the desired aesthetic value that is to be achieved. Olympic plates can be monogrammed with the organization's logo and dumbbells to reinforce the organization's brand identity.

One complete line of selectorized weight equipment should be included in the strength training venue. Typically, a complete line (11 to 18 pieces) will accommodate all major muscle groups. Selectorized equipment is ideal for beginners, women, and seniors because of the elimination of a balance component and reduces the risk found with the use of free weight activities.

Health Assessment and Testing Area

An organization truly having a vested interest in the physical well being of their membership will have a state-of-the-art fitness assessment, consultation, and educational seminar room.

Programmatic Considerations

The members' achievement of their fitness goals requires that they have a baseline to measure their progress prior to beginning their exercise programs. The health assessment process is an integral part in developing exercise plans. A determination must be made as to the scope of the health assessment process and the extent that educational and lifestyle programs will be offered, because these dimensions will dictate the amount of facility space required. Most health assessments include body composition analysis, blood pressure screenings, muscular strength and flexibility testing, submaximal cardiovascular testing, cholesterol screenings, health history appraisals, and nutrition consultations.

The following are specific fitness testing space and facility requirements:

- The scope of space required is ultimately dependent upon the scope of the health and fitness protocol completed. The fitness testing space requires a minimum of 100 to 180 square feet, consultation room (90 to 120 square feet), and a seminar room (20 square feet per participant) all with a minimum of an eight-foot ceiling with suspended acoustical panels; wall construction comprised of dry wall and painted with epoxy paint.
- The electrical outlets need to be strategically located in proximity to the exercise testing equipment and should be ground fault interrupters (GFI). Fluorescent lighting within this area should be at least 50 foot-candles of illumination at the floor surface.
- A sink in the facility is required.
- The emergency response system should include emergency lighting and audible alarms. This is necessary for the purposes of warning other facility personnel of a medical emergency in the area.
- Because of the function of the space, adhering to these standards is essential. The HVAC mechanical systems must have a temperature environment of 68°-72° F (22° to 26° C), humidity control of 55 degrees, and ventilation (8 to 12 exchanges per hour with a ratio of 40 to 60 outside to inside air).
- Size: The testing area includes a fitness testing space (100 to 180 square feet), counseling room (90 to 120 square feet), and seminar room (20 square feet per participant) all with an eight-foot ceiling (Peterson & Tharrett, 1997). There should be adequate space in this area to house two chairs, a desk, a file cabinet, a storage cabinet, a computer station, a bicycle ergometer, a flexibility tester, a treadmill, control console, crash cart, metabolic cart, 12-lead electrocardiogram (ECG), ECG defibrillator, cholesterol analyzer, examination table, double sink, spine board, and a storage cabinet for equipment such as skinfold calipers, stopwatches, and stethoscope(s).
- Walls: Simple drywall construction, epoxy painted with a pleasing color(s), appropriate graphics for the area, and a bulletin board.
- Floor: The floors should be carpeted with an antistatic and antifungal commercial-grade carpet, color coordinated with the walls and equipment in the room.
- Ceiling: A suspended acoustical panel ceiling is appropriate.
- Electrical: The electrical needs of the equipment in the room should be considered as well as the eventual location of the equipment. There should be numerous electrical outlets around the perimeter of the room. The outlets near the sink should be GFI. The recommended lighting for this area is fluorescent units that will produce at least 50 foot-candles of illumination at the floor surface.
- Climate control: The mechanical considerations for this space include heating and cooling (68° to 72° F [22° to 26° C]), humidity control (55 degree), and ventilation (8 to 12 exchanges per hour with a ratio of 40:60 outside to inside air). Due to the activities in this room, careful consideration to cooling, humidity control, and ventilation are necessary.
- Plumbing: A facility should ensure that every fitness-testing space either has a sink or access to a sink.
- Security: There should be emergency lighting and an audible emergency alarm to alert other personnel to a medical emergency in the testing area.

Equipment for the Fitness-Testing Area

The NSCA and ACSM suggests that a facility should ensure that its fitness-testing area has the following equipment (Baechle, 1994; Peterson & Tharrett, 1997):

- In the fitness-testing area—a bicycle ergometer, a treadmill or a fixed-step device (e.g., a bench) of a desired height, skinfold calipers or other body composition measurement device, sit-and-reach bench on goniometer, tensiometer or other device for measuring muscular strength and endurance, perceived exertion chart, clock, metronome, sphygmomanometer (blood pressure cuff), stethoscope, tape measure, scale, and first-aid kit.
- In the health promotion and wellness area—computer, overhead projector, video system, slide projector, conference table, and chairs.
- In the fitness-testing, health promotion, and wellness area—a system that provides for and protects the complete confidentiality of all user records and meetings.

Selecting and Purchasing Equipment

The selection and purchasing process is the key to securing top quality equipment. The planners of the facility should answer the following questions before selecting and purchasing equipment:

- What are the current equipment needs?
- What pieces would complement the new or existing facility?
- Will the selected equipment meet the programmatic objectives and needs?
- Will the clientele's needs be accommodated?
- Are ADA requirements being met in terms of type of equipment and placement?

The purchasing of exercise equipment is exciting; however, it is a time-consuming and involved process. With the numerous manufacturers of exercise equipment, the selection process is becoming much more difficult in trying to sort out which vendor to select. Purchases should be from reputable manufacturers that meet the fitness and industry standards for commercial equipment. Equipment for the home should never be considered for a public facility. To streamline the selection process, consider the following:

- Attend exercise equipment trade shows: This allows for the prospective buyer to use equipment and compare equipment vendors all at the same location. It is also an opportune time to establish rapport with vendors, particularly when planning to do business with them in the future.
- References: Call other fitness facilities to determine their level of satisfaction pertaining to a brand of equipment being considered for purchase. What do they like or not like about the selected equipment? What common maintenance issues have they had to address? What was response time for making repairs and the quality of service?

The following is a listing of selectorized equipment criteria:

- dimension of frames—floor space considerations
- shape of frames—oval, tubular, square—aesthetic value
- covered weight stack shrouds/sealed moving parts—avoid potential injuries
- ease of cleaning—labor savings
- color of frames and upholstery—aesthetic value
- ease of making seat adjustments—user friendly
- equipment instruction placards mounted on each piece of equipment

Delivery and Arrival of New Equipment Protocol

The arrival of new equipment is an exciting time for the respective facility and the membership. Proceed with the installation of equipment with caution and the utmost care.

- Establish a firm delivery date and time with the shipping company.
- Make an assessment to determine what entrance modifications, if any, need to be made to the facility when equipment arrives. Questions to consider include: Should the facility be temporarily closed; is the removal of door jams required; are pallet jacks or a four wheel cart required; will additional staff to assist with set up and installation be required or is this service included in the delivery and set-up process?
- Take pictures and write extensive notes pertaining to the condition of equipment upon arrival, specifically if it is damaged. Are upholstery colors and the models of equipment correct?
- Inventory the equipment immediately by securing the serial numbers from the delivery sheets or manually record the numbers off each piece of equipment. This is necessary because, when requesting future repairs, respective vendors will ask for serial numbers before processing equipment repair tickets.
- Sign off on deliveries, as long as items are acceptable. If equipment is not correct, an immediate call to the manufacturer or sales representative will determine the course of action to take, which may include the reloading of equipment onto the truck.

- Prior to allowing equipment to be placed into service, it should be thoroughly inspected as well as tested by the facility coordinator to ensure it is functioning appropriately.

To ensure the longevity of the facility and the equipment, the following criteria should be in place:

- Develop equipment and facility inspection systems.
- Establish equipment cleaning and maintenance schedules.
- Establish short- and long-term facility enhancement project schedules.
- Establish equipment replacement schedules.
- Establish staff cleaning matrix of assignments.
- Rules and regulations need to outline what the expectations are of members pertaining to cleaning cardiovascular consoles and upholstery after use, and so on.

Facility coordinators must be knowledgeable regarding manufacturers cleaning and maintenance requirements. Failure to adhere to these guidelines can jeopardize the warranty of equipment. Organizations must establish cleaning and maintenance manuals for the staff to use. The content should outline the cleaning materials, tools necessary to complete the task, the procedures for completing the cleaning or maintenance procedure; and the frequency of the cleaning or inspection to be done. Many small organizations and facility operations often require front desk or exercise floor staff to complete cleaning and maintenance functions. Greater accountability of staff is established when staff members are responsible for cleaning specific pieces of equipment and not just charged with the oversight of all equipment, especially if more than one person is involved in the cleaning and maintenance process.

Procedures for Maintaining Equipment

All strength and cardiovascular facilities, whether they are existing or new, should have a well-planned set of procedures for maintaining equipment in specified areas.

Aerobic/Anaerobic Fitness Area

This space contains rowing machines, bikes, sprint machines, stair machines, and skiing and climbing machines. In this area, surfaces that come into contact with human skin should be cleaned and disinfected daily. This not only protects participants from unsanitary conditions but also extends the usefulness and maintains the appearance of equipment surfaces. The moving parts of the equipment should be properly lubricated and cleaned when needed so that they are not stressed unnecessarily. Connective bolts and screws need to be checked for tightness or wear and replaced if needed. Straps and belts should be secure and replaced if necessary. Measurement devices such as revolutions per minute (rpm) meters should be properly maintained (this is usually done by the manufacturer, but the life span of the equipment can be extended by wiping off sweat and dirt regularly). Equipment parts such as seats and benches should be easily adjustable.

Machines Area

Isokinetic, variable resistance, single-station, and multistation machines are located in this space.

Rehabilitation and Special-Population Machine Area

The cleaning and maintenance of both the machines and rehabilitation areas are similar to those processes in the aerobic/anaerobic fitness area. Bench and machine surfaces that come into contact with skin should be cleaned and disinfected daily to provide a clean surface. Padded and upholstered areas should be free of cracks and tears. Moving parts should be cleaned and lubricated (guide rods on selectorized machines should be cleaned and lubricated two to three times each week). These areas should be free of loose bolts, screws, cables, chains, and protruding or worn parts that need replacing or removal. Pins that were designed for the machines and belts should be kept in stock. Chains and cables should be adjusted for proper alignment and smooth function. Machines should be spaced so that they are easily accessed with a minimum of two feet (61 cm) on all sides, preferably three feet (91 cm) (Baechle, 1994).

Body Weight Resistance Apparatus Area

This area contains sit-up board, pulleys, hyperextension benches, plyometric boxes, medicine balls, climbing ropes, pegboard climb, and jump ropes. It should have secured apparatus with well-padded flooring. If mats are used, they should be disinfected daily and be free of cracks and tears. The flooring below plyometric boxes and jumping equipment should be padded to protect the jumper from impact with a hard surface. The tops and bottoms of boxes should have nonslip surfaces for safe use.

Stretching Area

Equipment in this area includes mats, stretching sticks, medicine balls, elastic cords, and wall ladders. Mats in stretching areas should be cleaned and disinfected daily and be free of cracks and tears. Areas between mats should be swept or vacuumed regularly to avoid the accumulation of dust and dirt. The area should be free of benches, dumbbells, and other equipment that may clutter the area and tear mat surfaces. Medicine balls and stretching sticks should be stored after use and elastic cords should be secured to a base, checked for wear, and replaced when necessary.

Free-Weight Area

This area includes bench presses, incline presses, squat racks, dumbbells, and weight racks. Equipment should be spaced to allow easy access to separate areas. All equipment, including safety equipment (belts, locks, safety bars) should be returned after use to avoid pathway obstruction. Benches, weight racks, and standards may be bolted to the floor or walls. In the squat area, the flooring should be of a nonslip surface and cleaned regularly. Equipment such as curl bars and dumbbells should be checked frequently for loose hex nuts. Nonfunctional or broken equipment should be posted with "out of order" signs or, if a long delay in repairs is expected, removed from the area or locked out of service. All protective padding and upholstery should be free of cracks and tears and disinfected daily.

Lifting Platform Area

Equipment in this area includes Olympic bars, standards, bumper plates, racks, locks, and chalk bins. The cleaning and maintenance of the lifting platform includes ensuring that all equipment is returned after use to prevent obstruction of the area and hazardous lifting conditions. Olympic bars should be properly lubricated and tightened to maintain the rotating bar ends. If standards are used in the area, the base of each should be secure and each standard stored out of the way when not in use. Bent Olympic bars should be replaced and the knurling kept free of debris and chalk buildup by cleaning and brushing occasionally. All locks should be functioning, and wrist straps, knee wraps, and belts should be stored properly. The platform should be inspected for gaps, cuts, slits, and splinters (depending on the type of surface) and properly swept or mopped to remove chalk. The lifting area should be free of benches, boxes, and other clutter to give the lifter sufficient room.

Cleaning supplies should be kept in a locked cabinet located near the office or supervisor station. Supplies should be inventoried and restocked on a regular basis (once or twice each month). These items should be kept in stock (Armitage-Johnson, 1994): disinfectant (germicide), window and mirror cleaner, lubrication sprays, cleaning sprays, spray bottles (about four), paper towels, cloth towels, sponges, broom and dust pan, small vacuum cleaner, vacuum cleaner bags, whisk broom, mop and bucket, shower caps (for bicycle meter equipment), and gum and stain remover (for carpet and upholstery).

Maintenance supplies should be kept in a toolbox located in a locked cabinet. The toolbox should contain these items (Armitage-Johnson, 1994): file, hammer, pliers (standard and needle-nose), screwdrivers (Phillips and standard), allen wrenches, crescent wrench, rubber mallet, carpet knife, cable splicer parts and appropriate tools, chain splicer parts and appropriate tools, heavy-duty glue, nuts, bolts, washers, nails, and screws in various sizes, transparent tape, masking tape, duct tape, drill and drill bit set, lubricant spray, socket set, and vise grip.

Floor Cleaning and Maintenance

The life of any floor is directly related to the daily cleaning and maintenance of the surfaces. The floors should be cleaned regularly, especially surfaces near and around cardiovascular equipment. The established cleaning and maintenance schedule should indicate the type of solvents to use, cleaning process, and the frequency for completing daily or routine maintenance processes. Manufacturers will provide the guidelines, schedule, and tips for cleaning and maintaining the floors.

Disinfectant/Cleaning Schedule for Exercise Equipment

Selected solutions used to clean and disinfect equipment must comply with the manufacturer's recommendations. All upholstery, handrails, exercise mats, and cardiovascular equipment consoles, and especially any equipment surfaces that may come in contact with the skin, should be cleaned at least three times per day by a designated staff member. Members should be encouraged to wipe equipment after their use of equipment. Cleaning solutions should be applied to a soft cloth and then wiped on the unit, and not applied directly to any part of the equipment. The rails on ellipticals, treadmill bases, and footpads on stair-steppers as well as equipment housing units, will need to be vacuumed regularly.

Outsourced Maintenance Service Contracts

Establishing a maintenance service contract with an independent vendor is advisable for clubs or organizations that have numerous pieces of equipment or do not have the appropriate staff to service equipment. A Request for Proposal (RFP) for the servicing of equipment should be requested from vendors in order to secure the most competitive rates. Considerations included with the bid may include: service contract period, quarterly preventative inspection and maintenance schedule, hourly cost for service, trip charges, and the like. This formal approach may increase the likelihood of the organization's financial resources being maximized through a competitive bidding process.

In-House Maintenance Programs

Having a designated staff member responsible for servicing equipment increases the likelihood that repairs will be completed on a more timely basis and service interruptions for the members are kept to a minimum. Many equipment manufacturers provide training for in-house maintenance staffs. This service may be a variable when determining which manufacturer to consider when making future equipment purchases.

Once the warranty expires and the equipment ages, the frequency and number of repairs increase as well. Keeping the most common parts in stock minimizes the down time of broken equipment and the delay in receiving parts should they have to be ordered. It is advisable to have the following parts be in stock:

- treadmills—new running belts, decks, and motors
- ellipticals—ramp, wheels, and elevation assemblies
- stair climbers—alternators, cables and belts
- indoor Cycles—pedals, straps, water holders, crank arms, pads
- selectorized equipment—cables, Kevlar, weight stack pin replacements

Only certified trained staff should complete repairs on exercise equipment, especially when servicing electrical components.

Tools/Parts/Cleaning Supplies

The establishment of a comprehensive toolbox needs to reflect the tasks that will be completed by in-house maintenance programs versus outsourced service repairs. With each respective vendor using different size bolts and attachments, a survey of manufacturers' equipment manuals will delineate the necessary parts and tools necessary to make repairs. When an equipment catalog is not provided, it will be necessary to inspect the equipment attachments and fittings before making specific tool purchases. A word of warning is to make sure socket and Allen wrenches appropriately match metric or standard fittings. Lubricants for selectorized equipment rails must adhere to manufacturer's guidelines

Reporting Repairs

Establishing a formalized process for reporting repairs and for taking malfunctioning equipment out of circulation is a legal liability and necessary standard.

Facility coordinators have a duty to warn participants of any potential risk they assume in the general use of facilities, or pieces of equipment that are not operating efficiently, as well as when a respective facility area may be under repair. Equipment that is not operating should have a placard attached to it that states "DO NOT USE." Removing the equipment from circulation is a more prudent response to assuring the safety of participants.

The sample work order demonstrates the types of information that should be included.

Equipment Repair Work Order

Today's Date: _____

Name of Staff Member requesting repair: _____

Detailed Description of Item Broken: _____

Serial Number of the Product: _____

Organizational Inventory ID number (if used) _____

Was equipment taken out circulation or sign posted on equipment restricting use? (Please Circle). If no, describe what actions were taken!

YES   NO

_____

Date call was placed for repair?_____

Date Service was completed_____

Cost of Repair_____

Warranty of repair: 30   60   90   days

Strength Training Equipment Maintenance Checklists

The following are the standard inspections that should be included in a comprehensive maintenance program:

- Inspection of weight stacks, cables, and attachments—are they appropriately secured?
- Inspection of snap hooks—clasps close appropriately?
- No worn or frayed cables on equipment?
- Chrome end caps on dumbbells are not becoming jagged or flaking shrapnel pieces?
- Dumbbells tightened and secured?
- Bolts appropriately tightened on all benches?

Maintenance Records

At the time of installation of new equipment, a Maintenance Record Sheet should be established for each respective piece of equipment. This is necessary to track the maintenance inspection and servicing history and warranty schedule and to aid in decisions when a respective piece of equipment may need to be traded in or replaced. Extending the longevity of cardiovascular equipment can be enhanced if the pieces directly in front of entertainment sources are periodically interchanged with other pieces. Typical usage patterns are for cardiovascular equipment in front of entertainment venues to be the most frequently used. A review of the diagnostic tests to track usage patterns, specifically on treadmills is an excellent method to determine the number of miles as well as the frequency of starts and stops for each piece of equipment.

A safe-deposit box at an office site location should include a listing of all equipment, serial numbers, internal ID systems, as well as a video recording of the interior of the facility and the equipment. In the event of a fire or other catastrophic event, these records increase the likelihood of claims with insurance adjusters being settled much more quickly as a result of the detailed records being accessible.

Upholstery Repair

A common eyesore in facilities is worn upholstery. The process of repairing upholstery is a time-consuming process. Having the appropriate tools to complete the job and a skilled in-house staff member to perform this task is a challenging one; therefore, outsourcing this repair is recommended.

Summary

The development of strength and cardiovascular facilities requires a great deal of specific knowledge about the activities to be carried out within the facility. The planners need to be versed in the programs to be offered and the equipment used in the programs. Finally, the planners need to understand any specific requirements for programs or equipment.

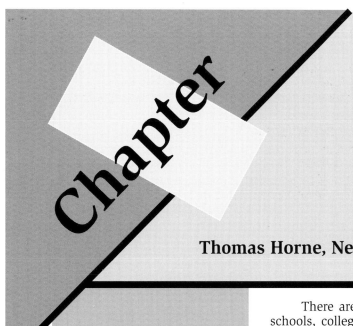

Adventure Programming Facilities

Thomas Horne, Ned Crossley, and Donald Rogers

28

There are literally thousands of adventure programs conducted in schools, colleges, summer camps, recreation programs, commercial adventure agencies, YMCAs, and fitness clubs. Adventure programs can be divided into three general categories: 1) Adventure Games, Initiatives Problems, and Trust Activities, 2) Adventure-Based Recreation Sports, and 3) Climbing Activities (Ropes Courses and Climbing Walls).

All three categories of adventure activities involve reasonable risk-taking activities designed to foster trust and cooperation, enhance self-image and confidence, improve physical skills, and be enjoyable. From a facilities standpoint, the least complex and structured category is Adventure Games, Initiatives Problems and Trust Activities. This category includes simple individual or group games, initiative problems involving group cooperation and innovation, or trust-building activities. Adventure-Based Recreation Sports Activities are traditional adventure-based recreation activities like mountain biking, kayaking, canoeing, hiking, skiing, and caving. All of these activities are also appropriate activities to meet adventure program goals; however, neither of these two categories of adventure activities have distinct facilities associated with them. Although these Adventure Games, Initiative Problems and Trust Activities and Adventure-Based Recreation Sports Activities include popular and effective adventure-oriented activities, they will not be discussed in detail in this chapter since they lack distinctive facilities and utilize a wide variety of equipment and support materials.

Adventure program activities categorized as Climbing Activities usually include challenge ropes courses and climbing walls. There are many variations of climbing walls and a wide variety of both high and low ropes elements. Despite the variety of climbing walls and challenge ropes courses, both have distinctive facility requirements and common features. Climbing facilities may be natural rock climbs, freestanding towers, indoor or outdoor climbing walls, or low bouldering elements that involve lateral climbing. All of these climbing activities involve climbing facilities with handholds, ropes, climbing hardware, and safety equipment. Similarly, ropes courses all have poles or trees as a base and use ropes, wires and wire hardware, pulleys, and safety equipment. This chapter will provide an overview of the common steps in a facility planning process, discuss the structures, equipment, and supporting materials needed for climbing walls and ropes courses, and identify safety and administrative considerations for those developing or conducting an adventure program.

Learning Objectives:

After reading this chapter, the student should be able to

- discuss the four design and construction planning steps used to develop adventure facilities,
- identify and compare the three categories of adventure programs,
- evaluate selection characteristics for a variety of climbing wall and challenge ropes courses components such as, support poles, ropes, helmets and climbing hardware, handholds, harnesses, and flooring,
- apply sound safety risk-management and administrative practices to building and operating adventure facilities.

The Planning Process

The initial step in planning is to establish program goals and determine what type of facility is needed to achieve these goals. In some cases this may require a formal needs assessment. Once a general facility concept is developed, a facility construction strategy is needed. The facility may be self-designed and built, or be designed and built by an outside architect or contractor, or a combination of the two. For example, installing a small bouldering wall (low climbing wall designed for lateral climbing) on an existing wall can be done in-house; however, building a large climbing wall or climbing tower is better left to professional climbing wall designers and builders. There are some excellent references that provide detailed information about self-built climbing facilities. For the more complex projects involving outside designers and builders, considerable planning and coordination will be required.

Many schools, colleges, recreation centers, fitness facilities, YMCAs, racquet clubs, commercial climbing centers, and even gymnastics clubs are building adventure program facilities to include ropes courses and climbing walls. Most of these adventure facilities support very popular, highly utilized adventure programs that achieve the goals and objectives of educators and operators. Ask any of the highly successful educators or operators what their secret to success is and almost every one will mention detailed planning and student-customer-focused programming. In short, they provide a quality product (the adventure facilities) and quality programs (safe, exciting adventure activities).

Whether in a school, community, or commercial setting, building adventure facilities and developing effective adventure programs requires planning. Every parent's guidance, "Do your homework!" is excellent advice for anyone involved in a large project like building and operating an adventure program facility.

Adventure programming is relatively new, so, until recently, there weren't many successful adventure programs for novice adventure programmers to use as facility design benchmarks. Today there are many successful adventure programs in operation at schools, fitness clubs, commercial adventure program facilities, and specialized climbing gyms. Lessons learned from both successful and failed programs are valuable planning guidelines for individuals considering developing or improving an adventure program facility.

No two adventure programs are exactly alike, but the planning process for developing and building an adventure facility or other athletic facility is similar. Whether building an indoor or outdoor climbing wall, high ropes course, low ropes course, comprehensive adventure facility, or any athletic facility, there are common planning steps (see Chapters 3 and 4).

This common recipe for design and construction in Chapters 3 and 4 can be applied to almost any athletic facility development project. The exact steps taken and the supporting tasks, coordination, and decisions required will vary with each application. A more detailed description of these planning steps will provide sound guidance on how to proceed with any design process. The next section of this chapter, Climbing Walls, is written in a facility planning format using the design and development of an indoor climbing wall as an example.

Climbing Walls

The design and construction steps used in this climbing wall example are similar to the steps that would be followed to design and develop a challenge ropes course or any other athletic facility.

Concept Development and Schematic Design

The initial idea leading to the development of an indoor climbing facility begins with a modest desire to build a simple wall. As the idea is discussed for possible action, it tends to grow. When the idea begins to receive serious consideration, the real homework begins by gathering information from as many knowledgeable sources as is feasible. Review recent climbing magazines, contact climbing wall builders, visit other facilities, talk to climbers, check local outdoor climbing sites, and surf climbing and climbing wall Web sites. Analysis of existing building codes is advisable at this point to avoid delays or costly changes. If the climbing wall is part of a multipurpose facility and the architectural engineer is unfamiliar with climbing wall design and construction (most are), the services of a climbing wall or adventure activity consultant may be needed. Most indoor climbing wall and adventure program equipment manufacturers and builders provide these consulting services. Using a professional adventure activities or climbing wall designer often speeds the planning process and results in a more efficient final design.

The motivation to develop a climbing facility is different in each situation; however, it is often desirable to:

- use the wall as part of an adventure program,
- have a climbing facility for personal use or use by a climbing group,

- include some high-profile architecture (usually in commercial fitness facilities or college recreation centers),
- more efficiently use an underutilized area of the facility (racquetball court, gymnasium wall, hallway, lobby, or storage area),
- provide a training facility for serious climbers, and
- add another fitness development opportunity.

Assessing why you want to build a climbing wall helps you determine who will be using the wall and how they will use it. This will guide many of your design criteria decisions. The design concept should meet current needs and provide flexibility for future program growth and development.

The climbing-wall concept will vary greatly depending on how the climbing wall fits into the overall facility design. The type of wall designed for a commercial indoor climbing gym may be very different from a wall designed for an outdoor adventure program in a public school. Determining how the climbing wall will be integrated into other program and support facilities will also have an effect on the design concept.

The location of the climbing wall in relation to entrances and exits, locker rooms, storage areas, offices, pro shops, water fountains, and other program areas such as the ropes courses, gymnasiums, pools, fitness rooms, racquetball courts, and classrooms will affect design concept decisions. Designers should consider general design criteria like visibility, control, and safety. Also, they need to decide if the climbing wall needs to be near to or isolated from any of the other features. Schematic drawings that show general size, location, and adjacencies will help refine concept development. More than one design option can be explored at this time.

Design Development

The design development phase is decision-making time. If more than one design concept was developed, a decision needs to be made on which design will go to full development. Full development requires decisions on:

- What is the scope of the project (including budget estimates, funding available, and space allocated for the climbing wall)?
- What heating, ventilation, and air-conditioning (HVAC) systems are needed?
- What features are needed for the walls, floor, and framework? (The wall, floor, and framework designs must meet Climbing Wall Industry Standards.)
- Which wall surface is desired (the real-rock look, seamless cement, prefabricated panels, wood, or doesn't matter)?
- How much wall height desired (a 12-foot high bouldering wall used primarily for horizontal climbing or a high top-roping wall)?
- Will a climbing treadmill meet program needs?
- What wall features are desired, especially the number, type, and location of handholds? Other surface features may be built into the wall such as cracks, arêtes (corner), depressions, over hangs, caves, ledges, and so on.
- How much wall security is needed? (Will the climbing wall be in a self-contained lockable area or will the wall be in an open area and require some way to limit access to the climbing surface?)
- What type of flooring is most appropriate? Bouldering walls and walls located in multipurpose locations like gymnasiums often have movable landing mats. Areas used exclusively for climbing usually have specially designed flooring such as thickly padded carpeting, six inches of rubber pieces, or six inches of gravel. Most new facilities are using the heavily padded carpeting because it provides better protection, is easier to maintain, and is cleaner than gravel or rubber pieces. Current practice calls for protective flooring to extend six feet out from the furthest protrusion of the wall surface.
- How much storage is required? A lot of equipment is required to operate a climbing program, ropes, climbing shoes, harnesses, helmets, and carabiners. The equipment needs to be located near the climbing wall so the storage areas for some of the newer climbing walls are built into the back of the wall.

Planning Summary

Failure to adequately plan (do your homework) and develop a comprehensive project concept often results in a climbing facility that does not have the desired features or meet programming requirements.

This may lead to a facility that is unpopular, unsafe, or prematurely obsolete.

Project planners must develop a comprehensive project concept that will guide specific design and operation decisions. Components of a comprehensive project concept for a climbing wall often address the following questions:

- Who are the target facility users? (Who will be climbing on the wall?) The design features for a bouldering facility to teach junior high school students will be very different from one designed to train lead-climbing mountain guides. Failing to identify the target facility users often results in an inefficient and ineffective climbing facility.
- Will the wall be a stand-alone entity, or will it be used with any other facilities? Climbing walls are often just one element in a comprehensive adventure program.
- What financial resources are available to fund the project?
- How many climbers will use the wall at any one time (peak load)?
- Is this a new build or retrofit of an existing area?
- How much space is available?
- How important are aesthetics? (Is a natural-rock look more important than having the maximum amount of climbing area?)
- What type of flooring will be best for the facility?
- Do the design features promote safety, minimize maintenance problems, and meet program needs?

Each climbing wall development project is unique and will require design and construction decisions not included in this planning model. This planning model does provide a template to guide the facility planners in developing adventure facilities or any other athletic facility.

Design Features

Building a climbing wall is, in many ways, like buying a car. Both are sizable investments that involve numerous decisions. Some of these decisions involve selecting which features and options are desired, which are affordable, which will be used, and which will provide the best value. When buying a car, decisions need to be made on the make and model of the car, engine size, color, and a variety of options like trim, floor mats, air conditioning, power steering, antilock breaks, and many others. When building a climbing wall, decisions need to be made on location of the wall (inside or outside), wall surface material, types and quantity of handholds, fixed wall features like overhangs, caves, or cracks, flooring materials, climbing equipment and hardware, and lighting.

Climbing Wall Types

Before selecting individual features of a climbing wall, a decision must be made on what general type of climbing wall is desired. Here is an overview of climbing wall types:

- Homemade—These are usually relatively simple walls made of framing lumber, plywood, paint, and handholds. Individual climbers build homemade walls for their personal use and institutions with limited resources build homemade climbing walls to support their program needs.
- Prefabricated panel system—Prefabricated panels are usually 4 feet by 8 feet plywood or fiberglass panels with predrilled holes for handholds.
- Portable walls—There are three general types of portable walls: disassemble and reassemble, assembled walls on a trailer, and the portable treadmill type wall.
- Steel structure wall systems—These systems are usually professionally designed and constructed walls with a structural steel frame and plywood surfaces. The surfaces may be coated with a cementitious, fiberglass, or

blown synthetic material. Some of the cementitious surfaces have natural features like cracks, ledges, and indentations that are troweled in while others replicate a real rock-style covering.

- Climbing towers—Towers are usually freestanding wooden towers built outside. They are often just one element of an outdoor adventure course.

The selection criteria most often used in making decisions on the general type of climbing wall to be built are program requirements, funding amounts, space available, and staff proficiency.

Climbing Wall Features and Equipment

Most new climbing walls have movable handholds that are attached to the wall with a T-nut insert. These T-nut inserts may be installed by the contractor as part of the construction, purchased as part of predrilled wood or fiberglass panels, or added to climbing panels as part of a homemade project.

Handholds may be simple wood blocks fixed to the wall surface with epoxy glue, wood screws, T-nuts, or a combination of these. Wooden handholds are relatively inexpensive, have a forgiving texture, and can be formed in a wide variety of shapes and sizes. Wooden handholds don't duplicate real rock shapes and textures very well. If a real rock shape or texture is desired, commercially manufactured handholds made of resin and fillers may then be the way to go. Serious builders of homemade wall can fabricate handholds from automobile body putty; however, this is a technical process not recommended for most wall builders. Most of the commercial handholds are designed for use with a T-nut system but some can be attached to the wall with epoxy cement. There are literally thousands of different types, sizes, and shapes of handholds. Handhold packages are available that include handholds that replicate natural features in rocks and require climbers to use specific grip and foot techniques. Handhold color and texture may attempt to duplicate natural rock, match the existing wall surface, or add color and flare to a climbing wall. Colored-coded handholds may be used to designate specific climbing routes or difficulty levels. Colored or numbered tags can also be attached to the handholds to mark specific climbing routes. The greatest benefit of having movable handholds is that the handholds can be moved, replaced, or simply rotated providing the climber with an infinite variety of climbing opportunities and route changing.

Climbing Equipment

The size and the scope of the climbing program and climbing wall will determine how much climbing equipment is needed. Magazines and catalogues are filled with a plethora of climbing gear and hardware. Standard equipment for general climbing programs include ropes, harnesses, helmets, belay system, and locking D carabiners. The Union of International Associations of Alpinists (UIAA) certifies that climbing equipment is safe and effective. Purchasing UIAA-certified climbing equipment is a sound practice. The specific selection criteria used to purchase equipment will vary with each application; however, the following are general selection criteria for standard pieces of climbing equipment:

- Ropes—Most climbing programs use 11 millimeter dynamic kernmantle ropes (continuous parallel nylon fibers surrounded by a nylon sheath) as their primary climbing ropes. They provide an excellent combination of strength, stretch, and suppleness. Kernmantle ropes are classified as "dynamic ropes," ropes that stretch so they can absorb some of the shock if there is a fall.
- Harnesses—The harness secures the climber to the climbing rope. Step-in premade commercial harnesses are recommended because they are more secure, comfortable, and convenient than self-made rope or tubular nylon harnesses, but they are more expensive.
- Helmets—Climbing helmets are essential pieces of safety equipment for many climbing and ropes course elements. Purchasing quality adjustable helmets will provide an extra margin of safety, make adjustments easier, and prove to be good investments since they will last longer.
- Belay system—There are numerous types of belay systems and all are designed to protect the participant from making an uncontrolled fall. Most belay systems are a rope threaded through some hardware (usually two carabiners or a shear reduction devise) or over a belay bar at the top of the wall. One end of the rope is secured to the climber's harness and the person belaying holds the other end, which is anchored, to the floor.

Notes

- Climbing shoes—Serious climbing programs should have climbing shoes available. Tight-fitting climbing shoes with high-traction rubber soles facilitate good footwork. Climbing shoes clearly make for a better climbing experience even when climbing on outdoor all-wood walls or when climbing on novice bouldering walls.
- 11 millimeter locking carabiners should be used for climbing and challenge ropes courses activities.

Purchasing, inspecting, and maintaining high-quality climbing gear is very important in protecting climbers from injury and owners and operators from costly litigation.

Climbing Wall Standards

The Climbing Wall Industry Group (CWIG) and the Climbing Gym Association (CGA), both sub-groups of Outdoor Recreation Coalition of America (ORCA), have helped establish enforceable climbing wall industry standards. CWIG and CGA standards are not presently required by law or government regulation, but a climbing facility, whether homemade or commercially designed and constructed, should comply with CWIG and CGA technical standards.

The American College of Sports Medicine (ACSM) has also established guidelines and standards for operating climbing facilities (Sol & Foster, 1992). The ACSM guidelines and standards focus much more on program and administrative procedures and less on technical design and construction features. ACSM recommends:

- Climbing wall areas must be supervised at all times by a qualified instructor.
- Supervisors should have CPR and First Aid certification and emergency equipment and supplies must be available.
- Climbing staff should undergo periodic in-service training.
- All policies and emergency procedures must be posted.
- Individuals participating in climbing activities must show proficiency in belay techniques, rope-handling skills, and climbing signals.
- All climbing equipment and facilities must be inspected on a regular basis and appropriate corrective actions taken.
- All climbing ropes must be UIAA static ropes.
- The climbing wall area must be allotted sufficient space.
- Negative air pressure should be maintained in indoor climbing areas as external air is drawn into the climbing area.
- The surface area of the climbing wall should have a moderately abrasive texture.
- Appropriate temperature (68° to 70° F), humidity (60% or less), and air circulation (8 to 10 changes per hour) should be maintained in indoor climbing areas.
- Mercury vapor or fluorescent lights are recommended with a lighting level of 50-footcandles at the surface of the floor.

Government laws and regulations do not currently cover adventure activity design, construction, and program operations. Everyone building or operating a climbing facility should follow CWIG, CGA, and ACSM guidelines. Local laws and regulations that governing zoning, construction, and safety must also be reviewed to ensure compliance.

Climbing Facility Operation

Climbing is an exciting activity that isn't nearly as dangerous as it looks, but certainly is not without risk. Owners and operators of climbing facilities must protect themselves and their organizations with insurance. Establishing sound standard operating procedures and conscientiously enforcing them will protect climbing participants and provide some legal protection for owners and operators. Each climbing program and facility will require custom made policies and procedures to maintain a safe and secure climbing environment. The following is a list of recommended policies and procedures for conducting climbing and adventure programs:

- Warn participants that climbing is a potentially dangerous activity. (The participant will then assume at least part of the risk of climbing.) Have climbers sign a waiver of liability prior to climbing.
- Post appropriate signage with safety warnings, policies, and procedures to be followed, emergency contact numbers, and any facility specific rules.
- Hire highly qualified instructors and keep their training current.
- Conduct regular formal equipment and facility inspections and keep documented records of inspections made and corrective actions taken.
- Supervise climbing activities with a qualified instructor.
- Secure the climbing area when not in use.
- Buy quality equipment and keep it well maintained.
- Train and certify belayers.
- Maintain a written set of policies and procedures operations manual.
- Keep emergency equipment and supplies available.
- No horseplay should be permitted.
- Warn participants about loose clothing or allowing long hair to hang loose because it may become tangled in the ropes or hardware.
- Always make a final equipment check before beginning a climb. (A buddy check is recommended.)
- Review communications procedures prior to starting a climb.
- Jewelry, including watches, should not be worn while climbing.
- Students must be given proper training and demonstrate appropriate skills before attempting the more difficult climbs.

This is not a comprehensive list of all risk-management issues associated with climbing but it does provide guidance on the kinds of issues to be addressed.

Challenge Course Adventures

This section of the chapter will define challenge courses, discuss the philosophy of challenge course programming, provide an overview of the industry, describe some challenge course elements, provide strategies for how to include people with disabilities, and provide guidance on how to develop and maintain challenge course elements for an adventure program.

"A Ropes Challenge Course is a series of individual and group activities designed to foster team-building, group cohesion, cooperation, leadership, problem-solving skills, communication skills, healthy risk-taking, and individual commitment" (Upward Enterprises, 2000). There are three basic types of challenge courses that meet the above-mentioned objectives and those are Teams Courses, low courses, and high courses. These and other adventure activities, including climbing walls/towers, are usually used in combination to achieve program, group, and individual goals.

At the core of adventure is risk taking. On challenge courses, participants are faced with physical, psychological, emotional and social risks. Of particular value with challenge courses is that the actual risk is low while the

participant's perception of risk can be quite high. This is helpful in situations where groups want to build the skills necessary to face actual risks in other activities or situations. When people are being asked to take risks, they should have the opportunity to at least co-create those experiences and have the option to control how they participate. The concept of "Challenge by Choice" was introduced by Karl Rohnke (1989) to address this need for freedom and self-direction within the challenge course adventure. It continues to be an important philosophical and programmatic guideline for most adventure programs.

The design of most challenge course programs fit within four categories: Adventure Recreation, Personal Growth and Enrichment, Developmental, and Treatment Services. While a program will have a predominant purpose that identifies it with one of these categories, it is typical to draw on approaches used in the other categories, depending on the needs of the group. In the fields of health, fitness, recreation and sport, most programs will be based on adventure recreation and personal growth and enrichment, or some combination of the two. Mental and physical health treatment programs such as psychiatric centers, stress-care clinics, and physical rehabilitation centers will utilize a treatment services approach. They too will blend treatment with the other categories. Challenge courses are often utilized in team or group development programs. These programs would use design components found in all but the treatment services area.

In order to provide effective programs, it is necessary to assess client/participant needs. Determining outcome and process goals plus individual needs establishes the foundation for program design. In fact, knowing as much as possible about the kinds of groups that will use the courses and what they will expect from the experiences is critical to courses' design.

Outside of the military, challenge courses were first used in Outward Bound to prepare groups for and supplement outdoor adventures. The first course, built at the Colorado Outward Bound School, was built with hemp rope, wood, and minimal safety systems (belays). About ten years later, in 1971, Project Adventure

built its first course in a Massachusetts high school. This course was used primarily within the physical education program but it led to applications in a wide range of settings, which today includes schools, camps, community centers, organizational development, and therapeutic settings (Rohnke, Wall, Tait, & Rogers, 2003).

The Association for Challenge Course Technology (ACCT) is the professional organization dedicated to developing standards for challenge course programs. The ACCT has developed challenge course standards for materials, construction, inspection, operations, and ethical behavior. The ACCT began as an organization for vendors who design and build challenge courses. It has since evolved into a full-service organization that has an associate membership option for programmers, managers, and operators. The challenge courses business has evolved into full-service vendors who build courses, provide customer staff training, recommend equipment purchases, and conduct annual inspections. Though not directly involved in design and building standards, both the Association for Experiential Education (AEE) and the American Camping Association have accreditation standards that address challenge course staffing, programming, and risk management.

Design and Development of Challenge Courses

The design and development process for challenge courses is the same as described in the previous section on climbing walls. In an ideal situation, the vision of the desired facility and program would be clearly stated and agreed upon by all involved parties. There would be adequate funding to plan and build the challenge course plus provide the necessary staff training. To locate a reputable challenge course vendor, contact the ACCT via their Web site, http://www.acctinfo.org. This site provides a list of vendor-members each of which has gone through a thorough screening process to determine the quality and reliability of their products and services.

Most organizations that want to build a challenge course do not have an ideal situation. They have to find a suitable location, struggle for adequate funding, promote the adventure facility and program, and search to find qualified people to staff the program. These are typical constraints that should not deter organizations from developing a course. There is considerable evidence that supports the value of using a challenge course. Challenge courses contribute to physical, emotional, and social development of the participants and are high visibility features that may be beneficial for program marketing and public relations. A well-run program with a quality staff can also be a productive source of revenue.

One approach to securing a challenge course is to build it with existing staff and the help of local talent. Many programs have done this in the past with considerable success. While this may be a tempting option, it is now strongly recommended that only experienced and qualified challenge course builders direct the process and build these courses. The designs, materials, and standards have become so very sophisticated that the do-it-yourself challenge course builder has gone the way of the wooden tennis racket. In addition to complex design and construction principles, there are substantial risk management and legal liability issues to consider. Insurance companies are very reluctant to cover a program with a challenge course that was not built by and is not being regularly inspected and maintained by a reputable vendor. Insurance companies still providing coverage for challenge courses have very specific criteria to assess the construction, inspection, maintenance, administration, staff training, clientele, and other risk management concerns. Course builders or the ACCT may be able to help locate an insurance provider. In lieu of a purely build-it-yourself course, some builders allow user assisted planning, design, and construction projects. Program staff may be able to assist with course design, layout, site preparation, basic carpentry, and even physical labor. Actually helping with the process is an effective way to foster staff buy-in and to help them learn about the course, how it works, maintenance needs, and programming potential.

For organizations with limited financing to build the desired challenge course, it may be necessary to develop a multiyear building and funding strategy that begins with short-term attainable goals and a limited course. Additional program support and funding will hopefully be made available as the program experiences success. With new ideas like a challenge course, those with decision-making power may be

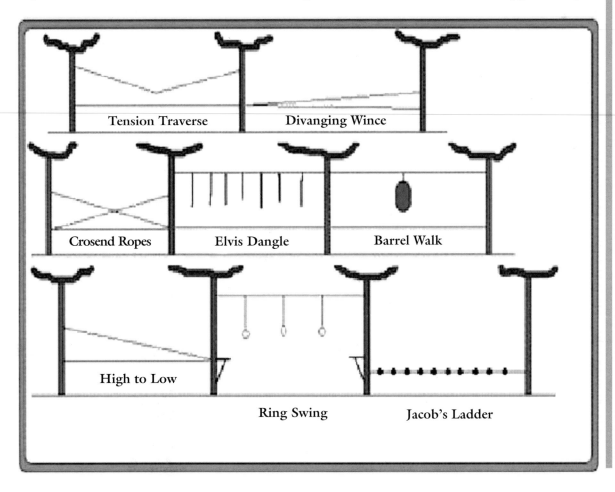

Tension Traverse   Divanging Wince

Crosend Ropes   Elvis Dangle   Barrel Walk

High to Low   Ring Swing   Jacob's Ladder

reluctant to commit resources until program benefits can be assessed. In this situation, starting with a small project, such as a Teams Course or a scaled-down complex, provides an affordable opportunity to demonstrate the viability of the program. Challenge course vendors can help with course planning and design that may easily be expanded in the future.

One of the first decisions is whether the challenge course will be an indoor course, an outdoor course, or a combination of the two. Many challenge course programs are part of a larger outdoor education program that may or may not have access to a multipurpose indoor facility. There are very creative designs available that utilize indoor spaces, both large and small. Having an indoor component provides options for rainy days, multiple groups, and possibly groups that would have difficulty using an outdoor course.

The next two decisions, site location and primary support structures, are often linked. A decision needs to be made whether the challenge course will be tree-based, using existing trees to support the challenge course, pole-based, which uses telephone type poles, a combination of trees and poles, or climbing tower-based course, where a tower is used as part of the support structure of the challenge course. A tower-based course may also use natural trees, poles, or both for additional support points. There are many new designs that combine these ideas with steel structures, tree houses, suspended yurts and gazebos, movable platforms, and prefabricated panel components. There is little to limit the types of designs that may be created.

The nature of the site available greatly influences the type of support structure used. If there are no trees at the proposed site, then poles or towers must be used. If appropriate trees are available to be used as the challenge course foundation, the amount of rock base, ground slope, erosion potential, natural water, and environmental sensitivity of the area are all factors to consider in selecting the type of support structure. Using natural trees is less expensive than using poles or towers, so financial considerations may also be a factor in both site location and support structure. Visiting a challenge course program that is operating in a similar setting, observing the program in action, interviewing the staff, and reading the operating procedures are all helpful in the early stage of planning. Be certain that local zoning regulations and building specifications are checked before making the final site and support structure decisions.

Selecting Challenge Course Designs

A challenge course is a set of tools that helps programs and participants achieve goals. As presented previously, outcome goals will fall within the Recreation, Growth and Enrichment, Developmental, and Therapeutic categories. When providing adventure recreation, participants are given safe but challenging opportunities to solve group initiative problems and climb on the higher elements. There is very little briefing or debriefing of the experience. The emphasis is on participants having fun while they are being challenged physically and mentally. As program goals become more diverse, course design becomes more complicated. In order to meet the programming needs of diverse groups, highly versatile and flexible courses must be designed. A higher degree of design specificity can be employed if the course will only be used with a specified clientele.

Among the programming areas, there may be similar outcomes or benefits although the means and reasons may differ. The positive outcomes that are possible with challenge course programs are enhanced

- self-respect and respect for others,
- communication skills,
- sense of physical and emotional exhilaration,
- personal comfort zone,
- leadership skills,
- fears management,
- teamwork and cooperation,
- conflict-resolution strategies,
- problem-solving skills,
- safety awareness,
- planning and organization skills,
- caring and compassion,
- physical fitness and coordination, and
- stress-management skills.

Achieving goals with a challenge course requires skillful application of a well-conceived plan. When planning a challenge course, consider the

- course lay-out,
- program goals,
- actions of facilitators (program staff), and
- needs and desires of the participants.

These four primary components are highly interrelated. Given the phenomenal nature of the experience, these factors could be described as having a synergistic relationship. In addition, factors such as environment, weather, and support facilities (restrooms, lodging) will have some influence on the process. The effectiveness of the course depends on the quality of the program and how skillfully it is administered. The course design is important, but it is just a means to an end within a dynamic cognitive, emotional, and social experience.

Any attempt to categorize challenge courses will be flawed in some way since challenge courses are such a versatile tool. Despite this limitation, courses tend to fall into three general types of courses, Teams Courses, Low Courses, and High Courses. Some adventure facilities, by design, include multiple types of courses, which are called challenge course complexes. Combining course types in a complex may be done because there is limited space available, to be clustered together, or simply to provide program flexibility. There are situations in a complex where staff can overlap, allowing economy of staffing. Building all the course elements in one central location may reduce building costs by allowing for the sharing of poles or trees among courses/elements. From a programming standpoint, there are important questions to answer before deciding on a complex approach. Some of those questions include:

- Will participants on other course elements be distracted?
- When running multiple groups, will the visual and audible overlap be a problem?
- Does a complex format create safety concerns with some groups?
- Will being able to see other groups on the course have a negative effect on accomplishing desired outcome goals?

Complexes tend to offer more logistical, staffing, and economic benefits than programming benefits. Challenge course planners and designers must decide if the benefits of a challenge course complex outweigh the possible negative impacts on the intended program.

Teams Courses

As the name implies, Teams Courses are designed to provide group experiences. The height of a course element should not create unsafe situations for user groups. Keeping elements close to the ground (usually two feet or less) is the primary factor that allows these elements to be used by the entire group without employing ropes, harnesses, or extensive spotting when group members or staff position themselves to provide support if someone falls. On Teams Course elements, spotting is provided as needed while the entire group negotiates the element.

Teams Courses are designed to have groups work together to solve problems. These problems or initiatives have a variety of physical and mental challenges that the group must overcome. During the process of planning and implementing solutions, the participants interact in ways that generate valuable group dynamics. Teams Courses are also called initiative courses, since they require the group to use a problem-solving approach to group learning and development.

Teams Courses are relatively inexpensive, which makes them a good option for adventure programmers wanting a challenge course, but have limited funds. They are also a good idea when space is an issue. Each element of a Teams Course is independent of the other so it is easy to locate them in many different configurations. Decentralizing the elements (i.e., placing them away from each other, out of sight and hearing distance) is a good strategy. It limits the "Hey, I wonder how that one over there works?" distraction within the group. Decentralizing also allows for multiple group programming by rotating groups from element to element without them coming into contact with each other. Decentralizing course elements is only one of many strategies that can be considered. Challenge course builders sometimes provide design, operation, training, and maintenance consultation service to program personnel.

Many of the well-known Teams Course elements are listed in *The Complete Ropes Course Manual* (Rohnke et al., 2003), which provides details about these and other challenge course elements.

Low-Challenge Course

A Low-Challenge Course incorporates elements that are normally about two to five feet above the ground. Low course elements are generally designed to present individual challenges within a group context. Individual group members negotiate the elements while the others provide spotting, performance feedback and encouragement. Since the elements are relatively low, participants perform most of the spotting and safety procedures without the aid of ropes and harnesses.

In recent years there has been a trend to make low course elements more team-oriented by creating situations where two people are on the element at the same time. These participants work together with the support of the rest of the group. Spotting is still provided by the group, though some incorporation of belay systems (a safety rope attached to the climber's seat harness) is being used. Having a belay system is very beneficial when programming with a diverse clientele. More information on programming for special populations is provided in the final section of this chapter, Accessible and Universal Designs.

No two low-challenge courses are exactly alike, but most have variations of common low-ropes elements. *The Complete Ropes Course Manual* is again a good resource to find examples of additional Low Course elements.

High-Challenge Course

The High-Challenge Course has challenged many since it was first developed. Innovative design components include steel structures, hydraulic auto belay devices, moveable platforms, suspended yurts/gazebos, shock absorbing systems, multiple levels, and improved safety equipment. With these and other cutting edge designs, High-Challenge Courses have become sophisticated, technical facilities. Elements on these courses range in height from between 20 and 60 feet. Additional safety systems and procedures are required for High-Challenge Courses. Each person negotiating the course must be connected to a belay system. There are variations to how these systems are set up, but generally they consist of a rope connected to a harness being worn by the participant. This rope is usually run through a pulley and then down to the ground where another participant or staff member is prepared to prevent a fall. Another approach is to employ a pair of short ropes that the climber clips onto cables or other approved anchor points. The ACCT has developed strict standards for belay system materials and construction.

Typically, a single participant negotiates his or her way through High-Challenge Course elements. Although this approach is still widely used, more programs are seeking designs that will allow multiple climbers or small groups on individual elements. Benefits are derived from the collaboration among participants on an element, sometimes called partner climbing. Partner climbing seems to more effectively capture and hold the attention of the group members who are on the ground observing. This also provides added value to the process with observers being supporters through encouragement and feedback.

High-Challenge Courses have administrative and financial factors to consider that are not as important for Team and Low Courses. High Course planners, builders, and operators must consider:

- Increased staffing requirements—One facilitator can manage a group of 12 to 15 on Team and Low Courses. On High Courses, a minimum of two or three staff would be needed depending on the design of the course and the needs of the group.
- Additional equipment costs—Typically, all the necessary start-up climbing equipment is part of the course package. This equipment will need to be replaced on a three-to-five-year schedule depending on usage and environmental factors.
- Possible higher insurance payments—Although the High Course is statistically safer than non-belayed courses, the majority of catastrophic injuries have occurred on High Courses.
- Access control—Preventing unauthorized access to the High Course can lead to an extra expense (fencing and other devices) and liability concerns.
- Staff training—Considerable staff training is needed to safely and effectively facilitate the High Course. The safety of everyone on the course, including staff, depends on having knowledgeable and experienced facilitators running the program. A year-round staff training schedule is recommended to maintain reliable skills and operating procedures.

This list is not intended to discourage agencies from adding a high course to their program. To the contrary, a high course adds features to a challenge program that are not available with the other types of courses. These features include a heightened sense of perceived risk, greater physical challenges, greater awareness of individual effort and concerns, greater sense of individual accomplishment, a visually striking apparatus, and a greatly amplified "WOW" factor. It also compliments other courses if available, by providing powerful individual challenges that serve to take the person's group-based learning to a higher level of commitment.

High Course elements are often similar to those included in Low and Teams Courses. This provides a chance to apply newly learned skills under greater stress and by adapting skills learned on the lower courses. Again a more detailed description of many High Course elements can be found in *The Complete Ropes Course Manual* (Rohnke et al., 2003).

Universal and Accessible Design Considerations

For the past 10 years, finding ways to make challenge courses accessible to participants with disabilities has been an industry priority. There have consistently been sessions on this topic at Association for Experiential Education (AEE) and ACCT conferences. The ACCT has published a position statement that supports the inclusion of individuals with disabilities in challenge course experiences. Standards within both organizations address inclusion and challenge course vendors have been incorporating accessible and universal designs into many of their products and training.

In an ACCT general membership survey (unpublished, 2001), the ACCT tried to assess the status of inclusion in adventure challenge courses. Those responding indicated that 48% of the courses had design and program features to include participants with disabilities. This number has increased since the survey. Nearly 84% of the respondents agreed or strongly agreed that it is important to continue researching, advocating, and reporting challenge course designs that provide opportunities for people with disabilities. While only about half of the respondents' courses are designed to include participants with disabilities, a significant majority of respondents support accessible challenge course design. The challenge is to incorporate designs that create relevant participation opportunities for participants with a wide range of physical and mental functioning.

The Universal and Accessible Design Committee of the ACCT (http:www.acctinfo.org/leadership_committees.html) and *The Complete Ropes Course Manual* (Rohnke et al., 2003) are excellent resources for additional information on making challenge courses accessible. A partial checklist of concerns/considerations is included below:

- Environment.
  — Are trail systems that lead to and link elements accessible? Planners need to consider slope, cross-slope, surface stability, and trail widths. Trail widths must be a minimum of 32 inches.
  — Are areas around individual challenge course elements level and firm with few obstructions?
  — Are drop-offs and steep embankments protected?
  — Are overhead clearances sufficient for participants with vision impairments?
- Elements.
  — Is independent access available to each element?
  — Are platforms, decks, and elevated walkways large enough and at heights that are usable by all participants?
  — Do transitions from element to element have options that consider the need for intermediate belay clip-ins and movement from one element to the other?
  — Are hand- and footholds of various sizes and shapes used to include enough large holds to improve access?
  — Are options for how individual elements can be negotiated (traversing, scooting, crawling, rolling, climbing) available?
  — Are access ramps handicapped accessible (a slope of 12:1)? Ramps that are part of the element do not have to meet accessibility slope standards.
  — Is edge protection used where participants with bony prominences might hit or have prolonged contact with a hard edge? Rounding edges and using foam to cushion edges and surfaces is recommended.
  — Are belay systems and elements designed so there are options for participants with mobility or balance concerns?
- Equipment.
  — Are mechanical advantage systems included to provide access to high courses? (A 3:1 or 4:1 pulley system is commonly used.)
  — Are full-body harnesses available and are course staff members trained to work with those who may need a harness? Many different harness configurations are available so handicapped climbers can minimize pain, support critical body parts, and make best of existing muscle function. Additional padding for harnesses may be needed when prolonged hanging in a harness is a concern. In most cases, no one should hang in a seat harness for more than 15 minutes. Harness suppliers will provide specific information on safe harness usage.
  — Are body protection systems available for participants with poor balance, diminished sensation or impaired muscle function? Areas to consider protecting include the head, elbows, hip-girdle, knees, and ankles. Padding used in other activities, such as skateboarding, works well in challenge course activities. Custom-fitting foam and other products to achieve a safe level of protection may be required.
  — Are hauling and counter-balance systems available to assist with access to high elements and climbing structures?
- Support facilities need to be accessible.
  — Do restroom facilities meet current accessibility standards?
  — Are storage facilities usable by all staff and participants?
  — Are debriefing areas, like the log circle, handicapped accessible?

When making decisions about how to make a challenge course experience accessible to participants with disabilities, it is important to understand that functioning levels and needs vary greatly. Conducting a needs and abilities assessment on each participant will help with activity selection and developing adaptations. When it is not clear how to include individuals with disabilities, it is best to ask them about their needs to assess their capabilities. Involving the individuals in the inclusion plan becomes a valuable part of the learning process. Providing a meaningful experience that maintains personal dignity for participants with disabilities may not be easy but with additional planning and a commitment to inclusion, challenge courses can provide exciting developmental experiences.

Challenge Course Operations, Administration, and Staffing

The overall safety record of challenge courses is impressive. They are among the safest of all physically demanding programs (Project Adventure, 2001). The ACCT has established safety and construction standards to provide guidelines for the safe and efficient operation of challenge courses. Even well-planned and operated challenge courses are potentially dangerous; therefore, all participants need to be informed of the potential danger and should sign a waiver of liability (Assumption of Risk). Other challenge course operation considerations can be divided into Administration and Staff, Equipment, and Maintenance issues. An overview of these operations issues is provided but is by no means a complete list of all operational considerations. Additional operational guidance is available in the ACCT Technical Operations and Inspection Standards.

Challenge Course Administration and Staffing
- Purchase and maintain liability insurance for the organization and the staff.
- Provide professional training for all staff members. Administrators must provide sufficient funding to ensure that staff members are up-to-date on current policies and operating procedures, including rescues and emergency response.
- Have a risk management plan that clearly indicates actions and responsibilities. Be certain all staff members are up to date on their responsibilities by providing periodic training. Monitor staff credentials regarding current first aid and CPR certification.
- Keep accurate records of staff training, program operations and procedures, annual and periodic inspections, maintenance and repairs, liability forms, insurance, student training records, and accident reports.
- Maintain a comprehensive equipment inventory and use equipment sign-out sheets to maintain property accountability.

Challenge Course Maintenance
- Inspect the entire challenge course and the supporting equipment on a regular basis depending on use rates, environment, and nature of the equipment. An ACCT vendor-member inspector should conduct a comprehensive annual inspection, preferably.
- Use pressure-treated lumber for outdoor challenge courses. Weatherproof wood parts as needed. (Annually is best, if feasible.)
- Use only healthy trees with a solid root system as support trees. Before building in trees, consult a qualified arborist about the condition of the trees.
- Use wood chips or bark mulch around the base of trees to protect the soil from compaction. Provide for drainage under the chips or mulch.
- Immediately replace dead or insect-infected trees. Trees are susceptible to weather, insects, disease, rotting, ground impaction and need to be checked regularly.
- Trim and clear broken or overgrowing limbs.
- Remove splinters and rough edges on all wood parts.
- Replace and repair all rotten or cracked wood.
- Peen down sharp metal edges and pad protruding bolt or metal ends that are in participant traffic areas.
- Reset protruding nails as necessary.
- Check for rotting of the poles in the ground.
- Use only corrosion resistant bolts, cable, cable locks, rapid links, and other metal parts.
- Critical cables such as belays, zip wires, and most guy wires should be 3/8 inch diameter galvanized aircraft cable (GAC) that is 7 x 19 (seven strands with 19 wires per strand).
- Tighten nuts and bolts, turnbuckles, and clamps as required.
- Temporarily cover all frayed cable ends with tape until they can be re-fitted with a serving sleeve.
- Inspect cables for smoothness and rust. Cables need to be smooth if a participant's hands or feet will touch the cable.

Challenge Course Equipment
- Use UIAA or European Community Norm (CEN) certified climbing ropes and locking gate carabiners.
- Install only stainless steel or galvanized hardware on outdoor challenge courses.
- Have participants wear an adjustable harness. A full-body harness is used instead of the seat harness when there are concerns about distribution of forces such as with the Pamper Pole activity.
- On static or self-belayed courses, maintain constant vigilance to assure that participants are using their "lobster claws" correctly when they switch from element to element. (Two locking steel carabiners are attached to the participant by two shock-absorbing lanyards.) One carabiner is locked onto the next element's belay cable before the other carabiner is unclipped from the previous belay cable.
- Minimize rope wear and damage by using a shear reduction device.
- Always have a first-aid kit available.
- Have a communication system in operation, such as two-way radios, as part of an emergency response plan.

- Store equipment in a cool, dry place, preferably adjacent to the challenge course.
- Include lightning protection on high-challenge courses.
- Require helmets to be worn on high elements and whenever anyone is beneath an active high activity.
- Keep a rope log that tracks hours of usage and falls taken on each rope. Also inspect belay ropes regularly for wear, cuts, discoloration, glazing, stiffness, soft spots, and any other changes in specifications. If you are not sure about the integrity of a rope, do not use it!

Summary

Adventure programs involve risk-taking activities designed to foster trust and cooperation, enhance self-concept and confidence, include all people, and improve physical skills while being fun, exciting, and safe. Adventure activities are usually done as games or problems, sports or recreational activities, or as climbing activities. These are technical facilities with standards for design and operations, which will necessitate the involvement of qualified designers and builders.

The planning, designing, and building process for these adventure program facilities is similar to that of most other athletic facilities. Common design and construction planning steps include determining its purpose, creating a schematic design, developing this design, establishing construction drawings, and contracting with a contractor to build the facilities. Throughout this process, a wide range of design, construction, and equipment decisions need to be made. Having a comprehensive vision for both the program and the support facilities will guide these facility and equipment decisions.

Skateparks and Winter Sports Areas

Thomas H. Sawyer

29

In the new millennium, there continues to be a skateboarding renaissance. Facility development, equipment quality, skateboarders' techniques and abilities, and participant attitudes and maturity levels have all reached new peaks. High-performance facilities and equipment for every style of skating are available. The abilities of professional skaters visibly advance each month, seeing athletes (yes, athletes) literally reaching new heights. Skaters have become less clique-oriented and more open-minded. All disciplines of skating are now respected.

These changes have made skating more accessible to many different people of varying ages. Presently, there are over 10 million skaters in the United States, making it the sixth largest sport (National Inline Hockey Association [NIHA], 2000). Skateboarding has become the third most popular sport among 6- to 18-year-olds (International Association of Skateboard Companies [IASC], 2001). Further, 1 in 10 U.S. teenagers owns a skateboard (IASC, 2001).

The popularity that skateboarding now enjoys is also reflected in the media. Skateboarding is regularly featured on major TV networks such as Fox, MTV, TSN, OLN, ESPN's notorious Extreme-Games (X-Games), and NBC's Gravity Games, thus bringing it into today's spotlight. Finally, this coverage, along with skating's appearance in marketing campaigns for Nike, The Gap, The National Fluid Milk Processor Promotion Board, Coca-Cola, and Nintendo has seen skateboarding appear on billboards, in magazines, and on television. All this exposure has greatly expanded public acceptance of skaters and skating.

Learning Objectives

After reading this chapter, the student should be able to

- develop a plan for a safe skateboard park, and
- design a safe sledding area.

Skateparks

History of Skateboarding

In the 1950s, surfers created skateboarding in order to pass the time when the ocean was flat. Roller-skate mounts and wheels were innocently nailed to 254s. This was the birth of the "sidewalk surfer." The earlier skateboard parks in the '50s and '60s reflected the surfer's passion for fluid, wavelike forms, and smooth sensations.

In 1970, the urethane wheel was applied to the skateboard. Skateboard-specific trucks appeared in 1973, which were followed by precision bearings in 1975. Being of higher performance than their predecessors, these new products allowed for an easier, more enjoyable ride. These improvements encouraged advancements in maneuvers and more challenging facilities and spawned a skateboarding boom that supported massive private skateboard parks across the United States and in Europe. The parks perfected the backyard pools, drainage pipes, and ditches that skaters had taken to riding. However, the demand for parks encouraged the development of poorly designed and constructed parks. This opened the door to insurance and liability problems. As a result, 80% of these parks were bulldozed in 1979, with the rest closing soon afterward. Some public parks remained, but basically skaters were left with nowhere to go, and many simply quit.

Yet during the '80s, the remaining dedicated and innovated skaters continued to push the value of the sport. Many changes took place in the design of facilities and equipment. The wooden backyard half pipe ramps began their evolution, which led to today's modern half pipes.

Presently, there is a resurgence in building skateboard parks. This has occurred because of the demand to remove skaters from city streets and public spaces. Skaters took to the streets because most of the skateparks had closed during the '80s, and they developed the "streetstyle" of skating creatively, adapting moves done in a pool or ramp in the defunct parks of the '70s to curbs, ledges, steps, handrails, and walls. Communities became concerned about the skaters, and some considered them rebellious and a public nuisance.

Skateparks have come a long way from the early, unsafe private parks to the well-designed safe public parks of today. The new facilities are larger and safer, and the skaters are using better designed equipment and safety gear. Skateboarding is fast becoming a very safe and exciting sport for young (ages 6 to 18) males (74%) to spend their spare time perfecting their skills.

Liability

Liability is always a question when dealing with sports in general. Therefore, it is paramount that owners (public or private) carefully plan for a safe facility for participants and spectators. Today most insurance companies do not view skateparks as a high risk for governmental agencies. They are no more dangerous than swings and slides. Yet it is advisable to make sure the facility is covered with the same blanket plan as the city or town. (See Figure 29.1 for a listing of insurance carriers)

Figure 29.1
Insurance Carriers

K&K Insurance Company 310-473-2522	Joint Powers of Insurance Agency 562-467-8720
Gelfand Newman Wasserman General Liability, Participant, and Event Insurance 310-473-2522	Association of Bay Area Governments, Pooled Liability Assurance Network 510-464-7900
City Securities Corporation 800-800-2489	Association of Washington Cities, Risk Management Service Agency 360-753-4137
International Special Events and Recreation Association 801-321-1493	

It is further advisable that the agency seriously consider safety when planning the skatepark. Signs should be posted to indicate hours of operations, pad and helmet requirements, and that the park is used at the participant's risk. The public agency needs to also consider the level of supervision that it should provide. Current common practice with skateparks is to leave the park open to "free play" with no supervision (i.e., similar to playgrounds). This practice will decrease the agency's liability. However, the operator must be certain that the area is safe, free of hazards, inspected regularly, and well maintained (i.e., similar to swimming pools at motels/hotels, where legislation protects those who have proper and adequate signage, a fence around the pool, safety equipment available, and the pool is maintained regularly).

The passage of numerous pieces of state legislation has allowed local public agencies to build unsupervised skateparks and post signs requiring safety equipment to be worn while skating. Unsupervised skateparks are very popular with skaters, but care has to be taken to build them in safe locations. If you do not have an ideal location, you may want to consider supervising the park or partnering with a private skatepark or other youth group, such as a church, Boys and Girls Club, or YMCA.

Immunity for Extreme Sports Parks

The Indiana General Assembly provided in Senate Bill 0141 (2001) that public and private owners and operators of extreme sports parks or recreation areas are immune from civil damages for injuries caused by extreme sports if 1) the extreme sports park or recreation area is designed or maintained for the purpose of extreme sports use, 2) a set of rules governing the use of the facility is clearly posted at each entrance to the extreme sports park or recreation area, and 3) a warning concerning the hazards and dangers associated with the use of the facility is clearly posted at the entrance to the extreme sports park or recreation areas; and they are immune from civil damages for injuries if the extreme sports park or recreation area is closed and has a warning against entry posted at each entrance. Other states have similar statutes and it is important for planners to pay attention to the three provisions outlined above when planning a skate park.

Safety Statistics

In 1968, the U.S. Consumer Product Safety Commission (CPSC) ranked sports and recreation equipment on a mean severity index that ranged from 10 to 2,516 (10 being the least severe). Swimming pools were given 335, bicycles 70, and skateboarding 34. There have been three deaths involving skateboarders in the United States since 1970 and these incidents involved motor vehicles. Table 29.1 provides the results of a recent survey conducted by the United States National Electronic Injury Surveillance System.

Table 29.1
Percentage of Injuries in Common Sports

Sport	Participants	Injuries	% of Injuries
Ice hockey	1,700,000	61,264	3.60
Football	14,700,000	409,206	2.78
Basketball	29,600,000	761,358	2.57
Soccer	10,300,000	146,000	1.42
Baseball	36,600,000	437,207	1.26
Volleyball	20,500,000	112,120	0.54
Skateboarding	6,200,000	27,718	0.49

Of those injured, 33% had been skating less than one week, 20% were people borrowing boards, and 95% received outpatient care. Most noteworthy is that 50% of the accidents occurred in unsafe areas where the skater struck an irregularity in the riding surface. Therefore, by providing and maintaining a professionally designed skate park instead of leaving these kids in the street, the above numbers would likely dramatically decrease.

General Planning Criteria

There are many sources of information on skateboard techniques and design of bowls, ramps, and other ancillary facilities. The following information is general in nature and provides the planners a place to begin this type of project.

Location

The planners should evaluate potential sites by considering the following issues: 1) potential usage of area (i.e., demographic analysis and a needs assessment), 2) size of site (i.e., how big is big enough), 3) access to public transportation, 4) drainage for the site, 5) access to public utilities, 6) noise pollution, 7) nuisance avoidance, 8) spectator seating, 9) parking, and 10) emergency access.

Safety

The following design features address safety issues that need to be considered by planners: 1) safe spectator areas, 2) low-maintenance site, 3) adequate sight lines of the area for supervision as well as viewing activities by spectators, 4) protective netting or barriers to guard against serious falls and to impede flying skateboards, 5) safety lighting, 6) emergency access, 7) exposure to environmental elements such as wind, rain, lightning, or sun, 8) shaded areas, and 9) drinking fountains.

Other Considerations

The following are a few additional considerations for planners to think about in the design of the skatepark: 1) adequate lighting for night activities, 2) facilities for skateboarding are suitable for other disciplines such as in-line skating or roller blading (e.g., recreational speed skating, in-line hockey, and freestyle or aggressive skating) and BMX bikes, 3) noise and light intrusion on neighbors, and 4) north or south orientation rather than an east or west setting.

Consulting Services

The services that are normally provided by consultants (i.e., architect, landscape architect, skaters, and safety experts) in this area include

- preparing a demographic survey of the local skate community,
- assisting in the site selection,
- determining designs and construction parameters (e.g., wood vs. concrete, size, budget [see Figure 29.2 for costs associated with the various types of parks], amenities),
- acting as an intermediary between owners and local skaters,
- organizing and establishing a pro shop (e.g., contacting vendors, preparing initial orders, etc.),
- preparing drawings for public venues, and
- developing design specifications for either wood or concrete skateparks.

Design Services

Skateparks are designed of either concrete, steel, or wood. The designs are unique and customized to the specific site, wishes of the local skaters, and the needs of the owners. The park should be designed to provide the skaters with a fun and safe place to skate. Skateparks should include elements for all levels of skating ability, from beginner to advanced with sufficient variety to challenge and keep them coming back for more. Elements are designed with the proper transitions and heights, and the layouts allow flow from one element to the next.

Figure 29.2
General Information on Skatepark Costs

Portable parks and wood parks—as little as $3,000 and up to $100,000 with the average park being 10,000 square feet and costing around $25,000; require regular maintenance; surfaces may be masonite, plywood, birch, skatelite, or skatelite pro.
Advantages—portable, movable, affordable.

Steel frame skateparks—steel frame with metal or skatelite surfaces; permanent parks; can be bolted to existing concrete pad; some maintenance; more expensive than wood, with a 10,000 square foot park starting at around $30,000.
Advantages—park can be reconfigured, weatherproof, affordable.

Concrete parks—concrete starting as low as $10 per square foot, averages $16 per square foot and can be as high as $20 per square foot depending on excavation, grading, drainage, irrigation, water table, and so on; average 10,000 square foot park costs $140,000, you must work with qualified builders and designers and make sure the concrete crew is experienced with mistakes made in concrete which are expensive and permanent and are happening too often, two bowls ($132,000) were built and the concrete crew brushed the finish making them unskateable.
Advantage—no maintenance, permanent park.

The designer of a skatepark should thoroughly understand skatepark design, site preparation (e.g., surveying, soil testing, etc.), and structural engineering (see Appendix AA for listing of builders, consultants, and designers). The designer selected should be able to provide the following services:

- Conducting preliminary consulting services appropriate to design considerations.
- Preparing custom concept designs for wood, concrete, or combination of the two.
- Developing detailed construction drawings for wood skateparks.
- Preparing detailed drawings for concrete parks.
- Providing budget estimates (see Appendix DD).
- Preparing detailed specifications for wood park construction.
- Consulting with concrete and steel contractors on design elements.
- Producing drawings in various formats using the latest version of AutoCad (see Figure 29.3 for samples of skatepark designs from http://www.skatedesign.com).

Specific Design Features

Wood Ramp Construction

Wood ramps can withstand many years of abuse by both skaters and the weather. The critical factors are that wood ramps are designed properly, built by experienced carpenters, and constructed of the right materials. The advantages of wood parks are that they are relatively inexpensive, easily built, and can be placed on an existing concrete or asphalt pad. In addition, most wood equipment can be moved to change the configuration of the park to create new challenges for the skaters to enjoy. (See Figures 29.4 and 29.5 for types of ramps)

Generally, specifications for outdoor wood parks include
(see also http://www.suburbanrails.com)

Photo by Michael Hypes

Various ramps at the YMCA skate park in Murfreesboro, Tennessee.

- All wood should be pressured treated.
- 3/4 plywood transition templates, on ends and every 4 feet or 6 feet.
- 2-inch x 6-inch joists, spaced 8 inches on center, 4-foot spans/double joists every 24 inches.
- Two layers of 1/2 plywood subsurface.

- 3/8 polyboard, 1/4 Skatelite, or 12-gauge steel ramp surface.
- 12-guage by 24-inch steel for all ramp bottoms.
- 1/4 Polyboard on ramp decks.
- Coping, 1 1/2 or 2-inch schedule 40 pipe (2 or 2 1/2-inch OD).
- Ramp joists fastened with #8 by 3-inch galvanized deck screws.
- Each layer of plywood is fastened by rust-proof decking screws on a 12-inch pattern.
- Ramp surfaces and bottoms fastened with #10 by 3-inch sheet metal screws.

Photo by Michael Hypes

Figure 29.3
Skatepark Design

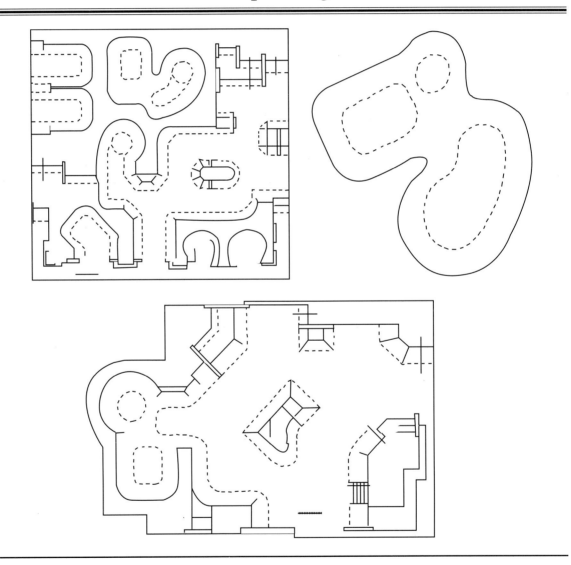

Figures 29.4 and 29.5 provide a few examples of ramps. They can be built with varying heights and widths. This list is far from comprehensive.

Concrete Skateparks

Permanent outdoor skateparks are constructed of concrete. The material is fluid and allows unlimited shapes to be integrated into the design. Objects can flow from one to another with no interruptions. Long, flowing designs that incorporate soft bumps as well as curbs, ledges, rails, and steps can be easily built to make interesting and challenging runs for skaters of all experience levels. If the owner has the budget, this is the way to go.

Figure 29.4
Sample Ramps

Figure 29.5
Sample Ramps

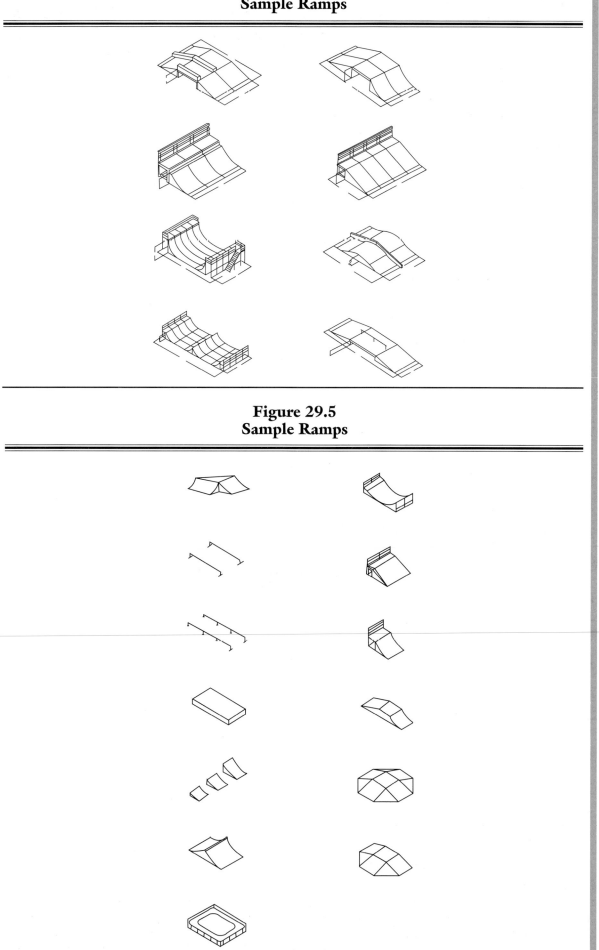

Concrete parks are built from the ground up. This allows for a more aesthetically pleasing park by incorporating varying elevations and by integrating grassy knolls, shade trees, flowers, and observation areas. Critical factors in concrete parks are the design and implementation of the transitions and placement of the coping. If a concrete park is poorly designed or built, the owner could be stuck with an area skaters will not skate.

Perfectly installed coping and forms act as guides for templates. The templates then guide a blade, called a fresno, which precisely cuts the concrete to shape. The template is then moved to the end of the trimmed section and the process is repeated. The concrete used is called shotcrete, which is also used for swimming pools.

Photos by Michael Hypes

BMX bike on the YMCA skatepark in Murfreesboro, Tennessee.

A grey coat is recommended for bowls, pools, or anything with transition. Working steeply inclined concrete with floats and trowels makes the concrete slump and compresses the transition, forming a kink. Cutting the concrete, then putting a finish coat on later, allows more control to achieve a precise shape and smoother finish.

Photo by Tom Sawyer

Concrete Skatepark in Green Castle, Indiana (above and below).

Photo by Tom Sawyer

Lighting

Most outdoor skateparks require lighting. Chapter 15 provides a great deal of detail regarding exterior lighting. Lighting for the park serves two main functions: to provide light for night skateboarding and for security when the park is not in use.

Indoor Skateboard Park

There are many locations in the United States that have a combined indoor/outdoor park because of climate. The actual design of the park will be the same except it will be indoors rather than out. The other components of an indoor structure such as heating, ventilation, air-conditioning, plumbing, electrical, and so on. are found in other chapters of this book.

Maintenance

Skateparks are generally constructed of concrete and repairs are rarely needed. Those that have steel and wooden structures will require regular inspection and maintenance. The facilities are kept clean by the skateboarders themselves. They do not want to trip on soda cans or other rubbish.

A major maintenance concern with steel is rust and loose bolts and screws. The wooden ramps also have problems with screws loosening and falling out. Weather can take a toll on both steel and wooden ramps. The major concerns with concrete are cracks and pooling water areas. The cracks need to be properly filled prior to winter. Frost can be very destructive to concrete.

Trees and other foliage enhance the visual beauty and provide shade for a park. However, trees require regular maintenance to keep them healthy. Areas around trees require regular cleaning to remove discarded limbs and leaves that could be a safety problem for the park. (See Chapter 19 for additional information regarding foliage, trees, and turf)

Other maintenance issues focus on cleaning restrooms, concession areas, offices, entrance and lobby areas, and the pro shop within the skate house. Further, exterior trash containers need to be regularly emptied and cleaned. Finally, the grass areas need to be mowed.

Concrete Skatepark in
Green Castle, Indiana
(left and below).

Photo by Tom Sawyer

Photo by Tom Sawyer

Winter Sports Areas

Sledding Areas

According to data provided by the CPSC, there were 115,000 emergency visits each year because of ski accidents but only 2.5% (3,750) are for head injuries. Sledding accidents account for 55,000 emergency room visits. Of those, 15% (8,250) are head injuries (CPSC, 2001). Most sledding accidents occur at a low speed between 10 and 20 mph.

Sledding Safety

Sledding is a great activity but results in many accidents each year, some of which are very serious and even fatal. The following safety recommendation should be considered when developing sledding areas:

- Avoid hills with trees, stumps, holes, fences, and rock walls.
- *Never* orient a sledding course toward a road, parking lot, pond, lake, river, railroad tracks, or raven.
- Allow for a sled return zone adjacent to the sledding course.
- Have all participants wear a helmet and mouth guard.
- Provide adult supervision.
- Pad all obstructions with hay bales.
- Use sleds that can be steered rather than snow discs.
- Do not allow participants to ride flat. Have the participants sit up and face forward.
- All participants should sled feet first, never head first.
- Do not allow inflatable tube sleds, they can bounce and throw children.
- Do not allow sitting or sliding on plastic sheets or other materials that can be pierced by objects on the ground.
- Be certain that the sledding area is well lighted during the evening hours.
- Post appropriate signage to warn participants of dangers of sledding and the do's of good sledding.

Designing a Safe Sledding Area

It is important to take into consideration the points made above when designing a safe sledding area for children. Sledding is a natural winter activity, and communities need to provide for safe sledding areas to protect the children.

A safe sledding area should include the following (see Figure 29.6):

- An entrance to the area.
- A wide, moderately sloped hill clear of stumps, trees, fences, and holes.
- The length should be between 50 to 150 yards.
- The runoff should be long and flat to accommodate deceleration of the sled.

Figure 29.6
Sledding Course Design

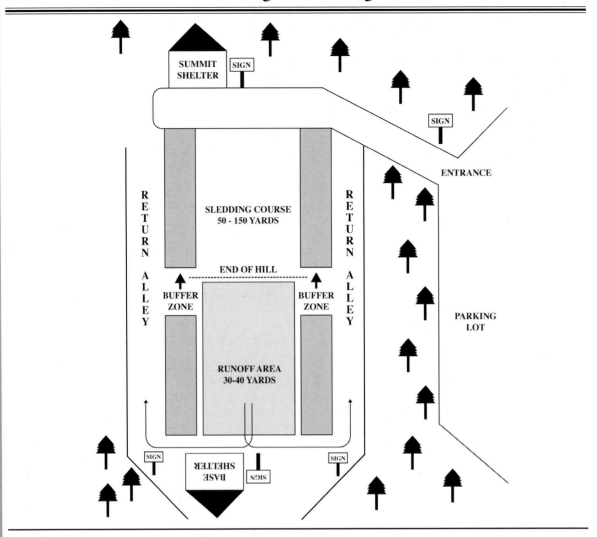

- The sledding course should be clearly marked.
- The return alleys for the sledders should be clearly identified on either side of the sledding course.
- There should be a buffer/safety zone of at least 10 yards between the sledding course and return alleys.
- The end of the course should not be compromised by roads, ponds, lakes, rivers, or parking lots.
- All obstructions must be padded by hay or straw bales.
- Lighting should be provided if the area is to be used in the evening hours.
- A shelter should be provided at the top and bottom of the course for sledders to use during resting periods with restrooms nearby.
- There should be appropriate signage placed at the entrance and shelters outlining the safety recommendations for sledders.

Snow Sports

Ski and Snowboard Hills

Skiing has become very popular. If climatic conditions are suitable and desirable topographic features are available, a school or a park and recreation department might look into the possibility of developing the facilities needed to foster this sport. A variety of artificial surfaces simulating real snow has brought skiing instructional opportunities to all sections of the country independent of climate.

The provision of skiing in a school or public recreation system should be approached from an instructional standpoint, the theory being to give participants some basic instruction so they can enjoy it as a leisure-time activity in the resort areas that have more ideal facilities. If the park system contains ideal skiing hills with plenty of room, regular ski courses may be developed. Some of the basic facilities required for skiing instruction include proper topographical features; a headquarters building for rental of equipment, a refractory, and similar purposes; a ski tow; and various slopes for instructional purposes.

Normally, the series of classes is broken into three units—beginners, advanced, and expert. It is the opinion of ski instructors that the beginners' ski class is by far the most important for recreation skiing. Basic instruction in skiing may be conducted in classes not exceeding 25 to 30 beginners. For this group, a gentle and short slope with a relatively large flat, run-out area is desirable because it permits a beginner to have complete control of him- or herself and allows him to gain confidence in the use of his skis. In the advanced group, classes are much smaller, and in the expert group, instruction becomes almost individualized. For each successive group, hills become longer and a little steeper.

The following criteria are recommended for the selection of facilities for beginners' classes:

- Flat-top hill area, 50 square feet per skier, 25 skiers per class.
- Slope about 75 to 100 feet long, drop in grade of 15 feet, or 4:1 ratio.
- Starting line at top of slope, 100 feet wide.
- Run-out at bottom of slope either flat or uphill.
- Slope facing east or northeast.
- Instructional area free of stones, woods, and other impediments.
- Protective cover, such as trees or brush, around the area.

The following criteria are suggested for advanced classes:

- Top of hill about the same as for beginners.
- Slope is most important: ratio about 3:1 and length 100 to 150 feet.
- Width of hill or slope, minimum of 150 feet because of speed and space required for turning movements.

The following criteria are recommended for the selection of facilities for expert classes:

- Either the same hill as advanced classes or, preferably, a longer and steeper hill.
- Enough downhill length to permit a minimum of three turning movements—for example, 250 feet on a 3:1 slope.
- Greater width than that of slope for advanced classes.

Cross-Country Skiing

Cross-country skiing has a broad popularity across the northern United States. Cross-country skiing, also known as ski touring, has attracted many people who cannot afford to keep up with "alpine" or "downhill" skiing price tags or do not want to stand in long lines at the lifts.

One of the attractive features of cross-country skiing is that a successful program can be developed with limited facilities. Existing trails can be groomed in the winter using homemade or purchased equipment that is towed by a snowmobile. Trail surfaces are best on a wood chip, grass, or gravel base. Asphalt bases do not work well. Trails can be carved out of almost any park area. If a golf course is used, the greens and tees should have a fence placed around them to keep skiers off of these sensitive areas. Trails should be signed with rules placed at starting points. The signs should indicate direction, distance, and level of difficulty.

Coasting and Tobogganing

Often a community has a hill or hills suitable for coasting, which become meccas after every snowfall for children with sleds, toboggans, and other coasting devices. In the absence of a natural coasting hill, some park and public works departments have built such a facility. These hills are usually located in a park safely guarded from the hazards of street traffic.

In developing local sledding (coasting) areas, care should be taken to incorporate adequate safety features. Sufficient space should be provided between sled runs and up traffic should be isolated from the down traffic. The area should be as free as possible from hazards, such as nearby trees, grills, benches, or other park paraphernalia. Municipal risk managers will provide input into the safety of the area.

Communities with an extensive response to sledding or skiing may want to counter adverse weather with the use of artificial snow equipment or improve the activity with a ski lift. Communities where there are not available hills have created their own sledding hills. They typically serve as a sledding hill in the winter and as part of a park in the spring and summer where multiple activities can be programmed.

Tobogganing is a thrilling sport that requires designed space. Occasionally, natural slopes are used if they are free from obstructions and have a long bottom run-off. The common practice is to select a hillside with a reasonable steep and even grade. A chute is constructed using a wooden trough. It can be permanent or built in sections. Some communities have created artificial toboggan runs with refrigerated chutes. They are expensive to develop and maintain.

Ice Skating

Ice skating facilities are feeling the impact of modern technology in more and more communities each year. With the advent of mechanical freezing, the skating season has been extended from a 20- to 60-day average season to a 140-day season and, depending on climatic conditions, to as much as 240 days.

While natural ice rinks have not gone out of style, artificial rinks are replacing them as central or regional facilities. Natural ice rinks are continuing to serve as a supplemental neighborhood facility in many communities. A considerable number of skaters still prefer the rugged pleasure of an old-fashioned skating experience.

Ice Hockey

Ice rinks may have a sports function as well as providing a recreation service. If ice hockey is to be part of the rink's activity schedule, goals will be needed and a 4-foot-high solid fence, called the dasher, will have to be installed to enclose an area as near to 85 by 185 feet as possible. Dasher boards are heavily reinforced to stand the shock of players being pushed against them and are lined on the rink side with either wood or plastic. There is normally a chain link or clear plastic barrier another 4 to 6 feet on top of the dashers to enable spectators to view games safely. The dasher board enclosure should have round corners, because square corners present a hazard. A kickboard, six to eight inches high, is fastened at the base of the dasher boards and is replaced as often as necessary.

Because dasher boards reflect sunlight and cause melting of the ice, they should be painted a dark color. However, it is difficult to follow the puck if the dasher boards are too dark, so a shade of gray is recommended. If the hockey rink is indoors, the dasher boards can be painted a light color without causing a melting problem.

Summary

In less than 50 years, skateboarding has become a large sporting industry. It started as a relief to boredom for surfers and has grown into a national pastime for thousands of young men and women ages 6 to 18.

Sledding is a natural winter fun activity but it is also dangerous if a few precautions are not taken. Municipalities and nonprofit organizations (e.g., Boys and Girls Club, YMCA, or YWCA) should consider developing a safe sledding area to protect the children of the community from sledding injuries. A safe sledding area can be a fun time for all if it is planned with safety in mind.

Section

V

Specialty Areas

Public School Health and Physical Education Facilities

Thomas H. Sawyer, David Hoffa, and Michael G. Hypes

30

In a public school building, the unit of primary importance is the room or space where teaching occurs. All other parts of the school plant are, in a real sense, secondary. In physical education, therefore, the determination of the number and character of the teaching stations is basic to the planning process. Further, it is important to locate these facilities in a separate wing for a number of reasons, including, but not limited to, noise, evening and weekend use, and non-school-sponsored uses.

The term "teaching station" is used to identify any room or space where one teacher can instruct or supervise the learning experience of a class or group of students. For instance, a gymnasium would constitute a teaching station and, if divided, could provide two or more teaching stations. Swimming pools, auxiliary physical education teaching stations, and dance rooms are examples of other types of teaching stations. The number of students accommodated by a teaching station is controlled by the nature of the specific activity, the size of the facility, whether the facility is indoors or out, and accessibility concerns.

The number of teaching stations required is dictated by enrollment, policies pertaining to instructional physical education, average class size, diversity of program, number of periods in the school day, and other uses of the facilities. Folding partitions and combinations of vinyl and mesh curtains can be effectively used for flexibility and to increase the number of teaching stations.

Planners should be aware that indoor facilities for physical education, athletics, and recreation are difficult and costly to expand at some future date. School planners should know the peak enrollment potential for each space. The anticipated enrollment 5 to 10 years after completion of construction should serve as a basis for determining the required number of original teaching stations. Long-range planning is imperative to provide for the logical and most economical expansion. The initial design should make provisions for the anticipated construction.

Learning Objectives

After reading this chapter, the student should be able to

- consult on the design of either elementary or secondary physical education facilities.

Common Planning Considerations

There are a number of common planning considerations for physical education facilities in public and private schools (see Chapters 3 and 4). These common planning considerations include surface materials (i.e., ceilings, floors, and walls), sound control and acoustics, electrical systems and service, climate control, security, climbing walls, ropes and cargo nets, storage, shower and dressing rooms, folding partitions or curtains, and office space for physical education teachers. Each of these common planning considerations is discussed in detail in the following pages.

Surface Materials

The selection of indoor surface materials for ceilings, floors, and walls becomes complicated because indoor facilities will be subject to hard usage, excessive moisture, and multiple uses. These surfaces must meet minimum standards in terms of acoustical and light-reflecting properties. Geographic location and the availability of certain surface materials are factors to be considered as well. (See Chapter 18 for greater details on indoor surfaces).

Floor Surfaces

The best floor surface to use may depend upon the number of different teaching areas. The main gymnasium area should have either a hardwood or synthetic surface. Wood, preferably maple, is an excellent all-around surface although it lacks the durability and flexibility that might be demanded by extensive community use of the facility. Synthetic surfaces have proven excellent for all normal game-type activities and also can better accommodate events that put additional stress on the floor such as setting up chairs, tables, booths, and the like. In an auxiliary teaching station, carpeting is often used but not recommend due to the low coefficient of slippage, which increases the chances of joint injury when quick movements are attempted (e.g., knee and ankle). Tile is also not recommended as a play surface due to the high co-efficient of slippage and the lack of adequate resiliency, which increases the chances of joint injury (e.g., knees and hips).

There are at least three distinct types of floor surfacing (e.g., hardwood, resilient synthetic, or common surfaces such as tile, ceramic tile, or rug) required in facilities described in this chapter. Floors in service areas such as locker rooms, shower rooms, toweling rooms, and toilet rooms require a surface impervious to moisture (e.g., concrete or ceramic tile). Classroom, corridor, and office areas may be grouped together for common surfacing (e.g., tile or rug).

Special activity areas require different treatments. For example, a dance gymnasium that is used for instruction in modern dance should have a finished treatment, which will allow dancers to slide or glide across the floor (see Appendix T for greater details on dance areas). In other areas, such as basketball courts, the finish should be of a nonslip nature. Careful consideration should also be given to the location of lines for various activities and floor plates for standards or gymnastic equipment.

Flexibility, durability, and cost are three criteria that have been instrumental in seeing synthetic surfaces challenge hardwood floors for installation in activity areas. The most popular synthetic surfacing materials can be classed into two types: plasticized polyvinyl chlorides (PVCs) and polyurethanes. The PVCs are primarily prefabricated while the polyurethanes are either poured in place or produced in factory-prefabricated sheets that are adhered down on the site. In general, the polyurethanes possess most of the desirable characteristics sought in a floor surface.

Walls

In addition to segregating specific areas, walls should serve as barriers to sound, light, heat, and moisture. In selecting wall surfacing, considerations should be given to the acoustical properties of the material. In general, moisture-resistant walls with good acoustical properties are recommended. Most modern gymnasiums have smooth surfaces on the lower portion of the walls so they may be used as rebound surfaces. Rough-surfaced walls collect dirt easily and are difficult to clean. Recently, there has been a trend to use color, murals, and graphics to add aesthetic appeal. However, in the elementary gymnasium, the need for walls to hold paper, posters, and/or decals should be considered as well.

In locker rooms, shower rooms, and toilet rooms where high humidity is often present, it is important to select wall surfacing that is moisture-resistant and has good acoustical properties. Walls serving as barriers between toilet rooms, handball courts, squash courts, and other areas where noise is a problem should have a minimum of sound transmission.

Ceilings

Roof design, type of activity, and local building codes should determine the ceiling construction. Ceilings should be insulated to prevent condensation and should be painted to provide pleasing aesthetics and to enhance light reflection. Acoustical ceiling materials are desirable in instructional and activity areas. Dropped ceiling panels susceptible to damage by objects or individuals will require considerable maintenance. False ceilings with catwalks above them have been effectively designed to permit maintenance and repair of lighting and ventilating systems.

Sound Control and Acoustics

The sonic, or audible, environment is the most difficult phase of the total environment to balance and requires the services of an acoustical engineer. In each room, attention must be given to reverberation time. This is influenced by the absorption and reflection qualities of all surfaces within the room. Hard surfaces reflect sound and produce excessive unwanted reflection and reverberations. Thus, the space may be "noisy." Soft or absorbable surfaces turn the sound into another form of energy and can produce areas that are too "dead." Therefore, most areas must have some materials with sound-absorbing qualities in order to balance the sonic environment for good hearing conditions.

Sound Insulation

Unwanted sound or noise may be transmitted into the room by means of ventilating ducts, pipes, and spaces around pipe sleeves. The transmission of sound through ducts can be reduced by the use of baffles or by lining the ducts with sound-absorbent, fire-resistant materials. The ducts may also be connected with canvas to interrupt the transmission through the metal in the ducts. Pipes can be covered with pipe covering and spaces in the pipe sleeves can be filled.

Sound can also be transmitted through the walls, floors, and ceilings. This can be reduced to a desirable minimum by the proper structural design and materials. In conventional wall construction, alternate studs can support the sides of the wall in such a manner that there is no through connection from one wall surface to another. This is sometimes known as double-wall construction. The space inside the walls can be filled with sound-absorbing material to further decrease the sound transmission. Sometimes, three or four inches of sand inside the walls at the baseboard will cut down the transmission appreciably. Likewise, sound absorption blankets laid over the partitions in suspended ceiling construction can frequently reduce the sound from one room to another.

Machinery vibration or impact sounds can be reduced by use of the proper floor covering and/or by installing the machinery on floating or resilient mountings. "Sound locks," such as double walls or doors, are needed between noisy areas and adjoining quiet areas. Improper location of doors and windows can create noise problems.

It is imperative to pay attention to the acoustical treatment of all areas. Gymnasiums, swimming pools, and dressing locker rooms are frequently neglected.

Materials for Acoustical Treatment

Care must be taken in the maintenance of acoustical materials. Oil paint reduces the sound-absorbing qualities of most materials. Surface treatment for different acoustical areas will vary. The most common treatment of acoustical fiber tile is a light brush coat of water-based paint. Most acoustical materials lose their efficiency after several applications of paint.

Electrical Systems and Service

All electrical service, wiring, and connections should be installed in accordance with the requirements of the National Electric Code of the National Board of Fire Underwriters and the state and local building codes and fire regulations. (See Chapter 15 for additional information.)

The capacity of each individual electrical system should be determined accurately for the obvious reasons of safety and economy. Full consideration should be given to present and future program plans when designing the electrical systems. The increasing use of electrically operated equipment, higher standards of illumination, and special audiovisual equipment should be anticipated.

Illumination

In addition to the amount of light in any given area, the quality of light is of equal importance. Providing efficient illumination is complicated and challenging and the services of an illuminating engineer are recommended in order to obtain maximum lighting efficiency. Gymnasiums, classrooms, corridors, and other specific areas have distinct and different lighting requirements. Planning for electric illumination requires that each area be considered relative to the specific use.

Important Lighting Considerations

In addition to the quantity and quality of light from the various kinds of lighting systems available, additional factors to consider in the selection of an electrical illumination system are maintenance, repair, replacement, and cleaning. The ideal lighting fixture has both an indirect and a direct component, throwing surface light on the ceiling to give it about the same brightness as the lighting unit itself.

There is less need, however, to provide high-ceiling areas with direct-indirect fixtures. In gymnasiums, swimming pools and similar activity areas, an even distribution of light is required to permit the individual to see quickly and distinctly in any part of the room. It is advisable to provide supplementary lighting on such specialized equipment and areas that may be provided in a main or auxiliary gymnasium. Even with careful planning, it is difficult to make adequate provisions without some compromise. In some activities, such as aquatics, the very nature of the activity necessitates a separate facility.

Night lights, sometimes known as safety lights, that burn continually are recommended for gymnasiums, swimming pools, handball courts, squash courts, and other indoor activity areas. Lobbies, corridors, and some classrooms should also be equipped with night lights. These lights are extremely important for safety and security purposes and should have separate controls.

Provisions for outside lighting should be considered. Exit lights must follow the prescribed codes of the local community and the state. Electrically illuminated exit lights clearly indicating the direction to the exterior should be provided over all exit doors from gymnasiums, combined auditorium-gymnasiums, multipurpose rooms, and other areas such as those containing goals or targets. Dimmers should be installed on the lighting in spectator areas. Supplementary light sources should be shielded from the eyes of participants and spectators in order to provide the proper brightness balance.

Transparent, nonbreakable plastic protective covers will protect lighting units in activity areas where balls may be thrown. Vapor-proof lighting units are recommended for damp areas such as toilets, showers, the dressing locker suite, and the swimming pool. Locker room lights should be spaced to the light areas between lockers.

Incandescent, fluorescent, mercury-vapor, sodium-vapor, and metal halide lighting systems are most commonly used in gymnasium buildings. The incandescent light is instantaneous, burns without sound, and is not affected by the number of times the light is turned on or off. Incandescent lights and fixtures are considerably cheaper in initial cost; are easier to change; and the lamp, within limits, may be varied in size within a given fixture.

Incandescent fixtures, however, have excessively high spot brightness and give off considerable heat, which becomes a problem when high levels of illumination are necessary. Fluorescent lamps have the advantage of long life and can be placed over all exit doors from the building and at the head and foot of exit stairways. Emergency (white) lighting systems should be provided for exits (including exterior open spaces to which the exits lead) in gymnasiums, multipurpose rooms, and other places of assembly or large group activity. This lighting should be on a special emergency circuit. All controls should be located so as to be under the supervision of authorized persons and all other aspects of the installation should meet the specifications prescribed by the Underwriters Exits Code and state and local fire laws and regulations.

Artificial Lighting System

A variety of trends in lighting systems have developed in conventional structures. One system utilizes primarily skylights and is supplemented with conventional artificial light. In such a system, a light sensor assesses the light level coming through the skylight in the working area just above the floor. At this point, the sensor signals that information to the artificial light system to shine from 0 to 100 percent of the wattage capacity depending upon how much light is coming through the skylights. The sensor in this system can raise or lower the intensity of the artificial light to an acceptable and predetermined candle power dependent on the activity. Installation of skylights plus a light sensor system will add an additional construction cost; however, this installation will reward the institution with energy conservation and cost savings. In addition, without the utilization of a light sensor system, a facility's lights would be required to be on full time whenever the building was occupied. Also, a high percentage of the total kilowatt hours used in a facility are conventionally designed for artificial lighting. A skylight and light sensor system will accrue a significant savings in energy cost. Artificial lights also generate considerable heat and, by reducing the amount of artificial light (heat), a skylight and light sensor system would have a significant impact on savings in air-conditioning cost. Such a system has an approximate theoretical saving projected to reduce air-conditioning costs by one-half and lighting costs by one-third.

Fire-Alarm System

Electrical fire-alarm systems should be separate and distinct from all program-signal or other signal systems and should be designed to permit operation from convenient locations in corridors and from areas of unusual fire hazard. All fire-alarm systems should meet the specifications prescribed by the Underwriters Laboratories and by state and local fire laws and regulations.

Program-Signal System

Gymnasium buildings can be wired for a signal system operated by a master clock or push buttons from the main administrative offices. Secondary controls may be placed in other administrative units of the facility.

Program signals should be independent of the fire-alarm system and should not be used as a fire-alarm system. Program signals usually include: buzzers or chimes in the classrooms; bells in corridors, pool, gymnasiums, fields, and dressing-locker suites; and large gongs on the outside of the building. In many instances, signals placed strategically in corridors rather than in individual classrooms are adequate. Electric clocks should be included in all indoor areas in the program-signal system.

Services for Appliances and Other Electrical Equipment

There are many needs for electrical wiring and connections, which require careful analysis and planning. The following are illustrative:

- Basic construction: motors to operate folding partitions, blowers for heaters and ventilating ducts, exhaust fans in gymnasium ceilings or walls.
- Custodial and maintenance services: receptacles for floor-cleaning equipment and power tools.
- Dressing locker rooms: wiring for hair and hand dryers and electric shavers.
- Lounges, kitchenettes, snack bars, and concessions: outlets for refrigerators, water or soft drink coolers, electric stoves, blenders, mixers, coffee urns, and hot plates.
- Office suites: wiring for individual air-conditioners, business machines, floor fans, and other mechanical and electrical equipment.
- Laundry rooms: wiring for washers, dryers, and irons.
- Pools: provision for underwater vacuum cleaners, pumps, and special lighting.
- Gymnasiums: provisions for special lighting effects, spot lights, and rheostats or controls to lower the illumination for certain activities.
- Health suites: receptacles and provision for audiometers, vision-testing equipment, floor fans, and air-conditioning units.

Climate Control

The engineering design of heating, systems should be based on the technical data and procedures of the American Society of Heating, Refrigerating and Air-Conditioning Engineers, Inc. The selection of the type of HVAC systems should be made with special consideration for economy of operation, flexibility of control, quietness of operation, and capacity to provide desirable thermal conditions. The design and location of all climate control equipment should provide for possible future additions.

Since the number of occupants in any given area of the building will vary, special consideration should be given to providing variable controls to supply the proper amount of fresh air and total circulation for maximum occupancy in any one area. Specially designed equipment and controls are necessary to ensure that climate control in some major areas can be regulated and operated independently of the rest of the facility.

All three mechanical systems—heating, ventilating, and air-conditioning—are interrelated and should be planned together. The services of a competent mechanical engineer should be obtained not only for design, but also for making inspections during construction and for giving operating instructions to the service department.

Some problems involved in the installation of HVAC systems include

- maintaining a minimum noise level;
- maintaining separate temperature control for laboratory areas;
- insulating all steam, hot water, and cold water pipes and marking them with a color code;
- exhausting dry air through the locker rooms and damp air from the shower room to the outside;
- providing a minimum of four changes of air per hour without drafts;
- installing locking type thermostats in all areas, with guards wherever they may be subject to damage;
- placing the thermostats for highest efficiency;
- zoning the areas for night and recreational use; and
- eliminating drafts on spectators and participants.

The geographical location of the proposed facility will dictate to some extent the type of climate control equipment selected for installation. Mechanical ventilation is preferred over open windows. Air-conditioning has been strongly recommended for southern climates; however, year-round uses of facilities make air-conditioning a desirable building feature in other areas. Special rooms such as locker rooms, shower rooms, swimming pools, and steam rooms need special consideration for moisture and humidity control.

Security

The athletic and physical education complex presents a unique security problem. The facilities and the programs attract large numbers of individuals who move at all times during the day and week and through many areas in different directions.

It is reasonable to believe that all students and visitors who come to the building have a distinct purpose in coming and should be welcome. This is the type of building which people enter through many outside doors and disperse to offices, classrooms, dressing rooms, activity areas, and spectator galleries. There should be some plan for pedestrian control and for the handling of visitors.

Security is accomplished in two ways:

- Constructing the facilities according to a plan, which allows for maximum security.
- Adopting an administrative plan for the direction and control of all persons using the building.

The physical layout will facilitate security but will not guarantee it. A good administrative plan will help. However, a good administrative plan cannot completely accomplish effective security if the physical layout does not lend itself to the attainment of such security.

Security Features of Construction

Entrance doors constitute the first barriers against illegal intrusion. Open and descending stairways, walled entries, and deep-set entrances should be avoided. The points of entrance to buildings should be well lighted from dusk until dawn. The corners of the buildings should have floodlights that light the face of the structure. So-called vandal lights should be installed and protected to make them vandal proof.

Corridors, which are continuous and straight, providing unbroken vision, add qualities of safety and security to the building, its contents, and its users. Corridors are best lined up with entrance doors to provide a commanding view of the doorway from the corridor and of the corridor from the entrance door. There should be an attempt to avoid angular corridors and to eliminate niches or cubbyholes.

The use of the night lighting within the building and at its entrances will assist in protection against vandalism and other forms of undesirable conduct. Night lighting will require separate wiring and switches in order to maintain a desirable amount of illumination. Switches for such lighting should be key-controlled to prevent their use by unauthorized individuals. A building chart for day and night "on" and "off" lights should be developed. There should be additional directions for "on" and "off" at every switch and such directions should be changed according to need. A key-station system for night watch checking is desirable.

Security of the Building

Securing the building and its component rooms against illegal entry is the first and most logical consideration in terms of building protection. Good door framing, substantial doors, and heavy-duty hardware and locks hold up against wear and abuse. In their long life and securing qualities, they constitute a reasonable investment. In reducing replacement costs for materials and labor, the installation of good hardware is economical in the long run. To reduce loss through breakage and theft, the additional security factor of quality hardware should never be overlooked at any cost.

A Lock-and-Key System

Enlisting the help of experts in the field of building administration will usually result in a plan which considers some of the following features:

- A building master plan including a lock-and-key system.
- The use of electronic locks with cards.

- Lock-tumbler adjustments so that an area may have its own control and authorization.
- Area division (vertical division) by responsibility or usage for key assignment; or "level" division (horizontal division) for key assignment; or a combination of both vertical and horizontal divisions.
- A policy of not lending keys is recommended. The person to whom the key is assigned signs a pledge to not lend it out. The keys for the facilities should be identified by a distinguishing mark, and a policy should be established with key duplicators in the areas that the duplicators will refuse to duplicate keys carrying such identifying marks.
- An annunciator system for outside or other doors of importance such as swimming pool doors.

Photo by Michael Hypes

Storage area.

Climbing Walls, Ropes, and Cargo Nets

The trend for the last decade has been to involve the elementary students in activities that allow them to develop upper-body strength (e.g., climbing walls [fixed and portable], climbing ropes, and cargo nets). The most recent addition to the elementary school gymnasium has been climbing walls and bouldering walls. These walls are either fixed to the gymnasium wall or portable. The fixed versions should have a resilient landing base and a safety rope system to protect the students from falls. See Chapter 28 for a listing of companies and detailed suggestions for construction of a climbing wall.

The traditional rope-climbing activities have not changed in great detail over the years. The important facility and safety issues include how 1) the rope is fixed to the ceiling, 2) the rope is stored when not in use, and 3) the landing base is established under the rope. Climbing ropes should be attached to a height of 24 feet and drop to about 3 feet above the floor. If the ceiling is placed below the structural members, the locations of suspended equipment should be planned and eye bolts provided during construction. Ropes should be placed 5 feet part, allowing one for each five students in class.

Cargo nets are great fun. The greatest concerns focus on how they are secured to the ceiling or wall and the landing base provided. The landing base should include either a landing pad, similar to those used in the jumping events in track and field, or a specially designed pit under the net filled with foam squares.

Storage

Two types of storage rooms are necessary for every physical education facility. The first is the storage of large pieces of equipment needed in the gym, items such as volleyball standards and officials stands, gymnastic equipment, chairs, mats and score tables, which, if left around the gym floor, are a safety hazard. This room should have easy access to the gym floor through a roll-up door. The room should be planned to provide for current equipment and future expansion and should be equipped with safety lights in case of power failure.

Storage rooms are needed for each of the different instructional areas. The room adjoining the gymnasium should be at least 1,000 to 1,200 square feet, 10 feet high, equipped with a roll-up door, and should be directly accessible from the gymnasium floor. Consideration must be given to community use of the facility and separately secured storage of related equipment. Ideally, there would be a separate storage room for each of the programs. The storage areas should have adjustable bins, shelves, racks, and hangers for the best utilization of space and the proper care of equipment and supplies. Space to store out-of-season equipment is essential to prevent loss or misplacement between seasons. An outside entrance assists in the handling of equipment that is used outdoors and/or in connection with a summer playground program.

The second type of room needed is for the storage and repair of small equipment and supplies. Special bins, racks, hooks and nets, with a work bench for making minor repairs, adds greatly to the efficiency of the room. Ideally this room should be located near faculty offices.

Shower and Dressing Rooms

Although it has been standard practice not to include shower, locker, and dressing room facilities in the elementary school, such facilities are essential if the gymnasium is to be used for intramural or interscholastic competition and community usage. The size, number of lockers, showers, and toilet facilities will be dependent on the extent of usage. (See Chapter 16 for greater detail on these areas.) If swimming pools are added as part of the school-community complex, such facilities are a must. Provision for outdoor restrooms is desirable if the general public is involved.

Folding Partitions or Curtains

Folding partitions make possible two or more teaching stations in the gymnasium. They should be power-operated, insulated against sound transmission and reverberation, and installed to permit compensation for building settlement. The control should be key-operated. The design and operation must ensure student safety. Partitions should extend from floor to ceiling and may be recessed when folded. Floor tracks should not be used. A pass door should be provided at the end of a partition. When partitions are installed in gymnasiums with open truss construction, the space between the top of the folding doors and the ceiling should be insulated against sound transmission.

Vinyl/mesh combination curtains have become very popular. The curtain is rolled to the ceiling when not in use. The curtains generally are vinyl for the first 6 feet to 8 feet with mesh for the remaining distance to the ceiling. The vinyl comes in a variety of colors.

Office Space for Physical Education Teachers

The office space for physical education teachers should be in close proximity to the gymnasium and locker room areas. It should range from 150 to 250 square feet and include an attached bathroom and shower facility. The office should have an observation window for the gymnasium and outdoor field spaces. Further, the office should be close to or attached to the storage space for the gymnasium. Finally, the office should be designed to include accessibility to a computer and a telephone.

Other General Considerations

It is important for planners to consider other uses of physical education teaching facilities for extracurricular activities for the students and the community in general at the end of the school day. These considerations include:

- Additional space will be necessary if all students are to be given an opportunity to participate in an intramural and/or interscholastic program.
- It is desirable to have such additional special facilities as dance studios (see Appendix T), gymnastics areas, swimming pools (see Chapter 23), and archery ranges in order to expand the offerings of the physical education program. Note: It may be possible for the school to obtain some of these facilities through the cooperative use of existing or proposed facilities owned and administered by some other agency.
- As planning for recreation is considered, the entire school plant becomes a potential space resource and all units should be scrutinized and planned with recreational adaptability in mind.

Specific Planning Considerations for Specific School Buildings

Elementary School

The elementary school is defined as follows for this book—kindergarten through fifth grade. These suggestions are based on input from experienced elementary practitioners and the Council on Physical Education for Children.

Indoor Activity Areas

The elementary school physical education program centers around the teaching of fundamental movement patterns, rhythmics or dance, fitness activities, games and sports, gymnastic activities, combatives, self-testing activities, and aquatics. The design and scope of physical education facilities should reflect the activities included in the elementary physical education curriculum. Additionally, the planners should refer to the National Association for Sport and Physical Education's Council on Physical Education for Children (COPEC) guidelines for facilities, equipment, and instructional materials in elementary physical education (2001). Finally, another good resource for planners is Chapter 33, Facilities, Equipment, and Supplies in Pangrazi and Dauer's *Dynamic Physical Education*.

Physical Education for Elementary School Children

A major consideration fundamental to the planning of an elementary school indoor activity area is the anticipated use by the community. Future years are expected to see more and more community use of these facilities.

Several of the standard planning principles apply particularly to the elementary facility. Such planning principles would include establishing priority use for the facility by giving basic consideration to the primary age group using the facility, allowing for use by children with disabilities, designing for the participants ahead of the spectators, and remembering considerations for maintenance of the facilities.

Location

Elementary schools are often more compact than other schools, and it is desirable to have the activity area apart from the classrooms to reduce noise disturbance. With the increasing use of such facilities by the community, consideration must be given to accessibility from the parking areas. In addition, it should be adjacent to the outdoor play fields. This allows for easier storage of equipment and increases the efficiency of the area to be used as a neighborhood playground in the summer months.

Teaching Stations for Physical Education

Elementary school physical education classes may be organized by a number of methods. The average class size is usually based on the number of pupils in the classroom unit. Because of differences in pupil maturation, physical education periods generally vary from 20 minutes for kindergarten and first grade to 45 minutes for fifth and sixth grades with the school average (for computation purposes) being 30 minutes per class. The formula for computing the number of teaching stations needed for physical education in an elementary school is as follows:

Minimum number of teaching stations equals the number of classroom students times the number of PE periods per week per class (Total number of PE class periods in a school week).

Example:

- Number of classrooms of students: school contains grades K to 6, three classrooms for each grade level, or a total of 21 classroom units.
- Number of physical education periods per week per class: one period per class for physical education each school day during the week equals five periods per week.
- Total number of physical education class periods in a school week: There are five instructional hours in the school day and the length of physical education period is 30 minutes. Thus, a total of ten 30-minute periods each school day may be scheduled for physical education, or a total of 50 periods for the five-day school week.

The teaching station needs would be calculated as follows:

Minimum number of teaching stations equals 21 classroom units times five periods per day, 50 periods per week, equals 105 divided by 50 equals 2.1.

In the above situation, if one classroom section has been dropped each week (bringing the total to 20), then the need would be two teaching stations. Therefore, requiring physical education five periods per week in the school used in the example would necessitate employing two physical education teachers each hour of the day.

In many school systems, the above situation would be too idealistic. More likely, only one physical education instructor would be available (either a specialist, or the classroom teacher, or a paraprofessional in collaboration with one of the other two). This would then drop the number of sessions per week for each classroom unit from 5 to an average of 2.5. One teaching station would handle this setup. If only one teaching station can be provided in the elementary school, then preferably it would be a gymnasium, despite the fact that some other type of auxiliary station might prove superior for instruction in the lower grades. The elementary gymnasium remains the preferred facility because of its heavy use by both the upper grades and the community. If the school system and the community were in need of an indoor swimming pool, this would be the choice for a second teaching station.

The next choice is an auxiliary teaching station, sometimes called a playroom. Particularly when heavy community use is anticipated, another alternative is to build a larger gymnasium and allow for dividing it by a folding partition or vinyl/mesh curtains. Such a setup would provide four possible teaching stations, two on each side of the divider. This area would also allow for two basketball intramural courts, one basketball interscholastic court, three volleyball courts, six badminton courts, and four multi-purpose game circles.

Multipurpose, Cafeteria-Gymnasium Combinations, and Self-Contained Classrooms

Multipurpose rooms and cafeteria-gymnasium combinations have been found to be most impractical for physical education, especially from the standpoint of scheduling. Self-contained classrooms are restrictive in the types of activities that can be offered and have an additional disadvantage. Furniture must be moved whenever activity takes place; but if there is no way to have a separate facility, make sure there is adequate storage space for the tables, chairs, and benches. This storage space should be separate for physical education equipment and for cafeteria equipment. Both spaces should have roll-up doors for ease of transfer of equipment between uses.

If used, such classrooms must provide an unobstructed area of 450 square feet, be of a nonskid surface, have no dangerous projections, and ideally have direct access to an adjoining terrace, part of which should be roofed for protection against rain. These self-contained classrooms would only be used in the lower grades.

The Gymnasium

In planning the elementary school gymnasium, a minimum of 110 to 150 square feet per pupil and a total of at least 4,860 square feet is recommended. Spectator seating (if provided) and storage rooms (ranging in size from 400 to 600 square feet with roll-up doors and a minimum ceiling height of 10 feet) require additional space. Many of the general considerations recommended for secondary school gymnasiums also apply to elementary school facilities.

The specific dimensions of the gymnasium should provide for a basketball court of 42 feet by 74 feet with a minimum safety space of 6 feet around the perimeter. An area of 54 feet by 90 feet (4,860 square feet) would be adequate. The ceiling should be at least 22 feet high. This space is adequate for activities normally included in the elementary school program and will serve the community recreation program. The gymnasium will be of a larger size if the decision is made to use it as a multiple teaching facility and include a folding partition or vinyl/mesh curtains as part of the design.

Special Floor Markings

The elementary gymnasium floor may have additional markings beyond the traditional game markings (e.g., basketball). These other markings may include, but are not limited to, circles of various sizes and shapes. Floor markings facilitate a variety of activities; however, the number of different markings should be limited to reduce confusion. The dominant lines should intersect the nondominant lines (e.g., game lines should intersect nongame lines). A nondominant line should be broken (two inches) prior to intersecting the dominant line, and lines should be in different colors.

Buffer/Safety Zones

All playing areas must have buffer/safety zones separating them from walls, bleachers, and adjacent playing areas. The distance should be at least 10 feet from the sideline to the nearest obstruction (e.g., wall, bleacher, stage, or adjacent playing area). Facilities without buffer/safety zones around playing areas will expose participants and/or spectators to serious injury.

Auxiliary Teaching Stations

If a second indoor physical education teaching area is built, it should be either a swimming pool or an auxiliary instruction room, sometimes called a playroom. Swimming pools are discussed elsewhere in this text (see Chapter 23). The auxiliary teaching station is most practical when the main gymnasium cannot fulfill all of the school's needs for teaching stations.

At least 80 square feet per primary pupil, with a total minimum of 2,000 square feet of space, is suggested for this unit. A ceiling height of 18 to 22 feet in the clear is preferred, although lower ceilings may be used. One wall should be free of obstruction to be used for target and ball games or throwing practice. A smooth masonry wall will provide an adequate rebounding surface. If included, windows should be of break-proof glass or be protected by a shield or grill and located high enough so as not to restrict activities.

The auxiliary unit should be planned to accommodate limited apparatus and tumbling activities, games of low organization, rhythmic activities, movement exploration, and other activities for the primary grades. Often a 30-foot circle for circle games is located at one end of this room allowing for permanent or semipermanent equipment at the other end. The equipment could include such items as climbing ropes and poles, ladders, mats, stall bars, rings, large wooden boxes, horizontal bars, and peg boards. These should be located so as not to interfere with other activities or so that they may be easily moved out of the way. A storage room for equipment and supplies should be included. A section of wall can be equipped with hangers for mat storage.

Electrical outlets are required for the use of sound equipment. This room will, for the most part, be used by the lower grades and should be accessible to those classrooms. If the area is to serve the after-school recreational program for pupils or community groups, toilet facilities should be accessible.

Use of Playroom

The area should be suitable for preschool and for grades K to 2 or K to 3 for fundamental movement activities including creative games and rhythms, relays, stunts, and climbing and hanging activities.

Size

The area should be a rectangle measuring approximately 50 feet by 40 feet providing 2,000 square feet of space.

Ceiling

The ceiling should be acoustically treated, 18 to 22 feet high (all beams and supports above the minimum height), with suitable fixtures attached to the beams to support hanging equipment.

Walls

Walls below 10 feet should be free from obstruction. A smooth concrete block sealed with epoxy paint works well. Above 10 feet, walls should also be free of obstruction but made of acoustic or slotted concrete block. A wall free from obstruction will provide practice areas for such activities as kicking, striking, and throwing, and a space for the placement of targets and use of visual aids.

Floors

Hardwood maple or synthetic surfaces provide the best floor for general activity use. Both have advantages and disadvantages. The decision should be based on how the floor is to be used. Careful consideration should also be given to the location of lines and the installation of equipment.

Lighting
Fluorescent lighting should supply 35 to 50 foot-candles on the floor and a switch should be installed at each door. Light fixtures should be guarded to prevent breakage.

Windows
If used at all, windows should be placed on only one side of the room to provide natural light. They should be covered with a protective screen. Window sills should be eight feet above the floor.

Electrical Outlets
Double-service outlets should be installed on each wall.

Equipment Storage Area
At least 400 to 600 square feet should be provided for storage. Cabinets and shelves should be installed. The equipment room should have a double door in order for wide equipment to be moved in or out easily. A telephone for emergency use should be placed in the equipment room.

Mirrors
Three full-length mirrors should be placed at one end of a wall, side by side, for visual analysis of movement.

Bulletin Board
Corkboard should be hung on the wall near the entrance for posting materials and schedules.

Chalkboard
A chalkboard can be wall-mounted to facilitate teaching if this will not interfere with wall-rebounding activities. Otherwise, portable chalkboards can be used.

Drinking Fountain
A drinking fountain should be placed on a wall in the corridor just outside the door to the playroom.

Speakers
Two matched speakers should be placed high on the wall or in the ceiling. A cordless headset with a mike and sound system should be built into a wall.

Paint
Walls should be painted off-white or a very pale color with epoxy paint. However, murals, accent colors, and designs can be used for aesthetics.

Other Items
If the building is equipped with closed-circuit TV, two outlets should be provided for the receiver. There should be a separate entrance for recreational use. The teaching station should be isolated from other parts of the building for evening functions.

Adapted Teaching Station
Local philosophy and state and federal laws vary as to the inclusion of students with disabilities in regular physical education classes. A separate adaptive teaching station would be an ideal setup; however, any special program for such students often has to be accommodated in the regular facilities. (See Chapter 14 for further details.)

Secondary Schools

A secondary school is defined as any of the following for this book—middle school (grades 6 to 8), junior high school (grades 7-8), high school (grades 9-12).

Teaching Stations

The type and number of indoor teaching stations for a secondary school depends on the number of students and the specific program of physical education and related activities. In all situations, a gymnasium is required. By determining the number of teaching stations essential for the formal program of instruction, planners will have a basis for calculating other needs. Computation of the minimum numerical requirement is achieved by the following formula:

Minimum number of teaching stations:
700 students times 5 periods per week equals 3,500
Teaching Stations
30 per class times 30 periods per week equals 900
3,500 divided by 900 equals 3.9 teaching stations

The fraction is rounded to the next highest number, making four teaching stations the minimum requirement. This number would also afford some flexibility of class scheduling.

In computing teaching station requirements for the secondary school, the desired class size must not be set so low as to require an impossible number of teachers and facilities, nor should it be so high that effectiveness is impaired. An average class size of 30 with daily instruction is recommended. However, if the physical education classes meet only two periods per week, the total number of class periods per week in the formula must be adjusted accordingly.

The next step for planners is to determine the degree to which the number of teaching stations for the program of instruction will meet the needs for voluntary recreation, extramural and intramural activities, and interscholastic athletics for girls and boys, as well as the possible use of facilities by the community. The needs must be based upon the season of the year representing the greatest demand for facilities.

The following guide can be used to determine the number of teaching stations needed for activities other than the formal program of instruction in physical education:

Minimum number of teaching stations, or fractions thereof, needed for interscholastic-team practice at peak load

Plus

Minimum number of teaching stations, or fractions thereof, needed for intramural and extramural activities

Plus

Minimum number of teaching stations, or fractions thereof, needed for student recreation

Plus

Minimum number of teaching stations, or fractions thereof, needed for community recreation

Equals

The total number of teaching stations needed for any specific after-school period.

To illustrate, assume a school has two interscholastic squads, an intramural program, a voluntary recreation group, and no community recreational use of facilities immediately after school during a specific season. The total needs are as follows:

Required teaching stations
equals
2 interscholastic
plus
1 intramural
plus
1 voluntary recreation
equals
4 stations

The need for four teaching stations for the after-school program must then be compared to the number necessary for the formal program of instruction in physical education. If the after-school needs are in excess of those for the regular periods of instruction, additional teaching stations should be provided. Careful administrative scheduling results in maximum utilization of facilities.

Variety of Teaching Stations

A wide variety of teaching stations are possible depending on the number of different activities that would appropriately be included in the physical education program. Among the possible types of indoor teaching stations that might be included are gymnasiums, rhythm rooms, rooms for gymnastics, adapted physical education rooms, wrestling rooms, classrooms, swimming pools, archery ranges, rifle ranges, and racquetball courts.

The problem for some schools is not the lack of an adequate number of teaching stations but rather the lack of facilities to accommodate the desired variety of activities. For a secondary school with 360 students, a divisible gymnasium will create an adequate number of teaching stations for the program of instruction in physical education but may not meet the peak load requirement for after-school activities. The facility must be planned and designed to serve all program needs as adequately as possible.

Whenever a school's teaching requirements are such that a basic gymnasium is inadequate, planners should consider special purpose stations such as auxiliary physical education teaching stations, a natatorium, or a dance studio.

Secondary School Gymnasium

The building or portion of the school that houses the gymnasium should be easily accessible from classrooms, parking areas, and the outdoor activity area. This also makes possible the use of the facility after school hours or during weekends or holidays without having to open other sections of the school.

Size and Layout

For general purposes, allow a minimum of 125 square feet of usable activity space for each individual in a physical education class at peek load. The space requirements and dimensions of a gymnasium floor are significantly influenced by the official rules governing court games, particularly interscholastic basketball and the extent of spectator seating. The minimum dimensions required of a gymnasium for basketball, however, should be expanded, if necessary, to accommodate other activities. In some instances, an entire gymnasium is not required for an activity. Folding, sound-proof partitions can be used to divide the area and provide two teaching stations.

Walls and Ceilings

The walls of the gymnasium should be of a material that is resistant to hard use, at least to door height. The finish should be non-marking and have a smooth, nonabrasive surface. All corners below door height should be rounded and there should be no projections into playing areas. Lower portions (10 feet) of the walls should be finished with materials that can be easily cleaned without destroying the finish. An epoxy paint on cement block makes a durable finish.

The ceiling should be 24 feet to the low side of beams or supports with fixtures attached to the beams to support hanging equipment. High ceilings are expensive, and a natural method for cutting construction costs is to minimize ceiling height. If this is in the area for basketball, volleyball, gymnastics, badminton, or tennis, it can be a critical error. However, in an auxiliary gym used for wrestling, dance, combatives, weight lifting, or table games, a 15- to 18-foot ceiling is acceptable.

All ceilings should be light in color and, if support beams are below the ceiling, they normally are painted the same color as the ceiling or background. Contrasting colors have been used effectively; however, such color contrast may make it difficult to follow the flight of an object.

Acoustical treatment of ceilings and walls is important where teaching is to take place. To obtain the best results, at least two adjacent surfaces should be treated. Many types of acoustical treatment are available. However, avoid those which will chip or break when hit with a ball.

Lighting

There are many types of lighting systems that will produce the 35 to 50 foot-candles needed for a good teaching and spectator area. For television, the foot-candles should be closer to 200 foot-candles and that requires more sophisticated lighting systems. When selecting a lighting system, compare initial costs, annual replacement costs, and operational or electrical expenses. Some are less expensive to install but very expensive to maintain or operate.

Windows

Windows should generally be avoided. When located to take advantage of the sun for solar heat, the glare may cause serious problems. When windows are on the north side, there is less glare, but the loss of heat may be significant. Vandalism is another disadvantage.

Wall Padding

Generally, at the end of the basketball competition courts, there is padding attached to the wall to protect the students from injury when running into the wall. This is true even when a 10-foot safety zone is provided at the end of the court. These pads can be permanently installed or made to be portable. They are generally 6 feet tall and 16 to 24 feet wide and attached approximately six inches off the floor. The pads can be designed with almost any kind of graphic desired by the school in a wide variety of colors.

Fixed Equipment

If suspended equipment is planned, provision for its attachment should be made before the ceiling is installed. Basketball backstops will need special care in their installation to ensure rigidity and safety. All basketball backstops should be attached to ceilings or walls and swing-up or fold-up models should be used where the backstops might interfere with other activities. In addition to the main court basketball backstops, provision should be made for other backstops on clear sidewalls. Hinged rims that collapse when grabbed are recommended for baskets used for recreational basketball play.

In the interest of safety, such suspension apparatus as bars, rings, and climbing poles and ropes should be so placed as to allow sufficient clearance from basketball backstops and walls. If wall apparatus is desired in the gymnasium, a strip of metal or hardwood firmly attached to the wall at the proper height is recommended. Wherever necessary, floor plates should be installed for fastening movable equipment such as horizontal bars and volleyball standards. If mats are to be hung in the gymnasium, appropriate hangers placed above head level to avoid any injury must be provided. Rubber-tired mat trucks, which may be wheeled into a storage room, are recommended. For safety reasons, padding should be installed on all walls in back of baskets.

Spectator Seating

The extent of the demand for spectator seating depends upon each school and the community it serves. Modern design uses power-driven folding or rollaway bleachers (see Chapter 21 for greater detail), which require little permanent space. If possible, the outer surface of folding bleachers should create a flat, wall-like surface so it may be used for ball rebounding.

The width of each seating space should not be less than 18 inches. Rollaway bleachers most commonly allow 22-inch depths for seats. The number of rows available in rollaway bleachers varies, with 23 rows being the maximum for standard equipment. In some instances, bleachers with 30 rows can be obtained by special order. Planners should investigate local and state codes.

Balconies can be used to increase the total seating capacity beyond the maximum permitted at floor level. The space at both levels should be considered as activity areas when the bleachers are closed. It may be desirable, in some instances, to provide less than maximum seating at floor level so a balcony will be wide enough to serve as a teaching station for specific activities. Balcony bleachers can be installed to telescope from the back to the front so that in the closed position they stand erect, creating a divider wall at the edge of the balcony. This arrangement affords partial isolation of the teaching station and enhances the safety of participants.

Traffic Controls

Good traffic control should permit the efficient movement of students to and from the gymnasium, locker rooms, and other related service areas. All traffic arrangements for spectators should provide direct movement to and from bleachers with a minimum of foot traffic on gymnasium floors. Spectators should have access to drinking fountains, refreshment counters, and toilets without crossing the gymnasium floor. Steep, high stairways should be avoided. Ramps with nonslip surfaces might be substituted in appropriate places. Local and state building codes and standards of the National Fire Protection Association should be consulted.

Foyers

Where finances and space will allow, foyers should be placed so they will serve as entries to gymnasiums and will guide spectators as directly as possible to seating areas. Toilet facilities for men and women, ticket-sales windows, ticket-collection arrangements, checkrooms, public telephones, a refreshment-dispensing room with counter, and lockable display case should be provided, opening directly to the foyer.

Spectator Restrooms

All athletic events that attract spectators require restroom facilities. Restrooms should be designed for proper light, ventilation, and sanitary care. State health codes will influence the number and location of restrooms.

Concessions

Concessions have come to be considered a necessary service for public gatherings. Appropriate space and distribution as well as adequate fixtures for concession stands within the fieldhouse should be planned. Since plumbing and electrical services are already available in the field house, the concession stand might be located as a part of or adjacent to the field house. The concessions area will include, but not be limited to, a double sink, garbage disposal, electric range, microwave, refrigerator, ice maker, popcorn maker, freezer, plenty of counter space, and signage.

Other Factors

Provisions should be made for the installation of electric scoreboards, a central sound and public address system, picture projectors, radio and television equipment, high-fidelity equipment, and cleaning machines. Special consideration should be given to locating floor outlets for scoreboards and public address systems adjacent to the scoring table. Wall outlets should be installed near cupped eyes to permit special lighting as needed. Controls for gymnasium lighting should be conveniently located, recessed, and keyed.

Drinking fountains and cuspidors should be accessible without causing a traffic or safety problem. It may be desirable to provide a drained catch-basin, grilled flush with the floor, to care for splash and overflow.

Cupped eyes can be installed in all walls at approximately 15-foot height and 10-foot intervals for decorating convenience. They may also be used for attaching nets and other equipment to walls at appropriate heights. Bulletin boards and chalkboards should be provided where needed. If wall space is available, such boards may be provided for each teaching station. Three full-length mirrors should be placed at one end of a wall, side by side, for visual analysis of movement.

The Auxiliary Gymnasium

Depending on the demands placed on a facility for classes, after-school athletics, intramurals, and student and faculty recreation, more than one gymnasium may be necessary. Careful program scheduling will determine what is best in each situation. However, most schools need at least one auxiliary gym. Room dimensions should be based on the anticipated uses with special attention to the need to accommodate standard-size wrestling mats.

The other type of auxiliary gymnasium closely resembles the main gym, except there is little or no need for spectator seating, and the floor dimensions may be smaller. A 75-foot by 90-foot gym will house two volleyball courts, three badminton courts, three one-wall handball courts, and space for some gymnastic equipment.

The auxiliary gyms can serve a variety of other activities in the instructional, intramural, recreational, or interscholastic program, which cannot all be accommodated after school in the main gymnasium. Some auxiliary gyms are large enough to be divided into two teaching stations. The characteristics of these facilities are similar to those in the gymnasium. A less-expensive type may have a ceiling as low as 18 feet. Activities as wrestling, tumbling, calisthenics, self-defense, and fencing may be conducted in such a room.

Adapted Physical Education Area

Federal legislation requires that special considerations be made for persons with disabilities. Schools must provide programs, which meet their special needs. The adaptive area, therefore, becomes essential (See Chapter 14 for additional information).

Gymnastics Area for the Gymnasium

By planning in detail, the equipment layout for gymnastics, attachment hardware for the floors, walls, and ceilings can be included in the original design and construction. The manufacturers of gymnastics equipment will supply details for the attachment of their equipment as well as suggestions for floor plans or layout for the apparatus with proper safety areas. Preplanning results not only in proper installation, but also in savings on the cost of doing the work at a later date.

Storage of gymnastics equipment requires special attention, for example a room adjacent to the gym with a roll-up door. Equipment left out or stored around the edge of the gym is a safety hazard and will shorten the life of the equipment. Mat storage requires either a mat truck or a hydraulic lift to ceiling. The use of light folding mats will, however, alleviate some of the storage problems.

Climbing ropes should be attached to a height of 24 feet and drop to about 3 feet above the floor. Apparatus may be attached to the exposed beams. If the ceiling is placed below the structural members, the locations of suspended equipment should be planned and cycbolts provided during construction. Ropes should be placed 5 feet apart, allowing one for each five students in class. The rings should be at least five feet from the walls. End walls at least 35 feet from the point of attachment will afford safety for the participants. Traveling rings are supported from a height of 18 to 26 feet and are located 7 feet apart along a continuous line. Lines should be provided for drawing ropes and rings not in use to the overhead so as not to interfere with other activities.

High bars require both floor and wall or ceiling attachments. Adjustable bars for class instruction can be arranged in a linear series. Bars vary from 6 to 7 feet in length and require 12 feet of unobstructed space extending perpendicular to their long axis. Bars for interscholastic competition are commonly located as individual units.

Free-Standing Gymnastics Area

Rarely will a free-standing gymnastics area be found in a secondary school. These facilities are either privately owned or part of a nonprofit agency (e.g., YMCA, YWCA, or Boy's and Girl's Club). The free-standing facility (Figure 30.1) will include:

- Entrance area.
- Lobby space.
- Small proshop.
- Concessions.
- Public restrooms.
- Day care area.
- Balcony for spectator seating for 300.
- Competition/practice area—boys: runway for vaulting with a landing pit, high bar (2) area with a landing pit, pummel horse area, parallel bars (2) area, rings area, and floor exercise area shared with girls; girls: runway for vaulting with a landing pit, uneven bar (2) area with landing pit, balance beams (3) area with a landing pit, and a shared floor exercise area.
- Trampoline area with trampoline flush with floor.
- Office space.
- A large storage area at least 600 square feet with a ceiling height of 10 feet and a roll-up door.

Strength and Cardiorespiratory Area

The current trend in physical education facilities is the addition of a strength and cardiorespiratory area. Student-athletes would use this area for physical education classes before and after school, and community programming after school hours and on the weekends. The details regarding this space can be found in Chapter 27.

Health Instruction

The purpose of health instruction is to provide health information and experiences that will lead to the establishment of attitudes and practices conducive to the conservation, protection, and promotion of individual, community, and world health. This section of the chapter is concerned with the facilities essential to the conduct of health classes, including first-aid and safety instruction.

Elementary School

For the elementary school, the general principle of the self-contained classroom is accepted. However, in order that there be maximum opportunity for health and safety instruction, it is important to have drinking fountains and handwashing and grooming facilities and that there be ready accessibility to toilets for the exclusive use of each room in the primary grades. In classrooms for intermediate grades, hand lavatories should be provided. In addition to the central storage space for equipment common to all rooms, each room should have storage space for health teaching aids especially suited to that class. A mobile laboratory table or a resource room equipped with facilities for demonstrations in health and science should be available.

Secondary School

The basic space allotment for the health instruction facilities in the secondary school should be in harmony with generally accepted standards for schoolroom size. However, due to the nature of activities

Figure 30.1
Sample Layout of a Free-Standing Gymnastics Area

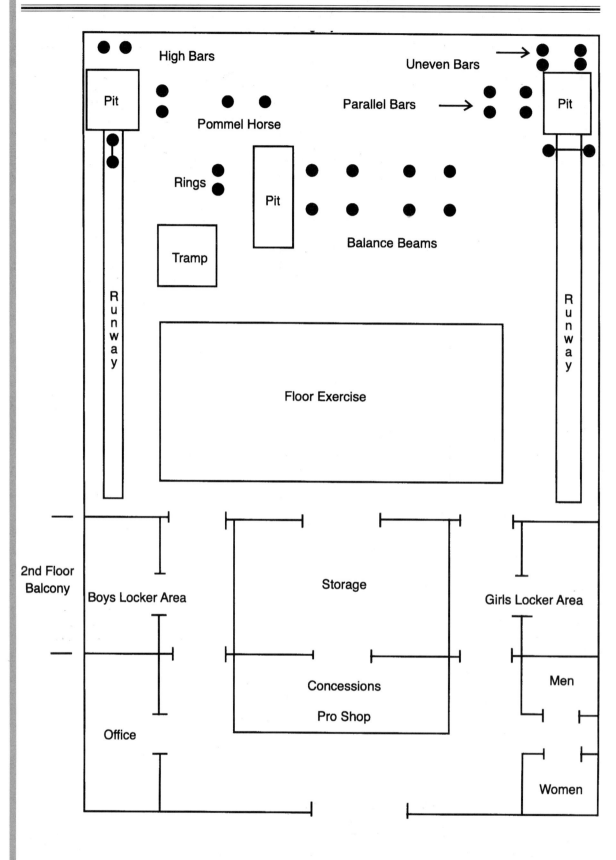

involved in health and safety instructional programs, it is recommended that the space allowed for such instruction be increased approximately 35% above requirements for the regular classroom. This will result in a space allotment of 35 square feet per student, including storage space.

The space allotment should be sufficient to allow for such activities as vision and hearing screening, first-aid and safety instruction and practical demonstrations, and for flexible teacher location. In addition to the conventional teacher's desk, provision should be made for laboratory demonstrations. This indicates the need for a laboratory-demonstration table, which will provide space and facilities for demonstrations. Thus, provisions should be made for water, gas, and electricity as well as storage space for heating devices, test tubes, flasks, beakers, and other equipment essential to such demonstrations. The diversity of teaching procedures requires that regular classroom arrangements (Appendix Q for additional information) be used at some times, but at other times floor space be available for practical instruction such as practice in artificial respiration, splinting, and emergency transportation.

The suggested laboratory method of teaching will require adequate storage space as well as display areas for charts, mannequins, models, and equipment. First-aid equipment such as blankets, bandages, splints, and stretchers will also be needed. For instruction in home nursing, such equipment as incubators, roll-away beds, pans, containers, and bedding will be required.

There should be a large amount of display space for the great variety of educational exhibits, literature, and pupil projects inherent in the health education program. This can be provided by allowing liberal space for tables and shelves and by using all available wall space for bulletin boards and tackboards.

The health instruction laboratory should provide for the optimum use of such additional audiovisual devices as still pictures, slides, motion pictures, radio, and television. This will necessitate a liberal allowance of appropriately located electrical outlets, shades, or curtains that will reduce the outside light and a screen that may be mounted above the chalkboard behind the laboratory desk.

It may be desirable that there be convenient access between the health instruction laboratory and the health service suite in order that each may augment the total health program. For example, when home-nursing classes are meeting in the health instruction laboratory, there will be times when it is desirable to have free but supervised access to both facilities. Similarly, when there is an occasion to have a large number of people using the health service suite, it may be desirable to have access to the health instruction laboratory for seating or other purposes. In some instances, it may be desirable to consider locating the health instruction laboratory near the science laboratories in order to facilitate joint use of equipment and supplies. In other instances, location in the area of the physical education facilities may be desirable.

The secondary school health instruction laboratory should be an example of the ideal classroom environment with special concern for color of walls, lighting, ventilation, temperature and humidity control, order, and cleanliness (see Appendix Q for additional information).

Recognition should be given to the desirability of joint planning of school health facilities with public health officials and other community groups who might need access to such facilities, thus strengthening the total community health program. Such arrangements can serve to strengthen the program of all who are concerned with health by providing for dual use of such facilities without duplication and with a minimum of expense.

The following is a checklist for health instruction facilities:

- space for 35 square feet per pupil, maximum of 30 pupils
- flexible teacher location
- provision for various teaching methods, including laboratory demonstration
- flexibility of seating
- hot and cold running water and gas outlet
- educational exhibit space
- storage space
- provision for using audiovisual devices (electrical outlets, window shades, screens)
- access to health service unit exemplary environmental features
- adequate handwashing facilities, drinking fountains, and toilets
- air-conditioning
- accessible to and usable by persons with disabilities
- planned jointly for community use

Health Services

Health services contribute to the school program by 1) facilitating learning, 2) encouraging pupils to obtain needed medical or dental treatment, 3) adapting school programs to individual pupil needs, 4) maintaining a healthful school environment, and 5) increasing pupils' understanding of health and health problems. Following the principle that program determines facilities, plans would include accommodations for:

- appraising the health status of pupils and school personnel;
- counseling pupils, parents, and others concerning appraisal findings;
- encouraging the correction of remediable defects and the proper adjustment of those identified as not remediable;
- assisting in the identification and education of pupils with disabilities;
- helping to prevent and control disease;
- providing emergency service for injury or sudden illness;
- maintaining a cumulative combined health and accident file for each student.

Health service personnel are not only charged with the responsibility for developing policies and procedures, but should also be consulted in planning programs and facilities. Policies and procedures are essential for the attainment of program objectives through the proper utilization of facilities and the protection of school populations under adverse or disaster conditions.

Health Suite

Whether in a small rural or a large urban school building, the health service suite will be used for a variety of activities. It may be the center for emergency care of injuries or sickness and health appraisals by nurses, physicians, dentists or dental hygienists, and psychiatrists or psychologists. Various types of systematized screening tests, such as tests of vision and hearing, may be conducted in this area.

The health suite is the logical place for conferences concerning a pupil's health problems involving the parent, teacher, doctor, nurse, and physical educator. A part of the suite should be used as a dressing room and another section should serve as a waiting room. Some space should be set aside for the isolation of a pupil when the situation warrants and accommodations should be provided for pupils on a prescribed rest schedule. The suite will also need to provide space for the health service personnel, plus the necessary space for records and equipment.

The common concerns of school health service personnel and guidance personnel suggest the need for a close, cooperative working relationship. This would indicate the desirability of locating the units in close proximity to each other and the possibility of using a common waiting room.

The school health suite may, in some instances, also serve the community. Thus, the health suite and the adjacent health instruction area may be for well-child conferences and other preschool health activities. They may accommodate classes for expectant mothers and other adult education activities. In those situations where the building and grounds are used for recreation purposes, the unit may serve as an emergency-care and first-aid station for those participating in the recreation program.

The fact that a health service suite is located within the school does not mean that programs for non-school groups will be administered or manned by school personnel. Usually, these community health activities will be under the direct supervision of the official health agency. If community usage of the health service suite is expected, then those who will provide the service should be involved in the planning.

Location

In locating a health service suite, consideration should be given to the variety of activities that will be carried on therein and to conditions that will permit those functions to be carried on conveniently and efficiently. Some factors to be considered in the location of a health service suite are:

- It should be located along a corridor near a main entrance to the building so that it may be completely isolated from the remainder of the building, yet remain conveniently accessible from all parts of the building.
- It should be located on the first or ground floor.
- The location should be in close proximity to the administrative suite. In situations where full-time health service personnel are not contemplated, direct access should be provided between the area and the administrative office, the teacher's lounge, or an adjacent classroom. In the secondary school, advantages will accrue from locating the health classroom and the service suite so that there is convenient access between the two areas. This is especially true when school health facilities are utilized for community health services.
- The location and acoustical treatment should be such that corridor and outside noises are kept to a minimum.
- A maximum amount of natural light should be available.

Rooms

All purposes for which the health service suite is designed may be carried out in one large unit, which may be subdivided into 1) waiting room, 2) examining room, 3) resting rooms, 4) toilet rooms, 5) counseling room, 6) dental health room, 7) isolation room, 8) special screening areas (e.g., vision and hearing), and 9) office area for health service personnel and records. Depending upon the size of the school and its health policies, various combinations of the above spaces may be planned without affecting the efficiency of the services. For example, in smaller elementary schools, all services may be cared for in one room provided proper screening is used and the administrative and health service suite are served by a common waiting room.

In larger schools, and especially in high schools, division of the unit into separate rooms is desirable. Thought should be given to the type of wall construction that provides for rearrangement of space allocation, since change in policies and school population will affect the nature and extent of health services. When remodeling old buildings, the same standards that apply to new structures should be maintained.

Guidelines based on accepted standards are recommended below.

Waiting Room

Schools with 10 or more classrooms or enrollments of 300 or more pupils should provide a waiting room, possibly in combination with guidance and/or administrative offices. It should be directly accessible to the corridor and the examining room. The waiting room should be separated from adjacent rooms by a full-height partition.

The decorations and furnishings should be designed to create a bright and cheerful atmosphere. The size is dependent upon enrollment and established health policies of the school (see Table 30.1).

Examining Room

Schools consisting of six or more classrooms or an enrollment of 180 or more pupils should include an examining room in the health suite. It should be directly connected with bathrooms and the waiting room, and should have access to toilets, the dental space, and any offices that are provided.

The location should provide for natural light and ventilation. The size and arrangement should be such that an uninterrupted distance of 20 feet is available for vision testing.

The room should be acoustically treated. If the examining room is to serve as a resting room (in small schools), screened cot areas should be provided. The space should be ample for proper arrangement or storage of the following equipment:

Table 30.1
Recommended Sizes in Square Feet of Health-Service Facilities for Schools of Various Sizes

ENROLLMENT	200-300	301-500	501-700	701-900	901-1100	1101-1300
Waiting Room	80	80	100	100	100	120
*Examining Room	200	200	200	240	240	240
**Rest room (total area for boys and girls)	200	200	200	240	240	240

Toilets.......... 48 square feet total area (provide one for girls and one for boys)

OPTIONAL AREAS

Dental Clinic	100 square feet for all schools
Office Space	80 square feet for each office provided
Eye examination	120 square feet minimum for all schools

* Examining room areas include 6 square feet for clothes closet and 24 square feet for storage closets.

** For determining the number of cots, allow one cot per 100 pupils up to 400 pupils, and one cot per 200 pupils above 400. Round out fractions to nearest whole number. Allow 50 square feet of floor space for each of the first two cots and 40 square feet for each additional cot.

*** In schools enrolling 901 to 1,100, a three-cot rest room is suggested for boys and a four-cot rest room for girls, and in 1,101 to1,300-pupil schools, a three-cot rest room is suggested for boys and a five-cot rest room for girls.
Note: For larger schools, add multiples of the above areas to obtain total needs.
\# State Department of Education, *School Planning Manual*, school Health Service Section, Vol. 37. November, 1954, Richmond Va.

- desk, chair, computer, and possibly a typewriter
- filing cabinets
- platform scale with stadiometer
- vision testing equipment
- movable spotlight
- blankets and linens
- folding screen
- sterilizer and instrument table
- cot or couch
- cabinet for first-aid supplies
- cup and towel dispensers
- wastebasket and foot-operated disposal can

- full-length mirror
- audiometric testing devices

The size of the examining room will be determined by enrollment, the types of activities to be conducted, and the extent of use by medical and other health personnel (see Table 30.1).

Resting Rooms
Resting rooms are essential in all schools. They should be directly connected with the examining room and toilets or be accessible to them from a restricted hallway. Separate resting rooms should be provided for each sex. A screened cot space may be a necessary arrangement in smaller schools.

The location should be such that natural light and ventilation and quiet atmosphere are secured. If there are no full-time health service personnel available, the location should be such that supervision of the area may be conveniently provided from the administrative office or an adjacent classroom. Adequate space should be provided for cots (see Table 30.1), bedside stands, wastebaskets, and blanket and linen storage.

Toilet Rooms
A toilet room with stool and lavatory should be directly connected, or be accessible by a restricted hallway, to the resting rooms in all schools with 10 or more classrooms or with an enrollment of 300 or more pupils. In smaller schools where the resting rooms are a part of the examining room or other space provision should be made for convenient toilet facilities. A toilet room with a minimum of 48 square feet should be provided for each sex (see Table 30.1).

Storage Closets
Storage space, opening off each resting room, should be provided for linens, blankets, pillows, and so forth. In the smaller schools without separate resting rooms, such storage should be provided for in the examining room.

A ventilated cloak closet should be provided for school health personnel. If built-in storage facilities are not feasible, space should be allowed for movable storage cabinets.

Isolation Room
An isolation room as an integral part of the health service suite is desirable to insure privacy when required. It should be directly connected with the examining room, but apart from the resting rooms. A space for one cot and the necessary circulation area is sufficient in most instances.

Vision and Hearing Screening Areas
Such areas should be included as a part of the examining room. An uninterrupted distance of 20 feet should be provided for vision testing. Audiometric testing will require an acoustically treated room.

Offices
The provision of office space for health service personnel will depend upon the time they spend in the school. If this facility is provided, it should be connected with the waiting room, the examining room and, if possible, the corridor.

The minimum recommended space for two people is 80 square feet. Provision should be made for maintaining health and accident reports.

Counseling Room
Although such space will not be in constant use, a room where the doctor, nurse, teacher, and parent can discuss a pupil's health is an important unit of the total health facility. Space large enough to accommodate a small table and four or five chairs is adequate. It may be used as office space for part-time health service personnel.

General Suggestions
The entire suite should present an informal and pleasant atmosphere. Flooring should be of a material that is nonabsorbent, easily cleaned, and light in color. Lavatories used by personnel functioning within the examining room should be operable by the wrist, knee, or foot.

Figures 30.2 and 30.3 are examples of some possible health suite arrangements.

Driver Education Areas and Facilities
The program of driver education is generally accepted as a responsibility of the school and, more specifically, as a function of health and safety and physical education departments. The guidelines outlined below are in keeping with approved standards and national recommendations.

Indoor Facilities
For the indoor program, there should be a classroom, a psychophysical laboratory with testing devices, a simulator laboratory, and an office.

Figure 30.2
Health Suite for Elementary School With Seven Classrooms

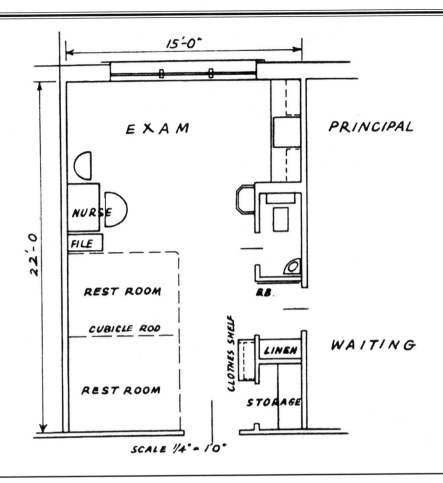

Figure 30.3
Secondary School Health Suite

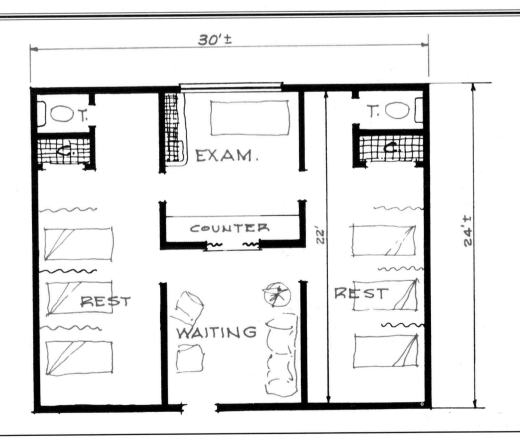

Location

All indoor facilities should be on the first floor of the building, near the garage or parking space for the dual-control cars, and near the driving range if one is used.

Classroom

Size

The recommended procedure is to combine the classroom with the laboratory for a combination room of 30 feet by 40 feet. Where separate rooms are used, the classroom should be of standard size.

Furniture and Equipment

In addition to the standard classroom facilities and equipment, such as chalkboard, bulletin board, desk, and chairs, the driver education classroom should provide facilities for the following special equipment:

- VCR and monitor
- bookcases and storage cabinets for videotapes, flip charts, testing equipment, models, and so on.
- demonstration table
- demonstration equipment, including magnetic traffic board, working models, flannel boards, model signs, and signals

Driver Education Laboratory

The laboratory contains equipment needed to test the student's physical, mental, and emotional qualifications required for safe and skillful driving.

Size

When the combined room is not used, the laboratory should be at least 24 feet by 30 feet.

Furniture and Equipment

The needed furniture and equipment will include a demonstration table, chairs, worktables, and spaces to accommodate equipment for testing visual acuity, depth perception, color vision, field of vision, reaction time, steadiness, night vision, and so forth.

Simulator Laboratory

Driver education simulators are accepted as a means of providing the preliminary steps to behind-the-wheel instruction. Because of the nature of the simulator units, facilities for them should be considered as permanent installations, preferably in a separate classroom.

Size

The size of the simulator laboratory will depend on the number of simulator cars to be installed. A typical eight-car installation will accommodate 450 to 500 students per year and a 16-car installation will accommodate 960 to 1,000. The room size for eight cars should be 24 feet by 33 feet and for 16 cars, it should be 30 feet by 40 feet.

Furniture and Equipment

The room should be clear of obstructions that might interfere with the projector beam and should be provided with the regular complement of chalkboard, bulletin board, tackboard, magnetic board, and so on.

Layout

The cars are arranged in a semicircular fashion with the first row a minimum of 8 feet, preferably 10 feet to 12 feet, from the screen and with the outside cars not exceeding an angle of 30 degrees from the screen. The first row should have the lesser number of cars.

A minimum of 24 inches should be allowed between the rows with a 30-inch aisle down each side of the room. Aisle spaces must comply with state safety codes. The projector should be located in the center at the extreme rear of the room, and a 6-foot by 8-foot screen should be placed in the front of the room.

Manufacturers' specifications for electrical requirements should be followed. Ordinarily, the standard 120-volt, 60-cycle alternating current is required. It should be supplied through a double outlet located in the vicinity of the recording unit.

Lighting

Soft white fluorescent-light tubes recessed in the ceiling with semi-translucent shields to provide 100 footcandles of light at desk height should be installed.

Color

Pastel colors should be used. The woodwork and finishing should be compatible with color used on the walls. A reflection factor of 80% is needed for the ceiling and 60% for the walls. The furniture should have a nonglare finish.

Heating and Ventilation

Heating and ventilation should conform to standards required throughout the entire school system.

Outdoor Areas and Facilities

Driving Area

Purpose

Behind-the-wheel instruction provides the skills necessary for safe and efficient driving.

Types

An on-street driving area is recommended for schools where traffic congestion is not a problem. First, driving maneuvers should be conducted in locations such as school driveways where there is no traffic. As ability develops, students get experience driving in situations that approximate normal driving conditions and then, finally, in actual normal traffic situations.

Blocked-off streets are sometimes used when street traffic is too heavy and school driveways are not available to teach the first driving maneuvers. Arrangements should be made with the residents of the area and with police officials. Since advanced driving skills are taught where other traffic is involved, streets should not be blocked off for an undue length of time.

An off-street driving range is recommended where land is available. Ranges should be laid out to simulate most physical situations associated with driving, such as: traffic signs, signals, and other control devices, parallel and angle parking, upgrade and downgrade situations, and simulated emergency situations. Space should allow for needed skill-test maneuvers. Different types of road surfaces should be provided. If night classes are conducted, the area should be lighted. The size of the driving range should be no smaller than 350 feet by 450 feet.

The multiple-car driving range (see Figure 30.3) has the advantage of accommodating several cars simultaneously under the supervision of one teacher, thus reducing the per-pupil cost. With this type of range, communication between the instructor and students is accomplished by means of a radio or public-address system.

Recommended Equipment and Facilities

* curbs for parking practice
* intersections for various turn maneuvers
* gravel area for driving and turn maneuvers
* streets marked properly
* streets that are both wide and narrow
* all signs—traffic, control signals, stop, warning, yield the right-of-way, regulatory, guide, and information

Figure 30.3
Multiple Car Off-Street Driving Range

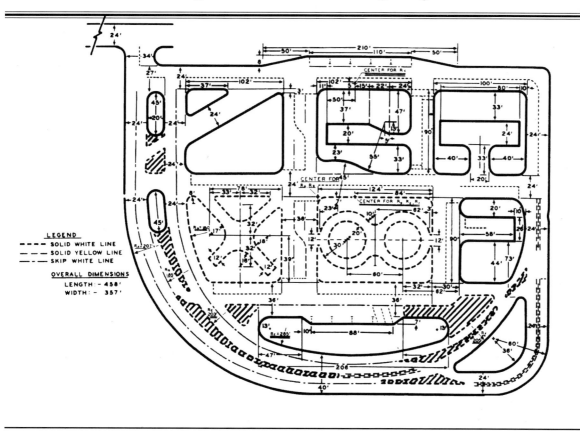

- upgrade and downgrade roadways
- simulated road surfaces—concrete, asphalt, and gravel
- muddy surface for emergency situations
- signboards found on normal roads
- stanchions, guide-on, and the like for maneuvers

Points to Remember
- Determine the needs of the student and the objectives of the program.
- Provide as many realistic situations as possible.
- Design the driver-training area equal to the best facilities available.

Summary

The unit of primary importance is the room or space where teaching occurs—the gymnasium. All other parts of the school plant are, in a real sense, secondary. In physical education, therefore, the determination of the number and character of the teaching stations is basic to the planning process for either an elementary or secondary school. Further, it is important to locate these facilities in a separate wing for a number of reasons, including, but not limited to, noise, evening and weekend use, and non-school sponsored uses.

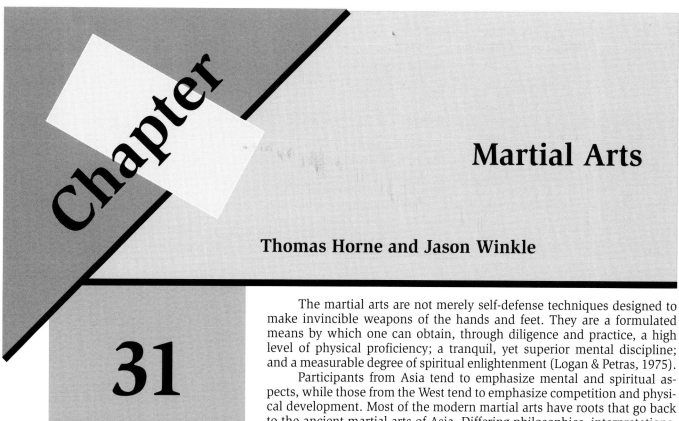

Martial Arts

Thomas Horne and Jason Winkle

31

The martial arts are not merely self-defense techniques designed to make invincible weapons of the hands and feet. They are a formulated means by which one can obtain, through diligence and practice, a high level of physical proficiency; a tranquil, yet superior mental discipline; and a measurable degree of spiritual enlightenment (Logan & Petras, 1975).

Participants from Asia tend to emphasize mental and spiritual aspects, while those from the West tend to emphasize competition and physical development. Most of the modern martial arts have roots that go back to the ancient martial arts of Asia. Differing philosophies, interpretations, and interests of instructors and students have produced the wide range of martial arts practiced today.

Building or renovating a martial arts facility requires extensive planning. This chapter will provide information to assist martial arts facility developers with design and construction decisions. Planners and developers of martial arts facilities must understand at least the general nature of martial arts if they are to make informed decisions. The major martial arts are summarized in this chapter to provide this knowledge base. A martial arts Web exercise is provided to familiarize readers with Web sites that may be helpful in developing a martial arts facility or program. A martial arts facility development case study that details a facility development effort is also included.

Learning Objectives

After reading this chapter, the student should be able to

- apply general facility planning principles to developing martial arts facilities,
- identify the two general types of martial arts facilities,
- identify the major martial arts styles and determine which of the two facility types is most appropriate for each style,
- list the equipment and key design features for each type of martial arts facility,
- access a number of Web sites to get additional information on martial arts facilities, and
- apply facility development concepts to a martial arts facility case study.

Facility Planning Concepts

The goal when constructing or renovating a martial arts facility is to produce a facility that is highly functional, cost effective, aesthetically pleasing, safe, and accessible to all. Failure to adequately plan often results in a facility that costs too much and delivers too little. Participatory planning (seeking information from all interested individuals, especially the representative user group) is the recommended planning strategy (Flynn, 1993). The first step is to conduct a needs assessment. The needs assessment solicits information from the owners and operators, the target facility users, and staff members. The owner and operator may be a person, a group of people, or an established organization. The owners and operators often provide all or some of the finances for the project, so they expect and deserve the opportunity to influence construction or renovation decisions. They are often the ones to provide a vision for the facility and leadership in organizing and executing both the planning and construction. Staff members provide an excellent source of information on which features should be included in a new martial arts facility. They have practical expertise and experience and can provide many useful recommendations. Gathering information from the target population provides valuable information to determine the demand for martial arts activities and identify which style is most popular. The users or customers are often the best source of information on the desired support facilities, such as parking areas, locker rooms, concessions, and administrative areas.

Armed with data gathered from the needs assessment the next step is to convince the higher authority or those providing the funding to support the construction or renovation project. It is important to present the data collected in a professional and persuasive manner. Failing to adequately prepare for this phase of planning could result in a poor presentation and the project being abandoned.

Once a project gets support from a higher authority, establish a planning group or a steering committee. This group will stay actively involved during the entire planning and construction process. They will provide guidance, and in some cases make decisions on such issues as:

- renovating an existing facility or building a new facility
- cost limitations and funding sources
- promoting the project
- gathering additional needs assessment data
- site location
- selecting an architectural firm
- approving, rejecting, or modifying architectural firm plans and proposals
- selecting construction contractors
- developing construction schedules and phasing
- specifying material and space requirements
- ensuring code compliance
- identifying and solving design and construction problems
- establishing and implementing maintenance and operation procedures
- determining requirements for support and competition areas

The scope of the project and the complexity of the administrative requirements will determine the magnitude of the planning effort. Whether planning a modest renovation of an existing martial arts room or constructing a new martial arts complex complete with all the support facilities, careful planning will avoid costly mistakes.

Overview of the Martial Arts

Martial arts can be defined as numerous systems of self-defense and offensive techniques that may emphasize sports competition, physical development, mental development, or a combination of these aspects. Initially, most martial arts taught in America were taught in wrestling rooms, gymnasiums, multipurpose rooms, or in the outdoors. This is still the case in most colleges, recreation centers, YMCAs, and other multipurpose facilities. Martial arts facilities, designed specifically for martial arts, are now being included in the design and construction of many of these multipurpose facilities. Many commercial martial arts programs are taught in specialized martial arts facilities called dojos (literally translated as "Place where one learns the way").

Whether designing a separate commercial facility or a martial arts area in a larger project, planners must decide if the new martial arts facility will be a general combative facility or a facility designed to accommodate a specific style of martial arts. In either case, a general knowledge of the major martial arts will help planners make important design decisions. There are almost as many types of martial arts as there are types of ball games. There are too many types and styles of martial arts to discuss the facility requirements for each one. Seven of the martial arts represent the major types and styles of martial arts. A brief summary of these seven major martial arts is provided to assist facility planners make informed design and construction decisions (Table 31.1).

Aikido

Aikido is the art of unarmed self-defense against either an armed or unarmed assailant. Mostly an art of spiritual enlightenment, a main focus of aikido is to develop a healthy mind, body, and spirit, free from bad habits. Aikidoists attempt to use their unlimited spiritual power called ki, internal energy, to redirect the energy of the attacker in a dynamic circle with joint manipulation and circular throws (Winderbaum, 1977). Most styles of aikido emphasize the art of self-defense and not the sport, so there is neither competition nor tournaments. One style of aikido, the Tomiki style, includes organized competitions.

Judo

Judo was adapted from jujitsu by Jigoro Kano. Kano retained the self-defense, flexibility, mental concentration, and self-improvement aspects of jujitsu and discarded dangerous techniques (Winderbaum, 1977). Judo emphasizes close-contact throwing and grappling techniques that include pinning, choking, arm locks, and striking techniques. Striking techniques are taught in formal instruction but not practiced in the sport aspects of judo.

Karate

Originally, karate was a form of deadly combat, but it is now practiced primarily as a sport. Karate is divided into six major areas, calisthenics, kihon (fundamentals), kata (forms of prearranged movements), kumite (sparring), and weapons training. Karate tends to emphasize kicks, punches, and a strong offense as a good defense (Trais, 1973).

Kendo

Kendo is a sport version of Japanese fencing. Contestants wear extensive protective armor and try to hit each other on designated parts of the body with simulated weapons (Goodbody, 1969).

Table 31.1
Martial Arts Summary

Art	Aikido	Judo	Karate	Kendo	Kung Fu	Tae Kwan Do	Tái Chi
Meaning	Way of devine harmony	The gentle way	The way of the empty hand	Way of the sword	Skill and effort or disciplined technique	The way of kicking and jumping	Grand ultimate boxing
Country of Origin	Japan	Japan	Okinawa	Japan	China	Korea	China
School	Aikidajo Dojo	Dojo	Dojo	Dojo	Kwoon	Do jang	Kwoon
Uniforms	Judogi	Judogi	Karetegi	Ilendogi	Dark top, sash pants and shoes	Dobok	Street clothes
Competitive	Most forms No	Yes	Yes	Yes	Traditionally no, some sport now	Yes	No
Facility Type	Grappling	Grappling	Striking	Striking (weapons)	Striking (weapons)	Striking	Striking
Flooring	Sub-mat with mat or tatami	Tatami	Wood/ synthetic	Wood/ synthetic	Wood/mat	Wood/ synthetic	Wood/ synthetic

Kung Fu

The two distinctive styles of kung fu are the "hard style" (Cho-li-fat) and the "soft style" (Sil-lum). The hard style emphasizes power and strength for debilitating offensive maneuvers. The soft style focuses more on speed and agility to deliver an effective attack on vulnerable areas of the body. Kung fu employs both the arms and legs to deliver kicks, blows, throws, holds, body turns, dodges, leaps, and falls. Weapons are used more often in kung fu than karate. Stylized movements are used, and some techniques are derived from animal movements.

Tae Kwon Do

Tae kwon do is the art and sport of self-defense that stresses kicking, aerial, and dynamic circular techniques. Like karate, tae kwon do consists primarily of two components, kata (series of preset movements) and kumite (sparring). With its Olympic recognition and worldwide disbursement, almost all tae kwon do school training now emphasizes the sporting aspects and competition.

Tái Chi

Tái chi is a Chinese soft art that emphasizes the harmony of the mind and the body (Perfetti, Internet). The qualities of slowness, lightness, clarity, balance, and calmness characterize tái chi movements. Never trained competitively, tái chi is the epitome of organized movement and is often practiced by more mature students for health and exercise (Logan & Petras, 1975). The fundamental moves of this graceful martial art can be practiced almost anywhere with little or no equipment.

Types of Martial Arts Facilities

Martial arts facilities tend to be simple structures with areas free from distractions. These training facilities are often called dojos. Most modern-day dojos maintain the standards of simplicity and beauty found in old school dojos (Urban, 1967).

There are many different styles of martial arts, and no two martial arts programs require the same type of facility and equipment. The major styles of martial arts emphasize primarily grappling techniques or striking techniques. Grappling martial arts emphasize throws, chokes, joint locks, wrestling, pushing, pulling, trips, and falling. Striking martial arts emphasize kicks, punches, strikes, and weapons. Martial arts facilities can therefore be divided into two types of facilities: grappling martial arts facilities and striking martial arts facilities.

Grappling Martial Arts Facilities

Aikido and judo are martial arts styles that involve throwing skills, joint locks, and wrestling-type activities. Aikido and judo require protective floor matting (Figure 31.1). The requirement of floor matting is the distinguishing characteristic of Grappling Martial Arts Facilities. Grappling martial arts often

Figure 31.1
Judo Competition Area

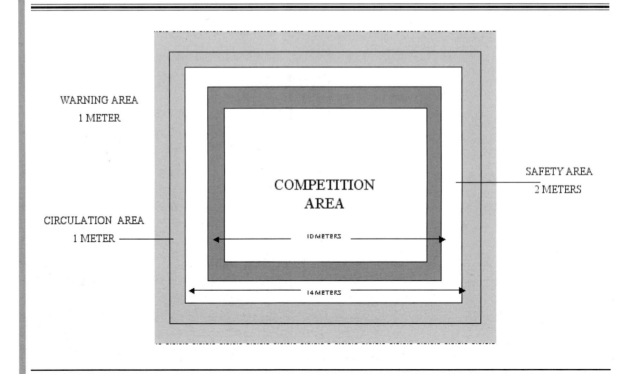

use traditional wrestling rooms with rubberized wrestling mats and padded walls. These wrestling rooms meet the minimum requirements for grappling martial arts, but a two-layer mat system is recommended for any of the grappling martial arts that require throwing. The standard wrestling mat alone does not provide sufficient protection for high-impact activities like throws. A two-layer mat system with a lower layer of foam-type matting and an upper-layer standard wrestling-type mat is a versatile option. Tatami mats, Japanese straw mats (modern tatami mats are made of compressed foam), over a spring-loaded base is ideal for judo and aikido.

When designing a dedicated martial arts facility, include specialized matting specifically selected for the intended activity. Most styles of aikido are non-competitive and only require a firm mat

Makiwara.

with shock-absorbing properties. The mat should not be slippery or too rough. The competitive judo mat is a minimum of 14 meters by 14 meters and a maximum of 16 meters by 16 meters. The top layer of matting is usually a green-colored tatami. Judo mats must have a smooth surface without gaps between sections. Competition mats have a competition zone surrounded by a one-meter danger zone marked in red. A three-meter zone on the outside of the danger zone is the safety zone. A resilient wooden platform is the preferred base for judo competitions. Competitive judo venues should also include two scoreboards and three timing clocks.

Striking Martial Arts Facilities

Karate, kung fu, tae kwon do, and kendo are martial arts that employ mostly striking techniques (Roth, 1974). Karate, kung fu, and tae kwon do all utilize a

Speed bag.

wide variety of kicks with the feet, punches with the hands, and striking skills with other body parts. The majority of these blows are delivered from the feet with full force and strike into a padded surface or stop just short of a human target. Kata, a prearranged series of skills, is also an important aspect for all of these styles. Normally, only the advanced students participate in contact competitions where they deliver full-contact blows against an opponent. Additional protective equipment is recommended when practicing striking techniques with an opponent and required for full-contact competition. The emphasis in each of these martial arts is body control, striking power, and precise technique. The punching, kicking, and striking techniques are delivered from either

Heavy bag.

a linear or a spinning and turning motion. Wrestling-type mats are not recommended when throwing circular techniques since the anchor foot must rotate freely. Flexible hardwood or smooth synthetic floors are preferred for striking martial arts.

Kendo is predominately a weapon-oriented art that is normally practiced in a striking-type facility. Both karate and some kung fus use weapons on a limited basis. Weapons-oriented martial arts require special protective striking gear and are normally practiced without mats on the floor.

Only a flexible hardwood or smooth synthetic floor is recommended for Striking Martial Arts. Small area mats may be used on an as-needed basis. Heavy bags and traditional striking posts, Makiwaras, are usually included in the facility to practice kicking and punching techniques.

Tái chi does not employ either grappling or striking techniques. Most tái chi movements are controlled and are performed in a slow, deliberate manner. Tái chi can therefore be performed in a Grappling Martial Arts Facility, a Striking Martial Arts Facility, or an open outdoor space.

General Features for Martial Arts Facilities

While the main distinguishing feature of martial arts facilities is the type of flooring and matting required, facility planners will also have other important facility features to consider.

Wall Coverings

The selection of appropriate wall coverings is critical. All martial arts facilities should have at least a portion of the wall covered with mirrors. Mirrors provide a valuable source of feedback for individuals participating in martial arts. Selecting the best location for the mirrors may be challenging because of conflicting priorities. Placing the mirrors too close to the activity area may result in the mirror being broken. Non-glass mirrors are safer and less likely to get broken, but scratch more easily and tend to give a distorted image. If glass mirrors are to be used, shatter-resistant glass mirrors are recommended. Placing mirrors too far from the activity area may make it difficult for participants to see themselves. Walls that do not have mirrors are often covered with protective wall mats, to a height of six feet.

Water Fountains

Martial arts activities are very demanding physically, and martial arts participants will need to keep hydrated. A recessed water cooler is recommended for all types of martial arts facilities. A recessed water spigot is often desired to make facility sanitation easier. The spigot may be located near or as part of the water cooler.

Ceiling

Martial arts facilities tend to be simple functional facilities with few distractions. The simplest and least expensive ceiling is an open ceiling, the roof or floor above and associated piping, conduit, and ductwork is left exposed. An open ceiling area is normally painted white to give the dojo an open-area feeling. The open ceiling has advantages for activities that involve weapons and throws. The longer weapons, bows and swords, may damage an acoustic tile ceiling. Acoustic tiles used in drop ceilings can be equipped with spring-loaded clips that will allow the tiles to be contacted without being knocked out of place. The open ceiling is not as aesthetic as an acoustical tile ceiling, nor does it have as good of acoustic properties. If the facility is to be used primarily as a teaching station, an acoustic tile ceiling may be the ceiling of choice and worth the extra expense. The minimum ceiling height is 12 feet for martial arts facilities, and a higher ceiling is recommended for a martial arts facility used primarily for weapons-oriented activities.

Lighting

The recommended lighting level for martial arts facilities is 50 foot-candles. Recessed lights that have some type of protective covering are recommended. If the facility will be used for martial arts demonstrations or shows, equip the lights with a dimmer switch.

Storage

Providing adequate storage space for the martial arts facility is an important planning decision. Like storage space in many other facilities, storage space in martial arts facilities is often overlooked or reduced as soon as finances become an issue. Specific storage needs vary with each martial arts program, but should include at least some storage for personal items and mesh-type lockers to allow stored gear to dry. The size and type of storage facility required depends upon:

- total space available for construction
- budget constraints
- type of facility (grappling or striking)
- class sizes
- whether the mats will need to be taken up and stored or not
- whether the uniforms will be stored or not
- the style of martial arts to be practiced (kendo with its weapons will require more storage space than tái chi)
- desire to include a trophy case to store and display trophies

If specific storage needs are not available during the planning phase, allow 8 to 10% of the total martial arts facility square footage for storage.

Scoreboard

A scoreboard with a clock is a practical feature for many of the martial arts, especially those that involve competition. The specific features of the scoreboard will depend on which style of martial art will use the scoreboard. If a scoreboard is desired, but funds are not available at the time of design, include the required power source in the plans. Including the power source in the original construction will cost very little and will save both time and money if funds become available to purchase a scoreboard in the future.

Custodial Closet

Martial arts facilities have a lot of skin contact areas that require regular cleaning and disinfecting. Locating a custodial closet in or close to the martial arts facility will facilitate cleaning and sanitation efforts. Rubberized mats require regular cleaning and disinfecting with a liquid disinfectant. A custodial sink is recommended, and a recessed spigot is the minimum source of water for cleaning the martial arts facility. The closet needs to have storage space for mops, buckets, cleaning and disinfecting supplies, and a vacuum cleaner (especially for carpeted facilities).

Summary

Planning and designing a martial arts facility is a difficult task, because there is no template for martial arts facilities. There are numerous types, styles, and variations of the martial arts. No two martial arts programs will have the same facility requirements. Martial arts programs are often conducted in multipurpose combative facilities, which makes the facility planning even more difficult. Facility planners and designers need to gather information from owners and operators, qualified martial arts instructors, staff members, and facility users to accurately determine program needs. Having a basic understanding of martial arts will help planners and designers make informed decisions concerning construction of martial arts facilities. Martial arts facilities can be classified as grappling-oriented facilities with matted floors or striking-oriented facilities with flexible hardwood or synthetic floors.

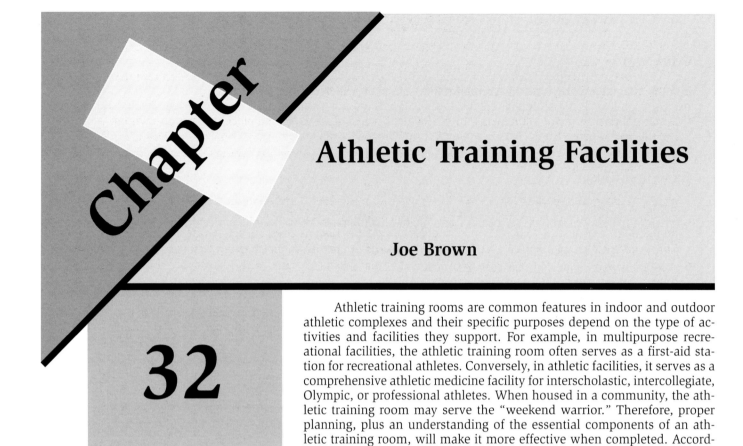

Athletic Training Facilities

Joe Brown

Athletic training rooms are common features in indoor and outdoor athletic complexes and their specific purposes depend on the type of activities and facilities they support. For example, in multipurpose recreational facilities, the athletic training room often serves as a first-aid station for recreational athletes. Conversely, in athletic facilities, it serves as a comprehensive athletic medicine facility for interscholastic, intercollegiate, Olympic, or professional athletes. When housed in a community, the athletic training room may serve the "weekend warrior." Therefore, proper planning, plus an understanding of the essential components of an athletic training room, will make it more effective when completed. Accordingly, athletic training room planners should regularly consult with staff athletic trainers during the planning phase to ensure the construction of a sound facility for treating and rehabilitating athletes (Ingersoll & Sawyer, 1999).

While the specific activities performed in an athletic training room are subject to institutional preference along with the availability of financial and facility resources, certain activities are performed in all such facilities. These include team preparation, injury evaluation, injury treatment, injury rehabilitation, and administrative functions. It is important, then, to understand these activities before building, retrofitting, or remodeling an athletic training room. To improve the planning process, general considerations for the athletic training room and/or the requirements of organizations concerned with athletic training facilities should be considered (Ingersoll & Sawyer, 1999).

Learning Objectives

After reading this chapter, the student should be able to

- outline the purpose of an athletic training room;
- list the general considerations for developing an athletic training room;
- describe the various spaces utilized in an athletic training room;
- discuss seven management factors for developing an athletic training facility;
- become familiar with the national standards for athletic training facilities recommended by the National Athletic Trainers' Association (NATA);
- describe the basic elements for renovating or retrofitting an athletic training room;
- discuss the various ways to determine the minimal size for an athletic training room;
- show the components of location, traffic flow, and structural needs with respect to an athletic training room; and
- list and describe the basic pieces of equipment needed in an athletic training room.

General Considerations for the Athletic Training Facility

Authors in the 1950s (Bevan, 1956; Morehouse & Rasch, 1958), 1960s (Morehouse & Rasch, 1964; Rawlinson, 1961), 1970s (Brown, 1972; Klafs & Arnheim, 1973), 1980s (Forseth, 1986; Penman & Penman, 1982; Sauers, 1985; Secor, 1984), 1990s (Arnheim & Prentice, 1997; Ingersoll & Sawyer, 1999; Lavoie, 1993; Rankin & Ingersoll, 1995; Ray, 1994), and 2000s (Sabo, 2001; Newell, 2003) have offered a number of options to be considered when contemplating an athletic training facility. While each author offers specific suggestions, a common thread is associated with each one. Generally, these authors agree that the athletic training room is a place specifically set aside for injury care. It has good lighting and ventilation; a constant temperature range; light-colored walls, ceilings, and floors; easily cleaned surfaces; adequate equipment; and ground fault interrupter (GFI) electrical outlets located on all walls. It is easily accessible by being near the dressing room, but is not a part of it, nor is it to be used as a passageway to the dressing room or showers. Moreover, these authors support the importance of a facility set aside specifically for the prevention, treatment, and rehabilitation of individuals who may incur injuries.

The Case for Athletic Training Facilities

It is important, then, for organizations without athletic training facilities to promote the need for an athletic training room.

First, these management promotion factors include a well-organized plan of action, which outlines why the athletic training room is essential to injury care. These three factors follow:

- Minor injuries often are not reported immediately, because there is no one place or person to whom the injured athlete should report. Moreover, the injured person is often reluctant to be treated for minor injuries in the presence of others. It also is difficult to give minor injuries proper attention during the confusion of dressing and undressing.
- A sanitary and comparatively private environment is generally helpful for treatment of injuries. Organizations are giving more attention to injury prevention, treatment, and rehabilitation because of the individual's privacy need from a practical and psychological point of view, because of the increased public attention given to sports injury problems, and because injuries adversely affect efficiency. Thus, the presence of an athletic training facility shows an interest in the welfare of athletes.
- A properly fitted athletic training room's cost is minimal when compared with costs incurred for lost time, uniforms, and other equipment (Brown, 1972),

Second, space needed for an athletic training facility must be determined. Forseth (1986) lists five general factors of facility development he obtained from Coates for determining the space needed for the athletic training room. These factors include:

- Program needs such as the number of sports and the type of sports offered at the institution.
- Projected institutional enrollment and the stability of the number of participants from one year to the next.
- Space needed for athletic training instruction.
- Cost per square foot estimates to determine what is feasible under the existing economic status.
- Communication with the architect early in the process to assure a functional athletic training room.

Third, the development of an athletic training facility requires the services of a certified athletic trainer. Such a person has requisite skills in the prevention, treatment, and rehabilitation of athletic injuries. Additionally, the certified athletic trainer has a working knowledge of the national standards for athletic training facilities (Newell, 2003).

Fourth, in retrofitting or remodeling facilities, the athletic training room size will be dictated by a number of unforeseen factors.

Fifth, make sure the athletic trainers are included during the planning phases.

Sixth, emphasize that the primary purpose of an athletic training room is to provide efficient service to large numbers of athletes at one time. Therefore, when building a new facility with a generous budget, the Arnheim and Prentice recommendation, the Penman and Penman formula, and/or Sabo's guidelines for minimal size should be followed.

Seventh, when possible, use the standards of the NATA and/or the American Academy of Orthopaedic Surgeons.

National Athletic Trainers' Association

The most important organization to consult is the NATA, especially if the athletic training room is in an institution that has a certification curriculum. According to Ingersoll and Sawyer (1999), the Commission on Accreditation of Allied Health Education Programs (CAAHEP) suggests specific guidelines for the development of an athletic training room. In this setting, the athletic training room components include team preparation area, injury evaluation/treatment area, rehabilitation area, wet space, maintenance area, storage space, office area, examination space, computer/study/conference area, and a classroom. The specifications for each of these areas are detailed to assist the planner in developing an appropriate floor plan for the athletic training room.

The *team preparation area* will have a tile floor with an appropriate number of floor drains, treatment cabinets with Formica tops, a recessed waste receptacle, drawers, and shelves. The ceiling height should be 11 to 12 feet, but not less than 10 feet. Further, fireproof tiles are a requirement for the ceiling. The walls should be constructed of blocks for durability and sound control and painted with an epoxy paint to seal the blocks so they will be easier to clean. A deep, double-basin sink is suggested. The direct lighting should be with fluorescent tubes. Electrical outlets should be located every 6 feet on all the walls and those electrical outlets around the sink should be GFI rated. Finally, this area should have a biohazard waste container and have double doors for entrance and/or exit.

The *injury evaluation/treatment area* requires different space and equipment needs for performing injury evaluations and treatments. This space has therapeutic modality applications, manual therapy, and treatment activities going on at the same time. Typically, this space includes numerous treatment tables that are used to examine body parts, do special tests on joints, and to treat various types of injuries. There should be a suspended curtain system that can, when necessary, be utilized for privacy.

Moveable carts between each table are used for transporting therapeutic equipment (e.g., ultrasound machine, muscle stimulator, etc.) and storing supplies (see Figure 32.1). The specific space needs of the injury evaluation/treatment area include:

- a ceiling with a minimum height of 10 feet (11 to 12 feet is desirable) that is covered with fireproof tiles
- cabinets for storage
- a deep double-basin, stainless-steel sink
- rubberized roll-out sports surface such as Mondo7®,
- block walls covered with epoxy paint
- GFI-rated electrical outlets at each treatment site and above the counter on either side of the sink,
- direct fluorescent lighting
- biohazard waste containers
- double doors for entering and exiting the area

The *rehabilitation area* includes space for therapeutic exercise equipment. This area should be separate from other areas in the complex because of the noise level and the movement of the exercising athletes. The needs of this area include:

- a rubberized roll-out sports floor surface such as Mondo7®
- free weights
- mechanized strength training equipment for exercising shoulders, arms, backs, hips, thighs, knees, and ankles
- electrical outlets on all walls spaced every 6 feet
- indirect fluorescent lighting
- a 10-foot ceiling equipped with fireproof tiles
- soundproofing in the epoxy-painted block walls
- double-door entrance and/or exit
- audio and video system
- space for running, jumping, and throwing activities

The *wet space (hydrotherapy) area* generally includes whirlpools, ice machines, therapeutic pools, refrigerator, and storage for large drink containers. The area should have:

- non-slip tiled floor
- a minimum ceiling height of 10 feet
- an appropriate number of floor drains
- recessed plumbing for whirlpools
- GFI electrical supply for whirlpools and ice machines
- storage area for drinking containers
- a deep double-basin stainless-steel sink equipped with storage
- extra ventilation and humidity control
- indirect fluorescent lighting
- close to the athletic trainer's office, so constant visual contact can be maintained

The *maintenance area* is where broken equipment is stored and repaired. The area needs are:

- shelves
- worktable
- concrete floor with a drain
- epoxy-painted block walls
- two eight-feet roll-up internal and external door entrances
- fireproof tiled eight-foot-high ceiling
- enhanced ventilation
- deep double-basin, stainless steel sink with storage
- GFI electrical outlets on all walls and an electrical strip above the workbench
- direct fluorescent lighting in the room and over the workbench
- storage space for an electric golf cart and its electrical charger

The *storage space* can never be too large. The storage space requirements include:

- humidity control to protect the stored tape
- lockable cabinets
- shelves of various heights and lengths
- concrete floor
- direct fluorescent lighting

Figure 32.1
Eastern Kentucky University Movable Cart

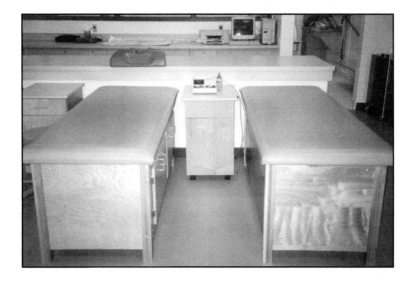

- epoxy-painted walls block
- double-door entrance, or at least a 36-inch door, or a roll-up door for easy access
- located close to the athletic trainer's administrative office area
- close to loading docks and/or delivery areas

The *office area* contains all medical records and serves as the administrative hub for the athletic training room. The space needs are:

- no smaller than 220 square feet
- located adjacent to the wet and storage areas
- a sight line to all other areas in the facility
- electrical, phone, and computer outlets on all walls
- lockable file and storage cabinets
- carpeted floor
- block walls with windows addressing each area of the facility
- a fireproof tiled eight-foot ceiling

The *examination space* is oftentimes the second office area that is used as a physician's examination room. The space includes those items in the athletic trainer's office area, an examination table, and single sink basin provided with storage above and below it. It should have a lockable door, and it could best be used for record storage, as there is less traffic.

The athletic training students will use the *computer/study/conference area*. This space should be no smaller than 220 square feet. The space needs include:

- tables for computers and printers
- a conference table
- shelving for a small library
- appropriate furniture for relaxing and studying
- storage lockers for the students' books, coats, and so forth located on the outside wall

The *classroom design* should include considerations outlined in Chapter 31. More importantly, the classroom must be dedicated for the use of the athletic training curriculum functions. Additionally, this room should have ample storage for instructional equipment and supplies used in athletic training instruction.

The American Academy of Orthopaedic Surgeons

While the NATA is the parent organization for athletic training standards, another good source is the American Academy of Orthopaedic Surgeons. Their publication, *Athletic Training and Sports Medicine (1991)*, contains suggestions useful for developing a training room when a curriculum is not a factor. The American Academy of Orthopaedic Surgeons suggests that each organization be obligated to provide athletic training room facilities sufficient for enhancing the athlete's health. Furthermore, this athletic training room facility is to be adequately sized; provided with utilities, supplies, and equipment; and staffed by qualified individuals. The services to be provided include preventive measures, assessment of injuries, first-aid administration, emergency care, routine evaluation and treatment, and rehabilitation of injuries. The academy's specific suggestions follow:

- The size and shape of the athletic training room should accommodate the number of individuals served by the facility.
- The athletic training room should be central to all of the activities provided by the organization. Also, the facility must be equally accessible to both men and women.
- The athletic training room should be equipped with the basic utilities of electricity, lighting, temperature control, ventilation, and plumbing.
- The walls in the athletic training room should have a minimum of two electrical outlets.
- The whirlpool area should have GFI electrical outlets.
- Light fixtures should produce a minimum of 30 foot-candles at four feet above the surface. When illumination varies in intensity, the brightest areas are to be used for evaluation and treatment of injuries or other conditions.
- Because of the use of warm water in the whirlpools and the hydrocollators, super ventilation must be present.
- The ideal athletic training room temperature is between 68° and 70° F.
- The basic minimum plumbing requirements include a deep sink with cold and hot water, a whirlpool, and a minimum of one to two floor drains.
- The athletic training room should have a number of lockable storage cabinets and closets. Additionally, a telephone, desk, computer, and file cabinet are necessary.
- The athletic training room traffic flow will be determined by the size and shape of the facility, placement of lighting fixtures, location of electrical outlets, site of phone/computer lines, and position of plumbing fixtures.

The athletic training room traffic-flow problems can be improved by:

- placing a bench outside a small athletic training room to reduce congestion in the treatment area,
- locating those services used less often away from the entrance,
- positioning taping tables nearest to the entrance, and
- stationing the trainer's desk so all ongoing activity can be observed.

Basic Elements for Renovating or Retrofitting an Athletic Training Room

Unfortunately, many organizations do not have the money or facilities for the development of an ideal athletic training room or to implement all the recommendations of national organizations. Therefore, it will be necessary to renovate or retrofit present facilities. While these two options do not make it easy to develop the ideal training room, it is still possible to provide a practical and efficient athletic training room. The elements to be considered when planning this facility include size, location, traffic flow, and structural components.

Size

LaVoie (1999) indicates the athletic training room designer, the administrative requirements of the athletic training staff, number of athletes, type of equipment, storage needs, and expansion possibilities should be considered in determining the initial size of the athletic training room. Furthermore, he states that a rule of thumb for the size and shape of the athletic training room is unnecessary. Instead, he relies on excellent communication between the designer and the athletic training staff to develop an athletic training facility that will be both productive and efficient. In a way, he agrees with the American Academy of Orthopaedic Surgeons (1991) who maintain that the size and shape of the athletic training room help determine an ability to accommodate large numbers of athletes at one time. Arnheim and Prentice (1997), however, contend that any athletic training room less than 1,000 square feet is impractical. Instead, they recommend that the facility be between 1,000 and 1,200 square feet, with 1,200 square feet being the preferred size. According to them, an athletic training room of this size accommodates large numbers of individuals along with the bulky equipment found in athletic training rooms.

Although minimum space requirements have been suggested, Penman and Penman (1982) provide a specific formula for determining a rough estimate of the minimum space needs for an athletic training room. This formula is based on the assertion that each taping or treatment table is sufficient for 20 athletes and occupies approximately 100 square feet including the table, work area around the table, and counter and storage space. Thus, the minimum space for the athletic training room can be determined by dividing the number of athletes expected at peak times by 20. This will give the number of treatment and/or taping tables needed. Then, by multiplying by 100, the total square footage can be obtained. The formula follows:

Number of athletes at peak ÷ 20 × 100 square feet =
Total square footage for treatment/taping tables

Sabo (2001) agrees that the athletic training room space needs can be determined by using the Penman formula. However, he suggests a more accurate means for sizing the athletic training room is by dividing the facility into eight functional areas: taping and first aid, hydrotherapy, treatment, rehabilitation, offices, physician's examination room, and storage. His specific recommendations for each of these areas follow:

- The taping and first aid areas are determined by using Penman's formula. However, Sabo does suggest that the minimum space requirements should be large enough for six taping tables to be used at the same time.
- The hydrotherapy area space is calculated by assessing the space needs of equipment in the area. Whirlpool space is based on the assumption that one whirlpool can accommodate three athletes per peak hour. Thus, the number of athletes to be treated during the peak hour is divided by 20 to determine the number of whirlpools needed. This number is multiplied by the square footage of the appropriate whirlpool to determine area needed. To calculate the square footage for the whirlpools, he uses the following guidelines: small whirlpool = 35 square feet, medium whirlpool = 56 square feet, and large whirlpool = 64 square feet.
- The treatment area should be large enough to house six treatment tables with two of these having privacy curtains. According to Sabo, one treatment table will accommodate three athletes per hour. Consequently, to obtain the number of tables needed, divide by three the number of athletes to be treated during the peak hour. Then, multiply the required tables by 100 to assess the square footage needed in the treatment area.
- The size of the rehabilitation area depends on the amount and kind of equipment housed in this area. The space required for each piece of equipment, working area around the equipment, further expansion, and storage are added together to give approximate space requirements for the rehabilitation room.
- The head athletic trainer's office should be a minimum of 120 square feet.
- The physician's office should be a minimum of 120 square feet.
- The storage area should have at least 100 square feet; however, a more accurate measure is that the room should be large enough to hold one year's worth of supplies.

Location

In locating the athletic training room, working space and traffic flow is of primary importance. When followed, the guidelines listed below will meet these criteria. Ideally, the athletic training room should be:

- Close to bathrooms.
- Close to dressing rooms, but away from the showers.
- Close to water and drainage.
- Easily accessible for both men and women.
- Easily accessible to emergency vehicle loading zones.
- Near participation areas.
- Located on an outside wall.
- Equipped with a street-level double door that can be operated automatically (similar to a handicapped entranceway).
- Provided with a janitorial closet that has a large sink, floor drain, and storage area. This janitorial closet should be adjacent to or within the athletic training room.

Traffic Flow

The layout of the athletic training room is designed to maximize the traffic flow of individuals who are using the various services of the athletic training room. Ideally, according to Arnheim and Prentice (1997), individuals should be able to enter and exit the athletic training facilities from an outside doorway and from the men's and women's locker rooms. The design shown in their textbook illustrates an ideal layout. Some of the characteristics of this design are:

- Saves unnecessary footsteps.
- Provides completely unhampered and uncomplicated traffic lanes.
- Places sensitive equipment away from the traffic lanes.
- Positions the athletic trainer's office in the center of the room so he or she can observe all ongoing activities.
- Locates the physician's office in a far corner so there will be privacy during the physician's examination.
- Furnishes the physician's office with a desk and chair, treatment table, sink, refrigerator, and storage space.

Figure 32.2
Main Entrance to the Eastern Kentucky University Building Where the Athletic Training Room Is Housed, Automatic Double-Wide Doors

Structural Components

To a large extent, structural features will dictate the configuration of the athletic training room. Accordingly, the following structural component guidelines will be beneficial in making the athletic training room as functional as possible.

- Ceilings should be a minimum of 10 feet in the treatment area so tall athletes can stand as they are being treated. Additionally, the ceilings should be constructed of material that will reflect light and deaden sound. Acoustical tiles are excellent for the athletic training room. For best results, the tiles should be white, ivory, cream, or buff color. These colors tend to reduce glare and provide good light reflection.
- Doors must be large enough to accommodate a wheelchair or a stretcher. Generally, a door 36 inches wide is sufficient for most athletic training rooms. However, if the budget is generous, double doors should be installed in at least one entrance. Figure 32.2 shows the outside double doors leading into the building where the Eastern Kentucky athletic training room is located. These doors have a full glass view and are wide enough for those in wheelchairs or on stretchers to enter or exit through them. Additionally, the surface under the doors is flat, so there will be no problem in moving injured athletes in wheelchairs or stretchers.
- Electrical outlets should be located three to four feet from the floor and spaced at six- to eight-feet intervals. Outlets equipped with ground fault interrupters (GFI) are required in areas where there is moisture. However, it is best if all electrical outlets in the athletic training room are GFI equipped because moisture could be present in all areas of the athletic training room.
- Equipment in the athletic training room should be a minimum of a desk and chair, bookcase, lockable file cabinet, one or two visitor chairs, a computer and printer, and a desk calculator. When possible, the computer should be connected to the internet.
- Floors should be sloped toward a drainage area, covered with a nonslip surface, moisture resistant, and easily cleaned and disinfected. Good materials for the floor include concrete, vinyl tile, ceramic tile, and poured liquid floors.
- Illumination in the athletic training room should provide even and efficient light on the work surface. Fluorescent fixtures with diffusers for elimination of flickering and that produce a minimum of 30 foot-candles four feet above the work surface are good choices. For evaluation and treatment areas, 50 to 60 foot-candles four feet above the work surface are recommended.
- Plumbing should follow all applicable building codes and the plumbing area must include at least one floor drain equipped with a trap to prevent odors from entering the athletic training room. The plumbing area has a concrete floor covered with a paint that has been modified to prevent slippage, rubber strips, pitted surfaces, or a rubberized liquid coating. The plumbing area should have a back flow device, a deep sink (preferably a double sink) equipped with hot and cold running water, and at least one whirlpool located in an area with a floor drain. Additionally, all electrical outlets must be GFI rated, and it is recommended that all equipment used in the plumbing area be approved by the Underwriter's Laboratory as safe for use in wet areas.

Figure 32.3
Austin Peay State University Taping Table

Figure 32.4
Austin Peay State University Taping Area Storage Cabinet

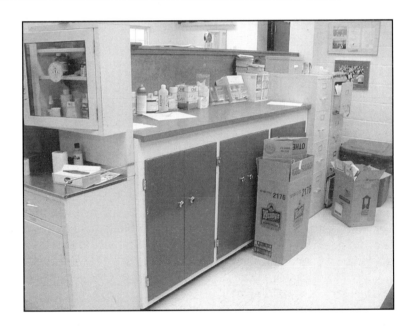

- Storage facilities are of prime importance and the storage area should include lockable cabinets, lockers, and closets. For best results, the storage facilities should be near the working space, but out of the traffic flow. Another storage consideration is that the storage area be designed so that it does not require excessive space. An example of efficient utilization of space is the taping and storage table at Austin Peay State Univesity. This taping table shown in Figure 32.3 is 42 inches high, 144 inches long, and 48 inches deep. It will accommodate four to five athletes for taping and it is located near the entrance to the athletic training room and adjacent to the Head Athletic Trainer's office. Beneath the tabletop are lockable cabinets that are used to store tape and other supplies. Directly across from the taping and storage table is a treatment storage cabinet (see Figure 32.4) which is 42 inches high, 84 inches long, and 26 inches deep. This cabinet is approximately six feet from the taping table, making it easy for the trainers to obtain the supplies they need for minor treatment and for preventive taping and wrapping activities. Another good feature of this taping and storage area is its close proximity to the athletic trainer's office and the fact that it facilitates preventing waste of materials and supplies while requiring very little square footage.

- Temperature control is provided with heating, ventilating, and air-conditioning (HVAC) units capable of maintaining a constant temperature range of 72° to 78° F and a humidity range of 40 to 50%. Additionally, the temperature control system must be sufficient to change the room air 8 to 10 times each hour so vapors from the warm water present in the whirlpools and hydrocollators can be exhausted continuously. Moreover, it is recommended, when possible, that the athletic training room temperature control units be separate from the rest of the building's temperature control units.
- Windows should be installed in such a manner that all activities in the athletic training room can be observed but, at the same time, maintain the privacy of individuals who may be conversing in the office area. One-way mirrors are good choices when privacy and adequate supervision are of primary importance.

Equipment Considerations for the Athletic Training Facility

Athletic training rooms contain a variety of equipment with the extent of the equipment being determined by the availability of financial resources and physical facilities. There are three categories of athletic training room equipment: basic, moderate, and ultimate (well-equipped).

Basic Equipment Needs

Basic equipment for the athletic training room consists of a dry and wet heat source, cold source, rehabilitation source, supply cabinet, treatment cabinet, training table, and whirlpool.

- Heat lamps provide dry heat for treatment of injuries. If a heat lamp is not available, a heating pad is a good substitute. Both of these dry heat devices are inexpensive and safe for use in the athletic training room equipped with GFI-equipped electrical outlets.
- A refrigerator is necessary for maintenance of an adequate supply of ice for use in treating injuries. A used refrigerator may be purchased in any locality at a reasonable price; however, just keep in mind that the main feature of this refrigerator is its capacity for making and keeping ice. It is also useful for storing ice bags and cold water.
- A double sink equipped with hot and cold running water, hooked to a trapped drain, and with under the sink storage and counter space of two to four feet is strongly recommended. Sinks are relatively inexpensive and can be purchased at home centers. Sinks may also be obtained from salvage yards or obtained when someone remodels a home or business.
- A supply cabinet is an essential piece of equipment for the athletic training room. The supply cabinet may be either metal or wood and it may be constructed or purchased secondhand. A suitable closet may be used, but it is important that any supply storage area be kept locked to prevent waste and misuse of athletic training materials. Figure 32.5 shows a suitable supply cabinet used in the Austin Peay State University athletic training room. The cabinet is 66 inches high (36 inches on the bottom and 30 inches on the top), 18 inches on the bottom section, 8 inches deep on the top section, and 30 inches wide.
- The treatment cabinet must have an adequate working surface and space for holding first-aid and other treatment supplies. It should be lockable to prevent misuse of supplies and to keep the supplies sanitary. A set of regular mason jars placed on the cabinet surface is recommended to keep dressing materials clean and available. The size of the treatment cabinet will vary among athletic training rooms; however, a treatment cabinet 78 inches high, 18 to 20 inches deep, and 36 inches wide is adequate for most basically equipped athletic training rooms.
- The training table is the most essential piece of athletic training room equipment, as it is used for examining injuries, applying treatment modalities, and applying protective taping and/or wrapping. The training table is usually constructed of heavy wood and measures 78 inches long, 24 inches wide, and 30 inches high. The top is covered with foam rubber or some other form of padding over which an easily cleaned cloth or other covering is applied. Figure 32.6 shows the pattern for a basic athletic training table.
- The whirlpool is another essential piece of equipment for the athletic training room for its use in applying wet, moving heat to athletic injuries. It is important that the whirlpool is on a concrete surface and that the area has adequate drains plus GFI-equipped electrical outlets. Figure 32.7 shows a whirlpool setup in the Eastern Kentucky University athletic training room. One way of improvising a whirlpool bath is to take an old bathtub and equip it with a portable agitator. Be certain the improvised whirlpool is properly grounded and connected to GFI electrical outlets.

Figure 32.5
Austin Peay State University Supply Cabinet

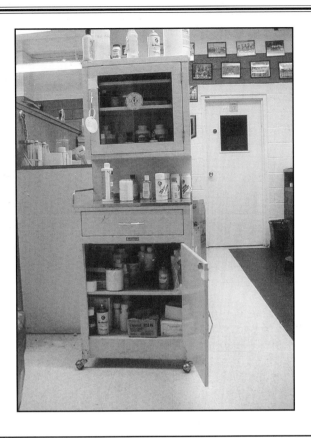

Figure 32.6
Athletic Training Table Pattern

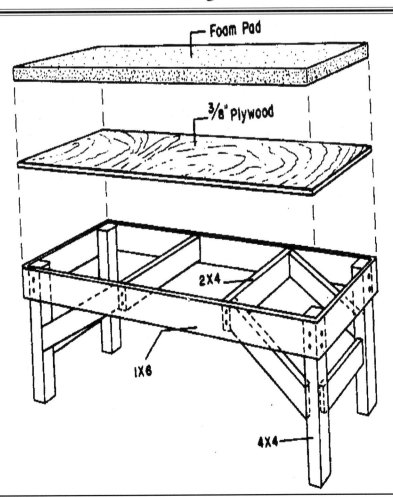

Figure 32.7
Eastern Kentucky University Whirlpool Setup

Examples of Moderately and Well-Equipped Training Rooms

Examples of a moderately and a well-equipped athletic training room are those at Austin Peay State University (APSU) and Eastern Kentucky University (EKU). One, APSU, is a retrofitted facility and the other, EKU, is a newly built structure.

Austin Peay State University

Austin Peay State University in Clarksville, Tennessee is typical of a moderately equipped athletic training room facility. It was retrofitted from a small athletic training room for football, two locker rooms, three shower rooms, a steam room, a large hallway, a sunken whirlpool and its deck, and an equipment issuing room.

The athletic training room contains 2,138 square feet and it is divided into seven components: head athletic trainer's office; assistant athletic trainer's office; team physician's office; treatment room; taping, wrapping, and weighing room; hydrotherapy room; and storage areas.

Head Athletic Trainer's Office

The head athletic trainer's office has 132 square feet (11 feet by 12 feet). It was retrofitted from an equipment issuing room and it has an entrance door from the hallway and a door leading to the taping table. The door leading to the taping table area has glass so it offers a direct sight line to the taping table area and a partial sight line to the treatment room. Yet the office design allows for privacy when it is needed. It contains

- a desk and chair,
- a chair for consultations,
- a computer connected to the internet,
- a printer for the computer,
- a telephone,
- a recording machine for voice mail,
- a calculator,
- two two-drawer and one four-drawer file cabinets,
- a large lockable double-door cabinet that has lockable drawers and file cabinets,
- a bookcase with adjustable shelves and a lockable cabinet and drawer, and
- a small bookcase with three shelves.

Assistant Athletic Trainer's Office

Two assistant athletic trainers share an office containing 110 square feet (10 feet by 11 feet). The office was constructed from an area in the rehabilitation area. It has two windows and a glass door with a clear sight line to the rehabilitation activities. This office is equipped with

- two desks and chairs,
- one computer with internet connection,
- one printer,
- a small worktable,
- two file cabinets, and
- bookshelves along one of the walls.

Team Physician's Office

The physician's office has 96 square feet (12 feet by 8 feet) and is located at one end of the treatment area. It has

- a solid door for privacy,
- a telephone,
- a desk and chair,
- an examination table,
- lockable storage cabinets along one wall, and
- a sink with hot and cold running water.

Treatment Room

The treatment room is located in a separate room that can be partially observed by the head athletic trainer from his office. It was once a locker room, and it has 345 square feet (23 feet by 15 feet) of space. It has the following treatment modalities:

- Orthotron KT1 exercise table
- Synatron 500 Electrotherapy CTL CTR
- Nemectron 2 ultrasound therapy unit
- Pentium Z station ZSK-8559
- Electrotherapy ultrasound modality
- Two Mettler electronic stimulators
- Z station
- treatment tables,
- examination tables,
- a hydrocollator and hydrocollator tree
- a computer with printer

Rehabilitation Room

The rehabilitation room was retrofitted from a dressing room. It has 448 square feet (28 feet by 16 feet) of space in which the following pieces of rehabilitation equipment are located:

- a Nemectrodyn Model V
- a Nemectrodyn MDL-2 nerve stimulator device
- an Orthotron II Fitron cycle-ergometer
- a Cybex 2450 upper body exerciser
- a Lifestep 1000
- a cable column rehabilitation device

Taping, Wrapping, and Weighing Room

The taping, wrapping, and weighing room has 228 square feet (19 feet by 12 feet) of useable space. It, like the rehabilitation room and assistant athletic trainer's office, was retrofitted from a room used for dressing and locker space. It has a taping table that is 144 inches long, 42 inches high, and 48 inches deep; a large weight scale; and a storage cabinet that is 84 inches long, 26 inches deep, and 42 inches high. The taping, wrapping, and weighing area is directly to the right of the entrance into the training room and is situated directly adjacent to the head athletic trainer's office. It is separated from the rehabilitation area by a five-inch-thick wooden partition wall that is 60 inches high and 145 inches long. This area is shown in Figures 32.3 and 32.4.

Hydrotherapy Room

The hydrotherapy room was once a shower room. It contains 60 square feet (10 feet by 6 feet), and it has a full body whirlpool and two extremity whirlpools. It is located adjacent to the treatment area, but it must be entered through a door from the treatment room, making it impossible to supervise its activities from any of the offices or other areas of the athletic training room. It has GFI electrical outlets and excellent drainage. Additionally, the area has a curb that will prevent overflowing water from entering the treatment or storage areas.

Storage Areas

The Austin Peay State University athletic training room has four retrofitted storage areas other than those already mentioned. One of these is a converted shower room containing 84 square feet of useable space (14 feet by 6 feet). It houses the ice machine, and it is where all the drinking and ice containers and the crutches are kept.

Another major storage area is located directly across from the hydrotherapy room in what was once a hall leading from the treatment room area to a steam room and a sunken whirlpool. This area contains 240 square feet (16 feet by 15 feet). It has lockable metal and wooden lockers that are used to store various treatment and rehabilitation supplies and equipment.

The area that was originally a large sunken whirlpool has 255 square feet (17 feet by 15 feet) including the large whirlpool, the whirlpool deck, and the hallway leading to the steam room. The area is utilized mostly for large boxes as well as a variety of protective and preventive equipment.

The former steam room is the most secure storage area, for it has a metal door and is away from any traffic flow. It has 180 square feet (15 feet by 12 feet). It is used to store old records and sensitive supplies and equipment. The room also has temperature and humidity controls not present in the other storage areas.

Eastern Kentucky University

Eastern Kentucky University's new athletic training room is an example of a well-equipped facility and it demonstrates what can be done when building a new athletic training room. It is located on the first floor of the 40,000-square-foot Harry Moberly Classroom, Wellness, and Conditioning Building. The first floor of the building houses the physical education activity/laboratory, the weight room, and the athletic training room. On the second floor, there is a wellness center, three large classrooms, human performance and computer laboratories, offices, locker rooms, showers, and dressing rooms. Primarily, the building houses the College of Health, Physical Education, Recreation, and Athletics plus the 16 intercollegiate athletic teams.

The athletic training room is located between the weight room and the physical activity/laboratory. It is entered from the main foyer through glass-enclosed double doors that do not have thresholds. The athletic training facility functional areas follow:

- a taping/treatment area (see Figure 32.8)
- a rehabilitation area (see Figure 32.9)
- a treatment/therapy area (see Figure 32.10)
- glass enclosed office (see Figure 32.11)
- treatment area storage (see Figure 32.12)
- hydrotherapy cooler storage area (see Figure 32.13)
- an in-ground hydrotherapy pool with a treadmill (see Figure 32.14)
- rehabilitation storage area (see Figure 32.15)
- treatment storage area (see Figure 32.16)
- hydrotherapy room (see Figure 32.17)

In addition to the areas depicted in Figures 32.8 to 32.17, the athletic training facility has three above-ground therapeutic pools in the hydrotherapy area, x-ray room with accompanying equipment and exposure control measures, and private examination rooms. All office doors have either full glass or partial full-length glass so activities can be observed from the office. There are artificial and natural light sources in all areas.

Figure 32.8
Eastern Kentucky University Taping/Treatment Area

Figure 32.9
Eastern Kentucky University Rehabilitation Area

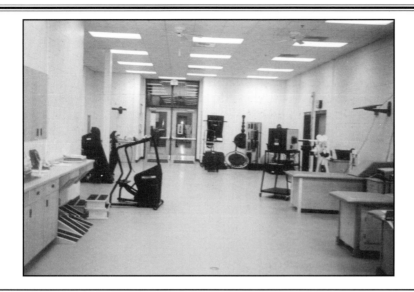

Figure 32.10
Eastern Kentucky University Treatment/Therapy Area

Figure 32.11
Eastern Kentucky University Office Area

Figure 32.12
Eastern Kentucky University Treatment/Therapy Storage Area

Figure 32.13
Eastern Kentucky University Hydrotherapy Cooler Storage Area

Figure 32.14
Eastern Kentucky University In-Ground Therapy Pool With Treadmill

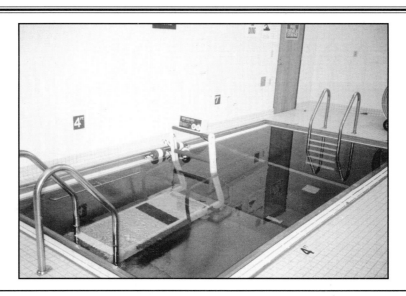

Figure 32.15
Eastern Kentucky University Rehabilitation Storage Area

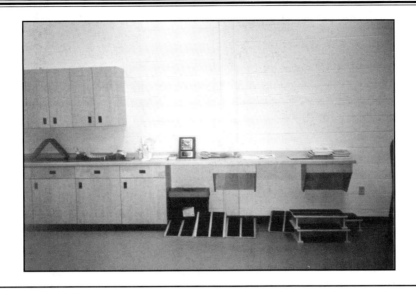

Figure 32.16
Eastern Kentucky University Treatment Storage Area

Figure 32.17
Eastern Kentucky University Hydrotherapy Area

Summary

The health of athletes and participants is extremely important for a successful athletic program for any organization—amateur, professional, or recreational. The planners for the athletic training room should regularly consult with staff athletic trainers during the planning phase to ensure the construction of a sound facility for treating and rehabilitating athletes.

Acknowledgments

Special thanks to Bobby Barton EdD (ATC), Head Athletic Trainer, Eastern Kentucky University; Leighton Brown (TSR), NEC, Inc., Nashville, TN; Chuck Kimmel (ATC), Head Athletic Trainer and Assistant Athletic Director, Austin Peay State University; and Jason Kizzee (ATC), Athletic Trainer, Naval Academy Preparatory School, Newport, RI.

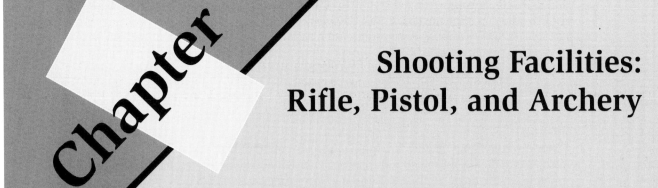

Shooting Facilities: Rifle, Pistol, and Archery

Jason Winkle and Thomas Horne

Shooting sports—rifle, pistol, and archery—started when early man began developing bows, arrows, and spears for protection and a way to gather food. Around 3500 BCE the Egyptians used archery as a weapon of war (*USA Archery*, 2004). Much of the early development of archery was based on designing archery equipment for a military application. In addition to using bows and arrows for weapons, they were also used for leisure activities and contests. Homer, in the *Iliad*, referenced archery contests where archers shot at tethered doves. During the 14th century in England, archery practice was mandatory for all able-bodied men (Van Dalen and Bennett, 1971). The advent of gunpowder led to the decline of archery as a tool of war and to the increased development of firearm activities. Organized firearms shooting began in Europe when the first shooting clubs were formed. Public shooting matches were first seen in Europe around the 16th century and in America in the early 1700s. The rules for shooting sports began to standardize when National Rifle Association (NRA) was founded in the United States in 1871 and the National Archery Association (NAA) was formed in 1879.

Numerous disciplines have developed for rifle, pistol, and archery sports; therefore, the facilities, equipment, and procedures used for shooting activities and competitions vary greatly. This chapter will focus on facilities, equipment, and operational procedures required when developing and operating competitive indoor rifle and pistol facilities and both indoor and outdoor archery facilities. The equipment, facility design, and risk management issues associated with these competitive shooting facilities can be applied or adapted to other shooting activities and facilities.

Learning Objectives

After reading this chapter, the student should be able to

- apply general facility planning and development concepts to building or renovating a rifle, pistol, or archery shooting facility;
- identify the key design features for competitive target archery, rifle, and pistol facilities;
- develop a standard equipment list to support each type of shooting facility;
- define terms associated with the design, operation, and management of shooting facilities;
- develop sound risk management policies and procedures for shooting facilities;
- access information from professional organizations that establish standards for shooting facilities and apply this information to design, develop, or operate a shooting facility; and
- adapt structured competitive shooting rules and procedures for instructional, recreational, and other less formal settings.

Planning and Designing a Shooting Facility

Whether planning and designing a shooting facility from scratch, remodeling an existing facility to accommodate shooting activities, or renovating an existing shooting facility, detailed planning will avoid costly design mistakes. The major factors that usually determine any facility design are the funding; availability of appropriate space; nature and scope of the program; and quality of the planners, architects, and engineers involved in the project.

Chapters 3 and 4 in this text provide an excellent guide for general facility planning and design. Since each planning and design situation is different, the relative importance of each design criteria will vary with each project. Based on guidelines for facility planning and shooting facility specific design criteria, the following are sound general guidelines for planning a shooting facility:

- Participatory planning—Involve the stakeholders in the planning process. This may include establishing a formal planning team.

- Needs assessment—Determine past, present, and future needs and desires as early and as accurately as possible in the design process.
- Site selection—A large, relatively flat area is ideal, since archery ranges are large facilities that usually require a flat shooting area. Consider the type and use of adjacent areas when selecting the shooting facility site. Use of natural land features such as hillsides may provide natural backdrops if available.
- Build to code—Be certain all construction meets governmental (local, state, and national) building codes to include Americans With Disabilities Act (ADA) requirements. If the shooting facility is to be used for competitions, be sure the facility specifications meet or exceed those required by sanctioning agencies. For target archery, the Federation Internationale de Tir a l'Arc (FITA) and the NAA are the recognized sanctioning organizations. These organizations publish detailed rules and specifications for sanctioned archery competitions.
- Support selection—A careful and judicious process should be used when selecting the architect, engineers, contractors, and any other consultants. Select individuals or organizations that have experience in building shooting or similar facilities and have good references. Do not hesitate to contact previous customers.
- Risk management—When planning a shooting facility, be certain to address security, access control, and buffer zones around shooting areas.

The specific design features for a shooting facility will depend on the availability of an appropriate site, the availability of funds, the type of shooting, and many other factors. Proper prior planning will help ensure a highly functional and efficient shooting facility.

Archery

According to *The American Heritage Dictionary*, "Archery is the art, sport, or skill of shooting with a bow and arrow." Although this may sound simple, many archery disciplines and activities have developed over the years. Competitive archery as we know it today originated in England in the 17th century. Most early competitions fell into one of three general categories of shooting: butt shooting, clout shooting, or roving. Butt shooting consisted of bowmen shooting from set distances at targets mounted vertically on earthen mounds or butts. Most modern competitive archery programs and competitions are based on butt shooting. Clout shooting involved shooting arrows into the air and having them land on a target mounted flat on the ground. The third type of archery was roving, where archers simulated hunting over rough ground and shooting targets representing animals. Roving is the forerunner of today's field archery programs that focus on hunting-oriented shooting. Field archery shots are often made uphill or downhill and may involve shooting around obstacles.

The most popular and numerous archery ranges are basic outdoor designs often referred to as "place-to-shoot ranges." These unmanned place-to-shoot ranges usually have target distances from 25 to 100 yards and cater to bow hunters. Some ranges include a field archery course that has targets placed in a natural setting and may even have tree stand stations to simulate bow hunting. Archers bring their own equipment and shoot unsupervised. Few specific design features other than a parking lot, outhouse, and possibly a covered pavilion are normally included. Most archery programs in schools, colleges, recreation settings, and the Olympics are based on early forms of butt shooting. The equipment, facilities, and risk management procedures used for this type of target shooting are well established and clearly defined by FITA and the NAA. This section will focus on facilities and equipment to support competitive target archery programs. Most of the facility and equipment issues for competitive target archery are applicable to other less structured types of archery shooting.

Outdoor Target Archery Competitions

Most major outdoor target archery competitions in the United States include a FITA Round followed by an Olympic Round. A FITA Round consists of 36 arrows shot at each of four distances (90, 70, 50, and 30 meters for men; 70, 60, 50, 30 meters for women) for a total of 144 arrows. Arrows are generally shot in groups of six (called ends) within a specified time period. Scores are then totaled to determine seeding for the Olympic Round. An Olympic Round is a direct elimination, head-to-head competition shot at 70 meters. The winner of each match advances until a champion is determined. All matches are 18 arrows, except the quarterfinals, semifinals, and finals, which are 12-arrow matches.

Indoor Target Archery Competitions

Indoor tournaments are held for the Recurve (Olympic) and Compound Divisions. Recurve Division events are generally held at either 25 meters or 18 meters. In a 25-Meter Indoor Round, archers shoot 60 arrows at a 60 cm diameter target face. In the 18-Meter Indoor Round, archers shoot 60 arrows at a 40 cm diameter target face. Championship events employ a Grand Indoor Round which starts off with a Combined Indoor Round (both 25-meter and 18-meter rounds) followed by a direct elimination competition for the top 16 archers. These direct elimination matches are 15-arrow matches shot at a special 20 cm diameter target face. Competitions in the Compound Division usually consist of a Combined Indoor Round of 60 arrows shot from 25 meters at 40 cm diameter target face. A Grand Indoor Round, used in championships, consists of a Double Combined Indoor Round. The top 16 archers advance to direct elimination matches made up of 15 arrows at 25 meters.

Target Archery Ranges

Competition target archery ranges must be designed and built to meet or exceed FITA and NAA specifications, the recognized sanctioning organizations for most archery competitions. FITA and NAA have also established standards for Field Archery and Ski-Archery; but these standards are outside the scope of this chapter.

Target archery ranges are often set up on multipurpose outdoor fields or in large multipurpose indoor areas. Some schools, clubs, camps, and other agencies have custom designed permanent archery facilities. Whether the shooting facility is a permanent facility or a temporary setup in a multipurpose facility, a classroom or meeting room is recommended if the shooting facility is to be used by a club or for educational purposes.

Outdoor archery ranges are most effectively laid out on level turf oriented north to south with shooting aimed to the north. The actual shooting length of the archery range will vary depending on the shooting event being contested but the range layout is basically the same for all events. The archers shoot from the Shooting Line at targets placed at the prescribed distance. The minimum spacing of the targets for competitions depends upon the number of shooters per lane. If shooters are shooting singly or in pairs, the minimum spacing between targets is 2.5 meters (8 feet, 2 inches) and 3.66 meters (12 feet) if the archers are shooting in threes. All targets should be clearly numbered. Shooting marks, consisting of discs or other flat markers, should be positioned opposite the targets at the shooting line. The shooting marks have the number that corresponds with the target for that lane. A line extending from the shooting line to the target line establishes shooting lanes. A waiting line should be placed at least five yards behind the shooting line. An equipment area may be marked off behind the waiting area. Behind the equipment area a space for athletes is recommended. A 50-yard buffer zone must be roped off behind the targets to keep spectators, competitors, and officials safe (see Figure 33.1).

Figure 33.1
Sample Archery Range Layout

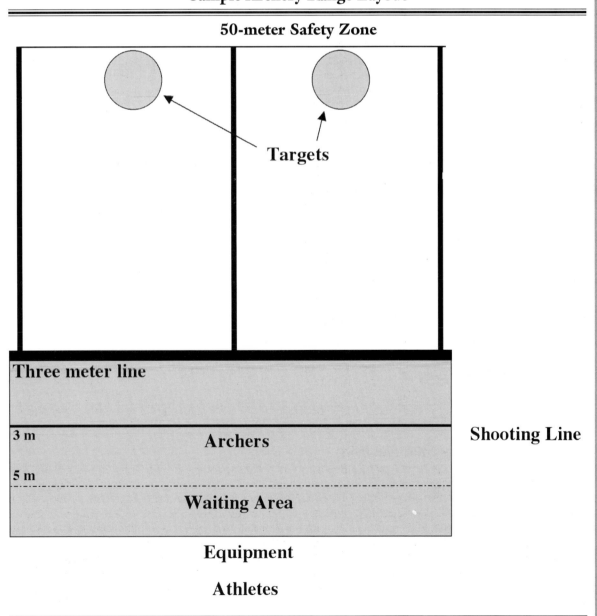

Targets

Targets have traditionally been a boss of tightly coiled roped straw about 4 inches thick and about 4 feet in diameter on which is stretched a target face. Targets for both indoor and outdoor target archery competitions are now often made of high density foam. Targets must be secured to target stands, called butts (buttresses), which are secured to the ground. For indoor archery, targets must be inclined, tilted back, between vertical and 10 degrees. For outdoor archery, targets must be inclined 10 to 15 degrees. The center of the target for both indoor and outdoor targets must be 130 cm (4 feet, 3 inches) (within 5 cm) above the ground for single target faces. All targets must be inclined at the same angle. The target face consists of 10 rings made out of five different colors. The scoring is 10,9 (gold), 8,7 (red), 6,5 (blue), 4,3 (black), 2,1 (white) from inner circle to outer ring. The rings all have the same thickness (except for the compound competitions where the 10 is made smaller). Target sizes vary at different distances and may be displayed as a single face (see Figure 33.2), triple faces triangular, or triple faces vertical.

Figure 33.2
Single-Faced Target

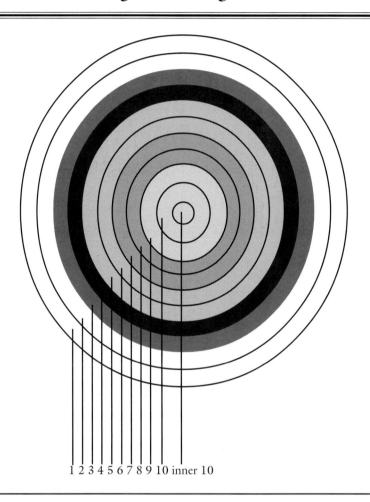

1 2 3 4 5 6 7 8 9 10 inner 10

Venue Support Equipment

If an archery range will be used for competitions, especially FITA- or NAA-sanctioned competitions, additional venue support equipment will be required. The following is a brief description of some of the additional equipment that may be required to host a sanctioned archery tournament:

- Barriers—Some type of physical restraint placed on the range to mark safety buffer zones to keep spectators out of the archer's competition areas and facilitate desired circulation patterns. The barriers may be as simple as a rope suspended between two poles or a fenced-in area with directional signage attached. The barriers must clearly designate safety zones and provide a physical obstruction.
- Scoreboards—Spectators, archers, meet officials, and competition organizers like to know how well the archers are shooting. As a minimum, one large scoreboard is needed for posting scores. For large sanctioned competitions, smaller scoreboards should be placed near the target butt to display a progressive score for each shooter. For less formal competitions and during match competitions, flip scoreboards may be used.
- Flags—Judges and officials are often separated from the archers and other meet officials. Flags or a similar device should be available for judges and officials for signaling or requesting assistance.

- Speaker system—Important announcements will need to be made during competitions to archers, coaches, officials, meet organizers, and spectators. A quality speaker system is needed to meet this requirement.
- Timing control equipment—Most archery competitions have time limits for the archers to shoot their ends. Enforcing the established time limits is essential in having a fair competition, so both visual and acoustic time signals are required for most sanctioned competitions. Visual time signals can be given with digital clocks, lights, flags, or other simple visual devices. The acoustical signals may be given with a whistle, air horn, or a similar device.
- Archer identification—Tournament officials, organizers, and spectators need to be able to identify archers competing in the competition. In championship tournaments, archers must wear a name tag and have a name plate displayed at the target area. Even at less formal tournaments, archers must wear some type of identification tag, number, or vest.
- Field glasses—Some type of visual aid is often necessary for competition administrators and officials to spot arrows. Providing field glasses or a telescope at the shooting facility is recommended.

Shooters Equipment

Bows used for target archery are held in one hand and drawn with the other. They may have an adjustable arrow rest on the riser. The bowstring is permitted to have a center serving to fit the arrow nocks, with one or two nock locators, and one attachment to serve as a lip or nose mark. An audible or visual draw checker (clicker) may be used as long as it is not electrical. Stabilizers and torque compensators are allowed, as long as they do not touch anything but the bow itself, and do not interfere with other competitors on the shooting line.

Recurve Bow

A recurve bow is a relatively short bow that was preferred over the longbow by archers who were forced into environments where long weapons could be cumbersome. A recurve bow used for target archery consists of a handle riser and two flexible limbs terminating in nocks supporting a single string. The distinguishing feature of the recurve bow is that the ends of the limbs curve away from the archer when in the shooting position (See Figure 33.3). This recurve shape reduces loading at full draw (let-off) and will impart more energy to the arrow than a standard longbow of similar top draw weight.

Figure 33.3
The Basic Recurve Bow

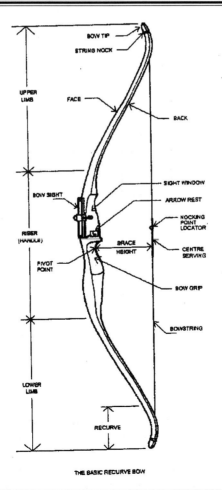

THE BASIC RECURVE BOW

Compound Bow

Compound bows have cams and cables, making the holding weight less than half of the draw weight. Bow hunters because of their greater accuracy, flatter arrow trajectory, and their ease of use. A compound bow with a peak draw weight of 60 pounds or less may be used for target archery competitions. Cables and cable guards are allowed (see Figure 33.4). The bowstring may contain a peep sight or hole for sighting. The bow sight may not have electrical components but may contain lenses and/or multiple aim points. A mechanical string release may be used, as long as it does not attach to the bow and has no electrical components.

Figure 33.4
The Compound Bow

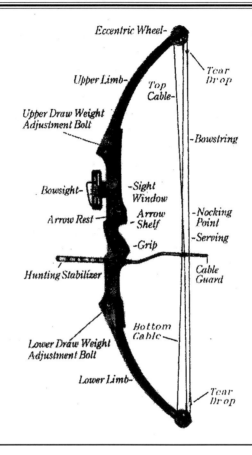

Strings

Strings are usually made by twining several strings of Kevlar, Dacron, or polyethylene to make a single cord. Dacron is relatively inexpensive, but prone to creep, meaning that it may stretch and make for inconsistent shots. Dacron is recommended for bows with wooden risers and older bows since the other string materials might put too much stress on the bow. Aramid fibers (Kevlar) have very little stretch, thus giving the arrow a flatter trajectory. The disadvantage of Kevlar is that these fibers cannot take much shear, so they tend to break more often, usually just below the nocking point. Kevlar fibers are also very susceptible to moisture; therefore, these strings have to be waxed carefully. Polyethylene fibers are the latest addition to string materials. Polyethylene strings last at least as long as those made of Dacron and are less susceptible to moisture than other string materials.

Sights

The sight can come in many forms, but the most popular sights have a circular sight with a cross-hairs or pin at its center. Some compound bows incorporate a "spirit level" which tells the archer if the bow is tilted.

Arrows

Wooden shafted arrows are still used with longbows and for recreational purposes but are rarely used for competitive target archery. For competitive target archery, arrows of any type may be used as long as the maximum diameter is 9.3 mm (.366 inch) or less. Arrows should be marked with the competitor's initials and all arrows used in an end must be of uniform color, shaft, fletching, and cresting. The most commonly used arrows for target archery are made of aluminum tubes, carbon fibers, or an aluminum/carbon combination (a very thin aluminum tube inside and carbon fibers on the outside). Aluminum tube arrows are more durable than either of the carbon fiber type arrows. Carbon fiber arrows and aluminum/carbon arrows are nearly impossible to repair if damaged. Aluminum/carbon arrows are the most commonly used arrow for outdoor shooting. All three arrow types are used for indoor shooting.

Vanes, also called the fletching, are the three featherlike attachments near the rear of the arrow that keep the arrow tracking. There are two options for vanes, either plastic vanes or real feathers. Plastic vanes are less affected by moisture and are recommended for outdoor shooting.

General Archery Equipment

A bow, arrows, and a target are required for target archery shooting, but experienced archers rarely shoot with only the bare essentials. Archers or those conducting an archery program, whether highly competitive or recreational, should consider purchasing the following general archery equipment:

- Arm guard—A piece of leather or other durable material that fits over the bow arm that keeps the string from contacting the arm when the string is released.
- Chest guard—Protects the chest and keeps loose clothing from becoming caught by the string.
- Finger protectors—One of a variety of protective finger stalls, gloves, tabs, or tape methods to protect the fingers on the draw hand.
- Quiver—An arrow-holding device that can be worn on the body or attached to the bow.
- Arrow straightener—A device that measures arrow bend and straightens arrows.
- Grip/arrow pull—A rubber grip that helps in removing arrows from the target.
- Fletching jig—Allows you to fletch a shaft, put vanes on it.
- Nocking jig—Allows you to accurately replace a nock on the arrow shaft.
- Stringer—Recurve archers use this device to string their bows. Compound bows are permanently strung and many longbows have built in stringers.
- Stringing rig—A device you can make your own strings with.
- String server—A device that allows you to create nocking points on the string.

Equipment Care and Maintenance

The Bow

The bow is the most important piece of equipment in archery, so keeping it in good working condition is essential. A sound practice is to never lay the bow on the ground. This can cause dust and other materials to damage or ruin sensitive parts of the bow. If a bow becomes wet for any reason, dry it off as soon as possible even if the finishes are waterproof. Metal bows may rust, reducing bow function. Apply bow wax to preserve the bow's finish.

Bow Strings

This vital part of the bow is perhaps one of the easier areas to damage. To avoid damage, archers should use bow string wax to keep the string waterproof. This will help keep the string in maximum performance condition and prevent it from becoming tangled.

Arrows

Although numerous and somewhat inexpensive, an arrow which has even the slightest malfunction can cause unexpected and unwanted results. Protect the fletching from getting wet or becoming damaged. Repair or discard any damaged arrows. Serious archers should only use arrows deemed to be in perfect condition.

Target Butts

To help prevent fungus growth, mold, and premature deterioration, do not place target butts on damp floors or leave them uncovered in the rain.

Target Faces

Target faces must be in good condition. Remove faces while moistening butts. If the face is torn, use masking tape to bind the tears.

Replacing a Plastic Nock

Nocks may become worn down and will need to be replaced, so inspect the nock regularly. If the nock needs to be changed, choose the same size and color nock as that of the other arrows. Place a small flame (perhaps from a lighter) under the nock and let the glue soften enough so it can be easily removed. Point the arrow up while heating to avoid damaging the feathers. Remove the old glue using fine sandpaper. Once the nock area is clear, apply glue and replace the nock. Wipe off any excess glue. Before the glue hardens, rotate the arrow while inspecting the nock alignment. An arrow with an off-center nock on an arrow will produce poor results when fired.

Replacing a Feather or Vane

Replacing a feather or vane is easy, but restoring an arrow to competition quality is difficult, and requires skill, experience, and the use of a feather jig. Feather replacement is only recommended for arrows that will be used for recreation or practice shooting.

Replacing Arrow Points

The condition of the arrow shaft directly behind the point should be checked when replacing points. If the shaft is damaged, the arrow cannot be repaired unless the shaft is shortened. These salvaged arrows may still be used for school, recreation, and practice purposes, but are no longer suitable for competition shooting.

Storage

The amount of storage required for an archery facility will vary based on many factors. If the archery facility is used for instructional and recreation programs where the program sponsors provide the equipment, well-secured storage will be necessary. If the archery facility is simply an outdoor facility that stocks limited personal archery gear, the storage requirements will be considerably less than a facility that provides equipment. If any bows and arrows are to be stored, they must be stored in a secure area since they could be used as weapons. Archery equipment, especially bows, arrows and targets, must be stored in a dry environment to avoid damage.

Risk Management

Establishing and maintaining sound risk management policies and procedures is especially important for shooting facilities since weapons are involved. Shooting facility design must consider risk management issues, including the following:

- Staffing—training, ratios.
- Insurance—waivers, liability.
- Emergency Procedures—first aid, emergency action plan.
- Equipment and supplies—safety checks, handling, storage.
- Facility—inspections, procedures.
- Post rules and signage.
- Shooting line.
- Be sure that safety inspections are performed regularly.
- Ensure that archers use appropriate protective equipment—eye protection, ear protection, and finger, wrist, and arm guards.
- Ensure that students use properly fitted equipment.
- Ensure that the equipment is properly set up, loaded, strung, and utilized as intended.
- Establish a systematic protocol for starting and ending the activity and retrieving arrows.
- Explain in clear, concise terms the safety rules of the archery range protocol before archers begin shooting.
- Properly locate the activity so that it does not pose a hazard to participants or spectators.
- Provide adequate spacing so that archery may be performed safely.

Rifle and Pistol

The first consideration when designing an indoor shooting facility is determining what type of shooting will be conducted. Firearm caliber, muzzle velocity, and the nature of the shooting all play an important role in the construction needs of the facility. Firearms commonly used in indoor ranges include air pistols, air rifles, handguns of various calibers, and rifles with muzzle velocities below 3,500 feet per second. Indoor ranges can also be used for a variety of shooting approaches from basic marksmanship to tactical shooting where participants practice defensive shooting skills. While each of the above-mentioned shooting variables have unique facility needs, they all share some common design characteristics. This section will examine these common design characteristics and design and construction standards for indoor shooting ranges.

Space Needs

Once the types of shooting that will be conducted in a facility have been determined, the focus can shift to designing a facility to adequately and safely house these shooting activities. The largest expense in range development is usually the real estate that comprises the shooting area. Thorough planning to determine space needs is critical to keep development prices from escalating dramatically. Most competition shooting can be accommodated with a range that provides 50 to 75 feet between the target and the firing line. Be sure to identify all space needs to include support functions such as parking areas, restrooms, storage, office space, lobby area, and circulation space.

Ceiling Height and Construction

An important space consideration is ceiling height in the range. A ceiling that is too low or too high can cause ricochet issues that must be addressed with baffling and other types of ballistic protection. A ceiling height between 10 and 12 feet is recommended. This height provides adequate overhead clearance for downrange shooting as well as keeping lighting, ventilation, and target retrieval systems costs to a minimum.

A slab ceiling is the industry standard. Slab ceilings require few baffles and guards, thus reducing costs. Guards are required, however, for any exposed light fixtures, ducts, conduits, and plumbing. For ceilings other than slab, baffles and guards must be placed at angles that are determined by the length and height of the facility.

Shooting Stalls

Shooting stalls function as protective dividers between shooters in the range by preventing interference from expelled casings, misdirected shots, and other distractions. In addition to their protective characteristics, stalls also provide a stable mounting position for range equipment. Stalls are typically equipped with a self-controlled target retrieval system. A stall width between 42 inches and 48 inches is suggested.

Shooting stalls are typically constructed of double-wall steel liners covered in a molded shell. While steel has been the industry standard, a new clear acrylic stall is becoming more popular. The acrylic stall is very popular in academic shooting ranges because of the unobstructed view the clear dividers provide range personnel.

Wall Construction

Range walls provide a protective shell between the interior of the range and the building exterior or adjacent spaces. In addition to their safety function, walls play an

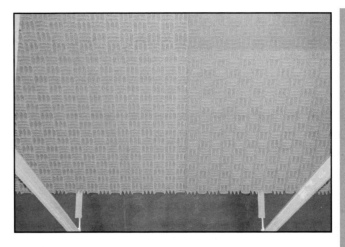

Back wall padding for shooting range.

important role in noise attenuation. Most range walls are constructed of poured concrete. Concrete block is also acceptable; however, the block should be filled with grout or cement. Unfilled block is sufficient in ballistic security but has poor sound-dampening qualities. Sound-dampening tiles are recommended for the walls from an area 10 feet forward of the firing line to 20 feet in front of the bullet trap.

Flooring

The flooring in shooting ranges needs to be durable enough to withstand the high volume of stray shots that will strike it and smooth enough to prevent erratic ricochets. Most ranges utilize a hardened concrete floor. A common mistake that is made in range construction is to include floor drains. Excluding floor drains and sloped floors in the

Absorbent material behind padding for back wall of shooting range.

shooting area is recommended. Environmental regulations stipulate that all floor drains located between the firing line and the bullet trap must contain filtration systems. These systems tend to be very expensive and require substantial maintenance.

The flooring from the firing line backwards should be covered with a non-slip surface. Moderate traction in these areas is suggested to prevent shooters from losing their footing. Many ranges have a vinyl floor cover in this area to prevent slippage.

Bullet Traps

Bullet traps have evolved substantially over the past 50 years. Environmental standards, particularly during the 1980s, have changed to accommodate environmental and safety concerns, but the object of the bullet trap has remained constant. The goal of any

Shooting stalls for shooters.

bullet trap is to provide a means of decelerating the bullet into a collection chamber. A brief description of the plate and pit trap, venetian blind trap, steel escalator trap, and the grandular rubber trap is provided below:

- Plate and pit trap—The first widely accepted bullet traps utilized a steel plate that was secured, at an angle, into a deceleration chamber. The bullet would strike the angled plate and break apart inside the chamber. While this method accomplished its purpose, it raised environmental concerns due to the generation of lead fragments and lead dust that accompanied a destroyed bullet. Other concerns with this type of trap include high noise levels from bullets striking steel, as well as erratic ricochets.

- Venetian blind trap—The first widely accepted improvement to the plate and pit trap was the venetian blind trap. The trap utilized a series of angled impact plates to direct bullets into a deceleration chamber. The bullet's velocity and energy is dissipated via friction. Typically this trap was a small freestanding trap, making it a popular model for shooting ranges.
- Steel escalator trap—The next evolution of bullet traps improved on the problem of bullets hitting the front edges of the venetian trap. This improvement was accomplished by designing a sloping plate that directed bullets into a deceleration chamber.
- Granular rubber trap—The latest development in high-tech, environmentally sound bullet traps is the granular rubber trap. This trap is constructed with an inclined skeleton of steel that supports a sloped mound of granulated rubber covered with a rubber blanket for containment. This design provides excellent sound attenuation as the bullets strike only rubber. Lead recovery is also simple and safer because the bullets are not destroyed upon impact. Bullets are decelerated and contained in the top 10 inches of the granulated rubber. Erratic ricochets resulting from hitting the trap itself are no longer a problem.

Range Lighting

Shooting range illumination entails general facility brightness and target specific lighting. Fluorescent fixtures typically generate general illumination. A soft light is preferable for general areas of the range. Target-specific lights need to be much brighter and have the ability to be moved to achieve a direct focus on a target. The industry standard in target lighting is two 150-watt lamps directed at each target face. These spotlights are typically mounted on the ceiling and surrounded by baffling and protective guards. Many shooting experts, however, prefer recessed floor spotlights. Shadowing is typically less of a problem with bottom-illuminated targets. It is important to have protective covers for floor lighting, since stray shots often strike the floor of a range.

Target Retrieval Systems

The purpose of a target retrieval system is to place the target downrange and retrieve it in a safe and convenient manner. Target retrieval systems allow the shooter to remain behind the firing line. The type of shooting that will be conducted in the range determines the type of retrieval system needed. Most target shooting consists of firing at a stationary bull's-eye target at predetermined distances and then retrieving the target to determine shooting accuracy. Two types of target retrieval systems are commonly used for this purpose, a guide wire system and a steel track system. These retrieval systems have the following features:

Communication equipment and target control.

- Guide wire system—This system utilizes a guide wire that is suspended between the bullet trap and the firing line. A target attachment travels along the tight guide wire to place the target downrange or for retrieval. The shooter typically controls the target's movement along the guide wire via a control switch located in the shooting stall. Many models of guide wire systems allow for intermediate target stops for various shooting distances. One limitation of all guide wire systems is that they do not accommodate any target oscillation.
- Steel track system—A steel track system is the most common target retrieval choice in commercial and law enforcement facilities. In addition to providing shooters with multiple stops, these systems offer 180-degree turning targets to present tactical situations. A steel track runs along the length of the shooting lane, providing the support structure for an oscillating target system.

Range Control

There are a variety of range control systems on the market, each with unique features. All of these systems, however, serve as the command center for target placement and retrieval. Some systems are controlled from the shooting stall while others utilize a central control booth. The level of sophistication and the capabilities of a control system are dependent upon the type of target system being used and the type of shooting desired.

High school and collegiate ranges typically only require a basic system that is controlled at the shooting stall. These systems contain a forward and reverse toggle switch for target placement as well as a rangemaster call intercom.

A computer-based control center is often utilized in military and law enforcement facilities. These systems offer sophisticated options for tactical training. Training scenarios can be created and downloaded into individual shooting stall systems to provide a personalized shooting session.

Range Ventilation

Exposure to lead in a shooting facility is a major concern for all range planners. Lead, when absorbed into the body in certain doses, can be toxic. When a gun is fired, lead dust and fumes are released. The amount of lead dust in the air is greatly increased in a range that uses steel bullet traps. When a bullet strikes a steel plate, it is destroyed, sending lead fragments and dust into the air.

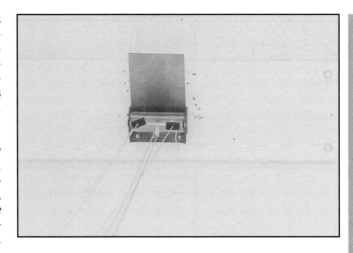

Target pulley with cables.

Federal and state health standards regarding permissible exposure to lead (PEL) must be adhered to when developing an indoor range. Ventilation systems should provide airflow from the firing line toward the bullet trap. Exhaust points should be located downrange from the shooter. Heating, ventilating, and air-conditioning (HVAC) systems are especially important in shooting facilities; therefore, shooting facility planners should enlist the services of an experienced HVAC engineer to ensure the ventilation system meets all safety and government standards.

As industry, state, and federal standards continue to tighten, the need to include a state-of-the-art ventilation system increases. Typically, a ventilation system is a large portion of shooting facility development costs. Professional developers recommend spending the money for a highly efficient and effective system rather than one that only meets minimum requirements. This may prevent the need to do a costly upgrade to meet governmental standards in the future.

The Occupational Safety and Health Administration (OSHA) established a PEL limit of 0.05 milligrams per cubic meter of air that is based on an eight-hour time weighted average. More information regarding permissible exposure to lead can be found in the National Institute of Occupational Safety and Health (NIOSH) publication 76-130.

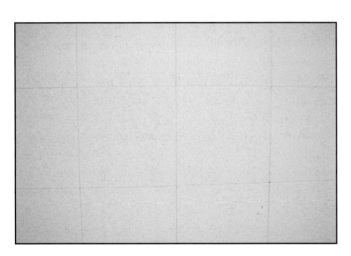

Sound-proofing for shooting range.

Ballistic Security

Range designers must be cognizant of potential ricochet threats and stray shots that may occur in a range. Misdirected shots can be extremely dangerous if protrusions in the range are not covered with protective baffling and guards. The three primary types of ballistic security used in indoor ranges include re-directive guards, air-space baffles, and steel guards. Each of these security devices has a particular function in the range.

Steel guards are most often used in facilities that have slab ceilings. These guards are positioned in a manner that directs any impact toward the bullet trap. Steel guards should be used to protect all protruding light fixtures and duct work.

Re-directive guards serve the purpose of deflecting stray shots in the direction of the bullet trap. These guards are typically located just in front of the bullet trap, as they are the guards that receive the greatest percentage of stray shots. Their composition should match the composition of the bullet trap. Steel bullet traps should utilize steel re-directive guards and rubber air-space guards should be earmarked for rubber traps.

Air-space baffles are a critical safety buffer for indoor ranges. These horizontally suspended panels reduce the risk of injury resulting from a vertically discharged shot by trapping the round in the panel. These baffles are constructed with a thin layer of rubber that is separated from a steel plate. A misfired shot passes through the rubber surface and strikes the steel plate. After striking the steel plate the bullet bounces back across the air space and re-strikes the rubber face. The baffle decelerates the bullet to where it no longer has the velocity to exit the baffle. The bullet is therefore trapped inside the air space. The danger zone for vertical shots extends from the firing line to 15 feet downrange. Air-space baffles should be hung at regular intervals for the first 15 feet and then where needed to protect protruding objects. Baffles should be installed with a 30-degree angle in relation to the floor.

Summary

The basic equipment needed to conduct an archery program is a bow, some arrows, and a target. FITA and the NAA have clearly established standards for archery equipment, archery ranges, and the conduct of competitions. If a competitive archery program or facility is desired, these standards should be followed. If a less formal program is desired, one that is more recreational or instructional, the FITA and NAA standards need not be followed, but they still provide sound general guidelines for archery programs at any level. No matter what type of archery program or facility is established, safety is paramount. A bow and arrow is a weapon and if mishandled could cause a serious injury or death. Archery program managers, administrators, and teachers must carefully analyze and manage risks.

Section

VI

Trends

Chapter 34

Trends in Stadium and Arena Design

Todd L. Seidler and John J. Miller

This chapter will present an overview and analysis of certain recent trends and innovations in stadium and arena design. It is by no means a complete look at these unique sports facilities; many additional trends and innovations are covered in other parts of this book. This chapter will merely try to highlight certain significant trends and concepts that should not be overlooked.

Learning Objectives

After reading this chapter, the student should be able to

- understand the importance of using luxury suites, naming rights, and personal seating licenses for maximizing revenue from spectator facilities;
- identify the new arena design features intended to speed the change-over from one event to another;
- be familiar with the concept of the retractable roof stadium and understand its advantages;
- identify the three main types of fabric structures and list the advantages and disadvantages of each; and
- identify the advantages of wooden domes.

Funding Arenas and Stadiums

Building stadiums and arenas today can be tremendously expensive, often running into the hundreds of millions of dollars. Of major concern to the owners of these facilities is the concept of maximizing the revenue generating potential (See Chapter 7). One of the most significant trends in revenue generation and financing of stadiums and arenas is the selling or leasing of luxury suites, personal seating licenses, and the naming rights to the facility.

Luxury Suites

One of the most dynamic trends that developed in the design of spectator sports facilities is the inclusion of luxury suites in professional as well as intercollegiate arenas and stadiums. Additionally, suites are now found at rodeo arenas; PGA, LPGA and Senior PGA events; the Kentucky Derby; the U.S. Olympic track and field trials; and ATP Tour tournaments, among others. This popularity may be traced to luxury suites becoming a significant tactic to take full advantage of cash flow per seat in most stadium construction projects (Howard & Crompton, 1995). In 1997, Funk estimated that the 114 teams belonging to the four major leagues (Major League Baseball, the National Football League, the National Basketball Association, and the National Hockey League) realized nearly $1 billion from luxury suite revenues.

This incredible increase in revenue can make a big difference in the profitability of an organization and can provide a huge competitive advantage over other organizations that do not have it. It also has become an essential part of the equation for financing a new facility. Thus, not only are luxury suites a design issue, but they are becoming of primary importance for any sports organization aspiring to maximize revenue.

Luxury suites are small, private rooms opening toward the court or field that are usually leased to individuals or companies who desire a semiprivate lounge area, typically large enough to accommodate 12 to 20 guests. Suites are normally leased on multiyear contracts and are often furnished and decorated by the tenant. The prevalence of these luxury suites is growing rapidly, primarily because they are such good revenue producers. Originally referred to as "skyboxes," luxury suites have become a foremost feature of the majority of new stadiums and arenas constructed since the early 1990s (Heistand, 1999). The Houston Astrodome is generally recognized as being the pioneer facility to include luxury suites in sports venues in the late 1960s (Fischer & Ozanian, 1999). However, while the inclusion of luxury suites is an acceptable, almost mandatory, feature of a spectator sports facility today, its revenue potential did not become fully recognized for 20 years (Heistand, 1999).

The impetus for the luxury suite trend was the tremendous success of The Palace at Auburn Hills in Detroit and Joe Robbie Stadium, now referred to as Pro Player, in Miami (Howard & Crompton, 2004). The Palace of Auburn Hills is a good example of how important suites have become to the economics of this type of facility. The original plans called for 100 luxury suites to be built as part of the arena. About one-third of the way through construction, all 100 suites had already been leased. Some quick design changes by the architect produced an additional upper ring of 80 suites, which were also leased by the time The Palace opened. Total construction cost for The Palace was about $70 million. The income from the lease of the suites alone was almost $12 million per year, which allowed for an unheard of six-year payoff (Howard & Crompton, 2004).

As for the Miami Dolphins, they took in gross revenues of nearly $20 million annually from the 216 luxury suites in their stadium. This amount equaled more than 50% of the entire team's 1990 gross revenues (Howard & Crompton, 2004).

The financial impact of luxury suites may be exemplified by the Dallas Cowboys who constructed 360 luxury suites which produced more than $23 million annually in potential revenue in the early 1990s (Gorman & Calhoun, & Rozin, 1994). Then, later in the 1990s, they increased the number of luxury suites to 398 which grossed about $29 million per year (Fischer & Ozanian, 1999). The Cleveland Browns' move to Baltimore was based on the assurance of a publicly funded stadium containing 108 luxury boxes that would be leased for between $55,000 and $200,000. As a result the Baltimore Ravens (formerly the Cleveland Browns) anticipated earning about $11 million annually from suite leases at the brand new Raven Stadium.

Professional sports teams are not alone in reaping the benefits of luxury suite sales. Despite uncertain economic times and criticism from university circles, major colleges around the country are constructing sports facilities at a tremendously fast pace primarily due to luxury suite income potential. It has been estimated that universities will invest between $800 million and $1 billion for new athletic facilities in the five-year period between 1999 and 2005 (Garbarino & Johnson, 1999). For example, Auburn University incorporated 71 executive suites into the football stadium renovation. This allowed Auburn University to entirely balance the $1-million-plus yearly debt created by the expansion. Once the facility construction debt is totally repaid, Auburn will realize an annual profit of close to $1.8 million (Simers & Wharton, 1999). Other prominent university facilities that have used proceeds from luxury suites for construction cost repayment include the University of Oregon's Autzen Stadium, the University of Texas's Darrel K. Royal Memorial Stadium, the University of Michigan's "Big House," Virginia Tech's Lane Stadium, and Texas Tech's Jones/SBC Stadium. Luxury suites have become a significant design feature and not only make the construction of future arenas and stadiums more economically feasible, but are becoming a necessity for many sports organizations to remain financially competitive.

Naming Rights

As with luxury suites, selling the naming rights of sports facilities has gained recent importance in sports facility construction. Naming rights deals are agreements made between stadium owners and large corporations that permit the sponsor to connect a brand name or logo to a stadium for a given period of time. The first naming rights agreement occurred in 1971 when the New England Patriots agreed to have the Schaefer Brewing Company pay $150,000 to rename Patriots Stadium, Schaefer Field. In 1973, the Buffalo Bills signed a 20-year agreement with a frozen food supplier, Rich Products, to rename War Memorial Stadium, Rich Stadium.

Between 1995 through 2000, the number and financial magnitude of sports facility naming rights grew dramatically. A primary reason for this escalation was due to the increased number of new sporting venues that were built in the late 1990s. For example, the period 1991 to 1995 had eight stadium or arena openings compared to a total of eight in the previous 15 year period between 1976 to 1990 (Waterman, 2002). In 1997, one third (41 of 113) of the sports stadiums or arenas used by teams in the NFL, NBA, NHL, or Major League Baseball had been named for corporations; however, by 2002, 80 of 121 teams were competing in sports venues that were named after large corporations (Waterman, 2002). According to a businessman who specializes in naming rights agreements there were three naming rights deals in professional sports totaling $25 million in 1988 (Maher, 2003). Presently, there are 69 pro teams, with anticipated significant increase of intercollegiate teams, who have naming rights deals that total in excess of $3.5 billion (Maher, 2003). Thus, this new strategy was implemented as a way of helping to ease the financial burden of stadium or arena construction.

On the next page are the names, naming rights sponsor, the name of the team, the average per year that the sponsor pays for the naming rights and the year the agreement will end for 69 professional teams associated with the four major leagues. The cost of naming rights for the professional teams listed on the next page ranges from $620,000 per year (Alltel Stadium) to $10 million per year (Reliant Stadium).

Stadium Name	Sponsor	Home Teams	Avg. $/Year	Expires
Air Canada Centre	Air Canada	Toronto Maple Leafs, Raptors	$1.5 million	2019
Alltel Stadium	Alltel Corp.	Jacksonville Jaguars	$620,000	2007
American Airlines Arena	American Airlines	Miami Heat	$2.1 million	2019
American Airlines Center	American Airlines	Dallas Mavericks, Stars	$6.5 million	2031
America West Arena	America West	Phoenix Suns, Coyotes, Mercury	$866,667	2019
Arco Arena	Atlantic Richfield	Sacramento Kings, Monarchs	$750,000	2007
Bank of America Stadium	Bank of America	Carolina Panthers	$7 million	2024
Bank One Ballpark	Bank One	Arizona Diamondbacks	$2.2 million	2028
Bell Centre	Bell Canada	Montreal Canadiens	N/A	N/A
Cinergy Field	Cinergy	Cincinnati Reds	$1 million	2002
Citizens Bank Park	Citizens Bank	Philadelphia Phillies	$2.3 million	2028
Comerica Park	Comerica	Detroit Tigers	$2.2 million	2030
Compaq Center	Compaq Computer	Houston Rockets, Comets,	$900,000	2003
Compaq Center at San Jose	Compaq Computer	San Jose Sharks	$3.1 million	2016
Conseco Fieldhouse	Conseco	Indiana Pacers, Fever	$2 million	2019
Continental Airlines Arena	Continental Airlines	New Jersey Nets, Devils	$1.4 million	2011
Coors Field	Coors Brewing	Colorado Rockies	N/A	INDEFINITE
Corel Center	Corel	Ottawa Senators	$878,142	2016
Delta Center	Delta Airlines	Utah Jazz, Starzz	$1.3 million	2011
Edison International Field	Edison Intl.	Los Angeles Angels	$2.5 million	2018
Edward Jones Dome	Edward Jones	St. Louis Rams	$2.65 million	2013
FedEx Field	Federal Express	Washington Redskins	$7.6 million	2025
FedEx Forum	Federal Express	Memphis Grizzlies	$4.5 million	2023
Wachovia Center	Wachovia Bank	Philadelphia 76ers, Flyers	$1.4 million	2023
Fleetcenter	Fleet Bank	Boston Celtics, Bruins	$2 million	2010
Ford Field	Ford Motor Co.	Detroit Lions	$1 million	2042
Gaylord Entertainment Center	Gaylord Entertainment	Nashville Predators	$4 million	2018
General Motors Place	General Motors	Vancouver Canucks	$844,366	2015
Gillette Stadium	Gillette	New England Patriots	N/A	2017
Great American Ball Park	Great American Insurance	Cincinnati Reds	$2.5 million	2033
Gund Arena	Owners	Cleveland Cavs, Rockers	$700,000	2014
Heinz Field	H.J. Heinz	Pittsburgh Steelers	$2.9 million	2021
HSBC Arena	HSBC Bank	Buffalo Sabres	$800,000	2026
Invesco Field at Mile High	Invesco Funds	Denver Broncos	$6 million	2021
Jacobs Field	Richard Jacobs	Cleveland Indians	$695,000	2014
KeyArena	Key Corp.	Seattle Supersonics, Storm	$1 million	2010
Lincoln Financial Field	Lincoln Financial Group	Philadelphia Eagles	$6.7 million	2022
M & T Bank Stadium	M & T Bank	Baltimore Ravens	$5 million	2018
MCI Center	MCI	Wash. Wizards, Caps, Mystics	$2.2 million	2017
Mellon Arena	Mellon Financial	Pittsburgh Penguins	$1.8 million	2009
Miller Park	Miller Brewing	Milwaukee Brewers	$2.1 million	2020
Minute Maid Park	Coca Cola	Houston Astros	$6 million	2030
Nationwide Arena	Nationwide Insurance	Columbus BlueJackets	N/A	INDEFINITE
Network Associates Coliseum	Network Associates	Oakland A's	$1.2 million	2003
Office Depot Center	Office Depot	Florida Panthers	$1.4 million	2013
Pacific Bell Park	Pacific Telesis	San Francisco Giants	$2.1 million	2024
Pengrowth Saddledome	Pengrowth Mgmt.	Calgary Flames	$1 million	2016
Pepsi Center	PepsiCo	Denver Nuggets, Colorado Avalanche	$3.4 million	2019
Phillips Arena	Royal Phillips Electronics	Atlanta Hawks, Thrashers	$9.3 million	2019
PNC Park	PNC Bank	Pittsburgh Pirates	$2 million	2020
Pro Player Stadium	Fruit of the Loom	Miami Dolphins, Florida Marlins	COMPANY BANKRUPT	N/A
Qualcomm Stadium	Qualcomm	San Diego Padres, Chargers	$900,000	2017

continued

Stadium Name	Sponsor	Home Teams	Avg. $/Year	Expires
Raymond James Stadium	Raymond James Financial	Tampa Bay Buccaneers	$3.1 million	2026
RBC Center	RBC Centura Banks	Carolina Hurricanes	$4 million	2022
RCA Dome	RCA	Indianapolis Colts	$1 million	2004
Reliant Stadium	Reliant Energy	Houston Texans	$10 million	2032
Rexall Place	Katz Group	Edmonton Oilers	N/A	2013
Safeco Field	Safeco Corp.	Seattle Mariners	$2 million	2019
Savvis Center	Savvis Communications	St. Louis Blues	N/A	INDEFINITE
SBC Center	SBC Communications	San Antonio Spurs	$2.1 million	2022
Staples Center	Staples	Los Angeles Lakers, Kings, Clippers, Sparks	$5.8 million	2019
St. Pete Times Forum	St. Petersburg Times	Tampa Bay Lightning	$2.1 million	2014
Target Center	Target	Minnesota Timberwolves, Lynx	$1.3 million	2005
TD Waterhouse Centre	TD Waterhouse Group	Orlando Magic, Miracle	$1.6 million	2003
Toyota Center	Toyota	Houston Rockets	N/A	N/A
Tropicana Field	Tropicana	Tampa Bay Devil Rays	$1.5 million	2026
United Center	United Airlines	Chicago Blackhawks, Bulls	$1.8 million	2014
U.S. Cellular Field	U.S. Cellular	Chicago White Sox	$3.4 million	2025
Xcel Energy Center	Xcel Energy	Minnesota Wild	$3 million	2024

Source: ESPN.com (Sports Business, 2004).

Three reasons have been identified as to why the Houston Texans were able to command $10 million per year. First, for the next three decades, not only will Reliant Stadium be the home of the Texans, each of three other facilities at the complex will bear the Reliant name. Reliant Park, as the Astrodome complex was renamed, consists of Reliant Stadium, Reliant Astrodome, Reliant Arena (formerly the AstroArena), and Reliant Center, a 1.4 million-square-foot exhibition center. Secondly, the 69,500-seat, retractable-roof stadium also annually holds the Houston Livestock Show and Rodeo, which attracts two million visitors during its two weeks of operation. Third, the stadium recently hosted the 2004 Super Bowl and is expected to become a part of the Super Bowl rotation. These value-added aspects significantly played an important part in Reliant's motivation to invest a large amount of money for the naming rights. The $10 million per year that Reliant Energy will pay breaks down in the following fashion: the Houston Texans NFL team will receive $7.5 million (75%), the Houston Livestock Show and Rodeo approximately $1.5 million (15%) and Harris County about $1 million (10%) annually until the agreement expires in 2032. Thus, the naming rights for Reliant Stadium will benefit not only the Texans, but also the Rodeo and the county as well in paying off the arena.

While naming-rights deals have become commonplace in professional sports, the trend has recently been seen in intercollegiate athletics. For many years, universities named buildings after munificent donors and prominent alumni. At the time of this writing, about a dozen have sold naming rights to major corporations. For example, Comcast Corporation has a $25 million, 25-year deal to have its name on the Terrapins' new arena in College Park at the University of Maryland (Weinberg, 2003). At Texas Tech University, SBC Communications is paying $20 million over 20 years to have its name on Jones SBC Stadium and United Supermarkets has a $10 million, 20-year naming rights deal for the United Spirit Arena, where the Texas Tech basketball teams play (Maher, 2003). The Ohio State University plays its basketball games at the Value City Arena, the result of a $12.5 million naming-rights deal with a discount department store chain. While these institutions possess impressive naming rights agreements, the largest intercollegiate deal to date has been a $40 million, 20-year deal for the Save Mart Center at Fresno State University. Most recently, the University of Memphis announced that the naming rights for the athletic director as well as the office of Memphis head basketball coach John Calipari had been sold for $100,000 (Tiger Athletics, 2004). As a result, collegiate sports are going to "be the next frontier." The only concerns are which schools are going to be first and how much will they receive (Maher, 2003).

It has been estimated that 80% of new stadiums or arenas will be named after a corporation in the near future (Brenner, 1999). As the prices of sports venues increase new sources of income must be recognized and used to the maximum that the market will bear. Therefore, the importance of naming rights to raise revenue to pay for sports stadiums and arenas will undoubtedly continue, if not increase in the future.

Personal Seating Licenses (PSL's)

A third revenue trend that developed significantly in the 1990s was the concept of personal or permanent seating licenses (PSLs). Personal seating licenses are to individuals what luxury suites are to corporations (Yeomans, 2001). They have been primarily associated with new facility construction and are used to assist in financing plans (Irwin, Sutton, & McCarthy, 2002). PSLs have given athletic organizations a tremendous benefit since they provide the opportunity to pre-sell seats in advance of the actual construction or renovation of the sports facility. This ensures that the organization responsible for the financing of the facility will not have to borrow as much (Irwin, Sutton, & McCarthy, 2002). Typically, PSLs allow the purchaser the right to buy season tickets in special seating areas such as club seats. Club seats are typically larger, more comfortable and have more leg room than regular seating. Also, they usually include special considerations such as a waitstaff who take orders and deliver food right to the seat and possibly access to certain restaurants or lounges.

First identified by the Dallas Cowboys in 1968, the concept of PSLs did not gain wide-spread recognition until the Carolina Panthers implemented a highly successful campaign in 1993. Using PSLs the Panthers were able to raise $125 million prior to playing in the National Football League. By 2002, nearly 30 professional, intercollegiate, and racecar speedways had adopted the PSLs concept (Howard & Crompton, 2004). For example, the Chicago Bears were able to raise approximately $60 million for 27,500 personal seating licenses to help pay for the recently completed renovation of Soldier Field. As stated earlier, other examples of the PSLs trend are not only limited to professional sports. The Ohio State University recently raised about $20 million from the sale of licensed seating in its new basketball arena while Texas Motor Speedway sold 30,000 PSLs generate $27.5 million of the $110 million construction costs.

It is important to note that the trend of PSLs is not without controversy. Because some critics have accused sports organizations of holding ticket holders "hostage" by forcing them to pay large upfront fees, some sports organizations such as the Pittsburgh Steelers have changed the PSL acronym to SBL (stadium builder licenses). This strongly expresses to the ticketholder that the money raised through personal license sales is going directly to construction of the stadium rather than to owners' pockets. Thus, whereas the corporate support and willingness to pay relative high prices for luxury suites and naming rights exists, the trend of PSLs, while an important component for paying for a sports facility, seems to be in an evolutionary, consumer-friendly stage.

Designing for Entertainment and Quick Changeover

The fundamental purpose and design of stadiums and arenas has changed radically in the last decade. These changes are so dramatic that many facilities have become obsolete, and even young ones 10 to 20 years old are facing the wrecking ball. The basic idea behind this change is that modern arenas and stadiums are no longer just places to watch an event, but are now designed to provide a total entertainment experience and optimally host as many different events as possible.

In order to maximize return on such a large investment as a stadium or arena, every effort must be made to ensure that the facility is able to accommodate as many events and different kinds of activities and generate as much revenue as possible. Recent trends include design features that allow a facility to change over from one event to another as quickly as possible. Whereas some older facilities would rely on 6 to 10 football games or 30 basketball games per year as their main source of revenue, some facilities now schedule from 250 to 600 events per year, including such varied activities as basketball, soccer, hockey, arena football, concerts, conventions, trade shows, rodeos, monster truck shows, and professional wrestling. It is not uncommon for older facilities to require up to a full day for a crew to change the setup from one event to another, whereas a well-designed facility can be transformed in a matter of hours. Not only can this provide significant cost savings in manpower, but also often means that more than one event can take place in the same day. Several aspects of design that allow a facility to accommodate a wide variety of events and also to quickly alter the setup for different events include:

- Versatile lighting and sound systems that are designed to adequately handle the wide variety of events.
- Heavy-duty lighting grids that can be lowered to the floor in order to enhance the placement of sound and lighting equipment for concerts.
- Loading ramps that allow semi-trucks to back all the way onto the floor. Even better, some facilities provide floor access for two or more trucks at a time so that one can be loading after a show while another is unloading for the next.
- Versatile, moveable sections of seats that can quickly change the configuration of a facility.
- Fixed, pre-wired camera positions that allow for quick and easy set-up for television broadcasts. Many new arenas are constructed with a full television production studio, which permits a television network to broadcast a game without bringing in their semi-trucks full of production equipment.
- Computerized curtain systems that can quickly change the layout and size of the facility.

Many sport organizations have made a shift in their fundamental mission and have gone from primarily trying to put a winning team on the court/field to providing a great family entertainment experience. This change in thinking has led to many design changes in the arenas and stadiums being constructed today. In general, this has caused a move toward more upscale facilities with greater service, entertainment and convenience for spectators. Some aspects of this trend include the following:

- Providing more restrooms, especially for women. In the past, many spectator facilities provided only enough restrooms to satisfy the local code requirements. This often resulted in long lines and frustration on the part of spectators. Many facilities are now being designed with more than twice as many restrooms as the minimum required. Since some events may draw a disproportionate number of men or women, consideration should be given to designing some rest rooms that can serve either gender simply by changing the sign on the door. Family restrooms are also becoming common in new stadiums and arenas.

- Taking into consideration the requirements of customers with disabilities. With the advent of the Americans With Disabilities Act, full accommodation of the needs of people with disabilities is now federal law. Recent lawsuits have established new standards for the placement of handicapped seating. All wheelchair-accessible seats should now be located so that users can see over the heads of the spectators in front of them even when the spectators stand.

- Building larger concourse areas and adding separate concourses to serve different levels. Improved access and less crowding make these areas more attractive. Some concourse areas are being designed to resemble a mini-mall by offering many different choices of food, novelty items, and entertainment opportunities. Some concession areas are designed so that customers standing in line still have a direct view of the field while others place closed-circuit televisions so that patrons will not miss the action while spending their money. Opportunities for amusement are becoming more common. These include things such as batting cages, merry-go-rounds, museums, and many types of electronic games. Many facilities strive to provide the atmosphere of an amusement park.

- Improving pedestrian traffic flow into, out of, and within the facility. People do not enjoy standing in long lines. This can be accomplished by providing more entrances/exits, as well as wider and more stairways and escalators.

Innovations in Materials and Methods of Construction

Recent innovations in the methods of enclosing large areas without support pillars and posts that interfere with spectator sight lines are providing many more options for the construction of stadiums and arenas. Stadiums with retractable roofs, tension fabric structures, air-supported fabric structures, cable domes, and wooden domes are examples of building designs that have been successfully used to enclose large sports facilities.

Retractable Roof Stadiums

One of the biggest innovations in stadium design is the concept of having a stadium that is open to the elements when the weather is nice but can be quickly covered when needed. The first attempt at a retractable roof stadium was Olympic Stadium in Montreal, built for the 1976 Olympic Games. The original plan was to build a huge concrete mast next to the stadium that would support a fabric roof supported by steel cables. The roof was supposed to have the ability to be lifted off the stadium and suspended from the mast, thereby creating an open-air stadium (Holleman, 1996). The roof could then be lowered back on top of the stadium to enclose it again when desired.

The design never has worked correctly, but this ambitious idea eventually led to the successful designs we are seeing today. It is estimated that adding a retractable roof to the design of a new stadium will increase the cost between $40 and $90 million.

Some examples of retractable roof stadiums are:

- SkyDome—Located in Toronto, Ontario, SkyDome was the first stadium to have a fully retractable roof. Opened in 1989, SkyDome can completely open or close the entire steel-trussed roof in 20 minutes. This is accomplished by three movable roof sections, two of which slide and another that rotates. The stadium seats 50,600 for baseball, 53,000 for football, and has different seating arrangements for concerts ranging from 10,000 to 70,000. It also contains 161 luxury suites, a 348-room hotel and health club, full broadcast facilities, underground parking, and a 110-foot-by-33-foot state-of-the-art video screen. Original estimates of the cost for

Photo courtesy of Ellerbe Becket
Toronto Skydome.

SkyDome were $184 million (Canadian) but it ended up costing about $585 million. Typically, the roof only has to be closed for about four or five games a season due to inclement weather (Gordon, 1990).

- Bank One Ballpark (BOB)— Opened for the 1998 season, BOB is the home of the Arizona Diamondbacks. Located in downtown Phoenix, it was the first retractable-roof stadium to be built since SkyDome. This air-conditioned, retractable-roof stadium is designed primarily for baseball and seats 48,500. It has a natural grass field and was built for a cost of $349 million with 68% coming from public financing. With a total of 69 private suites, 6 party suites and 5,592 club seats, there is something for everybody, including 350 bleacher seats that are sold for $1 per game. As with many of the new stadiums, it is more than just a

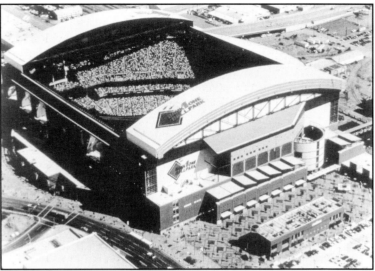

Photo courtesy of Ellerve Becket

Bank One Ballpark.

place to watch a ballgame. BOB contains two micro-breweries and two 10,000-square-foot beer gardens, a mini hall of fame fashioned after Cooperstown, a 4,000-square-foot team store, 110 picnic tables, 212 concession stands, and a swimming pool just beyond the outfield fence.

- Seattle Safeco Field—Opened in 1999, Safeco Field's retractable roof allows fans to stay dry during the rainy days of the season. While the retractable roof covers the entire ballpark, it does not enclose it, thus giving the stadium an open air feel. When opened, the roof sits above and behind the right field seats. There are many amenities at Safeco Field. There are three panels that glide on 128 steel wheels powered by almost 100 ten-horsepower electric motors. When fully extended, the roof encompasses almost nine acres in size and weighs 22 million pounds, yet, at the push of a button can close or open in 10 to 20 minutes depending on wind and other weather conditions. For protection against lightning the roof is self-grounded and is planned to hold up under six or seven feet of snow as well as winds of up to 70 miles per hour.

- Minute Maid Field—Originally named Enron Field, it was completed in time for the 2000 baseball season. In 2001, Enron declared bankruptcy and the naming rights were sold to the Minute Maid Company for an estimated $170 million for 28 years. Built for a relatively inexpensive $248 million, it seats approximately 42,000 and has a fully retractable steel roof. The roof covers 6.25 acres when closed and is made up of three moveable sections that can be opened in less than 20 minutes. The moving roof panels contain over 5,000 tons of steel as well as an acre of glass to allow for spectacular views even when the roof is closed. Also, the roof has been designed to withstand hurricane force winds. Special amenities within the stadium include a kid's play area, batting cages, more than 60 private suites and 4,850 club seats, a café, retail space, and even a 65,000-pound, full-size locomotive that moves along an 800-foot section of track after game highlights. The new stadiums are meant to provide a quality entertainment experience, not just a place to watch a game.

- Milwaukee Miller Park—Miller Park, which opened in 2001, possesses many unique features, the most obvious one being the retractable roof. The 12,000 ton, seven panel roof has a unique fan shape design. The moveable roof panels pivot from a point behind home plate and go along a semicircular track beam with 60-horsepower engines. The roof can open or close in 10 minutes and sits 175 feet above second base. Miller Park has no air-conditioning, but an air -circulation system keeps the ballpark comfortable when the roof is closed. The roof is able to withstand snow drifts of up to 12 feet.

- Reliant Stadium—The new 1.9-million-square-foot facility opened in August 2002 as the NFL's first retractable roof venue. It is also home to the largest rodeo in the world, the Houston Livestock Show and Rodeo and was built at a cost of $417 million. The roof is composed of two translucent Teflon-coated fiberglass fabric panels, which separate at the 50-yard line, slide on tracks, and rest over each end zone. It can open or close in just 7 to 10 minutes, depending on wind conditions. The super-trusses used to support the retractable roof transport system are 84 feet tall and 12 feet wide and weigh 3,750 tons (equivalent to the weight of more than 1,000 cars). The retractable panels move in opposite directions, similar to the Arizona Diamondbacks' Bank One Ballpark's roof but unlike the two moving panels at Houston's Minute Maid and Seattle's Safeco Field, which travel in the same direction. Miller Park in Milwaukee also has two moving panels, but they retract in a fan-shaped pattern. Even though Reliant Stadium's roof weighs an estimated 2,000 tons, high winds can create havoc. To counteract this, operable clamps hold the roof in place stabilize it.

- Arizona Cardinals Stadium—Construction of the Cardinals' stadium began in July 2003. Originally expected to be completed in time for the 2005 NFL season, it is now anticipated that the stadium will open in August 2006 at a cost of $355 million. Once completed, the facility will become the second NFL stadium to have a retractable roof. The roof will consist of two large panels that retract to uncover the entire playing field and has been designed to provide a balance of sun on the field and shade in the seats. An additional innovation will be a natural grass field contained on a moveable, 12-million-pound tray 234 feet wide by 400 feet long. The entire field will roll outside of the facility where the grass will absorb sunlight and receive nourishment, maintenance, and grooming. The facility will seat up to 73,000 with 7,000 club seats and 88 luxury suites.

Other professional teams that have stadium plans that will include a retractable roof are the Dallas Cowboys, New Orleans Saints, New York Jets, Minnesota Vikings, Minnesota Twins, New York Yankees, and the New York Mets. As of the time of this writing, several other teams are planning or considering construction of retractable-roof stadiums. It appears that the retractable-roof stadium is now coming into its own and we will probably see many new examples in the coming years.

Going "Green"

Another significant innovation of stadium and arena design will be the use of renewable and sustainable materials. The 2000 Summer Olympic Games in Sydney, Australia, exemplified the essence of going green on a global scene for sports facilities. Solar power was used for street lighting, water heating, and air conditioning. Bathing and kitchen water were treated on-site for reuse on gardens and for washing vehicles. Buildings facing north allowed for warmth in winter and cooling in summer, and there was a ban on environmentally harmful gases in insulation, refrigeration, and air-conditioning units. The 2004 Summer Olympics in Athens, Greece, followed the lead of the Sydney Games as many of the sports venues were made from materials that can be recycled after use. Additional concerns for the 2004 Summer Games that needed to be addressed by implementing green tactics was the potential of damaging the ancient ruins surrounding the sites. By incorporating ecologically friendly sports designs, the likelihood of excessive pollution protected the invaluable, historical monuments of Greece.

In regard to North American teams following "green" facility design, the new New York Jets stadium may be referred to as a truly "green" building in the truest sense of the term. The stadium will feature renewable technologies such as wind turbines, photo-voltaic panels to generate electricity, and collector tubes that may be integrated into the facade for solar heating of domestic hot water. Other advanced technologies make certain that water conservation and recovery and ultra low energy-use systems will be included. Through these innovations the Jets intend to become the leader in developing the New York Sports & Convention Center allowing the opportunity to host big-time events ranging from the Super Bowl to World Cup soccer matches to the 2012 Olympic Games.

Formed by the Washington D.C.-based U.S. Green Building Council (USGBC), the original standards for green design were mainly developed for privately built commercial buildings. However the Leadership in Energy and Environmental Design (LEED) standards are gradually gaining the awareness of city officials due to their potential energy and environmental saving costs. Five states, Washington, Oregon, Pennsylvania, New York, and Maryland, have introduced building programs that encourage LEED certification for state buildings. Additionally, cities of sporting note (Seattle; Portland, OR; and Austin, TX) require new public buildings to obtain LEED certification. Thus, individuals in charge of planning and/or construction of public sports and recreation facilities should be conscious of the rising attractiveness of a national voluntary movement to apply stringent "green building" standards to new construction and major renovation projects.

While approximately 40 projects in the United States have gotten one of the four levels of certification offered by the building council, more than 600 additional building projects, of which 150 were municipal building projects, have indicated their intent to apply for certification by the end of last year (Hammel, 2003). However, one of the primary concerns regarding whether to incorporate LEED standards into new building construction has been cost. Energy-efficient lighting systems have a greater initial cost but often lead to significant benefits due to reduced energy consumption. Among additional significant secondary savings available in a number of communities are tax credits for the construction of buildings that are environmentally responsible. Rebate programs have also been established in some communities; in the Seattle School District, each school gets back about 90% of its energy savings to purchase needed equipment and supplies (McCarron, 2001). Another example is the recent construction of a sports and recreation facility in Boulder, Colorado. The city of Boulder anticipates being able to recover much of the initial costs through an expected 37% annual reduction in energy costs (Hammel, 2003). Additionally, the significant cost of such items as solar panels were estimated to be recouped within 12 years (Hammel, 2003).

Through the adoption of LEED standards, a sports facility may recover much of the initial cost of the building without sacrificing sustainability. A well-designed building can decrease energy usage, increase indoor air quality, and utilize open areas better. When one considers the operating cost savings over the lifetime of a sports facility, the additional up-front cost is relatively insignificant. It is apparent, given the status of our environment that green design of sports facilities is and will continue to be an innovative trend.

Trends in Indoor Playing Surfaces

Due to the increase of retractable roofs or domed stadiums there needed to be playing surfaces that required either no or minimal amounts of sunlight. At first artificial turf fields were categorized as nothing more than carpets, often laid on hard, concrete bases. These surfaces presented a sports participant extensive opportunity for injury. Often, players would suffer injuries, sometimes career-ending ones such as Michael Irvin, as a result of being slammed to the ground. In other situations the footing was too good, thereby creating the potential for ankle, knee, and groin injuries when an athlete's shoe became planted in the carpet. The danger of friction burns when players slid on the carpet with bare limbs posed an additional risk of infection if these abrasions were not treated properly.

In response to these potentially unsafe situations, innovative indoor playing surfaces have evolved to the point that players actually prefer to play on some types of artificial surfaces. Approximately 40 Division I-A schools use synthetic turf on their playing fields, according to the NCAA. The majority of colleges still play on natural grass, but the percentage of artificial fields is the highest since 1997. In fact, a 2003 NCAA report showed baseball players experienced nearly identical injury rates on synthetic and natural surfaces. The following information will highlight the improvements of playing surfaces for retractable and/or domed stadiums.

New Breed of Synthetic Turf

The last decade has seen a tremendous improvement in the design and manufacture of synthetic turfs. Many of the old concerns about higher injury rates have been alleviated. The new designs are much softer to fall on and do not produce the friction burns of the previous designs. Most participants report that conditions are more similar to those found on good natural grass fields. The new turfs are typically filled with ground-rubber particles and sometimes with sand.

Recently the National Football League Player's Association conducted a survey of playing fields. The FieldTurf surface at Seattle Stadium finished as the third most popular playing surface in the NFL (Waterman, 2003). Additionally, the new FieldTurf playing surface at the Detroit Lions Ford Field ranked as the 11th most popular playing surface (Waterman, 2003). This despite the fact that only 9 of the 32 NFL teams had the opportunity to play on it. It is important to note that both of these fields were rated ahead of many natural grass fields and that no other artificial turf field rated higher than 20th. An added feature of FieldTurf is its ability to be installed for football, markings and all, in eight hours or less. The markings can be removed in the equivalent time frame as well. Therefore, it is also entirely possible that a field conversion from football to another sport may be accomplished in even less than eight hours. This would allow a stadium to stage a soccer game or tennis matches on it one day and a football game the next without the problem of tearing up the playing field that often exists on natural grass (Waterman, 2003).

Examples of professional football teams that have recently installed FieldTurf at their game or practice facilities are the Atlanta Falcons, St. Louis Rams, Kansas City Chiefs, Houston Texans, New England Patriots, Cleveland Browns, Green Bay Packers, Seattle Seahawks, Detroit Lions, Pittsburgh Steelers, New York Giants, and New York Jets. Additionally, the Florida Marlins have, of late, elected to install FieldTurf for their fields. It has becoming evident that the FieldTurf system is becoming the preferred design choice for the National Football League and major league baseball.

Removable Natural Grass

Another turf-related option that has become a facility design issue in sports stadiums is removable natural grass. This innovative concept was first used in the Silverdome for the 1994 World Cup Soccer Tournament. A hybrid grass was developed at Michigan State University that was designed to thrive in the low levels of sunlight that could enter through the fabric roof of the Silverdome. A system of nearly 2000 interlocking pallets was computer designed and built to provide the regulation soccer field. The pallets were set up in the parking lot where the grass received plenty of sunlight. Just prior to the first game, they were hauled by trucks and forklifts into the stadium and assembled. The process took two days to complete. The field was a

Photo by Todd Seidler
Pontiac Silverdome.

success and got very good reviews. Unfortunately, it was too large an undertaking to make it feasible to move in and out of the stadium on a regular basis, so the Detroit Lions continued to play on their Astroturf field.

The idea of using a removable natural grass field was also hotly debated during the construction of Reliant Stadium, since the field would accommodate both professional football and rodeo. A palletized natural turf field was seen as the solution. It integrates portable turf units of eight feet by eight feet, including a metal drainage base. The units incorporate a growing medium that is reinforced with Reflex mesh elements (small pieces of nylon mesh) that increase field stability, aids in water and air management, and provides a forgiving (non-hard) surface for the athletes (Thompson, 2001). The turf was designed so that any unit can be replaced without affecting the unit next to it (Valentine, 2003). They can be easily replaced so as to resist extreme wear as well as the effects of extended time in shade. The field is completely removed to an outside nursery once a year while the stadium hosts the Houston Livestock Show and Rodeo. While only Reliant Stadium possesses this turf, at the time of this writing, it is quite likely that this trend will continue in the future, given the propensity for multiple-use sports facilities.

In the new Arizona Cardinals stadium, the natural grass field will be contained on a movable, 12-million-pound tray that will be 234 feet wide by 400 feet long. The first field of its kind in North America, the entire tray will move from the parking lot into the stadium in about 45 minutes. The tray will rest on tracks and will roll out on steel wheel sets powered by small electric motors. When not needed for games, the field will move out of the stadium so the grass will be able to absorb more sunlight.

Fabric Structures

A fairly recent development in the area of physical education, recreation, and athletic facilities is the concept of fabric structures. The fabric used most commonly is a Teflon® -coated fiberglass material. The fiberglass fabric is, pound for pound, stronger than steel and is also less expensive. It can be designed to allow either a large or very little amount of natural light to penetrate. The fabric can withstand temperatures of 1,300° to 1,500° F and is not adversely affected by cold or the ultraviolet rays of the sun. Fabric structures offer a number of potential advantages and disadvantages when compared with standard construction.

Advantages

- Lower initial cost—Initial costs are usually lower than with conventional construction. Several factors contribute to this, the primary one being weight. A fabric roof is 1/30 the weight of a conventional steel-truss roof. This reduced weight means that the walls, footings, and foundations are not required to be nearly as strong as in a conventional building.
- Less construction time—The amount of construction time is directly related to the initial cost of the structure. The total time necessary to build a fabric structure is usually less than for a conventional roof.
- Natural lighting—Since the fiberglass fabric material that is used is translucent, it results in a large amount of interior natural lighting. Without using artificial lights during the day, the light intensity inside can vary anywhere from 100 to 1,000 foot-candles, depending on weather conditions, design, and choice of fabric. The interior light is considered to be of high quality, because it is nonglare and shadow-free.
- Possibly lower energy costs—In some climates or regions, energy costs may be substantially reduced by the fabric's translucency. The large amount of natural light may reduce or eliminate the need for artificial light during the daytime. This may also reduce the need for air-conditioning required to overcome the heat generated by the artificial lights.
- Less maintenance—The nonstick characteristics of Teflon® allow the fabric to be washed clean each time it rains.
- Full utilization of space—Depending on the fabric structure's configuration and support, the area that can be enclosed is almost limitless.

Disadvantages

- Life span—The fabric envelope in use today has a life expectancy of up to 25 years, with longer-life materials being tested. All other items such as the foundation, flooring, and mechanical equipment have the life span of a conventional building.
- Poor thermal insulation—In cold climates there may be an increase in energy cost when compared with conventional construction due to lower insulating properties of the fabric roof. The insulating value of a typical fabric roof is about R-2 but can be increased substantially (see Lindsay Park Sports Centre). The cost of heating is a significant factor and should be evaluated against that for a conventional building over time. During winter months when the heat is required to melt the snow or to cause it to slide off, a safe level of temperature will have to be maintained at all times, which has an impact on heating costs. If the bubble is not to be heated during inactive hours, it will have to be supervised constantly for the dangers of unexpected snowfall. In the summertime the heat gain of the air-supported structure may pose a cooling problem.
- Acoustic problems—The curved shape of the air-supported structure produces a peculiar acoustic environment. This large reflective surface magnifies crowd noise and can create undesirable noise conditions.
- Restriction due to wind—In winds of hurricane velocity, many codes require that the fabric structure be evacuated.

There are three basic types of fabric structures in use: 1) tension structures, 2) air-supported structures, and 3) cable domes. Tension structures are made by stretching the fabric between rigid supports and/or steel cables. Air supported structures are sealed buildings that, through the use of fans, maintain a positive internal air pressure that supports the roof. These structures are actually inflated like a balloon and must maintain the positive air pressure to remain inflated. Cable domes are the newest type of fabric structure. The cable dome is actually a modified tension structure that uses a complex network of cables and supports to suspend and hold up the fabric roof.

Tension Structures

Some projects lend themselves more naturally to tension structures than to air-supported structures or cable domes. Some of the conditions in which tension structures may be more favorable are as follows:

- Free and open access from the sides is desirable or required.
- A unique design or aesthetics are of importance.
- The facility will be largely unattended or not monitored.
- Possible deflation of an air structure would constitute a severe operational or safety problem.
- A retrofit to an existing building or structure such as a swimming pool or an outdoor stadium is desired.

Some examples of tension structures are:

- Knott Athletic, Recreation & Convocation Center—Located at Mount Saint Mary's College in Emmitsburg, Maryland, the Knott Center is a unique combination of standard construction and a fabric tension structure. Completed in 1987, most of the facility is built with standard brick construction, with the tension-structure field house connected onto one side of the building. The fabric roof covers 30,000 square feet of activity space including a multiple court setup and a 10-lap-per-mile running track. Rising to a height of 40 feet, the double-layered roof allows for almost exclusive use of natural light during the day. Also included within the facility are four racquetball courts, locker rooms, and a 25-yard pool.

Photo courtesy of Bohlin Cywinski & Jackson
Photo by Matt Wargo
Knott Center—exterior.

- Lindsay Park—The Lindsay Park Sports Centre in Calgary, Alberta, Canada, houses a 50-meter pool, a diving pool, a fully equipped 30,000-square-foot gymnasium, and a 200-meter running track. The roof is unique in that it was designed with insulation that is rated at R-16. This compares with a typical fabric roof that has about an R-2 rating. Despite the great improvement in insulating qualities, the fabric roof is still translucent enough to allow for an interior illumination of about 200 foot-candles. This facility was completed in 1983.

- McClain Athletic Training Facility—Completed in 1988, this field house is located at the University of Wisconsin at Madison. Due to site restrictions, this $9.5 million facility contains a 90-yard football field instead of a full-size

Photo courtesy of Bohlin Cywinski & Jackson
Photo by Matt Wargo
Knott Center—interior.

field. Most of the field is covered by a 42,000-square-foot fabric-tension roof that admits up to 750 foot-candles of natural light into the structure. When comparing the fabric roof to standard construction, it is estimated that the increased cost for heating and the reduced cost for artificial lighting result in an overall saving of about $21,000 per year. Below the synthetic turf field lies a full 64,320-square-foot basement that contains locker rooms for football, track, and coaches; weight room; training facilities; and therapy pool. The therapy pool is 15 feet by 40 feet and goes from 4 to 7 feet in depth. Also included in the facility are an auditorium, six meeting rooms, and a film room.

Air-Supported Structures

There are two basic types of air-supported structures: 1) large permanent structures and 2) smaller, more portable structures.

Air-supported fabric roofs are held up by a positive air pressure within a totally enclosed building. These facilities are actually inflated with positive air pressure that is produced by a group of large fans. In conventional buildings, the foundation, walls, and internal columns must support a roof weight of between 10 and 40 pounds per square foot. In air-supported structures, a roof weight of about 1 pound per square foot is transmitted directly to the ground by the increased air pressure. This increased pressure of about 4 or 5 pounds per square foot greater than ambient pressure is usually unnoticed by the building's occupants. Some of the instances when an air-supported structure may be preferable to a tension structure or standard construction are:

- When column-free spans of greater than 150 feet are desired.
- When large, column-free spans are desired at a cost that is greatly reduced compared to conventional structures. In fact, cost per unit area usually decreases as the size of the span increases.
- When a low silhouette is desired.

Some examples of air-supported structures are:

- Dedmon Center—Located at Radford University in Radford, Virginia, the Dedmon Center was constructed for a cost of $6,750,000 and opened in 1982. Encompassing 110,000 square feet, it has 5,000 temporary seats for basketball. Used for physical education, athletics, and recreation, the center provides five full basketball, courts, weight room, pool, locker rooms, and offices.
- Dakota Dome—Located at the University of South Dakota in Vermillion, South Dakota, the Dakota Dome contains five basketball/volleyball courts, two tennis courts, an eight-lane 200

Photo courtesy of Sasaki Associates
Dedmon Center.

meter track, four racquetball courts, a six-lane 25-meter pool, locker rooms, classrooms, and the offices for the athletic department. The main floor is a synthetic surface that is used for most court activities and has an artificial turf football field that can be rolled out for football, soccer, and other field events. When the facility is set up for football, there is seating for 12,000 spectators. The entire facility was built for the bargain price of about $51 per square foot in 1978.
- Carrier Dome—The Carrier Dome, located in Syracuse, New York, is the home of Syracuse University athletics. The stadium seats 50,000 for football and over 30,000 for basketball. Also a great bargain, total construction cost was $27,715,000, which figures out to $554 per seat. This is very inexpensive when compared to conventional covered stadiums. This facility was completed in 1980.
- RCA Dome—Originally called the Hoosier Dome, it first opened in 1984. The home of the Indianapolis Colts, the RCA Dome seats 57,890 for football and was built for a cost of $77.5 million. The versatile facility has been host to many national and international events including the Pan American Games, the World Track & Field Championships, the World Gymnastic Championships and several NCAA Final Fours.

- Steve Lacy Field House—Milligan College, Milligan, Tennessee–1974.
- Uni-Dome—University of Northern Iowa, Cedar Falls, Iowa–1975.
- Metrodome—Minneapolis, Minnesota—1982.

- B.C. Place Amphitheater—Vancouver, B.C., Canada—1983.
- Tokyo Dome—Tokyo, Japan—1988.

The primary disadvantage of air-supported structures is the need for the constant positive air pressure. Since this positive pressure is what supports the roof, if there is even a temporary loss of pressure, the fabric will hang down on the supporting cables. Although this alone should cause no damage to the facility, this is when the structural system is the most vulnerable. Even light winds, snow, or rain may cause extensive damage to a fabric roof in the deflated position. These facilities must be constantly monitored and all precautions must be taken to ensure that all systems are functioning properly. Since cable domes appear to have the same advantages as the large air-pressure structures but without many of the disadvantages, it is entirely possible that we have seen the last large air-supported structure that will ever be built (see Cable Domes on page 482).

Photo courtesy of Geiger Engineers

Metrodome.

Combining Air-Supported and Tension Roofs

Another development in the construction of fabric structures is the idea of combining both an air-supported roof and a tension roof in the same building. An example of this concept is the Stephen C. O'Connell Center. This physical education, recreation, and athletic complex is located at the University of Florida at Gainesville. This was the first structure to combine both air-supported and tension roofs in one building. The center or main arena is covered by a large air-inflated roof, while the outer areas of the building are the tension-covered spaces. The main arena has an indoor track and can seat 10,400 spectators for basketball. Located under the tension supported areas are a gymnastics area; dance studio; weight room; locker rooms; offices; and a 3,000-seat, 50-meter natatorium. Like most fabric structures, this facility was a bargain. The total construction cost was $11,954,418, which comes out to about $49 per square foot. This facility was completed in 1980.

The Sun Dome at the University of South Florida in Tampa is based on a very similar design. Following the same plans as the O'Connell Center, the Sun Dome initially was built with only the air-supported fabric roof main arena. It was not until several years later that the outer areas were enclosed by a tension roof and the building was completed.

Temporary Air-Supported Structures

This section will outline the merits of the smaller and more portable air structures. Air structures work well as environmental covers placed over existing recreational areas and, for many organizations, the 'bubble' is the answer to an increasing need for large covered activity areas at a nominal cost. Cost savings are in proportion to the size of the space to be covered. Spaces over 300 square feet usually bring a cost savings when compared to conventional roofing. Heat gain seems to present a more severe problem than heat loss and must be considered in warmer climates. There are numerous playing fields within communities and around schools and colleges that lend themselves easily to enclosure by a fabric air structure. Some of the additional advantages and disadvantages of using small air-supported structures are as follows:

- Speed of erection—Once in place, the actual erection of the structure usually takes only one or two days. However, additional time is required for the ground work, site services, foundation, anchorage, flooring, and installation of mechanical and electrical equipment needed in the initial installation. Only minimal field labor is needed.
- Ease of deflation, inflation, and repair—Deflation and inflation of the fabric bubble usually does not require skilled labor.
- Portability—When deflated and packed, the fabric envelope can be stored in a small space or easily transported elsewhere for storage or use. Depending on the size of the dome, deflation and packing usually require one or two days.
- Adaptability for temporary functions—For temporary use, the air-supported structure has definite physical and financial advantages over a conventional building.
- Long-span and high-ceiling features—Clear and unobstructed spaces are an inherent feature of the air-supported domes. Conventional long-span and high-ceiling structures are much more expensive.

• Integrated heating, ventilation, and air-pressure system—The integrated heating, ventilation, and air-pressure system is simple and less expensive than conventional systems. Lengthy duct work is not required.

Some examples of temporary air-supported structures are:

• Memorial Stadium—A portable inflatable fabric bubble is used to cover the entire football field at the University of Illinois in the winter. First erected in 1985, it was purchased for $1.5 million. With an average inside winter temperature of 55 degrees, the field is used heavily by several departments across the campus. The concept of a portable dome over the game field adds extra use to a facility that would otherwise sit empty much of the year.
• University of Santa Clara—The swimming pool at the Thomas E. Leavey Center is covered by a portable air structure. It is removed for use as an outdoor pool in the summer months and then reinflated for the winter to transform the pool for indoor use.
• Numerous tennis centers, golf driving ranges, pools, and fitness centers.

Cable Domes

Cable domes are the most recent innovation in fabric structure technology. Through a complex system of cables and girders, very large spans can be inexpensively covered by a fabric roof without the need for columns or fans to maintain integrity. Engineers predict that the cable dome concept is feasible for spans of at least 1,000 feet. Cable domes incorporate most of the advantages and fewer of the disadvantages of fabric structures when compared to standard construction. Many experts in fabric roof technology believe that cable domes will replace the air-supported structure as the fabric roof design of choice for the future. There will probably not be any more large air structures built because of the inherent advantages of the cable dome. Some of these advantages are as follows:

• Huge, column-free spans can be covered.
• There is no need for expensive, energy-consuming fans.
• A passive system means there is no need for someone to constantly monitor the facility.
• The structure has an extremely low silhouette.

Some examples of cable domes are:

• Redbird Arena—Opened in 1991, Redbird Arena is on the campus of Illinois State University in Bloomington-Normal, Illinois. This multipurpose arena can seat 10,500 spectators for basketball, with the ability to provide an additional 1,500 seats on the floor for concerts or commencement. The lower sections of seats are portable bleachers that can be removed to provide 36,000 square feet of space on the main floor. Built for a cost of $20 million, Redbird Arena was the first cable dome to be constructed on a college campus, but probably will not be the last.
• Tropicana Field—Tropicana Field is located in St. Petersburg, Florida, and was opened in 1990. This multipurpose stadium was designed primarily for baseball, yet with the flexibility to accommodate football, basketball, soc-

Photo by Todd Seidler
Redbird Arena.

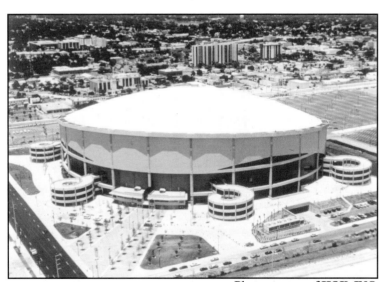

Photo courtesy of HOK, INC.
Photo by George Cott
Tropicana Field.

cer, and tennis, as well as concerts and trade shows. In addition to 50 private suites, a variety of seating arrangements allow the facility to function as an 18,000-seat arena or a 43,000-seat stadium for baseball. The unique movable grandstands contain built-in concession stands and public toilets.

The fabric roof is 688 feet in diameter and was constructed on a tilt of 60 degrees. This tilt is designed to allow more clearance for the trajectory of fly balls and allows the roof to reach a height of 225 feet in front of home plate. The cable truss roof system is capable of supporting 60 tons of lighting and sound equipment for concerts, yet weighs a mere six pounds per square foot. Tropicana Field was built for a cost of $132 million and is the home of the Tampa Bay Devil Rays.

Photo courtesy of Heery Architects & Engineers
Georgia Dome—exterior.

- Georgia Dome—Located in downtown Atlanta, Georgia, the Georgia Dome was completed in August 1992. This $210 million structure was the site of both the Super Bowl and the Olympics in 1996. The Teflon-coated fabric roof covers 8.6 acres, weighs 68 tons, and incorporates 11.1 miles of steel support cables. This multipurpose facility seats 70,500 for football and is the home of the Atlanta Falcons. A total of 202 luxury suites are located on different levels around the stadium that range in price from $20,000 to $120,000 per year for a 10-year lease. During the planning process it was estimated that changing the design from an open-air stadium to a fabric-covered dome increased the cost of the project by only 20% or less.

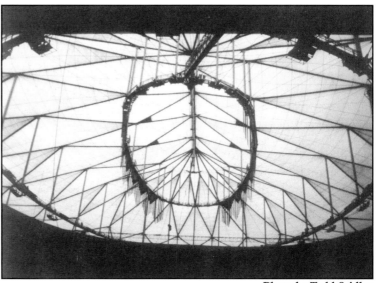

Photo by Todd Seidler
Georgia Dome—interior roof.

Wooden Domes

Another recent development in encapsulated spaces is the wooden dome. These spherical wooden structures have several advantages over conventional structures. Column-free spans of up to 800 feet are possible, and they are generally easier to build. There are several wooden dome structures around the country ranging from high school gymnasiums to very large stadiums. Some of the advantages of wooden domes when compared with standard construction may include

- efficient construction of huge column-free spans,
- lower initial cost when compared with conventional construction,
- less construction time,
- full utilization of space, and,
- good insulation and acoustical properties.

Some examples of wooden domes are:

- Round Valley Ensphere—Located in Eager, Arizona, this wooden dome is the only domed high school football stadium in the world. Opened in 1991, it was built for a total project cost of only $11.5 million and is unique in many respects. The 113,000 square feet of unobstructed floor space provides a full-size synthetic turf football field with seating for 5,000; a six-lane, 200-meter, synthetic-surface running track with 100-meter straight away; seven combination basketball, volleyball, or tennis courts; and a softball field; as well as offices, training room, and four full locker rooms. The wooden roof is insulated to a value of R-28 and is very energy and acoustically efficient. One of the most interesting features of the dome is that it contains a large skylight in the center of the roof. This skylight is made of clear Lexan and provides good illumination of the activity areas even on overcast days. At an elevation of over 7,000 feet, the Round Valley area experiences extremes in weather, including snow-packed winters. During these colder months, the skylight also acts as a solar collector, helping to make the Ensphere very energy efficient.

- Walkup Skydome—This laminated wood dome is located in Northern Arizona University in Flagstaff, Arizona. Opened in 1977, the Skydome is 502 feet across and covers 6.2 acres. It contains a full-size, roll-up, synthetic football/soccer field, a professional-size ice hockey rink, a 1/5-mile running track, a portable wood basketball court, and has seating for more than 15,000 people. The total construction cost was $8.3 million, or about $620 per seat.

- Superior Dome—Constructed on the campus of Northern Michigan University in Marquette, Michigan, this state-owned wooden dome was opened in the fall of 1991. With a diameter of 533 feet, the 14-story, $21.8-million structure was envisioned in 1985 as an Olympic training center. It has a 200-meter track, a full-size football field and is

Photo courtesy of Rossman, Schneider, Gadberry & Shay
Round Valley Ensphere—exterior.

Photo courtesy of Rossman, Schneider, Gadberry & Shay
Round Valley Ensphere—interior.

home to the NMU football team, with seating for 8,000 spectators. Designed to be constructed in phases as funding becomes available, the facility will eventually include an additional 5,000 seats; an ice rink for hockey, speed skating, and figure skating; locker rooms; sports medicine facilities; and public use areas.

Summary

The fundamental purpose and design of stadiums and arenas has changed dramatically in the last decade or so. These changes are so radical that many facilities built in the last 20 years have become obsolete. The basic idea behind these changes is that modern arenas and stadiums are no longer just places to watch an event but are now designed to provide a total entertain-

Photo courtesy of TMP Associates, Inc.
Photo by Balthazer Korab, Ltd.
Superior Dome—exterior.

Photo courtesy of TMP Associates, Inc.
Photo by Balthazer Korab, Ltd.

Superior Dome—interior.

ment experience and maximize the generation of revenue for the owner.

The cost of operating professional sports teams has grown dramatically over the past two decades and shows no signs of slowing. Therefore, it is imperative that professional sports venues include a variety of income-generating aspects. Luxury suites, naming rights, and PSLs are among the many new streams of revenue for the cash-hungry professional franchises. These concepts cater to big-dollar clients and may guarantee bonds used in funding the new facilities.

The retractable roof concept was born in the 1970s. The main advantage is fan comfort and being able to play during inclement weather.

The three main types of fabric structure include tension, air-supported, and cable domes. The advantages include lower initial cost, less construction time, natural lighting, possible lower energy costs, less maintenance, and full utilization of space. The disadvantages may include shorter life span, poor thermal insulation, acoustical problems, and restrictions due to high winds.

The advantages of wooden domes include huge column-free spans, lower initial costs, less construction time, full utilization of space, and good insulation and acoustical properties.

The new modern facilities are designed to accommodate a wide variety of events and also to quickly alter the setup for different events. The planners included such things as versatile lighting and sound systems; heavy-duty, moveable lighting grids; moveable seating sections; loading ramps with main floor access; and fixed, pre-wired camera positions to improve the changeover efficiency of these facilities.

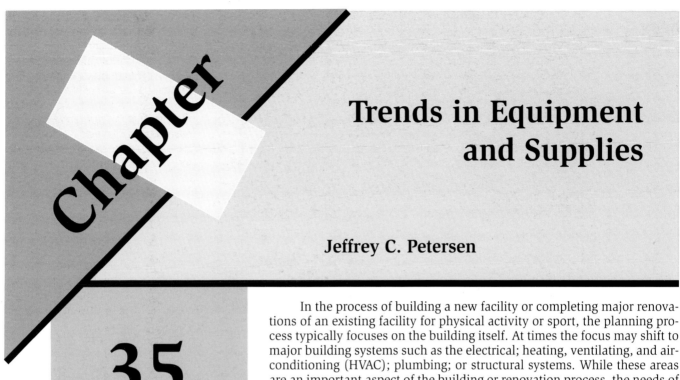

Trends in Equipment and Supplies

Jeffrey C. Petersen

35

In the process of building a new facility or completing major renovations of an existing facility for physical activity or sport, the planning process typically focuses on the building itself. At times the focus may shift to major building systems such as the electrical; heating, ventilating, and air-conditioning (HVAC); plumbing; or structural systems. While these areas are an important aspect of the building or renovation process, the needs of facility users must be the greatest consideration. Although the facility itself needs to be a high priority in the building process, it is also crucial that the equipment and supplies required within the facility are carefully considered and selected. The equipment and supplies are just as vital as the building itself if the facility is to fully serve its intended purposes for the users.

Consider, for example, a very basic health and fitness center. While a physical space for this center must be created, the space alone will never meet the expectations of the facility users without the procurement of the necessary equipment and supplies.

As the demand for these sports and recreation facilities increases so does the demand for necessary supplies and equipment. When considering the competitive nature of sports organizations (interscholastic, intercollegiate, and professional) as well as the pressure on fitness centers and health clubs to attract and maintain a customer base, it is not surprising that new equipment and supply innovations are regularly entering the sports marketplace. Each athletic program wants to provide the latest equipment innovation that may help their athletes or programs become more successful. Similarly, leaders in the fitness industry continually search to find the next "must have" exercise machine. Identifying trends becomes crucial for success because of both the large capital investments in equipment and the competitive nature of the fitness and sports market. Of course, predicting future trends is just as difficult as predicting a moneymaking stock or predicting what team will win the next Super Bowl. It is more typical to identify equipment or supplies that are experiencing rapid growth in use and popularity. The purpose of this chapter is to examine selected trends that impact the selection and use of equipment and supplies within several venue types. The discussion of various products should in no way be considered a blanket endorsement, because each facility operator or manager must develop his or her own selection criteria based on the wants and needs of the consumers.

Learning Objectives

After reading this chapter, the student should be able to

- differentiate between the terms *equipment* and *supplies;*
- analyze the balance between the user needs and the equipment costs;
- identify selected equipment trends for stadiums, arenas, and gymnasiums and the causes of those trends;
- identify selected equipment trends in fitness venues;
- define an Automated External Defibrillator (AED) and describe factors behind its growing placement in facilities;
- describe the impact of *extreme sports* on facilities and equipment;
- identify selected supply trends;
- describe storage options available for supplies and equipment;
- estimate space needs for storage of equipment and supplies.

Supplies and Equipment Defined

A case of athletic tape, a soccer uniform, hockey mouthpieces, football helmets, a case of tennis balls, portable bleachers, a baseball pitching machine, basketballs, wrestling mats, towels, and a pole vault landing pit are all items that might be necessary in a facility used for physical activity and sports. Which of these would be considered a supply and which would be equipment?

According to Merriam Webster's *Collegiate Dictionary*, equipment is defined as "all the fixed assets other than land and buildings of a business enterprise." A fixed asset is often considered an item with a worth or value above a preestablished dollar value. Equipment could also be defined as durable goods; these are items used repeatedly over a period of years. Items that have a short duration of use, typically one year or less, are classified as supplies. Many supplies have a one-time-only use, while others may be repeatedly used but do have a relatively short functional life. Equipment on the other hand will have a minimum of over one year of useful service.

The cost per item or unit is another method of differentiating between equipment and supplies. Items with higher costs are usually considered equipment. Therefore, something as large as a scoreboard and something as small as an external heart monitor are both considered to be equipment. Depending on the established policies of the organization, be it governmental, school, or private enterprise, a price standard may be set to distinguish between supplies and equipment. This may be set at the low end of perhaps $100 per item or at higher levels such as $250, $500, or even $1,000 per item. Items designated as equipment are more closely monitored through item tagging and annual inventory processes. Therefore, the two major considerations in differentiating between supplies and equipment are the cost of the item and the duration of its use.

Cost Considerations

The cost of supplies and equipment is a major consideration in both the initial creation and annual operation of facilities for physical activity and sports. When considering the costs for equipment and supplies, a balance must be maintained between the ultimate wants of the users and the total cost. There is usually a very significant portion of the project cost that should be allocated to properly equip and furnish a facility for sports or recreation. Without taking this into consideration, a beautiful facility could be constructed, but it would be useless without the necessary equipment and supplies.

Consider, for example, a fitness center. The greatest equipment cost factor for a new fitness facility would be the cost of the cardio and strength training equipment desired. According to a compilation of data from six recently completed facilities compiled by Kevin Stubbs of RDG Sports, a leading architectural firm, the fitness center equipment costs vary greatly (see Table 35.1). There was a rather large range of cost ($20.00 to $51.44 per square foot for equipment) depending on the specific requirements of the clients, but the average of the selected projects was found to be just over $30 per square foot. Note that these estimations only include the exercise equipment itself and a facility of this type would require other furnishings and operational supplies as well.

Table 35.1
Fitness Equipment Costs From Six Recent Building Projects

Facility Area (square feet)	Equipment Cost	Equipment Cost per square foot
1,200	$24,000	$20.00
2,000	$48,000	$24.00
2,500	$100,000	$40.00
6,000	$125,000	$20.83
7,270	$374,000	$51.44
15,000	$360,000	$24.00

K. Stubbs (personal communication, January 18, 2001)

Equipment Trends for Stadiums, Arenas, and Gymnasiums

With the 1990s having been a decade of unprecedented growth in professional sport venues in the United States, it is not surprising that many colleges as well saw the prosperous economic climate as a time to build or expand facilities. With such a high rate of growth in spectator sports venues, several equipment trends emerged. Most of the trends described in this section focus on enhancing the spectator comfort, the spectator sensory experience, or the use of creative management to reduce direct equipment expenses for the owner or operator.

The development of a myriad of seating options has been one major trend in large spectator facilities both indoor and outdoor. Gone are the days of standard bleachers with the minimal 18 inches per person seating-width allowance. The current trends are expanding not only the seat width, but also the legroom (tread depth) available. Stadium seating now commonly includes various seatback options, different levels of cushioning, custom color schemes, logo or graphic incorporations, armrests, and even cup holders.

Consider, as an example, Invesco Field at Mile High in Denver, the home of the NFL Broncos and the MLS Rapids. This new facility has an official seating capacity of 76,125 with a total facility size of 1,717,000 square feet. The previous home stadium of the both teams, Mile High Stadium, had an official capacity of only 2 fewer spectators at 76,123 but the total size was less than half the total of the new stadium at only 850,000 square feet. This increase of total square footage cannot be completely contributed to seating upgrades. The old stadium had an average seat width of 18 inches and legroom of 31 inches while the new facility has a 19-inch minimum seat width and 32 to 33 inches of standard legroom. The club seating area in the stadium boasts 20-inch-wide padded seating with 33 inches of tread depth. The new stadium seating also provides the added amenity of cup holders for every seat regardless of the seating section.

The continued trends of both luxury boxes and club seating areas also cater to the expanded desire to provide creature comforts such as food and beverage catering services, television monitors, and full climate control. There has also been increased emphasis in high-quality sound systems to enhance the live sports experience.

While watching a sporting event live at the venue was once considered the best place to view sports, television's use of instant replay (begun in the 1960s) has added a great deal to the viewing experience. Replays allow the spectator at home to see again plays that may be either spectacular or controversial in nature. Spectators attending an event at the stadium or arena may miss altogether key parts of the game due to lapses in concentration or their sheer distance from an actual play. However, the installation of big screen light emitting diode panels that serve as large video or television monitors can solve these viewing problems. The use of this video equipment now allows the spectators at the venue to view both the live action and have access as a whole to the replays, game statistics, close-up images, and other video information broadcast on the LED big screens.

The number of LED screen installations in sports venues increased enormously throughout the 1990s and this growth is likely to continue. LED displays are not the only video technology available, but other systems such as projection, liquid crystal display (LCD), and cathode ray tube (CRT) are at a significant disadvantage compared to LEDs. First, the power consumption for LED is lower than the previously mentioned systems. The second major advantage to LED displays is that they will typically operate for 100,000 hours before dropping to 50% of their original brightness (Dahlgren, 2000). The LED systems are also much lighter than the CRT display options, making them easier to suspend or mount. The major drop in production cost of the blue and green LEDs has also allowed the price for full-color displays to drop and become more affordable for collegiate programs (see Figure 35.1) and minor league professional venue use. The LED displays have even entered into the high school market with installations now in place at Emerald Ridge High School in Puyallup, Washington, and at Cicero North Syracuse High School in Cicero, New York.

Another reason LED video boards are expanding in use is that three different types of display manufacturing have been developed, each with its own specific applications. The lamp LED method uses a combination of reflector cups and epoxy lenses to intensify and focus the light. These are typically the brightest systems and can be used outdoors where more light intensity is needed (see Figure 35.2). The surface mounted lamp method utilizes a metal reflector frame that is mounted directly to the board. This method provides a higher resolution and allows for viewing from a wider range of angles. The drawback to the surface-mounted lamp LED display is that it lacks the brightness necessary to provide an optimal image outdoors. The chip on the board method places the LED directly on the board without any type of reflection or lens system. Of course this method is the least expensive, but it is the least light efficient of the three and it is often harder to maintain. The full-color displays in all three manufacturing options are obtained by the blending of light from the combination of red, blue, and green LEDs to create up to 16.7 million colors. The red LEDs continue to be the least costly to produce, so many scoreboard or marquee sign applications of LED technology continue to use red as the primary color.

A major factor in the growing popularity of the LED video display would be the competition between colleges and professional sports organizations. Each venue attempts to either keep up with or become the leader with the biggest or the best video displays available for their patrons. The inclusion of large video display screens is almost considered standard in new, large-scale venue constructions. Another advantage of the LED screens is that older venues can easily add these displays to upgrade the facility. This can have a major impact on spectators' impressions of the facility. The wide range of size options (from 6-foot-by-8-foot at the small end to the 27-foot-by-96-foot mammoth screen being installed at Invesco Field) allows each stadium to create a more customized fit for its particular needs. Other recent LED video innovations include the use of long narrow screens such as the two 300-foot-by-5-foot video displays located along the face of the upper deck of the US Cellular Field (home of the Chicago White Sox). These types of displays, installed in 2003, are used primarily for promotional and advertising purposes.

Another trend impacting equipment in spectator venues is contracting and outsourcing portions of the typical functions associated with the venue. According to Peter Bendor-Samuel, who is considered a leading outsourcing authority, outsourcing occurs when an organization transfers the ownership of a business process to a supplier. The key aspect is the transfer of control. Outsourcing differs from contracting, where the buyer retains control of the process and tells the supplier how to do the work. It is the transfer of ownership that defines outsourcing and at times makes it a challenging process. In outsourcing, the buyer does not instruct the supplier how to perform its task. The buyer clearly communicates the desired results and leaves the process decisions for accomplishing those results with the supplier.

Within stadiums and arenas, typical operational aspects that may be outsourced include services such as concessions, laundry, and facility maintenance. One of the advantages of outsourcing can be significant savings in major equipment expenditures. When organizations or teams owning or operating these facilities outsource, the equipment and supplies required can then be significantly reduced. For example, at a venue where concessions are outsourced, only a space allocation with water and electrical

Figure 35.1
Indoor LED Video Display at Nationwide Arena in
Columbus, Ohio, Featuring Four 9-foot-by-16-foot Video Screens

Figure 35.2
Outdoor Application of LED Video Technology at
Spartan Stadium at the Campus of Michigan State University in
East Lansing With a Video Display Size of 21 feet by 27 feet

supply would be provided. The outsourced supplier for concessions would provide all the necessary equipment for the preparation, storage, and sales of all products. Of course this would create a significant decrease in equipment and supplies expenditures in this aspect of operation. According to the Outsourcing Research Council (Raiford, 1999) operations and facilities outsourcing had an 18% growth rate in 1999 in the corporate sector. This trend will continue to impact the equipment needs for major venues in the future. The needs for equipment will not decrease, but outsourcing will shift the responsibility of equipment research and selection, purchase, and maintenance onto the outsourcing supplier.

Gymnasiums are facilities in secondary schools throughout the country that serve as both a primary activity space for physical education as well as a primary spectator venue for interscholastic sports. As spectator venues, gymnasiums require safe and ample seating; however as a teaching and practice area, the need is for maximum useable floor space. The most common solution to these two needs has been the telescoping bleachers unit. Most gyms have these seating structures; however, current requirements in the Uniform Building Code (UBC) and the Americans With Disabilities Act (ADA) are most likely not met if the bleachers were installed before 1990. The replacement of older models of bleachers has become a growing trend in the renovation and improvement of gyms.

The older model bleachers have some serious deficiencies in regard to safety and risk management. Many old bleacher models have open spaces between the seat and the foot rest or tread area. This is a space that small children can often fit through to fall under the structure, or where an adult could slip a foot or a leg into and be injured. Additionally, many old units lack designated aisles and require that the seating area itself double as an access route up and down the bleachers. The rails on many older units consist of a single or double bar that has a large open area where children could fall. Most older bleacher units also require manual operation to open and close; that can expose workers to the risk of injury during the process.

Because of the significant issues with many older bleacher units, it is not surprising that bleacher replacement is becoming more popular. Steel remains the primary structural component of the units; however, seats can be made of wood, vinyl-coated metal or, molded plastic for standard seating. Tip-up seating with either padded or unpadded chair backs is another option for telescoping bleacher units. The price for new bleachers ranges from the entry level of $90 to $100 per gross seat to as much as $350 per seat if fold-up padded seating with chair backs is selected (Kocher, 1996).

The specific UBC regulations impacting bleacher seating begin with row limitations. A maximum of 16 rows is allowed if the bleachers load only from the top or only from the bottom. No row limitations exist if the bleacher section can load from both the top and bottom. Whenever there are more than 11 rows of seating, aisles are required and no more than 20 seats can separate each aisle. Aisle steps cannot exceed 9 inches without providing an intermediate step; and since the typical bleacher rise between rows is more than 9 inches, these intermediate steps are almost always required. A minimum aisle width of 42 inches is necessary if servicing seating on both sides or 36 inches wide if seating is only to one side. When considering railings, the aisles require discontinuous rails that allow spectators to move laterally as well as up and down the aisle. These rails must also have an intermediate rail 12 inches below the top of the rail for shorter spectators (Scandrett, 1998). These "P-shaped" railings usually attach to the riser face in the center of the aisle and must be attached and removed each time the units are moved. The end railings prevent falls and must have no gaps greater than 6 inches.

The ADA requirements also specify that the seating areas provided for those with wheelchairs be spread throughout the facility rather than all congregated together. The number of wheelchair spaces should be reviewed carefully to maintain ADA compliance. For example, facilities with a capacity of 501 to 1,000 spectators must provide at least 1% of seating that is wheelchair accessible. For facilities with seating of 1,000 spectators and beyond requires that 20 accessible locations must be provided plus one additional spot for every 100 seats over the initial 1,000. So a gymnasium with a seating capacity of 5,000 would necessitate 60 wheelchair accessible locations (Uniform Federal Accessibility Standards, Internet).

Bleacher replacement (see Chapter 21) can improve a gymnasium facility not just by improving the facility's compliance with ADA and UBC but also by creating an improved facility appearance. Many models have color options to enhance the aesthetics image of the facility. The use of mechanical opening and closing greatly reduces the injury risk for personnel in facility setup and teardown. The risk management benefits and ADA compliance associated with bleacher replacement help make this improvement not only a desired trend but, in many cases, a necessity.

Equipment Trends for Fitness Venues

In 1999 a survey by the National Sporting Goods Association (NSGA, 1999) found that 46.45% of over 5,000 survey participants indicated a desire to increase their level of participation in activities utilizing exercise equipment. With this great desire of individuals to use exercise equipment, public and private institutions continue to focus efforts on meeting these fitness needs with their selection of exercise equipment.

One major consideration in the selection of fitness equipment is the cost. Table 35.2 identifies the average cost of 12 selected weight machines reported by Hasler and Bartlett (1995) compared to the average obtained from research of list prices from two lines of selectorized equipment in 2004. While cost is one major factor in equipment selection, the needs and wants of the users cannot be overlooked. According to the Fitness Products Council (Trend setting, 1999), four of eight major fitness trends identified related directly to equipment. One of the most significant trends is the explosive growth of the aerobic exercise equipment. A 63% increase in use for Americans was noted from 1987 to 1997 with 67.3 million people reporting regular workouts with cardio equipment. Within this increased use of cardio machines, the treadmill was still the highest used piece of equipment with 36.1 million regular users in 1997. The use of weight training among American women has increased by 127% from 1987 to 1997 to a total of 16.8 million. There can also be significant variance in the equipment preferences based on the demographic traits such as age and gender. This is evident in the results of a survey of nearly 1,200 collegiate recreation providers (see Table 35.3). The top preference of men at these colleges was free weights, while the top preference of women was treadmills.

Weight training has a variety of equipment options from free weights to plate loaded machines (Figure 35.3), to selectorized (weight stack and pin) machines (Figure 35.4). While novice lifters typically prefer the selectorized machines, there continues to be a significant amount of growth in the use of free weights as well as the plate-loaded systems. One trend within all of the strength training modes is a continued focus on safety and risk management. Some selectorized systems have incorporated shrouds that cover much of the weight stack and many moving parts to reduce to risk of injury (see Figure 35.5).

Table 35.2
Total-Body Weight Workout Sample Equipment Cost Sheet

Weight Equipment	Average Cost per Unit	
	1995	2004
Lower Body		
Leg press	$4,783	$4,510
Seated leg curl	$2,459	$2,975
Leg extension	$2,388	$2,663
Multi-hip	$2,406	$2,550
Mid Section		
Abdominal	$2,394	$2,713
Lower back	$2,729	$2,763
Upper Body		
Arm curl	$2,081	$2,563
Triceps extension	$2,256	$2,563
Chest press	$2,546	$2,813
Shoulder press	$2,414	$2,813
Rowing	$2,281	$2,813
Lat pulldown	$2,044	$2,663
Total Cost	$30,781	$34,398

Hasler, A.E., & Bartlett, M. (1995, September). Equipped for exercise. Athletic business, pp.47-54.

Table 35.3
Collegiate Fitness Center Preferred Equipment

Choice of Equipment	Men	Women
First choice	Free weights	Treadmills
Second choice	Bikes	Steppers
Third choice	Treadmills	Elliptical
Fourth choice	Steppers	Bikes

(Patton 1999, April)

On the free weight side, changes in the plate designs, such as the addition of openings for hand holds and/or the addition of flat surfaces on the circumference, have been made to reduce the number of accidents due to dropped or rolling plates (see Figure 35.6). Another major trend in weight training equipment is the continued integration of computer-chip technology on many selectorized systems. For example, some systems are able to read users' swipe cards or other input devices and can set resistance levels and record results based on a prescribed workout routine from a personal trainer. One additional trend impacting weight training equipment would be the adaptation of machines to special populations such as youths with smaller scale machines and smaller weight increments or senior citizens with smaller weight increments.

The increasing use of aerobic or cardio machines is another current trend. Since walking may be the most popular of all forms of aerobic exercise, it is not surprising that the treadmill is still a very popular piece of exercise equipment. Cycling machines have also been a mainstay of cardio exercise machines but have continued to diversify. Cycling equipment now includes many options such as the traditional exercise cycle (Figure 35.7), air resistance cycle, recumbent cycle (Figure 35.8), and spin cycle (Figures 35.9). Additional innovations such as steppers and elliptical machines are also popular cardio options that offer nonimpact-based aerobic training. While some cardio equipment users may exclusively train on one type of machine, other users tend to enjoy using a variety of machines to avoid stagnation or boredom in their exercise programs. Because of the varied use of aerobic exercise equipment, it is difficult to determine what machine might become the next "top choice" machine, but it is almost certain that there will continue to be other creative innovations.

Figure 35.3
Plate Loaded Smith Machine

Figure 35.4
Butterfly Chest Press as a Typical Selectorized Weight Machine

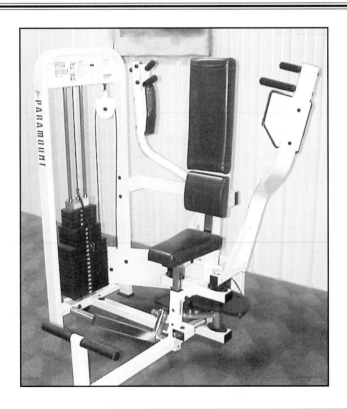

Figure 35.5
Selectorized Weight Machine With Shroud Providing
Protection From Many Moving Parts During Use

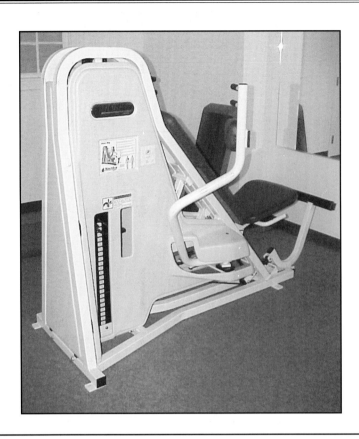

Figure 35.6
Free Weight Plates Designed With Risk Management Features

Figure 35.7
Typical Exercise Cycle With Electronic Control Panel

Figure 35.8
Recumbent Cycle With a High-Backed Seat

Figure 35.9
Spin Cycle Typically Used in Group Classes

The integration of computer technology within cardio machines is also a trend that should continue to expand in the future. The use of direct pulse monitoring while using the cardio machines began in the 1980s, but the development of computer programming that can alter the speed or resistance level of the machine to keep the person exercising within a specified target heart rate is definitely a great step forward in customizing workouts. The computerized workout routines that focus on optimal fat-burning pulse zones (typically 65% of maximal heart rate) or optimal cardiovascular benefit zones (typically 80 percent maximal heart rate) are becoming common options on many cardio machines. Additionally, many cardio machines contain other preprogrammed workouts such as interval or hill sessions and some manufacturers have installed fitness protocols used in military, law enforcement, or firefighting fitness assessments. Other cardio machine technologies emerging include "smart chips" that can be individually preprogrammed by a personal trainer for the creation and saving of customized workouts. These chips are plugged into ports on the control console of the equipment. One manufacturer, Star-Trac, has created a system where a personal digital assistant (PDA) device can be programmed by an exerciser with a personalized treadmill workout that can then be wirelessly transmitted to a treadmill immediately prior to the exercise session.

At the same time, there are many users of these machines who simply wish to get on and work out at a steady rate or pace without using these programming options. For those types of users, the manual operation or quick-start options are also available to allow a very basic workout. According to King (2003) approximately 80% of exercisers use these manual or quick-start settings; however, several factors contribute to the continued development of high-tech programming on cardio machines, including: catering to customer wants and needs, responding to more highly educated exercisers, and creating a unique sales tool for a manufacturer.

The entertainment of individuals using exercise equipment is a current trend that will likely continue to expand in the future as well. Cardiovascular exercise areas in the past may have provided reading material, a room-wide stereo system, and perhaps a television. More recent trends involve the use of multiple video display screens and FM band audio programming for individual headset listening of either the video programming or music. The addition of wireless broadband technology has also been adapted to fitness applications to allow institutions to customize audio and video entertainment and to include internal promotions as well. Numerous video monitors coupled with audio broadcasting systems are now trademarked as comprehensive systems such as Cardio Theater and Broadcast Vision. These systems meet users' needs by allowing them to select their own programming in news, business, or entertainment. In addition to the standard size or large screen video systems, there are also small-scale equipment mounted systems that provide small video screens in combination with cassette, CD, and DVD players. The video portion of these systems can play network or cable programming or they can play specific workout motivational or educational programming.

Figure 35.10
Elliptical Machine Providing a Nonimpact Cardio Workout

Figure 35.11
The Treadmill Is Still One of the Most Popular Cardio Machines

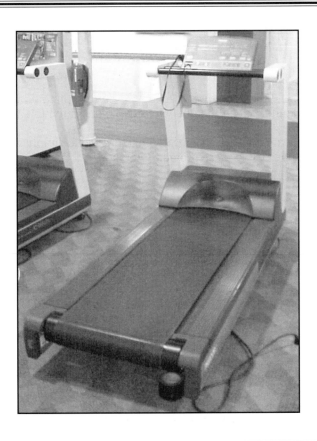

Entertainment while using cardio equipment has also moved into the interactive realm with options now available, such as stationary cycles combined with video gaming devices where the level of cycle performance directly impacts the performance in the video game. This video game system developed by Exertris has been developed for both individual applications and group competition where up to 16 riders can compete on the same system. Broadcast Vision has created a scenery simulation product that creates beach scenery, trails, or palm-lined streets, for example, that are projected on a video display. The landscape moves on the video monitor according to the rate of performance on the cardio equipment, and the virtual hills in the video are synchronized with the incline on a treadmill or the resistance level on a cycle (Brown, 2003).

In addition to the expansion of audio and video entertainment options while exercising, computers have been modified for ease of use while using many cardio machines. Computers and display monitors have been modified to allow for operation while exercising on an elliptical trainer, (Figure 35.10), treadmill (Figure 35.11), or stepper (Figure 35.12). This technology allows the exerciser to access the internet via a touch screen or modified mouse. These technology trends allow for an increase in individual choice in the entertainment options while exercising, and market forces will likely continue to drive an expansion of these trends.

Figure 35.12
Typical Stepper With Electronic Controls

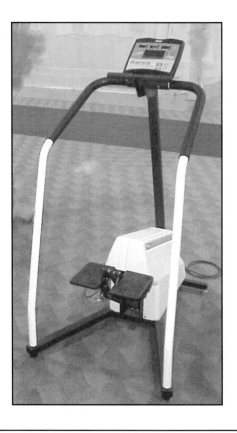

Automated External Defibrillators

Automated External Defibrillators (AEDs) are portable emergency medical devices that deliver an electric shock to the heart in order to halt sudden cardiac arrest (SCA). SCA is the onset of a chaotic and unproductive heart rhythm and the AED works to restore a normal heart rhythm. Published studies have proven that defibrillation within the first few minutes of cardiac arrest can save up to 50% of victims. Sudden cardiac arrest claims more than 350,000 lives outside the hospital setting in the United States annually (President Clinton Signs, Internet). The AED uses a two-electrode system, and once the electrodes are in place, the AED itself will analyze the heart rhythm and determine if an electric shock is necessary (see Figure 35.13). If the AED determines the victim is shockable, then the AED instructs the responder to push the button to activate the unit. The AED will also instruct the responder to repeat the procedure if necessary.

Much of the growing movement to place AEDs in facilities used for sports, recreation, physical education, and fitness has been in response to the passage of federal legislation, Cardiac Arrest Survival Act (HR 2498) in 2000. This federal law requires all federal buildings nationwide to provide an AED, and the law also provides nationwide Good Samaritan protection that exempts from liability anyone who renders emergency treatment with a defibrillator to save someone's life. This legislation has raised the standard for what would be considered customary treatment for a victim of sudden cardiac arrest. Many public facilities, such as airports, now have AEDs on the premises even though they are not mandated by law. Due to the large number of spectators present at sporting events, many professional stadiums and arenas have also added AEDs and trained personnel to use the devices.

In the school setting, AEDs are becoming more prevalent on campuses. In fact, the state of New York in 2002 became the first state in the nation to require automated external defibrillators in schools. This state statute requires school districts, boards of cooperative educational services, county vocational education and extension boards, and charter schools to keep at least one functional AED on their premises. It also requires that an AED be available at school-sponsored athletic events, whether on campus or at an off campus site (AEDs Now Required, Internet). It is likely that other states may soon follow New York in requiring schools to provide AEDs in the future. At the collegiate level there are similar AED needs for both large spectator events in sports as well as for campus fitness and recreation centers. In the private fitness club setting, the state of Illinois has proposed legislation that will require all clubs to provide at least one AED and at least one staff member trained in its use. Michigan, Rhode Island, and New Jersey also have similar bills in progress.

The cost of AEDs were approximately $3,000 per unit in 2000 when the federal AED legislation was passed. According to Richard Lazar of the Early Defibrillator Law and Policy Center in Portland, Oregon, the current cost for each AED is about $2,200 and training might run $100 per person (Kufahl, 2004). It would be expected that the increased placement of these devices might create market conditions that would allow for a further reduction in the price of the AEDs in the future so that more facilities can provide them for their users.

Figure 35.13
A Typical AED Device With Electrodes Displayed

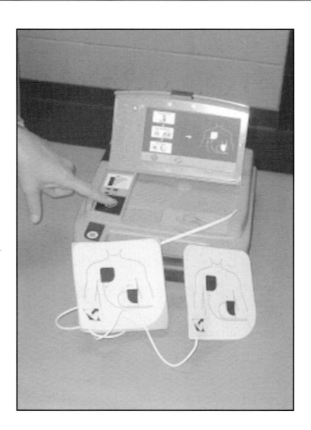

Extreme Sports

Adventure-oriented sports continue to grow in popularity and bring unique requirements for facilities and equipment. The media exposure of extreme sports through competitions such as ESPN's X Games and numerous other network imitations continues to help fuel interest in and give creditability to these activities. Although some of the events such as street luge may have limited appeal to mass participation, activities such as rock climbing and skating (skateboarding and in-line skating) have large levels of participation. In fact, these activities are attracting so many participants that instead of being viewed as extreme sports, it might be better to consider them extremely common.

The number of participants in skateboarding according to the SkatePark Association of the United States of America (SPAUSA) tops more than nine million regular users. There are approximately 650,000 serious climbers and perhaps tens of thousands of people starting the sport annually. Add to this the fact that in-line skating has over 75,000 members within the USA Hockey In-line with at least 2.5 million playing in-line hockey informally (Ahrweiler, 2001). Including the vast number of in-line skaters for cardiovascular exercise and the recreational street and skatepark skating, there is a significant population with sporting and recreational needs in this area.

Skateboarding and in-line skating opportunities can be enhanced through the creation of skateparks designated areas developed for safe, supervised, and exciting riding. More than 300 public skateparks were constructed in 1999 with double that number expected in 2000 (Ahrweiler, 2001). While some skateparks are elaborate concrete build-in-place systems, there are also modular park components available. These components could be considered the equipment necessary to create a skatepark from an available asphalt or concrete space. The modular components can be made out of concrete, wood, or a combination of steel framing, polyethylene, and zinc plating. These components combine elements such as angled and curved ramps, rails, curbs, and bumps to create fairly comprehensive parks suitable for both skateboard and in-line skate use. The modular components have even been assembled into portable units such as the "Flip Side" in Caledon, Ontario. This portable system of seven ramp structures and grind rails is transported to various locations throughout the summer in this Toronto suburb.

In-line hockey has allowed the expansion of the traditionally "northland" sport of hockey to be adapted to Sunbelt states without the requirement of ice. In-line hockey can be played indoors or outdoors and the facility space can often be converted for modified soccer use. Equipment needed to create a usable facility includes the dasherboards, goals, and a smooth base surface. The dasherboards are commonly constructed from wood, fiberglass, or plastic. One change is that the acrylic plastic upper portion of the boards seen in ice hockey is often replaced with coated fencing or netting for in-line hockey. The preferred playing surface is smoothly finished concrete; however, portable vinyl tiling systems such as Sport Court or other similar products can also provide a good playing surface.

The over 300 dedicated climbing gyms and the multitude of fitness clubs and recreation centers with climbing wall components have their own unique equipment requirements. The equipment required for the use of a climbing structure might consist of a variety of mountable holds (fiberglass or resin fixtures for hands or feet), belay systems (safety harness), ropes and rope hardware, helmets, and climbing shoes. Most climbing structures are custom built walls or free standing structures; however, in some instances, existing wall space of adequate height and structural soundness can be adapted into a functional climbing surface. Of course, the custom climbing areas are much more impressive in appearance and in realistic climbing features. Regardless of the climbing wall type, the ability to alter the holds creates immense flexibility for climbing walls to be configured for both novice and experienced climbers. This changeability also helps to keep climbers motivated and interested in the climbing experience.

Supply Trends

It is far more difficult to trace supply trends within sports facilities and sports and fitness organizations. Changes in the market for particular supplies, such as towels, athletic tape, or basketballs, would be more likely to be researched by the manufacturers and those practitioners in the field than those in the facility planning process. The specific supply needs also vary greatly based on the nature of the organization. A tennis club has far different supply needs than an arena league football team. Similarly, the maintenance department for a major stadium has far different supply needs than the baseball team that plays at the stadium.

One innovation that can now greatly influence the selection and purchase of supplies regardless of the program or department is the explosive growth of the use of the internet. The internet can be used to research products, obtain price quotes, and even place orders for almost any supply needed in the realm of sporting and recreation. The use of standard search engines can be used to locate supplies, but the development of sport-specific supply Web sites can also be effective. Athleticsearch.com can be used to research product information from a multitude of suppliers as well as access articles from trade magazines and other sources. The bidding and purchasing process can be facilitated through sites like AthleticBid.com that contact multiple vendors to allow them to place bids on your specified needs.

Supply and Equipment Storage

The storage space necessary for supplies and equipment is often one of the most overlooked areas in the facility planning process. An examination of the programs operating within a facility can help to determine the storage needs. It is important to gather input from those administrators, teachers, managers, coaches and others who will have to deal with the storage of equipment and supplies.

The arrangement of the storage space should also be considered. One option is to have one large centralized storage area. This type of storage is advantageous to large-scale programs that may have a full-time equipment manager and staff. With this arrangement, it may be easier to control the issuing, returning, and maintenance of equipment and supplies. One possible problem with the creation of a large centralized storage area is that it may become a target for renovation into a classroom, lab, office space, or other possible uses.

A second option is to have small separate storage areas. These storage spaces would be located near the individual team or program activity spaces. An advantage to this system is that individual coaches or program leaders would control their own access to equipment. This arrangement may allow for equipment to be stored closer to its point of use. The disadvantage to this system is that control of access to the multiple areas can be difficult to monitor.

In many instances, facilities do not have enough storage space or have outgrown their existing storage space. Utilization of "just-in-time" purchasing and delivery is one option to reduce the amount of storage space required. For example, rather than ordering and receiving your facility cleaning supplies in bulk for the year, the items could be purchased in bulk but delivered on a monthly or bimonthly schedule. This would reduce the amount of storage space that would need to be dedicated to these types of supplies. This form of purchasing, however, does not work well with large equipment or non-consumable items.

Regardless of whether the storage space is arranged in a large centralized space or in smaller "point-of use" areas, the total amount of space available must be adequate for the proper storage equipment and supplies. Proper storage would include keeping equipment secure and protecting it from inappropriate use or theft. Proper storage is also necessary to reduce liability for the facility operators and owners. In addition, proper storage should include adequate temperature and humidity controls for equipment that could be adversely impacted by environmental extremes. The use of overhead roll-up also can help maximize use and access of storage space.

How much storage space for equipment is enough? That is a question with no simple answer; however, there have been a number of facility studies conducted over time that have tried to approach this question in a systematic manner. Some of these studies have relied on the opinions of expert panels while others have relied upon data collection from selected facilities and input from facility administrators.

Table 35.4 traces the development of these recommendations over a period spanning more than 60 years. These recommendations provide an excellent starting point for consideration of storage space

Table 35.4
Equipment Storage Space Recommendations—A Selected Chronology

Date	Researcher(s)	Recommendation	Source and Level
1938	Evenden, Strayer, & Englehardt	400-square foot apparatus storage room	Expert Panel for collegiate facilities
1961	Sapora & Kenney	40% of total activity space dedicated to all ancillary areas including lockers, showers, drying areas, equipment storage, supply rooms and offices	Research of Big 10 Conference Universities
1967	National Facilities Conference	35% of activity area for all ancillary areas including lockers, showers, drying areas, equipment storage, supply rooms, and offices	Expert Panel for collegiate facilities
1968	College & University Facilities Guide	250 to 330 square feet of storage space for each exercise area	Expert Panel for collegiate facilities
1969	Berryhill	35% of activity area for all ancillary areas including lockers, showers, drying areas, equipment storage, supply rooms and offices	Research of one high school with expert panel input
1988	Strand	20 to 30% of all ancillary space within the facility	Research of Big 10 Conference Universities
1989	Walker	20 to 22% of all ancillary space within the facility	Research of 18 small colleges from two conferences
1997	Petersen	20 to 22% of all ancillary space within the facility	Research of 40 high schools

Adapted from Walker, M.L., & Seidler, T.L. (1993). Sports equipment management. Boston, MA; Jones and Bartlett Publishers

needs. Once an appropriate guideline has been selected for the proper level and facility, the recommendation for storage space can then be tested with the actual and projected needs specific to the programs to be served by the storage.

Summary

Supplies are typically items that are used only one time or that have a life span of a year or less. Equipment has a life span of one year or longer, and because of the fact that it is a type of durable good the cost is often higher than most supplies. For each purchase of equipment or supplies, facility administrators must balance the wants and needs of the users or programs with the cost of the desired items. The product quality level must be considered as well as the need to remain within the budgetary constraints of the organization.

A primary influence on trends in spectator venues is the comfort and entertainment of the spectators. These trends include upgraded seating options in gymnasiums, stadiums, and arenas, the addition of video and audio systems and the use of contracting or outsourcing.

Entertainment and technology enhancement are two major trends within fitness equipment. Workout monitoring via computer technology, improvements in video and audio options during aerobic workouts, and internet access are all major areas that are continuing to expand.

An AED is an emergency device that provides an electrical shock to restore a normal heartbeat to a victim of sudden cardiac arrest. Federal and state legislation is providing a major force behind the growing presence of these devices in facilities.

The continued growth of skating (both skateboards and in-line skates), rock climbing, and in-line hockey are impacting both the equipment and facility trends as more and more communities begin to fund the demand for facilities for these activities. Facility and recreation professionals must develop knowledge of the unique facility and equipment needs with these activities.

Supply trends are typically very specific to an individual product or product line, but the use of internet to research in obtaining bid and purchase information is a significant trend.

The storage required for supplies and equipment can be located in a larger centralized area or in smaller "point of use" areas. Regardless of where the storage is located, it is most important to provide sufficient space and proper storage to meet the program needs.

There have been numerous expert recommendations and research studies that have suggested space allocations for storage. Finding a recommendation appropriate to your facility or program creates a starting point for determining the storage space needed.

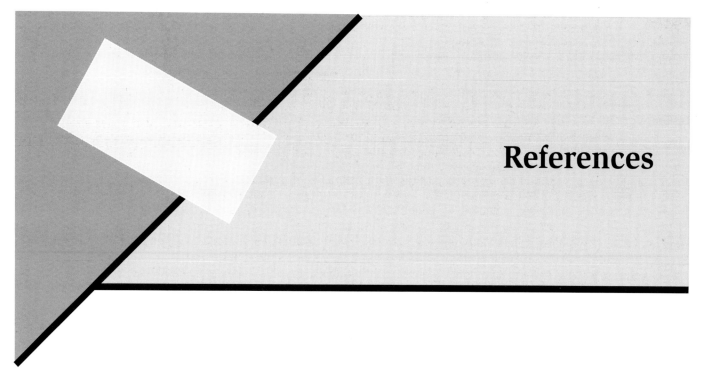

References

Access Board. (n.d.). Retrieved February 4, 2001, from http://www.access-board.gov/508.htm

Access Board. (n.d.). Retrieved February 6, 2001, from http://www.access-board.gov/ufas/ufas-html/ufas.htm#intro

Achampong, F. (1999). *Workplace sexual harassment law*. Westport, CT: Quorum Books.

AEDs now required in New York schools. Retrieved from Available: http://www.padl.org/articles.php3?id = aedsnyschools.htm

Agoglia, J. (2004, January). State of the industry: Taking the industries pulse for 2003-2004. Club Industry, 17-20.

Agron, J. (2001, April). Dwindling support. American School & University: Facilities, Purchasing and Business Administration, p. 24, 26-28, 30, 32.

Agron, J. (2001, April). Rising to the challenge. *American School & University: Facilities, Purchasing and Business Administration, 50b, 50d, 50f, 50h.*

Ahrweiler, M. (2001, January/February). Extremely mainstream. *Recreation Management*. 12-17.

American Society for Testing and Materials. (1995). Standard consumer safety performance specification for playground equipment for public use. (F1487). West Conshohocken, PA: Author.

Americans With Disabilities Act of 1990, Pub. L. No. 101-336, 2, 104 Stat. 328 (1991).

Ammon, R., Jr., Southall, R. M., & Blair, D. A. (2004). *Sport facility management: Organizing events and mitigating risks.* Morgantown, WV: Fitness Information Technology, Inc.

Ammon, R., & Unruh, N. (2003). Crowd management. In D. J. Cotten, & J. Wolohan, (Eds.), *Law for recreation and sport managers* (3rd ed.) (pp. 352-362). Dubuque, IA: Kendall/Hunt Publishing Company.

Andrus, S. (1990). Manual labor. *CAM Magazine, 2*(5), 61-64.

Anonymous (1998). Making indoor air quality work for you. P.M. *Public Management, 80*(8), A10.

Antoniou, P. H. (1994). *Competitiveness through strategic success*. Oxford, OH: Planning Forum.

Appenzeller, H. (2000). Risk assessment and reduction. In H. Appenzeller & G. Lewis (Eds.), *Successful sport management* (2nd ed.) (pp. 313-321). Durham, NC: Carolina Academic Press.

Armitage-Johnson, S. L. (1994). Equipment maintenance. In T. R. Baechle (Ed.), *Essentials of strength training and conditioning*. Champaign, IL: Human Kinetics.

Arnheim, D. D., & Prentice, W. E. (1997). *Principles of athletic training* (Ninth ed.). Boston: WCB/McGraw Hill.

ASLA (1998). Landscape Architecture. Retrieved from http://www.asla.org/asla

Atchison, J. (2003). Top 10 annuals for landscaping. *Sportsturf, 19*(7), 30.

Australia's Green Olympics. Retrieved May 17, 2004, from http://www.about-australia.com/spgreen.htm

Author. (1992, November). Blowing hot air. *Energy Ideas, 1*(5), 1-7.

Author. (1993, February). It's a small world after all. *Energy Ideas, 1*(8), 6-8.

Author. (1993, March). Sports vs. efficiency (OT). *Energy Ideas, 1*(9), 8-9.

Author. (2003). ASHRAE studies impact of IAC on classroom performance. HVAC/R Industry News. Retrieved from http://www.hvacmall.com/news/article_01180.htm

Author. (2003). CREON2000 disinfection unit studied under NIH grant. HVAC/R Industry News. Retrieved from http://www.hvacmall.com/news/article_01200.htm

Author. (2003). Sanuvox ultraviolet air purifier reduces school district air contaminants by 66%. HVAC/R Industry News. Retrieved from http://www.hvacmall.com/news/article_00973.htm

Azar, B. (1999). The top ten most common mistakes that retailers make. *Employee Services Management, 42*(3), 37-38.

Baechle, T. R. (Ed.). (1994). *Essentials of strength training and conditioning*. Champaign, IL: Human Kinetics.

Bannon, J. J. (1978). *Leisure resources: Its comprehensive planning*. Englewood Cliffs, NJ: Prentice-Hall.

Barkely, J. T. (1997). Surfacing. *A Fitness, Recreational Facility and Parks and Recreation Web Magazine* Retrieved from http:www.sandfordgroup.com/.

Bearman v. University of Notre Dame, 453 N.E.2nd1196 (Ind. Ct. App. 1999).

Bennis, W. (1989). *Why leaders can't lead: The unconscious conspiracy continues.* San Francisco: Jossey-Bass Publishers.

Bennis, W. (1994). *On becoming a leader.* Cambridge, MA: Perseus Books.

Bennis, W., & Nanus, B. (1997). *Leaders: Strategies for taking charge.* New York: HarperBusiness.

Berry, D. W. (1990). Maryland study shows simple signage works. *Aquatics, 2*(6), 16-20.

Bevan, R. (1956). *The athletic trainer's handbook.* Englewood Cliffs, NJ: Prentice-Hall, Inc.

Bishop, W. (1997). Athletic flooring. *Cornerstones: A Fitness Recreational Facility and Parks and Recreation Web Magazine.* Retrieved from http://www.sandfordgroup. com/

Boeh, Thomas. (1989). A program for selling. *CAM Magazine, 3*:10, 53-55.

Bower, M. (1980). *Foil fencing* (4th ed.). Dubuque, IA: William C. Brown.

Bowers, L. (1988). Playground design: A scientific approach. In L. D. Bruya (Ed.), *Play spaces for children: A new beginning* (pp. 22-48). Reston, VA: AAHPERD.

Brady, E., & Howlett, D. (1996, September 6). Economics, fans ask if benefits of building park outweigh costs. *USA Today,* pp. C13-C14.

Branvold, S. E. (1992). The utilization of fence signage in college baseball. *Sport Marketing Quarterly,* 1:2, 29-32.

Breems, M. (2001). Quality above depends on quality below. *Sportsturf, 17*(12), 10.

Brenner, S. (1999, July). Editorial column. Team Marketing Report, 2.

Bridges, F. J., & Roquemore, L. L. (1999). *Management for athletic/sport administration* (2nd ed). Decatur, GA: ESM Books.

Brinnell, Johann. (n.d.). Retrieved from http://www.fwkc.com/.

Bronzan, R. T., & Stotlar, D. K. (1992). *Public relations and promotion in sport.* Daphne, AL: United States Sports Academy.

Brown, B. J. (1972). *Complete guide to the prevention and treatment of athletic injuries.* West Nyack, NY: Parker Publishing Company.

Brown, G. (2003, August). Increased retention with entertainment systems. *Fitness Management,* 32-33.

Brown, M. T. (2003). Risk identification and reduction. In D. J. Cotten, & J. Wolohan, (Eds.), *Law for recreation and sport managers* (3rd. ed) (pp. 308-319). Dubuque, IA: Kendall/Hunt Publishing Company

Brownell, E. O. (1999). How to keep your service edge. *Employee Services Management, 41*(5), 39-40.

Bruya, L., & Wood, G. (1997). Why provide supervision on the playgrounds. In S. Hudson, & D. Thompson (Eds.), *Playground safety handbook* (pp. 38-48). Cedar Falls, IA: National Program for Playground Safety.

Bucher, C. A., & Krotee, M. L. (1993). *Management of physical education and sport* (10th ed.). Boston: Mosby Year Book.

Buisman, K., Thompson, A. F., & Cox, A. T. (1993). Risk management. *Athletic Management.* July, 1992. 3,10-16.

Busser, J. A. (1999). Conducting a needs assessment survey. *ESM Magazine, 42*(9), 28-31.

Byl, John. (1990). *Organizing successful tournaments.* Champaign, IL: Leisure Press.

Civil Rights Act of 1964; 42 U.S.C. §2000e-5–2000e-9.

Clement, A. (1988). *Law in sport and physical activity.* Indianapolis, IN: Benchmark Press.

Codring v. Board of Education of Manhasset Union Free School Dist., 435 N.Y.S.2nd 52 (App. Div. 1981).

Cohen, A. (1991). Back to the future. *Athletic Business, 15*(7), 31-37.

Cohen, A. (1993). Security check. *Athletic Business, 17*(3), 41-44.

Cohen, A. (1998, September). Beneath the Surface. *Athletic Business,* p.56-58, 60-62, 64, 66.

Cohen, A. (2000, July). Feet First. *Athletic Business,* 47-48, 50, 52, 54-55.

Cohen, A. (2002, May). Reflections. *Athletic Business,* 48-50, 52-55.

Cohen, A. (2002, November). Keeping up appearances. *Athletic Business,* 105-108.

Cohen, A. (2003, April). Out of the box. *Athletic Business,* 71-76, 78.

Conklin, A. R. (1999). Facility Follies. *Athletic Business, 23*(9), 28-30.

Conn, J. H. (1991). An open-book policy. *Athletic Business, 15*(2), 57-60.

Conn, J. H., & Malloy, B. P. (1989). *Organizing policy for interscholastic athletic programs.* Carmel, IN: Benchmark Publishing.

Cooper, Jay. (2004, July). The Changing Face of Sports Surface Selection. Retrieved from http://www.sandfordgroup.com/

Cotten, D. (2003a). Which parties are liable? In D. J. Cotten, & J. Wolohan, (Eds.), *Law for recreation and sport managers* (3rd ed.) (70-75). Dubuque, IA: Kendall/Hunt Publishing Company.

Cotten, D. (2003b). Waivers and releases. In D. J. Cotten, & J. Wolohan, (Eds.), *Law for recreation and sport managers* (3rd ed.) (pp. 105-113). Dubuque, IA: Kendall/Hunt Publishing Company.

Council on Physical Education for Children (COPEC). (2001). *Guidelines for facilities, equipment, and instructional materials in elementary physical education.* Reston, VA: National Association for Sport and Physical Education.

Crompton, J. L. (1999). *Financing and acquiring park and recreation resources.* Champaign, IL: Human Kinetics.

Crompton, J. L. (2004). Beyond economic impact: An alternative rationale for the public subsidy of major league sports facilities. *Journal of Sport Management, 18*(1), 41.

Crompton, J. L., Howard, D. R., & Var, T. (2003). Financing major league facilities: Status, evolution and conflicting forces. *Journal of Sport Management, 17*(2), 156-184.

Dahlgren, S. (2000, November). Making the grade. *Athletic Business,* 77-78, 80-82.

Dahlgren, S. (2000, September). LEDing the way. *Athletic Business,* 73-81.

Dethlefs, D. (1991). Multiple cheers. *College Athletic Management, 3*(3), 28-33.

Di Pilla, Steven. (2001, April). Minimizing 'slip & fall.' *Facilities Design and Management,* 48.

Dougherty, N. J., & Bonanno, D. (1985). *Management principles in sport and leisure services*. Minneapolis: Burgess Publishing Company.

Driscoll, Terri. (2000, October). In Goodman, J., *Cushion extends life: Facilities design and management*, p. 54, 56.

Eickoff-Shemek, J. (2002). Minimizing legal liability: Risk management for health fitness facilities (Part 2) [Videotape] *Risk Management for Health/Fitness Programs and Facilities. Standards and Guidelines*. Champaign, IL: Human Kinetics.

Ensman, R. G., Jr. (1999). Fun and games: Solving problems with playful brainstorming techniques. *Employee Services Management, 42*(2), 9-10.

Ensman, R. G., Jr. (1998). Angry customers: A step-by-step guide to turning things around. *Employee Services Management, 41*(1), 31-33.

Ensman, R. G., Jr. (1999). Nine steps to being a good buyer. *Employee Services Management, 42*(3), 39-40.

ESPN Sports Business. (2004). Retrieved May 5, 2004, from http://espn.go.com/sportsbusiness/s/stadiumnames.html

Evenden, E. S., Strayer, G. D., & Englehardt, N. I. (1938). *Standards for college buildings*. New York City: Teachers College, Columbia University

Ewing, S. (1999). Music influences consumers to buy. *Employee Services Management, 42*(3), 5-6.

Executive Order 11246.

Farmer, P. J., Mulrooney, A. L., & Ammon, Jr., R., (1996). *Sport facility planning and management*. Morgantown, WV: Fitness Information Technology, Inc.

Farmer, P. J., Mulrooney, A. L., & Ammon, R., Jr. (1999). *Sport facility planning and management*. Morgantown, WV: Fitness Information Technology. Inc.

Farrell, P., & Lundegren, H., M. (1978). *The process of recreation programming: Theory and technique*. New York: John Wiley & Sons, Inc.

Fischer, D., & Ozanian, M. (1999, October 20). Cowboy capitalism. *Forbes, 164*, 171-177.

Flynn, R. B. (Ed.). (1985). *Planning facilities for athletics, physical education and recreation* (seventh ed.). Reston, VA: American Alliance for Health, Physical Education, Recreation and Dance.

Flynn, Richard B. (1993). *Facility planning for physical education, recreation, and athletics*. Reston, VA: The Facilities Council of the Association for Research, Administration, Professional Councils and Societies.

Fogg, D. C. (1994). *Team-based strategic planning: A complete guide to structuring, facilitating, and implementing the process*. New York: American Management Association.

Forseth, E. A. (1986, Spring). Consideration in planning small college athletic training facilities. *Athletic Training*. 23-25.

Frost, R. B., Lockhart, B. D., & Marshall, S. J. (1988). *Administration of physical education and athletics: Concepts and practices* (2nd ed.). Dubuque, IA: Wm. C. Brown Publishers.

Frost, R. B., Lockhart, B. D., & Marshall, S. J. (1988). (3rd ed.). Dubuque, IA: Wm. C. Brown Company.

Frost, R. B., & Marshall, S. J. (1977). *Administration of physical education and athletics: Concepts and practices* (2nd ed.). Dubuque, IA: Wm. C. Brown Company.

Funk, D. (1997). *Economics of professional sports franchises: The role of luxury suites and club seats in the construction of sports stadiums and arenas in North America*. Paper presented at the annual conference of the North American Society for Sport Management, San Antonio, TX.

Future trends in fitness equipment. (1997, November). *Joe Weider's Muscle & Fitness, 26*.

Garbarino, E., & Johnson, M. S. (1999). The different roles of satisfaction, trust, and commitment in customer relationships, *Journal of Marketing, 63*(2), 70-87.

Girdano, D. A. (1986) *Occupational health promotion: A practical guide to program development*. New York: Macmillian.

Goodbody, J. (1969). *The Japanese fighting arts*. South Brunswick, NY: A. S. Barnes and Company.

Goodman, Julie. (2000, October). Cushion extends life. *Facilities Design & Management*, 54,56.

Goodstein, L. D., Nolan, T. M., & Pfeiffer, W. J. (1993). *Applied strategic planning: A comprehensive guide*. New York: McGraw-Hill.

Gordon, J. (1990). The suite smell of success. *Skybox, 1*(2), 6-9.

Gorman, J., Calhoun, K., & Rozin, S. (1994). *The name of the game: The business of sports*. New York: John Wiley & Sons, Inc.

Greenwood. Essential of strength training & conditioning. In *Strength and conditioning Professional Standards and Guidelines* (pp. 549-566). Retrieved from http://www.ncsa-lift.org/Publications/standards. Shtml

Gunsten, Paul H. (1978). *Tournament Scheduling: The easy way*. Winston-Salem, NC: Hunter Textbooks, Inc.

Hamar, Doug. (November 2000). In Dahlgren, S., Making the Grade. *Athletic Business*, 77-78, 80-82, 84.

Hamel, G., & Prahalad, C. K. (1994). *Competing for the future*. Boston: Harvard Business School Press.

Hammel, D. (2003, September). New green building standards are gaining popularity. *Recreation Management*. Retrieved May 17, 2004, from http://recmanagement.com/issuecontents.php?si=200309

Harassment cases soar in the nineties. (1999, April 1). *USA Today*, 1.

Hard Questions, Critical Answers. (March 1998). *Building Operating Management*. Retrieved from http://www.facilitiesnet.com/

Hasenkamp, T., & Lutz, B. (2001, March). The dash for splash. *Athletic Business*, 55-56, 58, 60.

Hasler, A. E., & Bartlett, M. (1995, September). Equipped for exercise. *Athletic Business*, 47-54.

Hauglie, J. (1997). A guide to benchmarking. *Employee Services Management, 40*(8), 9-12.

Heidrich, K. W. (1990). *Working with volunteers*. Champaign, IL: Sagamore Publishing.

Heistand, M. (1999, May 26). Skyboxes gain mass appeal. *USA Today*, p. 3C.

Helitzer, M. (1992). *The dream job sports publicity, promotion, and public relations.* Athens, OH: University Sports Press.

Helson, C. M. (1997). Keeping control when outsourcing your store. *Employee Services Management 40*(8), 30-31.

Helson, C. M. (1998). Employee stores keep growing. *Employee Services Management, 41*(3), 11-14.

Hendy, T. (1997). The nuts and bolts of playground maintenance. In S. Hudson, & D. Thompson (Eds.), *Playground safety handbook* (pp. 60-70). Cedar Falls, IA: National Program for Playground Safety.

Hewitt, C. N. (1997). Campus master planning. In Middleton, W. D., *Facilities planning, design, construction, and administration* (Part IV) (3rd ed.). Alexandria, VA: APPA: The Association for Higher Education Facilities Officers.

Hoffman, A. N., & O'Neill, H. M. (1993). *The strategic management casebook and skill builder.* Minneapolis/St. Paul: West Publishing.

Holleman, M. A. (1996). Scoring with stadiums. *Athletic Business, 20*(9), 45-49.

Holzrichter, Doug. (2001, January). Gymnasium makeovers. *Athletic Business,* 59-60, 62-65.

Horine, L., & Stotlar, D. (2003). *Administration of physical education and sport* (5th ed.). Dubuque, IA: Wm. C. Brown Company.

Horine, L., & Stotlar, D. (2003). *Administration of physical education and sport* (6th ed.). Dubuque, IA: Wm. C. Brown Company.

Howard, D., & Crompton, J. (2004). *Financing sport* (2nd. ed.). Morgantown, WV: Fitness Information Technology, Inc.

Howard, D. R., & Crompton, J. L. (1995). *Financing sport.* Morgantown, WV: Fitness Information Technology, Inc.

Howard, D. R., & Crompton, J. L. (2003). *Financing sport* (2nd ed). Morgantown, WV: Fitness Information Technology.

Howe, D. K. (2000, March/April). Nine trends of the 1990s. *American Fitness,* 12-13.

Huddleston, E. (2001, November). The sweet smell of success. *Athletic Business,* p. 63-64, 66, 68, 70.

Hudson, S., Olsen, & Thompson, D. (2004). *Playground safety.* Cedar Falls, IA: University of Northern Iowa.

Hussey, D. E. (1991). *Introducing corporate planning: Guide to strategic management.* New York: Pergamon Press.

IAAM. (1996). Emergency planning at public assembly facilities. Irving, TX: IAAM.

Illinois Park & Recreation Association. (1995). *A guide to playground planning.* Winfield, IL.: Author.

Ingersoll, C., & Sawyer, T. (1999). Sports medicine and rehabilitation. In *Facilities planning for physical activity and sport. Guidelines for development* (Ninth ed.). Dubuque, IA: Kendall-Hunt.

International Association of Skateboard Companies. [On-line]. Available: http://www.iasc.com

Jensen, C. R. (1988). *Administrative management of physical education and athletic programs* (2nd ed.). Philadelphia: Lea Febiger.

Jensen, C. R., & Overman, J. O. (2003). *Administration and management of physical education and athletic programs.* Prospect Heights, IL: Waveland Press, Inc.

Jewell, D. (1992). *Public assembly facilities* (2nd ed.). Malabar, FL: Krieger Publishing Co.

Johnson, D. K., & Patterson, D. S. (1997, December). Window and curtain walls: Out with the old? *Building Operating Management.* Retrieved from http://www.facilitiesnet.com/.

Johnson, R. (1991). All in one. *College Athletic Management, 3*(3), 28-33.

Jones, T. E (1990, April). Choosing Court Colors. *Athletic Business,* 70-71.

Kaiser, R., & Robinson, K. (1999). Risk management. In B. van der Smissen, M. Moiseichik, V. Hartenburg, & L. Twardzik (Eds.), *Management of park and recreation agencies* (pp. 713-741). Ashburn, VA: NRPA.

Kaplan, D. (1998). ABS: A new way to pay. *Sport Business Journal, 1*(1), 3.

Keller, I. A., & Forsyth, C. E. (1984). *Administration of high school athletics.* Englewood Cliffs, NJ: Prentice Hall, Inc.

Kennedy, M. (2000, October). A well-grounded plan. *American School and University: Facilities, Purchasing and Business Administration,* 30, 32, 34.

King, A. (1998). Maximize your sales dollars per square foot. *Employee Services Management, 41*(3), 15-19.

King, J. M. (2003, November). Cardio machine programming. *Fitness Management,* 34-37.

Klafs, C. E., & Arnheim, D. D. (1973). *Modern principles of athletic training* (Third ed.) (pp. 33-42). St. Louis, MO.

Kocher, E. (1996, April). Gymnasium facelifts. *Athletic Business,* 39-42.

Krenson, F. (1988). Crowd-pleasing arena design. *Athletic Business, 12*(9), 66-69.

Kroll, Karen. (2002, December). Steps to selecting the best floor. *Building Operating Management.* Retrieved from http://www.facilitiesnet.com/

Kroll, K. (December 2003). Ceilings—Blocking the talk: acoustics in the workplace. *Building Operating Management.* Retrieved from http//www.facilitiesnet.com/

Kufahl, P. (2004, January). Political push. *Club Industry,* 21-23.

Lavallee & Westervelt (2004). Retrieved from http://www.xsports.com/rehab.html

LaVoie, H. (1993). Ancillary Areas. In R. B. Flynn, (Ed.), *Facility planning for physical education, recreation, and athletics,* (pp. 147-148). Reston, VA: The Facilities Council of the Association for Research, Administration, Professional Councils and Societies: An Association of the American Alliance for Health, Physical Education, Recreation, and Dance.

Lewis, G., & Appenzeller, H. (1985). *Successful sport management.* Charlottesville, VA: The Michie Company.

Lewis, G., & Appenzeller, H. (2003). *Successful Sport Management* (2nd ed.). Durham, NC: Carolina Academic Press.

Lewis, W. (1994). Weeding out unwanted growth: Weed problems on athletic fields can be nipped in the bud by implementing a total week management program. *Athletic Management, 6*(3), 28.

Logan, W., & Petras, H. (1975). *Handbook of the martial arts and self-defense.* New York: Funk and Wagnalls.

Mack, M. G., Hudson, S., & Thompson, D. (1997, June). A descriptive analysis of children's playground injuries in the United States 1990-1994. *Journal of the International Society for Child and Adolescent Injury Prevention, 3,* 100-103.

Maher, J. (2003, June 28). What's in a name? American Statesman. Retrieved May 5, 2004, from http://www.utwatch.org/oldnews/aas_erwin_6_28_03.html

McArthur, S. (1992). Don't throw in the towel. *Athletic Business, 16*(7), 49-50.

McCarron, C. (2001, April). Reuse, recycle, rebuild. *Athletic Business, 25*(4), 55-62.

McPherson, D. (2004). Flooring your members. *Fitness Management, 18*(5), 43.

Meagher, J. (1985). Eliminating the negative in sports facility design. *Athletic Business, 9*(1), 32-35.

Meagher, J. W. (1995). Right on the money. *Athletic Business, 19*(8), 67.

Miller, L. K. (1997). *Sport business management.* Gaithersburg, MD: Aspen Publishers, Inc.

Minnesota Building Codes and Standards Division. (2001). Printouts: *Bleacher seating.* Retrieved from http://www.admin.state.mn.us/buildingcodes/printouts/bleachers.html

Molnar, D., & Rutledge, A. (1986). *Anatomy of a park* (2nd ed.). New York: McGraw-Hill.

Moore, A. L. (1995). What is risk management anyway? Vol. 6 no. 4, *Facility Manager.* Irving, TX: IAAM.

Moran, B. (1999, June). Mission essential: NIRSA conference highlights recreation's power to recruit and retain. *Recreational Sports & Fitness.* 14-18.

Morehouse, L. E., & Rasch, P. J. (1958). *Scientific basis of athletic training* (pp. 216-224). Philadelphia: W. B. Saunders Company.

Morehouse, L. E., & Rasch, P. J. (1964). *Sports medicine for trainers* (Second ed.) (pp. 214-223). Philadelphia: W.B. Saunders Company.

Moussatche, H., Languell-Urquhart, J., & Woodson, C. (2000, September). Life cycle costs in education: Operations & maintenance considered. *Facilities Design & Management, 20, 22.*

Mula, R. M. (1998). Employee vendor fairs. *Employee Services Management, 41*(10),31-32.

Mull, R. F., Bayless, K. G., Ross, C. M., & Jamieson, L. M. (1997). *Recreational sport management* (3rd ed). Champaign, IL: Human Kinetics.

Mulrooney, A., Farmer, P., & Ammon, R. (1996). *Sport facility planning and management.* Morgantown, WV: Fitness Information Technology, Inc.

National Facilities Conference. (1962). *Planning facilities for health, physical education, and recreation.* Chicago: The Athletic Institute.

National Facilities Conference. (1966). *College and university facility guide.* Washington, DC: The Athletic Institute and the American Association of Health, Physical Education and Recreation.

National Facilities Conference. (1966). *Planning facilities for health, physical education, and recreation.* Chicago: The Athletic Institute and the American Association of Health, Physical Education and Recreation.

NCAA Guides. (2004). Indianapolis, IN: National Collegiate Athletic Association.

National Inline Hockey Assocation (USA). [On-line]. Available: http://www.niha.com

NCAA Rule Books for Baseball, Football, Soccer, and Lacrosse. (2000). Indianapolis, IN: National Collegiate Athletic Association.

Neville, W. (1994). *Serve it up: Volleyball for life.* Mountain View, CA: Mayfield Publishing.

Nolan, T. M. (1993). *Plan or die: 10 keys to organizational success.* San Diego: Pfeiffer & Co.

Noyes, B., & Skolnicki, J. (2001) A modest proposal. *Athletic Business, 24*(8), 51-58.

Olguin, M. A. (1991). Vital marketing. *Fitness Management, 7:3,* 45-47.

Olson, J., Hirsch, E., Breitenbach, O., & Saunders, K. (1987). *Administration of high school and collegiate athletic programs.* Philadelphia: Saunders College Publishing.

Paley, N. (1991). *The strategic marketing planner.* New York: AMACOM.

Parkhouse, B. L. (1991) *The management of sport: Its foundation and application.* St. Louis, MO: C. V. Mosby Year Book.

Parkhouse, B. L. (2001). *The management of sport: Its foundation and application* (3rd ed.). Dubuque, IA: McGraw-Hill.

Patton, J. D. (1999, April). Fitness in flux. *Athletic Business,* 51-54.

Patton, R. W., Corry, J. M., Gettman, L. R., & Schovee, G. J. (1986). *Implementing health/fitness programs.* Champaign, IL: Human Kinetics.

Patton, W., Grantham, William C., Gerson, Richard F., & Gettman, L. R. (1989). *Developing and managing health/fitness facilities.* Champaign, IL: Human Kinetics.

Penderghast, T. F. (1999). Is your store ready for e-commerce? *Employee Services Management, 42*(7), 33-34.

Penman, K. A., & Penman, T. M. (1982, September). Training rooms aren't just for colleges. *Athletic Purchasing and Facilities.* 34-37.

Perfetti, R. & Ch'uan, T. C. [On-line]. Available: http://www.maui.net/ ~ táichi4u/overview.html

Peterson, J. A., & Tharrett, S. J. (1997). *ACSM's health/fitness facility standards and guidelines* (2nd ed). Champaign, IL: Human Kinetics.

Peterson, James A. (1991). Ten steps to effective publicity. *Fitness Management, 7:12,* 41.

Peterson, James A. (1991). The power and nature of publicity. *Fitness Management, 7:12,* 39.

Petersen, J. C. (1997). *Indoor activity space and ancillary space analysis for New Mexico high schools.* Unpublished doctoral dissertation, The University of New Mexico, Albuquerque.

Piper, J. (1998, March). Complete performances. *Building Operation Management.* Retrieve from http://www.facilitiesnet.com/

Piper, J. (2000, August). Flooring: The real bottom line. *Building Operation Management.* Retrieve from http://www.facilitiesnet.com/

Piper, J. (2003, December). Flooring for today, tomorrow. *Building Operation Management.* Retrieve from http://www.facilities.net.com/

Poirier, C. C. (1996). *Avoiding the pitfalls of total quality.* Milwaukee, WI: ASQC Quality Press.

Pollar, O. (1997). Effective delegation. *Employee Services Management, 40*(9), 13-16.

Popke, M. (2000, October). Skate nation. *Athletic Business.* 67-74.

Popke, M. (2001, May). Mixing it up. *Athletic Business*, 46-50, 52.

President Clinton signs cardiac arrest survival act. Retrieved from http://www.padl.org/articles.php3?id = newlegis005

Project Adventure. [On-line]. Available: http://www.pa.org

Raiford, R. (1999, June). Into uncharted territory: Outsourcing redirects the future of business for facilities professionals. *Buildings*, 40-42.

Railey, J. H., & Railey, P. A. (1988). *Managing physical education, fitness and sports programs*. Mountain View, CA: Mayfield Publishing Company.

Railey, Jim H., & Tschauner, Peggy Railey. (1993). *Managing physical education, fitness, and sports programs* (2nd ed.). Mountainview, CA: MayfieldPublishing Company.

Rankin, J., & Ingersoll, C. (1995). *Athletic training management: Concepts and applications*. St. Louis, MO: Mosby.

Rawlinson, K. (1961). *Modern athletic training*. Englewood Cliffs, NJ: Prentice-Hall, Inc.

Ray, R. (1994). *Management strategies in athletic training*. Champaign, IL: Human Kinetics.

Regan, T. (1997). Financing facilities. In M. L. Walker & D. K. Stotlar, (Eds.), *Sport facility management*. Sudbury, MA: Jones and Bartlett Publishers.

Rehabilitation Act of 1973; 29 U.S.C. §791.

Rigsbee, E. R. (1997). Finding your retail niche in the competitive '90s. *Employee Services Management*, *40*(10), 30.

Roberts, C. (2000, September). Ceilings: Form, function and ROI. *Building Operating Management*. Retrieved from http://www.facilitiesnet.com/.

Rohnke, K., Wall, J., Tait, C., & Rogers, D. (2003). *The complete ropes course manual* (3rd. ed.). Dubuque, IA: Kendall/Hunt Publishing.

Roth, J. (1974). *Black belt karate*. Rutland, VT. Charles E. Tuttle Company, Inc.

Rushing, G. (2000). A safety and legal liability self-appraisal instrument for athletic programs. In H. Appenzeller & G. Lewis. *Successful sport management* (2nd ed.). Durham, NC: Carolina Academic Press.

Russell, R. V. (1982). *Planning programs in recreation*. St. Louis: C. V. Mosby Company.

Russo, F. (2000). Marketing events and services for spectators. In Appenzeller, H. & Lewis, G. *Successful sport management* (2nd ed.), (151-162). Durham, NC: Carolina Academic Press.

Sabo, J. (2001, May). Design and construction of an athletic training facility. *NATA NEWS*. 10-22.

Samuelson, P. A., & Nordhaus, W. D. (1985). *Economics*. New York: McGraw-Hill.

Sandorti, C. C. (1995). Court cents, *Volleyball Magazine*, *6*(8), 114-115, 140.

Sapora, A., & Kenney, H. (1961). A study of the present status, future needs and recommended standards regarding space used for health, physical education, physical recreation and athletics. Champaign, IL: Stipes Publishing Company.

Sauers, R. J. (1985, September). Safety built into a flexible design. *Athletic Business*. 62- 63.

Saunders, K. (2001). Rotational field worth taking a look. *Sportsturf, 17*(11), 24.

Sawyer, T. H., & Smith, O. R. (1999). *The management of clubs, recreation, and sport: Concepts and applications*. Champaign, IL. Sagamore Publishing.

Schackter, D. (1983). Using advertising to help boost ticket sales. *Athletic Purchasing and Facilities*, 7:8, 38,40,42.

Schlosser, J., & Carter, D. (2001, April 2). TV sports: A numbers game. *Broadcast & Cable*, 32-33.

Schmader, S.W., & Jackson, R. (1997). *Special events: Inside and out* (2nd ed). Champaign, IL: Sagamore Publishing.

Schmid, S. (1993). Premium coverage. *Athletic Business*, *16*(4), 39-42.

Schroeder, C. L. (1999). Staffing your store. *Employee Services Management*, *42*(8), 37-39.

Schwabe, L. D. (2001, April). *Your store: The secret weapon*. Paper presented at the ESM Association Annual Conference and Exhibit, New Orleans, LA. April 8-12, 2001.

Secor, M. R. (1984). Designing athletic training facilities or where do you want the outlets? *Journal of Athletic Training*, 19:5, 19-21.

Seidler, T. (2000). Safe facilities: The facility risk review. In H. Appenzeller & G. Lewis (Eds.), *Successful sport management* (2nd ed.). Durham, NC: Carolina Academic Press

Severn, A. K. (1992). Building-tax abatements: An approximation to land value taxation. *American Journal of Economics and Sociology, 51*(2), 237-245.

Shaffer, A. L. (1999). Taking stock. *Club Industry, 15*(7), 49-51.

Shank, M. D. (2002). *Sports marketing: A strategic perspective*. Upper Saddle River, NJ: Prentice Hall.

Shaw, L. G. (1976). *The playground: The child's center learning space* (MH 20743034A1). Gainsville, FL: The Bureau of Research, College of Architecture, University of Florida.

Simers, T. J., & Wharton, D. (1999, October 10). How the game was played. *Los Angeles Times Magazine*, 28-31, 128-131.

Sol, N., & Foster, C., (1992). *ACSM's health/fitness facility standards and guidelines*. Champaign, IL: Human Kinetics.

Sol, N., & Foster C., (1997). Health/fitness facility standards and guidlines. American College of Sports Medicine, Champaign, IL: Human Kinetics Books.

Solomon, J. (2002). *An insider's guide to managing sporting events*. Champaign, IL: Human Kinetics.

Solomon, J. D. (2004, April 1). Public wises up, balks at paying for new stadiums. *USA Today*, p. 13A.

Stadiums & Arenas: Club Seat Breakdown. (2003, July 17-23). Street & Smith's *Sport Business Journal*, 10-11.

Staff. (1998). Stadiums: Today's bargaining chips. *Sports Business Journal, 1*(1), 19-36.

Staff. (1996). Scoring with stadiums. *Athletic Business, 20*(9), 51-54.

Staff. (2000). Key facility elements to meet the growing demands of multipurpose arenas. *Athletic Business, 24* (1), 37 - 41.

Staff. (2000). Stretched stadiums: Division I schools expand home venues. *Athletic Business, 24*(9), 44 - 47.

Steinbach, P. (2004, March). Sudden impact. *Athletic Business*, 51-52, 54, 56, 58.

Steinbach, P. (2002, July). Great plane. *Athletic Business*, 79-80, 82, 84, 86.

Steinbach, P. (2002, January). Beauty & brawn. *Athletic Business,* 58-65.

Sternloff, R. E., & Warren, R. (1984). *Park and recreation maintenance management* (2nd ed.). New York: John Wiley and Sons.

Stier, W. F., Jr. (1993). Project profit. *Athletic Business,* 4(2), 44.

Stier, W. F., Jr. (1994). *Successful sport fund-raising.* Dubuque, IA: EECB Brown & Benchmark Publishers.

Stoll, S., & Beller, J. (1989). *The professionals guide to teaching aerobics.* Englewood Cliffs, NJ: Prentice Hall.

Strand, B. N. (1988). *A space analysis of physical education activity areas and ancillary areas in big ten universities.* Unpublished doctoral dissertation, University of New Mexico, Albuquerque, NM..

Straus, D. C., & Kirihara, J. (1996). *Indoor microbiological garden: A microscopic line separates good and bad IAQ.* Retrieved from Available: http://www.facilitiesnet.com/

Tarlow, P. E. (2002). *Event risk management and safety.* New York: John Wiley & Sons.

Teach, E. (1997). Microsoft's Universe of Risk *CFO* 69-72.

Thompson, C. (2001, October 6). *First-class Reliant Stadium nears completion.* Retrieved on May 3, 2004, from http://www.chron.com/cs/CDA/story.hts/sports/fb/nfl/1077737

Thompson, D., & Hudson, S. (1996). *National action plan for the prevention of playground injuries.* Cedar Falls, IA: National Program for Playground Safety.

Tiger Athletics. Retrieved May 5, 2004, from http://gotigersgo.collegesports.com/genrel/042604aaa.html

Trais, R. A. (1973). *The hand is my sword.* Rutland, VT: Charles E. Tuttle Company, Inc.

Trend setting. (1999, February). *Joe Weider's Muscle & Fitness,* 23.

Turner, E. (1994). Vital signs. *Athletic Business,* 18, 65-67.

Uniform Accessibility Standards. Retrieved from http://www.access-board.gov/ufas/ufas-html/ufas.htm#4.1.1

U.S. Department of Justice. (n.d.). Retrieved from February 19, 2001, from http://www.usdoj.gov/crt/ada/enforce.htm

United States Consumer Product Safety Commission (2001). *Handbook for public playground safety.* Washington, D.C.: Author.

United States Professional Tennis Association, Rules Committee. (1996). *Tennis rules.* New York: USPTA.

United States Tennis Association. Retrieved from http://www.usta.com

United States Volleyball Association, Rules Committee. (1997). *Volleyball rules.* New York: USVA.

Urban, Peter. (1981). *The karate dojo* (12th ed.). Rutland, VT. Charles E. Tuttle Company, Inc.

Valentine, P. (2003, May). Out in front. *PanStadia International Quarterly,* 9(4).

Van Dalen, D. B., & Bennett, B. L. (1971). *A world history of physical education.* Englewood Cliffs: Prentice-Hall, Inc.

van der Smissen, B. (1990). *Legal liability and risk management for public and private entities: Sport and physical education, leisure services, recreation and parks, camping and adventure activities.* Cincinnati: Anderson.

Veterans Readjustment Assistance Act of 1974.

Viklund, Roy. (1995, July). High-performance floors. *Athletic Business,* 41-47.

Vocational Rehabilitation Act of 1973; amended 1974.

Walker, M. L. (1989). A space analysis of physical education activity and ancillary areas in selected small colleges and universities. Unpublished doctoral dissertation, University of New Mexico, Albuquerque, NM.

Walker, M. L., & Seidler, T. L. (1993). *Sports equipment management.* Boston, MA: Jones and Bartlett Publishers.

Walker, M. L., & Stotlar, D. K. (1997). *Sport facility management.* Sudbury, MA: Jones and Bartlett Publishers.

Waterman, S. (2003, February), Magic carpet. *PanStadia International Quarterly Report,* 9(3).

Waterman, S. (2003, November). The naming game. *PanStadia International Quarterly Report,* 10(2), 52-57.

Weinberg, A. (2003, March 23). Biggest college sports arena naming deals. Retrieved May 5, 2004, from http://www.forbes.com/2003/03/24/cx_aw_0320ncaa.html

Whalin, G. (1998). Effective store layouts. *Employee Services Management,* 41(2). 26-28.

Whalin, G. (1997a). Fourteen questions to ask before you buy a point-of-sale system. *Employee Services Management,* 40(9), 30-31.

Whalin, G. (1997b). Using cutting-edge retail trends in employee stores. *Employee Services Management,* 40(1), 26-27.

Which Dance Floor? (2001). Retrieved from http://www.stagestep.com/

Whitney, T. (1992). A house divided. *Athletic Business,* 16(3), 44-51.

Wilbur, R. A. (1999). Teams. . . friend or foe? *Employee Services Management,* 42(5), 9-11.

Wilkinson, H. T. (2002). Topdressing a baseball field. *Sportsturf,* 18(2), 27.

Wilson, S. (2000). Crowd pleasers. *Athletic Management.*

Winderbaum, L. (1977). *The martial arts encyclopedia.* Washington, D.C. INSCAPE Publishers.

Wolfe, R. (1987). Designing facilities to meet future needs. *Athletic Business,* 11(9), 48-55.

Wolkoff, M. J. (1985). Chasing a dream: The use of tax abatements to spur urban economic development. *Urban Studies,* 22, 305-315.

Wong, G. M. (2001). *Essentials of amateur sports law* (2nd ed.). Dover, MA: Auburn House Publishing Company.

Wong, G. M., & Masteralexis, L. P. (1998). Legal principles applied to sport management. In L. P. Masteralexis, C. A. Barr, & M. A. Hums (Eds.), *Principles and practice of sport management* (pp. 87-116). Gaithersburg, MD: Aspen Publishers.

Woodring V. Board of Education of Manhasset Union Free School Dist., 435 N.Y.S. 2nd 52 (App. Div. 1981).

Wright, P. L., Pringle, C. D., Kroll, M. J., & Parnell, J. A. (1994). *Strategic management: Text and cases.* Boston: Allyn and Bacon.

Yeomans, M. (2001, June 16). Heinz' naming rights deal. *Pittsburgh Tribune Review,* p. 1C.

York, R. O. (1982). *Human service planning.* Chapel Hill, NC: The University of North Carolina Press.

Index

VersaCAD 2005 by Archway Systems

The Practical, Versatile & Economical CADD Software for Production Design/Drafting in Every Discipline

VersaCAD by Archway Systems is the practical, easy-to-use yet affordable computer-aided design and drafting (CADD) software. It is logically structured and compatible with all computer-aided design software programs with versions for either Macintosh or Wintel-based platforms. Use VersaCAD for the seamless translation of any CAD system files by using its DXF, DWG, IGES translator.

VersaCAD's versatility allows for wide-ranging architectural, engineering and design applications including architectural and product engineering as well as facilities planning. In addition to your designs, use VersaCAD to create bills of materials, estimates and purchase orders or to create marketing and other operational documentation like catalogs, installation guides and computer network, wiring, and telecommunications schematics. You can even create office layouts, area calculations and furniture arrangements.

VersaCAD is the product designed for use where speed and efficiency are paramount. No other CADD software matches its processing speed or its versatility in creating computer-aided designs.

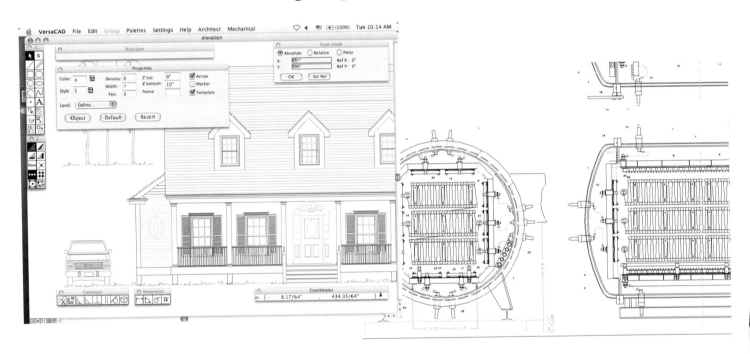

VersaCAD 2005 - The Practical, Versatile, Economical CADD Software

Archway Systems, Inc.
2134 Main St. #160, Huntington Beach, CA 92648
(714) 374-0440
www.versacad.com
sales@versacad.com